Politics and Policy

JAMES L. SUNDQUIST

Politics and Policy

The Eisenhower, Kennedy, and Johnson Years

THE BROOKINGS INSTITUTION
Washington, D.C.

Second printing April 1969
Third printing March 1970
Fourth printing April 1971
Fifth printing February 1973

ISBN 0-8157 8221-7 (paper)
ISBN 0-8157 8222-5 (cloth)

Library of Congress Catalog Card Number 68-31837

THE BROOKINGS INSTITUTION is an independent organization devoted to nonpartisan research, education, and publication in economics, government, foreign policy, and the social sciences generally. Its principal purposes are to aid in the development of sound public policies and to promote public understanding of issues of national importance.

The Institution was founded on December 8, 1927, to merge the activities of the Institute for Government Research, founded in 1916, the Institute of Economics, founded in 1922, and the Robert Brookings Graduate School of Economics and Government, founded in 1924.

The general administration of the Institution is the responsibility of a self-perpetuating Board of Trustees. The trustees are likewise charged with maintaining the independence of the staff and fostering the most favorable conditions for creative research and education. The immediate direction of the policies, program, and staff of the Institution is vested in the President, assisted by an advisory council chosen from the staff of the Institution.

In publishing a study, the Institution presents it as a competent treatment of a subject worthy of public consideration. The interpretations and conclusions in such publications are those of the author or authors and do not purport to represent the views of the other staff members, officers, or trustees of the Brookings Institution.

Foreword

THIS STUDY is an attempt to shed light on a question that has long intrigued observers of the American political and governmental scene: Why and how, in its policy-making processes, does the United States government alternate between spurts of creative energy and longer periods of deadlock and relative inaction? What lies behind the cyclical character of the political and governmental system?

To examine this question, James L. Sundquist has combined case study techniques with those of more general analysis. He has analyzed the response of political and governmental institutions to the major domestic issues of a fourteen-year period, from 1953 through 1966. Within that period—which covers one complete phase of the political cycle, from a peak of Republican strength in 1953 to a peak of Democratic strength in 1966—he observes the workings of the government under the leadership of three presidents, Dwight D. Eisenhower, John F. Kennedy, and Lyndon B. Johnson.

Part I presents the case histories of six problem areas—unemployment, poverty, education, civil rights, medicare, and the outdoor environment—and traces the institutional responses to the issues raised. Part II then synthesizes the findings and analyzes the performance of the party system, the electoral process, and the legislative processes of both the executive branch and the Congress.

Mr. Sundquist's study was planned and initiated under the guidance of George A. Graham, former Director of Governmental Studies at Brookings. Valuable suggestions were received from Gilbert Y. Steiner, Dr. Graham's successor, and from Stephen Horn and Herbert Kaufman, who read the entire manuscript. Many persons read and commented upon sin-

vii

gle chapters or sections, and in particular verified or corrected the narrative data.

The Brookings Institution and Mr. Sundquist are especially grateful to the organizations that made source materials for the study available—the Dwight D. Eisenhower Library at Abilene, Kansas; the Roper Center for Public Opinion Research at Williams College; the American Institute of Public Opinion at Princeton, New Jersey; the Survey Research Center at the University of Michigan; the United States Senate library in Washington; and a number of government agencies that permitted access to their legislative files.

Sandra Bennett undertook the basic research and prepared the initial draft of one chapter. Constance Holden carried out research assignments and provided secretarial services. The book was edited and the index prepared by Alice M. Carroll.

The conclusions expressed are those of the author and do not necessarily represent those of the trustees, the officers, or other staff members of the Brookings Institution.

KERMIT GORDON
President

July 1968
Washington, D.C.

Contents

Politics and Policy

of beautiful cities, and the advancement of knowledge."[8] Adlai Stevenson spoke of "the contrast between private opulence and public squalor," of "the shame of racial discrimination," of "urban decay and congestion," of the knowledge that "behind the shining child in the advertisement lurks the juvenile delinquent in the run-down slum."[9]

Some of the writers in that election year looked hopefully toward November. "We are waiting to be shown the way into the future," said Lippmann. "We are waiting for another innovator in the line of the two Roosevelts and Wilson."[10] James Reston put it in even plainer language: "The president of the United States is the one man who can get the attention of the American people. If he says the nation is in trouble, they will listen to him. . . . All the magazine articles on the national purpose, all the reports by all the foundations on all our manifold weaknesses . . . all the exhortations to return to the faith of our fathers—all are nothing compared to serious programs eloquently expressed and strongly pushed by a determined president of the United States."[11]

That winter, a new President took office—a determined President, surely, and one with "serious programs eloquently expressed." Yet more than two years after President Kennedy's inauguration, James MacGregor Burns could still write of "deadlock" as the normal state of American politics, broken only by brief intervals of activity. Said Burns:

> We are at the critical stage of a somber and inexorable cycle that seems to have gripped the public affairs of the nation. We are mired in governmental deadlock, as Congress blocks or kills not only most of Mr. Kennedy's bold proposals of 1960, but many planks of the Republican platform as well. Soon we will be caught in the politics of drift, as the nation's politicians put off major decisions until after the presidential campaign of 1964. Then we can expect a period of decision, as the voters choose a President, followed by a brief phase of the "politics of the deed," as the President capitalizes on the psychological thrust of his election mandate to put through some bits and pieces of his program. But after the short honeymoon between Congress and President the old cycle of deadlock and drift will reassert itself.[12]

Burns' prophecy proved too somber. By 1965, far more than "bits and pieces" of the President's program had been enacted. What happened? What broke the deadlock? One can identify two accidents of history that

[8] *Ibid.*, p. 133.
[9] *Ibid.*, p. 27.
[10] *Ibid.*, p. 127.
[11] *Ibid.*, pp. 112–13.
[12] *The Deadlock of Democracy* (Prentice-Hall, 1963), p. 2.

intervened—first, an assassination; second, a landslide presidential election that destroyed the normal balance of the two parties in the Congress. But is the American system of government so constructed that it must depend upon tragedy and political happenstance to render it capable of responding decisively to the nation's problems? Is the American constitutional system, bequeathed to the twentieth century by the eighteenth, so shackled with checks and balances that "deadlock and drift" are the normal and inevitable order? Or did the productive period of 1964–65 leave a legacy of institutional change that will make the system permanently more productive?

These are the questions that gave rise to this book. It was conceived and begun in 1965, the year of euphoria, against the background of the gloom and anxiety of the earlier years. How are national decisions made, in the American system? What is the capacity of the United States government to respond to national needs? How, indeed, should it respond? Is responsiveness to be judged solely on the basis of whether one likes or dislikes the governmental policies that are established, or are there objective criteria that can be applied in appraising a democratic political system?

To shed light upon these questions, I have chosen to examine the workings of the American system in response to certain specific national problems during a span of fourteen years, from 1953 through 1966. The issues are those that appeared to reflect the most pressing concerns of the people, as measured by the urgency and continuity of public and governmental attention, and that led to major innovations in national policy. They are six in number:

1. Jobs for the unemployed.
2. Opportunity for the poor.
3. Schools for the young.
4. Civil rights for minorities.
5. Health care for the aged.
6. Protection and enhancement of the outdoor environment.

These six issues have common characteristics that make them, collectively, a unified field of study. In each area, major new departures in national policy were initiated, refined, advanced, deadlocked, sometimes compromised, but ultimately adopted. In each area, then, the "deadlock of democracy" can be observed—first, as it developed; second, as it dissolved. Each of the issues arose from a fundamental need felt by a large segment of the population and, for that reason, became a *public* issue in the broadest sense of the term. Each engaged the organs of public opinion and citizen "public interest groups." Each was at or near the center of the policy-making processes of the executive and legislative branches; each received the personal attention of presidents and the active consideration of the whole membership of the Congress; each was an issue in political campaigns.

The list excludes, of course, a large part of the range of national policy. It omits issues where forces and events outside the country were the spur to action—foreign relations, national defense, and space exploration. It omits issues that arose primarily from the efforts of particular economic groups to improve their status in relation to other groups—issues of labor legislation, agricultural policy, aid to small business, regulation or subsidization of transportation. It excludes issues that were at the edge rather than in the center of the public debate of the period, as well as those concerned with enlargement or extension of established policies—increases in social security benefits, for example, or the raising of the minimum wage—rather than establishment of policies essentially new in character. Finally, it excludes consideration of certain problems, like "law and order," that welled up toward the end of the fourteen-year period but had not, by the close of the period, led to decisive action.

The period 1953 through 1966 covers a range of political climates and alignments—two years of Republican ascendancy, six years when the Republicans controlled the executive branch but the Democrats organized Congress, and six years of Democratic control of both branches. It extends through one clear phase of the American political cycle, beginning when the fortunes of one party—the Republican—were at their highest point in a generation and ending with the close of the Congress that represented a peak in the other party's strength. It covers periods of action and of relative inaction. The year 1953 is an appropriate starting point for another reason—it marks the year of transition between a time when the country was preoccupied with war, reconversion, and war again and a time when the country could turn once more to a consideration of its domestic ills. And the year 1966, as it happens, may have marked the end of that period of relative tranquility.

Part I presents, in seven chapters (two deal with unemployment), a narrative account of the way in which the country's political and governmental institutions responded to the six selected problems—how the problem was identified, how the remedial measures were developed and refined, how support and opposition were mobilized, how the parties and the politicians and private organizations conducted the national debate, and how that debate was finally resolved. The chain of events is recorded not only as a basis for the analyses in Part II, but also, as with all case studies, to provide data useful for analysis by others. Where possible, I have relied on earlier case studies of particular legislative events by political scientists or journalists. Where these did not exist—and they are all too few—I have made my own, less intensive case study, drawing upon public documents, journals of the period, government agency files and private papers, and more than one hundred interviews.[13] In some cases the narrative suffers from the inaccessibility of data; the complete record awaits the release of many papers still withheld from the public, the writing of memoirs, and the completion of such undertakings as the oral history projects of the Eisenhower and Kennedy libraries and eventually of the Johnson library.

In the narrative chapters, I have given the polemics of partisanship a prominence that some readers, I am sure, will feel they do not deserve. But while the language of politicians may embody hyperbole and outright inaccuracy—as well as insight and wisdom—the former as well as the latter are significant. It is in their own language, not in the restrained vocabulary of the experts, that politicians communicate with one another and with the electorate from whom they receive their mandates, and it is through the political processes that national policy is made. My purpose has been to trace the course of the policy and *political* debate that led to the ultimate national *political* decision—not to judge, at each stage of that debate, who was right and who was wrong.

Part II attempts to identify the patterns of policy formation to be found in the narrative data of Part I, and to analyze the role of particular governmental and political institutions in the policy-making process.

In democratic theory, the process by which a government responds to a problem is a simple one. Those among its citizens who advocate a course of action to cope with the problem organize for the purpose, through the mechanism of a political party. They present their solution to the people in an election. If they win, they have a mandate—and enact their program.

The narrative studies of Part I reveal, perhaps surprisingly, that amid all the complexity of politics and government in a vast nation with an enormous range of problems this simple process is still discernible. In the 1950's activist politicians, working in alliance with organizations out-

---

[13] These interviews were usually conducted on a "not for attribution" basis. Throughout this book, where sources are not indicated for information not available in published form, the confidential interview can be assumed to be the source.

side the government, *did* develop a program aimed at the solution of the country's major identified domestic problems, and with the Democratic party as their instrument in most cases, organized to present that program to the people. The Democrats received the electoral mandate. Then—after some delay—they enacted the program.

The first three chapters of Part II discuss the process, in these three stages. Chapter 9 reviews the response of the two major parties to the domestic issues as a group and examines particularly the mechanisms by which the Democratic party, during the Eisenhower years, assembled its party program. Chapter 10 explores the evidence from public opinion data as to the impact of the Democratic program, in its elements and as a whole, upon the outcome of the three elections that restored the Democrats to power—those of 1954, 1958, and 1960. Chapter 11 then analyzes the workings of the institutional system in enactment of the program.

There remains the question of criteria by which the policy-making process should be judged. Granted that the government did respond, during 1964 and 1965, to the problems identified earlier, did it respond quickly enough and smoothly enough, particularly in the Kennedy and Johnson years when the electorate had, presumably, given its mandate for action to the Democrats? Every democratic government seeks to strike a balance between the opposing principles of action and restraint, of innovation and stability. Incapacity to act can destroy governments, but so can rash and imprudent action; and minorities as well as majorities must be protected. Of all major democratic governments in the world, however, the United States government is the one that gives to minorities in the legislative process the most devices by which to obstruct and thwart majorities. One's judgment about those devices must rest upon one's view as to where the greater danger lies, in the long run—whether in a potential incapacity of government to act quickly and decisively or in the possibility that it may overact. For both groups, Chapter 12 discusses the major institutional obstacles that delayed the response of government to its domestic problems in the period covered by this study. For those who fear impulsiveness in government more than they fear lethargy, the bulwarks against action are described; for those (among whom I count myself) who fear most the incapacity of government to act, suggestions for weakening those bulwarks are reviewed.

Finally, it should be observed that the capacity of a government to make policy decisions is only one dimension of its capacity to govern. Other dimensions are substantive and administrative—the policies must be appropriate to the solution of the problems with which they deal, and they must be made effective through adequate appropriations and competent administration. This study does not attempt to deal with the latter two dimensions. As for substance, my object has been to trace the development of policies that appear *reasonably calculated* to solve, or lead to the solution of, the problem in question—not to pass judgment on whether they will in fact do so (although, at the conclusion of some of the narrative chapters, I have not refrained from introducing evidence that bears upon such a judgment). What is basic, after all, is the capacity to make the initial policy departure. In most of the fields of policy covered by this book, the initial action is not of a kind that is irreversible; if the capacity to make policy exists, then the capacity also exists to unmake or modify decisions that prove unwise. As for administration, there are many signs that the capacity of the United States government to make policies and establish programs in the domestic field has outrun its capacity, or its determination, to finance and administer them. This question, too, must be left to other studies. But again, it is the capacity to make the policy that is the basic dimension of capacity to govern. Administrative competence can make or break a national decision, but unless the decision can be made in the first place, the ability to make that decision effective cannot even be tested.

PART I

The Issues

CHAPTER II

For the Unemployed, Jobs:
An Activist Fiscal Policy

"WE HAVE PLEDGED OURSELVES," said the Senator from Illinois, "not to permit the great human suffering in the past which has accompanied economic recessions, panics, and depressions, by acting to prevent or to stop these economic maladjustments before they became too severe."

As Democrat Paul H. Douglas spoke[1]—in June 1958—one of every fourteen Americans in the labor force was unemployed. The country was mired in the third economic recession since World War II, and measured by that revealing index of human suffering—unemployment—this one was the worst. Not since the Great Depression of the 1930's had the American economy performed so badly.

Senator Douglas pleaded for an immediate temporary tax cut of $6 billion as the quickest way to create jobs for the five million men and women then out of work. But when the roll was called at the end of the afternoon's debate, only twenty-two senators stood with him. He was beaten, 65–23. Those who argued that it would be "fiscally irresponsible" to cut taxes at a time when the budget was already out of balance prevailed.

Yet, on February 7, 1964—less than six years later—seventy-seven senators voted for a tax cut almost twice as large, one that would be continuing instead of temporary, at a time when unemployment was less severe than in 1958 and the national budget even more heavily in the red. For the first time in history, the Congress in a period of relative prosperity

[1] *Cong. Record,* Vol. 104 (June 18, 1958), p. 11574.

13

created a substantial budgetary deficit as a deliberate, conscious step to put idle men and productive facilities to work and stimulate economic expansion. The phrase "fiscal responsibility" was given a meaning directly opposite to the sense it had conveyed in all the previous decades.

By 1965 the sponsors of that tax reduction were acclaiming it an unqualified success. The revenue reduction *had* stimulated the economy. It had increased production. It had helped to reduce unemployment to the lowest level in eight years. And the promised miracle of government finance had occurred—the government was actually collecting more revenue under the lower tax rates than it had a year earlier under the higher schedules. Secretary of Labor W. Willard Wirtz could confidently proclaim the tax cut "the ultimate triumph of the spirit of John Maynard Keynes over the stubborn shade of Adam Smith."[2]

Whether the triumph proved to be "ultimate" or not, it was clearly an historic victory for the practitioners of "the new economics"—a school of economic thought that traces its lineage and its inspiration to Keynes.[3] And it climaxed an economic policy debate between politicians of the two parties that had been carried on incessantly for a decade.

Since the electoral upheavals of the 1930's, few politicians have doubted the potency of unemployment as a political issue. In the 1946 postwar election, and again in 1952, it became clear that inflation also could sway a multitude of voters. The people hold the party in power responsible, the election returns showed, for steering the economy successfully between the shoals of recession or depression and the rocks of inflation. The party out of power can always be expected to stand in waiting, then, to exploit any veering of the economy from a steady course.

In the decade of the 1950's, it was unemployment that became the

[2] Commencement address, University of Iowa, June 4, 1965.

[3] The "new economics" was defined as follows by one of its critics, Raymond J. Saulnier, chairman of President Eisenhower's Council of Economic Advisers (CEA) from 1957 to 1960: ". . . the point of view, and the analysis underlying it, that the growth of the American economy in the last few years has been due not just primarily, but to all intents and purposes exclusively, to the aggressive use of fiscal policy and to a more or less continuously easy monetary policy, with attendant large increases in the use of credit. Fiscal and monetary expansionism is a perfectly good alternative term for it" (speech delivered June 24, 1965; reprinted in *Cong. Record*, Vol. 111 [July 9, 1965], p. 16299). Walter W. Heller, chairman of the CEA under Presidents Kennedy and Johnson, has pointed out that the term "new economics" relates not to a new body of doctrine but to "the swift and progressive weaving of modern economics into the fabric of national thinking and policy" (*New Dimensions of Political Economy* [Harvard University Press, 1966], Preface).

crucial economic issue. In two recessions, in 1953–54 and 1957–58, unemployment rose sharply above its previous levels—accompanied, of course, by fear of unemployment among many of those still employed, by lowered business profits, and by a slackening of growth throughout the economy. The Democrats, as the out-party, responded with vociferous demands for governmental action, if not with an agreed party position as to just what the course of action ought to be. Flailed by the opposition for "inaction," the Republican administration inevitably reacted by denouncing the Democratic proposals as overaction—as threatening the country with inflation. One party hurled the charge of "callousness" toward the unemployed; the other replied with accusations of "profligacy," "recklessness," and "waste." The shrill language may have been confined to the political arena, but in more temperate terms the editorial columns and the scholarly journals carried on the same debate—a debate that continued into the campaign of 1960. After the election of that year, the crucial discussions were those that went on within the Kennedy administration, as to the nature and timing of expansionary measures. Eventually the President cast his lot with the activists on fiscal policy, and the tax reduction act was recommended and adopted.

This chapter is an account of the political struggles over fiscal policy in the Eisenhower, Kennedy, and Johnson years, culminating in enactment of the Revenue Act of 1964. Governmental response to the unemployment problem through structural measures is reviewed in Chapter 3.

Fiscal Orthodoxy: The First Test   *(1953–54)*

To Dwight D. Eisenhower, the landslide election of November 1952 was a resounding mandate for fiscal orthodoxy—which, to Eisenhower, meant a reduction in governmental spending and in taxes, a balanced budget, and an end to "Democratic" inflation. As a candidate, he had made the Democratic record on fiscal policy a central issue of his campaign. In his opening speech at Abilene, he later wrote, "I put myself on record as an enemy of inflation and expressed the conviction that excessive taxation could destroy the incentive to excel."[4] To dramatize the inflation issue in the campaign, he displayed to his audiences a length of board, then broke off two pre-sawed pieces to represent the decline in buying power of the

---

[4] Dwight D. Eisenhower, *Mandate for Change* (Doubleday, 1963), p. 33.

dollar that had occurred since 1945 and that would "probably" occur in eight more Democratic years. "We expended a large pile of lumber in this lesson," he recalled, "but the point got across."⁵ When he assumed office, he said, "there was no one among my immediate associates not dedicated, in principle, to the proposition that both federal expenditures and the public debt must be reduced."⁶

The termination of active fighting in Korea gave them their opportunity. There were those who warned that the "danger signals" of recession were already flying, but the administration was more concerned at that time with reducing expenditures, as the precursor to a tax cut, and with putting a damper on inflationary pressures.⁷ A sharp reduction in military expenditures was ordered—and the pessimists proved correct. The economy slid into its second recession since World War II.⁸

The decline began in midsummer 1953. The Treasury and the Federal Reserve System had already acted to ease credit. On September 25, Arthur F. Burns, chairman of the Council of Economic Advisers, warned the

---

⁵ *Ibid.*, p. 127.

⁶ *Ibid.*

⁷ *Cong. Record,* Vol. 99 (March 12, 1953), p. 1906. Chairman Daniel A. Reed (Republican of New York) of the House Ways and Means Committee warned of recession danger in arguing for a tax cut in mid-1953. Sherman Adams, chief of Eisenhower's White House staff, later remarked that Secretary of the Treasury George M. Humphrey "was more interested at that particular time in putting a damper on spiraling inflation" (*Firsthand Report* [Harper, 1961], p. 160).

⁸ There appears to be wide agreement that the principal cause of the 1953–54 recession was the abrupt reduction in military expenditures. President Eisenhower reported that "the contraction reflected the efforts of businessmen to reduce inventories, and was aggravated by a large reduction in military expenditures" (*Economic Report of the President, January 1955,* p. iv). Alvin H. Hansen wrote: "The 1954 recession . . . was due almost entirely to the drop in government expenditures incident to the cessation of the Korean conflict. The decline in government outlays . . . in real terms amounted to $10.9 billion" (*Economic Issues of the 1960's* [McGraw-Hill, 1960], p. 146). Bert G. Hickman concluded that "the cutback in federal spending was the major deflationary force acting throughout the contraction"; he computed the drop in federal purchases at $12 billion between the second quarters of 1953 and 1954 (*Growth and Stability of the Postwar Economy* [Brookings Institution, 1960], p. 99). Wilfred Lewis, Jr., reached the same conclusion that spending reductions were "a major—if not the major—cause"; he notes that the Bureau of the Budget and the Labor Department in their internal memoranda anticipated the possibility of a downturn as military expenditures were reduced (*Federal Fiscal Policy in the Postwar Recessions* [Brookings Institution, 1962], pp. 182–83, 138–40). Sherman Adams placed more emphasis on credit policy: "The public finger was pointed at George Humphrey's attempt to tighten credit . . . a little too much. . . . The crisis passed, but it left its mark as an error in Humphrey's fiscal calculation. . . ." (*Firsthand Report,* p. 161).

Cabinet that while the situation was not critical, planning should be undertaken as a precaution against further decline. In the privacy of his Cabinet meetings, Eisenhower quickly abandoned the language of orthodoxy. The Republican party must be ready to use the full power of the government if necessary, he said, to prevent "another 1929."[9] And on November 18, when the recession was first mentioned in a presidential news conference, Eisenhower repeated his statement publicly: "When it becomes clear that the Government has to step in, as far as I am concerned, the full power of Government, of Government credit, and of everything the Government has will move in to see that there is no widespread unemployment. . . ."[10]

As the winter advanced, unemployment mounted. By February 1954 it had reached 5.8 percent of the labor force, with two million more persons unemployed than had been out of work the previous winter. Both Sherman Adams and Robert Donovan, in their accounts of this period, draw a picture of a President and an administration maintaining a constant vigil over the economic indicators, with intensive planning going on throughout the government under the supervision of CEA Chairman Burns. Adams describes Eisenhower as "ready to launch a public works program to ease unemployment if the emergency became dangerous" and reports that planning for a massive public works program went ahead.[11] Donovan was impressed with the "striking picture of a President and his government grappling with trouble in a vast, complicated economy."[12]

No massive spending programs were launched. Temporary income and excess profits taxes levied during the Korean emergency had already been scheduled, fortuitously, to expire on December 31 and the administration had recommended a tax reform measure that would bring the total revenue loss to $5.1 billion. Credit had been eased. Under these circumstances, the administration concluded that no decisive antirecession spending measures were necessary. A speedup of already authorized spending was finally ordered in a Cabinet meeting on May 14, 1954, but was not publicly announced, and Wilfred Lewis' analysis concludes that it could have had no significant fiscal impact until the October–December quarter of 1954, when recovery was already well underway. As he notes, the spending

[9] Eisenhower, *Mandate for Change*, p. 304; Robert J. Donovan, *Eisenhower: The Inside Story* (Harper, 1956), p. 209.
[10] *Public Papers of the Presidents, 1953*, p. 785.
[11] Adams, *Firsthand Report*, pp. 162–64.
[12] Donovan, *Eisenhower*, p. 213.

speedup order was not even mentioned in the recital of government anti-recession actions contained in the 1955 economic report of the President.[13]

To those inside the administration, the government's response to the winter unemployment crisis appeared, in Donovan's words, as one of "deep concern but not fright, of urgency but not rashness, of patience but not complacence, of a willingness to act if necessary, but a determination not to be stampeded."[14] Adams remarks approvingly that "there were no signs of panic around the Cabinet table," that Eisenhower "was unmoved by a call from Walter Reuther for a national conference on unemployment and by a demand for government action from a group of Democrats led by Senator Paul H. Douglas of Illinois." "That summer," he adds, "just as Eisenhower, Humphrey and Burns had predicted . . . the recession clouds blew away without . . . pump priming."[15] By October, unemployment had fallen to 2.7 million from its winter peak of 3.7 million.

But a skilful economic performance may be one thing and a skilful political performance quite another. What may appear from the inside as calm alertness amid crisis may look, to those affected by unemployment, like placidity or even unconcern in the face of human suffering. The Democrats were bound to seize the opportunity to remind the country, sometimes subtly and often less so, that the party Eisenhower led was, after all, "the party of depression." Concerned with stifling the alarmists and maintaining the confidence of businessmen in the economy, Eisenhower gave no public emphasis to the planning underway in his administration; his public stance was consistently, if often cautiously, optimistic. And the more his political opponents demanded action, the more Eisenhower by contrast appeared to be doing nothing at all. In the January 1954 economic report, prepared by Burns and his colleagues, the President acknowledged a "slight contraction in business" but predicted no "serious interruption" in economic growth.[16] On February 1, Eisenhower coldly rejected the proposal of Walter Reuther, president of the United Automobile Workers, for a national conference on unemployment and, in

[13] The administration's actions in countering the 1953–54 recession are reviewed in Edward S. Flash, Jr., *Economic Advice and Presidential Leadership* (Columbia University Press, 1965), Chap. 5, and in Lewis, *Federal Fiscal Policy*, pp. 142–70; Lewis also analyzes their fiscal impact (*ibid.*, pp. 177–87). See also *Economic Report of the President, January 1955*, pp. 18–20, and Arthur F. Burns, *Prosperity without Inflation* (Fordham University Press, 1957), pp. 30–31.

[14] *Eisenhower*, p. 213.

[15] *Firsthand Report*, pp. 163, 164. The reference is to Treasury Secretary Humphrey.

[16] *Economic Report of the President, January 1954*, pp. iv–v.

effect, rebuked Reuther for a lack of "confidence" and "perspective."[17] In a television speech on April 5 he disparaged talk about unemployment and declared he did "not intend to go into any slambang emergency program unless it is necessary." On May 5 he cautioned against overoptimism but found the economic outlook preponderantly favorable. On June 2, when a news correspondent quoted Sumner Schlichter, the Harvard economist, as saying that the executive branch had shown "a surprising lack of initiative and enterprise in fighting the recession," Eisenhower mildly referred his questions to "the chief of my economic advisers" to "get his side of the story." In August, with recovery underway but unemployment still at 5 percent—two million above the previous summer—he flew to the home state of Senator Douglas, then campaigning for reelection, to pointedly denounce the "prophets of gloom and doom."[18]

Other Republican spokesmen were less restrained in their response to Democratic prodding. House Speaker Joseph W. Martin, Jr., of Massachusetts attacked "left-wing eggheads" trying to "yell the country into a recession."[19] Representative Charles G. Oakman of a Detroit suburban district saw behind the clamor a communist plot: "We do know that there are those few within our shores who are happy at any time to do the bidding of the Russian masters." And he quoted Representative Jesse P. Wolcott of Michigan, the Republican chairman of the House Banking and Currency Committee, as saying that a "stabilization recession" was necessary.[20] Representative Carl T. Curtis of Nebraska told the House that "these calamitous speeches constitute a political conspiracy to throw the country into a depression."[21] And Defense Secretary Charles E. Wilson chose this as the year, and the labor stronghold of Detroit as the place, to compare unemployed workers to "kennel dogs."[22]

For its part, the Democratic opposition had nothing that could be called an antirecession program. Individual senators and congressmen variously advocated public works, tax reductions, cheaper money, broader social security, antimonopoly measures, housing bills, labor legislation, and miscellaneous other actions in a babel of voices and proposals. Perhaps the nearest thing to a party fiscal policy was the proposal for a $5 billion individual income tax cut advanced by seven Democratic members of the

[17] *Public Papers of the Presidents, 1954*, pp. 234–35.
[18] *Ibid.*, pp. 380, 456–57, 529–30, 732.
[19] Quoted by J. A. Livingston, *Washington Post*, Jan. 28, 1954.
[20] *Cong. Record*, Vol. 100 (Jan. 20 and 28, 1954), pp. 563, 970.
[21] *Ibid.* (Feb. 25, 1954), p. 2280.
[22] See Adams, *Firsthand Report*, p. 165, and Eisenhower, *Mandate for Change*, p. 437.

Joint Economic Committee in February 1954, but the party debate on the tax question subsequently centered not on fiscal policy as such but on the Democratic efforts to convert what they called a "rich man's tax bill" into one channeling greater benefits to lower-income groups. The out-party, however, can have a campaign issue without a program of its own; it can simply attack an attitude, as Adlai E. Stevenson did at the climax of the 1954 campaign: ". . . the election of a Democratic Congress on Tuesday . . . will chasten the administration's complacent attitude toward the millions of Americans who cannot find jobs."[23]

The Democratic Congress was elected. The party gained from the Republicans a net of two seats in the Senate and sixteen in the House, winning control of both bodies. Were the voters seeking to chasten the administration on the issue of unemployment? Or was the midterm loss of congressional seats merely the "normal" swing away from the party in power? The available survey data (which are assembled in Chapter 10) indicate that a decisive shift in voter sentiment occurred when the recession hit its low point in early 1954, and that the voters who then expressed their discontent to the pollsters did not return to the Republican side. Vice President Richard M. Nixon, reporting to the Cabinet after the election, said "such factors as unemployment in the coal fields" were among those contributing to the Republican defeat. When the test came, the principles of fiscal orthodoxy had been, at least tacitly, set aside. But in this case words may have been spoken louder than action. When one considers the narrow margins by which the Democrats captured Republican Senate seats in states that had experienced heavy unemployment (Senator Richard L. Neuberger won in Oregon by only 2,500 votes, Senator Patrick V. McNamara in Michigan by fewer than 40,000), it is hard not to conjecture that a more vigorous Republican show of concern with the unemployment problem during the winter of 1954—even if it were not accompanied by more aggressive action—would have enabled them to retain the majority of the Senate, at least, in the Congress that convened in January 1955.

Fiscal Orthodoxy: The Second Test   *(1957–58)*

The second, and sterner, test of fiscal orthodoxy came almost exactly four years later—coinciding by happenstance with another midterm congressional election. The contraction of 1957–58 was deeper, albeit shorter,

[23] Speech at Cooper Union, New York City, Oct. 30, 1954; reprinted in *What I Think* (Harper, 1956), p. 92.

than that of 1953–54. Between October 1957 and February 1958 unemployment more than doubled; in February it exceeded five million for the first time since the 1930's—7.7 percent of the labor force.[24]

The Democratic attack was bolder, sharper, and more confident than in 1954. As early as October 1957 the Democratic Advisory Council assailed "the theory, popular in Republican circles, that a little depression is a good thing."[25] On January 31, 1958, Senator Hubert H. Humphrey of Minnesota referred on the Senate floor to "the planned, premeditated, predesigned recession of this administration."[26] Senator Albert Gore of Tennessee, upon returning from a trip to Memphis, introduced a public works bill patterned on legislation of the 1930's and passionately told the Senate: "I have seen thousands of my fellow Tennesseeans, able-bodied men who want to earn a living, standing for hours in the cold to obtain a small allotment of surplus food commodities. That is a danger signal . . . I believe that this society of ours owes an opportunity for work to able-bodied men and women who want to work and earn their daily bread. . . . I am apprehensive that this situation may be galloping. I want Government to move, and to use its great resources to forestall a possible catastrophe."[27]

Next day, Senator McNamara declared that "if this is a 'recession as planned,' then someone is guilty of treason."[28] On February 10, Senator John A. Carroll, Colorado Democrat, quoted Federal Reserve Board Chairman William McChesney Martin, Jr., as saying that the recession was "deeper and sharper" than had been "anticipated."[29] On March 6 Senator Humphrey laid before the Senate a series of comments by columnists and administration spokesmen suggesting that the administration had consciously risked recession in its determination to moderate the inflation of 1957. "The administration's recession blueprint has come

[24] Seasonally adjusted, the percentage was 6.7 compared to 4.7 in October and a low of 3.9 in March 1957. However, the unadjusted figure more accurately reflects the actual hardship that gives rise to political reactions.

[25] Press release, Oct. 20, 1957. The council, formed in 1957 to coordinate the party's policy positions, is discussed in Chap. 9.

[26] *Cong. Record,* Vol. 104 (Jan. 31, 1958), p. 1446.

[27] *Ibid.* (Feb. 5, 1958), pp. 1721–22.

[28] *Ibid.,* p. 1828. The reference was to a comment in *Time* (Dec. 30, 1957, pp. 53, 55): "Many business men received the dip at year's end without alarm because they regarded it as a 'recession as planned.' . . . Though no one wants unemployment, coldly statistical economists can find some virtue in it, expect the U.S. to benefit through increased productivity. . . . Moreover, as jobs grow scarcer, wages will flatten out."

[29] *Cong. Record,* Vol. 104 (Feb. 5, 1958), p. 1951.

into full flower. . . . I trust that the Republican Party is pleased at its success," Humphrey said, and added: "The administration continues to sit on its collective hands."[30]

The administration did little to dispel the picture of complacency Senator Humphrey drew. As its economists read the indicators, no emergency fiscal measures were necessary—at least, not yet. They were convinced that the administration had been right in 1954—the economy had turned upward and recovered rapidly without the kind of "slambang emergency program" President Eisenhower had at that time condemned. If they could again weather the cries of alarm, they were confident of a similar upturn in 1958, possibly in the spring, without any massive new expenditures or cut in taxes. For the administration to "panic" or "get hysterical" would only jeopardize the public confidence necessary to assure recovery.[31]

Moreover, the struggle against inflation of only a year before was still fresh in the minds of responsible officials, and they took the long view that to overreact against the current downturn would be to store up trouble for later years. President Eisenhower, when asked about a tax cut at his news conference of February 5, acknowledged that it would be a stimulus to the economy but added: "On the other hand, this is something you can take hold of and, going too far with trying to fool with our economy, then you get something else started. And you just remember, all of you here a year ago, how we were always talking about inflation and the things we were trying to study."[32] In a speech to a Republican dinner in Chicago two weeks earlier he had denounced inflation as "one of the most sinister threats to prosperity" while not even mentioning recession or unemployment.[33]

Thus the Democrats were left free to ring the alarm and appear as the party of initiative and action. While denouncing Republican "inaction," they offered a rash of specific measures, as various as in 1954—tax reduction, public works, easier housing credit, liberalized unemployment compensation, increases in minimum wages and farm price supports, depressed areas legislation, and so on. But individual bills, sponsored by

[30] *Ibid.* (March 6, 1958), pp. 3578–83.

[31] This was the theme of a review of the economic situation by three Eisenhower Cabinet members with the Republican congressional leadership; see "Memorandum for the Record," Feb. 18, 1958, papers of Bryce N. Harlow (in Dwight D. Eisenhower Library, Abilene, Kan.).

[32] *Public Papers of the Presidents, 1958,* p. 147.

[33] *Ibid.,* p. 115.

individual senators or representatives, did not constitute a program. The Democrats had no party antirecession program nor even any machinery for making one. Activist senators from states with heavy unemployment pressed Senate Majority Leader Lyndon B. Johnson to take the lead, but he was caught between them and their organized labor and liberal allies, on the one side, and, on the other, the conservative committee chairmen upon whom he had to depend for legislative results. Moreover, he was evidently reluctant to take a highly partisan stand that would damage his image as a responsible and constructive legislative leader collaborating with the White House on measures for the good of the country. This posture had won Johnson and his fellow Texan, House Speaker Sam Rayburn, wide acclaim, particularly on foreign policy measures.

Under the pressure of an emergency legislative conference the AFL-CIO had called to convene in Washington a few days later, Johnson took the Senate floor on March 6 to explain his position: "I am aided by a cabinet made up of committee chairmen. I have conferred with them. I think they will expedite action." Specifically, he had talked to the chairmen about expediting reclamation, acquisition of stockpile materials, hospital construction, defense procurement, highway construction, housing, flood control, and farm legislation. But he refused to identify himself with those who demanded decisive, immediate action. On public works, he favored planning, so that "if the facts which will emerge later in the spring or in the summer or next fall indicate a need for a large public works program, something sensible and effective will be ready." On a tax cut, he had talked to many persons, including Henry Ford, II, who favored an emergency reduction measure, but he himself had not "reached a firm conclusion." A tax reduction measure would, in any case, originate in the House. But he predicted the economy would improve. "The reason it is going to get better is that in partnership the Congress and the Executive can march hand in hand to face up to the problem."[34]

Before that afternoon was over, however, Johnson had developed a plan calculated to appease his northern colleagues without disturbing his southern chairmen—and with probably no more than slight damage to the congressional-executive "partnership." He introduced, with the co-sponsorship of forty-six Democrats (of a possible fifty) and nineteen Republicans, two resolutions calling upon the President to accelerate all civil and military construction projects within the limits of existing au-

[34] *Cong. Record*, Vol. 104 (March 6, 1958), pp. 3509–11.

thority and appropriations. In introducing the measure, he said: "Congress is not the action arm of the government. We can grant authority and we can make appropriations. But we cannot administer the laws. . . . We can, however, express our feeling. . . ." "This is effective leadership," observed Hubert Humphrey. "This is action."[35]

Obviously stung by the resolution, with its implied criticism from Republicans as well as Democrats, the President dispatched a letter on March 8 to the minority leaders, Senator William F. Knowland of California and Representative Joseph Martin, saying, in effect, that the administration had already done what the resolution called for.[36] The budget director, he said, had directed federal agencies to "accelerate where practicable the construction of projects for which appropriated funds were available," which would advance the expenditure of nearly $200 million. He detailed a number of other steps already taken or in preparation, including release of $200 million for housing loans. But since the timing of these actions was left ambiguous and the administration had not bothered to bring them to public attention previously, the implication remained that whatever the administration was doing was in fact a response to the Johnson initiative. Thus the *New York Times* correspondent wrote that the Democratic proposals "got a jump on the administration which is preparing a proposal with the same objective."[37]

Moreover, the President took the occasion to play down his actions by warning the Congress against going too far. "The course of our huge, complex economy," he wrote, "mainly depends upon what individual citizens do. . . . The proper relation of government to the growth and vigor of such an economy must necessarily be to stimulate private production and employment, not to substitute public spending for private spending, not to extend public domination over private activity. I am concerned over the sudden upsurge of pump-priming schemes, such as the setting up of huge federal bureaucracies of the PWA or the WPA type."[38]

Retorted Johnson: "The President's recommendations for . . . pump-priming will be carefully examined."[39]

In one instance where Democratic activists happened to be in control of committee machinery, a $1 billion spending bill was conceived, ap-

[35] *Ibid.*, pp. 3570, 3573.
[36] *Public Papers of the Presidents, 1958*, pp. 208–11.
[37] March 7, 1958.
[38] *Public Papers of the Presidents, 1958*, pp. 208–11.
[39] *Acceleration of Public Works Programs,* Hearings before the Senate Public Works Committee, 85 Cong. 2 sess. (March 10, 1958), p. 4.

proved by both houses, and enacted in less than five weeks. Senator John J. Sparkman and Representative Albert Rains, the Alabama Democrats who chaired the two housing subcommittees, collaborated on a "quickie" housing bill whose principal provision authorized $1 billion in the equivalent of direct government loans at favorable terms for houses with mortgages up to $13,500. Senator Sparkman introduced the bill on February 27, held brief hearings March 4, reported the measure March 12, and passed it through the Senate by unanimous vote the same day. The House passed it March 19 and President Eisenhower reluctantly signed it April 1. In a statement, the President condemned the $1 billion lending program as simply substituting federal financing for funds that private investors would be willing to invest if the Congress would permit the interest rate on guaranteed mortgages to rise. He indicated he was accepting the bill because of other provisions that were in accord with his policies.[40]

The Johnson resolutions to expedite authorized public works were passed by both houses virtually without dissent, after the Republicans were appeased with an added sentence commending the administration for its antirecession actions. The Congress also agreed to expedite highway construction. But, beyond that, the Democratic Congress enacted none of the main emergency public works measures advanced by various of its members. A $1 billion community facilities lending bill made the most progress, getting as far as Senate passage, but it was killed on the floor of the House by a combination of Republican and southern Democratic votes.

By this time, however, the fiscal activists inside and outside Congress had begun to concentrate their energies upon tax reduction rather than public works as the most effective means of stimulating the economy— over and beyond the measures being taken to ease credit. Senator Douglas, a former economics professor, emerged as the leading advocate of a quick, temporary tax cut, arguing that the impact of public works if they were efficiently planned and executed would be far too slow. Repeatedly over a span of almost five months, he took the Senate floor for systematic presentations of the arguments for tax reduction, drawing upon staff of the Joint Economic Committee for assistance in preparation of the case. Support for the tax cut grew. The Democratic Advisory Council endorsed tax reduction on April 30. The Committee for Economic Development provided important advocacy from the business community. So did a Rockefeller Brothers Fund report issued in April. The president of the

[40] *Public Papers of the Presidents, 1958*, pp. 257–58.

U.S. Chamber of Commerce added his voice, [41] as did the president of General Motors and the chairman of the board of J. P. Morgan and Company.[42] AFL-CIO President George Meany, at his emergency conference on March 11, appealed for a tax cut ahead of public works as "probably the most important single weapon" in combating recession.[43] Budget Director Percival F. Brundage expressed a preference for a tax cut to public works if it came to a choice.[44] Former CEA Chairman Burns advocated a $5 billion cut and advised the President that a delay in cutting taxes would only lead to dangerous public works schemes instead.[45] Marriner S. Eccles, Utah banker and one-time chairman of the Federal Reserve Board, appearing before the Senate Finance Committee on April 16, stated the basic argument that was to prevail not then but six years later:

> If recovery can be hastened by a tax reduction, and I believe it can, it is reasonable to expect that even lower tax rates will soon be offset by the growth in the national income. Therefore, a balanced budget could be achieved through such recovery, whereas with higher tax rates and a depressed economy, the Government revenue would be diminished and a balanced budget impossible. I believe the Government deficit over the next 2 years, and hence the public debt, will be less if an adequate tax-reduction program is promptly adopted than would be the case if the country had to wait for the stimulating effect of increased Government spending.[46]

Douglas first moved his tax cut, in the amount of $5.2 billion divided between personal income and excise taxes, as a floor amendment to another bill on March 13. "It is better to act decisively, even if it turns out that we ultimately do too much, than to do nothing and later find disaster upon us," was his argument. "There is more to lose by not acting now than by acting."[47]

A clash between Republican Senators John J. Williams of Delaware and Charles E. Potter of Michigan captured the essence of the debate:

WILLIAMS: I do not believe a tax reduction should be financed with borrowed money. . . . A government cannot spend itself into prosperity any more than can an individual . . . erosion of the value of the dollar must be stopped.

[41] Quoted in *Cong. Record,* Vol. 104 (Jan. 28, 1958), p. 11597.

[42] Quoted in *ibid.* (Aug. 4, 1958), pp. 15980–82.

[43] Quoted in *ibid.* (March 11, 1958), pp. 3898–3901.

[44] Quoted at an Eisenhower news conference, Feb. 26, 1957, in *Public Papers of the Presidents, 1958,* p. 187.

[45] Dwight D. Eisenhower, *Waging Peace* (Doubleday, 1965), p. 309.

[46] *Investigation of the Financial Condition of the United States,* Hearings before the Senate Finance Committee, 85 Cong. 2 sess. (April 16, 1958), p. 1698.

[47] *Cong. Record,* Vol. 104 (March 13, 1958), pp. 4274–4302.

POTTER: It is rather hard to get the people of Michigan concerned about inflation when 350,000 of the people of Michigan are unemployed.

WILLIAMS: But a tax reduction is not what they want. What those men want are jobs. . . .

POTTER: But the tax reduction will put the economic machine back into operation, and in that way jobs will be provided.

WILLIAMS: No good will be done if the solvency of the Government is destroyed. . . .[48]

The amendment was defeated, 71–14.

On June 18, Douglas tried again, offering a $6 billion tax reduction amendment. This time he lost, 65–23. He had the support of a majority of the northern-western wing of the Democratic party, but of few others.

Among the factors holding down the Democratic vote was an agreement reached among three Texans—Secretary of the Treasury Robert B. Anderson, Speaker Rayburn, and Majority Leader Johnson—that neither side would try to gain political advantage over the other by "jumping the gun" on the tax cut issue. The President announced at his news conference on April 9 that the three had agreed "that there would be no tax cut proposed until after there had been full consultation" among them.[49] Rayburn discussed the arrangement with Democratic members of the Ways and Means Committee and won their concurrence. Douglas in the June 18 debate referred to the agreement flatly as one "to hold the line on taxes."[50]

The agreement may have reflected the Johnson-Rayburn strategy of "partnership" with the administration—facing the recession "hand in

---

[48] *Ibid.*, pp. 4285–87.

[49] *Public Papers of the Presidents, 1958*, p. 294.

[50] *Cong. Record*, Vol. 104 (June 18, 1958), p. 11574. Lewis points out that the prospects of a bitter fight over the distribution of any tax cut may have contributed to the decision not to seek one (*Federal Fiscal Policy*, p. 212). Eisenhower hints at this as a factor but makes clear that he was motivated primarily by the concern that "vast and continued deficits could become inflationary" (*Waging Peace*, p. 310). Lewis also notes, ironically, that while the President and the administration preferred stimulating private rather than public spending, "when the time came [they] accepted a variety of increases of government expenditures and opposed tax cuts"; not having developed a counter-recession program of its own, the administration could not resist piecemeal actions to increase expenditures; it was "carried along by the force of events" (p. 203). The consideration of tax reduction within the administration leading up to the President's truce with Rayburn and Johnson is recounted by Charles J. V. Murphy in *Fortune*, May 1958, pp. 106–09. Consistent with his agreement, Johnson voted "no" on both of the Douglas tax cut amendments.

hand," as Johnson had put it. But this may not be the whole explanation. One active participant in the 1958 tax cut struggle recalls that Rayburn, incensed over the continuing Eisenhower charges of "fiscal irresponsibility" and remembering the quarter-century of Republican attacks on his party for deficit spending, insisted that any action that could be labeled "irresponsible" must be initiated by the administration. "I can't put the Democratic Party's neck in a noose," Rayburn reportedly said. "It is no part of the Congress' duty to take Ike off the hook. If they won't move first, let them take the rap; let them answer for the recession in November."

Within the administration, Vice President Richard Nixon foresaw the same political consequences. Immediate tax reduction, he contended, was the only way to avoid "a Republican catastrophe" in the 1958 elections. But, "with Johnson and Rayburn on his side, Anderson was the undisputed winner over Nixon in the Cabinet."[51]

And the Republican catastrophe followed. Recovery began in the spring, spurred by the spending and credit measures that had been taken, and "the storm was over," writes Eisenhower.[52] As in 1953–54, the recession had been brief and once the bottom was reached, the upward climb was rapid. But as measured by unemployment, the hardship was greater than four years earlier; and during the recovery period, the effects on unemployment were felt slowly. Unemployment insurance was being exhausted, despite an emergency extension of benefits enacted in June. Savings were depleted. Unemployment dropped seasonally in the fall but, when adjusted for seasonal variation, remained above 7 percent through October. So the party in power did "take the rap" in November. The Democrats made a spectacular sweep, gaining a net total of thirteen seats in the Senate and forty-seven in the House, far more than any "normal" midterm gain by the party out of power. One of every four House seats held by a Republican was lost to a Democrat, and in the Senate the Democrats captured an extraordinary 60 percent of the Republican seats up for election. While unemployment and the recession were not the only issues, all analyses of the 1958 election—including Eisenhower's own—rate them as a major factor.[53]

[51] Rowland Evans and Robert Novak, *Lyndon B. Johnson: The Exercise of Power* (New American Library, 1966), p. 162.

[52] *Waging Peace*, p. 310.

[53] Chap. 10, pp. 456–62. Eisenhower lists the recession first among a series of reasons (*Waging Peace*, p. 310).

The Partisan Conflict Hardens (*1959–60*)

Once recovery was clearly underway, the Republicans ended their flirtation with expansionary economics and returned abruptly to fiscal orthodoxy. By the summer of 1958 and throughout the campaign, it was again inflation, not unemployment, that was the enemy. In his State of the Union message on January 9, 1959, President Eisenhower did not even mention unemployment, although it still remained at 4.7 million as he spoke—more men out of work than a year earlier. The recession, he said, "is fading into history, and this without gigantic, hastily-improvised public works projects or untimely tax reductions."[54] So he concentrated his attack upon inflation—although acknowledging that prices had been stable in recent months—and the big gun in his artillery was a balanced budget for the coming year, with a $4 billion reduction in expenditures. "If we cannot live within our means during such a time of rising prosperity, the hope of fiscal integrity will fade," he said. In his memoirs, he acknowledged that some of his advisers had cautioned against so rapid a return to a balanced budget, but the "overriding consideration" was the adverse balance of payments situation and the need to strengthen foreign bankers' confidence in the dollar. Secretary Anderson in particular argued for a balanced budget for that reason.[55]

During his last two years in office, the President did not waver from a pledge given at his 1958 postelection news conference to carry on the fight for fiscal responsibility "as hard as I know how." The budgets he sent to Congress were balanced with a surplus. He sought authority to veto individual items in appropriation bills and to curtail various lending and expenditure programs. He asked that price stability be made a specific objective of the Employment Act of 1946. He designated Vice President Nixon to head a Cabinet committee on price stability for economic growth, whose title reflected the emphasis given to the menace of inflation. He vetoed various spending measures that the heavily Democratic Congress served up to him. He stressed fiscal soundness in his speeches. And thus the Republican party entered the 1960 campaign united in support of a set of fiscal policies that met its ideological tests of prudence and responsibility.

But policies must also meet the pragmatic test of performance, and the Republican economic policies were made vulnerable by the failure of the economy to recover fully from the 1957–58 recession. Production did rise

[54] *Public Papers of the Presidents, 1959*, p. 9.
[55] Eisenhower, *Waging Peace*, pp. 385, 460.

rapidly in the last half of 1958 and the first half of 1959—more than
10 percent in the twelve-month period—but employment did not rise
correspondingly. Tens of thousands of men laid off in the recession were
not reemployed. In some large industries, such as steel, output spurted
upward with scarcely a noticeable dent in the unemployment rolls. All
through 1959, unemployment averaged 5.5 percent of the labor force—
a level that, for a presumably prosperous year, was only slightly less than
the recession year rates of 1949 and 1954. Fear of "automation," which
seemed to perpetuate unemployment amid prosperity, hung over the
unemployed and employed alike, and labor organizations began to clamor
for security against technological advance.

In March 1959 the Democratic majority of the Joint Economic Committee, led by Chairman Douglas, delivered a report that fractured the
sometime bipartisan harmony of that body. Inflation, said the majority,
was not the enemy. In fact, it hardly existed. Said the report:

> The consensus of the expert testimony presented to the committee in its
> hearings . . . was that substantial stability in the price level will be realized in
> 1959. . . . On the basis of the testimony and the facts, maintaining stability in
> the price level will probably require less emphasis in Federal economic poli-
> cies in 1959 than the other objectives of the Employment Act. . . . Since early
> 1958 . . . a high degree of stability in prices overall has been achieved.
>
> Examination of the facts belies the widespread impression that the economy
> has been persistently plagued since the end of the war with "classical" in-
> flationary pressures. . . . Until evidence of an imminent inflationary threat can
> be clearly seen . . . a reasonable and sane public policy aimed at promoting
> maximum employment and production and vigorous expansion of the econ-
> omy should not be unduly deterred by the possibility of future inflation.
>
> On the basis of the present economic outlook, principal emphasis in public
> policy this year should be placed on prompt and full recovery from the 1957–
> 58 recession.[56]

The majority emphasized the need for a higher rate of national growth.
While recognizing the desirability of a balanced budget "in times of
maximum employment," they did not find the national objectives "necessarily" dependent on "balancing a $77 billion Federal budget in fiscal
1960."

The Republican minority chided the majority for refusing to support
a balanced budget in the coming year and asserted that, with high levels
of economic activity in prospect, "failure to achieve a balance in the budget
can be expected to have prompt inflationary consequences." With a dissent

[56] *Report of the Joint Economic Committee on the January 1959 Economic Report of the President*, 86 Cong. 1 sess. (March 9, 1959), pp. 2–3.

from Senator Jacob K. Javits of New York, they termed inflation "the gravest potential obstacle to the achievement of high and rising rates of economic growth and improvement."[57]

Once that report was submitted, Senator Douglas threw his and the committee's energies into a massive study of *Employment, Growth and Price Levels,* hearing nearly 100 witnesses in forty days of testimony and producing a 3,500-page record and a 500-page study, submitted in December 1959. The study became known as the "Eckstein report" after its technical director, Otto Eckstein of Harvard University (who in 1964 was appointed a member of the Council of Economic Advisers).

The opening line of the Eckstein report—"the slow growth of the American economy of the last six years"—pointed a finger directly at the Eisenhower administration and phrased what became the central economic issue of the 1960 campaign. The report as a whole laid out what amounted to a Democratic alternative to Republican economic policy. That alternative was embellished and adapted for political use by politicians and economists working together, notably by the Joint Economic Committee and by John Kenneth Galbraith and other economists who were drafting the economic policy statements of the Democratic Advisory Council. By the time the Democrats met in Los Angeles in July, the party had achieved a working consensus on economic policy for the party platform and the fall campaign.

[57] *Ibid.,* pp. 33, 34. In retrospect, the majority seems to have had much the better of the argument about the seriousness of the inflation threat. As early as May 1961, W. Allen Wallis, who had served as vice chairman of the Cabinet group on price stability for economic growth, was quoted as saying in a speech: "The Federal Reserve Board tightened up the money supply in 1959 overvigorously and overpromptly as a move against inflation. But the inflation wasn't there" (*Cong. Record,* Vol. 108 [April 9, 1962], p. 6137).

Lewis concludes that the "excessive" tightening of budget policy in 1959 was "caused in part by faulty diagnosis of the state of the economy" (*Federal Fiscal Policy,* p. 241). In the summer of 1965 the Chase Manhattan Bank economic research division provided potent I-told-you-so ammunition by observing that "in the past seven years . . . there has been no real price inflation"; the gradual upward drift in prices had been offset by quality improvements in goods and services, the bank economists contended, and added: "Experience also shows that federal budget deficits within certain limits are not necessarily synonymous with inflation" (*Business in Brief,* No. 63 [July-August 1965]). Richard Ruggles of Yale University goes so far as to contend that quality increases have more than offset price increases since Korea, "so that we may actually have had declining rather than rising prices" (his argument is presented—and forcefully disputed by Ewan Clague, commissioner of the Bureau of Labor Statistics—in Arthur M. Okun [ed.], *The Battle Against Unemployment* [Norton, 1965], especially pp. 79–80, 86–87). J. M. Culbertson discusses the failure of price indexes to take account of qualitative changes and debunks the inflation fear in general in *Full Employment or Stagnation?* (McGraw-Hill, 1964), Chap. 6.

The Democratic case may be summarized as follows: The administration had fundamentally misinterpreted economic trends and events and was consequently fighting the wrong enemy with the wrong weapons. The overriding problem was not inflation, which the Republicans were flaying, but unemployment and the slow rate of economic growth. In overreacting to inflation, the Republicans had "stepped too hard on the fiscal and monetary brakes" (as the Eckstein report put it) thus reducing the rate of economic growth and throwing men and plant capacity into idleness. They had used the wrong weapons because such inflation as existed was due not primarily to excess demand, which fiscal and monetary brakes could curb, but to a variety of other causes beyond the reach of fiscal and monetary policy. The most important of these other causes was "administered prices"—that is, the ability of major firms, because of their market power, to raise prices even when demand was clearly not pressing upon supply.[58] What was needed now, in 1960, was growth-stimulating measures, particularly lower interest rates and increased public expenditures. Stimulation of growth would not add to inflationary pressures because the use of excess productive capacity would enable supply to keep pace with increased demand. The Democrats set a target of 5 percent annual growth, a figure taken originally from the report of a Rockefeller Brothers Fund panel in 1958. To protect their flanks against charges of "fiscal irresponsibility," they contended that a 5 percent annual increase in revenues would more than cover their proposed expenditures, leaving a surplus for debt retirement.

[58] The "administered price" theory of inflation was dramatically introduced into the economic debate by Gardiner C. Means, a leading economic theorist of the New Deal era living in semiretirement near Washington; on July 12, 1957, before the Senate subcommittee on monopoly and antitrust, chaired by Senator Estes Kefauver, Democrat of Tennessee, he presented a breakdown of the wholesale price index that showed the increases had occurred almost wholly in those sectors of the economy where prices are "administered" by firms holding substantial market power, rather than in those sectors where prices fluctuate freely in response to supply and demand. The Democrats seized Means' explanation as the answer to their political prayers, for at the same time it absolved "spending" as the cause of inflation it placed the blame on their ancient ideological foe—big business. Thereafter, the administered price theory found its place consistently in Democratic speeches and documents—for example, in the Eckstein report; the papers of the Democratic Advisory Council, which on December 5, 1959, said that "the most important inflationary force appears to be 'administered prices'"; and the 1960 platform, which promised "action to restrain 'administered price' increases in industries where economic power rests in the hands of a few." Means received support not only from economists identified as Democratic advisers but at least a measure of agreement from independent economists such as Woodlief Thomas and Ralph Young of the Federal Reserve Board (see Bernard D. Nossiter, *Washington Post*, March 16, 1959).

The Republicans, on the defensive, accused the Democrats of "inexcusable juggling of economic figures"[59] in attempting to prove that the economic growth rate was slower during the Eisenhower administration than in previous years. They charged the Democrats with "softness on inflation," as Nixon put it,[60] and condemned "the concept of artificial growth forced by massive new Federal spending and loose money policies," in the words of the 1960 GOP platform. They acknowledged that inflation resulted from "cost-push" as well as "demand-pull," but blamed the former on the power of labor unions to force excessive wage increases rather than on "administered prices." The 1957–58 recession was the result of the preceding period of inflation, not of the steps taken to combat it. In accounting for unemployment, the Republicans emphasized structural factors in the economy—the advance of technology and the barriers to labor mobility. They accused the Democrats of advocating public spending and other government action when encouraging free enterprise through a healthy business climate would stimulate economic growth more effectively.

Democratic charges of economic mismanagement were reinforced in midcampaign by another downturn in the economy—the third recession in six years and one that came even before the recovery from the last one was complete. As the Democratic candidate, Senator John F. Kennedy was cautious in leveling the "recession" charge, preferring to use the word "slowdown," but he did quote the *Wall Street Journal* after it published a front page article stating, "The question is not whether we are in a recession; the question is only how long it will continue."[61] Kennedy placed far more emphasis, however, on the "depressed areas" aspects of the unemployment problem (discussed in Chapter 3).

There is no hint, in the Democratic campaign and precampaign literature of 1960, of what was to become the keystone of the Kennedy economic program less than two years later—the deliberate unbalancing of the budget through tax reduction as a means of stimulating growth in relatively prosperous times. The majority of the Joint Economic Committee in its February 1960 report tried to outdo the Republicans by suggesting a surplus even larger than the $4.2 billion projected by Presi-

---

[59] Minority views accompanying the *Report of the Joint Economic Committee on the January 1960 Economic Report of the President*, 86 Cong. 2 sess. (Feb. 29, 1960), p. 39.

[60] *Daily News* (New York), Nov. 2, 1960.

[61] Remarks at Scranton, Pa., Oct. 28, 1960, and New York, N.Y., Oct. 27, 1960, *The Speeches of Senator John F. Kennedy, Presidential Campaign of 1960*, S. Rept. 994, 87 Cong. 1 sess. (1961), Pt. 1, pp. 798, 1203.

dent Eisenhower. The Democratic platform made its traditional pledge to a balanced budget "except in periods of recession or national emergency." And candidate Kennedy went even beyond the platform position, saying, "I believe in the balanced budget" except in times of "a *grave* national emergency or a *serious* recession."[62]

The evidence from 1960 polls suggests that the Democrats succeeded in capitalizing on the economic issue.[63] Sorensen notes that "the votes of newly unemployed workers alone in Illinois, New Jersey, Michigan, Minnesota, Missouri and South Carolina were greater than Kennedy's margin in those states, and their electoral votes were greater than his margin in the Electoral College. Nixon ran worst not, as many believe, in the cities with the highest proportion of Catholics but in the cities with the highest proportion of unemployed."[64] Perhaps the verdict of Robert Lekachman is not unfair: "By the criteria of the Employment Act of 1946, by the principles of public finance, and by the expectations of the general public, the Republican economic policy was a failure. In 1960 the party paid the appropriate electoral price."[65]

Economics Versus Politics   *(1961–62)*

As President Kennedy was inaugurated, the fourth postwar recession had not yet ended. In February and March, more men and women were out of work than at any previous time since World War II.[66] The new President's State of the Union message drew a bleak picture. "We take office," he said, "in the wake of seven months of recession, three and one half years of slack, seven years of diminished economic growth. . . . Our recovery from the 1958 recession, moreover, was anemic and incomplete. Our Gross National Product never regained its full potential. Unemployment never returned to normal levels. Maximum use of our national in-

[62] First debate, Sept. 26, 1960, *The Joint Appearances of Senator John F. Kennedy and Vice President Richard M. Nixon, Presidential Campaign of 1960*, S. Rept. 994, 87 Cong. 1 sess. (1961), Pt. 3, p. 83 (italics added). His wording throughout the campaign was consistently stringent.

[63] See Chap. 10, pp. 463–66.

[64] Theodore C. Sorensen, *Kennedy* (Harper & Row, 1965), p. 217.

[65] *The Age of Keynes* (Random House, 1966), p. 225.

[66] When allowance is made for the usual midwinter bulge in unemployment, the seasonally adjusted rates were slightly below the peaks of 1958.

dustrial capacity was never restored. . . . This Administration does not intend to stand helplessly by. . . ."[67]

The words were forceful, but the course of action the new President followed was more cautious than dramatic—and strongly reminiscent of his predecessor's course in 1954 and 1958. Like Eisenhower, he directed acceleration of authorized spending where it could be done without waste. Like Eisenhower, he asked a temporary extension of unemployment benefits, adding a proposal for liberalization of social security. He announced the distribution of more surplus food to the unemployed and the early payment of a National Service Life Insurance dividend. He proposed a tax reform measure designed to stimulate investment, but, like Eisenhower in 1958, he rejected a tax cut until the need were more urgently demonstrated. "We're going to make another judgment . . . in two to three months," he told his news conference on February 1.[68] Finally, like Eisenhower, he pledged allegiance to the balanced budget. "The programs I am now proposing," he told Congress, "will not by themselves unbalance the budget," which President Eisenhower had submitted.[69]

Yet, the economists of the "new" school were now *inside* the administration. Why did the President they counseled, while condemning the consequences of his predecessor's policies, move slowly in reversing them? Why did the President go out of his way to reaffirm, at the bottom of an acknowledged recession, the basic Eisenhower fiscal tenet of the balanced budget?

The answer lay not in Kennedy's economic understanding but in his appraisal of political considerations. For years the Republicans had been painting the Democratic party as the party of reckless spending and inflation, and throughout the autumn Kennedy had done his best to neutralize that issue by speaking in clear tones of fiscal soundness. Now he had won by the narrowest of margins, with a mandate far from plain. As he saw

[67] Message of Jan. 30, 1961, *Public Papers of the Presidents, 1961*, pp. 19–20.
[68] *Ibid.*, pp. 32–33.
[69] Special Message to the Congress: "Program for Economic Recovery and Growth," Feb. 2, 1961, *ibid.*, p. 43. In his State of the Union message three days earlier, he had carefully qualified his commitment: "Within that framework [the Eisenhower revenue and expenditure estimates], barring the development of urgent national defense needs or a worsening of the economy, it is my current intention to advocate a program of expenditures which, including revenues from a stimulation of the economy, will not of and by themselves unbalance the earlier budget." Heller recalls, "We counted seven escape hatches" (*New Dimensions*, p. 31).

it, his imperative duty in his first weeks of office was to demonstrate to the nation—and especially to the business community, which had given him substantial support and whose backing would be necessary in the future—that the Democratic party, under his leadership, was indeed fiscally responsible. Moreover, after his inaugural appeal to the people to ask what they could do for their country, not what their country could do for them, it would be anomalous to offer, in the next breath, a program of lower taxes and easy spending.

But the role of his economic advisers inside and outside the government was to supply economic, not political, advice. From their point of view, the restrictive Eisenhower fiscal policies had been folly in 1959, had been folly in 1960, and were still folly in 1961. While they were divided on whether expansion should be sought through higher spending alone or through a combination of higher spending and lower taxes, and while they had reached no agreement on the magnitude of the measures to be taken, there appears to have been little disagreement among them as to the desirability of expansionary measures that would further upset the budget. What followed was a vigorous, unremitting campaign by the Kennedy economists to make economics, rather than politics, the decisive influence in the fiscal policy of the government. Beaten at first, they were wholly successful two years later.

Their first encounter with political realities came even before inauguration. President-elect Kennedy had appointed a task force on economic prospects and policies headed by Paul A. Samuelson of the Massachusetts Institute of Technology and consisting entirely of economic thinkers of the new school. Their report, issued on January 6, 1961, reflected an uneasy marriage of economic logic and political caution. The report pointed to the existence of a recession and of chronic slackness in the economy, used strong language in advocating specific major expenditure increases totaling billions of dollars, suggested that budget deficits might at times be necessary, and denied that deficits were always inflationary. At the same time, it warned against "massive spending programs," and proposed a temporary tax cut only as a "second line of defense" if conditions did not improve as rapidly as anticipated. Samuelson has since made clear that the task force recommendations were tempered by noneconomic considerations. Two months after the report's appearance he acknowledged that from an economic standpoint a treasury deficit of $5 billion "is needed now." But politics, said Samuelson, "is the art of the feasible."[70] A year later he wrote: "Bluntly, the straight economics of the 1961 situation required a sizeable deficit. . . . Whatever the economic merits of a tax cut, it seemed politically out of the question. The President had run on a platform that asked sacrifices of the American people. How then could he begin by giving them what many would regard as a 'hand-out?' "[71]

In their struggle for the decisive voice in fiscal policy, the expansionists had to contend not just with the President's political advisers but with the conservative school of economic thought centered in the Treasury Department, and with President Kennedy's own less-than-complete understanding and acceptance of the new economics.

The last of these obstacles proved the easiest to overcome. The fiscal orthodoxy of Kennedy's 1960 campaign did not reflect unshakeable conviction. Sorensen reports that Kennedy "had no taste for economic theory."[72] He had been a member of the Joint Economic Committee in his last two years in Congress but had been inactive. He had voted against the first Douglas tax cut amendment in March 1958 but in favor of the second in June. The switch, he acknowledged, had been mainly on the advice of Seymour E. Harris, a Harvard economist.[73] When he assembled his academic advisory group in preparation for the 1960 campaign, he turned to the leading Cambridge economists of the new school for its economics component—notably Samuelson, Harris, and John Kenneth Galbraith. Most important, he turned to them for advice in selecting his first Council of Economic Advisers—Chairman Walter W. Heller, James Tobin, and Kermit Gordon. A political activist himself, he was clearly intellectually compatible with the economic activists.

Few among those activists had been more disdainful than Heller in debunking the balanced budget as a moral imperative. In 1959 Heller had accused the Eisenhower administration of an "obsession" with cutting expenditures and balancing the budget at a time when the country faced "the possibility of annihilation or humiliation," and when "much of our affluence is being frittered away in indulgences, luxuries, and frivolities." The result, he had said, was "as great a risk, calculated or otherwise, as this

[70] Comments on the television program, "Meet the Press," March 5, 1961, under questioning by Lawrence Spivak.

[71] "Economic Policy for 1962," *Review of Economics and Statistics*, Vol. 64 (February 1962), p. 4.

[72] *Kennedy*, p. 394.

[73] Seymour E. Harris, *Economics of the Kennedy Years* (Harper & Row, 1964), p. xi.

country has ever incurred in peacetime economic policy."[74] This was the point of view and vigor of expression to which Kennedy was now daily exposed. And Kennedy was receptive: even before the inauguration, he had charged Heller with educating the public as to "the desirable effects of a federal deficit in a recession."[75]

The council, says Sorensen, kept the President "buried under a tide of memoranda" and became "the most highly influential and frequently consulted Council of Economic Advisers in history."[76] Under its tutelage the President's public utterances on fiscal policy shifted steadily from the language of orthodoxy to that of the new economics. In his March 24 message on economic policy he still pledged a balanced budget "over the years of the business cycle."[77] But by summer he was extemporizing to his news conference about how the tax structure had "contributed to strangling the recovery after the '58 recession."[78] Heller himself, under the heading "Education of Presidents," has given a fascinating account of Kennedy's development as an economist. The President's "occasional doubts and concessions to prevailing economic sentiment," writes Heller, "stand out only as detours on his road to modernism. What was pleasing to his economic advisers, and fortunate for the country, was his responsiveness to *analysis*, the force of economic logic and fact; to *analogy*, the demonstrated success of Keynesian policies abroad; and to *anomaly*, the continued sacrifice of human and material resources on the altar of false concepts of 'sound finance.' "[79] But as Kennedy's economic views developed, he was always conscious that attitudes on Capitol Hill and throughout the country had undergone no corresponding evolution. The political barriers to fiscal activism remained as strong as they had been on inauguration day, and he was not yet in a strong enough position to tackle them head-on.

The second collision between Kennedy's economic and political counselors came in the summer of 1961, on the issue of a tax increase to offset the added military expenditures arising from the U.S.-Soviet confronta-

---

[74] *January 1959 Economic Report of the President,* Hearings before the Joint Economic Committee, 86 Cong. 2 sess. (Jan. 30, 1959), pp. 202–05. Kennedy had not yet been appointed to the committee and did not meet Heller until 1960.

[75] Quoted by Heller, *New Dimensions,* p. 26.

[76] *Kennedy,* pp. 264, 395. Heller says 300 economic memoranda went to Kennedy during the 34 months of his presidency (*New Dimensions,* p. 29).

[77] *Public Papers of the Presidents, 1961,* p. 221.

[78] News conferences of June 28 and July 19, 1961, *ibid.,* pp. 482, 516.

[79] Heller, *New Dimensions,* p. 35 (italics in the original); full account, pp. 29–36.

tion over Berlin. The tax increase proposal originated among the President's foreign affairs advisers, according to Sorensen, and was supported by the Treasury and some of the President's political staff. A tax increase, it was argued, would demonstrate America's determination at Berlin, protect the budget, prevent inflation, and symbolize the Kennedy theme of sacrifice. The economic advisers stood almost alone in emphasizing the slack in the economy and pleading that the needed expansionary effect of the spending not be wiped out by a tax increase. Sorensen writes that a tax increase "was tentatively approved by the President and came dangerously close to being announced."[80] But the council members stubbornly continued the debate. They enlisted the aid of allies outside the government. They arranged for Samuelson to fly from Massachusetts to Washington with the President. They met with Kennedy during the weekend and on the day and evening before the President was to address the nation on the Berlin crisis. By the time the President appeared before the cameras, on Tuesday evening, July 25, the proposal for an immediate tax increase was dead.

But the President went only half way. While he accepted the immediate deficit, he promised to submit a balanced budget in January 1962. Should an increase in taxes be necessary to achieve that balance, "those increased taxes will be requested in January," said the President.[81]

When January arrived, the President found it possible to balance the budget without new taxes, but only by predicting a 13 percent increase in receipts from existing taxes, which presumed an extraordinary 9 percent rise in the gross national product in 1962. By March it was already clear that no such rapid recovery was in prospect. In April the picture was even clearer. On May 28 occurred the "Kennedy crash" in the stock market. At his next news conference, on June 7, with the economy in a "pause" and recession fears rampant, the President opened the meeting with a long statement of economic policy.

The President said no word about a balanced budget. Instead he promised to submit to the Congress in January a bill incorporating "an across-the-board reduction in personal and corporate income tax rates which will

[80] Since the economic advisers did not participate in the Berlin crisis meetings, Sorensen represented their views; for his account of the debate within the administration, see *Kennedy*, pp. 399–400. See also Heller, *New Dimensions,* p. 32, and Flash, *Economic Advice,* pp. 201–06.

[81] *Public Papers of the Presidents, 1961,* p. 537

not be wholly offset by other reforms—in other words, a net tax reduction."[82]

For nearly a decade, since the Korean fighting halted, fiscal orthodoxy had had its trial. The results were in: three recessions, incomplete recovery from the last two, chronic unemployment and idle plant capacity, and now a leveling off of economic activity in the kind of slackness that Kennedy had attacked so vigorously in his presidential campaign. Now Walter Heller was to have his day. The new economics was finally to be given its test.

Fiscal Activism Prevails   *(1962–64)*

The commitment was made, but it was still a limited one and subject to differing interpretations. The size, the nature, and the timing of the tax cut had yet to be decided; the relation between tax reduction and tax reform had yet to be worked out; and the country and the Congress had yet to experience the same education and conversion the President had undergone.

The first question to be confronted was that of timing. If a tax cut made sense for January 1963, the economists argued, it made even better sense for the summer of 1962. During the next five weeks, as the "pause" continued, Heller pressed for a "quickie" tax cut—an immediate, temporary reduction that would be made permanent in the combined reduction-reform measure planned for 1963.[83] Heller had the support of other economists, including Samuelson and a group of twenty-five assembled by Seymour Harris, then economic consultant to Treasury Secretary C. Douglas Dillon. Both the U.S. Chamber of Commerce and organized labor were for it. So was Commerce Secretary Luther H. Hodges. But Dillon, whose limited tax reform proposal of 1961 had found rough going in the Congress, was eager to hold any tax reduction for use as a "sweetener" to make a much broader tax reform palatable in 1963, and in this position he was supported by such congressional advocates of tax reform as Arkansas Democrat Wilbur D. Mills, chairman of the House Ways and Means Committee, and Senator Douglas. The decisive consid-

[82] *Public Papers of the Presidents, 1962*, p. 457

[83] For accounts of the consideration of the quickie tax cut, see Bernard D. Nossiter, "The Day Taxes Weren't Cut", *Reporter*, Sept. 13, 1962, pp. 25–28; Sorensen, *Kennedy*, pp. 424–29; and Flash, *Economic Advice*, pp. 230–48.

eration appears to have been the weight of opinion that, whatever the merits of the quickie cut, the Congress would not act favorably—a view taken by Dillon and by the President's congressional relations staff. In July the President decided against the quickie cut, and on August 13 he publicly ruled it out—while going beyond his June statement in promising to recommend a major cut in January. Sorensen expresses the judgment that Kennedy, apart from believing the immediate bill could not pass, "was not convinced that a temporary cut at that time was essential, as distinguished from merely being helpful. . . ."

During the remainder of the year, the administration concentrated upon the simultaneous tasks of deciding how much tax reduction to recommend in January, designing a combination reduction-reform measure, and educating the country and the Congress to the need for the sharp departure from fiscal orthodoxy that was in prospect.

An examination of the *Congressional Record* for 1961 and 1962 reveals the magnitude of the latter task. Now, as in 1960, the Republicans saw deficit spending and inflation as their strongest domestic issues, and they were quick to center their attack upon any sign of looseness in the Kennedy fiscal policies. Nobody in either party rose to advocate deficit spending as such, and with one notable exception the language of the new economics was not heard on Capitol Hill. The exception was the majority of the Joint Economic Committee, which in May 1961 took the offensive against what it called the "too restrictive" fiscal policies of recent years. But even they only urged consideration of a tax cut, stopping short of a flat recommendation.[84] And the committee majority was strongly opposed by five members of the Republican minority, who submitted a carefully reasoned fourteen-page attack on the theoretical basis of the new economics. One member of the majority also dissented—Senator William Proxmire of Wisconsin, who earlier had dismissed the Samuelson report with the tart comment that "economic forecasting is about as advanced a science as phrenology."[85] Meanwhile, four senior members of the Senate (Republicans Styles Bridges and Norris Cotton of New Hampshire and Carl

[84] *Report of the Joint Economic Committee on the January 1961 Economic Report of the President*, 87 Cong. 1 sess. (May 2, 1961), pp. 29–31. The discussion is supported by an appendix (pp. 119–25) written by James W. Knowles, staff member, who as early as 1954 had prepared projections showing that tax cuts would be necessary by the mid-1960's if the budget were not to serve as a drag on economic growth and prevent full employment (see *Potential Economic Growth of the United States during the Next Decade*, prepared for the Joint Economic Committee, 83 Cong. 2 sess. [1954]).

[85] *Cong. Record*, Vol. 107 (Jan. 10, 1961), p. 489.

Curtis of Nebraska, and Democrat Harry F. Byrd of Virginia) once more introduced a constitutional amendment to outlaw unbalanced budgets except in times of grave national emergency. The Texas legislature memorialized Congress in support of its passage.[86] Federal Reserve Chairman Martin provided ammunition to the budget-balancers by contending that unemployment was due primarily to structural changes in the economy rather than deficiency of aggregate demand.[87] Senator Jack R. Miller, Republican of Iowa, declaimed that "I am even more convinced today that inflation is our greatest enemy, second only to world communism,"[88] and the Republican senator from Arizona, Barry Goldwater, contended that "deficit spending is not now and never has been the answer to unemployment."[89] Democrat Clarence Cannon of Missouri, chairman of the House Appropriations Committee, argued that "at the very heart of our national finances is a simple, inescapable fact, easily grasped by every Member. . . . It is that our Government—any government—like individuals and families, cannot spend more than they take in without courting disaster."[90]

Most important of all, Chairman Mills made clear that he was by no means a convert to the new economics. In August 1961 he told a reporter: "People think of me as a conservative and I guess I am. In the first place I believe that the function of taxation is to raise revenues. That may sound obvious; but I say it to make clear that I don't go along with economists who think of taxation as an instrument for stimulating, braking, or otherwise manipulating the economy."[91] Earlier, during a floor debate on a tax extension bill, he expressed agreement with former Treasury Secretary George M. Humphrey that "the time to reduce taxes as such is when you can foresee a surplus out of which those tax reductions can be made; and . . . you do not as a general principle reduce taxes in order to increase deficit spending."[92]

Not until the day after the "Kennedy crash" of May 1962 were voices raised in Congress to urge strong fiscal action. Senators Javits, Humphrey,

[86] *Ibid.* (Jan. 26, 1961), p. 1292.
[87] This episode is discussed in Chap. 3, pp. 57–59.
[88] *Cong. Record*, Vol. 107 (June 21, 1961), p. 11016.
[89] *Ibid.* (June 27, 1961), p. 11471.
[90] *Ibid.* (Sept. 26, 1961), p. 21541.
[91] Article by John R. Cauley, *Kansas City Times*, Aug. 22, 1961; inserted in *Cong. Record*, Vol. 107 (Aug. 28, 1961), pp. 17256–57, by Mills' Democratic colleague from Arkansas, James W. Trimble.
[92] *Cong. Record*, Vol. 107 (June 8, 1961), p. 9778.

and Eugene J. McCarthy (Minnesota Democrat) called for tax reduction.[93] During the debate that followed, the Republican position solidified that any tax cut must be accompanied by equal or greater reductions in expenditures to prevent inflation—still the "ever-present danger."[94] A Gallup poll inserted in the *Record* by Senator Proxmire showed the people to be 72-19 percent against a tax cut if it meant increasing the national debt.[95] The President suggested to reporters that the response might have been different if the question had been worded, "Do you believe in a tax cut as a means of preventing a recession at some future date, and unemployment which will bring potentially a larger deficit and a further increase in debt?"[96] But, assuming that the President was right, the task remained of educating a vast majority of the population to the new perspective from which he believed the tax cut should properly be viewed.

Such was the wall of conservative opinion the President had to surmount, once he had made his commitment of June 7. The campaign of public education began at once. On making his announcement, the President explained briefly but lucidly the theory of the full employment surplus[97]—a term used to measure the restrictive or expansionary impact of a budget. At Yale University four days later, he delivered a biting attack on the "truisms," "stereotypes," "cliches of our forebears," "stale phrases," and "myths" concerning the national economy. Among the "myths" were these: that the federal government is getting bigger, that federal deficits create inflation and that budget surpluses prevent it, and that the conventional budget is a sound measure of federal fiscal integrity.[98] But Kennedy, writes Sorensen, "did not become fully enthusiastic until December, and it was the convincing effect of one of his own speeches that helped convince him."[99] The speech was his address at the Economic Club of New York on December 14, in which he laid out fully for the first time the rationale for tax reduction. He said:

> The final and best means of strengthening demand among consumers and business is to reduce the burden on private income and the deterrents to private initiative which are imposed by our present tax system. . . .
> I am talking about the accumulated evidence of the last 5 years, that our

[93] *Ibid.*, Vol. 108 (May 29, 1962), pp. 9880, 9508, 9515.
[94] See remarks of Senator Frank Carlson of Kansas, *ibid.* (June 6, 1962), p. 9847; Homer Capehart of Indiana, *ibid.* (June 14, 1962), p. 10539; John Williams of Delaware, Wallace Bennett of Utah, Prescott Bush of Connecticut, and other senators, *ibid.* (June 28, 1962), pp. 12153–63.
[95] *Ibid.* (Aug. 1, 1962), p. 15260.
[96] *Public Papers of the Presidents, 1962*, p. 593.
[97] *Ibid.*, p. 457.
[98] *Ibid.*, pp. 470–75.
[99] *Kennedy*, p. 429.

present tax system, developed as it was, in good part, during World War II to restrain growth, exerts too heavy a drag on growth in peace time; that it siphons out of the private economy too large a share of personal and business purchasing power; that it reduces the financial incentives for personal effort, investment, and risk-taking.

Any new tax legislation enacted next year should meet the following three tests: First it should reduce net taxes by a sufficiently early date and a sufficiently large amount to do the job required. . . . Too large a tax cut, of course, could result in inflation and insufficient future revenue—but the greater danger is a tax cut too little or too late to be effective.

Second, the new tax bill must increase private consumption as well as investment. . . .

Third, the new tax bill should improve both the equity and the simplicity of our present tax system. This means the enactment of long-needed tax reforms, a broadening of the tax base and the elimination or modification of many special tax privileges. . . .

Our true choice is not between tax reduction, on the one hand, and the avoidance of large Federal deficits on the other. It is increasingly clear that no matter what party is in power, so long as our national security needs keep rising, an economy hampered by restrictive tax rates will never produce enough revenue to balance our budget just as it will never produce enough jobs or enough profits. Surely the lesson of the last decade is that budget deficits are not caused by wild-eyed spenders but by slow economic growth and periodic recessions, and any new recession would break all deficit records.

In short, it is a paradoxical truth that tax rates are too high today and tax revenues are too low and the soundest way to raise the revenues in the long run is to cut the rates now. The experience of a number of European countries and Japan have borne this out. This country's own experience with tax reduction in 1954 has borne this out. And the reason is that only full employment can balance the budget, and tax reduction can pave the way to that employment. The purpose of cutting taxes now is not to incur a budget deficit, but to achieve the more prosperous, expanding economy which can bring a budget surplus.[100]

Clearly, as Sorensen puts it, the President "had received a good education in economics in the White House."[101] But Wilbur Mills had not

[100] *Public Papers of the Presidents, 1962*, pp. 877–80.

[101] *Kennedy*, p. 433. Harris comments: "I do not mean to suggest that the President easily accepted modern Keynesian economics. He had to be shown. It was a long struggle. By 1963, he had clearly become a convert. . . . Not only did the President have to abandon the ideas of his early economic training, but he had in his cabinet Secretary Douglas Dillon. . . . The Secretary of the Treasury gradually accepted the tenets of Keynes, though with much less enthusiasm than the council members. . . . More than anyone else, the highly articulate and intelligent Heller won the President over to modern views of economics. . . . He accomplished this despite many obstacles, especially since the President in 1960 had not been convinced of the usefulness of budgetary deficits. Because he was confronted with a President who at first seemed allergic to modern economics, Heller deserves all the more credit" (*Economics of the Kennedy Years*, pp. 4–5, 23).

been subjected to the same intensive education. He read the speech "without commitment."[102] And already on the newsstands was a magazine interview with Mills entitled "Why a Tax Cut Is Unlikely in '63." A few passages from Mills' comments illustrate the difference between the presidential economics and those of the key congressional figure whose support would be essential for any tax reduction bill:

> The situation . . . would indicate that there has not been a deterioration in our economy and that there probably will not be a deterioration during the early part of 1963. On the basis of that projection, it would seem that there probably would be little justification at the moment for a "quickie" tax cut effective Jan. 1, 1963.
>
> Especially do I take that view when the net result would be to reduce revenues substantially in the year 1963 when they are already, without any reduction, apparently less than the rate of spending that may be projected in the budget for fiscal year 1964.
>
> I can't go along with the idea that you just cut taxes without regard to the deficit that is created. . . . All of us are aware of the desirability at any time of reducing the tax burdens upon the people. But, on the other hand, we have to take into account the effect on our public debt, whether or not we are providing those reductions in taxes out of a surplus of revenue. . . .
>
> I doubt that you could sell a tax cut alone for purposes of trying to do something to the economy until it's generally discernible that a downturn is coming. . . . It would be advisable, I think, if we are to try to reduce taxes, to have some assurance that there at least will be some better control over the rises in expenditures than we've had in the past several years. . . . It would lead to a greater acceptance of a tax reduction by the people generally and, I think, by Congress, if there were some reduction in expenditures accompanying it. . . .
>
> I haven't been able to reach the conclusion that we're justified in making temporary tax cuts effective Jan. 1, 1963. We all realize, of course, that those cuts would result in an increase in our deficit and, therefore, in our national debt. . . . We should think of tax-rate reduction accompanied by some reforms of the tax law that would give us a balance so that the entire amount of the reduction would not be reflected in increased deficit and increased debt.[103]

The President, in his Economic Club speech, quoted the Mills reference to "increased control of the rises in expenditures" and said, "This is precisely the course we intend to follow."

Government economists, working under the aegis of a Cabinet committee on economic growth, chaired by Heller, agreed during the fall that a net reduction of $12 billion was near the amount required to overcome

[102] *Kennedy*, p. 430.
[103] *U.S. News and World Report*, Dec. 17, 1962, pp. 42–45.

the "full employment surplus." The President's final decision, made at Palm Beach in December, was to recommend a reduction to be undertaken in several steps, in an amount that would hold the deficit to a smaller figure than the record $12.4 billion registered by the Eisenhower administration in 1958–59, and to make the tax cut contingent on tax reform. Nine months later, the bill was passed by the House of Representatives, by the overwhelming margin of 271–155.

The House Acts. No one will ever know how many of the 271 were intellectually converted to the new economics. After the victory, James Tobin said flatly, "There is not a Keynesian majority in Congress, and conscious deficit finance is still not respectable." He attributed the support for tax reduction to a "mixture of motives," which he did not attempt to define.[104]

Any analysis of the mixture of congressional motives should undoubtedly begin with the proposition that tax cuts are inherently appealing. Individual taxpayers, told by the President that as a patriotic duty they must accept an increase in their take-home pay, are apt to give their elected leader the benefit of any doubt. So are corporate taxpayers when told that they should retain a higher proportion of their earnings. Individuals and organizations who would react almost automatically against "deficit spending" as unsound and inflationary found themselves willing to take a second look at the soundness of a deficit produced by tax reduction rather than by increased spending. And they so informed their congressmen.

Offsetting the pressures of the "pocketbook" appeal was the weight of the popular belief in a balanced budget—not as a matter of economics but as a measure of public and political morality. One cannot read the continuing public debates over fiscal policy in the decade prior to 1963— or even the academic debates, for that matter—without being impressed with the extent to which the principle of the balanced budget had been not just an economic but a moral precept. The enemies of deficit spending not only attacked deficits as "inflationary," employing economic arguments, but associated them with patterns of personal conduct that bore a moral stigma—"waste," "profligacy," "recklessness," "spendthrift," "living beyond one's means," "insolvency," and even "immorality."[105]

104 "The Tax-cut Harvest," *New Republic,* March 7, 1964, pp. 14–17.

105 For example, Bernard M. Baruch testified before the Senate Finance Committee, April 1, 1958, that "to reduce revenues before our defenses are secure and our debt manageable is uneconomic and *immoral*" (*Investigation of the Financial Condition of the United States,* Hearings, p. 1636 [italics added]).

And they described the balanced budget in words that embodied a positive set of personal moral values—"responsibility," "prudence," "thrift," "soundness," "solvency." This was the language of political campaigns. The politicians who used these words were appealing not primarily to the economic judgment of the electorate but to its emotions—they were seeking to identify themselves with the voters' image of what constitutes virtue in public men. When the test came, in 1963, many members of Congress found themselves committed by their past dialogue with their constituents. Whatever respect for Keynesian economics they might reveal in private, it was in the *public* language that they had made their pledges and sealed their bonds with their supporters. If there were a "Keynesian majority" in the Congress, it would be in no position to say so openly.

But the leadership of the nation's business community was by no means so tightly bound to old positions, and in this circumstance is found the key to passage of the tax reduction measure. Ideological fixations among business leaders had faded with the passing of the generation that had waged the long quarrel against the fiscal policies of Franklin Roosevelt. And just as President Kennedy himself had been won over by his advisers to the concepts of the new economics, many business leaders had been similarly persuaded by the economists they had engaged to counsel them. Moreover, faith in fiscal orthodoxy as emphasized in Eisenhower's later years—and as initially espoused and carried on by Kennedy—had been shaken by a stubborn fact: it had not worked satisfactorily. Amid the clatter of campaign rhetoric in 1960, a sharp and serious debate on economic policy did take place between the parties and the candidates, and when it was over the winner had made his essential point: the economy was *not* growing fast enough—for full employment, for full production, or for maximum profits—and the interest of business in "getting the country moving again" was no less than that of labor. Finally, of course, those businessmen who still could not bring themselves to an intellectual acceptance of budget deficits as in themselves sometimes desirable could go along with the President at this time on the ground that high and "oppressive" taxes were an even greater evil.

Whatever the combination of all of these influences, the most important single business organization, the United States Chamber of Commerce, had in the early 1960's deserted the view that tax reductions should be made only out of surplus,[106] and its 1962–63 president, Ladd Plumley,

[106] Staff economists at the chamber in the late 1950's and early 1960's date the shift in opinion among the membership from about 1960 and attribute it to the impact of the recurrent postwar recessions and the economic debate that ensued.

was an all-out supporter of tax reduction. By the time of the Ways and Means Committee hearings, in 1963, it was joined by the National Association of Manufacturers, the American Bankers Association, the New York Stock Exchange, and an array of trade associations in testifying in favor of the measure.

From the beginning, the Kennedy administration had recognized that business support was crucial. In framing his specific tax reduction proposal, the President was careful to distribute the benefits in such a way as to retain his powerful business support, dividing them between corporate and individual income tax cuts and distributing the latter benefits through all the brackets of the tax structure. This balance was retained to the end, although the actual rates were adjusted slightly during committee consideration.

Thorough and aggressive organization clearly played a part in the bill's success. As soon as his program was announced, the President threw his personal resources and those of his entire administration into the educational lobbying campaign. All departments of government were mobilized under White House and Treasury leadership. The lead-off witness was a former banker and Republican with impeccable credentials among the businessmen whose support was being wooed—Treasury Secretary Dillon. Under Secretary Henry H. Fowler proceeded with characteristic thoroughness to mobilize outside support. Concentrating still upon the business community, Fowler was instrumental in forming a business committee for tax reduction in 1963, including such prominent names as Henry Ford, II, Roger M. Blough, and Stuart Saunders, which was "credited with the most diligent work on behalf of the measure."[107] He also initiated formation of a more broadly representative committee under the chairmanship of Howard R. Bowen, president of Grinnell College in Iowa. For those who would rely on expert advice, four hundred economists issued a strong statement supporting the President's position. Kennedy carried his personal advocacy to the country in a television speech just before the House voted, and the White House congressional relations staff "put the heat on" House members more than at any other time in the Kennedy administration.

Divided and leaderless, the opposition scarcely organized at all. No

---

[107] *Congressional Quarterly Almanac, 1963,* p. 491; it contains a complete and authoritative history of the tax bill during 1963 (pp. 470–99). For a detailed legislative history of any bill discussed in this book, see *Congressional Quarterly Almanac.*

group comparable to the business committee was lobbying against the tax cut bill. The Republicans, unwilling or unable to oppose tax cuts as such, centered their attack upon the failure of the administration to cut spending. But they joined the Democrats in abandoning the notion that the budget should be balanced. In their recommittal motion on the House floor, the Republican leaders proposed to make the tax cut—then measured by the Treasury at about $11 billion—contingent on a reduction in spending by the President of $1.2 billion in the fiscal year 1964 and $4 billion below estimates for the following year, which would still leave planned deficits of substantial size.

In every review of the struggle in the House, observers have credited much of the success to the floor leadership of Wilbur Mills. Ever since the inauguration, President Kennedy had assiduously courted Mills. He had brought Mills into the White House inner circle discussions of tax policy.[108] He had flown to Arkansas, as Mills' guest, to make a speech. "Slowly," writes Sorensen, "the President brought him around. Initially Mills agreed to a major tax reform bill, with a little tax reduction to help pass it. When presented, it was a tax reform and tax reduction bill. In testimony, it became a tax reduction and tax reform bill. And when it was finally reported out by Mills, the President had his major tax cut bill with a little tax reform."[109]

But, once converted to the President's position, Mills was a formidable advocate. Taking full advantage of his stature as a fiscally "sound" conservative, he maneuvered to disrupt the Republican-southern Democratic coalition that had been forming in opposition to other Kennedy domestic measures. When the "Boll Weevils," an organization of conservative southern Democrats, met to consider their position on the tax bill, a conservative member of the Ways and Means Committee was there to persuade them not to support the Republican recommittal motion.[110] When the time came, the chairman of the "Weevils," Omar Burleson of Texas, took the floor along with Mills to oppose the motion. So did such other southern stalwarts as A. Sydney Herlong, Jr., of Florida, member of the Ways and Means Committee, and George H. Mahon of Texas, ranking majority member of the Appropriations Committee. They did not dispute

[108] Sorensen, *Kennedy,* p. 432.
[109] *Ibid.*
[110] Randall B. Ripley, *Party Leadership in the House of Representatives* (Brookings Institution, 1967), p. 178.

the merit of cutting spending but argued, in Mahon's words, that the motion "constitutes a partial surrender of the power of the purse by the House . . . and by the Congress. . . ." It was also pointed out that business could make no definite plans if the tax cut were left to depend on an uncertain presidential action.

In leading the debate, Mills seized the initiative on the spending issue by painting the tax cut bill as an antispending and antideficit measure. Thus he provided an "out" to all those members who were long committed to opposing budget deficits on principle: a temporary deficit was necessary to achieve a balanced budget later, and it was better to incur that deficit through tax reduction than through increased spending. This was his theme:

> Let me readily confess, Mr. Chairman, that in the beginning I had perhaps more reservations about this matter than I have experienced with respect to most any other matter that has come up for consideration . . . before the House of Representatives. As the result of the initial concern that I had, Mr. Chairman, I devoted more thought and more study to the position that I have finally taken with respect to this legislation than I have with regard to any other bill that I have thought about or studied. . . . After that study I have reached the firm conviction that this legislation should be passed . . . by an overwhelming majority. . . .
>
> This is truly a crucial time in economic policy, for we face a series of problems which will not wait for a solution. Either we give our free enterprise system an opportunity to solve these problems for us, or we will find that an attempt will be made by others to solve them by more and more Government spending.
>
> It is an ironic twist of fate, Mr. Chairman, that those who in reality are opposing a tax reduction at this time—although they may think of themselves merely imposing a series of conditions—are in reality following a line which is almost certain to lead to more rather than less Government spending. . . .
>
> First, there is the problem of recurring deficits in the Federal budget. . . . For the economy to improve sufficiently for us to get rid of these plaguing deficits we must have a faster rate of growth generated by the private sector— as will occur if we free it from the present high tax straitjacket. A second problem to which I would like to direct your attention is the problem of unemployment. . . . The excess unemployment stems from a lack of sufficient growth in our economy. It is something that will not long be endured. If we do not find a way of stimulating the economy's growth through tax reduction, others will find an answer for it by increased Government spending. The unemployment problem is bound to get worse without some action in the years ahead, instead of better, as the size of the labor force increases. . . .
>
> . . . there are two roads the Government can follow toward the achievement of this larger and more prosperous economy. . . . One of these is the tax

reduction road. The other is the road of Government expenditures . . . **we want it understood that we do not intend to try to go along both roads at the same time.**

Section I of the bill announces very clearly that we are not rejecting a balance in the budget as the guiding criterion for management of the finances of the Federal Government. We are, indeed, emphatically reaffirming that criterion . . . the goal of a balanced budget in a prosperous economy. . . .

Failure to provide tax reduction and revision at this time would be fiscally irresponsible.[111]

Representative Thomas B. Curtis of Missouri, a senior Republican member of the Ways and Means Committee, contended that the Mills argument was not only a shift in style of presentation from that used by the administration—which was undeniable—but a shift in economic theory as well. "The gentleman from Arkansas does not share the economic theory which lies behind the Presidential presentation of this bill to the House," observed Curtis. "His statements here on the floor clearly demonstrate that he does not adhere to this theory nor does the Ways and Means Committee majority." Again: "The difficulty in debating this novel economic and fiscal policy publicly and here on the floor of the House lies in the fact that those who originated the tax cut were not originating it on the same philosophy advanced by the gentleman from Arkansas. . . . None of the advocates of this dangerous fiscal theory are here to support their theory and engage in straightforward debate. They hide behind the strength and character of the gentleman from Arkansas, Chairman Mills."[112] A month later, Curtis observed that "not a person supported the economic philosophy of planned deficit advanced by Dr. Heller and President Kennedy during the House debate."[113]

But the recommittal motion was defeated, 226–199, with only twenty-six Democrats defecting. The bill then passed, 271–155. Forty-eight Republicans deserted their party leadership to vote for tax reduction.

The Senate Concurs. On October 15, hearings opened in the Senate. Southern Democrats were beginning to suggest privately that Kennedy would have to choose between his tax bill and his civil rights bill, but there is no indication that they had the support of one of their number, Chairman Harry Byrd of the Finance Committee, in any delaying maneuvers. One report is that Byrd had made a firm commitment for committee

[111] *Cong. Record*, Vol. 108 (Sept. 24, 1963), pp. 17905–08.

[112] *Ibid.*, pp. 17912–13.

[113] Speech to the Associated Industries of Missouri, Oct. 30, 1963; inserted in *Cong. Record*, Vol. 109 (Nov. 4, 1963), pp. 21038–40.

action in December. Another report is that the commitment was for action in January but President Kennedy was insisting upon December.[114] Democratic Leader Mike Mansfield of Montana predicted the bill would be out of the Finance Committee shortly after January 1. Republican Leader Everett McKinley Dirksen of Illinois put his estimate as March 15.[115]

Lyndon Johnson, when he became President in November, "had some doubts about the Heller theory that the way to balance the budget eventually was to reduce taxes when there was a deficit," according to Jack Bell, his biographer of that period. "But he bought Heller's theories —and Heller." Then, whether or not he had to do so, he made what Bell calls a "deal" with Byrd, promising Byrd some expenditure cuts in exchange for a promise to speed action on the tax cut bill. The promise was to trim expenditures in the 1965 fiscal year budget to $97.9 billion—a figure even lower than the $98 billion sought by the House Republicans in their recommittal motion.[116]

The Senate took up the bill on January 30, 1964. No one could say afterward, as Representative Curtis had said following the House debate, that the Kennedy-Heller economic philosophy was not supported. Senator Russell B. Long of Louisiana, floor leader for the measure, made the most of the President's promises of expenditure control, but he also explained with clarity and candor the principles of the new economics.[117] The measure was passed, 77–21. Senate Republicans, unlike their House colleagues, did not fight the measure to the end. After supporting a losing motion to make the tax cut contingent on an expenditure limitation, they voted for the bill on final passage, 21–10. The final 77–21 roll call almost exactly inverted the last previous Senate vote on tax reduction as an instrument of fiscal policy, in June 1958.[118]

Both proponents and opponents called the Senate action historic. Senator Joseph S. Clark, Democrat of Pennsylvania, termed it "the first step toward the intelligent use of tax and expenditure policy to achieve full employment in the United States." Senator Proxmire agreed that "this 1964 tax cut inaugurates a brand-new era in American economic policy."

---

[114] Alan L. Otten, *Wall Street Journal*, Oct. 19, 1967.

[115] *Cong. Record*, Vol. 109 (Nov. 18, 1963), p. 22058.

[116] Jack Bell, *The Johnson Treatment* (Harper & Row, 1965), pp. 90–94. See also Evans and Novak, *Lyndon B. Johnson*, pp. 369–76.

[117] See especially *Cong. Record*, Vol. 110 (Jan. 30, 1964), p. 1501.

[118] Among the 21 negative votes were at least 2 whose opposition was based upon a belief that the unbalancing of the budget should be through expenditures rather than tax cuts.

The new policy, as he saw it, was "a principle-busting, financially irresponsible, inflationary, regressive monstrosity."[119]

Retrospect and Prospect. "It isn't often," said *Business Week* a year later, "that the United States can look back on a major change in Government policy and find absolutely no grounds for criticism."[120]

The annual rate of consumption expenditures rose by $45 billion in the first six quarters after the tax cut—an increase unmatched in peacetime history. The tax cut raised the gross national product by an estimated $25 billion annually by September 1965 and would ultimately provide the basis for an increment of $36 billion a year. As the tax cut advocates had predicted, the government took in more cash receipts at the lower rates— $4 billion more in the 1965 fiscal year than in the previous year. With this stimulus the economy continued through its fifth year without a downturn, and without any inflationary surge. Since the first quarter of 1961 the gross national product had been raised by about one-fourth (after adjustment for price changes)—for an annual growth rate of 5.3 percent, exceeding the optimistic 5 percent target set in the 1960 Democratic platform. Meanwhile, unemployment declined to 4.5 percent of the labor force, the lowest rate since October 1957.[121] And the economists predicted that the upward trend in the economy would continue—provided that Congress performed the happy duty of annually disposing of the year's increase in revenues, starting at $7 billion and rising, either through expenditure increases or further tax cuts. The Congress accepted this duty so readily in 1965 that a cut in excise taxes based upon the same economic reasoning as the Revenue Act of 1964 was passed promptly and almost without controversy. After that date, of course, the mounting costs of the Vietnam war absorbed the added revenues.

Does this mean that the economy is at last recession-free? Have the cyclical downturns that plagued the postwar years—and that had such a decisive impact on the political history of the period—become a thing of the past?

The answer of the economists is one of optimism—but cautious optimism. Walter Heller takes encouragement from the demonstrated success

[119] *Cong. Record,* Vol. 110 (Feb. 7, 1964), pp. 2393–94.
[120] Feb. 27, 1965, p. 160.
[121] Figures in this paragraph are from speeches by Gardner Ackley, chairman, and Arthur M. Okun, member, Council of Economic Advisers, before the American Statistical Association, Philadelphia, Sept. 9 and 10, 1965. The expansion was still continuing unchecked in 1968.

of the revolutionary tax cut of 1964, the growth of public confidence in the economists and the growth of their confidence in themselves, the improvement in the tools of their trade, and the change in public attitudes. He sees a growing acceptance of an active federal fiscal policy and an "ebbing" of old fears—"the fear that budget deficits necessarily spell inflation, insolvency, and irresponsibility; the fear that a growing national debt would burden our children and grandchildren and bring on national bankruptcy . . . the fear that fiscal planning, however prudent, necessarily spells growing centralization of power in Washington."[122]

To put it in other terms, the Revenue Act of 1964 may have marked the point at which the discussion of fiscal policy in the nation crossed the threshold from the realm of morals to the realm of economics. Fiscal policy may have come at last to be molded primarily by a cool assessment of its impact upon the various indices that reflect the economic well-being of the people—the rate of national growth, levels of employment and unemployment, the stability of prices—rather than by the force of moral absolutes. But assuming that "the Puritan ethic," as Heller once termed it, has faded, and assuming further that economic science has advanced to the point that the economists, at any moment in time, can devise the right antirecession measures, what then? Will the institutional structure of government permit the effective execution of well-designed antirecession measures?

As economic science has advanced, the institutional structure has advanced also. The Employment Act of 1946 provides the legal mandate for fiscal activism. Creation of the Council of Economic Advisers assures that fiscal economists will sit in the highest policy-making levels of the executive branch. The institution of the economic report of the President compels the chief executive to review and sign his name to a document his economists prepare. And, on Capitol Hill, the Joint Economic Committee, although it has no authority to act on legislative measures, provides a continuing and influential educational and communications link between the world of economic thought and the world of legislative action.

Nevertheless, there remain weaknesses in the institutional structure of government serious enough to suggest that the problem of cyclical unemployment is by no means finally solved. When Kennedy observed to Sorensen that "the British prepared, proposed, passed and put into effect a proportionately larger tax cut than ours, and are getting the benefits

[122] Walter W. Heller, "The Future of Our Fiscal System," *Journal of Business*, Vol. 38, No. 3 (July 1965), pp. 235–36.

from it, while we are still holding hearings,"[123] he defined a fundamental problem.

"The first principle," Arthur Burns wrote in 1957, "is that when the economy shows signs of faltering, prompt countermoves are required. Even mild measures on the part of government can be effective in the early stages of an economic decline. On the other hand, if action is withheld until a recession has gathered momentum, strong and costly measures may prove insufficient."[124]

To enable immediate action when a downturn threatened, standby authority for the President to accelerate public works was proposed in 1960 by the Senate special committee on unemployment problems. In 1962 and again in 1963 President Kennedy asked for standby authority both to initiate public works and to reduce taxes on a temporary basis.[125] In 1965 President Johnson suggested a modified approach, whereby Congress would merely alter its procedures to permit rapid action on temporary tax reductions if recession threatened. But Congress has shown little interest in these proposals.[126]

Once a fiscal policy emerges from the arduous relationships of the executive and legislative branches, it may or may not be in harmony with monetary policy made by an agency that is independent of both and very jealous of its independence—the Federal Reserve System. Yet fiscal and monetary policy tend either to reinforce or to neutralize each other. If the Congress and the executive branch, who must face the electorate, undertake an expansionary fiscal policy, their policies can be largely nullified by a board that does not have to account to the people for the consequences of its actions. Thus economic policy is placed in part outside the democratic process.

The Federal Reserve Board has, in recent years, sought to carry out

---

[123] Sorensen, *Kennedy*, p. 433.

[124] *Prosperity without Inflation*, p. 33.

[125] For a discussion of the unsuccessful attempt to enact a standby public works bill in 1962, see Chap. 3, pp. 93–97.

[126] CEA Chairman Ackley points out that undue comfort should not be taken from the fact that the 1965 excise tax cut was passed in 32 days, since full-scale hearings had been held earlier and the specific character of the changes was relatively noncontroversial (*Fiscal Policy Issues of the Coming Decade*, Hearings before Subcommittee on Fiscal Policy of the Joint Economic Committee, 89 Cong. 1 sess. [1965], p. 12). It should be noted that this chapter has been concerned only with the use of fiscal policy to stimulate the economy and eliminate excessive unemployment; experience since 1965 suggests that it may be much more difficult to use fiscal policy promptly and decisively for the opposite purpose of slowing the economy and checking inflation.

policies in reasonable harmony with those of the executive. The President has some leverage through his power to appoint and reappoint the board's members. Consultation has been systematized through regular meetings between Chairman Martin and the President or his top economic advisers. Yet Martin has zealously guarded his ultimate right to manage the country's monetary system without interference from the President or anyone else. The record seems clear that, on occasion at least, actions of the Federal Reserve System have been contradictory to the policy the rest of the government was pursuing at the time. And if the government pursues contradictory policies, then it has, in effect, no policy at all.

The people do not hold the members of the Federal Reserve Board responsible for the state of the economy. They hold the President and his party in Congress responsible, as the elections of 1954, 1958, and 1960 clearly demonstrated. And if the officials elected by the people are, in the present age, held accountable for maintaining prosperity and achieving maximum employment, should they have authority commensurate with their responsibility?

While these problems remained, the prospect that the American political and governmental system could steadily maintain the rate of economic growth necessary for full employment was far better as the 1953–66 period ended than it had ever been before. Three elections had taught the politicians that they *must* respond to the issue of unemployment whenever it appears. In a more positive sense, experience since 1964 had also taught them that a full employment economy provides the greater revenues from which politicians' dreams are realized—be they dreams of Great Societies or of tax cuts. Fiscal orthodoxy might not have been crushed for all time but it had assuredly been discredited—first by its own failures in the years of economic slowdown, then by the success of the new economics. If the economy were again to slump into recession, there is no doubt that the responsible politicians of both parties would turn quickly to their economists, and the advice they would receive would be Keynesian—as even Milton Friedman has said, "We are all Keynesians now."[127] Expansionary budget and revenue policies would not have to undergo again the long struggle for recognition and acceptance that was required in the years from 1958 to 1964.

[127] Quoted in *Time*, Dec. 31, 1965, p. 65. Friedman, an outspoken conservative, had served as an economic adviser in Senator Goldwater's presidential campaign.

CHAPTER III

For the Unemployed, Jobs: Structural Measures

CHAIRMAN William McChesney Martin, Jr., of the Federal Reserve Board had often described the board's policy as one of "leaning against the wind" to counter either inflationary or deflationary forces in the economy. Six weeks after the inauguration of President John F. Kennedy, when the Washington air was full of talk of new expansionary fiscal policies, Martin leaned against the political wind. Appearing before the Joint Economic Committee of the Congress, he dismissed cyclical unemployment in a single paragraph as "temporary" and devoted ten paragraphs to "another, structural type" of unemployment that he saw as worse.[1] Structural unemployment was manifest, he said, "in the higher total of those left unemployed after each wave of the three most recent business cycles, and in the idleness of many West Virginia coal miners, eastern and midwestern steel and auto workers, west coast aircraft workers, and like groups, in good times as well as bad."

"To have important effect," he warned, "attempts to reduce structural unemployment by massive monetary and fiscal stimulation of overall de-

[1] A simple and useful technical definition of structural unemployment is Barbara R. Berman's: "That part of unemployment which should be eliminated through labor market policies, except for that amount which could be eliminated by general demand-stimulation measures unaccompanied by other measures" ("Alternative Measures of Structural Unemployment," in Arthur M. Ross [ed.], *Employment Policy and the Labor Market* [University of California Press, 1965], p. 257). Structural unemployment is thus residual—the unemployment that remains after "cyclical" unemployment (which can be eliminated through demand stimulation) and "frictional" unemployment (which is the irreducible minimum that cannot be eliminated) are deducted from the total.

mands probably would have to be carried to such lengths as to create serious new problems of inflationary character—at a time when consumer prices already are at a record high." Instead, he advocated "specific actions that take into account the who, the where, and the why of unemployment, and, accordingly, go to the core of the particular problem."[2]

The committee took sharp notice. Only the day before, Kennedy's new Council of Economic Advisers had characterized as "false" Martin's basic thesis that structural unemployment had increased. The unemployment problem, CEA member James Tobin had told the committee, "is not a matter of the structure of the labor force or technological unemployment. . . . We have a problem of unemployment that we can defeat by fairly standard fiscal and monetary means provided these are applied resolutely enough."

"Maybe we are getting this difference of opinion out in the open," said Representative Thomas Curtis, Missouri Republican.

"To my ear," added Democratic Representative Henry S. Reuss of Wisconsin, "there appears to be a very basic conflict."[3]

"That is about as sharp and decisive a contradiction of economic policy as the Government can have," commented William Proxmire, Democratic senator from Wisconsin, when he inserted the contrasting statements in parallel columns in the *Congressional Record* two days later.[4]

But after a meeting with the President, the witnesses agreed there was no basic disagreement. "The apparent differences . . . are mainly ones of definition and emphasis," Martin subsequently told the committee. "The Council's statement recognized the importance of structural unemployment," said the council, while holding its ground in insisting that structural factors did not account for recent increases in unemployment.[5] "I do not see that there is a basic clash between these two views," the President told his news conference. "Some of it is structural and some of it is not."[6]

With the last statement, everyone could agree. And, as it turned out, the President's instinct that this was enough of a resolution as of early 1961 was sound.[7] Martin and the CEA agreed that total unemployment

---

[2] *January 1961 Economic Report of the President and the Economic Situation and Outlook,* Hearings before the Joint Economic Committee, 87 Cong. 1 sess. (March 6 and 7, 1961), pp. 464, 470.

[3] *Ibid.,* pp. 378, 417, 480, 485.

[4] *Cong. Record,* Vol. 107 (March 9, 1961), p. 3601.

[5] *January 1961 Economic Report of the President,* Hearings, pp. 486, 571.

[6] *Public Papers of the Presidents, 1961,* p. 187.

[7] For a commentary on the continuing dispute on this question in academic confer-

had both "cyclical" and "structural" components, and the Kennedy administration was committed to a simultaneous attack on both. As long as the attack on both components went forward successfully, it was not necessary to agree upon the exact size of each—which could never be computed with precision anyway. At some point, as full employment was approached, further expansionary fiscal and monetary policies would be inflationary, and unemployment would have to be reduced through structural measures alone. Nobody disagreed with Martin on that. He clearly felt that the danger point would be reached sooner, and the CEA later, but at a time when total unemployment was at the highest level in twenty years the point was, in either case, still a long way off. And the Federal Reserve Board, at the time, was pursuing an "easy" money policy.

The Martin-CEA clash did more than any previous event to dramatize the importance of structural unemployment, but the phenomenon was by no means a new discovery. Even during the hostilities in Korea, when employers everywhere frantically sought workers, unemployment averaged around two million—or about 3 percent of the labor force—and not all of this could be explained away as short-term "frictional" joblessness. From 1955 through 1957, during years of relative prosperity and of inflationary pressure, unemployment remained above 4 percent. Structural measures are those that, as Martin put it, "go to the core of the particular problem." What are the particular problems that prevent workers from being matched with available jobs at a time when jobs go begging?

There are three main problems: Some of the unemployed live in the wrong *place*—in areas lacking job opportunities. Some have the wrong *skill*, or none at all. And some are the victims of *discrimination*—because of race, sex, or age.[8]

---

ences and journals, see Richard G. Lipsey, "Structural and Deficient-Demand Unemployment Reconsidered," in Arthur M. Ross (ed.), *Employment Policy and the Labor Market* (University of California Press, 1965), pp. 210–55. Curtis C. Aller observes that most economists, too, are content with Kennedy's compromise: "True, there was a sharp, sometimes acrimonious debate between the structuralists and the aggregative theorists. But even for the professionals this seemed always to have an unreal quality and the more pragmatic politicians, as well as the American people, sensed early the conclusion that we need both, a position to which nearly all professionals have retreated as a happy compromise" ("The Role of Government-Sponsored Training and Retraining Programs," in William G. Bowen and Frederick H. Harbison (eds.), *Unemployment in a Prosperous Economy* [Princeton University, 1965], p. 126).

[8] This classification is consistent with that contained in the *Report of the Special Committee on Unemployment Problems*, S. Rept. 1206, 86 Cong. 2 sess. (1960), pp. 6–14. The report, with its 4,100-page "Readings in Unemployment" and its 432-page "Studies in Unemployment," remains the most comprehensive treatment of structural unemployment yet undertaken.

As the "who, the where, and the why" of hard-core unemployment were analyzed in the 1950's, the nature of the necessary remedial action for each of these categories could be at least broadly defined. For those living in the wrong place, either jobs should be brought to the workers or the workers should be relocated. For those lacking necessary skills, training and retraining opportunities should be provided. For victims of discrimination, private and public hiring policies should be changed.

As early as 1954, legislation designed to assist "depressed areas" was introduced in Congress. During the next dozen years, a series of measures were developed, introduced, refined, and enacted to deal with structural unemployment—progressively bolder, broader, and involving greater federal expenditures. This chapter traces the evolution of national policies to reduce unemployment through structural measures—except for measures to overcome discrimination in employment, which are discussed with other civil rights measures in Chapter 6.

The Area Redevelopment Deadlock   *(1955–60)*

"We don't want to see Carbondale, a typical God-fearing American city, die," the mayor of Carbondale testified. "The city and its people deserve a better fate."[9]

The plea of Mayor Frank P. Kelly of the small Pennsylvania city was the kind that could not go unheeded. Carbondale had made its living by digging anthracite coal. Now its mines were dead, their markets preempted by other fuels. Through no fault of its hard-working and "God-fearing" citizenry, a community was stranded. Able-bodied men idled their time away on street corners, business was withering, population declining.

What was true of Carbondale was true of the entire anthracite region of northeast Pennsylvania. It was true, also, of the soft-coal regions—the Appalachian belt running from western Pennsylvania through West Virginia and Kentucky all the way to Alabama, and the midwestern fields centering in southern Illinois. It was true, also, of the textile cities of New England, whose industry had been moving southward for decades. And it was true of lumbering communities, farm trading centers, and scattered

[9] Testimony before a subcommittee of the Senate Labor and Public Welfare Committee, at Wilkes-Barre, Pa., Feb. 10, 1956; inserted in *Cong. Record*, Vol. 102 (Feb. 20, 1956), pp. 2853–54.

industrial and railroad cities throughout the country where the economic base had, for one or another reason, declined or disappeared.

Emergence of the Depressed Areas Problem. When the Employment Act of 1946 was written, the emergence of depressed areas was not foreseen. The discussion leading to the 1946 act centered upon the Keynesian concepts and techniques for the planning and influencing of aggregates— the "national production and employment budget," the "aggregate volume of investment and expenditure," and so on. That full employment might also depend on measures to match individual workers with individual jobs was not recognized.[10]

As aggregate unemployment rose after the war, however, its concentration in certain depressed localities began to be apparent. The first economic report of President Harry S Truman, in 1947, noted the persistence of labor surpluses in certain areas. During the Korean period a policy was adopted that set aside a portion of certain military procurement items for negotiated contracts with employers in surplus labor areas, provided they could match the average of all bids submitted.[11] In July 1953, however, senators from regions that had lost contracts to the northeastern depressed areas joined in adding a rider to the defense appropriations bill prohibiting any kind of procurement preference. Senator Dennis Chavez, Democrat of New Mexico, expressed the argument simply: "Why should 250 widows in my state be thrown out of work, in order to give work to 250 widows in New England?" The anti-preference forces carried the Senate, 62–25, with only seven votes for the preference from outside the northeastern-midwestern industrial belt.[12] The rider was modified in the Senate-House conference to prohibit price differentials but permit preference where the employer in the labor surplus area could match the lowest bid from elsewhere.

[10] Stephen K. Bailey's case study of the history of that act contains no reference to structural unemployment (*Congress Makes a Law*, Columbia University Press, 1950); nor did the "Full Employment Bill," from which the quoted phrases in this paragraph are taken (for the text of the bill, which became the Employment Act, see *ibid.*, pp. 243–48). Interestingly Great Britain, the home of Keynes, had enacted a depressed areas bill as early as 1934, and in 1945 passed a Distribution of Industry Act, providing limited financial aid to firms locating in areas of above-average unemployment (see William H. Miernyk, "Area Redevelopment," in Joseph M. Becker, S. J. (ed.), *In Aid of the Unemployed* [Johns Hopkins Press, 1965], p. 162).

[11] Manpower Policy No. 4 of the Office of Defense Mobilization, issued in March 1952; originally it required the producer in the surplus labor area to meet the lowest bid submitted for that portion of the purchase not set aside, but the terms were subsequently liberalized (Miernyk, "Area Redevelopment," pp. 160–61).

[12] *Cong. Record,* Vol. 99 (July 22, 1953), pp. 9506, 9508.

As the national economy slid into the recession of 1953–54, the plight of the distressed areas worsened. In March 1954 the administration named a task force on local unemployment, and members of Congress began to design depressed areas bills.[13] First to introduce legislation embodying the central provisions of what became the Area Redevelopment Act was Democratic Representative Thomas J. Lane of the textile city of Lawrence, Massachusetts, in May 1954. Pointing out that "modern and diversified industries" could not be attracted to the "empty coal mines or ancient mill buildings" of the depressed communities, he proposed a $50 million federal loan fund to enable local nonprofit corporations to build modern, one-story factory buildings.[14] The following month, Republican Representative James A. Van Zandt of the Altoona, Pennsylvania, coal and railroad district proposed legislation for a special public works program for thirty-eight major industrial areas (almost 20 percent of the total) that he described as having unemployment over 12 percent.[15]

The decisive event, however, was the reelection campaign tour that autumn of Democratic Senator Paul Douglas through the coal fields of southern Illinois. Douglas returned to Washington convinced that the economic revival of depressed areas was a national problem requiring capital investment by the federal government. And, as chairman of both the Senate's labor subcommittee and the Joint Economic Committee in the new Congress, he was in a strategic position to obtain results.

In his economic report of January 1955, President Eisenhower suggested that special tax amortization benefits for new defense facilities be continued in labor surplus areas. Beyond that, however, he held that the federal contribution should be a "limited" one. The national government could help mainly by policies designed to bring about a "high and stable ievel of employment in the Nation at large." "A large part of the adjustment of depressed areas to new economic conditions," said the President, "both can and should be carried out by the local citizens themselves."[16]

This cautious approach gave Douglas a partisan springboard. The

[13] For a detailed history of the Area Redevelopment Act, see Sar A. Levitan, *Federal Aid to Depressed Areas* (Johns Hopkins Press, 1964), Chap. 1, and Roger H. Davidson, *Coalition-Building for Depressed Areas Bills: 1955–1965* (published for Inter-University Case Program by Bobbs-Merrill, 1966). Davidson's study appears in condensed form in John Bibby and Roger H. Davidson, *On Capitol Hill* (Holt, Rinehart and Winston, 1967).

[14] *Cong. Record*, Vol. 100 (May 12, 1954), pp. 6490–91.

[15] *Ibid.* (June 22, 1954), pp. 8674–75.

[16] *Economic Report of the President, January 1955*, p. 57.

Democratic majority of the Joint Economic Committee demanded a "positive program" to aid depressed areas. In general terms, they proposed a public works program, long-term credit for new industry or business, technical assistance, retraining of jobless workers, and allowances equivalent to unemployment insurance benefits for the workers undergoing retraining. When the Area Redevelopment Act finally became law in 1961, these were still its principal features, as refined and modified in six years of hearings and debate.

The Legislative Journey Begins. With seven Democratic cosponsors, including John Kennedy of Massachusetts, Douglas introduced on July 23, a few days before Congress adjourned, a bill embodying the proposals of the Joint Economic Committee majority report. Sar A. Levitan (who as a Library of Congress economist actually drafted the bill) observes that Douglas had originally intended to wait until 1956 before introducing the bill, in order to allow further time to perfect it, and conjectures that he moved up his timing when he learned that the administration might reverse its previous position and act first.[17] In October, as it turned out, the Eisenhower administration did reverse itself. CEA Chairman Arthur Burns presented a "point four program for America" to the President in his hospital room at Denver, and Eisenhower was, in his own words, "so pleased" that he had Burns announce the program as soon as he left the room.[18] The January economic report, in contrast to the one of a year before, asserted that "the fate of distressed communities is a matter of national as well as local concern" and urged "bolder measures" to be embodied in a new area assistance program.[19]

The administration bill was introduced in January 1956 by Senator H. Alexander Smith of New Jersey and nineteen other Republicans. The two measures now before Congress differed in important particulars: The Republican measure proposed $50 million for loans for industrial facilities in depressed areas; the Democratic measure, $100 million. The Democratic bill was more liberal in loan terms and in the definition of eligible areas; moreover, it proposed two programs not in the Republican bill: retraining of unemployed workers with subsistence allowances during retraining, and $125 million in loans and grants for public facilities neces-

[17] Levitan, *Federal Aid to Depressed Areas*, p. 4.

[18] Dwight D. Eisenhower, *Mandate for Change* (Doubleday, 1963), p. 553; also Davidson, *Coalition-Building for Depressed Areas Bills*, p. 5.

[19] *Economic Report of the President, January 1956*, pp. 61–63.

sary to enable a community to attract industry. For the next five years the depressed areas waited vainly for salvation while politicians of the two parties sparred and jockeyed over these points of difference—despite their agreement on objectives and on principles. Unable to compromise, and each unable to override the other, both parties took their cases to the voters in three national elections. In so doing, they magnified relatively minor differences of degree into major differences of principle. The Democrats, eagerly backed by organized labor, were able to convert area redevelopment into a powerful political issue in the affected areas, which symbolized —in their oratory—the contrast between Democratic compassion and Republican unconcern. The Republicans sought to recoup by using the bill as an example before the country at large of Republican fiscal prudence contrasted to Democratic profligacy.

Following hearings in early 1956, Douglas revised his bill—and a coalition was born. A measure designed for the textile and coal towns of the Northeast was broadened into a combined urban-rural bill with benefits also for the depressed agricultural regions of the South. The prime mover behind this development was Representative Brooks Hays, Democrat of Arkansas, who saw in the proposal a means of bringing industry to the rural South to offset the long-term decline in agricultural employment. In the Senate, Democrat John J. Sparkman of Alabama, who had just headed a Joint Economic Committee study of rural poverty, took the lead. The idea met little resistance. The memory of solid southern opposition in 1953 to procurement preference for depressed areas was still fresh in the minds of the bill's supporters, and Douglas and his associates quickly seized upon the Hays proposal.

To the $100 million authorized by the bill for loans for new industry in urban areas of heavy unemployment (now labeled "redevelopment areas" instead of "depressed areas"), Douglas added $50 million for the three hundred rural counties of greatest "underemployment" as measured by low income. Before the measure reached the Senate floor, however, another Arkansas Democrat, Chairman J. William Fulbright of the Banking and Currency Committee, challenged the jurisdiction of the Labor and Public Welfare Committee and, in so doing, won several concessions of major importance to the South. He succeeded in raising the $50 million rural loan fund to $100 million to attain "parity" with the urban areas, in deleting a provision that would have restored preference to depressed areas in government procurement, and in eliminating a labor-supported "antipirating" clause prohibiting loans where relocation of industry would result.[20]

In the brief Senate debate, only Republican Barry Goldwater of Arizona attacked the basic principle of area redevelopment—calling it "an unwarranted invasion of private rights" and describing depressed areas as "perfectly normal to the economic cycle of American enterprise." Other speakers differed only on the terms of the measure. Final vote for the Douglas bill was 60–30. The Republicans made no attempt to substitute their own measure, and sixteen of their number were willing to follow the Democratic leadership.

Meanwhile, at the House end of the Capitol, an odd drama was enacted. A companion bill to the Douglas measure, introduced by Democratic Representative Daniel J. Flood of the anthracite county of Luzerne, Pennsylvania, had been approved by the House Banking and Currency Committee but was bottled up in the House Rules Committee when Chairman Howard W. Smith, Democrat, disappeared in his Virginia district and refused to call a meeting. As adjournment approached, Flood sought to pass a bill under suspension of the rules, which requires a two-thirds vote. For this purpose Republican votes were needed, and Flood therefore agreed to accept the administration bill. He called Commerce Secretary Sinclair Weeks, who dispatched Assistant Secretary Frederick H. Mueller to the Capitol. Mueller conferred with Republican Representatives Van Zandt and Ivor D. Fenton, who represented another Pennsylvania anthracite district. The latter two, according to Flood, "advised me that the administration was adamant and against any bill whatsoever."[21] And so the bill was lost in the adjournment rush.

The administration had good reason to fear—as Flood doubtless had reason to expect—that if the House passed the Republican bill, the measure that would emerge from a House-Senate conference would be either the Douglas-Flood bill or one very close to it. But it is clear that the ad-

[20] Majority Leader Lyndon B. Johnson and Chairman Lister Hill (Democrat of Alabama) of the Labor and Public Welfare Committee acted as intermediaries in working out the agreement to accept Fulbright's amendments. Davidson (*Coalition-Building for Depressed Areas Bills*) credits the "activation" of Johnson to the Area Employment Expansion Committee, a small group formed in the spring by William L. Batt, Jr., director of the Toledo industrial development council, and Solomon Barkin, research director for the Textile Workers Union of America, to coordinate the efforts of labor and liberal organizations supporting the bill. Their group also took the initiative in persuading Senator Kennedy to assume responsibility for the bill when Douglas suddenly left the Labor and Public Welfare Committee in favor of a seat on the Finance Committee.

[21] *Cong. Record*, Vol. 102 (July 27, 1956), p. 15292.

ministration, taken as a whole, was less than wholeheartedly behind its "point four program for America." Eisenhower did not include the bill in his "must" list. His news conference comments were, at best, lukewarm.[22] When confronted at his August 1 news conference with Flood's story, the President replied: "You are telling me something now that I did not know . . . I was disappointed [the legislation] was not passed, and I don't know the reason lying behind it." In his memoirs, Sherman Adams admits that "the businessmen in the Cabinet were unenthusiastic about such new loan programs," and explains that Douglas "loaded [the bill] with subsidies and other provisions that Eisenhower and his more conservative associates would not accept." In his own memoirs, Eisenhower defines the unacceptable provisions as the inclusion of rural areas "where the problem was low incomes rather than unemployment" and inclusion of "urban areas of substantial unemployment regardless of whether that unemployment was temporary or chronic."[23]

Granting that Eisenhower personally favored the idea, he left the congressional relations to the "unenthusiastic businessmen," Weeks and Mueller. The President and the bill's advocates within the administration were not in communication with the bill's Republican supporters on Capitol Hill. No effort was made to strike a compromise or bargain with the Democrats on the bill's provisions. A few months later, in the state with the largest number of depressed areas, Republican Senator James H. Duff of Pennsylvania was upset by Democrat Joseph S. Clark by the slender margin of 18,000 votes out of 4.5 million, after a campaign in which Clark had made the most of the depressed areas issue. Since the Democrats organized the Senate in the Eighty-fifth Congress by only a single vote, it is at least open to speculation that if Mueller had said "yes" instead of "no" to Van Zandt and Fenton, Eisenhower would have had a Republican instead of a Democratic Senate to work with when he began his second term.

The First Eisenhower Veto. Despite the lopsided Senate victory in 1956, the going was not to be smooth when Douglas and Flood introduced their 1957 version of the area redevelopment bill. The jurisdictional rights of the Senate Banking and Currency Committee had been conceded during

[22] See, for example, his remarks of June 6, 1956, *Public Papers of the Presidents, 1956,* p. 562.

[23] Sherman Adams, *Firsthand Report* (Harper, 1961), pp. 361–62; Eisenhower, *Mandate for Change,* p. 553.

the 1956 negotiations and, while Douglas was on that committee, Fulbright was in control. He assigned the bill to a subcommittee headed by Douglas but appointed to that subcommittee a majority opposed to the measure. Among that majority was Fulbright himself, whose doubts of the previous summer had by now matured into outright opposition. Moreover, 1957 was the year of Eisenhower's and Treasury Secretary George Humphrey's challenge to Congress to cut the budget[24]—not a propitious year for any spending measure. Accordingly, while Douglas held hearings on his bill in 1957, he did not risk a subcommittee vote. In the House, where the budget-cutting fever ran hottest, hearings were not even scheduled.

In 1958, however, help came from a new quarter. A Republican member of the committee, Senator Frederick H. Payne of Maine, faced a difficult reelection campaign in a state dotted with depressed textile towns. Payne advised Douglas that he was ready to compromise whether or not he had the green light from Eisenhower. Douglas readily assented, and "the two gentlemen from Maine" (Douglas had lived in the state and had graduated from Bowdoin College) had no difficulty working out a bipartisan tactic. Payne introduced a new bill, with six other Republicans as cosponsors. When Fulbright on March 19 convened the committee for a hearing on his own antirecession measure, the community facilities bill,[25] Payne immediately moved that the group go into executive session to consider depressed areas legislation. Caught by surprise, Fulbright declined to put the motion and for the next forty minutes the spectators found themselves occupying ringside seats at a rare display of congressional in-fighting. Fulbright said Douglas should have put the matter to a subcommittee vote. Douglas retorted that he could not, because Fulbright had "stacked" the subcommittee. Fulbright denied the charge, called Douglas "derelict in his duty." Douglas called Fulbright a "deep-freeze artist." Fulbright termed the bill "special legislation for a few spots in Illinois, Pennsylvania, and few other places." Fulbright disparaged Illinois, and Douglas disparaged Arkansas. Presently, Payne inquired whether his own bill had been referred to subcommittee. When the committee clerk reported that the formal reference had not yet been made and the bill was therefore technically before the full committee, Douglas moved that it be made the "pending order of business" of the full com-

[24] See Chap. 9, pp. 424–26.
[25] See Chap. 2, p. 25.

mittee. The motion was carried, 8–5, with Payne and two Republican colleagues providing the necessary margin.

Douglas and Payne then put their heads together to merge their bills into a single measure. The new Douglas-Payne bill was essentially the Douglas proposal with minor concessions to the administration position. Seventeen Republican senators joined twenty-nine Democrats as sponsors. The committee approved it, 8–7, and the Senate passed it, 46–36, on May 13.

Republican support of the bill was slightly stronger than in 1956. Of forty-one Republicans voting, seventeen—or 40 percent—were in the affirmative. But erosion of southern Democratic support cut the bill's margin from thirty to ten. Eight southern votes, including Fulbright's, were reversed.

Fulbright argued that unemployment should be attacked nationally "without favoritism." The bill, he said, would limit its benefits to areas with only 12 percent of the nation's unemployed. Areas have deteriorated "because private investors have not considered them as attractive as other areas. . . . Here we have an attempt to substitute the judgment of the Federal Government for the judgment of our free enterprise system, regardless of the economic consequences." Democratic Senator Spessard L. Holland of Florida, another who reversed his position, referred to letters in opposition he had received from Florida business, industrial, agricultural, and municipal groups. He contended that if the bill proved helpful, it "would be an open invitation for an assault upon Congress the like of which we have never witnessed before" from the larger cities which accounted for the major portion of the nation's unemployed.[26]

Circumstances had changed since 1956. The proponents had had time to organize, but so had the opponents. In the antispending year of 1957, the U.S. Chamber of Commerce and other business groups had made the area redevelopment bill a particular target of attack, as Senator Holland noted. By 1958, southern senators usually responsive to the views of business groups had "heard from home." Fulbright, a southerner and chairman of the committee handling the bill, had assumed leadership of the opposition. The "antipirating" clause, deleted in 1956 as part of the price of Fulbright's support, had been reinserted. And, by the time the bill reached the Senate floor during the 1958 recession, the opposition could argue cogently that the unemployment problem was so widespread—with 86 of the nation's 149 major industrial areas suffering unemployment

[26] *Cong. Record*, Vol. 104 (May 13, 1958), pp. 8522–31.

over 6 percent—that a national rather than an area approach was needed.

The House Banking and Currency Committee reported the Douglas-Payne bill on July 1 with some amendments, one of which removed the ceiling of three hundred counties that could qualify for rural aid. The Rules Committee held the bill for six weeks but finally released it after the sponsors agreed to eliminate subsistence payments for workers undergoing retraining. Representative Hugh Scott, at that time the Republican candidate for the Senate in Pennsylvania, cast the deciding vote in the committee. The House defeated a Republican recommittal motion 188–170 and then passed the bill. Thirty percent of the Republicans, 49 of 165, voted against recommittal. The Senate accepted the House amendments.

But the President had other ideas. He overruled the entreaties of Senator Payne and many of his Republican colleagues, as well as those of Labor Secretary James P. Mitchell, and vetoed the bill. In his memorandum of disapproval, the President objected to the features of the bill that would "greatly diminish local responsibility" for solving the problem of depressed areas. In particular, he opposed a loan term of forty years instead of twenty-five, a loan limit of 65 percent of the cost of projects instead of 35 percent, "artificially low" interest rates, and public facility grants up to 100 percent. He also raised "serious question" as to whether the bill should be extended to rural areas. He urged Congress, which by then had ended its 1958 session, to pass early in 1959 a "more soundly conceived" bill that he could approve.

Two days later, Senator Payne was defeated in the September election in Maine.[27] Payne's defeat was too decisive (he received less than 40 percent of the vote) to be ascribed to this single cause, but the vote helped to dramatize the unemployment issue that became in November the strongest single factor in the Democratic landslide.[28] One Republican victor, Senator-elect Scott of Pennsylvania, observed that "Pennsylvania's areas

[27] At that time, Maine held its congressional elections in September rather than November.

[28] A scholar attached to the staff of Republican National Chairman Meade Alcorn has written: "The recession continued as a major factor throughout the campaign. In his appearances Alcorn normally incorporated the twin themes of pointing with pride to the administration's anti-recession program and attacking as irresponsible the more extreme Democratic proposals. But eloquent speeches about the inflationary irresponsibility of the Democrats seemed less persuasive with voters than Democratic charges that such things as Eisenhower's veto of depressed areas legislation showed Republicans to be heartlessly unconcerned with economic hardship and unemployment" (Philip S. Wilder, Jr., *Meade Alcorn and the 1958 Election,* Eagleton Foundation Case Studies in Practical Politics [Holt, 1959], p. 6). For a fuller analysis of the impact of the unemployment issue on the 1958 election see Chap. 10, pp. 456–62.

of chronic unemployment were made to feel by the Democrats that the situation which has existed with them for more than a generation has somehow been caused by the willfulness of the Eisenhower Administration. It was a phony issue, but it caught on, notably in the anthracite area."[29] One of the seats lost by the Republicans was in the anthracite area, centering on Scranton and including Mayor Kelly's Carbondale. Congressional Quarterly identified nine other Republican "depressed Districts" that were lost to the Democrats in 1958.[30]

The Second Eisenhower Veto. In 1959–60 the two parties replayed, with but minor variations, the scenario of the preceding Congress. If the Republican position had become frozen, the Democratic position was no less so. Organized labor had now made depressed area legislation a major objective. Groups interested in rural development, particularly the National Grange, the National Farmers Union, and the National Rural Electric Cooperatives Association, had become active supporters. So had a variety of other groups, including the influential American Municipal Association[31] and the U.S. Conference of Mayors—all loosely coordinated through the Area Employment Expansion Committee. Why should the Democrats give ground? The issue had proven potent in two elections. If an "adequate" bill—which meant a measure close to the Douglas bill— could not be passed, or if it were vetoed, then the Democrats would take the issue to the people in 1960.

So Douglas reintroduced his bill, with only minimal concessions to the administration—a thirty-year loan term, a slightly higher interest rate, and more restrictive requirements for eligibility. But the Eisenhower veto had established a Republican position; this time only five GOP senators joined as cosponsors, instead of seventeen. Douglas again held hearings in the depressed areas as well as in Washington. Again he bypassed his adverse subcommittee, but this time without any resistance on the part of the new committee chairman, A. Willis Robertson, Democrat of Vir-

---

[29] *U.S. News and World Report,* Nov. 4, 1958, p. 95.

[30] *Congressional Quarterly Almanac, 1958,* p. 147; Levitan (*Federal Aid to Depressed Areas,* p. 13) says about 80 percent of the 48 Republican seats captured by Democrats "were located in depressed areas," but the *Almanac's* lower figure appears to be closer to the number of districts where the area redevelopment bill had been well enough publicized to become a significant local issue. In the country as a whole, unemployment was identified with the 1957–58 recession rather than with area distress.

[31] Renamed, in 1965, the National League of Cities.

ginia. The committee approved the bill on March 11 and the Senate passed it twelve days later, 49–46.

The even narrower margin for passage, compared with 1958, is accounted for by the loss of Republican votes. Of the seventeen Republicans who in 1958 had voted for the Douglas-Payne bill, eleven were still in the Senate. Of these, seven changed their votes from affirmative to negative—although the remaining four, it may be noted, were the margin of victory. Even two of the five Republican cosponsors of the bill—Clifford P. Case of New Jersey and Jacob K. Javits of New York—voted against it on final passage.

The House Banking and Currency Committee approved the bill on May 5, after reducing the total authorization from $389.5 million to $251 million. But again it met a roadblock in the House Rules Committee. This time it languished in Rules for a solid year. Supporters of the bill bore down on Speaker Sam Rayburn of Texas for help in getting it dislodged. But the first half of 1959 was a period when the economy was looking brighter after the 1957–58 recession, and Rayburn considered the timing not propitious. He was adamant that the bill be put over until 1960,[32] which left the proponents no choice. Finally, in April 1960, the Rules Committee acted—but negatively. It rejected the bill by a 6–6 vote. Against the measure was the familiar lineup of the four Republican members and the two senior Democrats, Chairman Smith and William M. Colmer of Mississippi.

At this point, a newly organized bloc of northern and western Democrats known as the Democratic Study Group[33] decided that area redevelopment was an issue on which to test their strength. They considered alternative ways of overcoming the Rules Committee and concluded their best prospect lay in the rarely used "calendar Wednesday" procedure, a clumsy device that permits almost unlimited parliamentary obstruction if the opposition chooses to take full advantage of the rules. In this instance, the opponents yielded after over four hours of maneuvering and roll calls, and the bill did come to a vote.[34] It passed, 202–184. The Senate accepted

[32] Davidson, *Coalition-Building for Depressed Areas Bills*, p. 17.

[33] See Chap. 9, pp. 403–05.

[34] The maneuvering ended when the opposition coalition of Republicans and southern Democrats fell apart. Levitan refers to unconfirmed reports that the White House urged Republican leaders not to participate in obstructionist tactics to the point of preventing an ultimate vote. Davidson speculated that the southern Democrats who were joined with the Republicans did not want to push the matter to the point of depriving their party of an issue in the 1960 campaign, particularly in the light of the probability of a veto (Davidson, *Coalition-Building for the Depressed Areas Bills*, p. 19).

the House amendments, with Senators Kennedy and Hubert Humphrey, of Minnesota, dramatically flying back from their Democratic presidential primary campaign in depressed West Virginia to cast their votes. Vice President Richard M. Nixon reportedly favored approval of the bill, to remove a campaign issue. But, as in 1958, the veto came. Eisenhower termed the bill even more objectionable in some respects than the 1958 bipartisan measure. He emphasized that time still remained for the Congress to pass a satisfactory bill. Senator Everett McKinley Dirksen of Illinois and Representative William B. Widnall of New Jersey introduced a new Republican bill, drafted by the administration, with authorizations totaling $180 million—much nearer the $251 million in the vetoed bill than the $51 million in the original administration proposal.

But it was too late for compromise. The Democrats were in no mood to make a fresh start; another campaign was just ahead—this time with the presidency at stake. The Senate went through the motions of trying to override the veto but failed. Only five Republicans voted against the President's position.

Candidate Kennedy took the offensive on the area redevelopment bill in sixty-one separate campaign speeches or statements,[35] invariably reminding his audience that it was "twice vetoed by the Republicans" or "by the administration" (not "by President Eisenhower"). Kennedy referred to his role as the bill's floor manager in 1956. Nixon, forced on the defensive, could only contend that the Republican bill was superior and that the Democrats deliberately provoked the vetoes in order to "play politics" with the issue.

From city after city, as Kennedy campaigned, political leaders sent word to him: "When you speak here, talk about unemployment and automation, and especially the depressed area bill." Late in the campaign, on receiving this advice one more time, Kennedy asked one of his aides in exasperation, "Isn't there any place in this country that is not a depressed area?" But area redevelopment, by this time, was more than just a bill—it was a symbol. The election came at a time of high and rising unemployment. Throughout the industrial areas, the actual distress from unemployment was compounded by a deep-seated anxiety among employed workers over the advance of what was loosely called "automation." All a Democrat had to do to dramatize the response of his party to the insecurity of modern industrial society was to refer to an anti-unemployment bill—any such bill, whatever its specific content—that had been

[35] As counted by Roger H. Davidson (unpublished manuscript).

twice passed by a Democratic Congress and twice vetoed by "a Republican administration."

Other Measures Take Form *(1959–60)*

While the political spotlight focused upon the area redevelopment bill, other measures to deal with structural unemployment developed slowly in its shadow. The most important were two bills that sought to train or retrain jobless workers so that their skills would match the requirements of jobs, both within depressed areas and elsewhere. One was designed for the unskilled and inexperienced high school dropout, the other for the experienced worker whose skill had been rendered obsolete by the advance of technology.

The Youth Conservation Corps. Of all the categories of the unemployed, none aroused more concern than the out-of-school, out-of-work youth. Unemployment among youth was more than hardship for individuals and families; it could be a menace to the entire community, especially in the larger cities where jobless young people congregated in gangs. "Social dynamite" was to be James B. Conant's phrase for it.

In April 1959, nearly one-third of the unemployed were under twenty-five years of age—1,132,000 in all. For the labor force as a whole, one worker out of nineteen was unemployed, but for teenagers the ratio was one of seven. And among Negro teenagers, it was one of four—24.8 percent.[36] Dramatizing these statistics were others showing an upsurge in juvenile delinquency and youth crime. Clearly, to the activists, something had to be done. Judges, probation officers, social workers, and educators joined in the demand that young people who could not be held in the classroom be provided employment opportunities.

For the answer, what could be more obvious than one of the most popular of the New Deal experiments—the Civilian Conservation Corps? Two kinds of monuments had kept respect for the CCC alive two decades after its disbandment: the parks, artificial lakes, forest trails, campgrounds, and picnic sites that had been constructed all over America; and

---

[36] Testimony of Louis Levine, assistant director, Bureau of Employment Security, in *Youth Conservation Corps,* Hearings before the Special Subcommittee on Youth Conservation Corps of the Senate Labor and Public Welfare Committee, 86 Cong. 1 sess. (May 11–25, 1959), p. 245.

the "graduates" such as Democratic Representative John A. Blatnik of Minnesota, who could personally testify to the CCC's merits. As early as 1954, organizations identified with conservation of natural resources had begun to revive the CCC idea as one means of speeding development of recreational and other facilities in the national parks, forests, and wildlife refuges. They made no progress with the administration; the resource agencies were receptive, but Treasury Secretary Humphrey dismissed the proposal as so much "twaddle."[37]

Two forces generated by unrelated circumstances were moving toward the same end, and they converged in the office of Senator Hubert Humphrey. Responding to the pleas of both the conservationists and the urban youth welfare groups, Humphrey in 1957 introduced a proposal for a 500-man experimental work camp program as part of a series of bills making up a "youth opportunity program." A year later he joined with Blatnik to sponsor a full-fledged Youth Conservation Corps of 150,000— and a coalition to support it was born. To the juvenile court judges and the social workers, the YCC appeared as a hopeful means of keeping young men off the streets and out of trouble while teaching them the discipline of work. To the organizations making up the Natural Resources Council of America, the youth corps was manpower—an indirect means of augmenting the restricted budgets of the resource agencies. Humphrey combined it simply: "A Plan to Save Trees, Land, and Boys."[38] When he introduced the bill on January 29, 1959, his cosponsors reflected the coalition. They numbered seven members of the Interior Committee and three other westerners identified with conservation, four members of the subcommittee on soil conservation and forestry of the Agriculture Committee, four members of the subcommittee on juvenile delinquency of the Judiciary Committee, and four members of the Labor and Public Welfare Committee.

Both sides of the coalition appeared at hearings in May. Conservation spokesmen detailed the country's resource development needs and recounted the achievements of the CCC. Witnesses concerned with juvenile delinquency deplored the "tragically limited opportunities" for the jobless young.[39] Humphrey observed that the Eisenhower administration

---

[37] Letter to me from Spencer M. Smith, Jr., secretary of the Citizens Committee on Natural Resources, April 14, 1966.

[38] Title of an article by Humphrey in *Harper's*, January 1959, pp. 53–57.

[39] Testimony of David M. Crockett, probation officer of the Wayne County, Michigan, juvenile court, who testified that 16-year-old school dropouts were a major problem for his court (*Youth Conservation Corps*, Hearings, p. 14).

proposed a budget increase for prisons and commented, "I, for one, am a little tired of a government that knows how to build jails and does not seem to have the imagination to build bodies and minds and souls and spirits and personalities."

No adverse witnesses testified. The most thoughtful critical questions in the record were included, no doubt inadvertently, when a magazine symposium on youth work camps was reprinted in its entirety.[40] Dr. Kenneth Clark, psychologist at the College of the City of New York, asked

> . . . whether these camps do in effect contribute to the solution of the basic problems of young people or rather postpone more realistic and significant solutions. One may view these camps as temporary custodial facilities . . . wherein the society relegates for a given period of time those young people who reflect by their personal and social problems the society's most glaring deficiencies.
>
> "Realism" would argue that it would be easier for the society to send youth to work camps rather than to strengthen the schools and enrich their curricula; it would be more economical *in the short run* to send youth to work camps rather than to tackle the complex social and economic problems which are related to the deprivation and deterioration found in underprivileged communities; it would be less disturbing to send youth to work camps than to deal with the basic problems of prejudice and discrimination which blunt the motivation of a substantial proportion of the young people of our society. The fact remains, however, that these unsolved and difficult social problems will not disappear and will confront these same youth when they return to society.[41]

The bill split the parties clean. It was approved by committee on a straight party-line vote. On the Senate floor, only two Republicans supported it and only one Democrat outside the southern and border states opposed it. Fourteen Democrats from those areas voted in the negative, and the bill survived by just two votes, 47–45.

The opposition concentrated its fire on the cost of the measure—estimated to rise to $375 million a year—in view of the speculative nature of its benefits. "Inflationary," said the minority report; "there has been no clear showing that the bill would be effective in curbing juvenile delinquency" and "equally good or better conservation . . . can be achieved through present programs . . . at a mere fraction of the bill's cost." Said Senator Kenneth B. Keating, New York Republican: "At a time when our economy is booming and jobs are, on the whole, plentiful, we need not go off on budget-busting excursions such as this, which do not really get

---

[40] *American Child*, May 1959.
[41] *Ibid.*, pp. 92–93 (italics in original).

at the problems we are trying to solve." Concurred Herman E. Tal-
madge, Georgia Democrat: "The only question involved in this issue is,
Can we afford it? . . . Now is no time to be . . . spending money for ideal-
istic purposes."[42]

If the Senate could muster only a two-vote margin for the youth corps,
chances in the House were clearly slim—and an Eisenhower veto was
inevitable if the bill should pass. Supporters held two days of hearings
but did not press the bill in the election year of 1960. They had already
made their point. The bill had been well publicized. The White House
conference on children and youth, attended by 7,500 persons in the
spring of 1960, had endorsed it as one of many measures reflecting the
conference's belief in "a strong government role" in dealing with the
problems of youth.[43] Conservation organizations were solidly behind it.
The Democrats were satisfied to take into the campaign an issue made
clear-cut between the parties by the Senate vote, with their party aligned
on the side both of youth and of conservation.

Retraining of the Jobless. The little Susquehanna River town of Sayre,
in northern Pennsylvania, had just attained the goal sought by thousands
of small communities the country over. A shoe manufacturing concern
had chosen Sayre as the site for a new factory.

Why had the company bestowed its favor upon this particular dot on
the map? Among other advantages, Sayre could promise the employer
a labor force already skilled in shoe manufacture and ready to go to work.
The community had not been a shoe town, but ever since 1952 the Commonwealth of Pennsylvania had been saying to industries of every kind,
"Come to Pennsylvania and we will train your labor." In that year a Republican governor and legislature had launched the first state program
for training of the unemployed. Conceived initially as a means of helping
the jobless get off the welfare rolls, the program was subsequently publicized widely by the state department of commerce in its drive to bring
new industry into Pennsylvania.

At Sayre, 110 persons entered training to become shoemakers. Of these,
the factory hired 85 at total annual wages exceeding $230,000. Within
a few years, the state had recouped the $14,000 cost of the program
through additional taxes from the trainees alone—not to mention the
savings in the reduced costs of public welfare.

[42] *Cong. Record,* Vol. 105 (Aug. 13, 1959), p. 15792.
[43] *Congressional Quarterly Almanac, 1960,* p. 306.

In more than a score of other communities, unemployed adults were being trained in occupations ranging from airplane engine mechanics and polyethylene extrusion operators to typists. Of the trainees, 89 percent had jobs within a month. In some courses, as many as 98 percent were hired. "We have found that this job can be done and we are well aware of the need for it," testified William L. Cooper, supervisor of trade and industrial education in the state's vocational education program.[44]

Late in 1959, Cooper made a suggestion to Senator Clark of Pennsylvania, who was at that time impatiently waiting for the House to pass the area redevelopment bill and worrying about Pennsylvania's 400,000 unemployed. Why not provide federal funds to enable every state to retrain its jobless on the Pennsylvania pattern, and on a massive scale? "Draft me a bill," said Clark, and within a matter of hours Cooper sent him a measure that would add a new program of retraining for the unemployed to the state vocational education programs that had been assisted by federal grants-in-aid since 1917.[45] Like the area redevelopment bill, but unlike the Pennsylvania state program, the bill provided for payment of subsistence allowances to persons enrolled in retraining courses.

At this point, Clark and others had available to them the vehicle they had long been seeking to bring the problem of structural unemployment to the attention of the Congress and the country with a force that would compel action. That vehicle was the special Senate committee on unemployment problems, itself the product of an arduous history.

The Senate Special Committee on Unemployment Problems. After the election of 1958, in which the Democrats swept twelve Senate and forty-nine House seats held by the Republicans, Democratic leaders and their labor union allies from the North and East expected action on the paramount issue of that campaign—unemployment. But when the new Congress met, action was slow in coming. The Democratic party in Congress had no machinery for seizing the initiative from the President, writing its own anti-unemployment program, and enacting it. Majority Leader Lyndon Johnson was still dependent on his "cabinet" of committee chairmen, and no senator from the northern and eastern regions, which between

[44] *Training of the Unemployed,* Hearings before the Subcommittee on Employment and Manpower of the Senate Labor and Public Welfare Committee, 87 Cong. 1 sess. (March 21, 1961), p. 128.

[45] The bill was actually drafted in the Washington headquarters of the American Vocational Association, the professional organization and "lobby" for the vocational educators.

them contained more than half of the country's population, headed any committee with jurisdiction over any aspect of the unemployment problem.[46] Democratic senators from states with heavy unemployment pressed upon Johnson their demand for bold party action, with Patrick McNamara of Michigan, who still boasted his labor union membership, as their spokesman. But McNamara came away defeated.

Tension between the majority leader and the northern wing of the party boiled over on March 30 when the usually placid McNamara wrote Johnson a scorching letter and sent copies to thirty-eight other senators. The immediate cause was a double defeat on a bill providing an emergency extension of unemployment compensation to jobless workers whose benefits had expired. One defeat was suffered when a McNamara amendment was beaten on the Senate floor, the other when a milder amendment sponsored by Eugene McCarthy (Democrat of Minnesota) and adopted by the Senate was quickly rejected by a Senate-House conference committee. The letter, which is revealing of the frustration of McNamara and his allies on the one hand and of the majority leader on the other, said in part:

> The Senate has just completed an exercise in futility in connection with the emergency unemployment compensation legislation. . . . All this raises serious questions in my mind about Senate majority leadership—or the lack of it.
>
> As you will recall, I wrote you on March 12 to call to your personal attention the emergency extension program which I, with 17 other Senators, introduced. . . . I then called you on March 17, and you informed me that you would look into the matter but that you could not take a position until after the Senate Finance Committee had acted. . . . The Committee, on March 23, rejected our bill by a vote of 12–4. . . . That same day, Senator Clark and I talked to you in the Senate Chamber, again seeking to determine the position of the majority leadership. I think I indicated to you my surprise when you told us that since the Finance Committee had acted, the majority leadership could not go against the action. It seemed very strange to me that you would say you could do nothing *until* the Committee acted and then say you could do nothing *because* it had acted.
>
> In any event . . . we were able to pass an amendment liberalizing the House bill to a small degree by a decisive vote of 52–32. . . . This vote represented the first real results of what the voters did last November. It was the first stirring of what I hope will become the dominant group in the Senate. . . . However, this initial sign of Spring was quickly nipped by the frost of the old coalition which saw that our amendment was killed in the House-Senate

---

[46] The only chairman from the North or East was Thomas C. Hennings, Jr., of Missouri, chairman of the Rules Committee which had responsibility for little substantive legislation.

conference. I am convinced that this would not have happened had there been any exercise of the majority leadership's responsibility. . . .

The question is thus raised: Just where in this legislative process does the Majority Leader exercise his functions?. . . .

Johnson's reply to McNamara was a plaintive oral comment: "Pat, please don't send me any more letters." But the following week, Johnson was scheduled to face a "march on Washington" organized by the AFL-CIO. As he had done in like circumstances a year earlier, the majority leader devised a measure that could be passed quickly and overwhelmingly by the Senate. Supported by sixty-seven cosponsors, including eighteen Republicans, he proposed the creation of an eleven-member committee, made up of three senators, three House members, and five presidential appointees, who would "be charged with the responsibility of going to the areas of critical unemployment in this country . . . to feel and weigh the bitter despair which attends the lives of so many of our fellow Americans" and make recommendations within sixty days. The resolution was introduced on April 8, passed two days later by voice vote, and endorsed by President Eisenhower on April 14.

"I suppose it is much easier," the still bitter McNamara told the Senate next day, "to set up a study commission than it is to tackle realistically the problems that unemployment creates—and the problems that create unemployment. . . . It may be a convenient out; an opportunity to give lipservice to a situation without having to do anything about it."[47] The correspondent of the *Detroit Times* wrote that the rally's sponsors would claim to have accomplished their purpose "by wringing from a previously reluctant Lyndon Johnson . . . a vague promise of an investigation. . . ."[48]

But, oddly enough, the resolution never left the desk of Speaker Rayburn. House Republican Leader Charles A. Halleck of Indiana announced that his party would not oppose it, but Rayburn did not even send it to committee. No public explanation was ever given. One of Rayburn's confidants has commented that the speaker had a standing objection to joint Senate-House-presidential commissions for any purpose. The improvement in the unemployment picture, which influenced his views at that time on the area redevelopment bill, may also have been a factor. In any case, it gave the Republicans an opportunity to ask embarrassing questions, like that of Representative John J. Rhodes of Arizona: "The history of this unemployment commission bill is quite amazing. . . . Was it only

[47] *Cong. Record*, Vol. 105 (April 15, 1959), p. 5915.
[48] *Ibid.*, p. 5916.

suggested by the Majority Leader . . . as a sop to get the unemployed marchers out of town?"[49]

After five months, Johnson made good. On September 12 he created, by action of the Senate alone, a special committee on unemployment problems. He pointedly reached over the heads of the more senior senators who had been tormenting him on the question by appointing as its chairman the freshman McCarthy of Minnesota. But McNamara and Clark were among the nine members.

In twelve states, senators met and talked with the unemployed themselves. They did "feel and weigh the bitter despair" of the jobless, as these excerpts from the record show:

A West Virginia superintendent of schools:

> Another school weighed the pupils . . . and when Christmas came and the school was dismissed for Christmas, the average child had gained from 3 to 5 pounds. Then they were out for 2 weeks for the Christmas holidays. When the children came back to school they were weighed again, and most of them had lost the weight that they had gained while they were eating the hot lunches at school. I am positive this situation will be even worse at the Christmas season this year. . . . Very, very few of our college graduates ever come back to Fayette County, as there is no employment for them. The morale of the people of Fayette County is at its lowest ebb. The lack of material things is not the greatest problem—the morale, the attitudes, and other intangibles are really of greater importance. Busy people are happy people. But unemployed people take a defeatist attitude. We need above all industrial training and some diversified industry here in the mining area.[50]

A Kentucky editor:

> At about this time last year—2 weeks before Christmas—an unemployed coal miner in Letcher County whom I have known all my life shot and killed himself.
>
> The man was the father of eight children, stair-stepped from age 14 down to age 2.
>
> This man had been out of work for some 3 years. . . . I know that this man made every possible effort to find employment for himself. He made several trips into Ohio and Michigan, looking for work. But he was 55 years old, and he simply couldn't find a job. . . . And for some 2 years, he was forced to sit in idleness at home, watching the health of his children deteriorate from lack of enough food—watching their clothes wear out—with no money to replace them. . . .

---

[49] *Ibid.* (May 14, 1959), p. 8181.

[50] Testimony of A. L. Walker, superintendent, Fayette County, W. Va., schools, in *Unemployment Problems*, Hearings before the Senate Special Committee on Unemployment Problems, 86 Cong. 1 sess. (Nov. 17, 1959), pp. 2543–44.

The man watched this for some 2 years. He got to thinking about the situation and realized that if he were dead, then his wife and children could draw social security benefits. . . . They could eat, and they could buy clothes.

And so, as a Christmas present to his wife and his eight children, the man took out his shotgun and calmly shot and killed himself. It was the best Christmas present he knew how to give. Living he was of no help to his family. By dying he could feed them.[51]

An Indiana unemployed worker:

I'm an able bodied man; I would rather work than get unemployment, but when you go any place now . . . and when you tell them you're 61 years of age, regardless if you are able bodied, they seem to look at you and say, they don't tell you but they just give you the smile that you ought to have better sense than to ask and they will tell you if you are over 50, there's no need talking, so I think they should bring the old-age pension down and give it to people where people won't hire you.[52]

A Louisiana priest:

I refer . . . to the tens of thousands of migratory workers and to farm workers in general. Yes, these are little people—I use the expression in all reverence. Overwhelmingly they lack the protection of collective bargaining. Too often they are mere instruments for their employers to make money by. They make up a faceless mass of humanity for the most part, with few friends in Government or commerce. . . . Habitually they have to face the hazards of unemployment, underemployment, or overemployment and thus they are often forced to live in conditions unfit even for animals. The toll that these hazards exact in terms of human dignity is a shameful commentary on our lack of sincerity when we profess faith in the equality and inalienable rights of all men. . . .

And this is not to speak of an even greater national scandal. With cold, deliberate calculation we build into our employment practices discriminatory patterns, which reduce certain racial minorities to the role of drawers of water and hewers of wood. . . . I am here speaking of the objectively criminal abuse we are guilty of in exploiting the Negro, Puerto Rican, and Mexican-American manpower in our population.[53]

The nine volumes of testimony constituted an overwhelming demand for action on behalf of the structurally unemployed—the residents of depressed areas, the school dropouts, the older workers, the minorities victimized by discrimination. The area redevelopment bill was repeatedly endorsed. The Youth Conservation Corps was supported. And, for the first

[51] Testimony of Thomas E. Gish, editor, *The Mountain Eagle*, Whitesburg, Ky., in *ibid.* (Dec. 11, 1959), pp. 1994–95.

[52] Testimony of James Alderson, Evansville, Ind., in *ibid.* (Dec. 1, 1959), p. 2733.

[53] Testimony of the Rev. Louis J. Twomey, S.J., director, Institute of Industrial Relations, Loyola University, New Orleans, in *ibid.* (Dec. 11, 1959), p. 2065.

time, impressive testimony was gathered on the need for training or re-training of the unskilled. The manager of the Evansville office of the Indiana employment security division testified that in his community, with 6,100 unemployed, jobs were available and "difficult to fill" in 24 enumerated occupations, from mechanical engineer and legal secretary to hospital orderly trainee and snack-bar counter girl. The unemployed in Evansville could not meet the educational or skill requirements.[54]

Reporting in March 1960, the committee majority gave "highest prior-ity" to "an effective area redevelopment program." It endorsed the Youth Conservation Corps and "a nationwide vocational training program through Federal grants-in-aid to the States, including specialized courses for youth who have dropped out of school and for older workers who require retraining." While the special committee left the problem of cyclical unemployment to the Joint Economic Committee, which at that time had underway the Eckstein study on employment, growth, and price levels, it did propose one countercyclical measure—legislation authorizing public works and housing programs on a standby basis, to take effect automatically if rising unemployment indicated the onset of a recession.[55]

The three-man Republican minority—John Sherman Cooper of Ken-tucky, Winston L. Prouty of Vermont, and Hugh Scott of Pennsylvania—signed a 63-page minority report[56] which agreed more than it disagreed with the views of the majority. They termed the area redevelopment bill "a matter of prime importance" and, while they recommended a larger authorization than President Eisenhower's proposed $50 million, sug-gested that "it would be better to start in a modest way than not to start at all." They endorsed retraining of older workers and broader vocational training for the young. They saw "desirable aspects" in the Youth Con-servation Corps but felt that funds could be better used in ways "which strike at the heart of unemployment among the young."[57]

Senator Clark introduced a standby public works bill and, under a prearranged division of labor, Democratic Senator Jennings Randolph of West Virginia introduced the training bill originally drafted for Clark. Carrying out another McCarthy committee recommendation, Chairman Lister Hill (Democrat of Alabama) of the Labor and Public Welfare

[54] Testimony of John Ross, in *ibid.* (Dec. 1, 1959), p. 2804.

[55] The recommendations are summarized in *Report of the Special Committee on Unem-ployment Problems,* S. Rept. 1206, pp. 122–26.

[56] Prepared with the unofficial assistance of individuals within the Eisenhower admin-istration, particularly Secretary Mitchell's Labor Department.

[57] Cooper submitted individual recommendations for regional development programs. See p. 99.

Committee created a subcommittee on employment and manpower. Randolph became its chairman, with the understanding that Clark would assume the post after Randolph's reelection in November.

The area redevelopment bill, the Youth Conservation Corps, and manpower training and retraining all found their way into the Democratic platform of 1960. Senator Kennedy regularly advocated retraining, along with area redevelopment, in his battery of solutions to problems of unemployment and automation, and on a few occasions he mentioned the youth corps. The Republican platform endorsed aid to areas of chronic high unemployment and improvement of training opportunities. Nixon defended the administration's position on area redevelopment but did not advance in his campaign any affirmative program of the kind that might have been developed from the comprehensive recommendations of the Cooper-Prouty-Scott·minority report.

Kennedy Breaks the Deadlock   *(1961–62)*

If President Kennedy needed his "education in the White House" on the fundamentals of cyclical unemployment and Keynesian economics, he needed no such education on the nature of structural unemployment. He had encountered the hard-core unemployed of depressed communities many years before, in the textile towns of Massachusetts, and in 1960 he had spent a month seeking primary votes in the stricken state of West Virginia. "Kennedy's shock at the suffering he saw in West Virginia was so fresh that it communicated itself with the emotion of original discovery," writes Theodore H. White.[58] The unemployed coal miners and the subsistence farmers of that state had given him their confidence—and with it the presidential nomination—and he felt deeply his personal obligation "to do something for West Virginia."

Paul Douglas was already at work getting the area redevelopment bill ready for introduction on the opening day. Douglas planned to hold brief

---

[58] *The Making of the President, 1960* (Atheneum, 1961), p. 106; White continues: "He could scarcely bring himself to believe that human beings were forced to eat and live on these cans of dry relief rations, which he fingered like artifacts of another civilization. 'Imagine,' he said to one of his assistants one night, 'just imagine kids who never drink milk.' Of all the emotional experiences of his pre-Convention campaign, Kennedy's exposure to the misery of the mining fields probably changed him most as a man." Seymour E. Harris notes "the President's interest in the direct approach—that is, the treatment of structural unemployment" (*Economics of the Kennedy Years* [Harper & Row, 1964], p. 24).

hearings even before inauguration day, and get the bill to the Senate floor a few days after.[59] But the President-elect expected to lead, not follow, his Senate allies. In the course of a news conference, he announced that he would send his area redevelopment bill to Congress promptly after inauguration. When the news dispatch was handed to Douglas, the senator grumbled, "What does he mean, *his* area redevelopment bill. It was my bill before he ever heard of it."

But Kennedy found a device that would identify them both with the measure and dramatize and give it impetus as well. He appointed a task force on area redevelopment, with Douglas as chairman and six of its members from West Virginia. The group met in Charleston, West Virginia, and in Washington and reported to Kennedy at Palm Beach on New Year's Day.

While giving the area redevelopment bill major emphasis, the task force assembled other recommendations. It urged alleviation of distress through expanded food distribution programs, temporary extension of unemployment compensation, and broadening of public assistance. It suggested special provisions for depressed areas in the anticipated legislation for federal aid to education. And it recommended what was to become the essence of the Kennedy-Johnson program for Appalachia—funds for access roads, supplemental appropriations for development of natural resources, and a regional commission to coordinate the various resource development activities into a "broad regional development program."

The discussion at Palm Beach centered on the timing of the area redevelopment bill. Douglas won agreement to proceed on opening day, with a bill closely paralleling the one killed by the much-advertised Eisenhower vetoes. Accordingly, Douglas introduced S.1, with forty-three cosponsors. And "at high noon on the first minute of the first hour of the first day of the first session of the 87th Congress," Representative Flood introduced the companion House bill.[60] The Republicans were also prompt. Senator Dirksen and nine cosponsors introduced a bill slightly more liberal than the final Eisenhower compromise of 1960, and Senator Scott and Representative Van Zandt proposed one containing still higher authorizations.

Douglas proceeded with hearings January 18 and the bill reached the floor March 9. After adoption of an administration-sponsored amendment placing the Area Redevelopment Administration in the Department of

[59] This section again draws upon Levitan, *Federal Aid to Depressed Areas*, pp. 17–20, and Davidson, *Coalition-Building for Depressed Areas Bills*, pp. 22–28.

[60] *Cong. Record*, Vol. 107 (Jan. 4, 1961), p. 99.

Commerce (Douglas had proposed an independent ARA), the Senate approved the measure by an overwhelming 63–27. The Republican discipline of 1960 had vanished, and nearly half of the Senate GOP votes, fifteen of thirty-one, were cast in favor of the measure—compared to the five who had voted to override Eisenhower's second veto a few months earlier. Only eleven of fifty-nine Democrats voted in the negative. Bandwagon sentiment was also apparent in the House. There twenty-nine more Democrats and twenty more Republicans than in 1960 supported the bill. The final tally was 251–167, and the Area Redevelopment Act was signed May 1 as the first major legislative achievement of the Kennedy administration. That autumn, the first grant was made—not in Kennedy's West Virginia or in Douglas' Illinois, but for a water system to serve a shirt factory deep in the Ozark Mountains of Senator Fulbright's Arkansas. Even more ironic, from the standpoint of the labor organizations that had devoted so much effort to publicizing and supporting the bill, the factory was a nonunion, low-wage enterprise of the very type whose competition had been so keenly felt in the depressed manufacturing centers of the North.

While Senator Douglas was moving forward with the Kennedy blessing to enact his area redevelopment bill, Senator Clark waited impatiently for a corresponding presidential blessing for two other measures proposed by the McCarthy committee and left pending in 1960—the bill for retraining of the unemployed, and the public works bill offered originally as a standby measure to be used in event of recession. By February, unemployment reached 5.4 million—the highest total in twenty years—and almost 10 percent of these were in Clark's commonwealth of Pennsylvania. One worker out of nine in that state was jobless—and in some coal counties it was twice that ratio. Facing a hard reelection campaign in 1962, Clark was determined to make his subcommittee on employment and manpower (whose chairmanship Randolph had relinquished to him) the vehicle for these two measures which would bear his name and would attack Pennsylvania's overriding problem. In February he introduced revised versions of the bills and held hearings in seven cities. Thereafter, he could only wait, while the mills of the new administration slowly ground.

The Manpower Development and Training Act. The more vigorously politicians and economists disagreed over spending and tax reduction measures to counter the 1960–61 recession, the more they came to agree on the need for retraining of the unemployed. Those who favored an expansionary fiscal policy looked upon retraining as a necessary *supplement*. Those who opposed strong fiscal measures tended to seize upon retraining as a *substitute*. If the economy did not need stimulation to absorb the unemployed, they found themselves reasoning, then jobs for all must in fact exist or would exist if only the unemployed were competent to fill them. If the shortcomings were not in the economy, they could only be in the people. Thus, when the House Republican Policy Committee in 1961 set out on a study of "the structure of job making" in order to develop alternatives to what its members called the Democratic "spending spree," they emerged after six months with a report that placed heavy emphasis upon the upgrading of skills throughout the population. Representative Thomas Curtis of Missouri, director of the study, introduced bills to make training expenditures deductible for tax purposes and to assure that unemployed workers undergoing retraining would not be declared ineligible for unemployment compensation.[61] As one reporter observed, retraining legislation "fitted in perfectly with the conservative notion that nothing is basically wrong with the economy that cannot be solved by getting capital and labor to the right place at the right time."[62]

As officials and experts of all shades of opinion supported retraining, so did the general public. A Gallup poll showed 67 percent of the people "willing to sacrifice" to pay for retraining the unemployed. Only 28 percent, by contrast, would be willing to sacrifice for improvement of the armed forces—the purpose receiving the second highest measure of popular support.[63]

But if there was a national consensus on the objective, the new administration still had to make up its mind about the nature of the program. Unlike the area redevelopment bill, the retraining bill had not undergone six years of hearings, discussion, debate, and refinement. The idea was

[61] Curtis explained the origin and organization of the study in *ibid.* (June 28, 1961), pp. 11537–41. He inserted the list of participants (24 economists prepared papers, and 49 Republican congressmen participated in the review of them), the final report, a staff report, and four of the papers in *ibid.* (Aug. 14, 1961), pp. 15765–90. By 1965 his proposal for tax benefits for training costs incurred by business had developed into a full-fledged Republican party measure, entitled "The Human Investment Act of 1965," sponsored by 21 senators and 81 representatives. In referring to his bill, Curtis reiterated his contention that "there is a high incidence of people not working in our society, not working because of lack of incentive or lack of skills, not because of lack of jobs" (*ibid.*, Vol. 111 [Oct. 21, 1965], p. 27879).

[62] Julius Duscha, "Retraining the Unemployed: Little, Late and Limping," *Reporter,* Sept. 27, 1962, p. 35.

[63] Poll inserted, by Senator Proxmire, in *Cong. Record,* Vol. 107 (July 7, 1961), p. 12053.

scarcely a year old and had been before the Congress only since June of 1960.

Clark tried to speed the administration review of his bill by scheduling Washington hearings on March 20. Some Labor Department officials felt that the administration should grasp the opportunity, endorse the measure, and work out improvements later.[64] But others argued that the bill was so seriously defective that it should not be endorsed until rewritten. To gain time to consider the questions raised, Secretary Arthur J. Goldberg asked that his appearance before the subcommittee be deferred.

The central issue was whether retraining of adults should be organized and administered as a new category within the existing federal-state vocational education program, initiated by the Smith-Hughes Act of 1917 for vocational training in public high schools, or embody some major new departures. The Clark bill followed the Smith-Hughes pattern. It had been initiated, after all, by Pennsylvania vocational educators. But vocational education was being widely criticized as out of touch with the modern industrial world, as out of date in both equipment and curricula.[65] Should a mammoth new program for training experienced workmen be entrusted to the vocational educators when they were not even doing well by the nation's youth? The Department of Health, Education, and Welfare, administrators of the federal "vo-ed" grants, insisted that it should be—that the existing nationwide vo-ed structure could be adapted more readily than a new one could be created. The Labor Department was split between those who were ready to compromise and those who believed that Labor should insist upon authority to institute a broad and diverse program that would place a heavy emphasis upon on-the-job training and use school vocational education facilities only where these were the best means to a particular end.

The latter view was held even more strongly by the analyst responsible for the Bureau of the Budget's review of the bill, Michael S. March. March saw, on the one hand, the weaknesses of the decentralized vocational structure and, on the other, the successful experience with federally operated programs—the training-within-industry program of World War II and the vocational rehabilitation of veterans after the war. For several weeks, March and his Budget Bureau colleagues stalled action while they urged Secretary Goldberg to prepare a new bill that would place undivided

---

[64] This paragraph and those that follow relating to executive branch consideration of the bill are based upon interviews with participants and records in their possession.

[65] See, for example, Edward T. Chase, "Learning to Be Unemployable," *Harper's*, April 1963, pp. 33–39.

authority in his office and recast the program as a direct federal operation financed wholly by federal funds. The secretary could utilize public school facilities but would not be limited to them.

But the secretary was receiving opposite advice from other important quarters. For a relatively small group, the vo-ed lobby—the American Vocational Association (AVA)—wielded extraordinary influence in its field. Its executive secretary, M. D. Mobley, a Georgian, was skilled at translating a legislator's support for vocational education bills into support for that legislator back home—and vice versa.[66] Among legislators respecting both Mobley's views and his political power was Chairman Hill of the Labor and Public Welfare Committee. Samuel V. Merrick, counsel to Clark's subcommittee, knew that a bill opposed by Mobley would find rough passage through the committee and the Congress, and he made sure that Goldberg was well aware of "the Mobley problem."

The Labor Department attempted a draft that would reconcile, insofar as possible, the conflicting suggestions from the Budget Bureau, Capitol Hill, and HEW. But what appeared to the department as a compromise looked to March and his colleagues like surrender. The states were still to share the cost of training programs. Except for on-the-job training, the program would be administered by the states with the help of grants-in-aid distributed among them by formula. The whole undertaking appeared too closely associated with the public school systems and not sufficiently related to the counseling, placement, and other activities of the United States Employment Service designed to meet the needs of the adult unemployed. The consequence was another round of conferences, some of them at the White House, and a complete victory for March and the Budget Bureau. The bill sent to Congress by the President on May 29 placed control clearly in the secretary of labor, authorized complete federal financing, and provided for use of state vocational education facilities through individual agreements negotiated by HEW rather than through distribution of funds among the states by formula.[67] Those provisions of

---

[66] Chase wrote that Mobley "is (correctly) reputed to be Washington's most successful lobbyist" (*ibid.*, p. 35).

[67] The bill incorporated, as Title 1, a broad authorization for the secretary of labor to undertake research in the field of manpower, appraise the adequacy of the nation's manpower development efforts, and make recommendations. This proposal was taken from a bill introduced in 1960 by Senator Clark. Curtis C. Aller has predicted that the "most strategic and enduring contribution" of the Manpower Development and Training Act "will be found in the piggy-back beginning it provided for manpower planning" ("Government-Sponsored Training and Retraining," p. 128).

the Labor Department draft that represented concessions to the Capitol Hill viewpoint had been lost along the way.

But it was a simple matter to put them back. Mobley summoned to Washington a group of AVA leaders, who presented to Clark a demand for thirty-four amendments to the administration bill. The question, they said, was "who can do the job of training most efficiently and effectively to get the unemployed back into production."[68] The AVA proposed to modify those sections of the bill that appeared to authorize the secretary of labor to develop and conduct training programs without reference either to the states or to HEW. Negotiations resumed, with a new balance of forces. This time Merrick was at the head of the table, with Mobley on one side and the Labor Department representatives on the other. With all parties in a mood to compromise, agreement was reached to adopt twenty of the AVA amendments. In general, they put the program back into HEW-state vocational education channels, with the federal money to be distributed among the states by formula and matched by them after the second year. Clark and Merrick also accepted some amendments proposed by the Republican minority to provide safeguards against abuse.

When Goldberg learned of what had happened to his bill, he accosted Merrick and upbraided him. But he dispatched to the committee's chambers his under secretary, Willard Wirtz, and after Wirtz listened calmly to the explanation of each change, they were accepted and the storm passed. From that point on all was harmony. The committee review of the bill approached genuine bipartisanship. The members voted unanimously to report the bill—although one, Barry Goldwater, expressed reservations. It passed, 60–31, on August 23. Almost half of the Republicans—sixteen of thirty-three—voted for it. The Democrats backed it 44–14. Goldwater, in the end, was paired against it.

Meanwhile, a House Education and Labor subcommittee headed by Democratic Representative Elmer Holland of Pittsburgh had held two months of hearings in the spring on the general problem of unemployment and the impact of automation, had produced a staff report that recommended a retraining program, and had reconvened for quick hearings on the administration bill, which Holland introduced. The committee adopted several major amendments to meet Republican criticism that the bill gave the secretary of labor too broad a grant of power—a two-

[68] Testimony of William B. Logan, president, American Vocational Association, June 5, 1961, in *Training of the Unemployed*, Hearings, pp. 179–82.

year time limit on the legislation, a ceiling on appropriations, and a formula for apportioning funds among the states. But nobody was in communication with Mobley, and his amendments were largely ignored. The committee reported the amended bill August 10, with only four members opposing it. One Republican, Charles E. Goodell of upstate New York, even introduced the new bill under his own name. Nevertheless, when the bill reached the Rules Committee, there it stuck. The President at his August 30 news conference expressed hope for action, but when Congress adjourned the bill was still in Rules. "We helped," said Mobley; "We were in touch with every member of the Rules Committee."[69]

In November, Merrick became Secretary Goldberg's assistant for legislative liaison, with the manpower development and training bill his first priority when the Congress reconvened in 1962. Merrick felt he knew the combination that would unlock the Rules Committee safe. With the bipartisan-supported Senate bill in hand, he made contact with Holland and Goodell. The latter, he discovered, had studied closely the Senate amendments to the administration bill and had, in addition, some amendments of his own that had originated in a study by a House Republican Policy Committee task force headed by Representative Curtis of Missouri.[70] Merrick shuttled between Goodell and Holland, negotiating agreement on various of the Senate-approved and Goodell amendments—until Holland one day abruptly slammed the door on further negotiations, saying he refused to compromise the Kennedy bill further with the Republicans. But Goodell held the balance of power in the House; he could pry enough Republican votes away from the Republican-southern Democratic coalition to pass the bill, or decline to do so, and both he and the Democratic leadership knew it. So he went quietly ahead, using the Senate-passed bill as his model, to perfect his own bill. In due course,

---

[69] Interview with Mobley, December 1965. Duscha attributes the postponement to a decision by the Democratic leadership and the White House which he describes as "needlessly cautious" because the bill could have been passed ("Retraining the Unemployed," p. 36). Yet Duscha himself notes that amendments like those adopted by the Senate would have had to be accepted and that Holland did not like the Senate amendments. Even if the bill could have been pried out of the Rules Committee, the leadership did not have the means, in the final month of the Congress (adjournment came September 26), to rewrite the bill so as to reconcile the conflicts.

[70] See Charles O. Jones, *Party and Policy-Making: The House Republican Policy Committee* (Rutgers University Press, 1964), pp. 65–66, for a discussion of the task force's work.

Holland had to capitulate. He accepted the Goodell text in toto, saving nothing of his own bill but its number. With the understanding that the substitution would be made on the floor, the Rules Committee released the bill by an 8–7 vote. On February 28, 1962, the House passed the substitute, 354–62. The Republicans gave the bill a higher percentage of support than did the Democrats. What passed was the Goodell bill, but House records will always show that the body approved "H. R. 8399, by Mr. Holland, as amended." Not even the House records show that the Goodell bill, in turn, was essentially the Senate rewrite of the administration bill.

When President Kennedy signed the bill on March 15, he called it "perhaps the most significant legislation in the area of employment since the historic Employment Act of 1946." Subsequently, the effective date for state financial participation had to be deferred. In 1965, when the program was extended for four more years, the state contribution was set at a nominal 10 percent of the cost of training and none of the cost of the training allowances. By 1966 the cost had risen to $280 million a year. More than 370,000 workers had been trained or were in training, the administration reported.[71] The dropout rate was 25 percent—less than that of the nation's high schools. Seven out of ten graduates were placed in jobs for which they had been trained. Their federal income taxes would repay the cost of their training in five years. "The most important single fact which has emerged," said HEW Secretary Anthony J. Celebrezze, "is that the unemployed are not perforce unemployable."[72] No one could doubt that the Manpower Development and Training Act had become a permanent part of the country's full employment legislation. Not a single vote was cast against the 1965 extension act in a House of Representatives roll call, and only eight voted nay in the Senate.

[71] *The Budget of the United States Government, Fiscal Year 1967*, p. 122. The budget notes that 94 percent of those completing on-the-job training had been placed and that this type of training would be increasingly emphasized.

[72] James Clarke and Charles W. Phillips, "Manpower Training in a Changing World," *Health, Education and Welfare Indicators*, June 1965, pp. 17, 21, 24. An early critical analysis of MDTA experience was Aller's "Government-Sponsored Training and Retraining"; he suggests (p. 132) that the low dropout and high placement rates were due to the "natural inclination" of the employment service to "pick the best applicants for training" and that the hard-core unemployed—older workers, those with least education, those with low scores on aptitude tests, those with police records, etc., were being screened out of the program or not being reached. But Aller found that MDTA projects had demonstrated that, even of those, "very few are really unemployable."

The Accelerated Public Works Act. During the early months of 1961, while President Kennedy was deftly balancing the economics of expansion against the politics of prudence—and deciding in favor of the latter[73]— he received little sympathy or help from one important group, the nation's mayors. They were intensely aware of three facts: more men needed work than at any time in a generation; more work needed doing than could possibly be done; and the new President, in his campaign, had promised to "put our people, our resources, and our whole economy to work, to build the kind of America we want to live in and raise our families in."[74] When was the new Democratic President going to match the idle men with the $50 billion backlog of needed improvements through a public works program, as his Democratic predecessor, Franklin Roosevelt, had done in the 1930's?

A onetime colleague expressed their sentiments: "If Federal money is going to be spent, I urge that we put our emphasis on buying things of lasting value . . . rather than pay it out in the form of a dole which brings no tangible public benefit of any kind. There is hardly a community in the country that does not have a backlog of needed public works." So spoke Senator Clark, former mayor of Philadelphia, in introducing on February 20 a public works bill fashioned after the Public Works Administration of the Depression era.[75]

Clark's bill traced its lineage not only to the PWA but to the more recent Fulbright community facilities loan bill. That billion-dollar measure, with the strong support of mayors, governors, and other public officials, had attained more strength than any other Democratic fiscal measure of the 1957–58 recession period. It had passed the Senate, 60–26, with the support of forty of forty-four Democrats and nearly half the Republicans, twenty of forty-two. Doubled in amount by the House Banking and Currency Committee, it was defeated in the House by fourteen votes, but Democrats had supported it by a margin of 151–36.[76] Since then, the Senate special committee on unemployment problems had urged that such a program be enacted as a standby measure to take effect in any new recession.[77] Now, with that new recession acknowledged to be underway, Clark

---

[73] See Chap. 2, pp. 34–40.

[74] Remarks at Bethlehem, Pa., Oct. 28, 1960, *The Speeches of Senator John F. Kennedy, Presidential Campaign of 1960*, S. Rept. 994, 87 Cong. 1 sess. (1961), Pt. 1, p. 1210. The theme recurred, in varying language, throughout his campaign.

[75] *Cong. Record*, Vol. 107 (1961), p. 2373.

[76] See Chap. 2, p. 25.

[77] See p. 82.

had reason to regard community public works as an accepted part of a Democratic program to combat it.

Before introducing his bill in 1961, Clark had been persuaded by the energetic lobbyist of the American Municipal Association, Hugh Mields, that a loan bill on the pattern of Fulbright's would not accomplish the purpose. Cities that could accept federal loans could borrow privately just as readily, and a slightly lower interest rate under the federal program would not be enough to induce communities to step up their public works spending significantly. For that purpose, grants would be necessary. Accordingly, Clark's new bill provided $500 million for grants up to 45 percent of the cost of the public works, with another $500 million to be released by the President if he found the additional expenditure necessary to bring an end to the recession. The $1 billion of federal money would result in about $2.2 billion of new public works.[78]

Mields saw to it that the mayors and the state leagues of municipalities kept the members of Congress informed of their interest in the bill. But while a Democratic Congress could thrust an antirecession measure upon Eisenhower, it could not treat its own President that way. Clark prodded and encouraged those in the administration who were urging bolder fiscal measures, notably Labor Secretary Goldberg and Walter W. Heller, chairman of the Council of Economic Advisers, and in May 1961 his subcommittee heard a series of favorable witnesses—President George Meany of the AFL-CIO, mayors and county officials, and a panel of economists, including Paul Samuelson. But the President was not to be budged. He was still, in the spring of 1961, a year away from openly embracing the enlargement of the budget deficit as a calculated policy to end the business slump. On May 25, in his appearance before a joint session of Congress, he was categorical: "If the budget deficit now increased by the needs of our national security is to be held within manageable proportions, it will be necessary to hold tightly to prudent fiscal standards; and I request the cooperation of the Congress in this regard—to refrain from adding funds or programs, desirable as they may be, to the Budget. . . ."[79] Accordingly Goldberg had to testify against the bill. But Heller in particular remained dissatisfied. At the least, he felt, the Clark bill should be used as a means of getting standby authority. He persuaded the President to let the senator down easy with a letter promising to request a standby public works

[78] The bill contained provisions designed to assure that the federally aided works would be additional to a community's already-scheduled capital expenditures.

[79] *Public Papers of the Presidents, 1961*, p. 398.

measure in his 1962 legislative program and, if the authority were granted, to "use it resolutely against unemployment and economic recession."[80]

The request for standby authority went forward in February 1962 with modifications developed by the council. They raised the federal grant limit from 45 to 50 percent of project costs, made federal as well as state and local public works eligible for the funds, and refined the formula by which the standby authority would become automatically available when a rise in unemployment signaled a downturn in the economy. The standby bill was referred to the public works committee in each house.

But who, at a time like that, was interested in standby legislation? Unemployment was at its winter peak of 4.5 million, 6.5 percent of the labor force. This was an election year. A bill to take effect at an uncertain time in the dim future aroused no ardor in the Congress; what its members wanted was to see dirt flying in their districts before election day. The mayors, according to Mields, looked on the proposal as "a palliative that wouldn't cost money but would create the illusion that the Administration was doing something." Organized labor reacted similarly.

While the Congress contemplated the pallid measure before it, the economy continued in its winter doldrums. By March it was already clear that the optimistic predictions of the January economic report would not be realized.[81] The gross national product, in the first quarter, advanced barely 1 percent over the preceding quarter. Unemployment adjusted for seasonal variation was falling but slowly. The sluggish recovery was inevitably translated into intensified pressure upon the President—from the fiscal activists in the administration, from Capitol Hill, from public officials and Democratic Party leaders in unemployment areas, and in particular at this time from AFL-CIO President George Meany and other spokesmen for organized labor. The President yielded. On March 26 he asked Congress to authorize $600 million for immediate expenditure in areas of heavy unemployment.

The President proposed to limit the public works grants to areas of especially high unemployment on the ground that "our present problem is not . . . one of nation-wide recession,"[82] but the coverage was nevertheless broad. Included were all areas eligible for assistance under the Area Redevelopment Act plus those communities with unemployment above

[80] Letter reprinted in *Cong. Record,* Vol. 106 (Aug. 22, 1961), p. 16716.
[81] See Chap. 2, p. 39.
[82] Letter to the chairmen, House and Senate public works committees, March 26, 1962, *Public Papers of the Presidents, 1962,* p. 267.

6 percent for the past twelve months. Altogether, 958 labor market areas would qualify, including 38 percent of the country's population and more than half of the total unemployed.[83]

Both committees proceeded at once with hearings. Predictably, the amendment was far more popular than the original standby bill. The question, indeed, was whether the latter could ride to passage on the coattails of the former. Opponents trained their attack particularly upon the method chosen by the administration to finance the standby program. Recognizing that timing is crucial in antirecession measures, and that Congress might not even be in session at the critical time, the administration needed a source of funds that would not depend upon the regular appropriations process. The means it proposed was a grant of authority to the President to transfer unobligated balances of any funds already authorized by Congress. The proposal could be defended logically but not, as it turned out, politically. Committee Republicans indignantly demanded to know just whose funds the President proposed to divert if granted such unprecedented power, and the retreat began. The administration named five specific agencies—International Bank for Reconstruction and Development, Housing and Home Finance Agency, Federal Deposit Insurance Corporation, Federal Savings and Loan Insurance Corporation, and Federal Home Loan Bank Board—against whose authorizations there were substantial unobligated funds in the treasury. But this maneuver served only to transform a generalized anxiety into specific cries of anguish from the constituencies of the selected agencies. On May 1 the Senate Republican Policy Committee resolved unanimously to oppose the financing provisions "which set a dangerous precedent and strike at the financial stability of institutions in which the American public has great faith and confidence. . . . The four Federal agencies involved were established by the Congress of the United States to protect the homes and savings of

[83] Testimony of William L. Batt, Jr., area administrator, in *Public Works Acceleration,* Hearings before the Senate Public Works Committee, 87 Cong. 2 sess. (April 13, 1962); Batt gave this account of the March meeting at which President Kennedy made his decision: "We had been pressing for a public works program for depressed areas, and so had Secretary Goldberg—although he wanted to extend it to all areas of substantial unemployment. When we entered the President's office, I thought we had been called to discuss whether there should be such a program, but it soon became clear that the President's mind was already made up. He mentioned a letter from George Meany and one from Clark and Blatnik. We then began discussing amounts; the Budget Bureau was on the low side, and Goldberg and I were on the high side. The President came down on Goldberg's side both on the amount and on extending the benefits to all areas of substantial labor surplus. It was all over in about half an hour" (interview, December 1965).

American citizens. . . . This vast money scheme could jeopardize the financial stability of the agencies concerned."[84]

Senator Robert S. Kerr (Democrat of Oklahoma), floor manager of the bill, was compelled to accept an amendment subjecting the program to the regular appropriations process. This concession removed the central objection to the standby program by removing most of the substance from the concept. The amount had also been cut from $2 billion to $750 million (with the immediate authorization raised to a like amount). Even so, Kerr managed to save the standby program by only one vote, 37–36. Not a single Republican supported it. The minority argued that, since the standby authority would not be available in any case until after June 30, 1963, the Congress might as well reserve judgment until it met in that year and could see how the initial $750 million was spent.

Given the makeup of the Eighty-seventh Congress, any measure that cleared the Senate by just one vote was foredoomed in the House. Representative Blatnik of Minnesota, the House sponsor, abandoned the watered-down standby authority proposal and substituted an increase to $900 million in the authorization for the immediate program. Although House Republicans attacked the program as "a political boondoggle of the worst type," "the worst bill that has ever been voted out of our committee . . . a $900 million political slush fund for the President," "obviously politically conceived," "a 'Bundle for Bailey,' " and "a sham [which] will affect no more than 3 percent of the unemployed of the Nation,"[85] it passed the House by a voice vote after a recommittal motion was beaten comfortably, 221–192. The Democrats lost forty-four of their conservatives but picked up nineteen Republican votes, nine of them from Pennsylvania.[86]

The Senate quickly accepted the House amendments, and the President approved the Accelerated Public Works Act on September 14, assigning its administration to the Area Redevelopment Administration. The legislation, in the course of seven months, had traveled full circle. The original bill had been lost in its entirety; the amendment, increased by 50 percent,

---

84 For text of statement, see *Cong. Record*, Vol. 108 (May 2, 1962), pp. 7555–56.

85 Statements of William C. Cramer of Florida, Donald D. Clancy of Ohio, John W. Byrnes of Wisconsin, and John V. Lindsay of New York, *ibid*. (Aug. 28–29, 1962), pp. 17936, 17940, 17948, 18013. The reference was to John M. Bailey, chairman of the Democratic National Committee.

86 The Republicans also contributed a liberalizing amendment, sponsored by William W. Scranton of Pennsylvania, which authorized an increase in the federal share from 50 to 75 percent for communities unable to finance half the cost of their projects.

survived. A measure designed to combat cyclical unemployment in a future recession had been transformed into a companion measure to the Area Redevelopment Act, directed mainly toward reducing structural unemployment in the depressed areas of the country.

The Appalachian Experiment (*1958–65*)

"Coal has always cursed the land in which it lies," wrote Harry M. Caudill in his angry story of the devastated Cumberland plateau of eastern Kentucky.[87] "The capitalistic system which made America great has failed in eastern Kentucky," said his fellow townsman, Thomas E. Gish. "The failure is the fault of no one in particular, and yet is the fault of everyone."[88]

Of all the depressed areas of America, none was more distressed than the Cumberland plateau. It is not a land of ridges and wide valleys, like those parts of the Appalachian Mountains to the east, but a broad, wrinkled highland cut by narrow, twisting valleys wedged between steep hills. The turnpikes, the railroads, the highways, and the westward streams of migration went around, not through, the Cumberland barrier. Its early settlers carved out their tiny hillside plots, trapped and hunted, and their descendants lived for generations in isolation from the world. To this day, some "head of the holler" communities cannot be reached by automobile.

Without flat land for commercial farming or for factories, the Cumberlands were bypassed in the growth of modern industry and agriculture. Lumber brought prosperity, for a time. But then the virgin oak and poplar were gone. Coal brought another boom period. Then came mechanization. There remained a stranded population, exhausted resources, and a land denuded of cover to hold back floodwaters.[89] By every measure—

[87] *Night Comes to the Cumberlands* (Little, Brown, 1962), p. x.
[88] Testimony of Gish in *Unemployment Problems*, Hearings (Dec. 11, 1959), p. 1995.
[89] Gish gave a vivid account of conditions in eastern Kentucky: "Perhaps no area in the world has had a greater abundance of natural resources than eastern Kentucky—and with all of our natural wealth we should be a wealthy people. But to a degree that is shocking, eastern Kentucky was robbed by eastern financial interests, and the robbery goes on today. . . . Whatever profit—and the profits often have been fabulous—that has been made by coal operators in eastern Kentucky has been drained away. . . . They make their money and they move out—taking with them the wealth of the county. Letcher

poverty, unemployment, illiteracy, school dropout ratios, welfare costs—
the mountain people lagged far behind the rest of the nation.

On January 29, 1957, the waters came. Six inches of rain in seventy-two
hours sent the Big Sandy, the Kentucky, and their many tributaries over
their banks. The entire town of Pikeville was under water. Not a single
business building in Hazard was untouched.[90] Damage to the ribbon towns
strung through the narrow valleys reached $50 million.

In the autumn before the floods, John D. Whisman, a 35-year-old
businessman who was president of the Kentucky junior chamber of commerce, had taken the initiative in creating a thirty-two-county regional
development council in eastern Kentucky, with membership from the
"Jaycees" and other civic clubs, to formulate a long-range program for the
region's development. But when the flood waters receded, enormous new
problems of recovery had been added to the chronic problems of poverty
and underdevelopment. A firm of planning consultants engaged by the
Kentucky department of economic development recommended creation
of an official regional planning body, under existing state statutes, to
undertake the planning task the voluntary council had begun. Hearings
were held, petitions signed, and in August 1957 a nine-man eastern Kentucky regional planning commission came into being. Whisman was appointed its executive director.

By the time Senator McCarthy's committee on unemployment problems
arrived in Harlan and Pikeville, in December 1959, the commission had
completed its program. The furious battles among the politicians in Washington over whether the Area Redevelopment Act should offer $50 mil-
lion in loans to industry appeared to the eastern Kentucky planners as little
more than a noisy sideshow. Before the government could lend, an entre-
preneur must want to borrow, and what businessman would choose to put
a plant in a region that was lacking in flat land, subject to the ravages of
floods, remote from the main transportation systems of the country, de-

---

County has built some fabulous homes in Louisville, Lexington, Cincinnati, Pittsburgh,
on the French Riviera, and in Florida. But you won't find a single one in Letcher County.

"If only a fraction of the money made in eastern Kentucky was reinvested here, then
ample job opportunities would exist.

"Eastern Kentucky is 50 years behind the rest of the United States in development.
Our children still go to school much in the manner of Abe Lincoln—but they don't
receive as much education as Lincoln got. . . . There is at least a 50-year gap between this
area and the rest of the country—and it is to close that gap that we need outside help"
(*ibid.*, pp. 1995–97) ; see also pp. 80–81, above.

[90] Newspaper reports inserted in *Cong. Record,* Vol. 103 (Feb. 4, 1957), pp. 1497–
1502.

ficient in education and health and community facilities and services of every kind, and all compounded by a history of labor strife? "In the past 4 years," the president of the Harlan chamber of commerce testified, "I know of only one bona fide prospect that would be even interested in coming into our county. . . . We cannot generate any interest."[91]

Whisman told the committee that, in his opinion, eastern Kentucky would not "yield to the normal industrial or agricultural development efforts, but requires development of a broader, more basic type as a prerequisite to a direct approach to plant location and industrial development."[92] The commission's "broader, more basic" program—contained in a booklet entitled "Program 60"—called for coordinated action to improve highways, airports, education, health and welfare services, housing, planning and zoning, parks and other tourist attractions, forestry, and agriculture; to develop the region's water resources; and to provide plant sites and research and credit services to industry.[93]

The commission proposed that Kentucky ally itself with the other states containing portions of the Appalachian Mountain chain to form an Appalachian states development authority and press the federal government to create a corresponding regional planning body. It recommended to the newly elected governor, Bert T. Combs, that he call a conference of Appalachian governors for the purpose.[94]

Neither the majority nor the minority members of the McCarthy committee endorsed the Kentucky recommendation. It was reflected only in the individual views of Senator Cooper of that state. He argued that in addition to an area redevelopment act, "underdeveloped areas" needed preference in federal programs for highways, airports, and water resource development. He urged that the President appoint a task force of federal officials, headed by a full-time chairman, to work with the states in establishing programs "to develop the natural resources of the depressed areas, and to provide the basic industrial requirements which will attract industry."[95]

The next move came from neither Governor Combs nor President

---

[91] Testimony of Ernest Smith, in *Unemployment Problems*, Hearings (Dec. 10, 1959), p. 1823.

[92] *Ibid.*, p. 1915.

[93] A preliminary presentation of these ideas had been made by Whisman in *Area Redevelopment Act*, Hearings before Subcommittee No. 3 of the House Banking and Currency Committee, 86 Cong. 1 sess. (March 16, 1959), pp. 383–408.

[94] "Program 60" is reprinted in *Unemployment Problems*, Hearings, pp. 1854–1906.

[95] *Report of the Special Committee on Unemployment Problems*, S. Rept. 1206, pp. 190–92.

Eisenhower, but from an unexpected source. Governor J. Millard Tawes of Maryland, preparing to meet with a delegation from the Appalachian counties of his state, turned for advice to his state director of economic development, George Huebley, who had come to Maryland a few months earlier from a similar post in Kentucky. Huebley had with him a copy of "Program 60." He suggested that Tawes convene the conference of Appalachian governors that had been suggested to Combs. Tawes did so.

The governors, nine in number, met twice in 1960. At their second conference they adopted a "declaration for action" drafted by a staff committee headed by Whisman to inaugurate, with federal participation, "a special regional program of development." Meanwhile, Whisman and his allies found a target of opportunity in the task force on area redevelopment appointed by President-elect Kennedy and headed by Senator Douglas. The task force recommended the establishment of "regional development commissions" for regions "where economic problems are particularly deep-seated and severe" and proposed that the first such commission be set up for Appalachia.

The next step, clearly, was a meeting of the Appalachian governors with the President. It was scheduled for May, and the staff committee confidently prepared a memorandum for the governors to use in proposing to Kennedy the creation of a regional commission. By the time they assembled in Washington, however, circumstances had changed. The Area Redevelopment Act had been passed, and the Area Redevelopment Administration had just come into being. Those who had been heralding the ARA as the savior of the nation's depressed areas could hardly, at that moment, propose yet another new agency for the same purpose. Moreover, the governors were far from clear and united on just what kind of regional commission they wanted and on how great a financial commitment they themselves were prepared to make. Under the circumstances, before adopting any specific proposal for public presentation to the President, they decided to discuss the various alternative approaches with the President's representative, Myer Feldman of the White House staff. Out of that discussion came agreement that a small staff group would be established within ARA to concentrate upon Appalachia, working with a corresponding group representing the governors. At this meeting, also, the nine participating governors formally organized as the Conference of Appalachian Governors.

"Appalachia," says Whisman, "is the story of two floods. Each broke a dam of resistance to a comprehensive regional approach."

The second flood came in early 1963, coursing down the same Cumberland valleys that had been desolated six years before.

The "dam of resistance," however, had been undermined by the growing realization on all sides that the arrangement of two years before had failed. The staff groups created under the 1961 agreement had had no significant impact upon the poverty of Appalachia. The ARA had made some loans for mountain enterprises, but these served mainly to dramatize the Whisman-Cooper thesis that the region could not hope to achieve significant and sustained economic growth without first building, in the terminology borrowed by economists from the military, a solid "infrastructure." Yet no program of action toward that end existed—or was even in preparation.

The two lost years are variously explained. The Conference of Appalachian Governors looked to ARA to take bold leadership, making full use of its broad charter, its prestige—and its technical assistance funds. But ARA Administrator William L. Batt, Jr., and his staff were preoccupied with getting off to a sound start in administering the specific grant and loan programs with which they had been entrusted. Busy with organizing a new agency, establishing standards, and reviewing "overall economic development programs" and the first project applications, they were in no mood to embark on the high adventure of promoting vast new federal expenditures in Appalachia. Batt raised the banner of "states' rights" and urged the governors to develop specific proposals and make substantial financial and political commitments of their own. In short, the governors looked to Batt to run with the ball but he wanted to see them downfield blocking first. Neither was willing to make the first move.

In the early weeks of 1963, Feldman and Lee C. White of the White House staff, responding to the continuing pressure from the governors, summoned Batt and his deputy, Harold W. Williams, to discuss the possibility of a more intensive regional program for Appalachia. Williams began drafting a series of specific proposals, which included a plan for an Appalachian regional commission. This was the situation when the rains came.

The floods of March 11–12, 1963, were in much of the Cumberlands even worse than those of 1957—in some valleys the worst in history. Governor Combs turned to Washington for help, and Whisman, by this time thoroughly frustrated as chairman of the Conference of Appalachian Governors' staff group, saw another target of opportunity. As the last item on an agenda sheet for Combs' meeting with federal officials on

disaster relief, he revived the proposal for an Appalachian regional commission. Edward A. McDermott, director of the Office of Emergency
Planning and the President's disaster relief coordinator, responded affirmatively. Next day he notified Combs that the President, too, was
affirmative. By this time, Batt and Williams had their proposal ready.
They proposed a temporary joint federal-state commission, under the
chairmanship of Under Secretary of Commerce Franklin D. Roosevelt,
Jr., to prepare a development plan for Appalachia. Kennedy invited the
Conference of Appalachian Governors to meet with him in Washington
on April 9 and at the meeting announced establishment of the President's
Appalachian Regional Commission. The members represented fourteen
federal departments or agencies and nine Appalachian states.

After a flying visit to each state, Roosevelt established a network of
committees and subcommittees to consider virtually every form of aid
the federal government could offer. Each was headed by a federal official
and included representatives of the nine participating states. The states
knew what they wanted—highways first of all to open the mountain
valleys to the outside world, dams and reservoirs and other resource development projects, and preferential treatment in any other program area
where the federal government might be willing to extend it. The federal
officials had a presidential directive to cooperate, and to each agency that
became a directive to justify an expansion of its services wherever it could
do so. Appalachia was "in" in 1963; a federal agency that could not find
a way to help would have had to be singularly lacking in respect for its
own importance.

In every corner of the federal establishment, during the summer of
1963, ideas for the Appalachian program began to grow—usually in the
form of regional addenda to agency budgets. Often new legislation was
not even needed, just money. The highway planners alone developed a
regional network of access roads costing $1.2 billion, with the federal
government to finance the major share. It fell to Roosevelt and a small
central staff under John L. Sweeney, executive director of the temporary
commission, to try to assemble these proposals in some kind of balance,
respond to the priorities felt by the governors, develop the theoretical
rationale for giving Appalachia preferential (or differential) treatment,
plan the structure of a permanent Appalachian regional commission, and
draft a report.

As the work progressed, members of Congress from other depressed
regions paid closer and closer attention. Senators from the northern Great

Lakes states made inquiry. The Ozark states expressed an interest. Finally, shortly after the accession of President Johnson, the Bureau of the Budget also began to pay closer attention—and discovered to its horror that massive budgetary commitments were being made. The bureau hastily raised objections that the program was unbalanced, with far too much emphasis on highways, that it cost too much (keeping in mind the implications for other regions), and that funds for construction of specific projects should not be sought before a definitive development plan had been prepared.

Roosevelt responded that his commission was not just another federal agency, with its plans subject to the normal processes of budget review, but a federal-state agency. The report was intended to reflect the views of its members, including the representatives of nine governors, not the views of the administration as such. It represented the work of twelve hundred people over six months. Copies of the draft report had been distributed throughout the region. If it were now stripped of its substance, at a presidential directive, the governors would repudiate it and the whole enterprise would end in debacle.

For a time, President Johnson withheld approval. Rumors circulated that he was opposed to the regional approach to development. But it did not matter. By the history of the undertaking, he had been trapped. Had the commission been composed solely of federal officials, it could have been controlled and directed. Had it been made up of private citizens, it could have been repudiated. In either such case, the report might even have been, if necessary, suppressed. But a mixed federal-state commission, launched in a glare of publicity, operating in the open, and backed by the political and official leadership of nine states,[96] could not be subjected to any of these forms of discipline. President Kennedy, it turned out, had given away part of the administration's power to make its policy and budget decisions. Moreover, President Johnson wanted to dramatize his "war on poverty" by visiting some poor families, and how could he arrange a tour without including Appalachia—the very symbol of poverty? In the end, at a meeting with the Conference of Appalachian Governors at Huntington, West Virginia, he gave the enterprise his blessing.

The commission delivered its report in April 1964, its program and budget proposals uncensored. Three weeks later the President submitted a bill carrying out the recommendations of the report—with the exception

[96] Parts of Ohio, South Carolina, New York, and Mississippi were ultimately included in Appalachia, but these states did not participate in the early Conference of Appalachian Governors meetings or the President's Appalachian Regional Commission study.

that $200 million had been trimmed from the highway program. After hearings, two controversial minor sections were removed—and the $200 million restored. The bill contained more than $1 billion in federal funds for a single region. Despite opposition arguments that it was "hastily prepared" and "being rushed," that it was not based on a comprehensive plan, that the regional approach was discriminatory, that other regions would be applying next and "there would be no end to where the government could go if it is to hand out sugar plums indiscriminately,"[97] it passed the Senate on September 25 by an overwhelming margin, 45–13. In the House, however, the bill was scheduled twice for floor action but was still pending when Congress adjourned October 3. The Democratic leaders, said Congressional Quarterly, "reluctantly concluded they could not produce the necessary votes," at a time when many members were already at home campaigning, and the loss "constituted one of the Administration's few major setbacks of the session."[98]

After the landslide Democratic victory a month later, passage of the bill was almost perfunctory. The Senate, after the briefest of committee hearings, passed the bill before the new session was a month old. The debate centered not on the merits of the regional approach for Appalachia, but on how soon the same approach could be extended to half a dozen other regions. Amendments to create regional commissions for the northern Great Lakes states and the Ozarks were blocked only by assurance from the administration that a public works and economic development bill then in preparation would provide general authority for establishing such commissions anywhere.[99] New England Senators made clear they wanted one. Senator George McGovern, South Dakota Democrat, served notice that he supported the bill "with the full understanding that this is the first bill in a list of regional development programs that are to be implemented."[100] The final vote was 62–22. In the House, Republican William C. Cramer of Florida charged that his amendments were not being considered on their merits because the Democratic majority had been "instructed that the action of the other body be rubberstamped." "It now looks like we have the great stampede rather than the Great Society,"

[97] Speeches of J. Caleb Boggs of Delaware, Republican, and A. Willis Robertson of Virginia and William Proxmire of Wisconsin, Democrats, *Cong. Record*, Vol. 110 (Sept. 25, 1964), pp. 22903–15.

[98] *Congressional Quarterly Almanac, 1964* summarizes the legislative history and major provisions of the bill, pp. 288–94.

[99] *Cong. Record*, Vol. 111 (Feb. 1, 1965), pp. 1671–88.

[100] *Ibid.*, p. 1693.

observed Cramer.[101] The final vote was 257–165. One of President Johnson's few major setbacks of 1964 thus became his first victory of 1965.

The Public Works and Economic Development Act   *(1963–65)*

The experience of a decade of experimentation in stimulating the development of the depressed areas was consolidated, in 1965, in a single statute. The Public Works and Economic Development Act combined the three approaches that had been attempted—and, in doing so, solved three problems of legislative and political strategy.

First, it gave the Area Redevelopment Administration a new name and a new image, considered necessary after the House of Representatives refused to give the ARA additional funds in 1963.

Second, it responded to the pressure from Congress for resumption of the highly popular Accelerated Public Works Act, which had expired.

Third, it kept the commitment to senators from depressed regions outside Appalachia that they too could have regional development programs.

The House Repudiation of ARA. While the Area Redevelopment Administration had been created with a four-year life, funds for some of its programs were running low by the spring of 1963. In March of that year President Kennedy asked Congress to add $455.5 million to the agency's authorization, more than doubling its total resources.

But the ARA, from the beginning, had been the center of a swirl of controversy.[102] Initially, it was under enormous pressure from the depressed areas to begin providing jobs, and was criticized for being slow. Even Secretary of Commerce Luther H. Hodges joined in this criticism.[103] But as soon as ARA began approving projects, it was accused of favoritism and of making unsound expenditures.

The program was, by its nature, highly vulnerable to criticism. Virtually every business has competitors. A loan application from a soybean mill in Maryland brought down the wrath of the nation's entire soybean

---

[101] *Ibid.* (March 3, 1965), p. 4019.

[102] Levitan, *Federal Aid to Depressed Areas*, analyzes the many administrative issues that arose in getting the area redevelopment program underway. For a critique of the strengths and weaknesses of the program, see pp. 246–54; for a brief reply by ARA Administrator Batt, see pp. 257–58.

[103] Remarks at a press conference, Oct. 3, 1961 (*ibid.*, p 248).

processing industry and precipitated a congressional hearing—even though the application was never approved. ARA-financed motels in depressed areas were made to appear as threats to every existing motel for miles around. A technical assistance study of the feasibility of growing sugar beets in New York state drew the fire of established beet-producing areas. As Levitan points out, the slackness of the economy in 1961 and 1962 complicated the competition problems. "It is difficult to defend government financing of new capacity when established firms operate below their optimum level because of inadequate demand."[104] ARA denied many applications for loans where an adverse impact on competitors could be foreseen, but many other instances where its policies had led to "unfair competition" could be cited, and the opponents of ARA compiled these instances systematically.

Moreover, one aspect of the problem of competition had noticeably dampened the enthusiasm of organized labor—the source of most of the original bill's mobilized support. From the time of ARA's first grant, to assist the nonunion shirt factory in Arkansas, labor had felt betrayed. "With the gift of hindsight," Harold Williams has said, "it is easy to see that the program which labor espoused so vehemently was tailor-made to help organized labor's most direct enemies, businessmen who wanted to operate in low-wage, rural, hard-to-organize areas. It mattered little whether ARA refused to help with relocations as long as anyone could come in and start a new business in a low-wage area to compete against the high wage producers."[105] By this time, too, the accelerated public works program had superior attraction for the building trades and the manpower development and training program offered a better means for training the unemployed. To much of labor, then, the ARA seemed at best unnecessary and at worst dangerous.

On the day before the proposal to increase ARA's authorization reached the House floor, on June 12, the House leadership was confident. Its count showed the victory would be narrow but nonetheless secure, with 199 Democrats and an expected 25 Republicans favorable. But that night President Kennedy appeared on nationwide television, in response to the University of Alabama desegregation crisis, to charge Governor George C. Wallace with "unlawful obstruction" and to announce a civil rights

[104] *Ibid.*, p. 247. Miernyk lists first among ARA's handicaps the problem that "an area redevelopment program can be fully successful only if there is 'full' employment in the economy as a whole" ("Area Redevelopment," p. 170).

[105] Letter to me from Williams, former ARA deputy administrator, March 31, 1966.

legislative program to meet the nation's "moral crisis." "I saw my support melt away," says Batt. "Members who had personally given me their promise before the President's speech came to me to say they could not keep their pledges." On the morning of June 12, a rash of adverse reports came into the office of the Democratic whip. When it was over, the measure had lost, 209–204. Only 189 Democrats and 15 Republicans voted in the affirmative.

An analysis of the vote shows that 39 congressmen who had voted for the ARA in 1961 reversed themselves in 1963—20 Republicans and 19 Democrats, 18 of them from the South, 4 from Alabama.[106]

Seeing a chance to deal the Democratic administration a setback—and aware that most of the agency's programs did not actually need new money until 1964—the Republicans closed ranks. Three of the twenty who shifted their positions from 1961 offered their reasons in the House debate. Mrs. Florence P. Dwyer of Elizabeth, New Jersey, attacked ARA for retraining workers for a shoe plant in Hagerstown, Maryland, which had moved from her district. She accused the ARA of being "open-handed" in using subsidies to attract industry to areas "many of which cannot be considered depressed in the sense Congress originally intended."[107] John V. Lindsay of New York City also attacked "the piracy of industries" and hit the management of the agency from both sides, charging it with "stodginess" and "cumbersome red tape" on the one hand, and "waste" on the other. Foreshadowing the Economic Opportunity Act, he called for "something new, bold, and different. We should be working on education, vocational training, manpower retraining, school drop-out legislation, equal job opportunity legislation, housing legislation, and other basic measures. Pork barrel approaches are tired. They are the old approaches of the thirties that unimaginative people are trying to apply to the sixties." He also pointed out that withholding of additional funds would only chasten the agency, not kill it.[108]

Most significant of all appeared to be the opposition of Arch A. Moore, Jr., the only Republican from the state that was the very symbol of depressed areas—West Virginia—and an early and consistent supporter of area redevelopment legislation. Moore angrily accused the ARA of

---

[106] *Congressional Quarterly Almanac, 1963*, p. 565.

[107] *Cong. Record*, Vol. 109 (June 12, 1963), pp. 10694, 10693. Oddly, Representative Charles McC. Mathias, Jr., whose district included Hagerstown, was also among the 20 Republicans who shifted.

[108] *Ibid.*, pp. 10712–13.

political favoritism in language that every Republican could understand:

> Mr. Chairman, the funds of ARA without question were used in every way possible to bring about my defeat in the 1962 election, even to the extent of my opponent being permitted to announce preliminary approval of a project in my district. And when I countered with a preliminary approval of a project in another part of my district, I was greeted with wide denials in the press by ARA. . . . Every attempt was made by this supposedly qualified public servant to embarrass me. . . . All of this occurred one week before the general election in 1962. It had been planned for my opponent to announce it two days before the election. I might add, Mr. Chairman, that ten days following the general election, the preliminary announcement of the project which I made, even though denied by the Administrator as never about to occur, was finally given complete approval. To me this is a display of dishonesty that cannot be tolerated. For that reason, together with others, I intend to oppose with my vote H. R. 4996.[109]

If the man who represented the West Virginia unemployed did not want the bill, then why should his Republican colleagues from districts ineligible for ARA benefits support it?[110] In depressed Pennsylvania, Republicans from only the hardest-hit areas stuck by the bill; ARA received five GOP votes from that state, compared to thirteen two years before. Republican liberals who had broken ranks on many previous Kennedy measures, like Mrs. Dwyer and Lindsay, could find ample reason this time to give a vote to their own party leadership—which, scenting victory, was putting them under heavy pressure. On the final tally, only fifteen Republicans supported ARA, compared to forty-three in 1961.

Two weeks later, the Kennedy bill was passed intact by the Senate by a resounding majority, 65–30. Neither Republican nor southern Democratic supporters defected. Levitan attributes the disparity between the results in the two houses largely to the quality of the debate. It is unquestionably true that the opponents presented their case with far more vigor and persuasiveness in the House while the supporters marshalled their arguments most convincingly in the Senate, under Douglas' leadership and with important backing from Fulbright. Some other factors may be

---

[109] *Ibid.*; p. 10713. An account of the same incident, and of another involving Representative Clarence Kilburn of northern New York state, is in Levitan, *Federal Aid to Depressed Areas*, pp. 46–47.

[110] On the Democratic side, the loss of Representative W. Pat Jennings of Virginia's depressed 9th district, wholly located in Appalachia, was influential for the same reason. Jennings' defection was attributed to adverse local reaction to certain early ARA-financed plans for the region's development. One of the proposals is described by Levitan, *Federal Aid to Depressed Areas*, p. 218. See also Rowland Evans and Robert Novak, *Washington Post*, June 16, 1963.

mentioned: By the time the bill reached the Senate floor, the President's civil rights speech was fifteen days, instead of fifteen hours, old. Senators represent broader constituencies than congressmen, and virtually every state had been granted at least one eligible area. The Senate Republican leadership, with no prospect of winning, did not try to impose party discipline.

Throughout the rest of the session, supporters of the bill remained prepared for another effort in the House, counting on the fading of the civil rights issue and a reduction of $100 million in the authorization to bring them the necessary additional votes. But the Democratic leadership never felt sufficiently confident of its prospects to bring the issue to a showdown, and the bill was still in the Rules Committee when Congress adjourned. A rule was finally granted in the summer of 1964, just before the presidential nominating conventions, but the White House decided, for tactical reasons, to hold the issue over for yet another year.

Consolidation of the Depressed Areas Effort. Responsibility for figuring out how to salvage the Area Redevelopment Act fell largely upon the Bureau of the Budget as coordinator of the President's legislative program. But in a second capacity, as the President's agent for eliminating waste in government expenditures, the bureau was also highly sensitive to the charges heard in Congress, and presented in sophisticated detail in Levitan's study, that ARA funds were being spread too thinly over too broad an area to get significant results. It was also alarmed at the pressure behind renewal of the accelerated public works program and behind the "proliferation" of Appalachias. The bureau's economists therefore sought a program that would meet the political requirements but hold total expenditures in check and assure the most long-range benefits for the funds expended. To this end, they proposed to concentrate the funds upon areas with the greatest growth potential and into projects that contributed most directly to economic development. New courthouses, which in some areas had become a symbol of the Accelerated Public Works Act, might contribute to the morale of a dying community but they could not keep it from dying. In contrast, well-conceived infrastructure projects, located at the natural "growth centers" of a depressed region, could contribute to the revival of the entire region. As the means for channeling assistance into areas with true growth potential, the bill provided financial incentives for the states to organize multicounty "economic development districts" and prepare district development plans. A thriving community within a district would become eligible for benefits along with its depressed neighbors if it were identified in the plan as a logical "economic development center" for the entire district.

The bill created a new agency, the Economic Development Administration, to supplant the ARA. It put the accelerated public works program on a permanent basis, with $250 million a year for community projects contributing to economic growth. It authorized the secretary of commerce to designate regions, at the request of governors of two or more states, for comprehensive planning on the Appalachia pattern.[111] It also embodied various other refinements growing out of experience in the administration of the Area Redevelopment Act.

This careful consolidation of the three previous approaches sailed through the Johnson Congress of 1965. The Senate added language to assure that any new regional commissions would be equal in status to the Appalachian Regional Commission. The Senate raised the public works authorization to $400 million a year, and the House went $100 million beyond that. The House broadened the roster of communities eligible for public works. The Senate then accepted the higher figure[112] and the broadened eligibility.

In the Senate, only twelve members, nine Republicans and three Democrats, voted against the bill. In the House, the Republican Policy Committee formally opposed it, but after various Republican amendments were defeated, the leadership could not hold the line on the final vote. In all, one-fourth of the Republicans, thirty-one in number, voted with the Democrats on final passage.

A decade of conflict, groping, and experimentation with the problems of depressed areas appeared to have led at last to consensus—although whether the consensus measure was strong enough to provide the solution to those problems had yet to be demonstrated. "We are not helpless before the iron laws of economics," said the President on signing the bill. "A wise public policy uses economics to create hope—and not to abet despair."[113]

111 By the end of 1967, regional planning bodies had been established for the six New England states; the coastal plain of North Carolina, South Carolina, and Georgia; the Ozark region of Missouri, Arkansas, and Oklahoma; the cutover northern counties of Michigan, Wisconsin, and Minnesota; and the "four corners" area of Utah, Colorado, Arizona, and New Mexico.

112 In the budgets for both the 1967 and 1968 fiscal years, President Johnson held his request within the $250 million he originally proposed.

113 On Aug. 26, 1965, *Public Papers of the Presidents, 1965,* p. 931.

CHAPTER IV

For the Poor, Opportunity

"THIS ADMINISTRATION today, here and now, declares unconditional war on poverty in America," Lyndon Johnson told the Congress in his first State of the Union message.

Many Americans were inspired. "I was greatly moved," "I particularly applaud," "I especially commend," "it pleased me," or simply "I agree" —these were among the comments of senators who heard the President. "It will be good for us as a nation to be engaged in a cause again," wrote Walter Lippmann.

But other Americans were confused. "I thought we had been working against poverty since the beginning of this country," observed Republican Representative Robert Taft, Jr., of Ohio. "I thought many of the programs, the Manpower Development and Training Act, vocational education, unemployment compensation, all kinds of measures of this sort were trying to keep our economy strong. . . . Why, at this particular point, are we going ahead with a poverty program as such in an omnibus bill?"[1]

The question was appropriate. Was the "war on poverty" a new idea or simply a new name for old ideas? Had a new national problem really been discovered? Until the President's declaration on January 8, 1964, poverty had not even been included in the lexicon of America's recognized public problems. Presidents had not spoken, or sent messages to Congress, about poverty as such. Congressmen had not spoken, or introduced bills, on the subject. Until 1964 the word "poverty" did not appear as a heading in the index of either the *Congressional Record* or the *Public Papers of the*

[1] *Economic Opportunity Act of 1964*, Hearings before the Subcommittee on the War on Poverty Program of the House Education and Labor Committee, 88 Cong. 2 sess. (March 17, 1964), p. 99.

Presidents.[2] Two other headings did appear, with many entries: "unemployment" and "social security." These reflected a traditional dichotomy. The legislation of the New Deal era had separated poor people into two neat categories—the able-bodied unemployed, for whom jobs were the solution, and those unable to work, for whom financial assistance must be provided. This dichotomy led to the acceptance of two great national objectives. One of these, discussed in the preceding two chapters, was full employment for all who were able and seeking work—with minimum wage legislation to help assure that those who worked escaped poverty. The other was a minimum decent standard of living, through social security, for those in need and not able to work—the children of fatherless households, the old, the disabled. Meanwhile, social evils associated with poverty would be attacked directly through specific and piecemeal programs—urban renewal would clear the slums, youth work and institutional care would cope with juvenile delinquency, public housing would improve the shelter of the poor, and so on.

Sargent Shriver, President Johnson's director of the poverty war, responded to Representative Taft's puzzlement: "It is a question of timing. . . . There is a time when the timing is right to bring things together to go ahead and solve the problem."

The notion that the timing was right occurred first, apparently, to John F. Kennedy himself. The war on poverty did not arise, as have many great national programs, from the pressure of overwhelming public demand—the poor had no lobby. Nor yet was it proposed by the staff thinkers in government agencies who are paid to conceive ideas. It began when President Kennedy said to the chairman of his Council of Economic Advisers, Walter Heller, during the year-end review of economic conditions in December 1962: "Now, look! I want to go beyond the things that have already been accomplished. Give me facts and figures on the things we still have to do. For example, what about the poverty problem in the United States?"[3] That comment set in motion the staff work that, more than a year later, took concrete form as the war on poverty.

One can only speculate about the factors that influenced the President

[2] The word "poverty" does appear as a heading in *The Speeches of Senator John F. Kennedy, Presidential Campaign of 1960,* S. Rept. 994, 87 Cong. 1 sess. (1961), Pt. 1, but primarily in the context of "world poverty." At Hyde Park, N.Y., on Aug. 14, 1960, commemorating the signing of the Social Security Act, Kennedy observed that "the war against poverty and degradation is not yet over" (p. 18), but he did not repeat the phrase again in discussing domestic issues.

[3] Quoted by Heller in a speech at Indiana State College, Indiana, Pa., March 25, 1965.

in December 1962. Heller remembers that the President asked for copies of *The Other America*, by Michael Harrington, and a study of poverty by Leon H. Keyserling. Arthur M. Schlesinger, Jr., believes that Harrington's book "helped crystallize his determination in 1963 to accompany the tax cut by a poverty program" and that he was influenced also by John Kenneth Galbraith's *The Affluent Society*.[4] By the spring of 1963, writes Schlesinger, Kennedy "was reaching the conclusion that tax reduction required a comprehensive structural counterpart, taking the form, not of piecemeal programs, but of a broad war against poverty itself. Here perhaps was the unifying theme which would pull a host of social programs together and rally the nation behind a generous cause."[5]

The key words are those that express Kennedy's dissatisfaction with the nature, scope, and accomplishments of his, and his party's, program as it stood in 1962—his desire "to go beyond," his concern with "the things we still have to do," the reference to "piecemeal programs," the feeling that something "broad" was required. One can read in these phrases the normal yearning of an idealist for ideas and of an activist for action—or the accustomed search of a politician facing a reelection campaign for a measure that will dramatize his principles and bear his name. But they express also an attitude that had become pervasive in Washington as the Kennedy administration entered its third year—a feeling that the "New Frontier" was made up mainly of old frontiers already crossed, and that all of those old frontiers, all of the innovations conceived over the course of a generation and written into law would not, singly or collectively, change the gray face of the "other America." The Kennedy piecemeal programs, built upon those of his predecessors, were reaching toward the substratum of the population where all of the problems were concentrated, but the programs were somehow not making contact, not on a scale and with an impact that measured up to the bright promise of a "New Frontier" or to the specific pledges made by a presidential candidate in West Virginia. The measures enacted, and those proposed, were dealing separately with such problems as slum housing, juvenile delinquency, dependency, unemployment, illiteracy, but they were separately inadequate because they were striking only at surface aspects

---

[4] Michael Harrington, *The Other America* (Macmillan, 1962); Leon H. Keyserling, *Poverty and Deprivation in the United States* (Washington: Conference on Economic Progress, April 1962); John Kenneth Galbraith, *The Affluent Society* (Houghton Mifflin, 1958).

[5] Arthur M. Schlesinger, Jr., *A Thousand Days* (Houghton Mifflin, 1965), p. 1,009.

of what seemed to be some kind of bedrock problem, and it was the bedrock problem that had to be identified so that it could be attacked in a concerted, unified, and innovative way. Perhaps it was Harrington's book that defined the target for Kennedy and supplied the coordinating concept —the bedrock problem, in a word, was "poverty." Words and concepts determine programs; once the target was reduced to a single word, the timing became right for a unified program. That the word itself embodied various definitions, each leading logically to its own line of attack, only became apparent as the war on poverty developed.

Failure and Ferment   *(1954–63)*

The sense of failure had grown among participants in each of the major fields of public action that reached most deeply into the lives of the poor, among persons concerned, respectively, with how poor people lived, how they earned their livings, how they survived when they did not earn, and how they conducted themselves in relation to the rest of the community— in other words, housing, structural unemployment, welfare, and crime and delinquency. Welfare programs were not decreasing the incidence of dependency; indeed, it was often alleged that they were compounding it, as dependent daughters grew up to be dependent mothers in what Oscar Lewis has labeled "the culture of poverty." The rise in the volume and violence of youth crime revealed in terrifying terms that programs to fit slum children for the middle class world were falling short. Urban renewal was of little help; in most cities it was merely pushing the poor from one slum to another. The latest and most heralded of the measures to combat structural unemployment—retraining of the jobless—had already encountered the obstacle that many, perhaps most, of the hard-core unemployed lacked even the basic qualifications to enter training.

Traditionally, the reflex action to failure, on the part of each profession, had been to demand more and better-trained professionals—more teachers, social workers, counselors, policemen, probation officers, and all the rest. But somewhere, within or on the edge of each profession, were those who said that more of the same was not enough, that new methods, new approaches were needed, too. The private foundations, as well as federal agencies with funds for research, listened to those who urged that new ideas be tested, and the result was an interacting sequence of theory, experiment, and demonstration that produced new strategic and tactical concepts for what became the war on poverty.

In the atmosphere of dissatisfaction and criticism in each field, the streams of innovative thought and action arose, grew, and gained momentum. No one can say how much of the new thought and experimentation had made an impression directly upon President Kennedy by 1962 or 1963, but some of it had been sponsored or subsidized by the federal government, and as a senator and as chief executive he had undoubtedly encountered it. Certainly, many of his close advisers had—including his brother, Attorney General Robert F. Kennedy, who was chairman of the President's Committee on Juvenile Delinquency and Youth Crime. In any case, the sense of failure and the resulting ferment created the intellectual climate in which the war on poverty was born. They made the timing right. And when the war on poverty took form, those streams converged and provided most of the new program components that gave it substance.

Stream One: Mental Health Discovers the "Sick Community." When President Eisenhower first expressed the federal government's concern with juvenile delinquency, he did so in a presidential message to Congress on the subject of health.[6] That may seem odd, but in fact nothing could be more symbolic of the way in which the problem was regarded. Juvenile delinquents were, in one way or another, sick. They were deviants from the healthy norm. Their moral or emotional sickness should be, like a physical sickness, diagnosed and treated.[7] Early detection, as a means of prevention, was emphasized. But it was also noted that juvenile delinquents in the urban slums congregated in gangs, and that behavior patterns were consistent within gangs and even, to a degree, within the larger slum communities of which the gangs were a part. The question began to be asked, might the delinquent be not a deviant at all but a conformist? Might he be conforming to the culture of a community that was as a whole deviant, so alienated from the mainstream of American life that its values and habits were severely at odds with those of the larger society? To the extent that those battling juvenile delinquency came to focus their attention upon the "sick community"—the community of the urban poor—rather than upon the individual offender, their activities flowed out of

[6] Message of Jan. 31, 1955, *Public Papers of the Presidents, 1955*, pp. 216–23.

[7] This in itself was a shift from earlier thinking (still expressed occasionally on the floors of Congress) when delinquents were looked upon as "bad" rather than sick and the woodshed rather than the psychiatrist's couch was the symbol of the appropriate treatment. See John E. Moore, "Juvenile Delinquency Control: A Congressional-Executive Battleground, 1961–64," in Frederic N. Cleaveland (ed.), *Congress and Urban Problems* (Brookings Institution, 1969); this section relies upon Moore's study.

the original context of health into a new context that was one of the intellectual precursors of "the war on poverty."

In every year since World War II, the incidence of juvenile delinquency—as measured by juvenile court cases—had risen faster than the rate of population growth. Not only in the number but in the seriousness of youth crimes had the problem grown. Chief J. Edgar Hoover of the Federal Bureau of Investigation testified that "during the past decade, youth has led the criminal army in the United States."[8] And those who did not read congressional testimony could read in their newspapers about the gang warfare of the big cities.

The Children's Bureau of the Department of Health, Education, and Welfare saw a national interest, and a role for itself, in the growing problem of youth crime and delinquency. In the absence of an appropriation for the purpose, the bureau arranged for private foundation funds for a special staff within the bureau to be concerned with the problem. Out of their work grew a suggestion to HEW Secretary Oveta Culp Hobby that she call a national conference on juvenile delinquency. The conference, held in June 1954, in turn made a recommendation, which President Eisenhower accepted, for a national program of grants to the states totaling $5 million a year to assist them in combating juvenile delinquency. In his health message of January 31, 1955, President Eisenhower proposed the grants "as a vital part of our attack on a serious health and social problem." Meanwhile, congressional groundwork had been laid through a series of hearings by a Senate Judiciary subcommittee headed by Democrat Estes Kefauver of Tennessee, whose interest in youth crime was an outgrowth of his earlier investigation of organized crime in the United States. The administration bill was introduced in the Senate by a senior Republican, Alexander Wiley of Wisconsin, and a somewhat different bill was initiated by Kefauver.[9]

The combined support of the Eisenhower administration and leaders of both parties in Congress might suggest that a relatively minor bill, traveling under a banner as hallowed as that of child welfare, would have smooth sailing. Yet the history of the bill over the next six years was one of unending travail. As each obstacle was removed, another appeared.

In 1955–56 the bill became embroiled in substantive conflicts, primarily

---

[8] Quoted in *ibid*.

[9] Though both senators were from the Judiciary Committee, the body concerned with crime and punishment, their bills were referred to the Labor and Public Welfare Committee, which has jurisdiction over public health. Thus is marked the transition of a subject from an older to a newer context.

concerning the status of the Children's Bureau within HEW and the role of private welfare organizations in administration of the funds granted to the states. The conflicts were multidimensional—between the bureau and its parent department, between the private and the public welfare agencies, and between the Democratic Senate and the Republican administration. By the time they were resolved, through the ultimate acceptance by the Senate Labor and Public Welfare Committee of the essential administration position, the bill could pass the Senate—unanimously, by voice vote, on the final day of the Congress—but no time remained for consideration in the House.

In 1957–58 the decisive factor in preventing action was the opposition of North Carolina Democrat Graham A. Barden, chairman of the House Education and Labor Committee. However, this was also the period of the "battle of the budget" initiated by Treasury Secretary George Humphrey, and the climate was inauspicious for any spending measure—even one in the $5 million range. In 1959 the bill was delayed for a year when President Eisenhower withdrew his support as part of his anti-spending crusade—to the considerable embarrassment of HEW, whose officials had the job of explaining the retreat to the Democratic committees on Capitol Hill. Next year the President yielded to HEW to the extent of indicating his willingness to sign a bill limited to research and development—excluding the state grant program he had originally proposed. A compromise measure then passed the Senate, was approved by the House Education and Labor Committee, but died in the House Rules Committee. Barden could no longer control his reorganized committee[10] but he could, and did, help Virginia Democrat Howard Smith, chairman of the Rules Committee, to bottle up the bill, simply by exercising his chairman's option not to request Smith to hold a hearing.

Juvenile delinquency legislation was by no means a major campaign issue in 1960, or even a minor one, but it did find its way into the Democratic platform and Senator Kennedy's speeches. Kennedy condemned the "negative" Republican attitude toward helping the cities cope with the problem—which he described as lying "largely in the realm of public action."[11] In 1961 the Senate repassed its bill even before the new administration could decide what kind of program it wanted. The President sent his bill to the House in May, creating at the same time the President's

---

[10] See Chap. 11, p. 522, note 15.

[11] Speech before an urban affairs conference, Pittsburgh, Pa., Oct. 10, 1960, *Speeches of Senator John F. Kennedy*, S. Rept. 994, p. 551. Moore found four references to juvenile delinquency in Kennedy's campaign ("Juvenile Delinquency Control").

Committee on Juvenile Delinquency and Youth Crime, headed by Attorney General Kennedy. The bill was enacted in August but not without difficulty in getting an 8–7 clearance from the newly expanded Rules Committee.[12] The new law was patterned after the 1960 rather than the 1955 version of the Eisenhower program: the emphasis was upon federal assistance for research and demonstration projects; the proposal for grants to the states for improving their programs had been abandoned.

The shift in the bill's content during the six years between initiation and action reflected, in part, the shaping of a new philosophy and doctrine that were to have a profound influence upon the strategy of the war on poverty. Implicit in the 1955 bill had been the assumption that existing state and local programs of juvenile delinquency control were wisely conceived; all that was needed from the federal government was money to strengthen those programs and finance the training of their professional personnel—youth workers, probation officers, child welfare specialists. The Senate committee report of 1956 asserted that "existing programs . . . are shamefully weak" and that they would not be strengthened without federal financial assistance.[13] The emphasis was upon new institutions adapted to the needs of the individual child.[14] The language of juvenile delinquency prevention and control was the terminology of medicine— early detection, diagnosis, treatment.

As early as 1956, however, a countertheme was heard. Saul Alinsky, executive director of the Industrial Areas Foundation, testified: ". . . in the main, delinquency and crime arise out of inadequate, substandard housing, disease, economic insecurity, inadequate educational facilities, discrimination, and a series of social ills which combine to foster and relate to each other in a vicious circle with each feeding into the other so that frustration, demoralization, and delinquency mounts. . . . The job is one of community organization. . . ."[15]

On New York City's lower east side, those who believed that delin-

[12] Moore attributes the Rules Committee vote to the influence of Chairman John E. Fogarty (Rhode Island Democrat) of the House HEW appropriations subcommittee on two of the Rules Committee members, and to the "improbable friendship" that had developed between Chairman Smith and Robert Kennedy (*ibid.*).

[13] *Delinquent Children's Act of 1956*, S. Rept. 2765, 84 Cong. 2 sess. (July 21, 1956), pp. 6, 8.

[14] See, for example, testimony of the chief of the Children's Bureau, Katherine B. Oettinger, in *Juvenile Delinquency Prevention and Control*, Hearings before the Special Subcommittee on Education of the House Education and Labor Committee, 86 Cong. 1 sess. (March 18, 1959), p. 91.

[15] Quoted in *Delinquent Children's Act of 1956*, S. Rept. 2765, p. 6.

quency must be attacked through community organization had an opportunity to put their theories into practice. The Henry Street settlement house had been seeking funds for a comprehensive program that would "make use of everything we know" to get at the causes of delinquency. Concluding that money could be obtained most readily under the label of research, the settlement house approached the Columbia University school of social work late in 1958 for help in designing a project that could put the ideas into practice and then evaluate the results. Richard Cloward and Lloyd Ohlin of the school participated in working out the research design; the settlement house and other civic and social groups of the area formed an organization called Mobilization for Youth; the National Institute of Mental Health awarded the organization a two-year grant to plan its project, and Cloward and Ohlin continued as its consultants.[16]

The two sociologists were, at the time, completing a theoretical work that was to become the philosophical base of the federal juvenile delinquency program launched by the Kennedy administration. They saw delinquency not as individual pathology but as community pathology. Lower class youth have conventional goals but are faced with a disparity between what they "are led to want and what is actually available to them. . . . Faced with limitations on legitimate avenues of access to these goals, and unable to revise their aspirations downward, they experience intense frustrations; the exploration of nonconformist alternatives may be the result."[17] Discrimination, inadequate educational opportunity—these were the evils that must be diagnosed and treated.

They concluded their major work with these words:

> . . . services extending to delinquent individuals or groups cannot prevent the rise of delinquency among others. For delinquency is not, in the final analysis, a property of individuals or even of subcultures; it is a property of social systems in which these individuals and groups are enmeshed. The pressures that produce delinquency originate in these structures, as do the forces that shape the content of specialized subcultural adaptations. The target for preventive action, then, should be defined, not as the individual or group that exhibits the delinquent pattern, but as the social setting that gives rise to delinquency.
>
> It is our view, in other words, that the major effort of those who wish to

[16] This account is condensed from Peter Marris and Martin Rein, *Dilemmas of Social Reform: Poverty and Community Action in the United States* (Atherton, 1967), p. 20.

[17] Richard Cloward and Lloyd Ohlin, *Delinquency and Opportunity* (Free Press, 1960), p. 86.

eliminate delinquency should be directed to the reorganization of slum communities. Slum neighborhoods appear to us to be undergoing progressive disintegration. The old structures, which provided social control and avenues of social ascent, are breaking down. Legitimate but functional substitutes for these traditional structures must be developed if we are to stem the trend toward violence and retreatism among adolescents in urban slums.[18]

Leonard S. Cottrell of the Russell Sage Foundation put it even more sharply in congressional testimony in 1960. Referring to the work of Mobilization for Youth, he said:

> . . . the treating of a delinquent as a sick person who infects others with sickness is an important arm of treating delinquency. We have got to treat more people and finance more clinical guidance and better trained teachers. . . . But, beyond that, and what we have not yet learned to do, is to treat the sick community as such. That is to say, we need skillful persons who can mobilize the resources in the community.
> . . . It would be a grave mistake—and I repeat, a grave mistake—to think that you are going to deal or cope with this problem effectively if all that you can offer is an individual approach in psychology, psychiatry, and social work treatment.[19]

Within a week of the 1960 election, President-elect Kennedy and Robert Kennedy asked an old friend and campaign associate, David Hackett, to organize the administration's efforts against juvenile delinquency. Hackett arranged a conference of experts on March 16. Among those present was Ohlin. Hackett later remarked, "I quickly learned from the March meeting that you can't get consensus among professionals, so I had to pick one of the best and rely on his judgment." He picked Ohlin.[20]

By 1963 the work of the President's Committee on Juvenile Delinquency and Youth Crime had become, in the words of one observer, "a $30 million test of Ohlin's 'opportunity theory'."[21] The committee awarded grants to organizations in a dozen communities, including one to Mobilization for Youth, for developing comprehensive plans of community organization to attack the causes of juvenile delinquency. The plans were to be comprehensive because "since delinquency has many sources, it must have a variety of programs for solution. The varied sources of antisocial behavior must be attacked simultaneously."[22] The definition

---

[18] *Ibid.*, p. 211.

[19] *Report on Juvenile Delinquency,* Hearings before a Subcommittee of the House Appropriations Committee, 86 Cong. 2 sess. (March 10, 1960), p. 94.

[20] Moore, "Juvenile Delinquency Control."

[21] Quoted in *ibid.*

[22] Testimony of David Hackett, in *Economic Opportunity Act of 1964,* Hearings (April 22, 1964), p. 1235.

of comprehensiveness might vary among communities, but a community's program should "have identified many sources of the problem and have proposed to seek changes in many institutions."[23] No element of a comprehensive plan would be put into operation until all elements were ready to go.[24] Given the time required to create comprehensive organizations and prepare comprehensive plans, the committee by the end of 1963 had financed action programs only in New York City (Mobilization for Youth), New Haven, and Cleveland. The Mobilization for Youth demonstration included employment programs, work preparation, guidance, skills training, antidiscrimination activities, remedial education, home visits, and neighborhood service centers that provided an array of services.

Stream Two: Urban Renewal Discovers People. By 1959 the old city of New Haven, Connecticut, had already become celebrated as the country's pacemaker in urban renewal. Under the restless leadership of a mayor who was himself a product of the city's working-class neighborhoods, Richard C. Lee, New Haven had laid out a ten-year plan to become the nation's first city to be completely rid of slums. New Haven quickly achieved the distinction of winning more federal urban renewal grant money, on a per capita basis, than any other city. To the more timid of his contemporary mayors Lee demonstrated that the bold rebuilding of an entire city was good politics too: he had been reelected each two years with increasing majorities, and his 65 percent of the vote in 1957 was a margin even greater than the city had given Franklin Roosevelt.[25]

It was to be expected, then, that New Haven would emerge again as the most imaginative of American cities when Mayor Lee turned his attention to the deterioration of the social structure of New Haven's slums. As elsewhere, urban renewal had begun in New Haven as an effort to revive the city's economy and build its revenue base. Mayor Lee "wanted a new, vibrant downtown," wrote one reporter. "He had to keep the re-

[23] Policy guides issued by the President's Committee on Juvenile Delinquency and Youth Crime, September 1963, p. 3.

[24] Testimony of Hackett, in *Economic Opportunity Act of 1964*, Hearings, p. 1241. House sponsors of the legislation, particularly Edith Green, felt that in all of these respects Hackett had departed drastically from the intent of Congress. The conflict between the congressmen and the administration over administration of the 1961 Juvenile Delinquency Control Act is recounted in Moore, "Juvenile Delinquency Control."

[25] In recognition of these achievements, the American Municipal Association made Lee a member of its executive committee in November 1959. For an account of urban renewal in New Haven under Lee, see Robert A. Dahl, *Who Governs? Democracy and Power in an American City* (Yale University Press, 1961), especially pp. 115–40.

maining businesses and industries from moving out; he hoped to attract
new ones." But with the clearance of the first slum in 1956, "the 120
families who lived there thrust their miseries for the first time before the
eyes of the city. It was more achingly obvious than ever that it would not
be enough simply to provide housing and shelter and welfare payments."[26]
Lee obtained funds for a social worker to provide counseling services to
the displaced families, and he and the director of the city's redevelopment
agency, Edward Logue, began to talk of the need to combine with the
comprehensive physical redevelopment of the city an equally comprehensive and concentrated effort to deal with the social problems of the
slums.

Meanwhile, the thinking within America's largest philanthropic organization, the Ford Foundation, had undergone a corresponding evolution. The concern with urban problems of the foundation's public affairs
staff, headed by Paul N. Ylvisaker, had begun along lines that were
traditional enough. It took an interest in governmental reform, particularly in proposals for metropolitan government, and in urban planning
and renewal. But urban renewal had an "inherent weakness—it had little
or nothing to offer those whom it displaced, and only aggravated the social
distress it was supposed, ultimately, to relieve."[27] Ylvisaker began to protest "dealing with cities as though they were bricks without people . . .
trying with massive programs to perfect physical form and material function while merely dabbling and extemporizing with the city's humane and
civilizing purpose. . . ."[28] As early as 1957 he was looking for a new and
broader approach to the social as well as the physical problems of the urban
"gray areas."

Accordingly, when an organization of superintendents of the largest
city school systems asked the foundation for a grant to establish a secre-
tariat, the foundation invited them to come up with something bolder.
The superintendents responded individually. In 1960 and 1961, grants
totaling $6 million were made to ten of the participating school systems
for separate, unrelated experiments. Ylvisaker was still seeking ways "to

[26] Gregory R. Farrell, *A Climate of Change: Community Action in New Haven* (Rutgers
University, Urban Studies Center, 1965), pp. 3–4.

[27] Marris and Rein, *Dilemmas of Social Reform*, p. 15. This section draws upon their
account of the Ford Foundation's "gray areas" program and of the individual city projects.

[28] Speech before Citizen's Conference on Community Planning, Indianapolis, Ind.,
Jan. 11, 1963.

stimulate broader and more coherent community approaches,"[29] beyond what the schools could do alone.

Logue, hearing of Ylvisaker's interest, met with him in December 1959 and was encouraged to develop a specific proposal. New Haven's planning was delayed when Logue left the city for a position in Boston, but eventually, in April 1962, a grant to New Haven was approved. Ford also approved programs in Oakland, Boston, Philadelphia, Washington, D.C., New York City (Mobilization for Youth), and Pittsburgh, and a statewide undertaking in North Carolina initiated by Governor Terry Sanford.[30]

Except for Oakland, where the city was the recipient, each grant was made to a new corporation designed to coordinate all agencies in the community, public and private, whose activities impinged upon the poor. The specific activities to be financed were agreed upon by the community sponsors and the foundation staff. In theory, the communities made their own analyses of the problems and proposed the remedies, but in fact they had a sharp ear for suggestions as to what was most likely to be approved. "The programs which gained currency came to look very much alike, and they bore the stamp of the Public Affairs staff's analysis, more than the communities' first thoughts," write Marris and Rein.[31]

Nevertheless, the planning process within the cities had vitality and a value independent of its product. It broke down the insularity of established institutions and forced them to think about what they could do collectively. To illustrate from the experience in New Haven—which became, more than any other city, the model—the plan was developed by a staff group representing the redevelopment agency, the board of education, and the private social agencies, headed by Howard W. Hallman of the redevelopment staff. Through his appointments to the board of education, the irrepressible Mayor Lee had made that agency, too, an instrument of innovation and reform. Under the leadership of Mitchell Sviridoff, the young president of the Connecticut state AFL-CIO whom Lee had appointed to the board, the city was engaged in replacing one-third of its school plant, financed by a single $17.8 million bond issue. Ten of the new schools were to become "community schools," serving as

---

[29] As quoted in Marris and Rein, *Dilemmas of Social Reform*, p. 17.

[30] A Ford Foundation pamphlet, *American Community Development* (Oct. 1, 1963), outlines the origin and status of the "community development program" and the activities financed in each community.

[31] Marris and Rein, *Dilemmas of Social Reform*, p. 123.

community centers on an all-day, evening, and year-round basis.[32] The idea of community schools was not new—in fact, New Haven had established one in 1957—but only one city in the country (Flint, Michigan) was at that time operating a citywide network of such centers.

The staff group headed by Hallman asked themselves, he recalls, "If there were no limit on money, what would you do?" They seized upon the community school idea and proposed to establish in each such school a "neighborhood services director" who would "take a total approach to the social problems of the neighborhood" and integrate the work of the public health, public welfare, social service, legal service, and related agencies. The director's staff would include community workers who would "speak the language" of the neighborhood and serve as "a bridge between residents and service agencies." The poor themselves (although the words "poor" and "poverty" were not then used) would participate through neighborhood organizations.[33] Coordinating the entire structure would be a new corporation known as Community Progress, Inc., headed by a nine-man board representing the mayor (three appointees), the redevelopment agency, the board of education, the voluntary social agencies (two representatives), a citizens' group that had been created to back urban renewal, and Yale University. Community Progress was variously described, says Farrell, "as a coordinating agent, a catalyst, a solicitor and distributor of funds, and a force for innovation and reform."[34] Sviridoff became its executive director and Hallman his deputy. With the Ford funds in hand, New Haven had eighteen specific new programs underway by the spring of 1964 and five more planned. About half of its $2.5 million Ford grant was to be expended through the board of education.

All of the community programs emphasized education. But the range was as broad as the manifold and mutually reinforcing problems of the slum dwellers. In early 1963, Ylvisaker gave these examples of "social

[32] The construction program and the community schools were recommended in a report by Cyril G. Sargent, a professor of education at Harvard University. Sargent showed how the total cost could be reduced by $7 million by tying their construction to urban renewal, according to the newsletter of the National Committee for Support of the Public Schools, April 1965. Thus five of the fifteen new schools would be "free" to New Haven. Since Logue had prodded the board of education to initiate the Sargent study and since Logue's reputation as an expert in "milking" urban renewal funds is unsurpassed, it may be surmised that he had a hand in this part of the report.

[33] Quotations from "Opening Opportunities," Presentation to the Ford Foundation by the City of New Haven, Board of Education, and Community Progress, Inc., April 1962.

[34] *A Climate of Change*, p. 9.

inventions," which he said could be "procedural, physical, and mechanical":

> . . . building schools to double as neighborhood and social service centers; starting the education of Gray Area children at an earlier age; concentrating on improvement of speech, reading, and other communication skills among Negro children and other newcomers to the cities; adapting techniques borrowed from agricultural extension to the needs and circumstances of an urban clientele, involving health, family budgeting and home management, legal aid, credit use, and house repair and rehabilitation; combining work and study programs for school dropouts; relating (and even subordinating) physical to social planning; pooling local philanthropic funds for common programs . . .; recruiting industry and gearing vocational education to projections of technology and local manpower supply; early identification of urban newcomers; use of lay persons in school, recreation, welfare, and other programs; correcting bad practices in arrest, bail, defense, and other links in the chain of administering justice; finding constructive alternatives to present systems of high-density public housing and permanent-dependency welfare payments; and widening residential and occupational choice as a way of releasing individuals from the chains of ethnic, racial, and other attachments not freely chosen.

And he added that the community agencies had been created not deliberately but reluctantly:

> We would have preferred not to have been party to the creation of still another community agency. . . . But in three of the four culminating experiments we have helped launch . . . the only way open to fulfilling the broad objectives . . . was the building of a new instrumentality.
> There is some feeling that this decision to establish new instrumentalities is an attack on the present system of community health and welfare councils. If so, it came not by intent nor with malice, but as a commentary on the gap that exists between the job to be done and the capacity of our urban communities as presently structured to accomplish it.[35]

Stream Three: Public Welfare Discovers Rehabilitation. When Abraham A. Ribicoff was governor of Connecticut, he was as disturbed as every other budget-conscious governor by the steadily rising costs of public welfare. Since 1956, state and local expenditures classified under that heading had risen relentlessly at the rate of $300 million a year—from $3.1 billion to $4.7 billion in five years. Federal expenditures for public assistance had been rising at about the same 10 percent annual rate, going from $1.6 billion to $2.0 billion in the 1957–59 period alone.

[35] Ylvisaker, Indianapolis speech.

"I can tell you that from my own experience in 6 years as Governor that there were few problems that were as frustrating and as bothersome as the whole problem of welfare costs," Ribicoff told a House committee. "Welfare costs keep going up every year. They are open-end appropriations. . . ."[36]

During the hearing on his confirmation as President Kennedy's first secretary of health, education and welfare, Ribicoff had promised a complete restudy of the federal public assistance programs. President Kennedy reiterated the promise in his economic message of February 2, 1961.[37] They had a particular reason for emphasizing this intention: the President was requesting at this very time a further liberalization of aid to dependent children, the category of public assistance accounting for a large part of the increase in total costs.

The President's proposal was to eliminate an anomaly growing out of the distinction in New Deal legislation between the unemployed and the "unemployable." Unemployment insurance was designed for the former; other kinds of social security were carefully restricted to the latter, who were divided into categories—the aged, the blind, children deprived of support because of the death, absence, or disability of one parent, and (after 1950) the totally and permanently disabled. Anybody else in need would have to rely, as was the case before the New Deal, upon state and local public welfare programs or upon private charitable agencies.

In each recession, of course, a major new category of needy families appeared—families of men still jobless after their unemployment insurance benefits had expired. The anomaly was that if the family remained together it was ineligible for federally aided assistance, but if the father disappeared his wife and children could apply for aid to dependent children (ADC). "There are instances of fathers who are unemployed and desert because they see no other way to get their hungry children fed," the Advisory Council on Public Assistance asserted in 1960. "We are opposed to public assistance provisions that seem to put a premium on broken homes." They observed that "a hungry, ill-clothed child is as hungry and ill-clothed if he lives in an unbroken home as if he were

[36] *Temporary Unemployment Compensation and Aid to Dependent Children of Unemployed Parents*, Hearings before the House Ways and Means Committee, 87 Cong. 1 sess. (Feb. 15, 1961), p. 103.
[37] *Public Papers of the Presidents, 1961*, p. 47.

orphaned or illegitimate" and recommended extension of ADC coverage to "any financially needy children living with any relative or relatives."[38] Both the majority and the minority of the Senate's special committee on unemployment problems made the same recommendation two days later,[39] and it was proposed again by a task force on welfare appointed by President-elect Kennedy prior to his inauguration and headed by Wilbur J. Cohen of the University of Michigan.

Within a few days after his inauguration, Kennedy proposed legislation to extend ADC to children of unemployed parents, along with temporary extension of unemployment compensation benefits, as emergency measures. The ADC extension would be for a period of fifteen months, pending the proposed restudy of public assistance. On this basis it was passed quickly, without a recorded vote in either house. Secretary Ribicoff immediately appointed twenty-three leaders in the social welfare field to an ad hoc committee on public welfare.

The attention of the committee was focused suddenly and at once upon work relief. Under state and local legislation, more than 250 localities had been requiring the able-bodied unemployed to work on public projects to earn their assistance payments. But federal legislation, originally designed to assist only those unable to work, forbade any such requirement. When aid to dependent children was extended to families of the able-bodied unemployed, the federal requirement automatically applied, if federal aid were accepted for the purpose. The result was a rash of resolutions from the affected communities—often backed up by letters of protest from the unemployed themselves.

At this point the depressed Hudson River town of Newburgh, New York, attracted national attention with a thirteen-point crackdown on "welfare chiseling"—aimed largely at what were described as "undesirable newcomers" to the city. The Newburgh actions, announced by City Manager Joseph McD. Mitchell, were denounced by Governor Nelson A. Rockefeller's state board of social welfare as violating state laws and regulations, contravening the "cumulative wisdom and experience" of the years in welfare administration, and infringing the constitutional rights of welfare recipients. It accused Newburgh of embarking on a "publicity

---

[38] *Report of the Advisory Council on Public Assistance*, S. Doc. 93, 86 Cong. 2 sess. (March 28, 1960), p. 12. The council was a statutory body appointed by the secretary of HEW.

[39] See testimony on this point, Chap. 3, pp. 80–81.

campaign" and added caustically: "Newburgh may have some governmental problems but public welfare is not one of them." Governor Rockefeller backed up his welfare board with a statement endorsing "the human values underlying our social welfare laws."[40]

Caught in the middle, Senator Kenneth Keating, New York Republican, took the Senate floor to express what might be considered a middle point of view: "I personally feel that the townsmen of Newburgh have largely accomplished their major purpose in that they have focused widespread national attention on the need to tighten up many of our relief programs and on the concomitant need to stress getting people back to work, as opposed to building up the attitude that relief is and should be a way of life. . . . We need to help people help themselves, we must avoid structuring our relief programs in such a way that they become a rut, so that once you are in it, you never get out."[41]

Secretary Ribicoff's ad hoc committee saw a chance to turn the Newburgh ruckus to just such constructive use. As practitioners in the field of social work, its members were convinced that the road to reducing the incidence of family breakdown and dependency lay through the expansion, upgrading, and more intensive use of their profession. In 1956 the profession had succeeded in writing into the law a provision that covered within federal 50-50 matching provisions the cost of state services to help public assistance recipients achieve "self-support," independence, and more stable family life. But the provision had been little used by the states, except in experiments and demonstrations.[42] Now, in the glare of Newburgh, the committee took the occasion to place heavy emphasis upon the need to accompany financial assistance with adequate rehabilitative services. Otherwise, said its report, delivered in September, such expenditures "may actually increase dependency and eventual costs to the community." Individual states and localities had "convincingly demonstrated" that skilled rehabilitative services could return a large number of families to self-support. "The application of these findings should be extended to

<hr>

[40] Newburgh's "13 rules," Governor Rockefeller's statement, the statement of the state board of social welfare, and two *New York Times* articles of July 20 were inserted by New York Senator Jacob K. Javits (Republican) in *Cong. Record*, Vol. 107 (July 20, 1961), pp. 13052–54. See also Meg Greenfield, "The Welfare Chiselers of Newburgh, N. Y.," *Reporter*, Aug. 17, 1961.

[41] *Cong. Record*, Vol. 107 (Aug. 4, 1961), p. 14658.

[42] Charles E. Gilbert, "Policy-Making in Public Welfare: The 1962 Amendments," *Political Science Quarterly*, Vol. 81 (June 1966), p. 203.

recipients in all parts of the country. This cannot be done without greatly increasing the numbers of qualified staff."[43]

The committee resolved the difficult issue of work-for-relief by placing it in the same context of rehabilitation. Work-for-relief had long been anathema to organized labor, whose spokesmen saw a loss of jobs for union members, a lowering of wage scales, and the equivalent of "peonage." Many welfare officials shared their suspicion, but at the same time they recognized the value of work in the rehabilitation process. On August 11, in commenting on the Newburgh controversy, the American Public Welfare Association had endorsed work-for-relief for able-bodied persons, providing that the work was at prevailing wages, not competitive with private industry, and did not involve "the operation of public works programs by welfare departments."[44]

The committee similarly endorsed community work programs with these and other safeguards, and recommended federal aid for such programs. The jobs, it added, should offer "a chance for the worker to use his skill or to develop new skills; remuneration as a wage rather than as a return for charity; and the sense that the worker has been provided an opportunity to engage in useful work."[45] It also recommended that the temporary ADC legislation be broadened and made permanent.

During the fall the report's central ideas were incorporated by HEW into a bill. Rehabilitation was its focus. The "community work programs" of the report were converted under the guidance of Wilbur Cohen, now an assistant secretary, into "community work and training," with carefully worded safeguards to allay any misgivings that might remain in organized labor or the social work profession. The Bureau of Public Assistance became the Bureau of Family Services. The federal share of the cost of the rehabilitative services was raised from 50 to 75 percent. When President Kennedy sent the bill to Congress, he said that "public welfare . . . must be more than a salvage operation. . . . Its emphasis must be directed increasingly toward prevention and rehabilitation—on reducing not only the long-range cost in budgetary terms but the long-range cost in human

---

[43] *Report of the Ad Hoc Committee on Public Welfare to the Secretary of Health, Education and Welfare* (September 1961), pp. 10, 13. The most complete documentation of the results of intensified social work is a study by Winifred Bell (sponsored by the New York School of Social Work, dated April 20, 1961) included twice in *Public Welfare Amendments of 1962*, Hearings before the House Ways and Means Committee, 87 Cong. 2 sess. (February 1962), pp. 371–76, 410–15.

[44] *Cong. Record*, Vol. 107 (Aug. 29, 1961), p. 17351.

[45] *Report of the Ad Hoc Committee on Public Welfare*, p. 17.

terms as well. . . . The prevention of future adult poverty and dependency
must begin with the care of dependent children." Anticipating the rhetoric
of the war on poverty, he said the goal must be "to create economic and
social opportunities for the less fortunate." In communities where rehabilitation had been tried, he said, "relief rolls have been reduced."[46]

Speaking for the National Social Welfare Assembly, Robert E. Bondy
saw the shift in emphasis as epoch-making:

> . . . the Social Security Act, back in the mid-1930's, was a landmark, the
> opening of a new epoch in making minimum provision for the care of people
> in need. Likewise, the enactment of H.R. 10032 will open another epoch, the
> epoch of prevention and rehabilitation.
>
> This is a shift in emphasis from public assistance as the center of our
> American plan for care of people to that of helping people to help themselves
> to independence and self-sufficiency with public assistance as an indispensable
> resource to that end.[47]

Republican opposition to the bill, in the House, was based not upon
the change in concept but upon making permanent the federal responsibility for assistance to the unemployed and their children. Representative
Thomas Curtis of Missouri, the opposition spokesman, argued that "the
real estate property tax which does finance these programs is close to home
and . . . has stood up beautifully since World War II in providing the
funds to finance the programs at the local and State levels." Representative E. Y. Berry of South Dakota observed: "To me it seems that this is the
nucleus of eroding away the foundation of this Republic."[48] But the Republican motion to recommit was lost by a margin of 233–155, on a near
party-line vote, and the bill then passed, 320–69. In the Senate the measure was noncontroversial—once a proposed amendment for health care
for the aged was defeated—and was passed by a voice vote on July 17.
"The most far-reaching revision of our Public Welfare program since it
was enacted in 1935," President Kennedy called the measure.[49]

---

[46] Special Message on Public Welfare Programs, Feb. 1, 1962, *Public Papers of the
Presidents, 1962*, pp. 98–103.

[47] *Public Welfare Amendments of 1962*, Hearings (Feb. 9, 1962), p. 331. Gilbert
Y. Steiner contends that despite the greater financial incentives, the 1962 amendments
added little of substance to the language that had been written into the law in 1956.
"The great thrust on behalf of prevention and rehabilitation seems more gimmicky than
substantive," he writes, adding: "Somehow the 1962 amendments got oversold somewhere along the line" (*Social Insecurity: The Politics of Welfare* [Rand McNally, 1966],
pp. 40–47).

[48] *Cong. Record*, Vol. 108 (March 15, 1962), pp. 4272, 4271.

[49] On July 26, 1962, *Public Papers of the Presidents, 1962*, p. 580.

Stream Four: Retraining Discovers Illiteracy. Barely a year after enactment of the Manpower Development and Training Act, its warmest supporters were acknowledging that MDTA was failing in one of its major purposes: it was not reaching the long-term, chronic unemployed.

"We in South Bend are disturbed," an Indiana editor testified, "because at present we know of no way to train approximately 60 percent of our unemployed."[50]

A Michigan professor agreed. "A substantial portion of the 'hard core' unemployed are functionally illiterate and in the position where they cannot qualify for training," he told a House subcommittee.[51]

Labor Secretary Willard Wirtz described the retraining of the poorly educated as "one of the most intractable problems of unemployment." Twenty percent of all the unemployed had less than an eighth-grade education, but only 3 percent of MDTA trainees were drawn from this group. Among unemployed Negro workers, 44 percent had completed fewer than eight years of school, but only 5 percent of Negro trainees under MDTA came from this group.[52]

Accordingly, President Kennedy proposed in 1963 that MDTA be expanded to permit training in literacy and basic work skills in addition to the regular occupational training. The maximum period for training allowances would be extended from 52 to 72 weeks. His recommendation, significantly, was contained in a message on civil rights and job opportunities for Negroes, sent to Congress on June 19, after a series of White House conferences on racial tension. In the North it was recognized that these tensions had their roots in unemployment.[53]

In the hearings on this proposal, the director of the department of public aid of Cook County, Illinois, which includes Chicago, gave eloquent testimony of the success of a basic education program in that city. In March 1962 the department announced that all of the 50,000 to 60,000 able-bodied adults receiving general assistance would be required not only to participate in a work program but to enroll for basic education

---

[50] Testimony of Franklin D. Schurz, editor and publisher, *South Bend Tribune,* and chairman, St. Joseph County, Ind., manpower advisory committee, in *Manpower Development and Training Act,* Hearings before the Select Subcommittee on Labor of the House Education and Labor Committee, 88 Cong. 1 sess. (Aug. 15, 1963), p. 601.

[51] Testimony of Ronald W. Haughton, codirector, Institute of Labor and Industrial Relations, Wayne State University, in *ibid.* (Aug. 1, 1963), p. 399.

[52] *Ibid.,* p. 15.

[53] *Congressional Quarterly Almanac, 1963,* p. 524.

if they were functionally illiterate. The director, Raymond M. Hilliard, told the committee that compulsion was not necessary—"the response . . . to this proffer of education has been tremendous, in fact, overwhelming." Attendance was excellent. Discipline was no problem. The "eagerness to learn . . . amazed and gratified" the teachers. Hilliard went on:

> In carrying out this program, I have witnessed some deeply moving scenes. I think of the boy who brought his father for the first night and who helps him with his homework and also of the 50-year-old man writing his name for the first time and then writing it over and over again. Or there is the father of 13 who dropped out of school 38 years ago in the third grade and who entered our literacy program, and in the space of 5 months raised himself or was lifted to a point where he passed an eighth-grade examination and was awarded his elementary school diploma. On his graduation night, he remarked, "No kid of mine will ever drop out of school." He now has a good job and is also attending high school where in night classes he hopes to get a diploma in two years.
>
> . . . I wish that you could have been with me to see 25 men go off relief in a body, at a graduation exercise of a class where they had learned to become Yellow Taxi drivers; 266 former recipients have now received this training and 215 are currently employed.[54]

Hilliard urged a "massive attack" upon illiteracy as a basic cause of dependency. On Chicago's relief rolls, he said, were "the dropouts of yesterday. And our rolls of tomorrow are going to be made up of the school dropouts of today unless we do something abut it."

The opposition was little more than nominal. Republican Senators Barry Goldwater of Arizona and John G. Tower of Texas argued that extension of MDTA into literacy training was unnecessary because almost every community had adult education courses open to all. But the basic concept of MDTA as an alternative to "handouts" still commanded the wide bipartisan support of the year before, and the bill was passed by a voice vote in both houses in December 1963.

One provision of the 1963 amendments lowered from nineteen to seventeen the minimum age for the payment of training allowances, in order to induce more unemployed youth into MDTA courses. Originally, it will be recalled, the MDTA had been designed to meet the problems of settled older workers whose skills had suddenly become obsolete; for the young, another employment and training program had been conceived—the Youth Conservation Corps (YCC), patterned on the Civilian Conser-

[54] *Manpower Development and Training Act*, Hearings, pp. 444–48.

vation Corps of the 1930's. By 1963, however, it was clear that the youth employment bill had fallen upon difficult days. Upon sober second thought, influential persons in the Kennedy administration had come to share the reservations expressed in 1960 by the Republican opposition: would a YCC of up to 150,000 men—costing over half a billion dollars a year—be worth the investment? Was it, after all, the best approach to the problem of youth unemployment?

Awaiting President Kennedy and his budget director, David E. Bell, when they took office was a Bureau of the Budget staff paper suggesting that the CCC of Depression days was not a suitable model for the 1960's. The Budget staff was ready to recommend a small experimental camp program—a tiny fraction of the 150,000-man YCC of the Senate-passed bill of 1960—provided that it were supplemented by training programs more directly related to the work situations the young people would be likely to encounter after their camp days. The Interior and Agriculture departments championed the full-scale YCC, but the Budget Bureau found allies elsewhere in the government, and President Kennedy, in May, came down on the bureau's side. On June 7 he proposed to the Congress an experimental YCC of only 6,000, with another 50,000 to be employed in local public service and on-the-job training programs.

When hearings opened, the split within the administration was reflected at once on Capitol Hill. Speaking for the conservation groups, Spencer M. Smith, Jr., called the 6,000-man YCC "a great letdown, a most timid approach. . . . It is the kind of thing that causes our ardor to cool to the point of almost neutrality."[55] Spokesmen for youth welfare groups took the opposite view. Mrs. Agnes E. Meyer said a YCC of 6,000 was big enough. "I would prefer the emphasis at this time on the aid to the youngster who stays in the community," said Judge Mary Conway Kohler. Even the YCC camps should be near cities, she argued, so that "they could provide training for the kinds of work that the kid would have to come home to eventually."[56] Legislative strategists had to struggle to prevent the coalition formed in 1959 from falling apart in open warfare.

[55] Testimony of Spencer M. Smith, Jr., secretary, Citizens Committee on Natural Resources, in *Youth Employment Act—Youth Conservation Corps,* Hearings before the Subcommittee on Employment and Manpower of the Senate Labor and Public Welfare Committee, 87 Cong. 1 sess. (June 20, 1961), pp. 87, 89.

[56] *Ibid.* (June 22, 1961), p. 222.

The House Education and Labor Committee doubled the youth corps to 12,000 and made it permanent rather than experimental, but the bill died in the Rules Committee when the Congress adjourned in 1962.[57]

The conservationists devoted the fall months to a pressure campaign against the White House, and by January the White House reconsidered. The YCC was raised to 15,000 for the first year and 60,000 by the end of the fourth year, and the youth employment bill was raised to the top of the President's legislative program. The Senate bill was passed quickly and handily, 50-34, although a motion to delete the Youth Conservation Corps was defeated by only six votes. But, once again, the bill was stuck in the House Rules Committee when the year 1963 ended.

The War Is Declared   *(1963–64)*

By 1963 the streams of thought and action traced above had begun to flow together. The Ford Foundation and the President's Committee on Juvenile Delinquency and Youth Crime, in particular, were pursuing parallel courses. When David Hackett called his meeting of experts in March 1961 to consider the Kennedy administration's approach to juvenile delinquency, it was David Hunter of the foundation who prepared the basic discussion paper. Hunter was among those who had drawn Hackett's attention to the work of Mobilization for Youth and introduced him to Lloyd Ohlin, who became the committee's theoretician.[58] When the juvenile delinquency act was passed, the President's committee made grants to most of the community groups the foundation had brought into existence. The foundation in turn made a grant to Mobilization for Youth. Later, the Labor Department made grants to the same bodies for research and demonstration projects under the Manpower Development and Training Act.

---

[57] To have dislodged it would have required eight Democratic votes, including that of Carl Elliott of Alabama. Elliott, a special target of conservatives and segregationists in his state because of his pro-administration voting record, would have been further endangered by a vote for a program of integrated work and training programs and conservation camps. Whether because of his predicament, or because the Congress was moving toward a far larger YCC, or both, the White House did not press for a showdown. On Sept. 19, 1962, a group of House Democratic liberals led by Carl D. Perkins of Kentucky attempted to use "calendar Wednesday" procedures, but after two and a half hours of procedural delays gave up.

[58] Marris and Rein, *Dilemmas of Social Reform,* p. 21.

The committee and the foundation were agreed, too, upon the organizational approach to combating poverty: a coordinating body in each community that would have the power, through the leverage of money, to mobilize and redirect the energies of existing public and private bodies. By 1963 the new coordinating bodies—or "umbrella organizations," as they came to be called—were carrying out a concerted assault on poverty in several cities and preparing a statewide program in one state, North Carolina. The President's committee had made grants to a dozen other communities for the preparation of comprehensive plans. Meanwhile, demonstrations initiated in various places without benefit of community-wide organization were showing promise. The success of the Cook County welfare department with basic literacy training has already been mentioned.The results of retraining under MDTA were beginning to be reported. A dozen of the country's largest school systems had initiated projects, using Ford funds, for the improvement of slum schools. An educational experiment known as Higher Horizons was being acclaimed as "a model to be emulated," having "demonstrated convincingly that supposed uneducable children from lower socio-economic backgrounds can successfully learn and progress in a reorganized school environment."[59]

Thus, before the war on poverty was declared, some highly organized preliminary skirmishing was underway. Mobilization for Youth, New Haven's Community Progress, Inc., and their counterparts ultimately provided an arsenal of weapons for the war on poverty—although it is fair to say that the arsenal was not really discovered until after the decision to declare war had been made.

After President Kennedy's conversation with Walter Heller in December 1962, Heller assigned one of his staff, Robert J. Lampman, to assemble the available data on poverty in the United States.[60] In the press of current business—the tax cut battle was then beginning—the subject did not have high priority, but by May 1 Lampman had prepared an analysis of income statistics that revealed a "drastic slowdown in the rate at which the economy is taking people out of poverty." During the years between 1956 and 1961, the proportion of families with money incomes under $3,000 had declined by only 2 percentage points—from 23 to 21 percent. The

[59] Frank Riessman, *The Culturally Deprived Child* (Harper & Row, 1962), p. 98.

[60] Lampman, on leave from the University of Wisconsin, was author of *The Low Income Population and Economic Growth*, prepared for Joint Economic Committee, 86 Cong. 1 sess. (1959).

absolute number of families living in poverty had actually risen. Heller sent the memorandum to the President.

A month later Heller was stimulated to further action by an article in the *New York Herald Tribune* reporting that the Republicans were planning an antipoverty program. At that point he asked Lampman and others to consider what might constitute "a practical Kennedy anti-poverty program." He sent their preliminary ideas to the President and received encouragement, through Sorensen, to proceed. An informal interagency staff group that came to be known as the "Saturday club" was brought together during the late summer under the leadership first of Lampman and, when he left government service, of William M. Capron of the staff of the Council of Economic Advisers (CEA), to continue to analyze the problem of poverty statistically and conceptually. As early as August, Lampman had in draft a proposed chapter on the topic for the 1964 economic report of the President. Meanwhile, Heller had floated some trial balloons in a speech to the Communications Workers of America, in a discussion with reporters, and in meetings with other government policy makers; in all three cases, he recalls, the reactions were disappointingly cool.

Nevertheless, as the time came, in the fall, to crystallize the 1964 legislative program, the President's decision became firm. Sorensen says that Kennedy "started us working" on a "comprehensive, coordinated attack on poverty" more than a month before he went to Dallas—or some time in October.[61] Schlesinger details a series of specific instances in October and November indicating that the President had decided that an assault on poverty "would be the centerpiece in his 1964 legislative recommendations."[62] "By October," recalls Heller, "President Kennedy had given us a green light to pull together a set of proposals for a 1964 attack on poverty."[63] He believes that an article by Homer Bigart in the *New York Times* describing distress in eastern Kentucky[64] may have triggered the President's decision; at the least the article led Kennedy to initiate a "crash" program to mobilize federal resources to alleviate conditions in that region during the coming winter. Also pressing upon policy makers at all levels, particularly since the Birmingham demonstrations and violence in the spring, had been the demands of the civil rights movement. "The demonstrations that we are seeing in the streets today are ones

[61] Theodore C. Sorensen, *Kennedy* (Harper & Row, 1965), p. 753.
[62] *A Thousand Days*, p. 1012.
[63] Heller, Pennsylvania speech.
[64] *New York Times*, Oct. 20, 1963.

fostered by despair and hopelessness," was the way Whitney M. Young put it, some months later.[65]

On November 19, Kennedy gave Heller a flat "yes" to the question whether antipoverty measures would be in the 1964 legislative program and asked to see the measures themselves in a couple of weeks.

The Program Is Assembled: The Pre-Shriver Phase. Acting on the October "green light" from the President, Heller and Capron began to canvass the government for specific antipoverty proposals. They informally assembled fifty-eight ideas, largely from the departments of Labor and HEW, and these were attached to a memorandum of November 5 sent to the governmental departments and agencies principally concerned. Heller's memorandum identified three approaches—to prevent entry into poverty, to promote exits from poverty, and to alleviate the difficulties of persons who cannot escape from poverty. For the moment, the proposed program was labeled "Widening Participation in Prosperity"—a concession to those who thought the word "poverty" had a negative tone and would offend the people whom the program was designed to help. Budget Bureau, CEA, and White House staff were in the midst of a review of the departmental responses when they were interrupted by the news from Dallas.

President Johnson lost no time in restoring their momentum. At his first meeting with Heller, on November 23, Johnson said, "That's my kind of program. . . . Move full speed ahead."[66] There remained, however, the all-important question of what the legislation would contain. The staff of the Budget Bureau, which as the coordinator of the President's program assumed leadership at this stage, distilled out of the agency suggestions thirty-five major possibilities, some of which were already pending on Capitol Hill in one or another form. But well into December the bureau was still "floundering," as one participant put it, in search of a theme and a rationale that would distinguish the new legislation, as dramatically as possible, from all that had gone before—the Area Redevelopment Act, MDTA, Appalachia, the Public Welfare Amendments of 1962, the youth employment program, the pending proposal for a national service corps (the so-called "domestic peace corps" which Kennedy had proposed), and all the rest. What was the new element that would mo-

---

[65] Testimony of Whitney M. Young, Jr., executive director, National Urban League, in *Economic Opportunity Act of 1964*, Hearings (April 14, 1964), p. 634.

[66] Heller, Pennsylvania speech.

bilize all of these efforts into the "comprehensive coordinated attack" that Kennedy had been seeking? And how should the funds be concentrated to get the most results?

Into CEA's collection of ideas in November David Hackett, of the President's Committee on Juvenile Delinquency and Youth Crime, had tossed a suggestion that community organizations like those his committee had been assisting be utilized as instruments in the war on poverty. Hackett and his associate, Richard W. Boone, a veteran of the Ford Foundation's "gray areas" program, had subsequently discussed their idea with Heller and Capron, who in turn were in communication with Budget Bureau staff. But Hackett and Boone were thinking, at that stage, of a cautious start, with comprehensive studies to be made in a limited number of carefully chosen demonstration areas before legislation was even proposed.

After one Budget-CEA meeting during which the participants groped for the new idea that would distinguish and dramatize the antipoverty program, the realization came to William B. Cannon of the Budget Bureau staff that the Hackett-Boone proposal might contain the answer. Cannon suggested in a memorandum that ten demonstration areas be selected and that a "development corporation" be formed in each. In these areas, federal funds would be provided for a wide range of programs, with the corporations to plan the programs, expend the funds, and provide the coordinating mechanism. This scheme would solve several problems at once. It would introduce a distinctive and highly visible new element—the development corporation. It would resolve the immediate problem of selecting from among the battery of new programs being advanced by the competing government agencies—the corporations would make the selection. And it met a criterion advanced by Assistant Budget Director Charles L. Schultze that poverty funds, for maximum effectiveness, be concentrated geographically in "pockets of poverty" rather than spread thinly across the country.

In the course of a single week, in mid-December, aid to community organizations was transformed from an incidental weapon in the war on poverty into the entire arsenal. First the new program was assigned $100 million of the $500 million set aside in the budget to finance antipoverty legislation—then the whole amount. Schultze had endorsed the idea to Budget Director Kermit Gordon with a note that a better name than "development corporation" was needed. The phrase "action program" was found buried in Cannon's original memorandum; somebody put the word "community" in front, and the name was born. The advocates of community action, uneasy while the matter rested on Gordon's desk, turned to Paul Ylvisaker of the Ford Foundation for reinforcement. Ylvisaker called Gordon and argued from the Ford experience that, in effect, "this is the way you should spend your money," and he brought the administrators of several of the Ford-supported community action agencies to Washington for a breakfast meeting with the bureau staff. At that meeting the staff's acceptance of community action was clinched; they presently persuaded a skeptical Gordon, and he and Heller in turn convinced President Johnson that the community action concept was a solid one.[67] So the President, in his State of the Union message, declared "unconditional war," and the budget contained the original $500 million for community action plus about an equal amount that would be provided in other appropriations but spent through community action programs.

"I propose a program which relies on the traditional time-tested American methods of organized local community action to help individuals, families and communities to help themselves," the President said in his budget message. Locally initiated, comprehensive community action programs would be developed to "focus" federal, state, and local resources and services—health, housing, welfare, and agricultural services were specifically named—"on the roots of poverty in urban and rural areas."[68]

The report of the Council of Economic Advisers presented the statistics and economics of poverty, and the rationale of the proposed strategy, with an eloquence and passion unmatched in the two decades of economic reports.[69] Using an arbitrary standard of $3,000 in family income as its poverty measure, the report found that 20 percent of all families were poor. The proportion was much higher among Negroes, among the poorly educated, among the old, among families headed by women, among southerners, among rural residents. When some of these factors were found in combination, the proportion was still higher. Thus, of families headed by young women, nonwhite, with less than an eighth grade education, 94 percent were poor. Of comparable white families, 85 percent were living in poverty. And, as Lampman had pointed out in May, the proportions were shrinking but slowly.

[67] Rowland Evans and Robert Novak, *Lyndon B. Johnson: The Exercise of Power* (New American Library, 1966), pp. 427–28.
[68] Budget Message, Jan. 21, 1964, *Public Papers of the Presidents, 1964*, pp. 183–84.
[69] *Economic Report of the President, January, 1964; Together with the Report of the Council of Economic Advisers*, pp. 55–84.

The report described the "vicious circle" of inherited poverty:

> Poverty breeds poverty. A poor individual or family has a high probability
> of staying poor. Low incomes carry with them high risks of illness; limita-
> tions on mobility; limited access to education, information, and training.
> Poor parents cannot give their children the opportunities for better health
> and education needed to improve their lot. Lack of motivation, hope, and
> incentive is a more subtle but no less powerful barrier than lack of financial
> means. Thus the cruel legacy of poverty is passed from parents to children.[70]

As a "strategy against poverty," the council enumerated many measures—tax reduction, civil rights legislation, regional development programs, urban and rural rehabilitation, improvement of the federal-state
employment service, better educational services, the pending youth employment act, health measures, adult education and training, and medicare for the aged. But existing and new resources would be marshaled into
a "coordinated and comprehensive attack" through community action
programs.

Meanwhile, the Budget Bureau, CEA, and White House staffs were
laboring to refine the community action concept. When they discovered
the idea in mid-December—suddenly, fortuitously, and almost too late—
they did not know, and had no time to find out, exactly how community
action was in fact working in Manhattan, New Haven, and elsewhere.
They were sufficiently aware of a confusion of doctrine, however, to
recommend that the program begin on an experimental scale in a limited
number of communities. Marris has identified three distinct and conflicting "strategies of reform" that were then being followed.[71] One, exempli-
fied by the Ford projects, sought to work through existing institutions—
the local government, the school system, the private social agencies—
with the hope that they would be influenced through coordinated planning. Another, of which Mobilization for Youth was the prototype, went
behind the "power structure" to organize the poor themselves to assert
and defend their own interests—but "as Mobilization for Youth discovered . . . the support of protest can bring a crushing revenge from the
institutions upon whose cooperation the programs depend." The third
strategy, adopted by the President's Committee on Juvenile Delinquency
and Youth Crime, put its faith in the application of knowledge, through
comprehensive planning, with the risk that planning might never lead

---

[70] *Ibid.*, pp. 69–70.

[71] Peter Marris, "The Strategies of Reform" (paper delivered to the Conference on
Community Development, San Juan, Puerto Rico, December 1964).

to action. Along these three paths, community action was groping toward a doctrine. Some of the experiments had been set back severely by community controversy. The theory of community action could be described, in late 1963, as filled with promise but by no means either tested or proven. Both Ylvisaker and Hackett were moving with great care, city by city, with months of consultation and review preceding every grant.

The planners of the President's community action program did not choose among the divergent strategies—insofar as they recognized the divergence, they recognized also that no one pattern would fit all communities. An outline of staff thinking as of January 21 specified only that a community should have, preferably, a single organization or official with authority to coordinate public and private efforts. It did not specify how the organization should be created or whom it should represent. It made no mention of organizing the poor for self-assertion. It compromised the issue of planning versus action by requiring a comprehensive plan but permitting initiation, during the planning period, of some action programs. Of the $500 million, it set aside $50 million to finance planning, $275 million to finance grants to communities for new programs, and $175 million to supplement existing federal programs in community action areas. As for content, the emphasis was upon children and youth— where the poverty cycle could best be broken—and upon services that would help young people develop their capabilities, particularly improvement of health, education, training, welfare, rehabilitation, and related services.

This entire approach had at least one vigorous dissenter—Labor Secretary Wirtz. In a memorandum responding to the January 21 outline, Wirtz said that improvement of health and education services, while desirable, would produce no immediate, visible results. Poverty was, by definition, lack of income. Income came from jobs. To have impact among the poor, the war on poverty must begin with immediate, priority emphasis on employment. Fresh from another battlefront—the war on structural unemployment—Wirtz could find in the community action program few new jobs, apart from summer and part-time employment for students working their way through school.

Throughout December and January, also, the President's staff had been wrestling with a jurisdictional problem—who would administer the community action program? Among existing agencies, HEW would be the logical choice, but the other departments responded coldly to the notion of being coordinated by HEW. The alternative of an independent agency, headed by a director reporting to the President, gained support. Names were put on paper, including the name of Sargent Shriver, brother-in-law of the late President Kennedy and director of the Peace Corps. The President bought the idea of an independent agency—and Shriver.

The Program Is Reassembled: The Shriver Phase. Shriver moved into his new assignment with the same verve and energy he had brought to the Peace Corps. Notified of his appointment on Saturday, February 1, he arranged to be briefed on Sunday by Heller and Gordon and their staffs, and convened for Tuesday an all-day meeting of presidential advisers, departmental representatives, outside experts, and long-time friends upon whom he had been accustomed to try out new ideas. Wirtz and Heller were there, Gordon and Wilbur Cohen, Ylvisaker and Boone, Michael Harrington and Adam Yarmolinsky, whom Shriver had already tapped to become his deputy. Some of this group, plus others borrowed from other agencies and from private organizations on a catch-as-catch-can basis, remained for varying periods as members of Shriver's task force.

The community action idea was explained to the uninitiated, at the February 4 shakedown meeting, but it came out of the meeting in a modified form. Gone was the notion of a limited number of demonstration areas—it was simply not compatible with the President's rhetoric to fight an "unconditional war" on a pilot basis. Further watered down, for the same reason, was the idea that action programs should await the development of comprehensive, coordinated plans. The consensus was that individual action projects, called "building blocks," should go ahead where they would be consistent with the ultimate plan. At the meeting also, Secretary Wirtz presented forcefully his plea for job-creating programs.

Shriver quickly joined Wirtz in the view that community action alone was not enough. Its victories would not come quickly; the presidential election was but nine months away, and in a year Shriver would again have to face Congress and render an accounting. Moreover, the President and the press had by this time built up expectations so vast that a one-idea, one-title bill would be a serious letdown. The very idea of a massive, coordinated attack on poverty suggested mobilizing under that banner all, or as many as possible, of the weapons that would be used. Let the community action organizations coordinate as much as they could, but were there not other things that other organizations—including federal agencies—could be doing also?

Beginning on February 4, Shriver began the march back to the position that the Budget Bureau had left when Cannon wrote his memorandum in December. Not only were the departments and agencies given a chance to resurrect all of the proposals the Budget Bureau had buried then, but Shriver encouraged them to do so. Meanwhile, he cast a dragnet out to the business community, to the intellectual world, to state and local governments, and to private organizations of all kinds in the search for additional suggestions. People who might have ideas were brought in for conferences with the task force staff. Among them were Mayor Lee and Sviridoff and Hallman of New Haven, Governor Sanford of North Carolina, Mayor John Houlihan of Oakland, Hilliard of Chicago. In his testimony presenting the economic opportunity bill, Shriver listed 137 persons who had participated, he said, in the writing of the act.[72] And if a new idea was presented, the burden of proof was upon any listener who said it might not work.

In the ensuing weeks the one-title bill[73] gained five more titles—none of them, however, particularly novel. Two dealt with jobs. One, pressed by the Labor Department, embodied in modified form the youth employment program that was stalled in the House Rules Committee. The Youth Conservation Corps was renamed the Job Corps and the emphasis was placed upon large "urban" training and remedial education centers rather than on conservation camps. The local public service employment and training program was renamed the Neighborhood Youth Corps. A third section, borrowed from a pending education bill, authorized a work program to assist college students to earn their way. The second job title authorized 100 percent federal financing temporarily for the work and training programs for welfare recipients that had been authorized by the Public Welfare Amendments of 1962 but were moving slowly because of the requirement of state or local financial participation. However, a

---

[72] *Economic Opportunity Act of 1964*, Hearings, pp. 23–25. Much has been written on Shriver's personality and method of operations; see especially Murray Kempton, "The Essential Sargent Shriver," *New Republic*, March 28, 1964, pp. 12–14.

[73] During January the addition of a second title, for "special education," had been considered favorably in the Budget Bureau. In addition to the $500 million earmarked for antipoverty legislation, $200 million had been included for improvement of education in low-income urban and rural areas. While it was assumed that this amount would be administered by the Office of Education, at least a tentative decision had been made to request $140 million of the education funds in the antipoverty bill. The program was finally absorbed into the community action program and the funds requested in the antipoverty bill.

job-creation proposal reminiscent of the Works Progress Administration
of the 1930's, presented at a Cabinet meeting by Shriver, was rejected by
the President because it would have added to the budget (a tobacco tax
was proposed to finance it) at a time when taxes were being cut.

The Department of Agriculture, arguing that a "rural title" would
be tactically wise in an otherwise predominantly urban bill, won acceptance of a small loan program for farmers and rural businessmen, a supplementary grant program, and a "land reform" scheme to provide land
for poor farmers through subdivision of large tracts that might be offered
for sale. The Small Business Administration worked with the task force
in devising an "employment and investment incentives" title, including
a liberalized small loan program for low-income businessmen that had
been tested experimentally in Philadelphia Negro neighborhoods and a
second liberalized loan plan for employers who agreed to hire a majority
of workers from among long-term unemployed and low-income families.
Finally, the proposed national service corps, which had passed the Senate
by a narrow margin in 1963 but was blocked in the House Education and
Labor Committee, was incorporated under a new name, "Volunteers for
America" (subsequently changed to Volunteers in Service to America,
or VISTA).[74]

The bill was thus a composite of one central new idea—community
action—and long-discussed ideas, like the Youth Conservation Corps.
It had something for children, something for youth, something for the
adult poor. It offered something to the urban poor, and something to the
rural poor. It appealed to altruism with its bold objective of wiping out
poverty and to conservatism by emphasizing that this would be accomplished not through "handouts" but through opening opportunities for
people to escape poverty through their own efforts. (The bill was the
Economic *Opportunity* Act, administered by the Office of Economic *Opportunity*.) And, by incorporating funds provided elsewhere in the
budget, the bill added to the original $500 million another $462.5 million without increasing the budget total the new President had been taking
pains to portray as frugal. Thus, when Shriver appeared before the House
Education and Labor subcommittee on March 17, he was able to hail his
bill as both "new in the sweep of its attack" and "prudently planned" in

---

[74] Two more programs were added by the House committee: a basic adult literacy
program, taken from a pending education bill, and a program to provide services for
migratory laborers and their families, taken from a series of Senate-passed bills pending
in the committee. The Senate attached a temporary rider for payments to dairy farmers.

that "it does not raise the national budget by a single dollar."[75] The liberals' plaint that a war on poverty of barely $1 billion was a travesty was ignored.

The bill was deliberately drafted to grant the broadest possible discretion to the administrator. The nature of the community organization, the content of its program, the definition of the community itself were all left vague. The states were given no role in community action except that the director of the new Office of Economic Opportunity should "establish procedures which will facilitate effective participation of the states." Nor were the cities assured any role; the community action agency could be either public or private. The total authorization of $962.5 million was not divided among the programs in the act. Formulas for division of funds among states and communities were broadly drawn.

The Congress Affirms. Whatever history may judge to have been its legislative merits, the political merits of the war on poverty in 1964 cannot be denied. It gave the new President, whose legislative agenda consisted otherwise of leftover Kennedy proposals, a bold and attention-getting proposal on which he could put his personal stamp. And the issue itself was peculiarly suited to the personality of Lyndon Johnson, who could talk feelingly of his firsthand knowledge of poverty in the Texas hills and recall his experience as the Texas state director of Franklin Roosevelt's National Youth Administration. It gave him the excuse to stand on the same southern courthouse steps where Roosevelt stood[76] and pledge himself to carry on the war on want that FDR had started.

Moreover, it put the Republicans in a dilemma. As one ruefully put it, " 'War on Poverty' is a terrific slogan, particularly in an election year. It puts doubters under the suspicion of being in favor of poverty."[77] At no point did the Republicans attack the bill head-on. They condemned it as being "hastily drafted," as violating the principles of federalism, as duplicating existing programs, as granting too much discretion to a poverty "czar," and so on. They protested bitterly that Chairman Adam Clayton Powell, of New York, and his Democratic majority on the House Education and Labor Committee were "ramming the bill through"

[75] *Economic Opportunity Act of 1964*, Hearings, pp. 20, 22.

[76] At Gainesville, in the Georgia district of Representative Phil M. Landrum (Democrat), sponsor of the antipoverty bill.

[77] Representative Charles B. Hoeven of Iowa, *Cong. Record*, Vol. 110 (Aug. 6, 1964), p. 18315.

in an arbitrary and partisan manner as an "election-year gimmick." Peter H. B. Frelinghuysen of New Jersey, ranking Republican on the committee, drafted a substitute providing for a state-run program costing half as much, but it attracted little attention or support—not even from governors, who would have had to pay half the cost by the third year. The frustration of the Republican leaders in trying to find reasons why the Congress should reject a bill whose objectives they were compelled to endorse is evident throughout the five months' record of the congressional debate.

Once President Johnson had made the economic opportunity bill the "centerpiece" of his election-year program, it might have appeared foreordained that the Democratic Congress would pass it. Every new President, but especially one taking office suddenly under tragic circumstances, is entitled to a brief "honeymoon" with at least his own party in Congress. The northern Democrats could be counted on to embrace the program with enthusiastic unanimity. Would enough southern Democrats defect to deprive the first southern President in nearly a hundred years of his most cherished legislative objective? It seemed unlikely—yet the administration could not forget that southern Democrats in the House had joined the Republicans a few months earlier to defeat the extension of the Area Redevelopment Act and were still blocking the very youth employment program that had been reborn as the first title of the economic opportunity bill. The decision was to leave nothing to chance. The administration launched what newspapermen described as "some of the most intensive administration lobbying that Congress has ever encountered,"[78] and "the roughest White House lobbying since the Rules Committee fight of 1961."[79] Republicans protested the threats and pressures they claimed were being used upon individual congressmen, though they did not cite cases.[80]

Perhaps the most important single factor in unifying the Democrats was the decision of Representative Phil M. Landrum of Georgia to be the bill's sponsor. Committee Chairman Powell, Harlem's Negro congressman, introduced the administration bill but then stepped aside in favor of Landrum, whose credentials with the conservative southern

[78] Jack Bell, *The Johnson Treatment* (Harper & Row, 1965), p. 95.

[79] Rowland Evans and Robert Novak, *Washington Post*, Aug. 11, 1964; reprinted in *Cong. Record*, Vol. 110 (Aug. 11, 1964), p. 19020.

[80] See, for example, remarks of Representative Charles E. Goodell of New York, *Cong. Record*, Vol. 110 (Aug. 6, 1964), pp. 18262–63.

Democratic bloc were impeccable and whose parliamentary skills were considerable.[81]

Like the administration, the Republicans bore down heavily upon the southern Democrats—but with nothing to offer but arguments. They raised the banner of states' rights, traditionally popular in the South, pointing out that projects could be approved by Shriver over the opposition of governors. They demanded state approval of projects.[82] Representative Howard Smith (Democrat of Virginia), their long-time coalition partner, reminded his colleagues that antipoverty money could be turned over to the National Association for the Advancement of Colored People, as well as to the Ku Klux Klan or a "nudist colony."[83] Representative William H. Ayres, Ohio Republican, pressed a line of argument leading to the conclusion that "there won't be any white people in" the program, provoking Landrum to retort that "Negroes are not the only poor people in the world."[84] Representative Frelinghuysen repeatedly taunted the Georgian by referring to the measure as the "Powell-Landrum bill."

The Republicans sought by various other means to divide the proponents. They appealed to anti-parochial school sentiment by arguing that a compromise private-school provision agreed on in the House committee bill would "permit a direct grant to a church,"[85] then appealed to the Catholics by contending grants could be made to support birth control

[81] Landrum, who was about to become the hero of the Democratic liberal wing, had been best known as co-author of the Landrum-Griffin labor reform bill, which the liberals despised. Landrum's bid for a seat on the Ways and Means Committee had been blocked by Democratic liberals in 1963 because of his conservative record (Bell, *The Johnson Treatment*, p. 97). In 1965, after the Landrum-McNamara (Senator Patrick McNamara of Michigan) bill had become the Economic Opportunity Act, he won his seat on that committee. Bell credits Speaker John W. McCormack (of Massachusetts) with helping to convince Landrum. Landrum's own political sensitivity told him that the views of his constituency were changing and that it was safe in 1964—or, at least, no longer fatal—to be for measures that would have defeated him in earlier years.

[82] Minority views, *Economic Opportunity Act of 1964*, H. Rept. 1458, 88 Cong. 2 sess. (1964), p. 74. In the task force, any suggestion that the program be made subject to state control was instantly squelched by the use of a single word: "Wallace." Governor George C. Wallace of Alabama was then preparing to invade the northern presidential primaries on a segregationist platform.

[83] *Cong. Record*, Vol. 110 (Aug. 5, 1964), p. 18199.

[84] *Economic Opportunity Act of 1964*, Hearings, p. 322.

[85] *Cong. Record*, Vol. 110 (Aug. 6, 1964), p. 18265. The amendment was the result of a protest by Representative Hugh L. Carey of Brooklyn, backed by other committee Democrats, that parochial schools would be excluded from the act. In drafting the bill, the task force had been keenly aware that community action funds expended for educa-

clinics.[86] They reminded mayors that grants could be made to local private organizations that would bypass city hall. They tried to fan bureaucratic jealousies, during the hearings, by suggesting to Cabinet members that a poverty "czar" would be giving them orders. They appealed, similarly, to jurisdictional jealousies on Capitol Hill by suggesting that the omnibus bill should be split up and handled by various committees.

None of the opposition tactics proved availing. When the bill reached the House floor, Landrum countered the states' rights argument by accepting an amendment permitting state governors to veto any project other than those sponsored by institutions of higher education. At this point the Republicans reversed their field, charging Landrum with proposing a "segregationist amendment." Landrum countercharged that the Republican line of argument would "fill the *Record* with inflammatory material designed to build prejudice."[87]

The bill's sponsors made other concessions. An amendment offered by a southern Democrat, Basil L. Whitener of North Carolina, required that participating private organizations be limited to groups (again excepting institutions of higher education) with an already-established "concern" for the problems of poverty. Whitener sidestepped a question as to whether this would bar the NAACP but said "it is certainly not my intention to make them eligible." Three of the programs that bore the brunt of the criticism that the bill was "ill-considered" were eliminated—capital grants to farmers, the "land reform" proposal, and the liberalized loan program for businesses employing workers from low-income families. Authorization of funds was limited to a single year, thus providing for congressional reconsideration of the whole program in 1965, and the lump-sum authorization for the first year was divided among programs.[88]

---

tional programs could encounter the same church-state hazards on which general educa-tion legislation had been foundering for a generation. The bill sought a solution by providing for expenditures through public schools, with programs open to private school students. Carey forced a reconsideration, and a compromise was evolved that made private schools eligible for aid but only for "special remedial and other noncurricular educational assistance." The House committee minority commented in its report that this "would not prohibit a wide and completely undefined range of special aids for private schools. *These would be in the form of direct grants"* (*Economic Opportunity Act of 1964*, H. Rept. 1458, p. 75; italics in original).

[86] *Economic Opportunity Act of 1964*, H. Rept. 1458, pp. 76–77.

[87] *Cong. Record*, Vol. 110 (Aug. 6, 1964), pp. 18263–64.

[88] In addition, Democratic Representative Edith Green of Oregon won adoption of two important amendments. One made young women, as well as young men, eligible for the Job Corps. The other, reflecting her long-standing quarrel with the President's Committee

The President, at the insistence of the North Carolina delegation, agreed to jettison Adam Yarmolinsky, who was slated to be Shriver's deputy, an action the journalist-biographer Bell described as "an aspect of the Johnson treatment that was not comforting to look upon."[89] An amendment requiring that 40 percent of Job Corps enrollees be assigned to conservation camps soothed ruffled feelings among the conservationists who had seen their prized YCC swallowed up in a Job Corps that was to be dominated by the large "urban" training centers. The conservationists believed they "had the bill blocked" until this amendment was accepted.[90] Representative John P. Saylor (Pennsylvania Republican) was the sponsor of the amendment that assured his own support and that of other strong backers of the original YCC.

When the vote was tallied in the House, Johnson had held 60 of 100 southern Democrats and added 22 Republicans (20 from the Northeast) to his base of 144 solid northern and western Democratic votes. The margin was wider than expected, 226–185. The Frelinghuysen substitute could muster only 117 votes. In the Senate, where the issue was never in doubt, 10 of 32 Republicans supported the administration bill. The vote was 61–34. In the minority was Barry Goldwater, who underlined his opposition by signing a strongly worded, two-man minority report from the Senate committee. The Republican convention adopted a plank critical of the "so-called" war on poverty. Johnson "had demonstrated that he was a 'can-do' President," in Bell's words: he had his victory and the war on poverty was underway. But it was, as it had been when declared, the administration's war, not a national war behind which the country was united.

When the war on poverty was reviewed, in 1965, the lines held. Success stories were beginning to appear. Republican Senator Jacob Javits of New York credited the antipoverty measures in part for forestalling in 1965 the riots New York City had suffered in 1964.[91] In Los Angeles,

---

on Juvenile Delinquency and Youth Crime, eliminated a requirement that community action organizations be broadly representative, "with maximum feasible participation of public agencies and private nonprofit organizations primarily concerned with the community's problems of poverty." This left OEO free to make grants to agencies not associated with the communitywide "umbrella" organizations.

[89] Bell, *The Johnson Treatment*, pp. 98–99. Rowland Evans and Robert Novak recount the incident in "The Yarmolinsky Affair," *Esquire*, February 1965, and briefly in *Lyndon B. Johnson*, pp. 432–33.

[90] Interview with Spencer M. Smith, Jr., March 1966.

[91] *Cong. Record*, Vol. 111 (Sept. 24, 1965), p. 25125.

where the worst riot of 1965 exploded, the war on poverty had been
stymied. The program clearly had public support. In August, after the
Republican charges had been thoroughly aired, an Iowa poll showed 79
percent responding affirmatively to the question, "Do you think there is
need for such a program?" with only 12 percent against and 9 percent
with no opinion.[92] In February 1966, 72 percent of a national sample said
President Johnson should not reduce his domestic programs "such as
education, poverty, and health" because of the Vietnam war, with 22 percent in the affirmative and 6 percent undecided.[93]

The opposition centered the attack on "mismanagement" and alleged
use of poverty funds for political purposes, but it changed few votes. A
comparison of the 1964 and 1965 tallies showed not a single vote changed
in the Senate. In the House, twelve southern Democrats and one northern
Republican changed from "yes" to "no," the Democrats perhaps influenced by an amendment that permitted the director of the Office of Economic Opportunity (OEO) to override gubernatorial vetoes of community action proposals. On the other hand, one southern Democrat and
three Republicans switched in the opposite direction. The net shift of
votes against the bill was offset severalfold, of course, by the votes of the
Democratic freshmen elected in the Johnson sweep of 1964. Of the sixty-
five freshman Democrats, fifty-eight voted for the bill and only two—both
southerners—against. The margin in the House was thus increased to
245–158. In the Senate the vote on passage was 61–29. The 1966 authorization bills were approved by margins of 210–156 in the House and
49–20 in the Senate.

But All Is Not Settled. While the national decision of 1964 was confirmed in each of the two succeeding years, the significant aspect of the
vote lay not in the aggregate margin but in the continued united opposition of the Republicans to the Economic Opportunity Act as written, and
the weakening of southern Democratic support. In the 1966 House vote,
Republicans registered a majority of 105–15 against the bill and southern
Democrats a majority of 46–28 against. Unlike the Manpower Development and Training Act, as an example, or the economic development
programs, the war on poverty as then being conducted had not yet become

[92] *Des Moines Sunday Register*, Aug. 29, 1965; inserted in *ibid.* (Sept. 9, 1965), daily
ed., p. A5100.
[93] Louis Harris poll, *Washington Post*, Feb. 7, 1966; inserted in *ibid.*, Vol. 112 (Feb.
28, 1966), p. 4269.

part of the national consensus. The program which had been pushed through Congress in a singularly partisan atmosphere was fated to remain a partisan symbol, and it would accordingly find itself in special jeopardy whenever the swing of the political pendulum restored a conservative majority in the House.[94] At the same time, the "rubber stamp" role of the Democratic senators and congressmen in the enactment of the original bill had left, among some, a lingering resentment and, among all, an absence of the feeling of proud paternity that causes members of Congress to rise to the defense of programs when they are attacked.

Congressional support has also been weakened because the legislators, as well as the public at large, were surprised by the form the community action program, in particular, assumed in actual operation. Rarely has so sweeping a commitment been made to an institution so little tested and so little understood as the community action agency. And no time was accorded Congress to find out. As soon as the contents of the proposed economic opportunity bill were exposed to public discussion, on March 16, the bill was rushed into hearings, as the Republican committee members vigorously protested, and enacted within five months. On some of the most important sections of the act, little legislative history was written or none at all. One can search the hearings and debates in their entirety and find no reference to the language—which became so controversial later—regarding the participation of the poor in community action. The whole novel concept of community action—the definition of the community, the nature of the community action agency, the content of its program, all of which were to have a profound impact on federal-state-local relations and on the social and governmental structures of participating communities—was left to the Office of Economic Opportunity in an exceptionally broad grant of discretion. Shriver could not have told the committees, in any case, what community action would prove to be—advocates of each of the "divergent strategies" were on his staff and the contest for supremacy was yet to be fought. But when the series of clashes between militant leaders of the poor and "the power structure" erupted in the early

[94] In 1967, after such a conservative swing, the program survived. Observers said it was saved in the House by a "city hall" amendment designed to give local elected officials control over community action agencies where they desired to exercise it. With this amendment, a majority of House Republicans, for the first time, voted for the Economic Opportunity Act, 97–79. Southern Democrats were still opposed, but by only a 45–41 margin. The Senate vote was 60–21 for passage of the bill, even without the "city hall" amendment. Perhaps the poverty program, in 1967, *did* finally enter the national consensus—although the Republicans appeared committed at least to reorganizing it.

months of the program, members of Congress were bound to feel that in the haste of 1964 someone had pulled wool over their eyes.[95]

What was unsettled, essentially, was the issue that had been defined in the long debate on the strategy for combating juvenile delinquency. In the war on poverty, as in the war on youth crime, was the target the individual or the community? Could poverty be eliminated by providing opportunity, or resources, to the individual within the existing "social setting," in Cloward's and Ohlin's phrase, or was it necessary to alter that setting, as they concluded, to heal the "sick community," to shatter and remake the "culture of poverty"? If it were the former, then what was called for was community organization for the provision of individual services, in better but essentially traditional ways, an approach acceptable to the power structures of most communities. Even more simply, poverty could be erased by the provision of funds to raise incomes—an idea that, in the forms it has since taken, was not seriously advanced at any point while the economic opportunity bill was being debated. But if the problem is in the social setting rather than the individual, then the remedies are not so clear or so simple. Correction of personal deficiencies on the part of the poor must be accompanied—indeed, preceded —by changes in community behavior, both by the community of the poor and by the larger community. Those ends inevitably involve the organization of the poor under their own leadership for their own ends, and, also inevitably, some degree of challenge to, and confrontation with, the larger community. But can a national government maintain, for long, a program that sets minorities against majorities in communities throughout the land? Clearly it cannot, even if it should. The affluent majority will not be persuaded that tranquility is not also an objective of society—and one superior, if a choice must be made, to the eradication of poverty itself.

Another crucial ambiguity concerns the place of the war on poverty in the array of the country's national goals—a place that tends to determine the role of the Office of Economic Opportunity in the federal government structure and the role of the community action agency in the community. Did the nation establish an overriding objective to which other, and some-

---

[95] Adam Yarmolinsky, Shriver's chief aide when the bill was drafted and submitted to Congress, has indicated even the draftsmen of the act were surprised at the form that community action took. He understood "maximum feasible participation" of the poor to mean simply that services for poor people should "be carried out by poor people who lived in the area." "The concept of promoting control of the program by the poor did not surface during this early period of discussion" (*New York Times,* Oct. 29, 1967, quoting from *Social Sciences Forum,* a Harvard University student publication).

times long-existing, objectives were to be subordinated, or merely adopt one more government program known as "the poverty program," or something in between? President Johnson's message to Congress on March 16, 1964, defined the war on poverty broadly. The economic opportunity bill was the "foundation," but the President mentioned other proposals—from area redevelopment to medicare to aid to education—and said poverty "cannot be driven from the land by a single attack on a single front." To avert "a series of uncoordinated and unrelated efforts," he was proposing to create in the Executive Office of the President the Office of Economic Opportunity headed by his "personal chief of staff for the war on poverty . . . Sargent Shriver."

As the weeks went by, however, the concept underwent a gradual and subtle shift. Less was heard of the "war on poverty" and more of the "poverty program." And the latter had a much narrower definition, usually confined to the activities that happened to be authorized in the Economic Opportunity Act.[96] Then the phrase "war on poverty" began to take on the narrower definition. Facing innumerable difficulties in getting underway the three novel and controversial programs the OEO itself administered—the Job Corps, community action, and VISTA—Shriver had little opportunity to develop his role as coordinator of the "war" as a whole, whatever its total scope was conceived to be. The centrifugal forces within the government were stronger than the centripetal. Even the programs authorized in the Economic Opportunity Act but delegated to other agencies for administration tended to slip out of OEO's coordinating sphere. OEO became, essentially, one more among operating agencies of the government and the "poverty program" one more (or three more) in the long series of government programs.

In the communities, similarly, almost every community action agency had to wage a continuing fight for position against the various public and private agencies that it was designed to coordinate. While the pattern varied widely among communities, the new agency appeared in many areas to have simply divided the field with its competitors, becoming one more among community institutions. In some communities, it seemed clear, the community action agency was destined to become an element of

---

[96] This terminology varied too. In the entry entitled "poverty" in the *Encyclopedia Americana* of 1965, written by Sargent Shriver, the "war on poverty" is described as originally embracing "three major parts"—tax reduction, civil rights, and "the poverty program." The "poverty program," however, is defined more broadly than the Economic Opportunity Act. While the terms are general, the program would clearly include such related activities as Appalachia and MDTA.

city government—routinized as a new operating department taking its place among the old.

The distinctive contribution of the "war on poverty" as an idea lay less in what it added to the battery of governmental programs than in the unifying theme it provided for the activities of many governmental and private agencies and the coordinating devices that were created—OEO in the Executive Office of the President and the community action agency in each community. If the national decision was for such a unified "war on poverty," what resulted has been something less. Under the pressure of program operations, the movement has been almost steadily from the broader to the narrower conception, from the "war on poverty" to "the poverty program"—threatening ultimately only to add to the "series of uncoordinated and unrelated efforts" that the President had decried. And by 1967 the President and the administration appeared to be looking to a new program and a new device—the model cities program and the "city demonstration agency"—to fill the unifying and coordinating role for which the poverty program and the community action agencies had proved unsuited.

Finally the "unconditional war on poverty" declared by the President has proven to be highly conditional—dependent on limited annual appropriations. When budgets are tight, the hardest-to-reach are not reached. If the rate of expenditures per poor family by New Haven's community action agency were projected on a national scale, a sum of $10 to $13 billion annually would be required. If we accept Mitchell Sviridoff's estimate that to reach all of the poor families in New Haven, the effort in that city should be tripled, the national figure for community action alone in an *unconditional* war reaches $30 to $40 billion. Appropriations for community action are a tiny fraction of that figure—and, under the pressures of Vietnam spending, are not rising. While the ideal may be unattainable, the question remains whether a war on poverty that falls so far short of the presidential rhetoric that launched it will not, ultimately, add the disillusionment of its supporters to the strength of its opponents.

CHAPTER V

For the Young, Schools

"THE AMERICAN ANSWER" to the school classroom shortage, said General Dwight D. Eisenhower during the 1952 campaign, was federal aid.

Speaking to a nationwide television audience from Los Angeles in October, the Republican presidential candidate declared that 60 percent of all public school classrooms in America were overcrowded and "this year 1,700,000 American boys and girls were without any school facilities."

Eisenhower presented the solution as simply as he had stated the problem: "The American answer is to do in this field what we have been doing for a long time in other fields. We have helped the states build highways and local farm-to-market roads. We have provided federal funds to help the states build hospitals and mental institutions."[1] The schools could be aided, he made clear, without federal interference in their operation.

Federal aid to the public schools had been proposed before. It had been debated in the 1930's and again in the 1940's, but no bill had been enacted. Standing in the way had been the widely held conviction that federal aid would mean federal control of education, and federal control was a consequence far too dangerous to be risked. The very Republican platform of 1952 upon which General Eisenhower stood was clear on this point:

The tradition of popular education, tax-supported and free to all, is strong with our people. The responsibility for sustaining this system of popular

[1] Text of speech, Oct. 9, 1952, printed in *New York Times*, Oct. 10, 1952.

education has always rested upon the local communities and the states. We subscribe fully to this principle.[2]

To be sure, there were other obstacles. Most important was the issue of aid to parochial schools—the question on which an aid-to-education bill had foundered in 1949.[3] After 1954, with the Supreme Court school desegregation decision, came another, equally emotional issue—whether federal aid should be given to segregated schools. Finally, federal aid to education was opposed by those who objected on fiscal grounds to any avoidable increase in federal expenditures.

So it was to be a long and tortuous course from the simple problem of a national shortage of classrooms to the equally simple solution of federal aid. The public was overwhelmingly in favor of the general proposition of federal aid to education, when the question was asked by the poll takers in those terms. Most members of Congress, both Republican and Democratic administrations, and the major educational organizations were for federal aid in some form. Yet it was not until 1965—almost thirteen years after Eisenhower expressed "the American answer" to the school construction crisis—that the national government finally authorized aid for education on a large, and presumably a continually increasing, scale. Not until then was the state of the nation's education finally recognized and accepted as a matter of concern and responsibility for the nation as a whole, as distinct from its individual communities. This chapter traces the making of that national policy.

Years of Frustration   *(1953–57)*

In his first State of the Union message, in 1953, President Eisenhower asked for "prompt, effective help" for the nation's schools through "care-

---

[2] Earlier, Eisenhower himself had opposed aid to education. In 1949, when the Senate passed a federal aid bill, Eisenhower had gone on record against it with a warning against "paternalism" and "socialism" (*Congressional Quarterly Almanac, 1949*, p. 269). Ironically, his "conservative" opponent for the 1952 Republican nomination, Senator Robert A. Taft of Ohio, was one of the authors of the 1949 bill. The Democratic platform of 1952 supported federal aid for school construction, teachers' salaries, and school maintenance and repair, as well as federal scholarships and further aid to vocational education.

[3] For a summary of legislative struggles from 1870 through 1961, see Frank J. Munger and Richard F. Fenno, Jr., *National Politics and Federal Aid to Education* (Syracuse University Press, 1962), Chap. 1. Robert Bendiner, *Obstacle Course on Capitol Hill* (McGraw-Hill 1964), relates the history of various aid-to-education measures. This chapter draws upon both volumes.

ful congressional study and action"[4]—then did not publicly mention the subject again that year. He sent no further message to the Congress, transmitted no bill.

Nor did the Republican-led Congress attempt anything prompt or effective. No committee even held hearings. The Democrats, since they did not control the calendar, could exercise the initiative only by attempting to add an education amendment to a high priority administration bill dealing with another issue. They found their vehicle in an oil-for-education rider to the "tidelands" oil bill.

The rider, sponsored by Senator Lister Hill, the Alabama veteran of two decades of aid-to-education battles, provided that federal revenues from oil leases be placed in a trust fund for subsequent appropriation for educational purposes. By this device, such ticklish questions as aid to religious schools were bypassed. The Hill amendment carried the endorsement of the National Education Association (NEA), other educational organizations, and their farm and labor allies. The Republicans rightly contended that the measure would add nothing to the power of the Congress to appropriate money to aid the schools, which it could do at any time without a trust fund. The Democrats replied that it would add something significant—a commitment. They carried the day, in the Senate, 45–37, by winning nine Republican votes while losing only seven Democrats. But three of the five Senate conferees to whom the measure was entrusted—Republicans Hugh Butler of Nebraska, Eugene D. Millikin of Colorado, and Guy Cordon of Oregon—had opposed the amendment, and when the conference committee met, the Senate conferees yielded to the House. Cordon told the Senate they had discharged their duty to defend vigorously the Senate position, but Senator James E. Murray of Montana, a Democratic member of the conference committee, said he had heard no discussion at all.[5] Murray and Hill sought to send the measure back to conference, but they lost by two votes, 45–43.

The Cooper Bill—and the White House Conference. Meanwhile, the administration was deciding upon a course of action to propose to the Congress in 1954—a White House conference. Prior to the national conference, to be held late in 1955, a preparatory conference would meet in each state. President Eisenhower saw the conferences as the means of obtaining "the most thorough, widespread, and concerted study the

[4] *Public Papers of the Presidents, 1953*, p. 32.
[5] *Cong. Record*, Vol. 99 (July 30, 1953), pp. 10475–76.

American people have ever made of their educational problems."[6] But to the Democrats and their allies, the conferences looked suspiciously like a scheme for delaying action for three years while the school "crisis" worsened.

When Secretary of Health, Education, and Welfare Oveta Culp Hobby and Commissioner of Education Samuel M. Brownell appeared before the Senate education subcommittee on April 2, they testified to a national shortage of 340,000 classrooms—costing $10 billion to $12 billion— which, with a school population increase of a million a year, would rise to 407,000 by 1960.[7] A series of caustic exchanges with Senator Hill illuminated the philosophic differences between the administration and the Democratic activists:

SENATOR HILL: It is all good to have conferences but don't you think it is time for action?

SECRETARY HOBBY: If I had thought so, Senator Hill, I wouldn't have proposed the conferences. It is true that there are many types of information in the field of education, but nowhere . . . have all the problems been pulled together. . . . Some of the problems are in the local school districts, and some of the problems are at the state level. Therefore it seems to us, for the federal government to take a sound position, that there must be some consolidated thinking from the local school board straight through to the state department of education and straight on through to the national government.

HILL: Don't you think in the light of all the information we have that we ought to really be dynamic? The word "dynamic," as I understand it, implies action—action, moving forward—not simply killing maybe a year or a year and a half or two years, or longer, holding some more conferences. . . . Don't you agree with what President Eisenhower said on October 9, 1952, that we ought to move forward?

HOBBY: I think there are many ways to define the word "action." I believe we would get action in forty-eight states much faster . . . if all of the forty-eight states joined in the solution of these problems. Obviously the national government can't solve the educational problems of the nation. I do not believe the people of the United States . . . want . . . the federal government to control education. . . . I myself believe that we can solve these problems much faster by getting agreement as to what all levels of government can do. . . .

HILL: I am very, very much disappointed . . . your own charts today show the crying, compelling need for new school facilities, new school buildings.

---

[6] From his letter to state governors, Sept. 21, 1954, *Public Papers of the Presidents, 1954*, p. 851.

[7] *President's Recommendations Relating to Education*, Hearings before the Subcommittee on Education of the Senate Labor and Public Welfare Committee, 83 Cong. 2 sess. (April 2, 1954), pp. 14–15.

HOBBY: That is true. . . . I think we both want to do the same thing. . . . Our approaches are different.

COMMISSIONER BROWNELL: I recognize the concern on the part of the federal government.

HILL: Concern— you wouldn't use that word "responsibility?"

BROWNELL: . . . "Responsibility" is interpreted in a great many ways. . . . One of the things that we have to decide as American people is in what way the federal government proposes to recognize its concern, and, if you please, its responsibility. . . . I don't think that that is very clearly agreed upon . . . and . . . that is one of the important reasons for bringing people together in these conferences.

HILL: As the Commissioner of . . . Education would you not feel that you are in a position of leadership and should accept that leadership of helping to make clear what should be the concern or responsibility of the federal government in the field of education?

BROWNELL: . . . I would hope that the leadership would be not by my telling the people, but by my working with the people to help them to come to what is a reasonable solution. . . . I wish I thought that I had all the answers, but I am afraid I don't.

HILL: My dear doctor, do you think there is any problem to which we have all the answers?[8]

On the Senate and House floors the Democrats contented themselves with colorful language—"a pipsqueak program," "this tiny mite of a diminutive and altogether paltry program," "altogether unnecessary . . . 'talkfests' "[9]—then supported the proposal for the White House conference, which was duly held in November 1955.

As disappointed as any Democrat in the administration's position was the chairman of the subcommittee on education, John Sherman Cooper, Republican of Kentucky. Cooper represented a state where more than half the children were in overcrowded classrooms—many with more than sixty pupils—and where 7,881 of the state's 18,908 classrooms were "outmoded or unfit or should be abandoned." By national standards, only 122 school buildings in Kentucky could be rated satisfactory. In the next five years the state would need 10,590 new classrooms—and Kentucky was one of the poorest states.[10]

[8] Excerpts from *ibid.,* pp. 225–30.

[9] Representative Charles Howell of New Jersey and Senators Hill and Murray, respectively, *Cong. Record,* Vol. 100 (May 12 and June 17, 1954), pp. 6467, 8450, 8451.

[10] Testimony of Wendell P. Butler, Kentucky superintendent of public instruction, in *Construction of School Facilities,* Hearings before the Subcommittee on Education of the Senate Labor and Public Welfare Committee, 83 Cong. 2 sess. (May 17, 1954), pp. 181, 183.

As an interim measure pending development of the Eisenhower administration's position, Senator Cooper had introduced an emergency school construction bill on July 6, 1953, to provide $500 million in aid to the states over a two-year period. At the April 1954 hearing he tried to elicit a commitment of support from Secretary Hobby, but failed to get anything more than encouragement to hold committee hearings.[11] In the afternoon he was still hopeful: "I am not going to accept the assumption that the President didn't mean what he said. . . . I do not accept the assumption that the administration uses these [the White House conference and two minor accompanying bills] as a diversion."[12] But later in April Secretary Hobby made clear that those bills were indeed the entire administration program for that Congress. After discussion in Cabinet meeting, she sent the Senate committee a report recommending rejection of Cooper's bill and all other aid-to-education bills pending the White House conference. The Budget Bureau sent similar reports.

Senator Cooper nevertheless proceeded with hearings, as he had promised to do. He told the subcommittee that Commissioner Brownell "had said that he would be glad to come before the committee . . . and to give his views upon this bill."[13] But Brownell's appearance was repeatedly delayed, and on the last day of the hearings he was "out of the city." As Munger and Fenno point out,[14] this was a "lame" explanation, since the hearings could have been reopened. But Brownell was spared the embarrassment of testifying against a bill that—as clearly shown from previous Brownell statements which Senator Murray placed in the record—he personally favored.

On July 9 the committee reported the Cooper bill unanimously. But at that point the Senate Republican leadership declined to schedule it for action. Twenty national organizations, led by the NEA, appealed to President Eisenhower for support and sought a meeting with him, but two weeks later, when the President was asked at a news conference whether he was for the Cooper bill (and a corresponding House bill by Republican Peter Frelinghuysen of New Jersey, the education subcommittee chairman), he replied: "I do not know the details of that particular legislation.

---

11 *President's Recommendations Relating to Education,* Hearings, p. 33.
12 *Ibid.,* p. 47.
13 *Construction of School Facilities,* Hearings, pp. 41–42.
14 *Federal Aid to Education,* p. 86.

. . . I'd suggest you go to Secretary Hobby to find out where we stand. . . . I haven't seen any analysis of these bills."[15]

Finally, on August 19, the day before adjournment, the Senate Republican Policy Committee announced it had cleared the Cooper bill for action. Now, Senator Richard B. Russell of Georgia made clear he would delay adjournment and debate the bill at length if it were called up.[16] Cooper complained about the bill's having languished on the calendar for a month but emphasized that the objection to its consideration came from Democrat Russell. Loyal to the end, he concluded: "I want the responsibility to be fixed where it belongs—on the other side of the aisle."[17]

The Hobby Bill, the Kelley Bill—and the Powell Amendment. In January 1955 the President once again called upon the Congress for "positive, affirmative action"—but this time he had a bill. According to Robert J. Donovan, President Eisenhower personally "insisted" upon an interim school construction measure, overruling those of his advisers who continued to argue that any proposal should await the White House conference.[18] "Today we face grave educational problems," the President said in his State of the Union message. "An unprecedented classroom shortage is of immediate concern to all our people. Positive, affirmative action must be taken now."[19]

But the President could hardly have proposed a bill less likely to obtain action "now." The measure, which had been worked out by consultants from the New York investment banking community brought into HEW by Under Secretary Nelson A. Rockefeller, called for the federal government to assist states in establishing school building authorities patterned after those of Pennsylvania, Maine, and Georgia. The state authorities would borrow money to construct schools that would be turned over to local districts under lease-purchase agreements, the net effect being to pass on to all of a state's school districts the advantages of the lower interest rates the state could obtain. The federal government was to provide half the initial reserves of these authorities and guarantee repayment of their

---

[15] *Public Papers of the Presidents, 1954*, pp. 684–85. Frelinghuysen wrote the President offering to give him an analysis—and quoting the President's campaign language back to him—but the offer was not accepted.

[16] *Cong. Record*, Vol. 100 (Aug. 19, 1954), p. 15194.

[17] *Ibid.*, p. 15480.

[18] *Eisenhower: The Inside Story* (Harper, 1956), p. 316.

[19] *Public Papers of the Presidents, 1955*, p. 25.

bonds. The bill also provided $750 million for direct loans to districts with weak credit ratings, over a three-year period, and $200 million for grants over a three-year period to the poorest school districts.

To a budget-conscious administration, the use of school building authorities was an ingenious device to obtain a large volume of construction with almost no impact on the federal budget. It was estimated that $100 million in federal contributions would support $4 billion in construction; $150 million would support $6 billion. But the plan had two weaknesses. First, it required legislation in each state, and perhaps in some instances constitutional amendments. Second, it had not been drawn up in consultation with those who would carry the responsibility of winning support for it—either the educators who would be affected or the supporters of federal aid in the now-Democratic Congress—and those groups, it turned out, did not like it.

Edgar A. Fuller, representative of the Council of Chief State School Officers, charged that the bill was drafted "by people who were completely unacquainted with the local-state-federal relationships in education. . . . It is fantastically complex and . . . a bankers' bill rather than a bill that springs from the understandings that we have of educational finance."[20] He said officials of education organizations saw the bill only a week or two before it was presented. The National Education Association called an emergency meeting of its legislative commission and reached the conclusion, as reported to the House committee by Executive Secretary William G. Carr, that it "could not honestly say . . . the [President's bill] could do the job." Representative Frelinghuysen responded, "You sound a bit like the unsuccessful suitor who refused to kiss the bride out of sheer spite."[21] Fuller read into the record statements of indifference or outright opposition from state after state. The educators did not want encouragement to borrow. In most cases they already had that opportunity. They wanted federal grants to reduce the amount they would have to borrow. In innocent tones Democratic Senator Herbert H. Lehman of New York asked, "Am I not right in believing that when the federal government gives aid for the building of highways, it is done in the form of grants?" Senator Hill assured him he was correct.

[20] *Federal Assistance to Increase Public School Construction,* Hearings before the Senate Labor and Public Welfare Committee, 84 Cong. 1 sess. (Feb. 18–21, 1955), p. 214.

[21] *Federal Aid to States for School Construction,* Hearings before the House Education and Labor Committee, 84 Cong. 1 sess. (May 4, 1955), p. 830.

In the House hearing the estimated classroom shortage was suddenly and unexpectedly cut in half. As late as February 9, President Eisenhower had told a news conference that the shortage of school classrooms was 340,000, the previous year's figure. The rate of construction, he said, had risen to 60,000 a year but "at that rate we are never going to reach the objective of getting rid of the shortage."[22] But when Secretary Hobby appeared before the House committee, on March 29, she announced that the shortage of 407,000 previously projected for 1960 was now estimated at only 176,000 based upon new information received from state educational authorities in response to a telegram survey. The figures "clearly establish that the classroom situation is improving," she told the committee.[23] Carr of the NEA could only protest that the new figures could not be verified, because of the absence of detailed data, and that in any case a 176,000-room shortage meant 5 million children were ill-housed and $5 billion in construction was still needed. "The case for Federal assistance for school construction remains unshaken," he contended.[24]

On the Senate side of the Capitol the most important witness turned out to be Clarence Mitchell, director of the Washington bureau of the National Association for the Advancement of Colored People (NAACP). He asked for an amendment requiring that each state, before receiving aid, certify that school facilities in the state had been desegregated in conformity with the Supreme Court decision of the previous year.[25] Republican Senators Irving M. Ives of New York, William A. Purtell of Connecticut, and Gordon Allott of Colorado had raised the desegregation question at several points during the hearing and indicated their sympathy with the Mitchell position.[26] When Mitchell finished testifying, the issue was dead. Chairman Hill, who faced a reelection campaign in Alabama the following year, did not schedule an executive session of his committee to consider school construction legislation for the duration of that Congress.

Hill's fellow southerner in the House, Chairman Graham Barden (Democrat of North Carolina) of the Education and Labor Committee did allow his committee to meet,[27] but scheduled the hearings in the full

[22] *Public Papers of the Presidents, 1955*, p. 253.
[23] *Federal Aid to States for School Construction*, Hearings, pp. 281, 282.
[24] *Ibid.*, p. 798.
[25] *Federal Assistance to Increase Public School Construction*, Hearings, p. 368.
[26] *Ibid.*, pp. 143, 145, 314–16.
[27] In 1951 and 1952 he had refused to permit the full committee to meet to consider federal aid questions (Munger and Fenno, *Federal Aid to Education*, p. 128).

committee and dragged them out for nearly three months. At the end of May, fifteen pro-aid Democrats brought an end to the hearings by serving Barden with an ultimatum, but two more months were required before a bill could be reported.[28] Barden himself described the events as follows: "[the subcommittee] came up with a proposal to the full committee. . . . So we started as objectively as possible to give it the most careful consideration paragraph by paragraph and sentence by sentence. . . . People began to get impatient. . . . And this I did not agree with in my committee and, of course, they all know it. Suddenly about the time we had read 12 or 13 pages, the motion was made to report the bill out, and it was reported out."[29] The subcommittee bill, which carried the name of Augustine B. Kelley, a Pennsylvania Democrat, retained the proposal to help state school building authorities, but shifted the emphasis to outright grants, ballooning the $200 million in the administration's bill to $1.6 billion over a four-year period. The money would be distributed among the states in proportion to their school-age populations. The vote was 22–8, with six Republicans and two Democrats dissenting,[30] but it was late July and no time remained for action before adjournment.

The White House conference on education, convened in November, gave a resounding endorsement to federal aid for school construction. By a ratio of more than two to one, the participants approved the proposition "that the federal government should increase its financial participation in public education." Of those favoring federal aid, "the overwhelming majority" approved aid for school building. Only "a very small minority" opposed federal aid to education in any form. A majority agreed federal aid should be granted "only on the basis of demonstrated needs."[31] The committee that arranged the conference found that, of forty-one states reporting, only ten were gaining on their backlog of school construction

---

[28] *Ibid.* Also, Bendiner, *Obstacle Course on Capitol Hill*, p. 122.

[29] *Cong. Record*, Vol. 102 (June 28, 1956), p. 11302.

[30] *Congressional Quarterly Almanac, 1955*, p. 269.

[31] Committee for the White House Conference on Education, *Report to the President* (April 1956), p. 104. Munger and Fenno comment: "The outcome of the White House conference came as a surprise to many. Suspicions had been expressed that the conference would be stacked to produce a majority against federal aid" (*Federal Aid to Education*, p. 103). But education organizations and their allies moved into the state conferences in force and played a leading part in selecting the state delegations. Fred M. Hechinger said the endorsement of federal aid was not only unplanned but occurred "to the dismay of some of the top figures" (*New York Times*, July 25, 1965).

needs and another twelve were holding their own. Nearly half, or nineteen, were losing ground.[32]

With this backing—and with a new secretary of HEW, Marion B. Folsom, who was a far more convinced advocate of aid to education than was his predecessor—the Eisenhower administration went more than halfway toward the House committee's grant program. It proposed $250 million a year in grants for five years, compared to the committee's $400 million for four. The administration rejected the committee's simple per-child distribution formula in favor of a plan that took into account both the need and the effort of each state, but this too appeared to be within the range of legislative compromise. Nobody was advocating inclusion of private schools in a construction bill, and Representative Kelley, the bill's sponsor, was a prominent Catholic. All of the auguries were favorable, except for two things: first, 1956 was a presidential election year; second, it was the year of the Southern Manifesto, the resolutions of interposition by southern legislatures, the declarations of "massive resistance" to school integration—and the Powell amendment.

The events of the previous year, when the proposed antisegregation amendment had immobilized Senator Hill and his Senate committee, made clear the danger. Advocates of federal aid frantically sought to hold their lines against the amendment, which now carried the name of Harlem's congressman, Adam Clayton Powell. Twice in the summer of 1955 President Eisenhower denounced it as "extraneous."[33] The House committee rejected it, 17–10.[34] The AFL-CIO opposed it. So did the Democratic presidential candidate, Adlai Stevenson. So did former President Truman. The NEA and other education groups argued strenuously that it would "kill the bill," either in the House or through a filibuster by southern senators. In the words of Senator Richard L. Neuberger, Oregon Democrat, the amendment would provoke "a bitter and hopeless debate over enforcing an amendment to a bill which would not become law, to restrict the use of funds which would not be appropriated, to prevent segregation in schools which would not be built."[35] Said Powell: "Negro people have waited many, many years for this hour of democracy to come and they are willing to wait a few more years rather than see a bill passed

[32] *Report to the President*, p. 27.

[33] News conferences, June 8 and July 6, 1955, *Public Papers of the Presidents, 1955*, pp. 584, 678.

[34] Statement by Representative Cleveland Bailey, Democrat of West Virginia, during House debate, *Cong. Record*, Vol. 102 (July 3, 1956), p. 11761.

[35] *Ibid.* (Feb. 17, 1956), p. 2784.

which will appropriate federal funds to build a dual system of Jim Crow schools in defiance of the law."[36]

When the vote came on the House floor in early July, neither the northern Republicans nor the northern Democrats were willing to follow the education organizations or their own national party leaders. From its national convention at the end of June, the NAACP delivered an ultimatum: "Any vote against the Powell amendment is a vote in favor of segregation."[37] For the northern Republicans who opposed aid to education in any form, the choice was easy—they could vote on the side of civil rights and, if it killed the school bill, accomplish that purpose at the same time. But Democrats and Republicans who supported school aid were forced to choose between objectives—and most chose civil rights. One by one they expressed themselves: "The issue before us is a very simple one because it is a moral one." "I shall be found on the Lord's side." "We cannot avoid our responsibility." "This amendment involves a principle so fundamental, so basic . . ." "Now is the time to stand up and be counted—on this . . . moral issue." "A matter of principle . . . that we cannot dodge." "A question of principle upon which there should be no compromise."[38] Only 46 of 194 Republicans supported the President's position on that vote, and among the defectors were the party leaders—Minority Leader Joseph Martin of Massachusetts and Whip Leslie C. Arends of Illinois. On the Democratic side the big city delegations were overwhelmingly with Powell—every member from New York, all but one from Chicago, all from Philadelphia, Pittsburgh, and Baltimore, and all but two from New England, including Democratic Leader John McCormack of Massachusetts. Significantly, the lone vote against the amendment from the Chicago delegation came from that delegation's only Negro—Democrat William L. Dawson, who said, "I can never do anything that I conscientiously believe will deprive any child of an education."[39] The amendment was adopted, 225–192.

Meanwhile, the money differences had been compromised by acceptance of a Republican amendment reducing the amount from $400 million to $300 million a year for five years. That left one other major issue: the

[36] *Ibid.* (Jan. 24, 1956), p. 1193.

[37] As quoted by Powell during the House debate, *ibid.* (July 3, 1956), p. 11757.

[38] Democrats Thomas J. Dodd of Connecticut and Sidney R. Yates of Illinois, and Republicans Dean Taylor, Henry Latham, and Albert H. Bosch of New York, John F. Baldwin of California, and Kenneth B. Keating of New York, respectively, *ibid.* (July 3 and 5, 1956), pp. 11766–73, 11876; all voted for the Kelley bill.

[39] *Ibid.* (July 3, 1956), p. 11771.

formula for distribution of the funds. Republican Representative Samuel K. McConnell of Pennsylvania presented a modified version of the administration plan that would grant more funds to the poorer states, mainly in the South, and require states to participate in the matching. Defenders of the Kelley formula argued that such a move would win no votes from southern members, who could not support any bill containing the Powell amendment, while it would lose votes in the North. The amendment was defeated, 262–158.

Then the bill itself was killed, 224–194. Every vote but one in the eleven southern states was lost.[40] Some of the staunchest of aid-to-education supporters over the years, like Democrats Carl Elliott of Alabama and Brooks Hays of Arkansas, were forced into opposition. Joining them were some border state Democrats, two northern Democrats,[41] and 119 Republicans. The 119 Republican opponents were more than half again as many as the 75 voting for the bill.

Before and after the vote, recriminations flew. Senator Hubert Humphrey was quick to blame the President. "The White House," he said, "failed to rally Republican votes. . . . A majority of Republicans turned against their own President's recommendation and first voted for inclusion of a civil-rights rider, and then flip-flopped to vote against the final bill. . . . Cynical opponents of school aid have been at work to use us, to split and divide us. . . ."[42] The President, in the campaign, blamed the Democrats. Only nine Democrats, he pointed out, had supported the McConnell amendment to revise the formula. Most Republicans voted for it. After the amendment lost he said, "I wasn't doing anything to get their bill through. . . . I am perfectly ready to stand up and say I take responsibility for not allowing that."[43] James Reston of *The New York Times* blamed "racial politics"—a "combination of fierce emotional feeling among Southern Democrats and determined Republican action to win back the Negro vote."[44]

[40] The sole favorable vote was cast by Representative Howard H. Baker, Republican of eastern Tennessee.

[41] Fred Marshall of Minnesota and Francis E. Walter of Pennsylvania.

[42] *Cong. Record*, Vol. 102 (July 9, 1956), p. 12147. The senator's reference to "a majority" of the Republicans slightly overstates the case. Of the 194 Republicans voting on the two questions, 96 voted for the Powell amendment, then against the bill (*Congressional Quarterly Almanac*, 1956, p. 411).

[43] News conference, Oct. 11, 1956, *Public Papers of the Presidents*, 1956, pp. 893–94; his explanation in various campaign speeches was similar.

[44] *New York Times*, July 8, 1956.

There is no disputing Humphrey's point that the President failed to rally the Republicans. But it is more difficult to join Humphrey in placing all the blame upon the President. Of the two votes to which the senator referred, the vote on the Powell amendment was the more crucial—because the amendment, if it had not killed the bill in the House, would surely have precipitated a hopeless end-of-session filibuster in the Senate. On this vote the Democrats were not being rallied either. Could the President fairly be asked to help pass a school bill for which the Democrats would be able to claim most of the credit, by asking Republican congressmen to vote in a campaign year "in favor of segregation" while Democrats were left free to oppose it?

But the President's position cannot be wholly credited either. Blaming the Kelley distribution formula for his withdrawal of support and hence for the defeat of the bill was an ingenious way of shifting the onus to the Democrats, but it was disingenuous too. It suggested that the McConnell amendment to alter the formula rather than the Powell amendment was the key to passage of the bill (but in his memoirs Eisenhower himself acknowledges that adoption of the Powell amendment had made defeat "inevitable"[45]). Moreover, it suggested that, if the McConnell amendment had been passed, the President could and would have switched at least sixteen Republican votes. Conceivably so, but so many of the Republicans were irreconcilable opponents of aid to education in any form, and had been on record for so many years, that only the strongest White House leadership could have brought them around—and the President, as Reston put it, "with his own party divided and wavering on what to do, . . . did not send a single word to the Congress during this week's debate."[46]

Among supporters of "action" to meet the "critical" classroom shortage, as the President portrayed himself in his campaign[47] as well as in his memoirs, the President was virtually alone in taking an all-or-nothing position on his distribution formula. Few others saw the issue as being that significant. The plan in the Kelley bill had been worked out in bipartisan collaboration in the Education and Labor Committee. Republican Carroll D. Kearns of Pennsylvania called it "the only approach we had which met the approval of all the educational interests of America as a

[45] Dwight D. Eisenhower, *Mandate for Change* (Doubleday, 1963), p. 552.
[46] *New York Times*, July 8, 1956.
[47] The quoted words are from his Lexington, Ky., speech of Oct. 1, 1956, *Public Papers of the Presidents, 1956*, p. 845.

fair approach."[48] It was simpler and it involved less federal interference in state financial practices. Democratic Representative John E. Moss of California, for example, said the McConnell plan for state matching would require two constitutional amendments in his state. Moreover, possibility for further compromise remained during Senate and House-Senate conference consideration. Republican supporters of aid to schools—seventy-five in all, or 39 percent of those voting—were able to back the Kelley bill, on final passage, as better than none at all. For the President to have withdrawn support, upon such a narrow ground, from the first general aid-to-education bill to reach the House floor in the twentieth century contradicts his self-portrait. More nearly accurate is Munger's and Fenno's appraisal of the President's attitude: "actively hostile" at the beginning and "never more than lukewarm."[49]

No one, at the time, made the point later brought out by J. W. Anderson that the timing of the Kelley bill "was fatal" because it preceded House floor consideration of the civil rights bill. The Rules Committee had considered both bills on June 14, but it cleared the Kelley bill while only scheduling hearings on the civil rights measure. The Powell amendment, he argues, "could have been defeated only if liberal House members had been given an earlier opportunity to go on record for the more comprehensive administration civil rights program." He holds "the conservative majority in the Rules Committee" responsible for the order in which the two bills reached the floor. The actions of June 14 were in fact taken by a coalition of liberal Democrats and Republicans who seized control of the committee, but the conservative Democratic chairman, Howard Smith of Virginia, used his position to obstruct the bill he opposed more strongly— the civil rights bill. Anderson does not argue that the consequences of putting the Kelley bill ahead were clearly foreseen and prearranged by Smith but he reasons that if the Rules Committee had been in friendly hands, the order of consideration of the two bills would no doubt have been reversed and the Powell amendment would, under those circumstances, have been defeated.[50]

In analyzing the defeat, two other factors should be noted. One was the limited popular appeal of the school construction issue. Parents and teach-

---

[48] *Cong. Record*, Vol. 102 (July 3, 1956), p. 11751.
[49] *Federal Aid to Education*, pp. 103, 129.
[50] *Eisenhower, Brownell, and the Congress* (published for Inter-University Case Program by University of Alabama Press, 1964), pp. 66–74. But see Chap. 6, p. 229, below, for evidence that liberal Democrats were also a party to the civil rights delay.

ers in areas of overcrowding, notably the suburbs, were expending their political energies at the state and local levels, organizing bond campaigns and appealing for state aid. They were not accustomed to looking to Washington for help in building schools; the Kelley bill was not translated into specific help for local districts, and the congressmen, waiting to hear from home, heard little. The voice of the NAACP rang far louder, during the hectic week of the debate, than the voice of beleaguered school districts. The second factor was the lack of cohesion, discipline, and influence of the Education and Labor Committee.[51] Some committees, after negotiating their compromises in executive session, then close ranks to defend their product against amendments offered during floor debate. But the Education and Labor Committee has been notorious for carrying its disputes to the floor. Its bipartisan majority worked well in defending the Kelley bill against the traditional charges of "socialism" and "federal control," but it fell apart on the complex tactical issues presented by the Powell and McConnell amendments.[52]

The Second Kelley Bill—and No Word from Eisenhower. The 1956 fiasco was repeated, with variations, in the heat of the next midsummer. As he had promised in his reelection campaign, President Eisenhower proposed to make up the lost year by compressing his five-year building program into four years and raising the level of annual grants from $250 million to $325 million. The Democrats countered with $600 million a year for six years in a new Kelley bill, whose priority they emphasized by assigning it the number H.R. 1. When the storm broke over the budget,[53] the President stood fast. While emphasizing that federal aid should be temporary, he said of his school bill: "I believe it is a necessity; and the longer it is neglected, the more we will suffer as a nation in the long run."[54] Next day he told the NEA convention, "It is my firm belief that there should be federal help to provide stimulus to correct an emergency situation."[55]

[51] This circumstance is particularly well elaborated in Munger and Fenno, *Federal Aid to Education*, Chap. 5, especially p. 130, and Chap. 6, pp. 146–48.

[52] Representative Cleveland Bailey said during the House debate that committee supporters had agreed upon a "nonpartisan-bipartisan" defense of the bill against "crippling amendments" and accused McConnell, the ranking committee Republican, of a breach of faith in proposing his revised formula (*Cong. Record,* Vol. 102 [July 3, 1956], p. 11751).

[53] See Chap. 9, pp. 424–26.

[54] News conference, April 3, 1957, *Public Papers of the Presidents, 1957,* p. 243.

[55] *Ibid.,* p. 267.

Representing Secretary Folsom, Assistant Secretary Elliot L. Richardson of HEW worked with the House subcommittee to bring forth a compromise, and within a month they were successful. The $325 million was raised to $400 million, and the disputed distribution formula was resolved by splitting the difference—half the money to be apportioned by the administration formula and half by that of the Kelley bill. The compromise was approved on May 9 by a strong bipartisan majority of the full committee, 20–9. Representative McConnell said the President gave the compromise his full support, and Secretary Folsom said he hoped the President would "get on the phone" on its behalf.[56]

But the President did not do so. When the House debate opened, on July 23, the opponents centered their case at first on the progress being made by states and localities toward solving the school construction problem. They used Secretary Folsom's own figures against him—he had testified that the construction rate was up to 69,000 a year and the backlog down to 159,000—and they filled the *Congressional Record* with statistics on how their own states and districts were meeting their own school construction needs without federal help.[57] By the third day of debate, the absence of presidential activity on the bill's behalf was so marked (and the dispute over the statistics, perhaps, so confused) that the question of whether the bill had Eisenhower's support became the central issue. "Is the President back of the committee bill or not?" Stewart L. Udall, Arizona Democrat, demanded to know. "Because if he is not, then the work of the committee is a shambles, and none of us know where we are. We are adrift here."[58] But no Republican could say for sure. Peter Frelinghuysen had earlier offered a letter from Eisenhower saying, "I earnestly hope.... that legislation will be enacted at this session" but declining to "pass judgment on all the details of this bill" and asking further attention "to that portion of the bill which allocates funds on the basis of need."[59] Republi-

[56] *Congressional Quarterly Almanac, 1957,* pp. 590, 592. See also Eisenhower's account of his talk with McConnell, *Waging Peace* (Doubleday, 1965), pp. 139–40.

[57] The effective use of statistics by the opposition—and, to some degree, the accelerated progress indicated by the statistics—can be credited largely to the leading foe of the school aid measure, the U.S. Chamber of Commerce. In opposing federal aid the chamber had urged its local affiliates to demonstrate that states and local communities could raise funds for school construction without help from Washington. The response of local business leadership in many localities contributed to raising the rate of school building to the record height. The state conferences preparatory to the White House conference had also been a force to mobilize state and local effort, as the President had predicted.

[58] *Cong. Record,* Vol. 103 (July 25, 1957), p. 12723.

[59] *Ibid.* (July 24, 1957), pp. 12607–08.

can Leader Martin had said the President was "not entirely satisfied" but would accept the bill, and Press Secretary James C. Hagerty had confirmed the Martin statement.[60] The Associated Press reported that the President was considering sending the House a statement clarifying his views.[61]

With the House "adrift" and the scheduled hour of voting imminent, Republican William Ayres of Ohio stepped forward with a substitute bill incorporating the distribution formula the administration had offered through McConnell the previous year. The Ayres substitute bill not only met all of the President's expressed reservations but removed as well a "Powell amendment" offered by Republican Stuyvesant Wainwright of Long Island, an avowed opponent of the bill, in Powell's absence. The Wainwright amendment had been adopted by teller vote, 136–105, but Ayres assured the House it would not be reoffered as an amendment to his bill.[62]

Charles Halleck of Indiana, assistant Republican leader, greeted the Ayres substitute with enthusiasm: "It is President Eisenhower's program. I voted for it last year and I shall support it this year."[63] At this point the leading Democratic supporters of school aid rose, one by one, to announce that they too would join the Ayres bandwagon in order to pass a school aid bill. But victory was still not to be theirs. Halleck, after an "anxious conversation" with Leslie Arends, the Republican whip, suddenly left the floor. Five minutes later[64] Representative Howard Smith, the Virginia Democrat who usually acted as coleader with Halleck of the Republican-southern Democratic coalition, moved to strike the enacting clause and thus kill the bill. The motion was carried on a teller vote, 153–126. But there was still time to reach the President before the vote was confirmed in a roll call. McConnell and his Republican allies tried but failed. The administration forces lobbying for the bill could not get through to the White House either. On the roll call, 111 Republicans (or 59 percent of those voting) joined with 97 Democrats (or 43 percent of those

60 *Congressional Quarterly Almanac, 1957*, p. 592.

61 *Cong. Record,* Vol. 103 (July 25, 1957), p. 12745.

62 *Ibid.,* p. 12750.

63 As reported by Bob Hoyt of Knight newspapers; Halleck's comment was edited out of the *Record*, presumably by Halleck, but at the next meeting of the House the Democrats read it back in (*Cong. Record*, Vol. 103 [July 29, 1957], pp. 12929, 13061). Other reporters had similar versions; see Bendiner, *Obstacle Course on Capitol Hill,* p. 136.

64 As reported by Don Irwin in New York *Herald Tribune* and quoted by Bendiner, *Obstacle Course on Capitol Hill,* pp. 136–37. Representative Richard Bolling (Missouri Democrat), in *House Out of Order* (Dutton, 1965), p. 87, says Smith and Halleck "hastily conferred on the floor—in the open."

voting) to bury the school construction issue for one more year, 208–203. Among those voting to kill the Ayres substitute was Halleck, who had hailed it before the Democrats made it their own.[65]

Not only did McConnell fail on July 25 to get through to the President, but six days later Eisenhower professed that news of the event had not even reached him. Told at his news conference that Democrats were complaining that he "failed to go to bat" for his own bill after the Democrats came round to support it, he responded: "I never heard that. . . . If that is true, why you are telling me something I never heard."[66] He went on to say he had "never wavered" in supporting his school construction proposal, but after sending a program to Congress, "I try to win their votes over but I don't get up and make statements every twenty minutes. I don't think that is good business." Although the bill he "thoroughly favored" was the Hobby proposal of 1955, he would have signed the committee compromise, he said.[67]

Year of Consensus: The National Defense Education Act *(1958)*

"I ask you, sir, what are we going to do about it?"

With this blunt question, Merriman Smith of the United Press opened President Eisenhower's news conference of October 9, 1957, five days after the Soviet Union launched its first sputnik into orbit.[68] The Presi-

[65] Eisenhower's explanation of the bill's defeat in *Waging Peace* is itself inexplicable. He blames the Wainwright amendment, saying simply, "This rider again consolidated the opposition" (p. 140). But the House understood that the antisegregation amendment was effectively eliminated by the Ayres substitute, as evidenced by the fact that thirteen southern and border state Democrats, including seven from Alabama, voted against Smith's motion. This bill would have survived if, of the seventeen northern and western congressmen who had voted for the Kelley bill in 1956 but voted with Smith in 1957, even three had been willing to accept the President's bill. The seventeen who switched included twelve Republicans, seven of them from New York, and five Democrats. All but two of them had voted for the Powell amendment in 1956, so they were hardly "consolidated" into the opposition by the segregation issue.

[66] *Public Papers of the Presidents, 1957,* p. 576.

[67] The 1957 incident may shed further light on the President's contention, the year before, that if the Democrats had been willing to accept the McConnell amendment, the 1956 bill would have passed. But their announced readiness in 1957 to accept the Ayres amendment did not bring over any large body of administration supporters. A comparison of the two votes shows only nine Republicans who opposed the Kelley bill in 1956 were willing to support the Ayres substitute, by defeating the Smith motion, in 1957. Those nine votes would not have been enough.

[68] *Public Papers of the Presidents, 1957,* p. 719.

dent's response that day did not mention education. But later, in two television addresses to the nation, he referred to the shortage of highly trained manpower in scientific and engineering fields as "one of our greatest, and most glaring deficiencies,"[69] and "according to my scientific advisers . . . the most critical problem of all." The Soviet Union, he said, already had more persons in these fields than the United States and was currently "producing graduates . . . at a much faster rate." The problem was one for the whole country but, he promised, "the Federal government . . . must and will do its part."[70] Under the menace of the orbiting sputniks, the raucous partisanship of the school construction debate dissolved, and within a year the Congress had enacted the most important piece of national education legislation in a century.

Congressional consideration of the National Defense Education Act (NDEA) began with two bills introduced almost simultaneously at the end of January 1958—one a Republican bill written within the Department of Health, Education, and Welfare, the other a Democratic bill written on Capitol Hill under the supervision of two close friends from Alabama, Senator Hill and Representative Elliott. Both bills provided scholarships for college students, with preference to those in specified defense-related fields, and assistance to educational institutions to improve instruction in those fields.

On the administration side, "the origins of the NDEA are traceable back at least as far as the 1955 White House Conference on Education," according to Elliot Richardson, who as assistant secretary of HEW was responsible for developing the administration version of NDEA.[71] He might have gone back further. A year before the White House conference, President Eisenhower himself had advanced the idea of scholarships. Asked at a news conference about reports that the Soviet Union was outstripping the United States in training scientists, the President responded: "Here is one place where the government should be very alert, and if we find anything like that . . . I believe the federal government could establish scholarships. . . . I am just saying what could be done, and, possibly, will have to be done. I don't know."[72]

When the decision was made to limit the White House conference to elementary and secondary education, those interested in higher education

[69] Address of Nov. 7, 1957, *ibid.*, p. 794.
[70] Address of Nov. 13, 1957, *ibid.*, p. 814.
[71] Letter to the editor, *Reporter*, July 23, 1959, p. 6.
[72] News conference, Nov. 10, 1954, *Public Papers of the Presidents, 1954,* p. 1040.

proposed a separate study. The President responded by creating a President's Committee on Education Beyond the High School, headed by Devereux C. Josephs, a life insurance executive and former president of the Carnegie Corporation, and the question of federal scholarships became a part of its agenda. That committee estimated that 100,000 able high school graduates each year were not going on to college for primarily financial reasons, but recommended that the federal government stay out of the scholarship field (except for an experimental "work-study" program for 25,000 to 50,000 students) until other sources had a "fair trial" to see whether they could multiply existing scholarship funds several-fold.[73]

In June 1957, as soon as the Josephs report was available, Secretary Folsom appointed a task force within HEW headed by Commissioner of Education Lawrence G. Derthick to review its recommendations and draw up a legislative program. Rejecting the caution of the Josephs committee, the task force proposed federal scholarships. It also emphasized the early identification of talent through strengthening of testing, guidance, and counseling services in secondary schools. The Derthick program was in draft form at the time of sputnik. At that point, a major new program was developed for grants to the states for improvement of high school science and mathematics instruction.

On the congressional side, support for a program of federal scholarships had been steadily rising. Early in 1956 Democratic Representative Melvin Price of Illinois, chairman of a Joint Committee on Atomic Energy subcommittee, published a Library of Congress study with a warning "that the United States is in desperate danger of falling behind the Soviet world in a . . . life-and-death field of competition" and called for a "crash program" for the training of scientists and engineers.[74] Citing data from that report, Senator Earle C. Clements of Kentucky, the Democratic whip, introduced a bill for 5,000 federal scholarships in science and engineering. The following year, more than a dozen scholarship measures were introduced in both houses, and Representative Elliott, the sponsor of one of them, scheduled a series of Washington and field hearings during the late summer and fall. It was in the midst of these hearings that the news of sputnik came.

[73] President's Committee on Education Beyond the High School, *Second Report to the President* (July 1957), pp. 56–57.
[74] Harris Collingwood, *Engineering and Scientific Manpower in the United States, Western Europe, and Soviet Russia,* prepared for the Joint Committee on Atomic Energy, 84 Cong. 2 sess. (March 1956), p. v.

On that date, Lister Hill was in Berlin. When he returned, on top of the papers awaiting his attention was a memorandum from the chief clerk of his committee, Stewart L. McClure, suggesting that sputnik be made the vehicle for carrying an aid-to-education program through the Congress. Hill agreed. He told a staff group headed by John S. Forsythe, committee counsel, to assemble a bill that, besides linking education to defense, would "steer between the Scylla of race and the Charybdis of religion." This they did, piecing together suggestions from individual scientists and educators and their organizational representatives in Washington and taking what they liked from the drafts of the administration bill that Richardson supplied them—making bigger and better, of course, the more appealing sections of the administration proposal. In accepting the title "national defense education act," Hill observed that his colleagues would not dare vote against both national defense and education when joined in the same bill.

The administration bill, called the "educational development act of 1958," was introduced on January 28 by Senator H. Alexander Smith of New Jersey and Representative Carroll Kearns of Pennsylvania. Two days later, the national defense education bill was introduced by Hill and Elliot. The Democratic bill was broader and considerably more generous in the student aid provisions, the Republican bill more generous in its aid to schools. The Hill-Elliott bill called for 40,000 new four-year scholarships a year, at a flat $1,000 stipend; the administration bill provided less than one-fifth as much money for the program, but since the stipend would be variable depending upon need, perhaps one-third as many scholarships. The Hill-Elliott measure also authorized $40 million a year for student loans and $25 million a year for work-study programs. For graduate fellowships the administration bill provided a slightly larger program.

Considering that the two bills were defended as national defense measures, it is noteworthy that neither restricted its assistance to students in defense-related fields. The Hill-Elliott bill required only "special consideration" for students with preparation in science, mathematics, or modern foreign languages; the administration bill had "preference" for those prepared in mathematics or science. Once chosen, however, the students could study what they pleased. The administration bill put no limitations whatever on its fellowship program.

Both bills authorized funds, to be matched by the states, for improvement of guidance and counseling in the secondary schools and for the training of counselors, with no striking dissimilarities in scope and purpose. In aid to the states for the improvement of instruction in defense-related fields, the administration bill provided $150 million a year and permitted aid for teacher salaries, while the Democratic measure provided only $40 million and restricted its use to purchase of equipment and minor remodeling of facilities.

During this period, other bills were foundering on partisan differences much narrower than these. But Hill and Elliott, on the one hand, and Folsom and Richardson, on the other, had no intention of letting that happen to the education bills. They had established informally a collaborative relationship during the period when the rival but parallel proposals were being drafted, and once both bills were in, the formal negotiations could begin.

The two bills by no means met with universal acclaim. The National Education Association, in December, had proposed a general aid bill both for school construction and for raising teacher salaries, providing $1 billion in the first year and $4.5 billion by the fourth year, and was rallying professional support behind it. Congressional supporters of federal aid were cool to the long-term and technical nature of the educational development bill; they wanted a more spectacular "crash" response to the challenge of sputnik. But these critics had no choice; they knew that they would get, in 1958, a combination of the Hill-Elliott and administration bills or nothing at all.

Scylla and Charybdis were successfully skirted. The NAACP[75] again proposed a "Powell amendment" but it was not pressed in either committee. Protestants and Other Americans United for Separation of Church and State expressed "apprehension" that scholarships for use in sectarian institutions of higher education might set a precedent for similar scholarships in elementary and secondary schools. They were also "apprehensive" at the eligibility of private colleges for teaching equipment and materials.[76] But the points were not pressed. When Senator Purtell offered an amendment suggested by the National Catholic Welfare Conference authorizing loans to private schools for teaching equipment in science, mathematics, and modern foreign languages, it was accepted by the committee without opposition and survived unnoticed through the floor debate.

[75] Testimony of Clarence Mitchell, in *Science and Education for National Defense,* Hearings before the Senate Labor and Public Welfare Committee, 85 Cong. 2 sess. (March 5, 1958), pp. 878–79.

[76] Statement, undated, submitted in *Science and Education for National Defense,* Hearings, pp. 1351–52.

By midsummer the two committees, working in an atmosphere of rare harmony both internally and with the administration, produced their separate compromises and approved them by lopsided bipartisan majorities. Only three members of the House committee—Republicans Ralph W. Gwinn of New York, Clare E. Hoffman of Michigan, and Donald W. Nicholson of Massachusetts—signed a minority report. Of the Senate committee, only Barry Goldwater, Arizona Republican, and Strom Thurmond, then a Democrat, of South Carolina, said it went too far. Goldwater's minority report follows in all its eloquent simplicity:

> This bill and the foregoing remarks of the majority remind me of an old Arabian proverb: "If the camel once get his nose in the tent, his body will soon follow." If adopted, the legislation will mark the inception of aid, supervision, and ultimately control of education in this country by federal authorities.[77]

The debate, in both houses, centered upon the student aid provisions. Republican members of the committee, with Stuyvesant Wainwright of New York as their spokesman, had taken the precaution of checking the amended bill with President Eisenhower and found he had two objections—the number of scholarships had been increased by the committee compromise, and half the stipend, or $500, was to be granted regardless of need. The members of the bipartisan committee bloc agreed to yield to the President's terms, and the changes were made in the House bill when the debate opened. With that change, Wainwright assured the House that "the President supports" the bill.[78] Nevertheless, Walter H. Judd, Minnesota Republican, proposed to strike the entire scholarship section, retaining only the student loans from the Elliott bill. "Any boy or girl bright enough to merit a scholarship is good enough to be able to pay a low-interest loan back without difficulty or hardship in an 11-year period after his graduation," he argued. "Any boy or girl who is not sufficiently competent to be able to pay back such a loan . . . is not good enough to deserve a free scholarship."[79] The amendment carried on a division vote, 109–78. On signing the bill, President Eisenhower complained that Congress "did not see fit" to approve his scholarship proposal, but later, in his memoirs, he wrote that the Judd amendment

[77] *Cong. Record,* Vol. 104 (Aug. 13, 1958), p. 17290.
[78] *Ibid.* (Aug. 8, 1958), p. 16727.
[79] *Ibid.,* p. 16728.

"was, I thought, a good one."[80] The Senate accepted, 46–42, an amendment by John Sherman Cooper, Kentucky Republican, limiting scholarships to $250 a year, with any aid above that amount in the form of loans. In the Senate-House conference, the Senate gave up the truncated scholarship program entirely.

What began as a scholarship bill, now devoid of scholarships, breezed through both houses. The vote was 62–26 in the Senate and, on a recommittal motion, 233–140 in the House. Comparing the House vote on the National Defense Education Act with the vote by the same Congress to kill the school construction bill in 1957, the major difference lay in the return of thirty southern and border state Democrats to the support of aid to education.[81] Folsom and his staff, as well as Hill and Elliott, had entreated the liberal forces not to kill this bill with an antisegregation amendment, and Powell had responded by agreeing to limit his anti-discrimination amendment to the student aid provisions of the bill, to which nobody objected; he did not propose to disqualify segregated schools from the school aid provisions. The Republican vote showed a net shift of five members to the favorable side, but a majority of Republicans were still in opposition, 95–86. In the Senate, a clear majority of both parties supported it.

"An historic landmark," Majority Leader Lyndon Johnson termed the bill just before the Senate vote; "one of the most important measures of this or any other session."[82] Subsequent appraisals agree—not so much because of the specific provisions of the NDEA but because of the psychological breakthroughs it embodied. It asserted, more forcefully than at any time in nearly a century, a national interest in the quality of education that the states, communities, and private institutions provide. "The Congress hereby finds and declares," said the preamble to the act, "that the security of the Nation requires the fullest development of the mental resources and technical skills of its young men and women. . . . The national interest requires . . . that the federal government give assistance to

[80] Statement of Sept. 2, 1958, *Public Papers of the Presidents, 1958,* p. 67, and *Waging Peace,* p. 243. James McCaskill, chief of the NEA legislative staff, offers evidence that the latter was Eisenhower's true view; while the NDEA bill was pending, he said, the President in a private conversation expressed himself against scholarships on the ground that "everyone should either work or pay his own way."

[81] The comparative figures used in this paragraph consider only the 294 members who were recorded on both votes.

[82] *Cong. Record,* Vol. 104 (Aug. 13, 1958), pp. 17331, 17330.

education for programs which are important to our national defense."
Henceforth, as Elliot Richardson put it, "discussion . . . no longer centers
on the question of whether or not there will be federal aid. Rather, the
debate has shifted to the two factions who agree that there should be
federal aid but who divide sharply over the form in which it is to be
provided"—that is, short-term aid for specific needs, as in NDEA, or a
permanent sharing of the total costs, as proposed by the National Education Association.[83]

The NDEA experience also demonstrated how a consensus for national
education legislation could be formed. Once these thresholds were crossed
—or, from Senator Goldwater's point of view, once the camel's nose was
under the tent—other and bolder measures could, and did, follow. But
before they followed, several more years of frustration were to intervene.

More Years of Frustration   *(1959–62)*

Arthur S. Flemming, who became secretary of HEW in August 1958,
took office at what, for an advocate of aid to education, was a most un-
propitious time. The National Defense Education Act did nothing to
solve the school construction "crisis" that the Republican administration
and the congressional Democrats both acknowledged. The backlog of
school building needs remained. But politics, which had been adjourned
long enough after sputnik to permit passage of the NDEA, resumed with
doubled force when the question of general aid for construction or teacher
salaries was again considered.

"History will smile sardonically," said Robert Maynard Hutchins, "at
the spectacle of this great country's getting interested, slightly and temporarily, in education only because of the technical achievements of Russia,
and then being able to act as a nation only by assimilating education to
the cold war and calling an education bill a defense bill."[84] But that was
the way it was. The political deadlock made the country, whether "interested" or not, powerless to act.

The Flemming Bill—and the NEA-Democratic Alliance. In the 1958
campaign President Eisenhower centered his attack on what he called the

---

[83] Richardson letter, *Reporter*, p. 6.
[84] Quoted in *New York Times*, Jan. 22, 1959; reprinted in *Cong. Record*, Vol. 105
(March 2, 1959), p. 3123.

"spending wing" of the Democratic party, using such epithets as "left wing government," "extremists," and "political radicals."[85] At the same time he issued a stringent directive to all departments to hold down their spending proposals for the coming year. So when Elliot Richardson set out in midcampaign to put together a 1959 education bill for Flemming, the ground rules were clear—whatever was done must be accomplished, for the most part at least, outside the budget. Moreover, Richardson was by this time convinced that the school construction crisis had now moved up to the college and university level, and a public school grant program on the scale of the 1957 administration bill—even assuming the President would support it—would leave nothing for higher education. The compromises he had negotiated with the House committee in previous years were now out of the question, and he launched a search for alternatives. Out of this reexamination came a complicated proposal to offer federal grant assistance to needy districts—those that could not, with a "reasonable tax effort," finance their own schools—but to spread the budgetary impact over twenty to thirty years by letting the districts borrow and then making an annual federal contribution, matched by the state, to debt repayment. Thereafter, the districts, insofar as possible with the same tax effort, would repay the federal and state "advances." Even this proposal violated the President's "no new spending programs" edict, but with an assist from Vice President Richard M. Nixon—who reportedly argued in Cabinet meeting that the Republican party could not afford to go into the presidential campaign with no education program at all—Flemming won the President's grudging assent. The proposal was submitted to Congress by Flemming, unheralded by any word of support in any presidential message. This was the first time since 1954 that the President had not personally recommended an education bill—a "visible waning of support," in Representative Udall's words,[86] that was noted by Republican as well as Democratic members.

Virtually isolated within the administration, Flemming was even more

[85] Campaign speeches, *Public Papers of the Presidents, 1958*, pp. 760, 822, 758. See also Chap. 9, pp. 425–27, below.

[86] Stewart L. Udall, "Our Education Budget Also Needs Balancing," *Reporter*, June 25, 1959, pp. 23–25. Perhaps a more convincing expression of Eisenhower's withdrawal of support was his extemporaneous comment at his July 31, 1957, news conference, in reference to construction proposals (his own as well as the Kelley bill): "But I am getting to the point where I can't be too enthusiastic about something that I think is likely to fasten a sort of albatross, another one, around the neck of the Federal Government—I don't believe it should be done" (*Public Papers of the Presidents, 1957*, p. 576).

isolated on Capitol Hill. Still smarting from the President's campaign attacks on spending, and buttressed by their landslide victory and by repeated polls showing strong public support for federal aid to education, the congressional Democrats had no intention of accepting a program that saved President Eisenhower's balanced budget by spreading the spending out over two or three decades of his successors' budgets. They simply refused to take the proposal seriously. On the floors of both houses and in hearings reminiscent of those on the Hobby bill of 1955—but more heavily laden with partisan acrimony—they ridiculed the measure as an unworkable subterfuge.[87] As in 1955, educational organizations likewise could see no merit in it. Among the dwindled ranks of Republicans, some sought a bill along the lines of the 1956–57 compromises while a large bloc wanted no legislation at all. That left only a handful of Republicans —who, under the circumstances, were without influence—to fight for Flemming's measure.

The majority of congressional Democrats had, by this time, joined in open alliance with the NEA—which could claim to speak for over 700,-000 voting teachers. Two Montana Democrats, Senator Murray and Representative Lee Metcalf, had introduced the NEA's bill for a multibillion-dollar program of aid for school construction and teacher salaries, and that bill was rapidly achieving the status of a party program measure among northern and western Democrats. Metcalf, in a blunt speech to the NEA's annual convention in 1958, had told the teachers they would have to enter the arena of political action if they were to get federal legislation. They had been bested by the U.S. Chamber of Commerce and its affiliates, he told them, because the businessmen had actively supported congressmen who opposed federal aid while too many educators took the "peculiar attitude . . . that political action is somehow not a proper activity of good citizens."[88] The NEA tacitly accepted the challenge. More vigorously and systematically than before, it identified to its members the congressional "friends" and "enemies" of the Murray-Metcalf bill. Their bill, because it gave the states the option of using part or all of their

[87] The case against the bill is summed up in a speech by Democrat Lee Metcalf of Montana in the House on February 24; he called it "feeble and ineffectual," labeled it "deferred deficit financing," said sixteen states could not participate without constitutional amendments and others would require referenda, and argued that it would be no help to school districts—some or all of the districts in thirty-one states—that had reached their legal debt limits (*Cong. Record*, Vol. 104 [1958], pp. 2888–94). See also Munger and Fenno, *Federal Aid to Education*, pp. 89–90.

[88] Speech inserted in *Cong. Record*, Vol. 104 (July 3, 1958), pp. 13020–22.

federal funds to raise teacher salaries, had far more appeal to NEA's membership than did the earlier Kelley construction-only bills. Congressmen began receiving mail from teachers and resolutions from their local organizations,[89] and one by one the supporters of school aid became committed to that specific measure.

In June 1959 the House Education and Labor Committee reported the Metcalf bill, scaled down to about $1 billion a year, as a strictly Democratic measure opposed by all the committee Republicans.[90] Senate committee Democrats were, however, split. Four, along with Republican Cooper, had joined Murray in sponsoring the NEA measure. But others argued that only a construction bill could be passed; the National Catholic Welfare Conference had made clear that aid for teacher salaries, which it regarded as "inherently nonterminable," would raise the issue of aid to private schools which the temporary emergency construction measures had successfully skirted.[91] Chairman Hill felt that aid for teacher salaries, likewise, was much more likely to raise the aid-to-segregated-schools issue. Until he was sure his view would prevail, he exercised his chairman's prerogative not to call a meeting. Bendiner notes that Majority Leader Johnson's "considerable powers" were also used to limit the bill to construction.[92] Finally, as the session approached its end in September, the committee did meet and approved, by the vote of all the Democrats and three Republicans,[93] a $1 billion construction bill sponsored by Senator Patrick McNamara, Michigan Democrat.

The House Democrats who reported the Metcalf bill knew it had no chance of clearing the Rules Committee. Solid Republican opposition in the Education and Labor Committee assured equally solid Republican opposition in the Rules Committee, and without at least one Republican vote the bill could not win approval, since two of the eight Democrats on the eight-to-four committee—Chairman Smith and William M. Colmer

[89] See, for example, comment by Representative John P. Saylor, Republican of Pennsylvania, on the mail he had received in support of the Metcalf bill (*ibid.,* Vol. 105 [Aug. 10, 1959], p. 15408).

[90] See Munger and Fenno, *Federal Aid to Education,* pp. 117, 128, 130–31.

[91] *Federal Grants to States for Elementary and Secondary Schools,* Hearings before the Senate Labor and Public Welfare Committee, 86 Cong. 1 sess. (1959), p. 528. Cited by Munger and Fenno, *Federal Aid to Education,* p. 59.

[92] *Obstacle Course on Capitol Hill,* p. 162.

[93] Cooper, Clifford P. Case of New Jersey, and Jacob K. Javits of New York. Cooper and Javits reserved the right to offer a substitute embodying some features of the administration bill.

of Mississippi—were sure to vote, as they always had, against any general school aid bill. So the bill languished in Rules for the remainder of the year[94] and, when Congress adjourned, the indefatigable Cleveland M. Bailey (Democrat of West Virginia), the subcommittee chairman, set out to draft a compromise that would command enough bipartisan support to both pass the House and win President Eisenhower's approval.

In March, Bailey brought forth his compromise—a three-year emergency, construction-only measure like those of 1956 and 1957, but with each state permitted a choice between receiving its funds as flat grants or as federal commitments for debt service on the pattern of the administration bill. He claimed no administration support, however, and only Frelinghuysen among the Republicans voted for the bill in committee.

While the House committee was reversing its field to exclude teacher salaries from its bill, the Senate had moved in the opposite direction. The NEA, in November, had made clear its lack of interest in any bill that contained no funds to increase the salaries of its members. Calling the McNamara construction bill "unwise and unsound" and opposing the administration bill outright, the NEA promised that if a bill "embodying the principles of the Murray-Metcalf bill" were not enacted, it would "endeavor to make this matter a major issue in the political campaigns of 1960 so that the American people may again express their mandate for the enactment of such legislation in 1961."[95]

Senate Democrats relished the prospect of their party's entering the 1960 campaign as the staunch and proven friend of three-quarters of a million teachers. Senator Joseph Clark of Pennsylvania agreed to sponsor an amendment to revamp the McNamara bill on the lines of the Murray-Metcalf measure by permitting the bill's funds to be used for teacher salaries as well as for construction. Without difficulty, he lined up twenty-one Democratic cosponsors.[96] When the roll was called on the amendment, the result was a 44–44 tie, and Vice President Nixon ultimately cast the deciding vote in opposition. Some said that Majority Leader Johnson prevailed on a Democratic opponent of the bill to switch his position to the favorable side to assure a tie vote, so that Nixon would be forced to personally kill the amendment.[97] In any case, the vote solidi-

---

[94] Bendiner suggests that opposition by Speaker Sam Rayburn, of Texas, contributed to its death in the committee (*Obstacle Course on Capitol Hill*, p. 163).

[95] Statement of Nov. 29, 1959; inserted in *Cong. Record*, Vol. 106 (May 26, 1960), pp. 11286–88.

[96] And one Republican, Thomas E. Martin of Iowa.

[97] Democrat J. Allen Frear, Jr., of Delaware, an opponent of the amendment, voted for reconsideration, creating the tie vote that Nixon broke.

fied the Democratic-NEA alliance. Only five of the thirty-two Republicans voted for the Clark amendment, while the northern and western Democrats were unanimous except for J. Allen Frear, Jr., of Delaware, Carl Hayden of Arizona, and Frank J. Lausche of Ohio. And the Nixon vote served further to dramatize the sharp partisan division.

In the debate on the amendment the Democrats accepted also the new rationale for federal aid to education. The Clark amendment was not premised on the assumption, explicit in all school aid debates since 1955, that the federal government could solve the school "crisis" by pumping money into school construction for a few years and then retreat to its previous position of unconcern. "Let us not kid ourselves, let us be candid, let us face the facts," said Clark. "This educational crisis is not going to be with us merely for next year or for only 5 years from now. It is going to be with us for the rest of the lives of those of us in the Senate. . . . Mr. President, the educational gap will not be closed until we undertake a massive Federal aid to education program."[98] State and local debt, he pointed out, had more than quadrupled in the thirteen years since 1946, rising from $13.6 billion to $55.6 billion, while the federal debt had risen only 4 percent. Similarly, state and local tax revenues had increased 232 percent in twelve years while federal budget receipts had climbed but 74 percent and, in relation to the gross national product, had actually declined. Without federal aid, Clark contended, the states and localities could not raise the $1.5 to $2 billion additional required every year for the next ten years.[99]

After Nixon's vote killed the Clark amendment, Senator A. S. Mike Monroney, Oklahoma Democrat, came forward with a modification that would reduce the funds by 20 percent and authorize the program for four years only.[100] These concessions picked up support from seven Democrats, including Lister Hill, and three Republicans. In this form the bill was passed.

At the other end of the Capitol, it required a threat by school aid supporters to resort to "calendar Wednesday" procedures[101] before Howard

---

[98] *Cong. Record*, Vol. 106 (Feb. 3, 1960), p. 1945.

[99] *Ibid.*, pp. 1943–45. As it happened, the states and local governments did prove able to increase their expenditures for education by those amounts during the first half of the decade. The increase was $14.5 billion in the six years from 1960 to 1966 and the total reached $33.3 billion in the latter year (not adjusted for price changes); see *Economic Report of the President, February 1968*, p. 289.

[100] Because of parliamentary technicalities, the amendment was actually offered by Clark and is sometimes, like the earlier amendment, identified by his name.

[101] A complex procedural device for bypassing the Rules Committee, which had been used successfully to dislodge the area redevelopment legislation. See Chap. 3, p. 71.

Smith would agree to call a meeting of his Rules Committee to consider the Bailey construction-only bill. When it met, the balance had shifted just enough to clear the bill; one Republican, B. Carroll Reece of eastern Tennessee, who had heard from educators in his district, voted with the six pro-aid Democrats to provide a 7–5 majority for sending the bill to the House floor.[102] Compared to previous engagements there, the debate was mild. A Metcalf amendment to substitute the Senate-passed bill, with the funds cut in half, was ruled out of order as not germane. The Powell amendment was adopted. As in 1956, Republicans who had supported the Powell amendment—seventy-eight in all—then voted to kill the bill. But this time they lost. The bill passed, 206–189.

The victory was accounted for entirely by the changed composition of the House since the 1958 election. A comparison of the 1960 vote with that of 1956 (when the Powell amendment was also in the bill) shows an actual loss of support among the congressmen who voted on both occasions. The Democratic votes were stable, with a net shift of one to the favorable side, but the Republicans recorded a net switch of eleven from yes to no. The percentage of support within the dwindled Republican minority thus fell from thirty-nine to thirty-two. But these losses were more than offset by the almost unanimous support of Democrats who replaced Republicans in 1959. Of these, forty-three voted for the bill and three against.[103]

For the first time in the twentieth century, then, both houses of Congress had passed a general aid-to-education bill. The outlines of a compromise in a Senate-House conference seemed clear: the Senate would drop its teacher salary provision and the House would give up the Powell amendment. But the conference never convened; the House Rules Committee refused permission—thus overriding the expressed will of both houses. Reece of Tennessee and James W. Trimble, Arkansas Democrat, switched to the opposition in a 7–5 vote against the bill on June 22. In the ten remaining weeks of the session, positions only hardened.

Several factors influenced the Rules Committee decision. At a meeting of Republican congressional leaders with the President on June 9, it was agreed that the Republicans would not accede to a conference unless they were assured in advance that the conference committee would report a bill the President could sign; otherwise they would suffer the embarrassment of an Eisenhower veto of an education bill at the outset of the 1960

---

[102] See Bendiner, *Obstacle Course on Capitol Hill,* p. 166, and Munger and Fenno, *Federal Aid to Education,* p. 134.

[103] Munger and Fenno, *Federal Aid to Education,* p. 162.

campaign.[104] The failure to obtain any such assurance accounts, presumably, for Reece's vote. Trimble may have been influenced by the Powell amendment. A third factor was the lukewarm support of the bill by the NEA. With the conference committee foreordained to give up the aid for teacher salaries won on the Senate floor, the organized teachers, as they had said in their November statement, preferred to take their chances in the coming election. A new president, with a fresh mandate, might get them the bill they wanted; if they settled for a "half a loaf" construction bill, many years might elapse before they would have another chance as favorable for aid for salaries. Liberal Democrats likewise "preferred a campaign issue to a watered down bill," according to Munger and Fenno.[105] Some of the Democrats also welcomed the Rules Committee action as a powerful argument to be used in attempting a reform of that committee in 1961.[106]

The Kennedy Program—and the Church-State Issue. As the campaign progressed, Senator Kennedy exploited the education issue with increasing zest. In speech after speech he read the record of Republican votes against school construction bills, climaxing each assault by denouncing the vice president's "tie-breaking vote killing a Democratic bill giving the states money to increase teachers' salaries."[107] In the first Kennedy-Nixon debate, Nixon had been asked about that vote. "We want higher teachers' salaries; we need higher teachers' salaries," Nixon responded; "but we also want our education to be free of federal control. When the federal government gets the power to pay teachers, inevitably, in my opinion, it will acquire the power to set standards and to tell the teachers what to teach." Not so, said Kennedy in rebuttal; the amendment had proposed aid "without any chance of federal control" because the money was paid in a lump sum to the states.[108] The NEA stopped just short of endorsing Kennedy, giving wide distribution to literature that made clear that Kennedy supported the

[104] Papers of Henry Roemer McPhee, Jr. (in Dwight D. Eisenhower Library, Abilene, Kan.).

[105] *Federal Aid to Education*, pp 164–67.

[106] Bendiner, *Obstacle Course on Capitol Hill*, p. 171.

[107] See *The Speeches of Senator John F. Kennedy, Presidential Campaign of 1960*, S. Rept. 994, 87 Cong. 1 sess. (1961), Pt. I; quoted phrase is from his Los Angeles speech, Nov. 2, 1960 (p. 1235). Sorensen observes that in the campaign, as well as throughout his presidency, "he devoted more time and talks to this single topic than to any other domestic issue" (Theodore C. Sorensen, *Kennedy* [Harper & Row, 1965], p. 358).

[108] *The Joint Appearances of Senator John F. Kennedy and Vice President Richard M. Nixon, Presidential Campaign of 1960*, S. Rept. 994, 87 Cong. 1 sess. (1961), Pt. 3, pp. 84–85.

NEA position on federal aid while Nixon did not.[109] As the campaign was closing, Kennedy devoted an entire speech to education, boldly promising that "in 1961, a Democratic Congress—under the leadership of a Democratic President—will enact a bill to raise teachers' salaries ..." as well as pass "an adequate bill for school construction."[110]

But it was not to be. The debacle of 1961 was a worthy successor to those of 1956, 1957, and 1960. The legislative process depends not only upon readiness to compromise but upon room for maneuver in consensus-building, and by 1961 important forces became "locked in" to fixed and diametrically opposed positions on an issue that had been quiescent during the 1950's—aid to parochial schools.

Because he was the country's first Catholic president, John Kennedy was locked in from the beginning. In his climactic confrontation with the Greater Houston Ministerial Association, he had said: "I believe in an America where the separation of church and state is absolute—where no Catholic prelate would tell the President (should he be a Catholic) how to act . . .—where no church or church school is granted any public funds or political preference."[111] After the campaign, in which Kennedy's Catholicism had been the single most important issue, Kennedy remarked that whether the "unwritten law" against a Catholic president was to be permanently repealed—rather than temporarily set aside—would be determined by his administration. If he appeared to yield to the church hierarchy in the conduct of his office, the religious issue would be used against any future Catholic candidate.[112] Accordingly, when he sent his education bill to Congress on February 20—essentially the construction-salary bill passed by the Senate in 1960 scaled down to $2.3 billion over a three-year period—he was categorical: "In accordance with the clear prohibition of the Constitution, no elementary or secondary school funds are allocated for constructing church schools or paying church school teachers' salaries."[113]

But the Catholic hierarchy had likewise become locked in. During the Eisenhower period the religious issue had remained abeyant as long as legislative activity centered on short-term aid for school construction; but now, with a very real possibility that a president strongly committed to

[109] Munger and Fenno, *Federal Aid to Education*, p. 183.

[110] Los Angeles speech, Nov. 2, 1960, *The Speeches of Senator John F. Kennedy*, S. Rept. 994, Pt. 1, p. 1235.

[111] Speech of Sept. 12, 1960, *ibid.*, p. 208.

[112] Sorensen, *Kennedy*, p. 358.

[113] *Public Papers of the Presidents, 1961*, p. 109.

school aid could succeed in inaugurating a permanent and growing flow of federal funds to education, the stakes were high and the church moved rapidly to rally its political power. Three days before the inauguration, Francis Cardinal Spellman of New York denounced the recommendations of President-elect Kennedy's task force on education, which proposed aid only to the public schools, as "unfair," "blatantly discriminating," and "unthinkable," as making Catholic children "second-class citizens," and as embodying "thought control" by compelling a child "to attend a state school as a condition for sharing in education funds."[114] Catholic diocesan newspapers took up the cry. On March 1 the National Catholic Welfare Conference declared its opposition to any federal aid program "which excludes children in private schools." The bishops did not seek grants but, said Archbishop Karl J. Alter as their spokesman, "we hold it to be strictly within the framework of the Constitution that long-term, low-interest loans to private institutions could be part of the federal aid program. It is proposed, therefore, that an effort be made to have an amendment to this effect attached to the bill."[115]

Reacting to the vigor of the Catholic demands, non-Catholic organizations quickly became locked in also. On February 22 the general board of the National Council of Churches, whose constituents claimed 38 million members, adopted a statement saying: "We do not . . . consider it just or lawful that public funds should be assigned to support the elementary or secondary schools of any church. The assignment of such funds could easily lead additional religious or other groups to undertake full scale parochial or private education with reliance on public tax support." The statement expressed flat opposition only to "grants" for nonpublic schools, but Gerald E. Knoff, in presenting the board's statement at House subcommittee hearings, said he was "very sure that a great majority" would be opposed to loans also, "deeming such loans to be an outright departure

---

[114] Quoted by Hugh Douglas Price, "Race, Religion, and the Rules Committee: The Kennedy Aid-to-Education Bills," in Alan F. Westin (ed.), *The Uses of Power* (Harcourt, Brace & World, 1962), pp. 22–23; this section relies on his definitive case study of the 1961 aid-to-education struggle (pp. 1–71). The story is told in briefer style by Bendiner, *Obstacle Course on Capitol Hill*, pp. 180–89, and the chronology of events is recounted in *Congressional Quarterly Almanac, 1961*, pp. 215–46. The Price case study, abridged, is included in his article, "Schools, Scholarships, and Congressmen," in Alan F. Westin (ed.), *The Centers of Power* (Harcourt, Brace & World, 1964).

[115] Such an amendment had been offered to the school bill by Senator Wayne Morse, Democrat of Oregon, in 1960 but it was easily defeated. Significantly, Kennedy was the only Catholic senator recorded against it (he was paired). A similar amendment in the House was ruled "not germane" to a public school bill.

from long-cherished principles of separation of church and state." "Un-happy accumulated experience," he said, showed that concessions such as those made in the college housing program, the National Defense Education Act, and various state enactments inevitably led to other con-cessions. For that reason, "what may be constitutional may not be wise."[116]

The two parties in the Congress, it should be added, also had taken fixed and irreconcilable positions on aid for teacher salaries. Once aid for salaries became a major partisan issue in the campaign, dramatized by the first Nixon-Kennedy debate, Democratic and Republican campaigners—which included all House members—became committed to the views of their respective presidential candidates. Even the bipartisanship of 1956 and 1957 in the House was impossible now. The Democratic bill had to aid salaries as well as construction, and that assured the administration a solid bloc of opposition votes no matter how it might resolve the religious controversy.

The President appeared surprised and irritated by the forcefulness of the attack on his program by his own church. "I do not recall that [during the Eisenhower administration] there was a great effort made . . . to pro-vide across the board loans to an aid to education bill," he complained to a news conference, "and I am concerned that it should be made an issue now in such a way that we end up the year with, again, no aid to secondary schools."[117] If the Congress wanted to consider the question, he made clear, it should be in a separate bill.

While Catholic and non-Catholic organizations devoted their energies to generating a flood of emotion-laden mail to members of Congress, the administration sought a way out of the dilemma. HEW Secretary Abraham Ribicoff and Special White House Counsel Theodore Sorensen opened conversations, through an intermediary, with the bishops, and out of these talks a strategy emerged: the public school bill would proceed as planned, but the Congress—not the President—would initiate a private school loan program as an amendment to a measure extending the life of the National Defense Education Act.[118] That act had already breached the aid-to-private-schools barrier in providing loans for equipment for science, mathematics, and foreign language teaching, and the new program would

---

[116] *Federal Aid to Schools*, Hearings before the General Subcommittee on Education of the House Education and Labor Committee, 87 Cong. 1 sess. (March 16, 1961), pp. 392–95.

[117] News conference, March 8, 1961, *Public Papers of the Presidents, 1961*, p. 156.

[118] Sorensen, *Kennedy*, p. 360.

merely extend the aid to the construction of facilities for the same purposes. An HEW brief had indicated that aid in this form would be constitutional. Accordingly, on April 25, President Kennedy formally recommended the extension of NDEA, with the pointed suggestion that "it is
also appropriate that the Congress consider other proposals" as amendments. But by no means were all Catholics ready to compromise on any
terms that provided their aid in a bill separate from the one that carried
aid for the public schools. Ribicoff swung over to their position. On the
day debate opened in the Senate, May 16, he and Lawrence F. O'Brien of
the White House legislative staff, supported by Majority Leader Mike
Mansfield of Montana, argued for combining the two bills. But Wayne
L. Morse of Oregon, manager of the President's public school bill, felt
that such a tactic presented the greater danger, and the two-bill strategy
prevailed. Senator Morse then skilfully steered the public school bill to
passage, 49–34. The division was almost identical with that of the year
before.

In the House the intransigent positions of the opposing religious groups
were reflected far more sharply in the positions of individual members
than was the case in the Senate. Hugh Douglas Price has suggested the
basic reason: Almost every senator, save those in the South and one or two
western states, must represent both Catholics and Protestants, but many
House members have constituencies made up almost wholly of one or the
other religious group. Thus, on the parochial school issue, "compromise
was accomplished *within* most senators themselves, but would have to be
negotiated *between* members in the House."[119] The Boston district represented by Majority Leader John McCormack was almost wholly Catholic,
the rural district represented by Speaker Rayburn almost wholly Protestant. As it developed, more significant was the fact that three of the eight-
man administration majority on the Rules Committee[120] were Catholics
representing heavily Catholic districts (James J. Delaney of Queens
Borough, New York City; Thomas P. O'Neill, Jr., of the Boston-Cam-
bridge district once represented by John F. Kennedy; and Ray J. Madden
of Gary, Indiana) while three others were Protestants from southern

[119] "The Kennedy Aid-to-Education Bills," pp. 51–52.

[120] The committee had been "reformed" early in the year, after a torrid floor fight, by
increasing the membership from twelve to fifteen and adding two administration Democrats—Carl Elliott of Alabama and B. F. Sisk of California—and one Republican; the
administration could count on eight of the ten Democrats for support on most issues
(see Price, *ibid.,* pp. 13–20; Bendiner, *Obstacle Course on Capitol Hill,* pp. 171–80). Also
see Chap. 11, pp. 472–73.

districts with few Catholics and strong sentiment against aid to parochial schools (James Trimble of Arkansas, Homer Thornberry of Texas, and Carl Elliott of Alabama). Even a House member who becomes majority leader still represents his district—it was McCormack who assumed generalship of the legislators seeking aid for parochial schools.

The House Education and Labor Committee approved the public school bill in May, with the Republicans now unanimous in opposition. The apportionment formula was revised, but the committee avoided every other hazard. Powell himself led the fight in committee against the "Powell amendment," sponsored this time by Republican Frelinghuysen.[121] The spotlight now centered on the fifteen members of the Rules Committee. Delaney and O'Neill first voted with the seven opponents of federal aid to delay action until the NDEA bill with its private school loan provision was ready for action. But on July 18, when the latter bill was also before the Rules Committee, Delaney cast the deciding vote with the opposition coalition to kill them both. Describing the loan program as "just a little bit of a sop" for the Catholics, he demanded a truly "nondiscriminatory" grant bill. Moreover, he had no confidence that, if he approved the public school bill, the private school-NDEA bill would survive as a separate measure.[122] Many members were happy to be relieved of the responsibility of recording their votes on the two bills, which by then had generated hundreds of thousands of messages to representatives from their constituents. *Time* quoted a southern member as saying, "when Delaney cast his vote, you could hear the sigh of relief all over the Capitol," and congressmen were shaking Delaney's hand for hours afterward.[123]

In an attempt to salvage something, the administration retreated to a 1961 version of the old Kelley bill—a one-year program of aid for school construction, but not for teacher salaries—and its sponsors on August 30 attempted "calendar Wednesday" procedures. But this was a bill almost nobody liked. "Woefully inadequate," the NEA called it. The Republicans, former supporters as well as consistent opponents, saw no reason to back it. The solidification of their opposition, as compared with previous

121 Bendiner, *Obstacle Course on Capitol Hill*, pp. 185–86.

122 Sorensen says Delaney "concluded—and no doubt rightly—that once he agreed to the public school bill, the NDEA bill would be mutilated or killed" (*Kennedy*, p. 361). *Congressional Quarterly Almanac, 1961* (p. 214), notes that Elliott, Trimble, and Thornberry of the Rules Committee "reportedly would have voted to table the NDEA bill" and that, had they done so, the public school bill would not have survived. See also Munger and Fenno, *Federal Aid to Education*, p. 135.

123 Bendiner, *Obstacle Course on Capitol Hill*, pp. 194–95.

votes on school bills, made the difference. Only 6 of 166 Republicans voted to take up the bill (compared to 44 of 136 voting for the school construction bill in 1960). The Democrats managed to attract 17 southerners who had voted against the 1960 bill—while losing 6 nonsoutherners (only 2 of them Catholics)—but it was not enough. The Republican-southern Democratic coalition prevailed, 242–170, on a vote not to take up the bill on the House floor.

The following year President Kennedy went through the formality of again recommending his school legislation. But nobody had any stomach for another round of religious warfare. Neither committee gave the matter any serious consideration.

In the postmortems the blame was well distributed. Each side of the religious argument, of course, charged the other with intransigence. But could the parochial school issue have been avoided somehow, or resolved before it reached the fever point? Nobody has explained how. "They expected a miracle and I couldn't produce a miracle," was Ribicoff's summation. "It was impossible to bring together a majority for a bill when most members didn't want one."[124] Bendiner concluded, "There is no reason to suppose that without the trickery of the Rules Committee an agreement would not have been reached in 1961."[125] But this seems too easy a conclusion. The Rules Committee, by the time the religious feud had boiled up, was not an unrepresentative sample of the full House. Seven of its fifteen members were opposed to both the bills before the committee—reflecting closely the division of the House. Of the other eight, three were reportedly insisting upon *no* aid to parochial schools, and Delaney and O'Neill were demanding *some* aid as the price of support for the public school measure. If Delaney had not killed the bill in committee, would not many Delaneys among the eighty-eight Catholics in the House (not to mention non-Catholic Democrats with Catholic constituencies) have joined with the Republican-southern Democratic coalition to provide the margin of difference on the House floor? There is no mathematical way to compromise between *none* and *some,* and the impossible would have been even harder to accomplish on the House floor than in committee.

The New York Times editorially blamed "legislative irresponsibility and inept executive leadership."[126] Price, unlike Bendiner, absolves the

[124] Munger and Fenno, *Federal Aid to Education,* p. 169.
[125] *Obstacle Course on Capitol Hill,* p. 199.
[126] *New York Times,* Sept. 1, 1961.

Rules Committee with the comment, "a bill could always be brought to the floor by other means," and observes that "the one point on which all could agree was the lack of presidential leadership." The President "apparently decided to knuckle under," he says, but also adds that Kennedy could have prevailed on this issue "only at the cost of disaster for much of the rest of his program, sharpened religious cleavage in America, and seriously endangering his own reelection prospects." Even a strong president, Price concludes, "must choose his showdown battles with care."[127]

But even this balanced judgment as to presidential power evades the substantive question: For precisely what kind of measure could the President have battled successfully? Price does not tell us, saying only that it would have embodied the President's "national" view of the matter. Yet the President tried two different positions, each presumably a "national" view. He began by offering the Catholics *nothing*; some Catholics responded by demanding *equal* treatment, others by asking for at least *something*. He then offered them *something*—and only intensified the Protestant insistence that the Catholics be given *nothing*, while leaving the Delaneys among the Catholics still demanding *equal* treatment. The switch of positions did not help, and laid his administration open to charges of duplicity and ineptness, but it is not clear how remaining adamant in the original position would have succeeded either. Every president has found that there are limits to the effectiveness of the tactics of pressure and coercion that Price suggests Kennedy could have used successfully; they were at least tested, without avail, on Delaney. "He had no interest in bargains or trades," writes Sorensen.[128] Perhaps a Protestant president-elect, if he could have fully anticipated the fury of the religious controversy, would have been able to find and include in his original program the *something* that would satisfy the preponderance of Catholics while not arousing the preponderance of Protestants. This had been accomplished, after all, in the National Defense Education Act— and was to be accomplished again in the education legislation of 1965. But the *something* could only have been found through conversations with the interested parties, including the Catholic bishops, and how could Kennedy—given the circumstances of the campaign—begin his tenure as the first Catholic president by opening negotiations with the hierarchy over ways to breach the wall of separation between church and state? Moreover, a bill that could have averted the religious quarrel would, in

127 "The Kennedy Aid-to-Education Bills," p. 69.
128 *Kennedy*, p. 361.

all probability, have had to be a measure other than the NEA general aid bill to which the Democratic party, as a matter of political inevitability, had become wedded.

Perhaps the fairest judgment is that the 1961 experience was both unavoidable and necessary. For the leadership on all sides—Catholics, Protestants, NEA, tacticians in the administration and in Congress—and for supporters of school aid among the general public, the 1961 debacle was a chastening ordeal from which they gained both wisdom and humility. It shattered the locked-in positions and gave all parties room for maneuver in designing a school aid measure that could win, under a Protestant president, in 1965.

The Education "Crisis" Reaches College (*1956–62*)

When Devereux Josephs assembled his Committee on Education Beyond the High School, in 1956, most of the members were predisposed against any massive federal financial intervention in the field of higher education. Enlargement of the federal government and its budget had no more inherent appeal to them than to any other group of Eisenhower appointees.

But when they finished their work, a year later, they recommended—by at least a "substantial consensus"—grants by the federal government for construction of classrooms, laboratories, libraries, and other facilities at colleges and universities throughout the country.

What converted them? Those who participated in the committee's work answer simply: "the facts." With the assistance of the American Council on Education and its constituent organizations representing colleges and universities, the committee projected the figures on college enrollment and translated them into costs, which they found would rise from $3 billion a year to $7.5 billion by 1970. Then they appraised the potential support from all sources—states, local governments, private gifts, endowment earnings, student fees. After making maximum allowance for increases in support from all these sources, they found that a gap remained, and only one additional source of funds could be identified—federal aid.

"Josephs started out being quite negative to the idea of federal aid," recalls one participant. "His conversion took place in the committee meetings in front of all the other members. When he swung over, so did the other members who were open-minded."

The gap between the nation's educational needs and its effort "is widening ominously," said the committee in its summary report in 1957. It did not measure precisely the size of the gap that should be filled by federal funds, but it was specific as to priorities and purposes. The "absolute highest priority" was raising faculty salaries. Here federal aid should be through tax credits to encourage private gifts rather than through direct grants, since the latter carried the possibility of federal control. Second priority was construction and remodeling of facilities, estimated to require about $1.3 billion annually through 1970; for this purpose, federal matching grants similar to those provided for hospital construction should be authorized "to assist as many types of nonprofit higher education institutions as possible." Third priority was aid to students; federal action in this case should be deferred to give other sources of support "a fair trial."[129]

The men and women who had faced the hard facts of the education gap disbanded, leaving their recommendations in the hands of a man who categorically rejected them. President Eisenhower has included in his memoirs excerpts from a letter written in 1958 in which he explained his opposition to any general program of aid to colleges:

> (a) The United States government can obtain no money for this purpose that is not already in the hands of its citizens, corporations, states, and localities. Consequently, the process of taking the money away from citizens to return it to localities for special purposes implies a centralization of wisdom in Washington that certainly does not necessarily exist.
>
> (b) The more that our institutions, in general practice, lean on the federal government for this kind of help, the more they invite a kind of federal influence and domination that could have very bad effects. These I do not need to elaborate. . . .[130]

The President did not face the question, with which the Josephs committee had struggled, of how money in the hands of citizens, corporations, states, and localities would be gotten to the country's institutions of higher education if the federal tax structure were not employed. But the budget policy was clear, and when the Eisenhower proposals for what became the NDEA went to Capitol Hill in 1958 they inverted the priorities of the Josephs committee. The administration bill, like the Hill-Elliott measure, proposed aid to students, none to colleges.

The Clark Bill—and Two Eisenhower Vetoes. When it became clear that the administration did not intend to act on the Josephs committee's

---

[129] President's Committee on Education Beyond the High School, *Second Report to the President*, pp. 1, 6, 56–57, 88, 89.
[130] *Waging Peace*, p. 217.

proposal for aid to colleges, Senator Clark of Pennsylvania moved into the vacuum. He first sought to have drafted a college aid bill patterned after the Hill-Burton hospital construction act as the Josephs committee had suggested. But the hospital act could not be directly adapted. So Clark retreated to a simpler approach—to make available for academic buildings the assistance of the well-established college housing loan program, under which public and private institutions had borrowed nearly $1 billion at low interest rates for dormitories and related income-producing facilities. If the government could lend for buildings in which students ate and slept, why could it not lend for the buildings in which they were taught? Moreover, as a member of the housing subcommittee, Clark was in a position to pilot such a program through the Senate.

Clark introduced a bill authorizing $250 million in loans, at the college housing interest rate (about 3 percent) for terms up to fifty years, and had no difficulty incorporating it as a section of the housing bill of 1958. During debate on the Senate floor, not a voice was raised against it.[131] But when the bill reached the House floor, in August, Democrat Albert Rains of Alabama, chairman of the housing subcommittee, said he was "astounded that this new proposed program has touched off so much opposition,"[132] though he did not specify its source. In the debate, which centered on the broad issue of "spending," the section came in for no particular attention. But it was lost in any case when the House fell narrowly short, 251–134, of the two-thirds margin necessary to suspend the rules and pass the housing bill.

The vote demonstrated that a college aid program, in the form of loans, could readily pass both houses on the initiative of members of Congress alone, without the support of the administration or any organized and unified backing from the institutions of higher education. In hearings during 1958 the representatives of college and university organizations had given only tentative opinions. In general, the private colleges looked favorably upon a loan program but the public institutions sought grants, if anything, and were skeptical of loans. "The very existence of this federal loan program . . . might encourage some of our State legislatures not to do the job that they ought to be doing," the president of the University of Arkansas testified as spokesman for the state universities and land-grant

---

[131] As part of an amendment cutting the authorizations for various of the bill's programs, the $250 million was cut in half.

[132] *Cong. Record*, Vol. 104 (Aug. 18, 1958), p. 18246.

colleges.[133] Since the public institutions could not commit their legislatures to pay off the loans, the cost of amortization might have to be placed upon student fees, and the students would ultimately pay for their academic buildings, just as they paid for their housing.

By the next year, however, the higher education organizations were ready to accept what the Congress was willing to do. The five major organizations went formally on record in favor of the loan program. The private colleges endorsed it with restrained enthusiasm; the public colleges went along mainly out of a spirit of fraternity since they expected to make little use of the program themselves.[134] The Office of Education was emboldened, too, by the congressional attitude and incorporated a loan program in its legislative proposals for the new Congress, along with grants for junior colleges. This was the year, however, when Secretary Flemming was restricted to his ill-fated debt service proposal for assisting elementary and secondary school construction; his proposal for aid for college construction emerged as a parallel debt service plan—calling for grants of $500 million over a twenty-year period to help the institutions pay off private loans—and met the same hostile reception by the Democratic Congress. The higher education community was also cool to the Flemming bill, some of its spokesmen wary of the church-state issue that would be raised by grants to private schools. For more than a year neither education subcommittee even bothered to call a hearing on the Flemming plan. Instead, the Democratic-controlled Congress again incorporated in its housing bill a reduced version of the Clark college loan program that both houses had approved in 1958.

Unfortunately for their plans, however, the housing bill as a whole became the focus of the "spending" debate of 1959. Twice Eisenhower dramatized his views on spending and inflation by vetoing Democratic

---

[133] Testimony of John T. Caldwell, in *Housing Act of 1958,* Hearings before the Subcommittee on Housing of the Senate Banking and Currency Committee, 85 Cong. 2 sess. (May 21, 1958), p. 647. HEW Assistant Secretary Richardson testified that at meetings of university representatives called by HEW in the fall of 1957, "there was very little support ... for a loan program" (*ibid.,* pp. 210–11).

[134] Organizations endorsing the program were the American Council on Education, Association of American Colleges, Association of Land-Grant Colleges and State Universities, Association for Higher Education of the National Education Association, and American Association of Junior Colleges; see *Housing Act of 1959,* Hearings before the Subcommittee on Housing of the Senate Banking and Currency Committee, 86 Cong. 1 sess. (Jan. 26, 1959), and *Federal Assistance to Higher Education,* Hearings before the Subcommittee on Education of the Senate Labor and Public Welfare Committee, 86 Cong. 2 sess. (June 17 and 20, 1960).

housing bills, and finally the Democrats capitulated by passing a scaled-down third bill which he accepted.

In vetoing the first housing bill as "extravagant" and "inflationary," President Eisenhower included the $62.5 million college loan program among those provisions to which he objected. Because the loans would be made at "subsidized interest rates," he argued, they would "substitute public for private financing."[135] But, in putting together a second bill, the Senate housing subcommittee refused to strike the program entirely; it merely cut the figure by 20 percent, to $50 million. The administration thereupon made clear, through Senator Prescott Bush of Connecticut, that the college loans were one of the two or three most objectionable features of the bill. On the issue of public as against private financing, Senator Morse protested: "We have never yet evaluated the educational system of the country on a profit motive basis. . . . Whether any profit is derived from them [the classrooms] is far less important than whether they are actually built in sufficient number."[136] A motion to strike was defeated in the Senate, 53–40, with only three Republicans supporting the program and two nonsouthern Democrats against it. In the House, a similar Republican motion was defeated by a teller vote, 146–133.

In his second veto message, Eisenhower condemned the program directly and sharply. It would, he said, "tend to displace the investment of private funds in these projects. This is federal aid to education in a highly objectionable form."[137] In their third housing bill the Democrats tried no further.

During all this time Senator Clark had grown increasingly impatient with the higher education community. The major organizations in the field had testified in favor of his loan bill, but they had made no evident attempt to arouse public support or bring pressure upon the administration. Moreover, while spokesmen for public institutions—which would have to provide most of the new facilities—had repeatedly said that they needed grants, not loans, they had not even drafted a grant proposal nearly three years after the Josephs committee had paved the way for them. Clark suspected that the reason was the division of opinion among and within the existing organizations, none of which was created for lobbying purposes and all of which included in their leadership at least some persons ideologically opposed to federal aid. He suggested the formation

---

[135] *Public Papers of the Presidents, 1959*, pp. 503–06.
[136] *Cong. Record*, Vol. 105 (Aug. 17, 1959), p. 16015.
[137] *Public Papers of the Presidents, 1959*, p. 640.

of a new single-purpose organization, made up solely of those committed to the federal aid cause, that could propose a grant plan and then campaign for it—just as the NEA was at that time campaigning, in single-minded fashion, for the Murray-Metcalf bill. Clark proposed the idea, first, at a Washington meeting of organizational representatives and, when that evoked no response, attempted shock treatment in May 1960 at a conference of the American Assembly at Harriman, New York, in which much of the national leadership in the field of higher education participated:

> The idea put forward by the Josephs committee three years ago died as completely as if it had never been born. Why did higher education drop it? Wasn't there anybody in the field with interest or initiative enough to pick up the thought, refine it, agitate for it, and eventually get it seriously considered by both the President and the Congress? Apparently not.
>
> I don't know myself whether the suggestion of the Josephs Committee is feasible, but the higher educational community should know and, if it does not, it ought to find out. . . .
>
> I wonder whether existing organizations in the field of higher education are set up to do the needed job of working out a proper plan for Federal aid and then lobbying vigorously for it? I suspect that, to some extent, they are immobilized by internal divisions on the basic questions; first, of whether Federal aid in any form is desirable and, second, if so, who should get it? . . . Would it not be desirable to organize an ad hoc committee of leading educators and other citizens who are convinced of the need for Federal aid so that, when they meet, they need not argue whether, but only how?[138]

Clark had barely returned to his office when a delegation of Washington representatives of higher education organizations sought an appointment. The shock treatment had worked—they had heard from members of their governing boards who had been in the American Assembly audience. They agreed to draft a grant bill quickly and barely a month later had succeeded. The difficult question of distribution of the funds was bypassed by delegating broad discretion to the commissioner of education

---

[138] The speech is included in *Federal Assistance to Higher Education*, Hearings, pp. 47–52. Homer D. Babbidge, Jr., and Robert M. Rosenzweig describe the speech as a "dressing down" of the educators present. They also detail some of the internal conflicts that plagued the organizations. "The desire for harmony in a number of organizations has caused a clear majority to fall prey to a stubborn, articulate minority," they conclude (*The Federal Interest in Higher Education* [McGraw-Hill, 1962], pp. 104–13). Other members of Congress were also critical. See Representative John Brademas, Democrat of Indiana, "Higher Education and the 87th Congress," *Higher Education*, Vol. 57, No. 7 (April 1961), pp. 5–7.

and a national advisory council.[139] Clark introduced the bill on June 29, but it was too late for Congress to initiate so bold a proposal. Flemming made a final appeal to Eisenhower, in August, to support a program of matching grants, but was rebuffed. The two-year struggle had simply enabled both parties to add to the image they sought to establish for the 1960 campaign: the Democrats as champions of federal action to meet national problems, the Republicans as enemies of "spending" and "inflation."

The campaign itself, in tone if not in substance, confirmed these images. Vice President Nixon actually went further than Senator Kennedy in endorsing aid for college construction. In a "study paper" issued September 25 and based on Secretary Flemming's recommendations, he said specifically that the college housing program should be "greatly expanded into a program of both loans and matching grants for classrooms and laboratories and libraries as well."[140] But he did not develop this proposal in his speeches, and the party platform did not support it. Senator Kennedy, while at no time specifically endorsing grants, argued aggressively for federal assistance in general and deplored the Eisenhower vetoes of the college construction loan programs. In their comments on education, however, the college expansion issue was muted. Both candidates stressed instead their positions on aid to elementary and secondary schools and to college students.

The Colleges' Bill—and the NEA. During the fall of 1960 the major organizations in the field of higher education finally hammered out a consensus on a construction program, in a series of meetings convened by the American Council on Education. "All the major studies," the conferees agreed, "show that after traditional sources of income, including student tuition and fees, have been stretched to the limit, there will still be a large gap that can be filled only by greater support from the Federal

---

[139] This plan may have been inspired by the University Grants Committee in Great Britain, which had made grants to universities since 1919 on behalf of the government but with a large degree of autonomy. The British scheme had been commended to the American Assembly conference by John A. Perkins, president of the University of Delaware and under secretary of HEW in the Eisenhower administration, and Daniel W. Wood, "Issues in Federal Aid to Higher Education," in American Assembly, *The Federal Government and Higher Education* (Prentice-Hall, 1960), pp. 169–75.

[140] *The Speeches of Vice President Richard M. Nixon, Presidential Campaign of 1960,* S. Rept. 994, 87 Cong. 1 sess. (1961), Pt. 2, p. 283.

Government."[141] In a spirit of live and let live, the public and private institutions joined to support both grants and loans, with each institution to choose its form of aid. They recommended $1 billion a year in federal funds, 70 percent for loans and 30 percent for grants, as the federal share of construction needs estimated to total about $2 billion a year. A poll by the council of its members—146 organizations and 1,065 institutions, including nearly all accredited institutions of higher education in the country—showed 89.5 percent in favor of the dual grant-loan plan.[142] President-elect Kennedy's task force on education, headed by Frederick L. Hovde, president of Purdue University, endorsed the same plan but under pressure from Kennedy's staff suggested the authorization be held to $500 million for the first year.[143]

The new President, however, was just as locked in politically on grants to Catholic colleges as on grants to parochial schools. He proposed only the simple loan scheme of 1958–59, still further reduced to $300 million, and another try for federal scholarships. The Association of Land-Grant Colleges and State Universities in its newsletter said Kennedy's program showed "little relationship to the basic needs of higher education at this juncture in history."[144] A matching grant program was a "must," testified Arthur Flemming, now enjoying a President he could quarrel with publicly; "I cannot understand why the administration did not recommend such a program."[145]

To the higher education community and its supporters, however, the word was passed that—as in the case of the elementary and secondary school bill—what the President could not initiate the Congress could. Among those who received the message was Representative Edith Green of Oregon, chairman of the special subcommittee on education. When the bill emerged from her subcommittee, 60 percent of the $300 million total had been converted from loans to grants, and in this form the mea-

---

[141] The agreement growing out of the conferences, entitled "A Proposed Program of Federal Action to Strengthen Higher Education," appears in *Aid to Higher Education,* Hearings before the Special Subcommittee on Education of the House Education and Labor Committee, 87 Cong. 1 sess. (March 16, 1961), pp. 145–49.

[142] Testimony of Everett Case, president of Colgate University, on behalf of the American Council on Education, in *ibid.,* pp. 143, 150.

[143] The Hovde task force recommendations are in *Saturday Review,* Jan 21, 1961, pp. 94–95.

[144] Circular letter, dated Feb. 24, 1961.

[145] *Aid to Higher Education,* Hearings, p. 126.

sure reached the Rules Committee. The Education and Labor Committee said flatly that the changes had the approval of the administration.[146]

No education bill could have gone further in assuring equal benefits for Catholic institutions, yet when Representative Colmer moved in the Rules Committee on July 18 to kill the elementary and secondary school aid bills, he included the college bill as well—and Representative Delaney voted for the motion. The administration and Mrs. Green felt that her bill had met death as an innocent bystander in the feud over the other measures and determined to try again—but in 1962, when tempers presumably would have cooled. They also decided to delete from the construction bill the proposal for federal scholarships, on which the House had expressed itself adversely in 1958.

Mrs. Green's new attempt came at once when the Congress reconvened in January 1962, and within three weeks of the opening session the college aid bill reached the House floor.[147] Impressed by the near-unanimity within the quarrelsome Education and Labor Committee (the vote had been 22–6, according to Chairman Powell) and among institutions of higher education, public and private alike, the House passed the measure by an overwhelming vote of 319–80. The conservative leadership, including Minority Leader Halleck and Chairman Smith of the Rules Committee, voted with the liberals. Edith Green assured her questioners that there were many precedents for federal grants to church-related colleges, such as research grants from the National Institutes of Health and the National Science Foundation, and the religious issue kindled barely a flicker of the fire that had consumed the elementary and secondary school bills a few months earlier.

The Senate committee made only one significant alteration in the administration bill—the addition of a $50 million annual grant program for public two-year community colleges, originally proposed by Senator Clifford Case, New Jersey Republican. In a debate no less placid than that in the House, the measure was passed by an equally lopsided majority, 69–17. An amendment to limit the construction loans to public institutions drew only fifteen supporters. An amendment to convert the scholarships into

---

[146] *College Academic Facilities and Scholarship Act*, H. Rept. 440, 87 Cong. 1 sess. (1961), p. 4. Seven Republicans who supported the measure took occasion to chide the Kennedy administration for presenting a loan bill that would largely fail to accomplish the necessary objectives (*ibid.*, pp. 22–27).

[147] Congressional action on higher education legislation in 1962 is narrated in Price, "Schools, Scholarships, and Congressmen," pp. 83–96.

loans, similar to the one that had carried the Senate by a four-vote margin in the National Defense Education Act, lost this time, 50–37. The shift in sentiment was accounted for by the 1958 election. Senators who voted on both occasions split their votes exactly the same, but new Democratic senators cast eleven votes in 1962—and all were in favor of scholarships.

Two bills passed with such powerful four-to-one bipartisan support would appear to be easily compromised. Yet such was not to be the case. For three months the House Rules Committee refused to let the House bill go to a House-Senate conference. Finally, after extracting a promise that under no circumstances would the House conferees accept a scholarship provision,[148] it released the bill by a vote of 8–6. But by this time a new factor had entered the picture—groups opposed to aid to parochial schools had discovered the House provision for grants to Catholic colleges, which had passed almost unnoticed in January, and saw in it a fearful precedent for legislation assisting elementary and secondary schools. On June 16 the National Congress of Parents and Teachers, the National School Boards Association, the American Association of School Administrators, the American Vocational Association, and the Council of Chief State School Officers notified congressmen of their opposition to the House bill.[149] According to one congressman, the National Education Association "flew its state representatives to Washington to help lobby against the bill."[150] On June 25 the Supreme Court aroused a new storm of religious controversy with its decision outlawing a state-prescribed prayer in New York schools. As the summer wore on, passions rose almost to the pitch of the year before, and the conferees seemed irreconcilably divided. In an attempt to salvage something, a compromise was put together in September. The House conferees agreed to restrict the contested college grants to facilities to be used for defense-related purposes like those aided under NDEA—science, engineering, and libraries.[151] The Senate conferees agreed to convert their scholarships to "loans" except for 20 percent that could be forgiven in whole or in part for "exceptionally needy" students who could not otherwise afford to be in school. Of the conferees, only three found the compromise unacceptable: Senator Goldwater, who had opposed the Senate bill; Senator Hill, who was en-

---

[148] *Ibid.*, pp. 92–93.

[149] *Congressional Quarterly Almanac, 1962*, p. 235.

[150] Bolling, *House Out of Order*, p. 134.

[151] Aid for facilities to be used for religious instruction or worship, as well as for athletic events, had been ruled out by both houses before their bills were passed.

gaged in a close reelection race in Alabama; and Representative Kearns, who contended that Chairman Powell's promise to the Rules Committee not to accept any form of scholarship provision had been violated.

In the House the debate centered on the scholarship issue. But Mrs. Green referred to what was probably a more decisive influence: "I regret with all my heart the telegrams which have been sent to the Members of this body by the National Education Association opposing this bill on the basis of the religious issue."[152] Congressional Quarterly cited still another reason: The University of Mississippi had been ordered by a federal court to enroll James Meredith, a Negro. The "exceptionally needy students" who would benefit from federal scholarships in the form of loan forgiveness looked to some southerners like so many Merediths.[153] Senator Hill crossed the Capitol to "rally the southerners," one participant-observer summed it up, against a bill that was dangerous to them on both racial and religious grounds. Having been burned the year before on the parochial school issue, the White House shied away from any active intervention. The final vote was 214–186 for recommittal. Only 30 of 160 Republicans supported the bill. Of 240 Democrats, 84 voted for recommittal—all but 8 of them southerners.

Education Becomes a National Responsibility (1963–65)

By the end of 1962 the years of frustration had produced a pervasive pessimism. William V. Shannon wrote that "religious and philosophical antagonisms engendered by school questions are so bitter that a solution through normal . . . methods is no longer possible."[154] Congressional Quarterly concluded its review of the 1962 college aid struggle with the comment, "Several education aid backers said they felt that the entire subject was dead for the foreseeable future."[155] Yet, less than a year later, Lyndon Johnson was proclaiming that "this session of Congress will go down in history as the Education Congress of 1963."[156] And, by 1965, resistance to federal aid to education had been shattered and the Congress was preparing to pour more than $4 billion a year into the national educa-

---

[152] *Cong. Record,* Vol. 108 (Sept. 20, 1962), p. 20138.
[153] *Congressional Quarterly Almanac, 1962,* p. 237.
[154] Quoted by Bendiner, *Obstacle Course on Capitol Hill,* p. 199.
[155] *Congressional Quarterly Almanac, 1962,* p. 238.
[156] Statement of Dec. 16, 1963, *Public Papers of the Presidents, 1963–64,* p. 57.

tion system at all levels from preschool classes to graduate school—more than 10 percent of all public expenditures for the purpose.

The sudden turnabout reflected, perhaps most of all, a simple fact: people *do* learn from experience. First, both sides of the religious controversy had learned. The NEA and its public school allies now knew that an all-or-nothing attitude would mean, for the public schools, nothing. Likewise, Catholic leaders now understood that an equal-treatment-or-nothing position would mean, for the Catholic schools, nothing. For each side the question was whether it preferred to maintain the purity of its ideological position or receive some tangible benefits for its schools. The Washington representatives of organizations on both sides were, with a few exceptions, cautiously on the side of accommodation: they were acclimated to the legislative world of practical compromise and, besides, they had a common need to produce results for their members. Accommodation was supported by public opinion polls, which showed that a majority of Americans no longer opposed aid to parochial schools.[157] Second, the tacticians had learned. The National Defense Education Act had shown that special-purpose aid, carefully designed, could be enacted at a time when general-purpose aid could not be. A special-purpose approach would make it possible for the tacticians to probe, jockey, negotiate, and compromise on a wide range of separable and lesser programs, and the antagonists could move quietly away from the irreconcilable positions they had assumed—and would be compelled to maintain—on general aid.

President Kennedy sent to Congress early in 1963 the widest range of programs he could assemble—two dozen in all, mostly in the form of special-purpose grants and loans. As a device to encourage educational organizations to work together for one another's programs—in other words, to hold the NEA in line on the college aid program—all of the proposals were embodied in a single omnibus bill. Public school aid was converted from "general" to "selective" aid, to be used in areas of greatest need in accordance with state plans, but it would still be limited to public

---

[157] Frank J. Munger emphasized the importance of the public opinion shift in "The Politics of Federal Aid to Education" (paper presented at the 1965 annual meeting of the American Political Science Association); he quotes the findings of the American Institute of Public Opinion that the proportion of adults supporting aid for parochial as well as public schools rose from 39 percent in 1961 to 55 percent in 1963 and 1965 (excluding those respondents—7, 8, and 8 percent, respectively, in the three polls—expressing no opinion). Conversely, Philip Meranto, *The Politics of Federal Aid to Education in 1965: A Study in Political Innovation* (Syracuse University Press, 1967), pp. 46–50, discounts the importance of the public opinion factor.

schools and would still finance the teacher salary increases and classroom construction to which the President was committed. Kennedy asked for $1.5 billion for the purpose, to be spread over four years. Proposals for college construction followed the conference committee compromise of 1962—loans would be generally available but grants, except in the case of public community colleges, would be limited to facilities for training of scientists, engineers, mathematicians, and technicians, for libraries, and for graduate centers. Scholarships were abandoned, but the NDEA loan program would be expanded and new programs of insurance of private loans and part-time employment of college students would be instituted. With all these were combined the extension of other NDEA programs, an expansion and recasting of aid for vocational education, and new programs of aid for adult literacy training, expansion of university extension courses, and urban libraries.[158]

The Easier Measures Come First. The committees in their hearings tested the political winds on all the Kennedy proposals and made their choices. Breaking the omnibus bill into segments, they acted first on those that aroused least controversy. In June the House committee approved a vocational education bill combining some proposals of the administration with others from the American Vocational Association. Here the principle of federal aid was not in dispute—the federal government had been aiding vocational education for nearly half a century. The House Democrats had to beat back a Republican antisegregation amendment that they claimed would "kill the bill" (only twenty-three Democrats voted for the amendment, only six Republicans against it), but then the measure was easily passed, 378–21.[159]

Meanwhile, Edith Green's subcommittee, with jurisdiction over higher education, had carefully repeated the steps that had led to the easy passage of her college construction bill in January 1962. In collaboration with Peter Frelinghuysen of New Jersey, the ranking Republican, Mrs. Green again converted most of the President's proposed loan program to grants, without limitation to specific fields of instruction, and in this form the committee approved the bill. President Kennedy had made no secret of

[158] Special Message on Education, Jan. 29, 1963, *Public Papers of the Presidents, 1963,* pp. 105–16.

[159] Douglas E. Kliever, *Vocational Education Act of 1963* (Washington: American Vocational Association, 1965). Kliever centers his attention on the vocational education bill but covers all education legislation enacted in 1963; this section relies upon his careful chronology.

his acquiescence in the bill's transformation, but Frelinghuysen could not resist needling the chief executive. "Had our committee followed his advice," Frelinghuysen told the House, "the program . . . would be of little significance. . . . Apparently his advisers failed to read the testimony of experts before our committee."[160] A motion to limit the bill's benefits to public institutions was defeated, 136–62. The mood of the House had mellowed since the previous September. There was no scholarship issue this time. The NEA sent no telegrams, flew no representatives to Washington. Chastised both by its friends in Congress and by its own members —who, as one NEA official put it, "could not understand why their organization had defeated a school bill, *any* school bill"—the NEA in its 1962 convention officially softened its opposition to aid to private schools. In August of 1963 it simply looked the other way while a college bill with equal treatment for Catholic institutions passed the House handily, 287–113.[161]

The Senate subcommittee on education approved both the vocational education and the college aid bills, but with important modifications. The vocational education fund authorization was increased, and an equalization feature introduced to give greater benefits to the poorer states. Two new programs, proposed by President Kennedy in a civil rights message received after the House committee had acted, were added—$50 million for part-time employment of high school youth, and an experimental plan for residential vocational schools. The vocational education program, thus revised, was incorporated in a bill that also extended the NDEA, with increased funds for student loans, and the program of aid for school districts serving large numbers of federal employees' children (referred to as the program for impacted areas).[162] The bill passed easily, 80–4.[163] The college construction bill was restored to essentially the administration version. Senator Morse, chairman of the Senate education subcommittee,

---

[160] *Cong. Record*, Vol. 109 (Aug. 14, 1963), p. 14957.

[161] A factor in the softening of the opposition of public school organizations, as well as of Protestant church groups and the public generally, was undoubtedly the consistent position of President Kennedy against aid to parochial schools. As the country's first Catholic president consistently made clear that he was indeed independent of his church on public policy questions, concern aroused in the 1960 campaign regarding the breaching of church-state barriers died down. Munger, in his 1965 paper, observed that the President's staunch opposition to aid to parochial schools, by reassuring non-Catholics, may have contributed to a swing in public opinion which in turn made possible the passage, in 1965, of the kind of legislation Kennedy opposed ("The Politics of Federal Aid to Education").

[162] Public Laws 815 and 874, 81 Cong. 2 sess. (1950).

[163] Four senators, including Goldwater of Arizona, were paired against it.

had not planned to bring it to the floor at once, but Representative Delaney sent word from the House Rules Committee that the vocational education bill, with its all-public benefits, would not be allowed to go to a Senate-House conference until the college bill, containing its grants for private institutions, went with it. Accordingly, the latter bill was also passed, and with nearly equal ease, 60–19.

The conference committee settled the higher education issues quickly, in early November. It retained the Senate proviso that grants, except in the case of public community colleges, could be made only for facilities designed for instruction in particular subjects or for other specified purposes. But it dropped the requirement that the facilities *designed* for teaching of the approved subjects must also be *used* for them. Legislators quickly noticed, says Kliever, that "this made the Senate categorical approach meaningless" but it was "slurred over" in the conference report.[164]

The vocational education bill, however, was deadlocked on three changes the Senate had made in the House version: the equalization formula inserted to favor the poorer states and the two new programs—work-study and residential vocational schools—on which the House had held no hearings. The five House Republicans, joined by Mrs. Green to make a majority of the eleven House conferees, were adamant for the position of their chamber and Morse dared not yield on the equalization issue for fear of driving Senator Hill into his 1962 role of active opposition to the college bill.[165] The stalemate continued through November. President Johnson, in his first address to the Congress, on November 27, pleaded for action on the deadlocked bill. Then he personally entered the negotiations. Mrs. Green accepted a modified equalization scheme. She also accepted modified versions of the two new programs. The House Republican conferees announced they would carry their fight to the House floor. When the report was before the House, they moved for recommittal to eliminate the two new programs, described by Frelinghuysen as "novel, expensive, and quite possibly unwise." The new President, by a 193–180 vote, narrowly escaped his first defeat. Kliever, on the basis of his extensive interviewing, concluded that two factors made the difference: First, Phil Landrum, the Georgia Democrat who was the voice of southern conservatism on the Education and Labor Committee, stuck with his northern Democratic colleagues and carried some southern-

---

[164] Kliever, *Vocational Education Act of 1963*, p. 54.
[165] *Ibid.*, pp. 57–59.

ers with him. Second, the bill carried as a hostage the renewal of aid to federally impacted areas, which was the subject of pleas from school superintendents throughout the country.

Neither bill proved troublesome in the Senate. On December 16 and 18, President Johnson happily signed the first two major pieces of legislation produced by "the Education Congress of 1963."

Next year, the Congress completed work on aid to libraries and again renewed the NDEA. In the latter bill it increased the authorization level for student loans to $195 million by 1968, raised the number of graduate fellowships from 1,500 to 7,500 a year by 1967, extended aid for instructional equipment to include English, reading, history, geography, and civics, and broadened various other programs—thus illustrating the strategy of moving toward large-scale aid through gradual expansion of special-purpose legislation.

Then Come the Harder Measures. There remained to be tackled the one element of the Kennedy program that the committees had found too explosive to handle—"selective" but large-scale aid for elementary and secondary schools. Chairman Morse of the Senate education subcommittee saw little chance that the Kennedy proposal of 1963—which limited aid to public schools—would fare any better in the House of Representatives than had the Kennedy bill of 1961, and he and his aide on the subcommittee staff, Charles Lee, began probing for a new approach. Openly espousing the special-purpose strategy, they suggested as a new special purpose "the education of children of needy families and children residing in areas of substantial unemployment." The Congress had, after all, acknowledged a federal responsibility for assistance to families on welfare and for aid to depressed areas. Assistance to school districts "impacted" by federal activities was also long-established; would it not be as logical to assist "poverty-impacted" districts? To make the logical relationship doubly clear—as well as to take advantage of the propulsive power of the popular program for impacted areas—Morse proposed to enact his new program as an amendment to the impacted areas legislation. His bill would authorize about $218 million a year, to be distributed among school districts on the basis of unemployment and welfare statistics.

By the time Morse introduced his bill, in February 1964, the President's declaration of war on poverty provided still another context for the Morse approach. But the administration was skeptical. Preoccupied with other legislative issues, HEW neither endorsed the Morse bill nor devised an alternative. Finally, in July, Morse called a hearing. Commissioner of Education Francis Keppel agreed that "the broad, massive educational assault on poverty" required aid "on a larger scale and scope" than was contemplated in the economic opportunity bill then pending. But he found many technical flaws and administrative complications in Morse's bill and asked time for further study. Morse could only castigate the administration, through Keppel, for "stalling" and "dragging its heels."[166] But a few weeks later Keppel advised him, "The President wants us to tell you that we are for your bill. We are even going to expand it."[167]

Under the leadership of Assistant Secretary Wilbur Cohen, HEW staff had been "going over and over" the Morse bill and the questions it raised. Out of these discussions came a proposal for solution of the vexing religious issue. If the special purpose were the education of poor children, then could not the programs that would be financed be considered as benefits to children rather than aid to schools? If so, the courts would uphold extending the benefits to children attending church-related and other private schools—just as they had upheld publicly provided school lunches and bus service for children in private schools. President Kennedy might have been barred by his commitments from recommending such assistance to Catholic children, but President Johnson would not be. The HEW lawyers concluded that the proposed new programs for poor children could be classified as "child benefits." Keppel and his colleagues began exploratory talks with the NEA, the National Catholic Welfare Conference, and other groups, and even brought the NEA and the Catholics into communication. It became evident that the formula for accommodation might have been found.[168]

When Johnson sent his program for "full educational opportunity" to the Congress on January 12, 1965, it was clear that he had indeed expanded the Morse idea. Morse's $218 million (and Kennedy's $375 million) had become a round $1 billion a year, to be spent for "the special educational needs of educationally deprived children." The formula for distribution had been simplified; instead of welfare and unemployment

---

[166] *Expansion of Public Laws 815 and 874,* Hearings before the Subcommittee on Education of the Senate Labor and Public Welfare Committee, 88 Cong. 2 sess. (July 30, 1964), pp. 100–01, 96–97.

[167] Quoted by Morse in a speech before the American Personnel and Guidance Association in Washington, June 2, 1965.

[168] Meranto, *The Politics of Federal Aid to Education in 1965,* p. 70. Also Stephen K. Bailey, *The Office of Education and the Education Act of 1965* (published for the Inter-University Case Program by Bobbs-Merrill, 1966), p. 5.

statistics, the readily available census data on income would be used. The money would be distributed in proportion to the numbers of children in families with incomes under $2,000 a year. In addition, President Johnson proposed a series of measures, some old and some new—some of the latter having originated in a task force on education appointed by the President and headed by John W. Gardner, president of the Carnegie Corporation (and later to be named secretary of HEW). He asked for more aid for college construction, 140,000 scholarships a year, $100 million a year for aid for libraries, textbooks, and other instructional materials, another $100 million a year for a variety of new services to be provided centrally to supplement what individual schools could offer, funds for research and demonstration activities aimed at "educational reform," and aid to state departments of education to upgrade their capacity to administer the new and expanded federal programs.

Since the proposed aid to elementary and secondary schools was massive in amount, and since virtually all of the nation's school districts would benefit, the President's program was identified at once by all concerned as the old idea of general aid to education in a new form—a form carefully designed to circumvent previous constitutional barriers to benefits for parochial and other private school children. H. B. Sissel, speaking for the United Presbyterian Church, called the bill "a fantastically skillful breakthrough . . . in the stalemate which has been hung up on the church-state dilemma for so many years."[169] An opponent made the same point with a touch of bitterness; it offered "just enough aid to parochial schools to push away the veto of the Roman Catholic Church but not enough to drive away the support of the National Education Association. . . ."[170] And he was right. The official Catholic spokesman gave it qualified approval because "all children in need will benefit."[171] The NEA offered "wholehearted support" and found no violation of the principle of separation of church and state.[172] The National Council of Churches on February 26 officially adopted the child-benefit theory, with carefully stated safeguards.

[169] *Aid to Elementary and Secondary Education,* Hearings before the House Education and Labor Committee, 89 Cong. 1 sess. (Jan. 28, 1965), p. 784.

[170] Speech by Rabbi Maurice N. Eisendrath, Jan. 30, 1965, quoted by *Congressional Quarterly Weekly Report,* Feb. 5, 1965, p. 204.

[171] Testimony of Monsignor Frederick G. Hochwalt, in *Aid to Elementary and Secondary Education,* Hearings, p. 804.

[172] Testimony of Robert E. McKay, chairman of the NEA legislative commission, in *ibid.* (Jan. 25, 1965), p. 235.

The American Jewish Committee also endorsed it.[173] Some Protestant and Jewish groups maintained their opposition, but they represented fewer members. Organizations representing the preponderance of both Catholics and non-Catholics, as well as public school groups, had been either won over or neutralized until they could see exactly how the child-benefit theory was to be interpreted and applied as the legislation progressed.

Kelley and La Noue, in their authoritative review of the church-state issue as it developed during consideration of the bill, observe that the favorable response was influenced by three factors:

> For one thing, the great wave of public support for the President's message on education combined with Johnson's personal prestige and the overwhelming Democratic congressional majority made it difficult to criticize, let alone oppose, the bill. Second, in this ecumenical era discussion of the church-state aspects of the bill had to be undertaken with great restraint on all sides, since a considerable portion of both the secular and religious press regards exhibitions of religious rivalry and conflict as being in poor taste. Finally, although the major interest groups had been briefed about the general trends in the proposed legislation, the bill itself with all its novel provisions was not made public until ten days before the House hearings began. This was not nearly enough time for large national organizations to study the bill, to report to their constituencies, and to prepare careful commentary. The administration hoped (successfully as it turned out) to inhibit controversy by rushing the bill through.[174]

The Republican opposition saw that its main chance to defeat the bill lay in prying apart the new and extraordinary Catholic-Protestant-NEA coalition, whose members surely retained some measure of the old suspicion and hostility, by raising doubts as to how the child-benefit theory would work in practice—as to whether, on the one hand, the benefits would truly go to *all* children and, on the other, whether they would not in fact go to the private schools rather than to the pupils in those schools. The House committee corrected some ambiguities in the administration bill that raised these kinds of questions. For instance, where the original bill left open the possibility that title to equipment and materials, includ-

---

[173] Dean M. Kelley and George R. La Noue, "The Church-State Settlement in the Federal Aid to Education Act," in Donald A. Giannella (ed.), *Religion and the Public Order—1965,* Annual Review of the Institute of Church and State of the Villanova University School of Law (University of Chicago Press, 1966), p. 114.

[174] *Ibid.,* p. 119. In regard to the final point, the administration in its discussions with the key groups on the general outline of the bill had obtained a tacit agreement that they would emphasize their support of the measure as a whole and deemphasize their disagreement with particular provisions.

ing textbooks and library materials, would pass to private schools, the committee incorporated an assurance that materials would remain in public ownership on "loan" to the private schools—even though the loans might be understood to be permanent.[175]

But the committee changes still left enough ambiguities for Republican exploitation on the House floor. On the opening day of debate, March 24, Representative Charles Goodell of New York sought to drive a wedge into the coalition on the question of whether, in order to provide benefits on an equal basis to all children, the public school authorities could send a teacher to teach in a private school. He pressed the bill's sponsor, Carl D. Perkins of Kentucky, for a "yes" or "no" answer. Democratic Representative B. F. Sisk of California, a Protestant, observed that if the answer were "yes" he would vote against the bill. Republican James J. Cahill of New Jersey, a Catholic, responded that if the answer were "no" he would vote against the bill. Goodell finally pushed Perkins into saying the answer was "no." Goodell then turned to Democrat Hugh L. Carey of Brooklyn, a Catholic subcommittee member,[176] to ask whether he agreed with Perkins. Carey replied that "we do not plan to put teachers in the private schools" but "they might be in the building." Goodell concluded that Carey's answer was "yes." Perkins corrected him: "There are special services as to which I would say 'yes,' but generally 'no.' " What was a "special service," Carey had explained earlier, "would be determined by pedagogy."[177] Later, Representative Frank Thompson, Jr., Democrat of New Jersey, drafted a statement designed to establish a clear legislative history that the services "must be special as distinguished from general educational assistance" and that the decision about the special services to be provided would be left to each local school district, operating under the constitution and laws of its state. Given this kind of "yes and no" answer, and with the controversy shifted to the communities, the coalition held. Both Sisk and Cahill—and the blocs, or potential blocs, for whom they had been speaking—voted for the bill. The final tally was 263–153. The landslide election of 1964 had foreordained the outcome: of the fifty-six freshman nonsouthern Democrats who voted, every one was recorded in favor of the bill.

In the Senate, debate centered upon the allocation formula, and numer-

[175] *Ibid.,* pp. 129–30.

[176] Kelley and La Noue refer to Carey as the member "who speaks for parochial schools on the Committee" (*ibid.,* p. 124).

[177] *Cong. Record,* Vol. III (March 24, 1965), pp. 5747–48.

ous amendments were offered. But to avoid the hazards of another Senate-House conference, where so many education bills had foundered, the administration and the bill's managers had agreed to fight off all amendments, no matter what their merits, and Senator Morse, the bill's manager, had the votes to defeat every proposal. In response to the outraged cries of the Republicans that the Senate was becoming a "House of Lords" which could only delay but not amend legislation, he explained calmly that the bill could be amended next year if found defective. When the bill passed, only eighteen senators voted nay. The bill was signed two days later, in a Texas schoolhouse.

Many members of Congress saw the sun upon the horizon. Some hailed a sunrise. "We are finally at the threshold of a breakthrough," exulted Senator Ribicoff of Connecticut, the former HEW secretary. "Now we stand at the moment of beginning. . . . We have . . . finally put behind us the years of travail and controversy. We have opened ahead of us years of greatness and fulfillment."[178] "This is the precise moment in history for which we have waited," said Adam Clayton Powell. "Let us ring our bells of freedom and liberty throughout the land."[179] Wayne Morse was more matter-of-fact: "Let us face it. We are going into federal aid for elementary and secondary schools . . . through the back door."[180]

Others saw a setting sun. "We apparently have come to the end of the road so far as local control over our education in public facilities is concerned," said Howard Smith of Virginia. "I abhor that . . . but I think I see the handwriting on the wall. This is the day that the bureaucrats in the Education Department have looked forward to. . . ."[181] "Make no mistake about it," warned John Williams of Delaware. "This bill, which is a sham on its face, is merely the beginning. It contains within it the seeds of the first Federal education system which will be nurtured by its supporters in the years to come long after the current excuse of aiding the poverty stricken is forgotten. . . . The needy are being used as a wedge to open the floodgates, and you may be absolutely certain that the flood of Federal control is ready to sweep the land."[182]

The Congress still had a lone piece of unfinished business from the Kennedy twenty-four-point program of 1963—scholarships. President

[178] *Ibid.* (April 8, 1965), pp. 7531–32.
[179] *Ibid.* (March 24, 1965), p. 5735.
[180] *Ibid.* (April 7, 1965), p. 7317.
[181] *Ibid.* (March 24, 1965), p. 5729.
[182] *Ibid.* (April 9, 1965), p. 7710.

Johnson asked for 140,000 scholarships a year, averaging $500 each. This once highly inflammatory proposal was absorbed almost without notice into the new consensus—Republicans on the House committee accepted it with the single stipulation that a scholarship could not cover more than half of a student's need for financial aid. The President also proposed that the government insure $700 million in private student loans, with a proviso for federal subsidy of the interest rate—the 1959 Flemming approach to public school and college construction which the Democrats at that time had ridiculed as a "subsidy for bankers." These and other aids to colleges (for library materials and teaching, for general or "urban" extension and community service programs, and for assistance to smaller colleges) were approved in the House with only twenty-two dissenting votes.[183] In the Senate, only three votes were cast against a corresponding bill that included an additional innovation, a national teachers corps. The final bill also doubled the amount available for construction grants under the 1963 act, which the President had not requested, and removed the restrictions imposed at that time that the facilities must be designed for certain specified fields of instruction.

In one year, said President Johnson, Congress "did more for the wonderful cause of education in America than all the previous 176 regular sessions of Congress did, put together."[184]

Some Consequences. By the end of 1965 Senator Hill and former Commissioner of Education Brownell could look back upon their 1954 colloquy and agree that the question Brownell posed to the American people at that time had been decided by the people—the national "concern" for education had become, after a decade, a national "responsibility." The most important domain of traditionally exclusive state and local responsibility was now to be shared with Washington. The question would be, henceforth, not *whether* the national government should give aid but *how much* it should give, for what purposes—and with how much federal control. Already, in volume terms, the aid was substantial. By 1968, federal expenditures for education had multiplied more than ten-

183 In 1966 a $2.9 billion expansion of college programs passed the House by a voice vote, with less than forty minutes of debate and no opposition at all (*New York Times* and *Washington Post*, May 3, 1966).

184 Speech at San Marcos, Texas, before signing the Higher Education Act of 1965, Nov. 8, 1965, *Public Papers of the Presidents, 1965*, p. 1103.

fold in a decade—from $375 million in 1958 to an estimated $4.2 billion.[185] The federal share of all expenditures for education by all levels of government had risen during the decade from less than 3 percent to about 10 percent. And it is safe to predict that the trend will not be reversed: federal assistance once given, accepted, and built into the ever-rising annual budgets of local school districts cannot later, as a practical matter, be withdrawn. The ease with which the combined political power of local school districts has defeated proposals by three presidents, of both parties, to reduce the funds for federally impacted areas testifies to that.

Yet the exigencies of politics had channeled the funds into a complex structure of special-purpose assistance which, a decade earlier, almost nobody would have recommended. Before the National Defense Education Act of 1958, and afterward as well, most advocates of federal aid for elementary and secondary education sought to deliver federal funds to the states and local school districts under the broadest definitions of purpose, with no—or almost no—strings attached. President Eisenhower had sought the funds for construction of buildings, the NEA and Kennedy to finance construction and raise teacher salaries. Ironically, with all the federal funds being poured into the nation's education in 1968, very little went for either of these purposes. One of the earliest advocates of federal aid, Senator Cooper of Kentucky, raised the basic question with regard to the neediest districts of his state: "Supplemental projects, however desirable, are not fundamental, it seems to me, and in many of these neglected areas should follow and build upon improvements made in the regular, basic educational program. . . . The needs of these schools . . . surely can not be met simply by superimposing special-purpose projects, important as they are, on a foundation fundamentally weak in facilities or staff." If the pressing needs were for classroom construction or higher teacher salaries, he suggested, that is where the federal funds should go.[186]

The backlog of school construction needs, which formed the heart of the argument for aid to education in the mid-1950's, has not appreciably diminished. The outmoded buildings in the urban slums that were in need of replacement then are now ten years older; few cities have made ap-

---

[185] These figures, for fiscal years, include funds for activities classified under "education" in the functional tables of the federal budget, *The Budget of the United States Government, Fiscal Year 1969,* p. 540.

[186] *Cong. Record,* Vol. 111 (Aug. 10, 1965), p. 19114.

preciable inroads on them.[187] The question of aid for the basic requirements of construction and teacher salaries must inevitably arise again.
This will be particularly the case when and as a leveling off or reduction
of military expenditures releases federal revenues for other purposes. To
the extent that additional resources can be made available for elementary
and secondary education, will the expansion of special programs—rather
than an upgrading of established programs—be the best utilization of
the funds?

The special-purpose approach also leads, inevitably, to a considerable
measure of the very federal "control" of education that federal aid advocates have consistently disavowed. Under the Elementary and Secondary
Education Act of 1965, it is true, authority for approval of the special
programs planned by local districts is delegated to the states. The federal
criteria are general enough—the programs must be designed for the "edu-
cationally disadvantaged" and they must extend to private school children
in a form that will not constitute aid to the private schools themselves.
But even though the federal government does not approve projects, its
funds influence local school programs in directions chosen for the local
boards of education by the federal government—and where is the boundary between influence and "control"?

It is perhaps significant that those who designed the Elementary and
Secondary Education Act of 1965 have been among the principal critics
of the quality of American education. John Gardner and Francis Keppel
have not been among those who contended that, in the oft-repeated phrase
of the early advocates of federal aid, "there is nothing wrong with American education that more money won't cure." The Gardner task force of
1964 devoted much of its discussion to the need for "innovation"—in
other words, qualitative improvement. Even if the task force had not been
compelled by the religious issue to adopt the special-purpose approach,
it may be doubted whether its members would have been willing to propose general aid to the states without assurance that the aid would achieve
certain priority objectives to be defined by the federal government. In his
1965 message President Johnson was specific about some objectives:

---

[187] The *Digest of Educational Statistics, 1965* (Office of Education), pp. 46–47, shows
a total of 104,400 classrooms estimated by local officials to be needed to relieve overcrowding and another 309,200 in buildings built before 1920 or "combustible." Assuming
that schools built before 1920 are obsolete, the total need is 413,600 classrooms—or more
than the 340,000 originally estimated by HEW Secretary Hobby as the national shortage
when the debate began in 1954.

to equalize educational opportunity for the disadvantaged, to improve libraries, to do more for the gifted and the slow learners, "to put the best educational equipment and ideas and innovations within the reach of all students."[188] Two paragraphs later he reasserted the familiar phrase, "federal assistance does not mean federal control"—but will "the best" always be left to state and local definition? And should it be? It is the national interest in education that justifies, in the first place, the expenditure of federal funds in aid to schools; how will the national interest be served unless the federal government defines what that interest is and then channels its funds in a way that is designed to serve it? Keppel has said that "we cannot any longer separate our local goals from our national goals" and "our approach . . . must be unified . . . by coordinated plans." How can approaches be unified, plans coordinated, and the national goals achieved without a central influence or "control"? Keppel further points out that the 1965 act requires reporting on what the federal money has been used for—and Congress and the President will expect "not just a fiscal accounting but an educational accounting."[189] If they are not satisfied with the state and local decisions reflected in those accounts, will they not make national decisions by statute the next time funds are authorized?

Ironically, the conservatives who opposed "federal control" most strongly could have minimized the federal influence by supporting measures like the Kelley bill or the Murray-Metcalf bill which offered aid with virtually no strings attached. But they chose instead to deny the need for federal aid of any kind, and so forfeited their opportunity to participate in deciding what form the aid would take. When it was ultimately provided, it was cast in a pattern least compatible with their principles.

The decisions of 1965, in any case, took the issue of federal "control" out of the realm of ideological debate and thrust it into the area of practical administration. Some measure of federal leadership, influence, and control is now with us. Federal money is now being used, and will continue to be used, as a lever to alter—qualitatively as well as quantitatively—the American educational scene. Federal "control" has been authorized by Congress—almost inadvertently, to be sure, under the pressure of other considerations, within very real practical limits, and in a rhetorical context of hostility to that objective, but nonetheless authorized. The

---

[188] Message of Jan. 12, 1965, *Public Papers of the Presidents, 1965*, p. 26.
[189] Address to American Association of School Administrators, Atlantic City, Feb. 14, 1966.

meaning of the decision will be written in the processes of legislation and administration over the years as the product of national pressures and local resistance, of federal assertion and federal self-restraint—all as part of a new structure of federalism that is evolving, so far, without benefit of any enunciated and accepted theory.

CHAPTER VI

For Minorities, Equal Rights

ON CHRISTMAS NIGHT in 1951 a bomb was thrown into the home of Harry T. Moore, the Florida state secretary of the National Association for the Advancement of Colored People, and Moore and his wife were killed. They had been engaged in a campaign to get Negroes registered to vote. Nobody was ever arrested for the crime.

"The state of Florida for political reasons does not try to stop that kind of thing," Clarence Mitchell of the NAACP told a House committee, "and when any state in the union does not try to give protection to its citizens, it seems to me the federal government has an obligation to step in. . . ." "The colored people of the United States are tired of being studied," he said, "they want action."[1]

The Florida murder was one of a long series of racial crimes that had gone unpunished. President Truman's Committee on Civil Rights, in 1947, had detailed a series of actual or attempted lynchings in the year preceding its report—in Georgia, a mob killed four Negroes; in Louisiana, a young Negro was beaten to death; in South Carolina, a Negro youth was taken from jail, beaten, and shot; and in North Carolina, another Negro youth was removed from jail but escaped his kidnappers.[2]

Throughout the South, Negroes were systematically being denied the right to vote. Throughout the South and the border states, they were

[1] *Commission on Civil Rights,* Hearings before the Subcommittee on Constitutional Rights of the House Judiciary Committee, 83 Cong. 1 sess. (Jan. 26, 1954), pp. 45–47.
[2] President's Committee on Civil Rights, *To Secure These Rights* (1947), pp. 22–23.

segregated in schools, hospitals, public housing projects, public accommodations of all kinds. Throughout the country, hiring policies of "whites only" denied them job opportunities.

"We have learned much that has shocked us," the President's committee reported, "and much that has made us feel ashamed." Yet not since 1875 had Congress acted to lessen the shame. Indeed, when President Roosevelt took executive action to create a fair employment practices commission, Congress killed it. When President Truman sent to Congress a battery of bills to carry out the recommendations of his civil rights committee, few of his measures emerged from committee and none passed. The one insurmountable obstacle was the Senate filibuster, which killed two bills passed by the House. Negroes could protest, presidents could recommend, party platforms could endorse, the House of Representatives could act; but no civil rights bill could become law without a change in the Senate rule requiring a two-thirds majority to end debate—and the rules could not be changed because any proposed rules change, too, could be filibustered to death.

Yet the stalemate was broken. In 1957 Congress passed its first civil rights bill in eighty years, and in the next decade went on to pass three more. Even the barrier of the Senate rules could not restrain the momentum of the civil rights movement—propelled by the Supreme Court decision outlawing school segregation, by the nonviolent "Negro revolution," and by instances of white brutality witnessed by an entire nation on television. By 1966 the Negroes' right to equal treatment in most aspects of the national life was established in law—with the notable exception of fair housing legislation, which was not enacted until 1968. After that, there remained the harder problem of converting equal rights into truly equal opportunity.

The First Civil Rights Act: Historic Breakthrough   *(1953–57)*

In 1953 Senator Hubert Humphrey of Minnesota and a half dozen Democratic colleagues introduced the entire range of Truman civil rights measures, ten bills in all, but Humphrey was willing to retreat to the barest possible beginning. He offered to abandon, for the time being, any attempt to define new crimes or to impose any compulsion or enforcement upon the South and to settle for what seemed the most innocuous of all the Truman measures—a five-man commission to gather information, make studies, and report.[3] Senator Everett Dirksen of Illinois, for the Republicans, offered a similar bill which gave the proposed commission, in addition to its general mandate, a specific charge to investigate complaints of discrimination in employment and make recommendations.

It was these two proposals that prompted Clarence Mitchell to demand not studies but action. "Today the Negroes of the United States are in the position of asking for bread, and the Congress is in the position of offering them a stone," he said. "Neither of these bills would effectively remedy the basic problems in the field of civil rights."[4] But the Congress did not offer even a "stone." Two civil rights action bills did clear their committees, but neither went further. A House bill to prohibit segregation in interstate transportation died in the House Rules Committee, and a bipartisan Senate bill to outlaw discrimination in employment was never scheduled for floor debate. "The forces in Congress supporting civil rights are less zealous and resolute today than they have been in the past," commented Senator Herbert Lehman, Democrat of New York, a few months later. "Even among some of unquestioned and unquestionable good will, there is a strong tendency to put the civil rights issue aside for another day. Others are resigned to making only token progress...."[5]

Evolution of the Brownell-Eisenhower Program. President Eisenhower, in his first three years in office, asked for no civil rights legislation—and, indeed, positively resisted such proposals. Tactical considerations alone might suffice to explain the new President's position. Not only had President Truman failed to obtain a civil rights program from Congress, but his efforts to do so had poisoned his relations with the southern Democratic leaders of Congress throughout his remaining years in office. "In their eagerness to see the federal government on a new and more profitable course, the Eisenhower men had little interest in spending their energy blowing on the embers of their predecessors' disasters," observes J. W. Anderson in his case study of the 1956 civil rights bill. "At the Cabinet level, the incoming Republicans tacitly ratified their party's old compact with the Southern Democrats."[6] But Eisenhower's news con-

---

[3] *Cong. Record,* Vol. 99 (Jan. 16, 1953), p. 408.

[4] *Commission on Civil Rights,* Hearings, pp. 42, 45.

[5] Speech at Stephen Wise Award Dinner of the American Jewish Congress, Washington, May 12, 1955; inserted in *Cong. Record,* Vol. 101 (May 13, 1955), p. 6320.

[6] J. W. Anderson, *Eisenhower, Brownell, and the Congress* (published for Inter-University Case Program by University of Alabama Press, 1964), p. 1. This section relies on Anderson's research, particularly for events during 1956.

ference remarks over a period of several years suggest that his position was more than a matter of tactics; it rested also on his commitment to the goal of a limited central government—a goal he stressed in his first State of the Union message. "I believe there are certain things that are not best handled by punitive or compulsory Federal law," he said in 1954, in the course of disavowing Labor Secretary James Mitchell's support of an equal employment opportunity bill.[7] Later in that year, asked about bills to prohibit segregation in interstate travel, he commented, "I believe in progress accomplished through the intelligence of people and through the cooperation of people more than law, if we can get it that way."[8]

But while he opposed new federal law, the President was sternly determined to eliminate discrimination wherever the federal authority already extended and states' rights were not involved. In his memoirs he chides his predecessors for vainly expending their efforts on legislation while neglecting what could be done without it. "The very least the Executive could do would be to see first that the federal house itself was in order," he wrote.[9] Accordingly, he promised to use all his authority to end segregation in the District of Columbia, in the armed forces, and elsewhere in the federal establishment. He takes pride, in his memoirs, that orders to the executive agencies were "issued quietly" and "with much care to avoid making an open issue of things,"[10] but his achievements through executive action were sufficiently impressive to draw encomiums from Negro Representatives Adam Clayton Powell of New York City and Charles C. Diggs, Jr., of Detroit, both Democrats. Diggs admonished his party colleagues that many Negroes, in 1956, would support Eisenhower "unless the Democratic members of this body wake up and match the executive and judicial departments in civil rights accomplishments."[11]

But the Democrats did not overlook the opportunity that the Eisenhower view on legislation afforded them. In 1955, when the administra-

[7] News conference, March 3, 1954, *Public Papers of the Presidents, 1954,* p. 48.
[8] News conference, June 16, 1954, *ibid.,* p. 143.
[9] Dwight D. Eisenhower, *Mandate for Change* (Doubleday, 1963), p. 234.
[10] *Ibid.,* pp. 236, 235.
[11] *Cong. Record,* Vol 101 (Feb. 2, 1955), pp. 1084, 1086. For the specific achievements of the administration in ending discrimination in the District of Columbia, in schools on military bases, in veterans' hospitals, and elsewhere in the federal establishment, see Eisenhower, *Mandate for Change,* pp. 234–36; Robert J. Donovan, *Eisenhower: The Inside Story* (Harper, 1956), pp. 154–61; Sherman Adams, *Firsthand Report* (Harper, 1961), pp. 333–35; and *Cong. Record,* Vol. 102 (March 28, 1956), p. 5805.

tion declined to send witnesses to a House Judiciary subcommittee hearing on fifty-one bills,[12] Emanuel Celler, the chairman, took aim at his fellow New Yorker, Attorney General Herbert Brownell, Jr.: "The Attorney General has stated that he cannot take action in many cases because the existing laws are too weak. Now . . . it is difficult to comprehend why he would not appear and indicate his views as to what laws are necessary to effectively enforce presently recognized civil rights."[13]

As the northern Democrats stepped up their fire, events conspired with them against the President's objective of keeping the civil rights issue quiet. It was now clear that the southern states were not going to submit calmly and quickly to the Supreme Court's school desegregation decision of May 1954. Southern leaders were calling for "massive resistance" and talking of closing their public schools. The White Citizens Councils, first organized in Mississippi, were appearing in other states, as agencies of intimidation through economic pressure. In the fall of 1955 the school segregation issue came to a head in the little town of Hoxie, Arkansas, when the school board voluntarily desegregated its schools without waiting for a court order but the community—under considerable outside pressure—organized a boycott, and the schools were temporarily closed.[14] What was to become the nonviolent "Negro revolution" of the next decade began in December with a boycott of the Montgomery, Alabama, bus system by Negroes led by an obscure minister, Martin Luther King, Jr. Meanwhile, instances of violence continued to stir the northern conscience. The most publicized was the case of Emmett Till, a fourteen-year-old Chicago Negro whose body was found in the Tallahatchie River in Mississippi after he allegedly whistled at a white woman. Nobody was convicted of his murder.

In the late fall of 1955 Clarence Mitchell initiated a meeting of congressmen of both parties sympathetic to civil rights. Democratic Representative Richard Bolling of Kansas City, Missouri, a participant, wrote that the consensus favored a bill to guarantee the right to vote, as the civil

---

[12] One agency head, Administrator Albert M. Cole of the Housing and Home Finance Agency, did appear, but only to say that the administration had no position on the bills affecting his agency.

[13] *Civil Rights*, Hearings before the Subcommittee on Constitutional Rights of the House Judiciary Committee, 84 Cong. 1 sess. (July 13, 1955), p. 181.

[14] Cabell Phillips, *New York Times Magazine*, Sept. 25, 1955; quoted by Anthony Lewis and contributors to *New York Times, Portrait of a Decade* (Random House, 1964), pp. 33–36. The book was republished as *The Second American Revolution* (London: Faber and Faber, 1966).

right most difficult for southerners to oppose and as the means for assuring the Negro political power to attain other rights. Bolling presented this proposal to Speaker Sam Rayburn, and Representative Hugh Scott, Philadelphia Republican, discussed it with Attorney General Brownell.[15] By this time, Brownell and others within the administration who, for reasons of philosophy or tactics or both, disagreed with the President's opposition to civil rights legislation were already preparing to force the issue. The President's heart attack in 1955, which opened the possibility he might not run for reelection, enhanced the need for the Republicans to strengthen their political position in the northern states with large Negro populations. While the President was recuperating, late in the year, Brownell presented the question to the Cabinet and won its agreement that he should proceed with the drafting of an administration civil rights program. The President, at Key West, concurred in the decision and approved inclusion in his 1956 State of the Union message of a promise to recommend soon "a program further to advance the efforts of the Government, within the area of Federal responsibility, to accomplish these objectives."[16]

The President specifically proposed the bipartisan civil rights commission that had been discussed, and derided, in the 1954 hearings. Beyond that, the content of the program had yet to be decided. But the career lawyers of the Justice Department, who had prepared and defended the Truman administration measures, could do the staff work quickly. Some of the old measures needed to be redrafted in the light of recent court decisions, but basically the question was one of selection. On March 9, after more than two months of discussion within the department, Brownell presented four proposals to the Cabinet.

Two were organizational measures. They would create the Civil Rights Commission and elevate the civil rights section of the Justice Department to divisional status under an assistant attorney general. The other two were extensions of federal power. One, which was to be known for a decade as "Part III," would authorize the attorney general to seek injunctive remedies where civil rights were violated. The other applied to voting rights, which the Bolling-Scott congressional group had recommended be given priority. It extended the election provisions of the criminal code to cover primary and special elections as well as general elections, and it authorized either the aggrieved individual or the attorney general to sue for injunctive relief in voting rights cases.

[15] Richard Bolling, *House Out of Order* (Dutton, 1965), pp. 176–78.
[16] *Public Papers of the Presidents, 1956,* p. 25.

Sherman Adams has given an account of the reactions of the Cabinet members at the March 9 meeting and at another session two weeks later.[17] He lists only Labor Secretary Mitchell and Arthur Flemming, then director of defense mobilization, in support of Brownell. HEW Secretary Marion Folsom supported creation of the Civil Rights Commission but argued that all other measures should be left to the commission to study and recommend. Defense Secretary Charles E. Wilson agreed with Folsom and "said that the racial issue was hot enough without adding more fuel to it." Ezra Taft Benson, secretary of agriculture, urged delay. Harold E. Stassen, the foreign aid administrator, was negative. So was Secretary of State John Foster Dulles. Anderson writes that the President's personal views also collided with those of Brownell, and that a factor in the President's position may have been a protest that the Republican leader in the Senate, William Knowland of California, delivered when he read newspaper accounts of what Brownell had in mind.[18] In any event, the President deferred decision, while the White House staff negotiated with Brownell. The latter was willing to modify his proposed extensions of federal power but not to drop them to accord with the majority view of the Cabinet. As the negotiations wore on through March and into April, congressional civil rights leaders grew increasingly restive. A House Judiciary subcommittee headed by Democrat Thomas J. Lane of Massachusetts approved a comprehensive bill sponsored by Chairman Celler. To force a decision, Celler scheduled a hearing of the full committee on April 10 and invited Brownell to testify. Under this pressure the White House was forced to a decision—and decided against Brownell. The President cleared only the two organizational bills. He denied approval to the voting rights bill and Part III.[19]

Thus rebuked, Brownell embarked on a course that Anderson describes as "astonishingly bold tactics" and "insubordination."[20] The attorney general transmitted the two approved bills but left in his transmittal letter the arguments for all four. At the hearing, by apparent prearrangement,

[17] Adams, *Firsthand Report*, pp. 337–38.

[18] Anderson, *Eisenhower, Brownell, and the Congress*, p. 28.

[19] The Republican congressional leaders were told on April 9 that "the Attorney General will shortly send to Congress a letter recommending establishment of a Commission of Inquiry and the creation of an Assistant Secretaryship in the Department of Justice" (letter, L. A. Minnich, Jr., of the White House staff to Percival F. Brundage, budget director, April 9, 1956, in papers of Gerald D. Morgan [in Dwight D. Eisenhower Library, Abilene, Kan.]).

[20] Anderson, *Eisenhower, Brownell, and the Congress*, p. 43.

Republican Representative Kenneth Keating of Rochester, New York, asked Brownell whether he could put his two additional proposals into legislative form. Brownell replied it could be done "easily" and he would be "very happy" to oblige.[21] The bills reached the committee by messenger that afternoon. Brownell said he "personally" supported the measures. Pressed by Celler as to whether he spoke for the administration, he replied: "Yes. I think I am authorized to say, as the letter in fact points out, that these are submitted for the consideration of the Congress. I also say that if the Congress doesn't pass them at this session, important as we think they are, then we certainly want them considered by the Commission." The word "we" must have meant the Justice Department, but congressmen would be justified in assuming it referred to the administration. The press, reading Brownell's letter recommending four measures, which were promptly introduced, could hardly be blamed for assuming they were all administration bills.[22]

But the President was consistent. A list of "must legislation" released by the White House at the end of May contained only the two approved bills. Representative Diggs telegraphed the White House: "Are we to take the announcement . . . as meaning that you will push for only two of the original . . . proposals contained in the civil rights package? If this is true, it is a tremendous blow to the more important phases of the package. . . . It is a matter of massive importance that should be clarified immediately, or the administration subjects itself to legitimate criticism that it is insincere in its stated position." Bryce N. Harlow of the White House staff passed the telegram on to Gerald D. Morgan, the President's special counsel, with the question, "Shouldn't we categorically support the *whole* package?" and Maxwell M. Rabb, the Cabinet secretary, added, "I feel strongly that we should review this policy so as to put a better front on."[23] Their counsel went unheeded. The President did clarify his position at his next news conference but not in the way Diggs desired. Questioned about the civil rights bills, the President responded: "There were only

[21] *Civil Rights,* Hearings before the House Judiciary Committee, 84 Cong. 2 sess. (April 10, 1956), p. 19.

[22] A careful reading of Brownell's transmittal letter might, however, have made it clear. Not only were the bills not transmitted, but the letter urged their consideration "by the Congress *and* the proposed bi-partisan commission" (italics added). This language would hardly have been chosen if the administration had been recommending enactment of the two measures in the act that created the commission.

[23] Bryce N. Harlow to Charles C. Diggs, Jr., June 7, 1956 (attachments) (papers of Dwight D. Eisenhower [in Dwight D. Eisenhower Library, Abilene, Kan.] OF 102–B–3).

two that I ever did send down as legislation. The other two I said I thought they should instantly study and see whether they wanted to put them in legislative form."[24]

It was a foregone conclusion that a civil rights bill, even a moderate one, introduced in mid-April of a presidential election year could not be passed. Some Democrats, and others, saw the timing as a political plot to put the Republican party on the side of civil rights legislation and pin responsibility on the Democratic Congress for failure to pass it. As an earnest of the Democratic position, the party's leaders agreed that House approval was necessary—and there was tacit agreement between Speaker Rayburn and his Rules Committee lieutenant, Bolling, that the bill should be "unobtrusively" delayed in the House till the session's end so that it would reach the Senate too late to precipitate a "brawl" there.[25] Celler, whose own subcommittee-approved bill was far stronger than the Brownell proposals, yielded to the latter in the interest of getting action. With both wings of the Democratic party pursuing delaying tactics for different reasons, the Brownell bills (now combined into a new Celler bill) passed the House, 279–126—but not until adjournment week.[26] Paul Douglas, Illinois Democrat, made a futile attempt to bring the House bill up for consideration on the Senate floor (the Senate bill, of course, never having emerged from Mississippi Democrat James O. Eastland's Judiciary Committee), but the question was left for action by the next Congress.

In mid-October, Eisenhower for the first time endorsed all four points of the Brownell program, in a letter to the American Civil Liberties Union.[27] But the endorsement did not become an important part of his campaign. In his references to civil rights in his speeches, he put his emphasis on his administrative record. "We have erased segregation in all those areas of national life to which federal authority clearly extends," he declared. He not only ignored the opportunity to chastise the Democratic Congress for defeating his civil rights bill but actually continued to downgrade the importance of legislation. "The final battle against in-

[24] News conference, June 6, 1956, *Public Papers of the Presidents, 1956*, p. 567.

[25] Bolling, *House Out of Order*, pp. 179–80, recounts that he proposed these delaying tactics to Speaker Rayburn and, when Rayburn did not disagree, pursued them in the Rules Committee.

[26] The bill was dislodged from the Rules Committee after Bolling and his allies seized control of the committee from Chairman Howard W. Smith, Virginia Democrat, in their coup of June 1956. See Chap. 5, p. 169, above, and Bolling, *ibid.*, pp. 180–81.

[27] Anderson, *Eisenhower, Brownell, and the Congress*, pp. 134–35.

tolerance," he repeated, "is to be fought not in the chambers of any legislature—but in the hearts of men."[28] But other Republicans were not so reticent. In New York and other cities the GOP slogan in Negro areas was, "a vote for Stevenson is a vote for Eastland." Vice President Richard Nixon told his Harlem audience that if Republicans were elected "you will get action, not filibusters. . . ."[29] And the Negroes swung heavily to Eisenhower. His share of the vote, compared to 1952, rose 17 percentage points in Powell's Harlem district, 11 points in Democrat William L. Dawson's Chicago South Side district. In the fourteen congressional districts with more than 20 percent Negro population, Eisenhower averaged a gain of 6 percentage points—more than double his 2.3-point gain nationally.[30] "Democrats are digging their own grave by inaction in the field of civil rights," said Hubert Humphrey.[31] Republicans were encouraged to redouble their efforts, and Negro civil rights leaders saw the opportunity to play the two parties against each other. At last, in his 1957 State of the Union message, President Eisenhower gave emphatic endorsement to civil rights legislation. He listed the four points of the program he said "the Administration recommended" in 1956 and urged their enactment.

The Fight on the Senate Rules. From the beginning it was clear that the House, which passed the Brownell bill in 1956, would do so again in 1957 and the Senate—with its filibuster rule—would be the crucial battleground. The House did indeed pass the four-point program, with a couple of softening amendments, by a vote of 286–126, on June 18.[32] All but fourteen members from districts outside the South and the border states supported it.

The Senate civil rights advocates faced a complex procedural problem. Rule 22 of the Senate, which required the vote of two-thirds of the Senate membership (as distinct from those voting) to close debate, could not be changed through ordinary procedures, since one of its provisions exempted from any kind of debate limitation any motion to change the rules.

---

[28] Both quotations are from his Beverly Hills, Calif., speech, Oct. 19, 1956, *Public Papers of the Presidents, 1956*, pp. 175–76.

[29] *Congressional Quarterly Almanac, 1957*, p. 555.

[30] *Ibid.*, p. 808, as computed by Congressional Quarterly.

[31] Statement made Nov. 9, 1956 (*ibid.*, p. 555).

[32] Since the bill came before the Rules Committee in early April, Chairman Smith could not avoid a vote indefinitely, but he did manage to delay committee action until May 21 (Bolling, *House Out of Order*, pp. 183–85).

To change the rules required a procedure that somehow circumvented the rules themselves.

The proponents of the rules change hit upon a tactic that ran against the grain of a Senate that venerates tradition but that was the only means at hand. They contended that the Senate in each new Congress was not bound by the rules of the past but could adopt new rules by majority vote. According to Senator Richard Russell, Democrat of Georgia, the idea was first broached by Walter Reuther of the CIO in hearings in 1951, but others discovered that it had been formally proposed to the Senate in 1917 by Senator Thomas J. Walsh, Democrat of Montana.[33] In any case, at the opening of the Eighty-third Congress in 1953, Senator Clinton P. Anderson, Democrat of New Mexico, made a motion that the Senate proceed to the adoption of rules. Senator Robert A. Taft of Ohio, the Republican leader, announced that the Republican caucus had instructed him "by a very large majority," to present the view that the Senate was a continuing body whose rules were therefore continuous. It was not a civil rights question, he said, but a constitutional question. He moved to table the Anderson motion and won easily, 70–21. Only five Republicans joined sixteen Democrats against him.

But in 1957, when the Anderson bloc planned another try, the scene had changed dramatically. Civil rights organizations had been extracting pledges from senators and senatorial candidates to support a change in the filibuster rule. They were lobbying heavily among uncommitted senators as the Congress opened. Senators of both parties who felt the compulsion to enact civil rights legislation found that Senator Taft's constitutional argument had paled; moreover, the Anderson bloc had assembled respectable constitutional arguments, too. And Vice President Nixon gave them powerful aid with an advisory opinion from the chair that any rule by one Congress that purported to bind its successor was itself unconstitutional. Civil rights backers could vote their convictions on the issue with assurance that they were not violating their oath to uphold the Constitution. "A vote to table Senator Anderson's motion is . . . a vote against civil rights," Senator Douglas put it bluntly.[34] Republican Senator Charles Potter of Michigan, who as a freshman had supported Taft in 1953 but who faced reelection in 1958, explained why he had reconsidered: "The people of the state of Michigan who have communicated with me resent the fact that their senators are prohibited by a talkathon from voting on

[33] *Cong. Record*, Vol. 99 (Jan. 6, 1953), pp. 201, 203.
[34] *Ibid.*, Vol. 103 (Jan. 4, 1957), p. 187.

any issues, major or minor. . . . I respectfully remind my Republican colleagues that many of them ran for election on . . . the program of President Eisenhower. A vital part of that program is the proposed legislation dealing with civil rights. I say to my colleagues that they will never have an opportunity to vote on a civil rights measure in the Senate unless rule 22 is changed."[35]

But the leaders of both parties assured them otherwise. The Republican leader, Senator Knowland, promised that if the Anderson motion were defeated, he would sponsor a change in rule 22 to reduce the majority required for cloture to two-thirds of the number of senators present and voting. Then the Democratic leader, Lyndon Johnson of Texas, delivered a passionate closing plea that defended rule 22 and, in effect, promised the enactment of civil rights legislation in spite of it.[36] He said:

> I cannot agree . . . that rule 22 prevents the Senate from acting on any subject. . . . It has been my experience that a truly determined and united majority cannot be blocked from exercising its will. . . .
> I cannot see the prudence of now opening the Senate to a prolonged and chaotic period by making a decision which would deprive us of all of our rules. . . . If we were to find ourselves in such a situation . . . I am afraid we might lose our power to act—and the loss might be more than temporary.
> I am well aware of the problems that have arisen in our country. . . . I agree . . . that effective methods should be found to solve those problems. . . . But there is no solution in abandoning a rule that was designed specifically to protect minorities.
> Mr. President, it is my belief that this Congress can act effectively on any proposed legislation that is within its legitimate sphere. . . . I have great faith in the ability of reasonable men to find a solution to any problem, no matter how grave it may be. And the solution does not require that a majority have the right to ride roughshod over a minority.[37]

Johnson and Knowland held their majority, but a switch of only seven votes would have reversed the result. The tally was 55–38 on Johnson's motion to table the Anderson resolution but the three absentees were announced for the resolution. Outside the South, the rule change claimed a decisive majority. Democrats from the North and West were almost solid against their leadership; in addition to his southern bloc, Johnson held only the venerable Theodore Francis Green of Rhode Island and Carl

[35] *Ibid.*, p. 159.
[36] Knowland had made a similar promise at the end of the 1956 session; Johnson had not committed himself. See Anderson, *Eisenhower, Brownell, and the Congress*, p. 107.
[37] *Cong. Record*, Vol. 103 (Jan. 4, 1957), p. 214.

Hayden of Arizona, Alan Bible of Nevada, and three votes from the
border states of Oklahoma and Delaware—and he lost one southerner,
Estes Kefauver of Tennessee. Moreover, eleven Republicans had switched
their votes from 1953, all from states east of the Mississippi; a clear majority of Republicans, and virtually all the Democrats, from the politically
decisive Northeast were now on record for civil rights even if it meant
altering the hallowed Senate rules. Finally, rule 22 was sustained by the
elder senators who had reached the Senate before the year 1948, when
the Truman program and the Democratic convention fight had made
civil rights a preeminent national issue. Of the fifty-six senators of both
parties first elected in 1948 or since, a majority of thirty were for the rules
change. Clearly, the strength was gathering so that, if Johnson proved
wrong and the southerners successfully filibustered once more, rule 22
itself might be overturned. The interest of the southerners in 1957 was
therefore *not* to filibuster but to accept as weak a civil rights bill as they
could get away with—as the means of preserving rule 22 as a barrier
against stronger or, as they phrased it, "more punitive" legislation in the
future. As Howard E. Shuman concludes in his study of the 1957 parliamentary maneuvering in the Senate, the rules struggle in January was
"crucial" in producing "a climate in which . . . a meaningful bill could
pass." [38]

The Senate Acts. For the Senate civil rights bloc the first problem was
to get a bill to the floor. The Senate Judiciary Committee had reported no
bill. Chairman Eastland simply declined to recognize the subcommittee
chairman, Thomas C. Hennings, Jr., Missouri Democrat, to make the
necessary motion in committee. After reviewing various alternatives, civil
rights strategists of both parties, led respectively by Douglas and Knowland (who, despite his stand on rule 22, was wholly committed to the
Eisenhower civil rights proposal), reached the conclusion that the best
prospect lay in trying to intercept the House bill when it arrived at the
Senate and bring it directly to the floor without reference to committee.
Douglas was able to enlist only ten other Democrats in thus defying their
party leadership, but Knowland delivered an almost solid Republican

[38] "Senate Rules and the Civil Rights Bill," *American Political Science Review*, Vol. 51
(December 1957), pp. 955–75. Shuman, who was legislative assistant to Senator Douglas
at the time, goes on to argue that the fight produced a climate in which a bill could have
been passed "much stronger than that which was actually passed" (p. 958).

party and the Knowland-Douglas strategy prevailed, 45–39.[39] The bill
was then before the Senate.

For the southerners the problem was to achieve the objective of a bill
too weak to require filibustering—yet to do so without attacking head-on
the principle of civil rights, which they knew commanded overwhelming
support in the Senate as in the House. Their opportunity grew out of the
extraordinary history of the bill. Since Parts III and IV of the bill—dealing, respectively, with general civil rights enforcement powers and with
voting rights—had been "bootlegged" to the House committee by
Brownell, they had never been made the subject of a full and forthright
explanation in a presidential message or anywhere else. The press had
come to refer to the entire bill as the "voting rights" bill and this mis-
apprehension had never been corrected.[40]

The opening southern volley was fired by Georgia's Senator Richard
Russell in a dramatic speech on the Senate floor on July 2. Quoting various
newspaper stories that described the bill as a measure to protect voting
rights, he condemned what he called "a propaganda campaign to deceive
the American people as to the true purposes and effect" of the measure.
"The bill is cunningly designed," he charged, "to vest in the Attorney
General unprecedented power to bring to bear the whole might of the
federal government, including the armed forces if necessary, to force a
commingling of white and Negro children in the state-supported schools
of the South. . . . The great organs of the national press chorused this
flagrant misrepresentation of the true character of the bill." The reason
that the "sweeping powers" conferred by the bill were concealed was
that millions of people outside the South "would not approve of another
reconstruction at bayonet point of a peaceful and patriotic South."[41] Re-

[39] Some of the Democratic senators who followed Majority Leader Johnson rather
than Douglas did so out of faith that, with Johnson implicitly committed to a civil rights
bill, he would find a way to bring it to a vote if they followed his leadership on procedural
questions. His reputation for parliamentary wizardry was already well established. For
example, Senator John F. Kennedy, one of those who voted with Johnson, argued that to
follow the usual course of referring the bill to committee would mean only one or two
additional cloture votes—three or four instead of the two required under the alternate
procedure. See *Cong. Record*, Vol. 103 (June 20, 1957), p. 9805. Also Shuman, "Senate
Rules and the Civil Rights Bill," pp. 961–66.

[40] Anderson puts it this way: "To get the bills through the White House, or more
accurately around it, he [Brownell] had been forced to conceal their import; and none
but a few specialists quite understood them until a moment of appalled enlightenment
was to burst on the congressional debate fifteen months later" (*Eisenhower, Brownell, and
the Congress*, p. 43).

[41] *Cong. Record*, Vol. 103 (July 2, 1957), p. 10771.

publican Everett McKinley Dirksen of Illinois responded that "seldom . . . have I seen within the frame of a single speech so many ghosts discovered under the same bed,"[42] but from that time on Russell had the civil rights forces in full retreat.

Asked at his news conference next day about the Russell statement, President Eisenhower said his objective "was to prevent anybody illegally from interfering with any individual's right to vote, if that individual were qualified under the proper laws of his state, and so on." He said he had been reading the bill that morning and found "certain phrases I didn't completely understand." He intended to ask the attorney general "exactly what they do mean."[43] Some of the Republican leaders were surprised by the President's "air of doubt and hesitation," writes Adams, but on July 9 they advised him that some compromise would be necessary.[44]

Meanwhile, Senator Douglas had also emphasized that the civil rights forces were concerned "primarily" with the right to vote. "If this right is guaranteed," he argued, "then many other abuses which are now practiced upon the disenfranchised will be self-correcting."[45] *The New York Times* editorially acknowledged that Senator Russell had "discovered in the pending bill terminology that may indeed be fairly interpreted in the way he chooses to interpret it." The *Times,* which had viewed the bill "primarily as a 'right-to-vote' bill," advised that it be restored to that form. "One step at a time," said the editorial.[46]

Finally, on July 17, the President completed his repudiation of the bill as written—specifically, of Part III. He answered "no" when a news conference questioner asked him whether he believed the attorney general should be empowered to bring school desegregation suits where local authorities did not request his aid.[47]

While Eisenhower, Brownell, and Knowland were reviewing substitute language for Part III, Senator Anderson took note of reports that it would be "substantially altered" and observed that the most substantial

[42] *Ibid.,* p. 10780.
[43] News conference, July 3, 1957, *Public Papers of the Presidents, 1957,* p. 521.
[44] Adams, *Firsthand Report,* p. 341.
[45] *Cong. Record,* Vol. 103 (1957), p. 10988. But Douglas did not speak for all of the Senate's civil rights bloc. Senator Morse described as "so much nonsense" the idea that "all that needs to be done is to give the Negro the ballot and the abuses and denial of civil rights will vanish" (*Cong. Record,* Vol. 103 [July 23, 1957], p. 12458).
[46] *New York Times,* July 11, 1957.
[47] *Public Papers of the Presidents, 1957,* pp. 555–56.

alteration would be its deletion. He joined with Republican George D. Aiken of Vermont in moving to strike it. "I take this step not because I love civil rights less but because I want to see this bill enacted and become effective," Anderson told the Senate. "If this bill is a voting rights bill, Part III has no proper place in it. It is a section of dubious parentage, of uncertain effect, and of mysterious purpose. How it got into this bill is a mystery; how it would operate is . . . a riddle. . . ."[48]

It remained for Republican Senator Jacob Javits of New York, at this late stage, to give for the first time an authoritative exposition of Part III —and, in so doing, to confirm that some at least of Senator Russell's "ghosts" were indeed real. On the very day that Eisenhower expressed his lack of support for legislation permitting the attorney general to initiate school desegregation cases where the local authorities did not ask for federal intervention, Javits was telling the Senate the bill had been designed for that purpose. "If a school board does not act, because of its own feelings," he explained, "the Supreme Court decision dictates that we should authorize an agency of the United States to act for it, if we are going to be sincere about it." Going far beyond school cases, said Javits, Part III would enable the attorney general to go into court and enforce any right to which a citizen is entitled under the Constitution. He enumerated twenty-four such rights. This section, he asserted, was more important than the provisions, in Part IV, dealing with voting rights alone.[49] If a clincher were needed, the Javits speech provided it. A majority of the Senate was not ready to approve so sweeping an extension of federal power when the consequences were so little understood—particularly since they clearly would not have the votes to invoke cloture on the issue.[50] "The Senate stands at a crossroads," said Mike Mansfield of Montana, the assistant majority leader. "One path leads to interesting—and lengthening—oratory. The other path, in my opinion, can lead to a meaningful

---

[48] *Cong. Record*, Vol. 103 (July 17, 1957), p. 11974. For a discussion of Majority Leader Johnson's role in working out what the South would accept without a filibuster, and for an intimate account of the maneuvering in the Senate, see Rowland Evans and Robert Novak, *Lyndon B. Johnson: The Exercise of Power* (New American Library, 1966), pp. 119–40.

[49] *Cong. Record*, Vol. 103 (July 17, 1957), pp. 11997, 12080.

[50] Shuman, "Senate Rules and the Civil Rights Bills," pp. 970–72, outlines the plans of the Knowland-Douglas forces to try to make Part III acceptable to a majority by modifying amendments. The plans bogged down on procedural obstacles. But once the original language had been repudiated by virtually everyone concerned, it can be doubted that the Senate would have accepted any hastily contrived substitute.

conclusion."[51] The vote for the Anderson-Aiken amendment was 52–38, with the Democrats splitting 34–13 against Part III and the Republicans 25–18 in favor of retaining it. A subsequent hotly contested amendment assured the right of trial by jury to persons cited for criminal contempt under the voting rights legislation.[52]

Vice President Nixon raised with civil rights organizations the question of whether the eviscerated bill should be allowed simply to expire. The Leadership Conference on Civil Rights, a coordinating body representing more than a score of organizations, debated that question for a full day before concluding that it should support the amended measure as a break-through that could be built upon in future years. The influence of Roy Wilkins of the NAACP, the chairman, and Joseph L. Rauh, Jr., the counsel, was probably decisive. Partisan Democrats in the group (and these included Rauh) were not unaware that if the bill died, the issue would be presented to the country by the Republicans—including Nixon —as an Eisenhower civil rights bill killed by the Democratic Congress.

Now that the bill had been restored to what most of its supporters, with the notable exception of Javits, had called it all along—a voting rights bill—they deplored its limitation. "The Senate is now conducting a wake over the corpse of the civil rights bill," said Senator Patrick McNamara, Democrat of Michigan, on the day of passage. "The defenders of segregation have won a great defensive victory." To Republican Clifford Case of New Jersey it was "the pitiful remnant of a civil-rights bill." "I shall vote for this bill," said Gordon Allott, Republican of Colorado, "but I shall do it with a broken heart."[53] Russell, in contrast, called it "the sweetest victory in my twenty-five years as a Senator."[54] "I am aware of the fact," said Lyndon Johnson in summation, "that the bill does not pretend to solve all of the problems of human relations. But I cannot follow the logic of those who say that because we cannot solve all the problems, we should not try to solve any of them. . . . The bill now before the Senate seeks to solve the problems of 1957—not to reopen the wounds of 1865."[55]

[51] *Cong. Record*, Vol. 103 (July 24, 1957), p. 12520.
[52] This provision was modified in conference, after difficult negotiations, to exclude instances where penalties were less than a $300 fine or a 45-day jail sentence. Prior to the conference compromise, Eisenhower felt strongly enough on this issue to threaten a veto of the bill. See Adams, *Firsthand Report*, pp. 342–43. Also see Bolling, *House Out of Order*, pp. 188–89.
[53] *Cong. Record*, Vol. 103 (Aug. 7, 1957), pp. 13844, 13865, 13883.
[54] *Ibid.* (Aug. 30, 1957), p. 16661.
[55] *Ibid.* (Aug. 7, 1957), p. 13897.

There was no filibuster—except for a record-breaking twenty-four hour oration by Democratic Senator Strom Thurmond of South Carolina, which was termed a "grandstand play" by his southern colleagues. The bill was passed, 72–18. Five senators from the States of the Confederacy —two from Texas, two from Tennessee, and George Smathers of Florida —voted with the majority. The vote of one of the Texans—Lyndon Johnson—and his part in steering the bill successfully through the Senate transformed him from a southern regional politician to a national leader and made him eligible for national office.

The Second Civil Rights Act: Victory For "Moderation"   *(1959–60)*

Majority Leader Johnson was only half right in appraising his, and the Senate's, handiwork. The Civil Rights Act of 1957 may have reopened no wounds—it was too mild for that—but neither did it seek to solve the problems of 1957. The overriding civil rights problem of that year was school desegregation in the South, and the bill, once Part III was excised, did not even deal with the school issue.

Fifteen days after President Eisenhower signed the bill, he found himself compelled to order federal troops into the South for the first time since Reconstruction. The soldiers enforced the integration of Central High School at Little Rock, Arkansas, that year, but the next fall Central and three other Little Rock schools were closed. When the new Congress convened in 1959, nine others in Norfolk, Charlottesville, and Warren County, Virginia, were also shut. A million student-days of education had already been lost. Encouraged by the decisive defeat of Democratic Representative Brooks Hays of Little Rock, who had tried to mediate the crisis in his city, southern politicians were vying with one another in postures of defiance against the Supreme Court. Southern legislators were competing in the design of legal means to maintain segregation, with school-closing as the last resort. An estimated 300,000 persons belonged to resistance groups—mainly White Citizens Councils, which had spread across the South from their 1954 beginning in Mississippi, and various branches of the Ku Klux Klan. By the end of 1958, church groups had counted 530 acts of racial violence in four years, including six Negroes killed, twenty-nine persons shot, forty-four beaten, five stabbed, thirty homes bombed, eight burned, seven churches bombed, one burned, and four schools bombed, including a blast at Clinton, Tennessee, so powerful that it damaged thirty nearby homes as well.[56]

Civil rights activists planned another try for Part III and some additional measures as well, but first they had to attack once more the Senate's filibuster rule. Again, as the Senate convened, debate was joined on another Anderson motion. Senator Javits used the Civil Rights Act of 1957 as evidence of the need for a change in rule 22, blaming the threat of a filibuster for the loss of Part III.[57] Majority Leader Johnson took the opposite view—"I, for one, have never accepted the proposition that the Senate could not work its will"—and cited as his "conclusive" evidence the same Civil Rights Act of 1957.[58]

Johnson and Everett Dirksen, who had become Republican leader when Knowland left the Senate, took the initiative by proposing to reduce the requirement for cloture from two-thirds of all senators to two-thirds of those present and voting[59]—a concession that opponents of the filibuster regarded as virtually meaningless on any crucial issue when absentees would be few or none at all. But with this concession, the leadership proved stronger on the question of adopting new rules than it had been two years earlier. Of the sixteen new nonsouthern Democrats, on whom the rules change advocates had been counting, eight voted with Johnson; all had been importuned on the issue by the leadership, and the newcomers were especially vulnerable to the "Johnson treatment" because they had not yet been assigned to committees. In addition, six other Democrats, five of them from the mountain states, switched to Johnson. The result was a 60–36 vote against the Anderson motion.

Three Competing Approaches. As soon as the rules fight was out of the way, Johnson stepped forward to assume personal leadership of a drive for civil rights legislation. While the Johnson bill can be characterized as mild, he nevertheless became the first southern member of Congress since

[56] Report compiled by the southeast office of the American Friends Service Committee, the department of racial and cultural relations of the National Council of Churches, and the Southern Regional Council; inserted by Senator Javits in *ibid.*, Vol. 105 (June 17, 1959), pp. 11024–25.

[57] *Ibid.* (Jan. 8, 1959), pp. 125–26.

[58] *Ibid.* (Jan. 12, 1959), p. 493.

[59] The proposal also eliminated the provision of rule 22 that had exempted rules change resolutions from cloture under any circumstances and provided that the Senate rules would thereafter continue from one Congress to another. However, under the Nixon advisory opinion, the latter provision would be unconstitutional and the Senate could by majority vote so hold.

Reconstruction to sponsor a major civil rights bill of any kind. His measure included four provisions: to create a community relations service to mediate in tension-torn communities, to extend the life of the Civil Rights Commission, to outlaw transportation of explosives across state lines for purposes of bombing or intimidation, and to grant the attorney general subpoena powers in voting rights cases.[60]

In introducing his bill, he denounced "punitive legislation" and stressed the community relations service as embodying the alternative approach of conciliation:

> There is no question involved of the right of the majority to govern. We all concede that. The only thing at stake is whether the majority shall have an unrestricted right to govern.
>
> On this issue, I believe the American answer is no. . . .
>
> For many years, I have had the feeling that the inability to secure action on civil rights is due to the fact that the problem is being approached from the wrong direction. It is being pushed in a manner which the American people will not buy.
>
> Far too many of the measures that are proposed are efforts to punish people for the sins of their fathers. There is in many of the proposals an underlying tone almost of blood guilt.
>
> . . . Punitive legislation may satisfy the souls of those who feel outraged. But it aggravates, not heals, the gaping wounds.
>
> . . . The outward manifestations of tolerance can be enforced by guns, clubs, and bayonets. But understanding does not exist until the people themselves will it to exist.
>
> The conciliator would perform the most important of all services—keep people in communication with each other. And I have a deep and abiding faith in the ability of people to solve any problem—so long as they are in communication.
>
> Mr. President, I can sympathize with those who feel that everything should be done at once—or nothing. . . . Rome was not built in a day. And compared to the promotion of human understanding, the building of Rome was a minor and relatively simple job.[61]

Senator Douglas answered nine days later:

> . . . Conciliation that has no stated purpose to bring compliance with the Constitution and the law of the land or a cessation of the denials of constitutional rights will have a very limited utility, if any, in the school situation. And it is there that we find such pressing challenges to law and order, and to national leadership.

[60] Senator Sam J. Ervin, Democrat of North Carolina, had earlier joined John F. Kennedy as a cosponsor of an antibombing bill.

[61] *Cong. Record*, Vol. 105 (Jan. 20, 1959), pp. 875–77.

Peaceful relations among citizens . . . are obviously desirable in every community. But the Supreme Court has properly pointed out that this is not the only essential objective or indeed the primary one. . . .

Indeed, if the conciliation is free to try to maintain peaceful relations which in fact violate the constitutional principles, it may set back the progress of desegregation. . . .

In the so-called conciliation proposal we have neutrality toward the fourteenth amendment as the guiding principle. . . . To be neutral on such a central point of national policy is not a compromise. Instead, it is a surrender. . . . Congress must not be concerned merely with disruptions of the peace. Congress must also be concerned with denial of rights; and it must be concerned with equal justice under the law. . . .

The test of the filibuster rule will not be whether some noncontroversial, ineffective measure—dressed up and disguised as a civil rights bill, but ignoring the primary problems of desegregation—may be passed. The real test of Senate rule 22 will be whether some meaningful bill like a carefully drafted Part 3 . . . can get past the obstacle of prolonged debate . . . or the threat of such debate.[62]

Douglas and sixteen colleagues put in a bill dealing directly with school desegregation. It endorsed the Supreme Court decision as the law of the land, and authorized the secretary of HEW to provide both technical assistance and funds to facilitate desegregation and to initiate desegregation plans where conciliation, assistance, and other measures failed. And it again proposed the old Part III authority for the attorney general to initiate suits to safeguard civil rights.

President Eisenhower, meanwhile, had repeatedly made clear his skepticism about the possibility of changing "the hearts and minds of men" through legislation.[63] Asked at his first 1959 news conference, on January 14, whether Congress should pass legislation dealing specifically with school segregation, he replied:

I think when we get into the field of law, here we must be very careful. I do believe in the law concerning voting, and I think we should have whatever correctives are necessary in the law in order to make certain that a qualified citizen's privilege of voting is not taken away from him for such inconsequential things as race, or creed, or origin. That to my mind is the first thing to do.

Now, when we get the Federal Government working by law in things that are known to be primarily State, we run into difficulties. One of them is the closing of schools. To my mind this is tragic. . . .

[62] *Ibid.* (Jan. 29, 1959), pp. 1367–68.
[63] See his comments of Oct. 3, 1957, *Public Papers of the Presidents, 1957*, p. 707; March 26, July 2, Aug. 6, Aug. 20, and Aug. 27, 1958, *Public Papers of the Presidents, 1958*, pp. 238, 514, 588, 626, 647.

So I would say, first, I would like to see this problem of voting solved with whatever laws may be necessary. I would like to see extended the life of the Civil Rights Commission. I would like to see power more clearcut to make certain that they can examine into the difficulties about voting, the bars to it, and to get some kind of procedures that will make this privilege stand so it will not be violated. And if this is done, it is my belief that now voters themselves—local voters, State voters, and national voters—will have a greater and finer opportunity to proceed with, you might say, the proper observance of their other rights.

But I do say that until all of us take again as a standard, a standard of living by the concepts of the Constitution, and try by our teaching, our example, our beliefs, expressed convictions—we are not going to get too far just by laws that operate specifically upon a State-supported activity because, as I say, if the State ceases that activity, then what do we do? That, to my mind, is a problem that takes time, dedication, but I do say this: it must be solved.[64]

Accordingly, the President rejected a proposal by the attorney general for a modified Part III. When the administration bill was sent to Capitol Hill, on February 5, its proposals to deal with school desegregation contained only financial and technical assistance to state and local agencies to help them make the adjustments required by desegregation. The President proposed to define as a federal offense the use of force or threats of force to obstruct court orders in school desegregation cases.[65] He asked for an antibombing provision, which would give the Federal Bureau of Investigation additional investigative authority by making flight across state lines to avoid detention or prosecution for bombings of schools and churches a federal crime.[66] In regard to voting, he requested legislation requiring local authorities to preserve federal election records and empowering the attorney general to inspect them. He also requested extension of the life of the Civil Rights Commission and creation by statute of the Commission on Equal Job Opportunity under Government Contracts, which had been established by executive order and was headed by Vice President Nixon.[67]

[64] Answers to questions at National Press Club, Jan. 14, 1959, *Public Papers of the Presidents, 1959*, pp. 22–23. Anthony Lewis attributes the slowdown in initiation of desegregation by school boards to the President's attitude, noting that both judges and school officials respond to "the mood of Washington." In the last three years of the Eisenhower administration, only 49 school districts desegregated (Lewis, *Portrait of a Decade*, p. 119).

[65] Before passage, this provision was broadened to cover all court orders.

[66] Before passage, this provision was broadened to cover all racial bombings and to outlaw the interstate transportation of explosives for use in such bombings.

[67] Special Message to Congress, Feb. 5, 1959, *Public Papers of the Presidents, 1959*, pp. 164–67.

A Year of Procedural Travail. In the House, Chairman Celler of the Judiciary Committee moved promptly. He referred all civil rights measures to a subcommittee headed by himself—a subcommittee that southern congressmen charged had been "stacked."[68] When hearings closed in May, the subcommittee approved a measure combining the administration bill, which had been introduced by the ranking Republican, William M. McCulloch of Ohio, with a Part III from Celler's own bill. But if the subcommittee were "stacked," the full committee, nearly half of whose Democratic members were southerners, was not. It removed not only Part III but two of the provisions of the Eisenhower bill—the technical and financial aid to desegregating school districts and the statutory authority for Vice President Nixon's committee on government contracts, the latter deletion being attributed in part to a Democratic desire not to build Nixon's stature. The truncated bill then went to the Rules Committee. In Berman's words, "a stone wall was promptly erected. It soon became apparent that the chairman did not even intend that the committee should meet and discuss the matter."[69] Celler promptly filed a discharge petition to release the bill from the committee, and signatures were still being sought when Congress adjourned.

The Senate hearings likewise extended into May, but after they closed the Hennings subcommittee was unable to take action throughout May and June. Southern members absented themselves, one member was ill, and the other members had difficulty maintaining a quorum. During May and June, five scheduled meetings had to be canceled.[70]

On July 1, Javits took the floor to call attention to "the alarming lack of time now left" and fix the blame on the Democratic leadership. Johnson in his turn blamed the Republican senators who had failed to attend subcommittee meetings, and Hennings pointed the finger at President Eisenhower, suggesting that "a strong statement or two" from him would help.[71] The latest Eisenhower statement had again disparaged legislation. "I happen to be one of those people who has very little faith in the ability of statutory law to change the human heart, or to eliminate prejudice," the President had said.[72]

[68] See Daniel M. Berman, *A Bill Becomes a Law: The Civil Rights Act of 1960* (Macmillan, 1962), p. 13. Berman's case study is relied upon for the chronology in this section.

[69] *Ibid.*, p. 22.

[70] Chairman Hennings inserted a chronology of his tribulations in *Cong. Record*, Vol. 105 (July 1, 1959), p. 12401.

[71] *Ibid.*, pp. 12388–95.

[72] *Public Papers of the Presidents, 1959*, pp. 447–48.

Finally, on July 15, Hennings was able to report a limited bill from subcommittee but then ran into a filibuster in the full committee, which civil rights supporters discovered had no cloture rule.[73] Both Hennings and Kenneth Keating, New York Republican, announced they would seek to initiate the legislation on the Senate floor by amending a bill on the calendar—since the Senate has no rule of germaneness. Keating selected a peanut bill of particular interest to the South, Hennings a minor measure, but neither was called up for action. Newspapers began to speculate that Johnson would fulfill his promise of a civil rights bill by enacting a "token" measure. "We urge the friends of civil rights not to be stampeded into accepting a token civil rights bill," the Leadership Conference on Civil Rights telegraphed its Senate supporters.[74] Finally, just before adjournment, Johnson resolved the deadlock by obtaining a suspension of the rules to extend the Civil Rights Commission and announcing that on February 15, 1960, a civil rights bill would somehow reach the Senate floor. Minority Leader Dirksen indicated that he would cooperate.

A New Issue: Federal Registration of Voters. The Civil Rights Act of 1957, designed and defended as a voting rights law, had not by 1959 added a single southern Negro to the voting rolls. But if the voting rights provisions had less impact than expected, another section of the 1957 act—the one creating the Civil Rights Commission—had far more than had been anticipated. Discounted by action-minded civil rights advocates as a mere study group—and one that would be immobilized by its three-to-three division between northern and southern members[75]—the commission in hearings and in its first report, in September 1959, dramatically exposed the facts about voting discrimination in some southern states.

In Lowndes County, Alabama, not one of the county's 15,000 Negroes was a registered voter; in Wilcox County, not one of 18,500; in Bullock County, 5 of 11,000; in Dallas County, 163 of 18,000. The varied means by which Negroes had been intimidated in these and other counties to keep them from applying, and the pretexts used by election officials to reject those who did apply, were detailed in the commission's report with

---

[73] The techniques of delay used by the southerners, principally the filibuster, are detailed in Berman, *A Bill Becomes a Law,* pp. 30–31. They are also alluded to by committee members in a discussion on the Senate floor, *Cong. Record,* Vol. 105 (Aug. 19, 1959), p. 16308.

[74] Letter inserted in *Cong. Record,* Vol. 105 (Sept. 4, 1959), pp. 18048, 18230–31.

[75] See Senator Douglas' remarks on Senate floor, *ibid.* (Jan. 29, 1959), p. 1367.

names, dates, and places.[76] Moreover, in Lowndes, Wilcox, and Dallas counties the commission had encountered "repeated obstructions and delays" that prevented access to the voting records.[77] And Alabama had just passed legislation by a unanimous vote of both houses authorizing registrars to destroy within thirty days the applications and questionnaires of rejected applicants for registration.

In Louisiana, four parishes with large Negro populations had no Negro registered voters; five others had fewer than 100. Moreover, Louisiana officials had been systematically removing Negro voters from the rolls: between 1950 and 1959 the proportion of Negroes of voting age registered to vote had dropped from about 30 percent to 13 percent. Louisiana dramatized its intransigence by obtaining a court order enjoining a commission hearing in that state.[78]

"Some method must be found," five of the six commission members concluded, "by which a federal officer is empowered to register voters for federal elections. . . ."[79] They recommended legislation authorizing appointment of federal registrars to enroll voters in cases where the Civil Rights Commission certified that complaints of discrimination were valid.

The three northern members of the commission went so far as to propose a constitutional amendment that would outlaw all qualifications for voting except age, length of residence, and freedom from legal confinement, but on this suggestion all three southerners dissented.[80]

It should have been clear, from the 1956 election-year experience, that before 1960 was past the Democrats and Republicans would be vying for civil rights credit, yet the administration did not embrace the proposal of its own commission. The President, in a pallid civil rights section in his 1960 State of the Union message, reendorsed his 1959 bill with a recommendation that the commission's proposals also be "seriously considered." But a few days later he told a news conference that what he was really interested in was his 1959 proposals. "Let's get this bill already proposed

---

[76] *Report of the United States Commission on Civil Rights* (1959). See pp. 69–97 for description of situation in Alabama.

[77] Among those participating in the procedural delays was Circuit Judge George C. Wallace, who was elected governor at the next election, in 1962. The commission said Wallace had played "an elaborate game of hide and seek" with voting records and had threatened to "lock up" agents of the commission if they came to get the records (*ibid.*, pp. 88, 71).

[78] *Ibid.*, pp. 98–106.

[79] *Ibid.*, p. 141.

[80] *Ibid.*, pp. 143–45.

... acted on," he said; and as for the registrar plan, "I don't even know whether it is constitutional."[81]

This left the initiative to the Democrats. Senator Hennings, chairman of the Committee on Rules and Administration, which had jurisdiction over election legislation, announced early hearings and invited Attorney General William P. Rogers to testify. Rogers delayed his appearance for a time; then he came forward with a new proposal that he presented as an improvement over the commission's plan. It provided for court-appointed "referees" rather than presidentially appointed "registrars"; appointment would follow a judicial finding of a "pattern or practice" of discrimination, state as well as federal elections would be covered, and the referees would supervise the actual voting as well as the registration process. The President gave his approval. He later defined his goal as a "moderate" bill.[82]

If the administration had scored a point by improving on the registrar proposal, it was up to the Democrats to score their point by finding flaws in the referee plan and devising still another approach superior to both. Hennings and his staff, in consultation with civil rights lawyers, contended that the referee plan would entangle prospective Negro voters in cumbersome legal proceedings that would discourage their applying. Chairman John A. Hannah of the Civil Rights Commission, a Republican, joined in arguing that an administrative procedure was necessary to serve the "overriding need for speedy action."[83]

To meet this objection, Hennings presented a plan for registration of voters by "enrollment officers." As in the Rogers plan, state as well as federal elections would be covered and action would be initiated by an attorney general's suit. But once the judge had found a pattern of discrimination, further proceedings would be administrative.

"A Victory for the South." While the merits of the respective plans were being argued, the procedural obstacles of 1959 still remained to be overcome. On the day of the promised Johnson-Dirksen action, February 15, Johnson called up a minor bill to authorize the leasing of an army building to a Missouri school district and announced that the bill was open to amendment. Dirksen responded by offering as an amendment the

[81] *Public Papers of the Presidents, 1960*, pp. 27, 26.

[82] News conference, March 16, 1960, *ibid.*, p. 93.

[83] In a letter to the Hennings committee, quoted by Berman, *A Bill Becomes a Law*, p. 48.

administration civil rights program, consisting of the 1959 bill plus the Rogers plan for voting referees. Then the southerners began to talk.

In the House, civil rights activists were attacking their own procedural obstacle, the Rules Committee, through the means that Representative Celler had chosen the previous summer—the discharge petition. Organizations making up the Leadership Conference on Civil Rights launched a systematic drive to press each congressman to sign, but even though the petition had the tacit support of Speaker Rayburn, the necessary 219 signatures could not be obtained. The Democrats alleged, in a series of speeches on January 27, that the Republicans were deliberately holding back in a revival of the old Republican-southern Democratic coalition.[84] As in 1956, the political benefits would be to the Republicans if the Democratic leadership proved incapable of passing the Eisenhower civil rights program. The circumstances were right for a new organization of Democratic liberals, the Democratic Study Group, to test its potency.

House rules specify that signatures on a discharge petition shall remain secret, but any member of the House can, of course, examine the document when affixing his own name—or refreshing his memory as to whether he had signed or not. An "epidemic of forgetfulness" broke out among members of the Democratic Study Group.[85] One by one they carefully perused the document, memorizing names, and presently the list of 175 signatures appeared in *The New York Times*. The list put the onus for blocking the Eisenhower bill squarely on the Republicans; it showed 145 Democratic signatures and only 30 from the minority. "The public pressure generated by such spot-lighting caused the Republican minority leadership to wilt," wrote Representative Bolling.[86] Three Republicans on the Rules Committee joined the northern Democrats, and the Celler bill was cleared in the form approved in 1959 by the Judiciary Committee.

The bill was kept in its "moderate" mold when Representative Francis E. Walter of Pennsylvania, a maverick among northern Democrats whom Rayburn had designated to preside over the House proceedings, declared various strengthening amendments to be nongermane. On this ground, Part III was ruled out. So were amendments to restore the original pro-

---

[84] Celler had charged earlier that the withholding of signatures was directly related to southern Democratic support for the 1959 Landrum-Griffin labor reform bill (*Cong. Record*, Vol. 106 [Jan. 12, 1960], p. 310).

[85] The phrase is Berman's. For his account of the incident, see *A Bill Becomes a Law*, pp. 72–78.

[86] Bolling, *House Out of Order*, p. 209.

visions of the administration bill lost in committee—creation of a statutory commission on discrimination in government contracts and provision of technical assistance to desegregating school districts. When Celler appealed the first of these rulings to the House members, they upheld their presiding officer on the procedural question. A modification of the Rogers plan for voting referees, which the Rules Committee had exempted from points of order, was added as an amendment. The bill then passed, 311–109, on almost a purely sectional division. It received one vote from Florida (Miami), two from Tennessee (eastern mountain districts), and four from Texas.

By the time the House acted, on March 24, the Senate had been debating civil rights for more than five weeks. Johnson had ordered the Senate into around-the-clock sessions on February 29, but eighteen southerners had no difficulty in holding the floor in teams. Civil rights supporters complained, indeed, that the physical burden of the filibuster fell most heavily on them. Southerners could sleep between shifts, but northerners had to be on hand for quorum calls to prevent the Senate from adjourning. Senators slept in their offices and on cots set up in the Capitol, and often appeared for early morning quorum calls in something less than dignified attire. While the press lampooned the spectacle, the civil rights bloc was bitter toward Johnson. If at the beginning of the session he had supported their plea for an easier cloture rule, or if he supported them now, debate could be ended. Early in March, they took matters into their own hands and filed a cloture petition. The issue was not so much the bill itself—which the President had described as "moderate"—but the innumerable strengthening amendments that were to be offered, particularly Part III to enforce the desegregation of schools. Johnson argued that the cloture motion was premature before two-thirds of the senators—or enough to invoke cloture—had agreed on the contents of a bill. In his own view, that would be a limited bill:

> I consider safeguards of the right to vote to be paramount to all other considerations in this debate; and I cannot understand the reasoning which seems to say that the Senate should not pass voting rights legislation unless we tack onto it other types of legislation. . . .
> A man with a vote has his destiny in his own hands, and he can do far more to help himself than we can do to help him.[87]

[87] *Cong. Record*, Vol. 106 (March 10, 1960), p. 5117. Johnson's management of the 1960 civil rights debate is reviewed by Evans and Novak, *Lyndon B. Johnson*, pp. 220–22.

Dirksen, reminded that he had supported Part III in 1957, when it had been recommended by Brownell, justified his switch by pointing to the additional provisions in the administration's new program—those dealing with obstruction of court orders, with bombing, and with voting referees. The cloture motion did not even win a majority, much less two-thirds. It gained forty-two votes against fifty-three, although Douglas took comfort in reminding the Senate that the forty-two votes represented 60 percent of the population and 70 percent of the voters in the last presidential election.[88]

With this expression of the temper of the Senate, opponents of Part III brought it to a vote and defeated it, 55–38. The tally was close to the 52–38 margin by which Part III had been deleted from the 1957 bill, but the party lineup was markedly different. Republican support fell from 58 to 32 percent, now that the President and the attorney general were unambiguously opposed to it, while Democratic support rose from 28 to 45 percent as the result of the increase in northern and western members following the 1958 election. Of the sixteen new nonsouthern Democrats, thirteen voted for Part III[89] but their strength was more than offset by the Republican reversals.

A "moderate" consensus was now established. There were no more around-the-clock sessions and no last-ditch filibuster. When the House bill was passed, it was substituted for the Senate bill. Various strengthening amendments, one by one, were tabled on motion of the leaders. Even amendments to restore those parts of the administration bill that the House had deleted were tabled, one on a motion by Republican Leader Dirksen. When Hennings offered his enrollment officer plan, he was swamped, 58–26. "Weakening" amendments offered by southerners were defeated by even larger votes. Thus protected from major amendment by either side, the bill was passed, 71–18, in a vote paralleling that of three years earlier.[90] The House accepted the minor Senate amendments without a conference.

Senator Spessard Holland, Florida Democrat, called the bill "relatively moderate" and a "vast improvement."[91] Harry Byrd, Virginia Democrat,

---

[88] *Cong. Record,* Vol. 106 (March 10, 1960), p. 5180.

[89] The three recorded against it were Oren E. Long of Hawaii, Robert C. Byrd of West Virginia, and Gale W. McGee of Wyoming.

[90] One southern vote changed sides, that of George Smathers, Democrat of Florida, who had voted for the 1957 act.

[91] *Cong. Record,* Vol. 106 (April 8, 1960), p. 7804.

said that "in the main the result has been a victory for the South."[92]
Northerners agreed. Democrat Joseph Clark of Pennsylvania called
the bill a "crushing defeat" and added: "Surely in this battle on the
Senate floor the roles of Grant and Lee at Appomattox have been reversed. . . . But I, for one, believe we are approaching the end of an era;
that the national mood will change; that new and vigorous leadership
will arise. . . ."[93] Paul Douglas quoted Senator Eastland as saying the bill
would permit only a few Negroes to vote and agreed with him. Said
Douglas:

> The bill sets up an elaborate obstacle course which the disenfranchised
> Negro in the South must successfully run before he will be permitted to vote
> at all. At every strategic point there are high technical walls which he must
> scale, and along the course there are numerous cunningly devised legal pitfalls
> into which he may fall. . . .
> Every move to strengthen the bill, however mild, has been defeated by a
> coalition—operating with the threat of a filibuster—of the southern op-
> ponents of any legislation, of the overwhelming majority of administration
> Republicans, and of the Democratic leadership with its 12 to 15 hard core
> supporters. . . .
> We shall carry this issue to the public and be back again. . . .[94]

From the standpoint of the activists the 1960 bill dealt ineffectively
with voting rights, it dealt not at all with the old questions of employment
and school integration, and it did not touch upon a new issue—access to
public accommodations—which a series of "sit-in" demonstrations that
began in Greensboro, North Carolina, in February and spread quickly
throughout the South had brought to the forefront of public concern.

The Rejection of "Moderation"   *(1960)*

If the roles of Grant and Lee at Appomattox had been reversed on the
Senate floor in April, they were reversed once more in the heat of summer.
The civil rights forces who lost in the Senate, as Douglas had noted, represented 60 percent of the population and 70 percent of the presidential
vote. In the national party conventions there is no filibuster rule—the
majority governs. Both conventions resoundingly repudiated the "moderation" of their congressional leadership and wrote the strongest civil

[92] *Ibid,* p. 7814.
[93] *Ibid.,* p. 7768.
[94] *Ibid.,* p. 7805.

rights platforms in history. Then both parties nominated as their presidential candidates men identified with activism on civil rights.

Senator Clark had predicted that the national mood *would* change, but the conventions made clear that it already *had* changed. Delegates from not only the northern big-city states but also the plains and mountain states which had provided the Johnson-Dirksen leadership with its margin of victory were ready, in the summer of 1960, for a strong commitment to civil rights. The bayonets at Little Rock, the bombs at Clinton, and perhaps most of all the revelation in the lunch counter demonstrations of the depth of Negro feeling had transformed the issue of racial discrimination from, in Anthony Lewis' words, a "matter of tepid righteousness" to "a vital concern."[95]

The strength of the Democratic platform reflected the will of the party's national chairman, Paul M. Butler. A departure from the tradition of nonideological chairmen whose specialty under Democratic presidents had been patronage,[96] Butler had deep convictions on civil rights. In arranging the 1956 convention he had, according to custom, entrusted its platform to the congressional elders by naming House Majority Leader John McCormack chairman of the platform committee. The committee wrote a conciliatory civil rights plank, and when the civil rights forces tried to strengthen it in a floor fight, they were overwhelmed. Butler was determined that the Democratic party in 1960 would not again defeat its civil rights activists in the full view of the national television audience. Passing over the senior members of Congress, he chose as platform committee chairman a freshman congressman and former governor of Connecticut, Chester Bowles, who had established himself as a leading spokesman for the party's intellectuals. From that moment on, a strong civil rights plank was assured. In consultation with Harris L. Wofford, Jr., the civil rights specialist on the Kennedy campaign staff, Bowles drafted language endorsing virtually all of the legislative proposals seriously advanced by the civil rights bloc on Capitol Hill—from Part III to elimination of literacy tests and poll taxes as requirements for voting, to "ma-

[95] Lewis, *Portrait of a Decade*, p. 114.

[96] Butler's occupancy of the post can be traced back to the Stevenson influence. Adlai Stevenson in 1952 had bypassed the political professionals to choose a national chairman not identified with organization politics, Stephen A. Mitchell, a Chicago lawyer. Mitchell sought as his successor a man who would continue to support the reform, "antimachine" elements of the party and found him in Butler, who at the time was Democratic national committeeman from Indiana and an opponent of what had been the "regular" party organization there.

jority rule" in the Senate—and added some new ideas of his own. Besides legislation, the platform promised "effective moral and political leadership" by the President and his administration to assure "equal access . . . to . . . voting booths, schoolrooms, jobs, housing, and public facilities." The platform approved the sit-in demonstrations.

Bowles wrote what he regarded as a "maximum" draft, from which he was prepared to make concessions in the platform committee. But when Senator Sam Ervin of North Carolina, the former judge who had marshaled the legal and constitutional arguments for the South in two Senate debates, presented his case inside the committee, he found no support outside his region. Here no two-thirds vote was required to close debate, and when the votes came, there was no bloc of moderate allies from the sparsely populated states—the South stood alone. The only change in the plank was one to strengthen it, by adding a specific promise to create by law a fair employment practices commission. On the convention floor the amendments were offered this time not by the civil rights forces but by the southern delegations; some of their spokesmen were booed,[97] and when the vote was taken the South again stood alone.

In contrast to Bowles' careful control at all stages of the Democratic civil rights plank, the Republican statement became the subject of a three-way struggle that arose when Governor Nelson Rockefeller of New York revolted against what he felt was the complacent tone of the White House platform draft.[98] While the national defense plank was his main concern, civil rights was a second point at issue. When Vice President Nixon flew to New York to settle the platform issues with Rockefeller, civil rights was one of the fourteen points on which Nixon accepted revised language as proposed by Rockefeller.

At Chicago, however, a Rockefeller ally who was chairman of the civil rights subcommittee of the platform committee, Joseph F. Carlino of New York, had let the leadership of that group pass to Senator John Tower of Texas.[99] When Carlino presented the Nixon-Rockefeller plank to the subcommittee, that group rejected it by an 8–7 vote in favor of an alternate version presented by Tower. The full committee formally ap-

[97] *Official Proceedings of the Democratic National Convention, 1960* (Washington: National Document Publishers, 1964), pp. 84–86.

[98] Theodore H. White, in *The Making of the President, 1960* (Atheneum, 1961), pp. 193–205, gives a complete account of the Republican platform dispute.

[99] Paul Tillett, "The National Conventions," in Paul T. David (ed.), *The Presidential Election and Transition, 1960–61* (Brookings Institution, 1961), p. 39.

proved the subcommittee recommendation. There matters stood until Nixon arrived in Chicago and took charge. "One by one," writes White, "he summoned key members of the platform committee and their masters to his presence and insisted that the civil rights plank be rewritten to please Rockefeller and match the Democrats."[100] This was done the next day, although some concessions in language were made to the Tower draft.[101] On one of the major points at issue—the sit-ins by Negroes at southern lunch counters—the platform made clear its support of the demonstrators, as had the Democratic document two weeks earlier. It endorsed Part III legislation but only for school desegregation "in appropriate cases." It promised a federal-state program for fair employment in somewhat less categorical language than that of the Democratic platform, but it promised legislation in a field the Democrats had ignored— "to end the discriminatory membership practices" in labor unions. On Senate rule 22 it promised only a "change" compared to the Democratic pledge of "majority rule."

Whatever one may conclude about the relative strengths and weaknesses of the two platforms, one point stands out: Both documents, hammered out in arduous sessions by the elected delegates and the rising leadership of the two parties, were far more responsive to the civil rights movement than either the Republican administration or the Democratic Congress had been a few months earlier. The "moderation" of the established leaders of both parties, of Eisenhower and Dirksen, Johnson and Rayburn, was repudiated. The new era had arrived far sooner than those who predicted it in April had dared to expect. It is one of the ironies of history, however, that the final affirmation of the great national decision embodied in the two platforms was not to come until the presidency of the very man who had done most to thwart the activists' endeavors and who, with Eisenhower, most personified the rejected course of "moderation"—Lyndon Johnson.

[100] White, *The Making of the President, 1960,* p. 204.

[101] Tillett reports that in seven votes the Nixon-Rockefeller language was adopted in four instances and the southerners' language in three; he does not say, however, what the issues were or indicate their relative importance ("The National Conventions," p. 40). White, who was also in Chicago, states categorically that the Nixon-Rockefeller plank was adopted (*The Making of the President, 1960,* p. 204). Tillett says "neither Nixon nor the southerners on the subcommittee won." White reports only the southern disappointment. Judging by the strength of the platform language, it seems likely that the White version is more nearly correct and the concessions to the southerners were not of major substance.

Campaign Promises—and Legislative Priorities   *(1960–63)*

The platforms set the tone of the campaign. When Congress reconvened after the conventions, President Eisenhower challenged it to enact
those minor parts of his civil rights program it had failed to pass earlier.[102]
The Democrats were quick to condemn this as a political maneuver, in
view of the crowded calendar and the desire to adjourn for the campaign,
and when Dirksen offered the Eisenhower proposals they were tabled on
a nearly party-line vote. After some hesitation, Kennedy was persuaded
that, under the circumstances, he had to take steps to make his stand on
civil rights legislation unmistakably clear. He called his first major press
conference of the campaign, announced he was appointing a two-man
committee consisting of Senator Clark and Representative Celler to prepare a comprehensive civil rights bill embodying the Democratic platform
position for introduction "at the beginning" of the next session, and
promised to seek its enactment "early" in 1961.[103] During the campaign,
however, he placed less emphasis upon legislation than upon the responsibility of the President to provide "a moral tone and moral leadership" in
the field of civil rights.[104] Seizing upon a recommendation of the Civil
Rights Commission, he repeatedly promised to wipe out discrimination
in federally aided housing "by a stroke of the Presidential pen." He
promised more vigorous action to protect voting rights, under the 1957
and 1960 laws, and to eliminate discrimination by government contrac-
tors.

In midcampaign Kennedy had an opportunity to illustrate even more
concretely what he meant by moral leadership when Martin Luther King,
Jr., was sentenced to four months' imprisonment for participating in a
sit-in at an Atlanta restaurant. At the suggestion of Wofford, Kennedy
telephoned the distraught Mrs. King and offered to intervene if necessary.
"In the Negro community the Kennedy intervention rang like a carillon,"

---

[102] Message to Congress, Aug. 8, 1960, *Public Papers of the Presidents, 1960*, p. 616.

[103] Statement of Sept. 1, 1960, *The Speeches of Senator John F. Kennedy, Presidential
Campaign of 1960*, S. Rept. 994, 87 Cong. 1 sess. (1961), Pt. 1, p. 72. See also,
statements of Senator Kennedy and 23 Democratic senators, and Kennedy press conference,
Sept. 1, 1960, *ibid.*, pp. 68–70.

[104] The phrase is from the second Kennedy-Nixon debate, Oct. 7, 1960, in which he
developed at some length his conception of the President's responsibilities for leadership
in the field (*The Joint Appearances of Senator John F. Kennedy and Vice President
Richard M. Nixon, Presidential Campaign of 1960*, S. Rept. 994, 87 Cong. 1 sess. [1961],
Pt. 3, pp. 149–52).

White reports.[105] The campaign organization printed a million pamphlets describing the episode,[106] and they were distributed at Negro churches on the Sunday before election. Since the heavy Negro margins for Kennedy were enough to swing the balance in several close states that determined the outcome of the election, Kennedy's strong civil rights position must be counted as a key factor in his victory.[107]

Enactment of the Kennedy campaign pledges on civil rights still depended, however, upon modification of the Senate filibuster rule. Backed by the platform, by the President-elect's past votes, and by the rulings of Vice President Nixon, who was still in the chair, the civil rights forces had high hopes for victory in 1961. When the Senate convened, Senator Anderson offered a motion to amend rule 22, but the new majority leader, Mike Mansfield of Montana, made the first test of his leadership the avoidance of what he called "a time-consuming, emotion-filled, disunifying, disrupting struggle" at the beginning of the new administration.[108] Mansfield therefore moved to refer the question to the Committee on Rules and Administration, which he headed. Kennedy took no public position on the question and privately supported Mansfield—although he was openly engaged at this time in a successful fight, on the other side of the Capitol, to enlarge the House Rules Committee. Mansfield's motion carried by four votes, 50–46, with the Democrats divided 32–31 and the Republicans 18–15. Mansfield found himself leading only the southern bloc of his party plus a dozen senators from the border states and the Rocky Mountains. Not a single Democrat from the belt of states east of the Rockies and north of the Mason-Dixon line, or from the Pacific Coast—regions containing most of the country's population—supported him. But Republicans from the Northeast were divided; enough Republicans from big-city states, led by Dirksen of Illinois, voted with Mansfield to give him his narrow margin.

---

[105] *The Making of the President, 1960,* p. 323.

[106] This is White's figure (*ibid.*). Lewis puts the number at two million (*Portrait of a Decade,* p. 116).

[107] See White, *The Making of the President, 1960,* pp. 321–23; Arthur M. Schlesinger, Jr., *A Thousand Days* (Houghton Mifflin, 1965), p. 930; and Lewis, *Portrait of a Decade,* p. 116. White's account of Nixon's "indecision" on civil rights in general, and on the King episode in particular, is on p. 315. According to White, the Justice Department had prepared a draft statement in support of King's application for release from prison, but it was killed either by the White House or by Nixon's headquarters. Nixon, in *Six Crises* (Doubleday, 1962), pp. 362–63, makes clear that he favored issuance of the statement, but Attorney General Rogers could not get White House approval.

[108] *Cong. Record,* Vol. 107 (Jan. 10, 1961), p. 520.

Surveying his prospects in the new Congress, Kennedy abandoned whatever plans he may have had to seek civil rights legislation "early" in the 1961 session. Republican civil rights advocates branded this decision a "breach of faith with the public" taken to "appease" southern legislative leaders.[109] According to his biographers, Kennedy regarded the question as one of timing and priorities, not of principle. "There was no indifference to campaign pledges," writes Sorensen. "But success required selectivity. . . . He would take on civil rights at the right time on the right issue."[110] Schlesinger puts it this way: "He had at this point, I think, a terrible ambivalence about civil rights. . . . He had a wide range of presidential responsibilities; and a fight for civil rights would alienate southern support he needed for other purposes (including bills, like those for education and the increased minimum wage, of direct benefit to the Negro). And he feared that the inevitable defeat of a civil rights bill after debate and filibuster would heighten Negro resentment, drive the civil rights revolution to more drastic resorts and place a perhaps intolerable strain on the already fragile social fabric. He therefore settled on the strategy of executive action."[111] All Kennedy said publicly was, "When I feel that there is a necessity for a congressional action, *with a chance of getting that congressional action,* then I will recommend it to the Congress."[112]

Kennedy maintained his stance for two and a half years. When Clark and Celler, having waited in vain for the President to request the bills he had asked them to draft, introduced them in May 1961, the White House disavowed them.[113] When civil rights forces attempted on the Senate floor in August to attach Part III and other amendments to a simple measure extending the life of the Civil Rights Commission, they received no White House support.[114] When the Civil Rights Commission in a series of five reports in 1961 made more than a score of legislative recommendations, Kennedy ignored most of them; he sent to Congress only a bill to prohibit the arbitrary use of literacy tests in qualifying voters in federal elections—

[109] Comments of Representative Lindsay and Senator Javits of New York, *ibid.* (May 4 and 11, 1961), pp. 7422, 7821.

[110] Theodore C. Sorensen, *Kennedy* (Harper & Row, 1965), p. 476.

[111] *A Thousand Days,* pp. 930–31.

[112] News conference, March 8, 1961, *Public Papers of the Presidents, 1961,* p. 157 (italics added).

[113] *New Yorks Times,* May 10, 1961. The disavowal came in the form of a comment from the White House press secretary, Pierre Salinger, that the measures were not "administration bills."

[114] Even without Kennedy's help and with Mansfield leading the opposition, the Javits amendment to approve Part III lost by only five votes, 47–42.

a measure that did not attract much support and was killed by a Senate filibuster—and he endorsed a constitutional amendment outlawing the use of poll taxes in federal elections, which was adopted. When the civil rights bloc moved in January 1963 to reduce the majority required for cloture from two-thirds to three-fifths, Kennedy at the request of Mansfield[115] did not intervene and the rules change was again defeated, 53–42. When Kennedy sent his first civil rights message to Congress, on February 28, 1963, it was devoted mainly to reporting what had been accomplished by executive action and the minor bills it recommended were not even all introduced before May.

During all this time, civil rights groups withheld their fire. "I am filled with wonder," remarked Republican Senator Keating of New York, "as to how so many who criticized President Eisenhower for not going far enough in this field can sit by silently accepting every excuse for this administration's glaring failure to move forward one inch toward the goal of fair treatment for all Americans."[116]

The explanation appears to lie in many factors. Civil rights leaders were sophisticated; they were no more sanguine than the President about prospects on Capitol Hill. Kennedy was accessible to civil rights leaders, candidly explained his strategy, put to rest any doubts that he was committed to their goals, and, according to one participant, "won them with charm." He "stole" Lincoln's birthday from the Republicans in 1963 by inviting several hundred Negro leaders to the White House. The President and, to an even greater degree, Attorney General Robert Kennedy made clear their sympathies with the sit-in demonstrations and with the "freedom riders" who set out in May 1961 to challenge segregation at bus terminals in the South. Where Eisenhower had refused to endorse the wisdom of the Supreme Court's desegregation decision, Kennedy did so.

Moreover, the "strategy of executive action" began to show results.[117] The President appointed Negroes to high positions and announced his

[115] According to Lawrence O'Brien, head of Kennedy's congressional liaison staff, Kennedy stayed aloof from the battle because the Senate Democratic leadership "reiterated . . . that . . . they did not feel this was of any concern to the President, that the Executive branch was not involved, and the President acted accordingly because that was the desire of the leadership . . ." (*Congressional Quarterly Almanac*, 1963, p. 373).

[116] *Cong. Record*, Vol. 107 (May 4, 1961), p. 7340.

[117] Sorensen details the administration's actions (*Kennedy*, pp. 473–82). See also the report of Attorney General Kennedy for 1962, inserted in the *Cong. Record*, Vol. 109 (Jan. 29, 1963), pp. 1385–87, and President Kennedy's civil rights message of Feb. 28, 1963, *Public Papers of the Presidents*, 1963, pp. 221–30.

intention to elevate one of them, Housing and Home Finance Administrator Robert C. Weaver, to the Cabinet if a department of urban affairs were created. The civil rights division of the Justice Department, under Burke Marshall, initiated thirteen voting rights cases in 1961 alone. The pace of school desegregation was speeded in quiet ways.[118] In May 1961 Robert Kennedy dispatched 600 United States marshals to Alabama to protect the "freedom riders" after they had been attacked by mobs in that state. A year later, federal marshals escorted James Meredith when he registered at the University of Mississippi and troops were sent to put down riots on the campus. Late in 1962, after two years of delay that vexed the civil rights groups, Kennedy issued his "stroke of the pen" order on housing discrimination (although, as will be noted later, it covered only a small part of the housing supply). Finally, the Negroes themselves had removed the focus from legislation. Senator Javits warned that, by refusing to legislate, Congress would "invite them . . . to take the law into their own hands."[119] But the reverse was also true. By taking matters into their own hands, they had lifted the pressure from the President and Congress. The objectives of the demonstrations in southern cities were immediate and concrete—the privilege of voting, jobs in downtown stores, access to lunch counters and amusement parks and the front seats of buses, removal of "white only" signs from bus terminal waiting rooms, appointment of Negroes to police forces—privileges that could be won, and often were won, without the intervention of Washington at all. The Negroes were in the streets; they were not writing letters to congressmen.

Yet demonstrations were not enough. Progress was made, but many demonstrations failed; others produced only token results. Nonviolence threatened increasingly to turn into bloody racial warfare. As long as Congress did not act to require what the demonstrators sought, the legal order was the local, not the national, order. And in southern localities, those who held the power to grant or withhold equal status—the employers, the restaurant proprietors, the mayors, the police, the voting registrars, even judges and juries—were arrayed against, not with, the Negroes. Suddenly, in the late spring of 1963, in Birmingham, it became clear—to the President, to Congress, to the nation at large—that the country could not wait for an endless series of local decisions, produced only by agony

[118] The voting rights cases are listed in Burke Marshall, *Federalism and Civil Rights* (Columbia University Press, 1964), pp. 25–27. On school desegregation, see Lewis, *Portrait of a Decade*, pp. 118–20.

[119] *Cong. Record*, Vol. 107 (Aug. 30, 1961), p. 17513.

in the streets of city after city across the South. The Negro cause demanded, and justified, a sweeping national decision that would settle the question of equal rights for all cities, for all regions, and for all time.

Birmingham—and the Third Civil Rights Act (1963–64)

"Police clubs and bludgeons, firehoses and dogs have been used on defenseless schoolchildren who were marching and singing hymns." Emanuel Celler thus expressed his outrage as he opened hearings May 8, 1963, on eighty-nine civil rights bills before his Judiciary Committee.[120] "Turmoil is a sign of birth, as well as decay," hopefully added the ranking committee Republican, William McCulloch of Piqua, Ohio.

In the preceding five weeks, 2,200 Negroes had been jailed in Birminghim, Alabama.[121] Martin Luther King, Jr., and his Southern Christian Leadership Conference had begun demonstrations on April 3 in Birmingham, the largest southern city still to maintain with absolute rigidity the segregation customs of the past. The demonstrators, mostly schoolchildren, marched daily in the downtown area demanding access of Negroes to restaurants and lunch counters and jobs in downtown stores. "If we can crack Birmingham, I am convinced we can crack the South," said King. "Birmingham is a symbol of segregation for the entire South."[122] But Birmingham police under the direction of Police Commissioner T. Eugene (Bull) Connor, the Democratic national committeeman from Alabama, met nonviolence with the force of authority. From the Negro community of 140,000, more hundreds came forward to replace those who were arrested.

No federal law was being violated. Negroes had no federally guaranteed right to eat at Birmingham lunch counters, work in Birmingham stores, or even demonstrate on Birmingham streets in defiance of local ordinances. "In the absence of such violation or any other federal jurisdiction," said President Kennedy in opening his news conference of May 8, "our efforts have been focused on getting both sides together to settle in a peaceful fashion the very real abuses too long inflicted on the Negro

[120] *Civil Rights*, Hearings before the House Judiciary Committee, 88 Cong. 1 sess. (1963), p. 907.
[121] *New York Times*, May 9, 1963.
[122] *Congressional Quarterly Almanac, 1963*, p. 336.

citizens of that community."[123] Republicans were quick to point out—indeed, had already pointed out—that the President had not asked for legislation to establish federal rights; and they had introduced bills of their own that went far beyond the President's mild proposals. "The sad part is that the administration must seek a truce, and cannot fully enforce the substantive rights for which Negro citizens are marching and demonstrating, because the administration has failed to seek legislative action which would give it statutory authority and means," Senator John Sherman Cooper, Kentucky Republican, had told the Senate.[124]

A truce was, however, achieved. By early May the business community, sensitive to the adverse national publicity, was ready to yield, and on May 10 an agreement was reached for desegregation of downtown eating places, hiring of Negroes in downtown stores, release of Negroes still in jail, and establishment of a biracial committee to mediate further grievances. But the new tranquility was shattered two days later by bombs that blasted the motel where King had been staying and the home of his brother, the Reverend A. D. King. The Negro response this time burst the limits of nonviolence. Rocks were thrown. "Bull" Connor's police met force with even stronger force. National attention was riveted on Birmingham with more intensity than in any civil rights crisis since Little Rock in 1957; thousands of vivid words and scores of action pictures flowed through the national news channels. Wrote Eric Sevareid: "A newspaper or television picture of a snarling police dog set upon a human being is recorded in the permanent photo-electric file of every human brain."[125] President Kennedy dispatched troops to military bases near Birmingham and sent Assistant Attorney General Burke Marshall to mediate. And, speaking in the South, he made the Negro cause his own. "No one can gainsay the fact that the determination to secure these rights is in the highest traditions of American freedom," he said at Vanderbilt University.[126] He also announced that additional legislative proposals were being considered.[127] During the week of May 25, according to the Justice Department, demonstrations took place in thirty-three southern and ten northern communities, and voluntary steps toward desegregation were taken in 143 cities of the South. Unmistakably, the nation as a whole re-

---

[123] *Public Papers of the Presidents, 1963*, p. 372.
[124] *Cong. Record*, Vol. 109 (May 6, 1963), p. 7782.
[125] *Evening Star* (Washington), May 14, 1963.
[126] On May 18, 1963, *Public Papers of the Presidents, 1963*, p. 408.
[127] News conference, May 22, 1963, *ibid.*, p. 423.

sponded. In the House of Representatives, 127 civil rights bills were introduced between May 13 and June 20 alone. The northern press took up the cry for legislation. "The great need now," said *The Washington Post*, "is for dynamic national leadership to tell the country of its crisis and to win public opinion to support the dramatic changes that must take place."[128] "The cause of desegregation," wrote Walter Lippmann, "must cease to be a Negro movement, blessed by white politicians from the Northern states. It must become a national movement to enforce national laws, led and directed by the National Government."[129]

Most important of all, perhaps, was the commitment of the nation's churches. In 1963, for the first time, they entered the civil rights struggle in force. Even before the Birmingham eruption, in Chicago in January, seven hundred delegates from sixty-seven major religious bodies had met in the first conference on race and religion ever held and issued "An Appeal to the Conscience of the American People." It read in part:

> We Americans of all religious faiths have been slow to recognize that racial discrimination and segregation are an insult to God, the giver of human dignity and human rights. Even worse, we all have participated in perpetuating racial discrimination and segregation in civil, political, industrial, social, and private life. . . . With few exceptions we have evaded the mandates and rejected the promises of the faiths we represent.
>
> We repent our failures and ask the forgiveness of God. . . . We call for a renewed religious conscience on this basically moral evil. . . .
>
> We affirm our common religious commitment to the essential dignity and equality of all men under God. We dedicate ourselves to work together to make this commitment a vital factor in our total life.
>
> We call upon all the American people to work, to pray, and to act courageously in the cause of human equality and dignity while there is still time, to eliminate racism permanently and decisively, to seize the historic opportunity the Lord has given us for healing an ancient rupture in the human family, to do this for the glory of God.[130]

On June 5, Republican senators met for five and a half hours late into the evening and reached a consensus that further legislation was needed to achieve the equality of rights and opportunities promised by the Fourteenth and Fifteenth amendments. "The conference crystallized sentiment in my party," reported Senator Javits, and Senator Cooper added:

[128] Editorial, May 26, 1963; inserted in *Cong. Record,* Vol. 109 (May 27, 1963). p. 9545.
[129] *Washington Post,* May 28, 1963.
[130] *Civil Rights,* Hearings (1963), p. 2011–12.

"Our party yesterday took a historic step. . . . I am proud and happy."[181] In the House, Republican civil rights activists discussed proposed legislation in a session that—with delays occasioned by southern-demanded quorum calls—lasted until nearly ten o'clock.

The stage was set for presidential leadership. And Governor George Wallace of Alabama provided the immediate occasion. On June 11 he defied a federal court order by "standing in the schoolhouse door" to prevent two Negroes from registering at the University of Alabama. The President ordered the Alabama national guard into federal service and, three hours later, the governor stepped aside. The students were enrolled, but Kennedy, who had planned to address the nation on the crisis at the university, decided to use the time even though the crisis had passed. In a speech that was in part extemporaneous and in part a Sorensen draft,[132] Kennedy said:

> We are confronted primarily with a moral issue. It is as old as the scriptures and is as clear as the American constitution. . . .
> We preach freedom around the world, and we mean it, and we cherish our freedom here at home, but are we to say to the world, and much more importantly, to each other that this is a land of the free except for the Negroes; that we have no second-class citizens except Negroes; that we have no class or caste system, no ghettoes, no master race except with respect to Negroes?
> Now the time has come for this nation to fulfill its promise. The events in Birmingham and elsewhere have so increased the cries for equality that no city or state or legislative body can prudently choose to ignore them. . . .
> We face, therefore, a moral crisis as a country and a people. It cannot be met by repressive police action. It cannot be left to increased demonstrations in the streets. It cannot be quieted by token moves or talk. . . .
> Next week I shall ask the Congress of the United States to act, to make a commitment it has not fully made in this century to the proposition that race has no place in American life or law.[133]

Counsels of Caution. The decision to ask for legislation had been made May 31.[134] Clearly the new proposals had to center upon the issue that had given rise to the three years of demonstrations climaxed at Birmingham—equality of access to restaurants, hotels, theaters, and other places of public accommodation. But beyond that, little was settled; the program could be as bold or modest as Kennedy chose to make it. To the Leadership

131 *Cong. Record*, Vol. 109 (June 6, 1963), p. 10262.
132 Sorensen, *Kennedy*, pp. 492–95.
133 *Public Papers of the Presidents, 1963*, p. 469.
134 Sorensen, *Kennedy*, p. 494.

Conference on Civil Rights, which by this time represented half a hundred organizations and had opened a Washington office, the spring of 1963 was the time everyone had been waiting for, when anything the President was willing to propose could be swept to passage on the tide of public indignation. But to those who were concerned with the fate of the tax reduction bill and all the rest of the Kennedy program, the reasons for caution were nearly, if not fully, as compelling as they had been since 1961. Initially, the civil rights groups learned, the administration was not planning even to cover all public accommodations in the new bill, and it was considering a Part III applying only to school desegregation. Through every channel the civil rights groups and their allies on Capitol Hill pressed the White House to expand its program. Their demands included a fair employment practices title, a complete Part III, total coverage of public accommodations, a universal "Powell amendment" forbidding federal aid to any activities practicing discrimination, and federal registration of voters through administrative rather than court procedures. The Kennedy program as planned was "inadequate," Representative John Blatnik of Minnesota and a dozen other members of the Democratic Study Group wired the President after Attorney General Kennedy had briefed them on the administration's plans. "All-out fights are made on all-out measures," argued Roy L. Reuther of the AFL-CIO.

When the program was sent to Congress, in a June 19 message, it was clear that the counsel of caution had, on the whole, prevailed. The President had accepted the proposal to cut off federal aid where discrimination was practiced, but he wanted such action left to the discretion of the executive branch rather than made mandatory. While still omitting fair employment practices from his bill, he compromised by endorsing legislation then pending. He picked up the proposal for a conciliation service from Vice President Johnson. But the public accommodations proposal was limited to enterprises having a "substantial" effect on interstate commerce; Part III was limited to schools, and then only in cases where an aggrieved citizen filed a written complaint and could demonstrate that he lacked the means to press it himself; and there was no new voting rights proposal. The President "was looking for a law, not an issue," explains Sorensen.[135] And the civil rights groups had to agree that, with all its weaknesses, Kennedy's program was still by far the boldest and most comprehensive ever proposed by any President to advance the cause of civil rights.

[135] *Ibid.*, p. 408.

At a White House meeting, the President and the vice president explained to the spokesmen of the Leadership Conference on Civil Rights that the balance of power in the Senate, under the two-thirds cloture rule, lay with senators from the sparsely populated mountain and plains states where civil rights had never been a burning issue and that these senators could be alienated if they felt too much was being asked.[136] The civil rights groups expounded their strategy of asking for the strongest possible measures and then compromising only as necessary. The meeting closed with an understanding that prospects for the President's bill would not be harmed, and might even be helped, if the civil rights groups denounced its imperfections and demanded they be remedied. The Leadership Conference then set out to mobilize its member organizations. Meanwhile, the President himself met with several thousand persons—religious leaders, businessmen, and such specifically affected groups as hotel, restaurant, and theater owners—in a series of White House sessions. Among other consequences, one participant relates, Kennedy "energized the churches." The southern opposition organized, too, but since the legislation would have an impact upon the legal and social order only in the South, organized opposition did not develop outside that region.

Parliamentary strategy called for action first in the House, where Celler's Judiciary Committee provided a favorable forum. The division of House Democrats was a foregone conclusion: the large bloc of southerners wanted no bill at all, while almost all nonsouthern Democrats would support the strongest bill they could get. That left the decisive voice with the Republicans, particularly McCulloch—who had said in May that he believed in a "moderate, but ever forward-moving, program"—and Minority Leader Charles Halleck of Indiana. When the hearings ended, on August 2, Attorney General Kennedy entered into negotiations with McCulloch and Halleck.

Meanwhile, pursuing its strategy, the Leadership Conference—now expanded to seventy-nine organizations—bore down upon the members of the Judiciary Committee. For civil rights legislation, Celler used his antitrust subcommittee, renamed "Subcommittee No. 5." Over the years this panel, which Celler himself chaired, had been carefully constructed as a group favorable to civil rights. None of the committee's senior southerners were members; in 1963 its Democratic majority consisted of Celler, five other northerners, and a southerner favorable to civil rights—

[136] Schlesinger, *A Thousand Days*, pp. 968–71.

Jack Brooks of Beaumont, Texas. By the end of September the subcommittee was out of the administration's control. It approved a measure embodying virtually all of the Leadership Conference's demands—extension of the public accommodations section to all state-licensed businesses, a complete Part III, a fair employment practices section, extension of voting rights protections to state as well as federal elections, and a mandatory cutoff of federal funds to activities practicing discrimination (the last of these had been approved by the administration). The southerners on the full committee, as the administration had predicted, saw that their chance of defeating any bill lay in putting before the House a bill that appeared extreme, and they rallied to the support of the subcommittee. The administration, alarmed, persuaded Celler to defer the full committee meeting. President Kennedy personally entered the negotiations the attorney general had been carrying on with Halleck and McCulloch and a bipartisan compromise was reached. Robert Kennedy took the political risk of testifying before the full committee on behalf of weakening the subcommittee bill, and Celler and three of his subcommittee followers retreated. Thus, when the vote came on October 29, the subcommittee measure was opposed by the subcommittee's own leaders but supported by an odd combination of southern opponents of civil rights and last-ditch supporters of the Leadership Conference strategy. It was defeated, 19–15. The committee then approved the bipartisan compromise.[137] But while weaker than the subcommittee bill, it was on balance stronger than the original administration proposals. Robert Kennedy called it "a better bill."[138] A fair employment practices title was included. So was a broadened version of Part III, authorizing the attorney general to intervene in any civil rights suit initiated in federal court by private parties. Offsetting these in part was a weakening of the voting rights provision.[139]

The bipartisan bill had just reached the Rules Committee when Kennedy left for Dallas.

"We Have Talked Long Enough." President Johnson moved at once to set at rest any doubt that a southern President was as firmly committed

---

[137] For the committee votes and the detailed provisions of the various bills, see *Congressional Quarterly Almanac, 1963*, pp. 349–51.

[138] Schlesinger, *A Thousand Days*, p. 973.

[139] The eliminated provision would have authorized federal referees, after a suit was filed under the 1960 act, to begin registering voters immediately under state standards in certain counties. See Marshall, *Federalism and Civil Rights*, pp. 38–39, and Alexander Bickel, *Politics and the Warren Court* (Harper & Row, 1965), p. 119.

to civil rights as his northern predecessor. In his brief address to Congress on November 27, he listed first among "immediate tasks" the passage of the civil rights bill. "We have talked long enough in this country about equal rights," he told Congress. "We have talked for one hundred years or more. It is time now to write the next chapter, and to write it in the books of law...."[140]

Chairman Howard Smith of the House Rules Committee said a few days later that he planned no hearings. Celler then filed a discharge petition, and Johnson said he would give the petition his full support. Smith responded by promising hearings early in January.[141] With unanimous Republican and northern Democratic support, the measure easily cleared the Rules Committee. The "most intensive, extensive, and effective lobby assembled in Washington in many years"—as Senator Russell ruefully called it[142]—helped the leadership and the Democratic Study Group make sure that committed congressmen were in Washington and on the floor for teller votes,[143] and with this support Celler and McCulloch defeated every major amendment and the bill coasted to passage, 290–130. In the opposition were twenty-two Republicans and four Democrats from outside the South, but offsetting these were eleven southern Democratic votes.[144]

---

[140] *Public Papers of the Presidents, 1963–64*, p. 9.

[141] *Congressional Quarterly Almanac, 1963*, p. 334. Also Jack Bell, *The Johnson Treatment* (Harper & Row, 1965). Evans and Novak refute what they call "the myth that Johnson saved the civil rights bill from slow death" (*Lyndon B. Johnson*, p. 378). They argue that the "great breakthrough" came when President Kennedy won a commitment of support from House Republican Leader Charles Halleck just before the assassination.

[142] *Cong. Record*, Vol. 110 (March 9, 1964), p. 4743.

[143] In the House, votes on amendments are made in Committee of the Whole by "teller votes" in which members pass down the aisle to be counted. To make sure that the 220 congressmen who were committed to the bill delivered on their promises to oppose weakening amendments, the organizations making up the Leadership Conference posted watchers in the galleries. Since no writing is permitted in the galleries, enough watchers were posted to enable them to observe and memorize the conduct of each congressman. This system received its accolade from Representative James A. Haley, Florida Democrat, who said that what he called "this monstrous bill" could not have been passed without the "vultures in the galleries" (*ibid.* [1964], p. 2503). Joseph L. Rauh, Jr., general counsel of the conference, commented on the organization's work in rounding up absent congressmen: "When the Tuesday-to-Thursday eastern congressmen, even including Congressman Buckley of New York, answered present to a quorum call on a Saturday, old-timers began talking about miracles" (unpublished manuscript of the history of the Civil Rights Act of 1964).

[144] This breakdown, used by Congressional Quarterly, defines as southern the eleven states of the Confederacy plus Kentucky and Oklahoma. The eleven southern votes for

In the Senate as in the House, the Republicans held the key to the final outcome—and they held it even more tightly, because a two-thirds vote to break a filibuster would require the almost solid support of senators of both parties from the North and West. Minority Leader Dirksen, who was also ranking Republican on the Judiciary Committee, occupied the central position as leader of his party's uncommitted "moderates." Initially, Dirksen had declined to support the public accommodations section of the Kennedy program, and he had never supported a fair employment practices bill that had enforcement features. For the next three months he was the pivotal figure in the civil rights debate and the focus of the most intensive pressure by the civil rights groups.[145]

As in 1957 and 1960, the House bill was intercepted and placed directly on the Senate calendar without referral to committee. On March 9, Majority Leader Mansfield moved for the bill's consideration—and one of the longest filibusters in the history of the Senate began.[146] The southerners were, as before, organized in teams to hold the floor as long as necessary, but the nonsoutherners were organized too. Majority Whip Hubert Humphrey was designated as floor leader, with Minority Whip Thomas H. Kuchel of California as his opposite number. Individual senators on both sides were assigned responsibility for mastering particular titles of the bill and defending them in floor debate. Floor duty was scheduled. A daily information bulletin was published. The senators and their staffs met daily with Justice Department representatives, and twice a week with spokesmen for the Leadership Conference.

The Humphrey-Kuchel strategy was to avoid a cloture motion until they could count the necessary two-thirds vote to end debate. President Johnson made clear that time did not matter—all other Senate business could wait

---

the bill included four from Texas, three from Oklahoma, two from Tennessee, and one each from Florida and Kentucky. One of the two Tennesseeans supporting the bill, Ross Bass, was elected to the Senate in November 1964 after defeating Governor Frank Clement in the Democratic primary. His civil rights stand was believed to have won him more votes, including almost solid support from Negro voters, than it lost him.

[145] The paragraphs that follow draw upon the careful account of the Senate struggle in *Congressional Quarterly Almanac, 1963*, pp. 354–68, as well as upon Rauh's manuscript.

[146] The bill was before the Senate until June 19. Senator Russell computed that the debate consumed 82 working days, filled 6,300 pages of the *Congressional Record*, and amounted to ten million words (*Cong. Record*, Vol. 110 [June 18, 1964], pp. 14299–300). See also *Congressional Quarterly Almanac, 1964*, p. 366, for a comparison with previous filibusters. No bill had tied up the Senate for so long a period since the Smoot-Hawley tariff debate of 1929–30.

three months, if necessary, to get the civil rights bill passed. The leadership held Saturday sessions, and met morning and afternoon, but avoided the all-night sessions that might irritate potential supporters. Once the southerners had had unquestionably ample time to present their case—and as the civil rights groups did their work on the uncommitted senators—the votes for cloture grew.

By all accounts the work of the churches was decisive. "Washington has not seen such a gigantic and well-organized lobby since the legislative days of Volstead and the Prohibition amendment," complained Georgia's Senator Russell early in the debate. "Groups of ministers from all over the nation arrive in relays. . . ."[147] Three months later, he compared "the philosophy of coercion by the men of the cloth" to the doctrines of the Spanish inquisition and observed: "We have seen cardinals, bishops, elders, stated clerks, common preachers, priests, and rabbis come to Washington to press for passage of the bill. They have sought to make its passage a great moral issue. . . . They have encouraged and prompted thousands of good citizens to sign petitions supporting the bill. . . ."[148] Douglas said "the active participation of the church people . . . is . . . the decisive venture in the civil rights struggle.[149] Religious bodies of many faiths organized in large part the historic nonviolent March on Washington that was televised to the nation in August 1963. Clergymen were prominent in demonstrations everywhere; they were among the jailed and the killed. The chief executive of the United Presbyterian Church, Eugene Carson Blake, was arrested for trying to integrate a Baltimore amusement park. The churches supplied a civil rights constituency, for the first time, to senators from the Rocky Mountain and Great Plains states where Negroes are few and civil rights sentiment had in the past been weak—and whose senators had traditionally voted against cloture motions. And despite the "white backlash" that was apparent in some primaries, there was no organized opposition to the bill in the North to offset the church influence.

Meanwhile, Humphrey and his colleagues and the Justice Department negotiated intensively with Dirksen; President Johnson "never let him alone for thirty minutes," as one White House staff member put it. The

---

[147] *Cong. Record*, Vol. 110 (March 26, 1964), p. 6455.

[148] *Ibid.* (June 10 and 18, 1964), pp. 13309, 14300.

[149] *Ibid.* (June 19, 1964), p. 14448. Joseph Rauh put it this way: "When the House Judiciary Committee members used to troop in for a civil rights vote, they met just Clarence Mitchell and me and that was a pretty weak rag-tag army. In 1964, when twenty Episcopal clergymen were standing there, you could feel the difference."

Kuchel bloc of Republican activists kept him under pressure—and also kept Humphrey under pressure not to concede too much. McCulloch and other House Republicans let Dirksen know they were not abandoning their bill. Public opinion polls showed overwhelming support for action. And Dirksen moved steadily toward a compromise. In mid-May, when the compromise was announced, it was clear that he had come far more than halfway. He accepted an enforceable title on employment practices, with relatively minor modifications: Suits would be brought by the attorney general, rather than the equal employment opportunity commission, and only in cases where he found a "pattern" of discrimination; and an aggrieved individual could not sue until he had exhausted state or local remedies. The minority leader accepted the public accommodations title with those same limitations on the attorney general and individual complaints. Explicit language was written into the school desegregation section making clear that it did not affect the de facto segregation that had become an issue in northern cities. All of these provisions, taken together, enabled senators from northern states that had already enacted civil rights legislation to tell their constituents that the bill would not affect their states.[150] The "compromise," introduced jointly by Mansfield and Dirksen, made seventy other changes in the House bill, but most were technical and minor. The House bill remained basically intact.

"An Idea Whose Time Has Come." The show of negotiations with Dirksen and the concessions made to him, however minor, won the entire center bloc of uncommitted Republicans, and the leaders were now ready to try for cloture. Now it was too late for the southerners to seek concessions.[151] The cloture petition was filed June 6, with Dirksen's name leading its thirty-seven signatures, and the vote was taken four days later. For the second time in twenty-nine years—and for the first time ever on a civil rights bill—the Senate voted cloture. The tally was 71–29. The

---

[150] Senator Russell alleged that northern senators had so written in their newsletters (*Cong. Record*, Vol. 110 [1964], p. 13309).

[151] Congressional Quarterly said flatly that the southerners committed a "strategic error" in demanding "unconditional surrender." Had Russell bargained early, he could have "extracted some teeth from the bill." Had he permitted amendments to come to a vote before Dirksen became committed, some might have carried. The southerners apparently assumed that time would be on their side, but it worked the other way. Congressional Quarterly had high praise for Humphrey's management of the bill (*Congressional Quarterly Almanac, 1964*, p. 355). For an account of the role that Dirksen played, and the manner in which he played it, see Murray Kempton, "Dirksen Delivers the Souls," *New Republic*, May 2, 1964, pp. 9–11.

opponents included twenty-one southerners, and three Democrats and five Republicans from outside the South, including Barry Goldwater. As pending amendments were then voted upon, only a few minor changes were accepted; ninety-nine amendments were defeated on successive roll call votes in six days. A motion to strike each title was defeated in turn, the highwater mark for the opposition being thirty-three votes against the fair employment title. The bill then passed, 73–27. This time, only one non-southern Democrat (Robert C. Byrd of West Virginia) and Goldwater and four other nonsouthern republicans voted in the negative. Goldwater said he found "no constitutional basis for the exercise of federal regulatory authority" over employment practices and public accommodations. "To give genuine effect to the prohibitions of the bill," he added, "will require the creation of a federal police force of mammoth proportions."[152]

George Smathers, Democrat of Florida, said the bill was being passed in an "emotional binge," powered by "the propaganda of police dogs, bully sticks and mass jailings." Dirksen quoted words attributed to Victor Hugo: "Stronger than all the armies is an idea whose time has come." "America grows, America changes," said Dirksen. "In the history of mankind there is an inexorable moral force that carries us forward."[153] To Douglas the act was "a substantial measure of atonement for three and a half centuries of wrongs."[154]

When the bill was accepted without change in the House, one more southern voice was added to the eleven who had voted for civil rights in February. Charles L. Weltner, Atlanta Democrat, told the House: "Change, swift and certain, is upon us, and we in the South face some difficult decisions. We can offer resistance and defiance, with their harvest of strife and tumult. We can suffer continued demonstrations, with their wake of violence and disorder. Or, we can acknowledge this measure as the law of the land. We can accept the verdict of the Nation. Already, the responsible elements of my community are counseling this latter course. . . . I shall cast my lot with the leadership of my community. . . . And finally, I would urge that we at home now move on to the unfinished task of building a new South. We must not remain forever bound to another lost cause."[155]

Jacob Javits, in his closing speech, had expressed a wishful thought:

---

[152] *Cong. Record,* Vol. 110 (June 18, 1964), p. 14319.
[153] *Ibid.* (June 10 and 19, 1964), pp. 14446, 13319, 14510.
[154] *Ibid.* (June 19, 1964), p. 14447.
[155] *Ibid.* (July 2, 1964), p. 15894.

"It is now clear that the mainstream of my party is in support of civil rights legislation, and, particularly, support of this bill."[156] But his party nominated for president one of the half dozen Republican senators who stood outside the mainstream in the Senate voting, while Lyndon Johnson underlined his own unflagging support of the strongest civil rights bill in a century by taking as his running mate the senator who had been the Democrats' floor leader in the long struggle, Hubert Humphrey.

Selma—and the Fourth Civil Rights Act *(1965)*

After a victory like the Civil Rights Act of 1964, some men might rest. But Lyndon Johnson's style was otherwise. "Great social change tends to come rapidly in periods of intense activity before the impulse slows," he told the National Urban League in December 1964. "I believe we are in the midst of such a period of change. Now, the lights are still on in the White House tonight—preparing programs that will keep our country up with the times."[157]

He had asked the Justice Department what more could be done for civil rights before the impulse slowed. They responded that in the field of voting rights—the one section of the Kennedy bill that had been weakened by Congress—new law was needed. The provision of the 1960 act authorizing federal judges to appoint referees to enroll Negro voters had not been utilized, except in one minor instance, and Negro applicants were still encountering the procedural obstacles described in elaborate detail in the Civil Rights Commission's first report.[158] Accordingly, the President inserted in his State of the Union message of January 1965 a general sentence urging "elimination of barriers to the right to vote," and the Justice Department proceeded to consider specific legislation.

Thus, when Martin Luther King, Jr., began his voting rights demonstrations in Selma, Alabama, on January 18, the President had anticipated the crisis that would develop. By early February two thousand Negroes, including King, had been jailed for "parading without a permit" when they marched to the Dallas County courthouse demanding that eligible Negroes be registered. King failed to open the voters' rolls to Negroes in

---

[156] *Ibid.* (June 18, 1964), p. 14291.
[157] *Public Papers of the Presidents, 1963–64*, pp. 1653–56.
[158] See Bickel, *Politics and the Warren Court*, p. 118, for a discussion of judicial reluctance to apply the referee provisions of the 1960 act.

Selma, but as in Birmingham two years before, he accomplished his other purpose—he attracted national attention. Fifteen congressmen, seven of them freshman Democrats elected in the Johnson landslide, spent four days in Alabama and reported to the House their findings. In Dallas County, Negroes outnumbered whites, but the registration figures were 9,800 white voters to 325 Negroes (up from 163 in 1959)—70 percent of voting age white persons registered against only 2 percent of the Negroes. In the adjacent counties of Lowndes and Wilcox, not a single Negro had yet registered. White applicants were helped to fill out the literacy test questionnaire but Negroes were not. Six voting rights lawsuits had been filed in Dallas County beginning in April 1961, but only in February 1965 had Federal Judge Daniel H. Thomas enjoined use of some of the more complicated provisions of the literacy test.[159] Democratic Representative Charles C. Diggs, Jr., of Detroit, leader of the delegation, quoted the mayor of Selma as stating that if outsiders would leave town, things would return to normal. "That is what we were afraid of, that things would return to normal," commented Diggs. The delegation agreed that some kind of new legislation on voting rights was needed.[160]

President Johnson repeated his promise of new legislation when King visited the White House February 8.[161] Republicans promised their support. As Justice Department lawyers continued to ponder the terms of an administration bill, a group of Republican leaders—five governors, four senators, and twenty-two representatives—prodded the President: "How long will Congress and the American people be asked to wait while this administration studies and restudies Dr. King's request for new federal legislation. The need is apparent. The time is now. . . . Despite abuse, threats, and beatings, Dr. King and his people walk the streets of Selma in protest. Republicans march with them."[162] This time the unpredictable Dirksen was out in front; he announced that he was drafting a bill, and Attorney General Nicholas deB. Katzenbach, through Majority Leader Mansfield, entered into negotiations in the hope of producing the "consensus" bill, this time, before it was introduced.

King meanwhile assembled his forces for a Sunday march from Selma to Montgomery. Governor Wallace ordered the march halted. At the end

[159] Bickel says that in at least one instance Judge Thomas "actively obstructed the government's lawsuits" (*ibid.*, p. 118).

[160] *Cong. Record*, Vol. 111 (Feb. 8 and 9, 1965), pp. 2150, 2422–37.

[161] *New York Times*, Feb. 9, 1965.

[162] Inserted in *Cong. Record*, Vol. 111 (March 1, 1965), pp. 3746–47.

of the long bridge over the Alabama river leading out of Selma, reported *The Washington Post*, "state troopers and mounted deputies bombarded 600 praying Negroes with tear gas . . . and then waded into them with clubs, whips, and ropes, injuring scores." Then they "chased the screaming, bleeding marchers nearly a mile back to their church, clubbing them as they ran."[163] The scene "resembled that in a police state," said *The New York Times*.[164] The next day a white Unitarian minister from Boston, the Reverend James J. Reeb, was beaten to death by white men in Selma.

Once again, through television and news pictures, the nation became an eye-witness to southern violence, and the outrage was instantaneous. "Telegrams from horrified citizens—neighbors of mine—pour in to me," Democrat John O. Pastore of Rhode Island told the Senate. "The citizens of Minnesota . . . can no longer tolerate the trampling of human rights by southern law enforcement officers," said Democratic Senator Walter F. Mondale. "Shame on you, George Wallace," cried Senator Ralph W. Yarborough, Texas Democrat, "for the wet ropes that bruised the muscles, for the bullwhips which cut the flesh, for the clubs that broke the bones, for the tear gas that blinded, burned, and choked into insensibility." Yarborough called on Wallace "to atone for the shame he has brought . . . to my beloved Southland."[165]

On March 15, when the Katzenbach-Dirksen-Mansfield consensus bill was ready, the President went before an extraordinary evening session of the two houses of Congress so that all the nation could see and hear. Listing Selma with Lexington, Concord, and Appomattox as places where "history and fate" had met "to shape a turning point in man's unending search for freedom," he climaxed his address by uttering as his own the refrain of the civil rights marchers' hymn, "We Shall Overcome."

The bill he presented made the voting provisions of the three previous acts look like pale compromises. It was a frankly regional measure. It singled out seven southern states for attention by limiting its application to areas where literacy tests were used and where fewer than 50 percent of the voting-age population voted in a presidential election.[166] In those

---

[163] *Washington Post*, March 8, 1965.

[164] *New York Times*, March 9, 1965.

[165] *Cong. Record*, Vol. 111 (March 8 and 9, 1965), pp. 4545, 4351, 4335.

[166] The bill thus covered all of six southern states—Alabama, Georgia, Louisiana, Mississippi, South Carolina, and Virginia—and numerous individual counties in North Carolina. It also technically applied to Alaska, but the low voting percentage there was attributed to the large number of military personnel in the voting-age population and to distances and climate rather than discrimination, and the act was not applied there.

areas, it provided for federal registration of voters, not through "tedious, unnecessary lawsuits" but by examiners appointed by the executive branch. It did not merely propose to stop the abuse of literacy tests but swept such tests away. It covered state and local as well as federal elections. It protected not just the right to register but the right to vote itself. In short, it removed from state to federal control the effective supervision of elections and provided a simple and uniform national standard the attorney general could enforce.

Said the President:

> Every American citizen must have an equal right to vote. There is no reason which can excuse the denial of that right.
> Yet . . . every device of which human ingenuity is capable has been used to deny this right. . . . The fact is that the only way to pass these barriers is to show a white skin.
> . . . No law that we now have on the books—and I have helped to put three of them there—can insure the right to vote when local officials are determined to deny it.
> In such a case our duty must be clear to all of us. . . .
> And we ought not and we cannot and we must not wait another 8 months before we get a bill. We have already waited a hundred years or more, and the time for waiting is gone.
> Their cause must be our cause too, because it is not just Negroes but really it is all of us, who must overcome the crippling legacy of bigotry and injustice. And we shall overcome.[167]

The President did not have to wait eight months for his bill—or twelve months, as in 1963–64. It was passed in five. From March to August the civil rights forces never lost momentum. The Leadership Conference and its member organizations pressed to strengthen the bill at every point where they could detect a compromise. When the bill reached the President's desk, they could hail it as stronger than the one originally proposed.

Much of the legislative struggle centered on the poll tax. Although outlawed by the Twenty-fourth Amendment for use in federal elections, poll taxes remained as a barrier to voting in state and local elections in four southern states. The administration opposed, on constitutional grounds, trying to remove these barriers by statute, but the House voted to do so anyway, and the Senate, on an amendment offered by Edward M. Kennedy, Massachusetts Democrat, came within four votes of doing likewise. In a compromise solution, Congress approved a congressional declaration that poll taxes abridged the right to vote and a directive to the

[167] *Public Papers of the Presidents, 1965,* pp. 282–84.

attorney general to bring suit to test their constitutionality. The suits were filed immediately after the act was signed, and the poll taxes were outlawed by the courts.

Yielding to criticism from House Republicans, the Congress also extended the impact of the act beyond the states originally affected to include "pockets of discrimination" anywhere the attorney general demonstrated their existence to a federal court. The final bill also contained a provision, inserted by committees in both houses, authorizing poll watchers in any subdivision where examiners had been assigned.

The two parties shared the credit, although the Republicans were embarrassed when southern opponents embraced their substitute measure as "relatively moderate" and "far preferable" to the bill that was finally approved.[168] The vote in the House was 333–85. Among those voting for it were eight representatives from Texas, six from Florida, four from Tennessee, two each from Georgia and Louisiana, and one from Virginia. In the Senate, cloture was voted, 70–30, after twenty-five days of debate, and then the bill passed, 77–19. Two days after the bill became law, federal examiners assumed their voter registration duties in Selma, Alabama, and eight other counties in three southern states.

"They came in darkness and they came in chains," said the President on signing the bill. "Today we strike away the last major shackle of those fierce and ancient bonds." And a year later federal examiners had certified 124,000 new voters in forty-two counties in four states, and Negro registration in the six southern states wholly covered by the act had risen from 30 to 46 percent of those eligible.[169] Negro voters defeated Sheriff James G. Clark, Jr., of Dallas County, Alabama, in the Democratic primary.

"Black Power"—and the Bill That Failed   *(1965–66)*

But there were yet other shackles. Foremost among the areas of discrimination still untouched by federal legislation was housing. As early as 1959, the Civil Rights Commission had devoted more than a third of its first report to housing discrimination, which it found resulted in "high

---

[168] See remarks of House Democrats William M. Tuck of Virginia and William M. Colmer of Mississippi, *Cong. Record*, Vol. 111 (1965), pp. 15151–52, 15155.
[169] Figures compiled by Southern Regional Council (*New York Times*, Aug. 5, 1966). By 1967 the proportion exceeded 50 percent, according to the Department of Justice (*Washington Post*, July 7, 1967).

rates of disease, fire, juvenile delinquency, crime and social demoralization" among those confined to ghetto slums.[170]

In November 1962, after a long delay,[171] President Kennedy issued the "stroke of a pen" executive order that the commission had recommended, but the order was by no means all-inclusive. It was limited to housing guaranteed or insured by the Federal Housing Administration (FHA) and the Veterans Administration (VA),[172] and it contained no retroactive feature. Thus, it excluded all existing homes and about 80 percent of new housing. To enforce the order and to encourage voluntary fair practices in the sale or rental of housing not covered, Kennedy established the President's Committee on Equal Opportunity in Housing under the chairmanship of former Governor David L. Lawrence of Pennsylvania. At its second meeting the committee concluded that the order that established it was too limited. It was supported by builders using FHA insurance, who complained at being covered while their competitors were not.

As long as the 1964 civil rights act was pending, the committee did not press its demand for a broader order. But after that act was signed, and after the 1964 election, it made a formal recommendation to President Johnson. The President asked Vice President Humphrey to review it and to consider, with Attorney General Katzenbach, the legal problems involved. While this review was underway, the President and Humphrey were faced with a danger—reported in a newspaper column[173]—that several of the committee's members, including its Negro members, would resign if the President rejected its recommendations. This, said the columnists, would mean "the virtual dissolution of the Lawrence committee" and "would trigger recriminations from responsible civil rights leaders."

Counsels of Boldness. Perhaps the President's decision was never in doubt, but when he made it he went all the way. Instead of issuing a new

---

[170] *Report of the United States Commission on Civil Rights* (1961), Bk. 4. Findings and recommendations are summarized on pp. 144–53.

[171] See Sorensen, *Kennedy,* pp. 480–82, for a discussion of the reasons for the delay.

[172] The administration cited legal and administrative reasons for the limitation. In the case of FHA-insured and VA-guaranteed housing, the nondiscrimination requirement could be (and was, under the order) made a simple feature of the insurance or guarantee agreement, but for conventionally financed housing the legal authority would have to be found in the general powers of the Federal Home Loan Bank Board and the Federal Deposit Insurance Corporation and enforcement carried out through these agencies. The authority would be subject to challenge in the courts, and neither agency was well suited to the administrative task.

[173] Rowland Evans and Robert Novak, *Washington Post,* May 14, 1965.

executive order—which at best could only cover new housing and would be on dubious legal grounds for some of that—he would ask for legislation. That course would plunge him into one more fight on Capitol Hill and one more Senate filibuster, but if it were successful he would have covered *all* housing, on a secure and permanent legal foundation, with suitable enforcement machinery, and with the superior moral suasion that attaches to a solemn congressional enactment as distinct from a presidential decree.

In the South the right most forcefully demanded was the right to protection of life itself—specifically, protection of the lives of persons asserting other rights. In 1964, at Philadelphia, Mississippi, three civil rights workers had been slain upon their release from jail, but state and local officials apprehended no one for the crime, and when the Federal Bureau of Investigation arrested a score of suspects—including the sheriff and deputy sheriff who had custody of the civil rights workers before their release—Federal District Judge Harold Cox dismissed the case against them on the ground that murder was not a federal crime. A similar case was dismissed, for the same reason, in Georgia. The accused killers of two northerners who had participated in civil rights demonstrations in Alabama were quickly acquitted by all-white juries in October 1965. In that state not one conviction had been obtained in twelve recent civil rights slayings, either because nobody had been arrested or because of what northern newspapers called "sham" and "mock" trials.[174]

In November 1965 the Civil Rights Commission, in a 188-page report on law enforcement in the South, charged that violence was used in that region "with implicit legal sanction . . . to maintain and reinforce the traditional subservient position of the Negro." In Mississippi alone, the commission found, more than 150 serious incidents of racial violence had occurred between 1961 and 1964, including at least six murders, but "in only a few cases were those responsible arrested or prosecuted by local authorities."[175]

The Justice Department was already publicly committed to request legislation to attack discrimination in jury selection, and the President went on record on this subject in November. Civil rights groups, in drafting legislation for the coming session of Congress, made clear that physical protection for southern Negroes and civil rights workers would be

[174] See Neil Maxwell, *Wall Street Journal,* Oct. 22, 1965, and Fred Graham, *New York Times,* Oct. 31 and Nov. 14, 1965.
[175] *Law Enforcement, a Report on Equal Protection in the South* (United States Commission on Civil Rights, 1965), p. 13. Recommendations are presented on pp. 177–82.

a major objective. The planning session for the White House conference on civil rights, meeting in November,[176] urged a broad "civil rights protection act of 1966."

In his State of the Union message in January, the President asked for action in three areas—juries, physical security, and housing. By late April the specific proposals were ready, and they left little for civil rights groups to criticize. The housing recommendations were all-embracing, covering all sales and rental transactions. The recommendations relating to juries covered state and federal juries alike. The physical security provisions made it a federal crime for any person to interfere, by threats or force, with the exercise by others of their fundamental rights—and voting, education, housing, employment, jury service, and travel were enumerated among those rights. At last, racial murder would be a federal offense. The President added two other recommendations. He proposed to remove the limitations in the 1964 act upon the powers of the attorney general to initiate suits to enforce desegregation of schools or other public facilities.[177] He also endorsed a measure, already passed by the House, to grant enforcement powers to the Equal Employment Opportunity Commission created by the Civil Rights Act of 1964.

On those provisions aimed at segregation and violence in the South, the consensus of 1964 and 1965 held firm. The House Republican Policy Committee endorsed those titles. The House Judiciary Committee added, with no discernible struggle, the entire Part III authority, which had been debated and enacted in bits and pieces over the past decade. All of these titles went through the House with ease. When a motion was made to strike the title setting federal standards for state jury selection, only thirteen votes were mustered to defend states' rights.

Housing, however, was another story. Here for the first time in the long history of five proposed civil rights acts, northerners were asked to strike at practices of discrimination that were all but universal in the North itself. The 1964 act had been amended in the Senate to enable northern senators to assure their constituents that the act would not affect their states. But the 1966 bill would destroy the sanctity of the all-white suburb, an institution more characteristically northern than southern. Only seven-

---

[176] See pp. 283–85.

[177] The 1964 act had two limitations the administration sought to remove: the attorney general could act only when (1) he received a signed complaint by an aggrieved person and (2) he found that person lacked means to finance his own suit. The House, in acting on the administration bill, retained the requirement for a signed complaint.

teen states had fair housing laws, and few covered all housing. Such large states as Illinois and Michigan had no legislation, and California voted overwhelmingly to repeal its law in a referendum in 1964.[178]

Under these circumstances, the 1966 debate proceeded in an atmosphere dramatically altered from that of 1964 and 1965. The impact of mail from home upon northern and western congressmen was reversed. The National Association of Real Estate Boards rallied its 83,000 member firms and their business allies to "generate an immediate wave of indignation" against the bill's alleged threat to property values and free enterprise, and took credit for arousing what they reported was the heaviest flow of mail on a single issue in the memory of "many senior members of Congress."[179] In contrast, the Leadership Conference on Civil Rights deplored the absence of mail on behalf of equal housing opportunity.[180] Negro demonstrations, too, had a different impact. When Martin Luther King, Jr., led a band of Negroes into a white residential area of Chicago and engaged a white mob, he stirred up indignation in the North not unlike that aroused by Birmingham and Selma—but this time directed against, not for, his cause. "I have never seen such hatred—not in Mississippi or Alabama," said King. The church delegations so conspicuous in Washington in 1964 stayed home in 1966. "The music has gone out of the movement," wrote Mary McGrory.[181] Emanuel Celler was led to remark upon the hypocrisy of "some northern civil libertarians" whose ardor for civil rights paled when it was their own institutions that were challenged.[182]

The Chicago riots, subsequent bloodier clashes in Cleveland, the memory of last summer's Watts and the previous summer's Harlem, the ominous slogan of "black power" that appeared in 1966, overhung the debate. Roy Wilkins of the NAACP said that an uncompromised open housing title was necessary to prevent further "heartbreaking developments that could be ugly as well."[183] Southerners repeatedly expressed the opposite view—that violence in the North was the direct result of

---

[178] The repeal action was ruled invalid by a court decision, but the sentiment was unmistakable.

[179] *New York Times*, July 29, 1966.

[180] *Ibid.*, June 9, 1966.

[181] *Evening Star* (Washington), Aug. 5, 1966. See also, *New York Times*, July 26 and 27, 1966, and *New Republic*, July 2, 1966, p. 9.

[182] *New York Times*, June 23, 1966.

[183] *Ibid.*, July 27, 1966.

civil rights acts already passed. "We tremble in our seats and yield to the fear of the Negro revolution," said Howard Smith of Virginia in opening the House debate for the opposition. "If that is the kind of spirit that has come to this country and we are going to operate in the Congress on the theory of fear, on the theory of violence, on the theory of mobs, and so forth, then this is not the place to which I was first elected."[184] Responded Charles McC. Mathias, Jr., Maryland Republican: "We are not yielding to threats. Rather, we are responding to conditions—conditions which have been forced to our attention convulsively and dramatically, perhaps because we failed to apprehend dangers expressed in more placid ways. . . . We are not responding, essentially, to protests, but to the causes of those protests. . . ."[185]

By only the narrowest of margins did the housing title survive the House. It cleared the Judiciary Committee by two votes, 17–15, after a "Mrs. Murphy" clause had been inserted exempting small apartment houses where the owner occupied one of the apartments and after an amendment by Mathias, backed by McCulloch and several Democrats, exempting sales by homeowners of their own homes. On the floor the test came on an amendment by Mathias to his own amendment to make clear that it exempted sales by homeowners of their homes through brokers. The administration and the Republican leadership saw the parliamentary situation in the same way—without the clarified Mathias amendment the title as a whole would be defeated. The administration therefore supported the amendment, which weakened its bill; and a large majority of Republicans, whose policy committee had gone on record against any fair housing title, joined southern Democrats in opposing the exemptions. They were joined by a few last-ditch supporters of the original administration bill who contended that the Mathias exemptions were, in effect, a "codification of prejudice."[186] The amendment carried on a teller vote, 180–179. Once the amendment was adopted, the title as a whole was preserved by a more decisive margin, 198–179 on a teller vote and 222–190 on the roll call vote. On the latter tally it received only eight southern votes—all from urban centers—compared to the thirty-one cast for the Voting Rights Act of 1965, and thirty-one northern and border state

[184] *Cong. Record*, Vol. 112 (July 25, 1966), p. 16054.
[185] *Ibid.* (July 27, 1966), p. 16378.
[186] The phrase of Representative William Fitts Ryan, New York Democrat, *ibid.* (Aug. 3, 1966), p. 17328.

Democrats defected.[187] Nonsouthern Republicans barely supported the title, 62–61. Then the act was passed, 259–157.

"Some People Are in an Undue Hurry." As in 1964 and 1965, the key to Senate cloture was held by Everett Dirksen. Northern and western Democrats could be counted on to vote for cloture, southern Democrats against; therefore, if two-thirds of the Senate were again to be mustered to shut off debate, northern and western Republicans would again have to provide the margin, and Dirksen's influence was crucial.

As in 1964, too, Dirksen took an initial stance of outright opposition to one feature of the bill, this time to the open housing section—"absolutely unconstitutional," he called it. But as the 1966 bill moved along its course, he found no reason to alter his position. No tidal wave of public opinion arose this time to overwhelm him. Indeed, the trend of opinion *against* the bill that had developed during House consideration intensified, if anything, in the weeks after the House acted in early August. New riots broke out—in Atlanta, Omaha, and a dozen other places. The image of the Negro in 1966 was no longer that of the praying, long-suffering, nonviolent victim of southern sheriffs; it was of a defiant young hoodlum shouting "black power" and hurling "Molotov cocktails" in an urban slum. And the white neighborhoods that might have opened their doors to a Martin Luther King of 1964 would only bar and shutter them at the thought of Stokely Carmichael as a neighbor. A survey by the Louis Harris organization, published in *Newsweek* in August, showed that 46 percent of the entire white population would object to having a Negro family next door and 70 percent thought the Negroes were "trying to move too fast."[188] Another Harris poll, in September, listed civil rights violence among the factors that had brought President Johnson's popularity to the lowest point since he entered office. The *Wall Street Journal* reported a "heavy preponderance" of congressional mail against the bill.[189] And just before the cloture vote, on September 13, George P. Mahoney rode to an upset victory in the Democratic primary for governor of Maryland on the single issue of "Your home is your castle—protect it." The message was clear.

[187] Only about half of these were northern or western by strict definition; the others were from border states or districts, the exact number varying according to how the boundary is drawn between northern and border. The term "southern" is restricted here to the eleven states that made up the Confederacy.

[188] *Newsweek,* Aug. 22, 1966, pp. 25–26.

[189] *Wall Street Journal,* Sept. 7, 1966.

Supporters of the civil rights bill did little more than go through the motions of a Senate debate, and opponents did not need to. What counted were the backstage appeals to Dirksen, and these were unavailing. "I think some people are in an undue hurry," Dirksen told the Senate, and added, "we have been talking a long time about color, when in fact we should also be talking about conduct." It was a "frightening argument," responded Edward Kennedy, that "because the actions of some Negroes deserve condemnation," all should be denied the full rights of citizenship.[190]

After a week of dispirited discussion, which was cut short on three occasions when the Senate could not maintain a quorum, Majority Leader Mansfield scheduled the vote on cloture. A majority of the body voted to shut off debate, but not two-thirds. The vote was 54–42. Of those opposed, nineteen were southerners, four were nonsouthern Democrats, and nineteen were nonsouthern Republicans. Twelve Republicans, led by Dirksen, and one Democrat (Frank Lausche of Ohio) who had supported cloture on the 1964 and 1965 civil rights acts opposed it in 1966. A week later, Mansfield again attempted cloture but not a single vote was changed. The bill was shelved. If the prospects for civil rights legislation were to be improved, said Mansfield, "the question of riotings, marches, shootings, and inflammatory statements . . . will have to be faced frankly and bluntly."[191]

"The problem is not going away," was Roy Wilkins' comment. "The Negro is not going away. . . . We will be back in this or another Congress."[192] Paul Douglas and others noted that the will of the Senate majority was thwarted by rule 22 and promised to continue their fight on the filibuster issue. Lyndon Johnson told his press conference he was happy that a majority of both houses supported the bill—"in a democracy where majority rules should prevail."[193] It is ironic that, had Lyndon Johnson spoken those words a decade earlier, majority rule would almost surely have come to prevail in the Senate.[194]

---

[190] *Cong. Record,* Vol. 112 (Sept. 14 and 19, 1966), pp. 21691, 21693, 22082.

[191] *Ibid.* (Sept. 19, 1966), p. 22115.

[192] *New York Times,* Sept. 21, 1966.

[193] *Ibid.,* Sept. 22, 1966.

[194] An act containing physical protection and antiriot provisions like those of the defeated 1966 bill, but with stronger open-housing provisions, was passed in 1968. The Senate action came when Senator Dirksen once more reversed himself and supplied the needed margin of Republican votes to invoke cloture, and the House accepted the Senate bill in the aftermath of the assassination of Martin Luther King, Jr.

Beyond Opportunity to Achievement

Before the 1966 setback to the cause of civil rights, the President had already announced the next stage of the struggle—"the more profound stage," he called it—in an address to the 1965 graduating class of the leading American university founded for Negroes, Howard University in Washington, D.C.

Said the President:

> The voting rights bill . . . as Winston Churchill said of another triumph of freedom—"is not the end; it is not even the beginning of the end. But it is, perhaps, the end of the beginning."
>
> That beginning is freedom. . . . But freedom is not enough. . . . it is not enough just to open the gates of opportunity. All our citizens must have the ability to walk through those gates. This is the next and the more profound stage of the battle for civil rights.
>
> . . . the great majority of Negro Americans—the poor, the unemployed, the uprooted and the dispossessed— . . . still, as we meet here tonight, are another nation. Despite the court orders and the laws, despite the legislative victories and the speeches, for them the walls are rising and the gulf is widening.
>
> For Negro poverty is not white poverty. Many of its causes and many of its cures are the same but there are differences—deep, corrosive, obstinate differences—radiating painful roots into the community, and into the family, and the nature of the individual.
>
> These differences are not racial differences. They are solely and simply the consequence of ancient brutality, past injustice and present prejudice.
>
> Perhaps most important—its influence radiating to every part of life—is the breakdown of the Negro family structure.[195]

Part of the answer, said the President, lay in jobs, in welfare and social programs, in the poverty program, in education, training, and medical care. "But there are other answers that are still to be found, nor do we fully understand even all of the problems," he went on. To define the problems, and find the answers, he announced a White House conference of scholars and experts, officials and Negro leaders, to be held in the fall of 1965. Its theme would be "to fulfill these rights," and its objective to help the Negro move "beyond opportunity to achievement."

It was unique, observed two scholars who have studied the origin and consequences of the Howard University speech, to find the product of three decades of social science research so central to a major presidential

[195] *Public Papers of the Presidents, 1965,* pp. 636–39.

address.[196] It was equally remarkable, they might have added, that echoed in the speech, too, was the anguish expressed by a generation of Negro novelists, essayists, and poets. As in his "We Shall Overcome" speech, the President again, and even more deeply, committed himself to the Negro cause—but in a context of far more conceptual complexity and practical difficulty.

In the first stage of the civil rights battle, the problem and the remedies could at least be readily defined. Constitutional rights, while they evolve, are at all times written in the language of statutes and judicial interpretations. When the people of the North and West, watching the events of Birmingham and Selma on their television screens, resolved to make real in the South the Negroes' constitutional rights, the statutes could be drafted handily—though their effect through enforcement might, in many cases, be slow and gradual. But when the same people, watching the events of Watts and Cleveland on the same television sets, were stirred to demand action, there was no body of settled doctrine to which to turn. The two major parties, building upon their separate traditions, responded with quite different remedies.

Democratic leaders saw the solution in expensive programs to relieve the sordid conditions of the slums. When the Hough area of Cleveland exploded in violence, Democratic Senator Stephen M. Young of that city demanded "federal action on a large scale. . . . The housing program is too small. The poverty program is too small. The program for slum schools is too small. . . . It is clear that the elimination of slum misery will require new programs and much money."[197] Vice President Humphrey a week earlier had been more graphic. He said "the National Guard is no answer to the problems of the slums" and—while not condoning lawlessness—predicted "open violence in every major city and county in America" as long as people were forced to "live like animals . . . in . . . filthy, rotten housing . . . with rats nibbling on the kids' toes . . . with garbage uncollected . . . with no swimming pools, with little or no recreation. . . ." If he lived in such conditions, he "could lead a mighty good

[196] Lee Rainwater and William L. Yancey, "Black Families and the White House," *Trans-action*, July/August 1966, p. 6. They credit Daniel Patrick Moynihan, then assistant secretary of labor, and Richard N. Goodwin, then a presidential speech writer, with being the draftsmen of the Howard University speech. Its theme followed that of a report prepared by Moynihan and his staff, *The Negro Family: The Case for National Action* (Department of Labor, March 1965).

[197] *Cong. Record*, Vol. 112 (July 26, 1966), p. 16246.

revolt" himself, he added.[198] Said the administration's top-ranking Negro, Secretary of Housing and Urban Development Robert Weaver: "Society has to act effectively to redress the deprivations of the environment that occasion despair. We must diagnose the ills of our ghettos and move to heal their sickness before they explode."[199]

The White House conference that the President heralded at Howard University reached the same conclusion. Meeting in June 1966 (after a postponement from the previous fall), it endorsed in general the recommendations of its preparatory council, headed by Ben W. Heineman, which proposed low-cost housing construction at the rate of a million units a year, public works, guaranteed jobs for all workers, free junior colleges, improvement of slum schools, higher welfare benefits, and the strengthening of a host of other services.[200] The council did not put a price tag on its recommendations, but a group subsequently convened by A. Philip Randolph, honorary chairman of the conference, and other civil rights leaders proposed a "freedom budget" of $185 billion over a ten-year period.[201]

Republicans, preparing to exploit both "crime in the streets" and inflation-spending as central issues in the off-year elections, could hardly advance spending as the solution to riots. Their demand was for "law and order." To Barry Goldwater the solution to racial unrest lay not in legislation but in better police forces and stronger public support for their efforts.[202] "How long," asked House Republican Leader Gerald Ford of Michigan, "are we going to abdicate law and order—the backbone of any civilization—in favor of a soft social theory that the man who heaves a brick through your window or tosses a fire bomb into your car is simply the misunderstood and underprivileged product of a broken home?"[203] A Republican-sponsored amendment to the civil rights bill would have made it a crime to cross state lines or use interstate facilities with intent

[198] *New York Times* and *Washington Post*, July 19, 1966.

[199] Address delivered in Philadelphia, Aug. 1, 1966; *Vital Speeches*, Sept. 1, 1966, p. 675.

[200] White House Conference "To Fulfill These Rights," *Council's Report and Recommendations to the Conference* (June 1-2, 1966). The conference did not formally vote on the recommendations, but reporters covering the meeting agreed that the proposals reflected the consensus. Moynihan describes the conference as "a lifeless affair" and comments that "nothing whatever came of it" ("The President and the Negro: The Moment Lost," *Commentary*, Vol. 43, No. 2 [February 1967], pp. 31–45).

[201] *New York Times*, Oct. 27, 1966.

[202] *Ibid.*, July 28, 1966.

[203] Speech at Illinois State Fair, reported in *New York Times*, Sept. 21, 1966.

to incite or participate in riots. The Republican Coordinating Committee pointed out that under the Kennedy and Johnson administrations the number of crimes had increased 46 percent and, in an obvious reference to Humphrey's statement, charged that "high officials of this administration have condoned and encouraged disrespect for law and order."[204]

The "law and order" issue unquestionably contributed to the Republican landslide of 1966. The election added forty-seven Republicans to Ford's minority in the House. And the defeat of such southern liberals as James A. Mackay of Atlanta and George W. Grider of Memphis gave civil rights supporters no cause to expect reinforcements from the Democratic south. Yet, in Roy Wilkins' simple phrase, the problem was not going away and the Negro was not going away. As the Negro's aspirations rose, his frustrations—if jobs, housing, and opportunity for full participation in American life were not open to him—would mount, and the ghettos would become ever more explosive. And each explosion, as the experience of 1966 made clear, would increase the demand for "law and order" and the resistance to the use of tax money for any program that might seem to reward the rioters. In the words of Tom Wicker of *The New York Times,* "There is at work a tragic cycle."[205]

The urban ghetto had become, indeed, the crucial testing ground of the President's conception of his "Great Society." There all of the programs devised by the activists to cope with unemployment, with poverty, with delinquency, with the shortcomings of educational systems, would undergo their trial by ordeal and succeed or finally fail. The urban ghetto had become the central challenge, in the nation's domestic affairs, to every element of the political community—to the intellectuals, who must analyze the problems and develop the solutions; to the government administrators at all levels, who must overcome incredible obstacles to make their programs effective; but most of all to the politicians whose job it was to select appropriate measures, organize the consensus for their enactment, and raise the money to finance them. At the end of 1966 no one could say that the country's political institutions were responding on a scale and with a tempo that matched the magnitude of the challenge that confronted them.

---

[204] Republican National Committee press release, Oct. 3, 1966. A notable exception in Republican ranks was Mayor John V. Lindsay of New York City, who estimated that his city alone needed $50 billion in state and federal funds over a ten-year period (*Federal Role in Urban Affairs,* Hearings before the Subcommittee on Executive Reorganization of the Senate Government Operations Committee, 89 Cong. 2 sess. [Aug. 22, 1966], p. 582).

[205] *New York Times,* Sept. 30, 1966.

CHAPTER VII

For the Old, Health Care

"Us PENSIONERS are not asking for charity," the 69-year-old retired steelworker insisted. But he insisted also that pensioners needed help. Waving a sheaf of bills and receipts before the microphone, he explained: "I pay $38.70 hospitalization. My wife was in St. Francis Hospital last spring. I got a bill of $576 which Blue Cross does not pay. ... Here is a bill that I pay an average of $450 a year, drugstore bills."[1]

Another steelworker stepped to the microphone with another file of papers. One, he said, was a bill "from one of our members" for $925.65 for four weeks' hospitalization for a heart condition. The member's income was $114 a month from social security. "How is he going to pay that? If anybody can figure that out I don't possibly know."[2]

The pensioners were speaking at a "town hall" hearing conducted by the Senate subcommittee on problems of the aged and aging at Pittsburgh in the fall of 1959. That year the subcommittee held hearings in seven cities as part of the first congressional inquiry ever conducted into the entire range of problems confronting the country's older citizens. Two years later the same body—promoted to the status of a special committee of the Senate—visited another thirty-one cities. In the two sets of hearings Chairman Patrick McNamara, Democrat of Michigan, and his colleagues heard more than three thousand witnesses and compiled over seven thousand pages of testimony.

[1] Testimony of Wesley C. Collard, District 15, United Steelworkers of America, in *The Aged and the Aging in the United States,* Hearings before the Subcommittee on Problems of the Aged and Aging of the Senate Labor and Public Welfare Committee, 86 Cong. 1 sess. (Oct. 23, 1959), p. 720.

[2] Testimony of Joseph Reynolds, in *ibid.,* p. 722.

The testimony was not always couched in elegant language but it drew for the senators a vivid self-portrait of the unhappy and often bitter aged. It was a picture of millions of old people who had worked hard for a lifetime but were nevertheless spending their retirement years in, or on the edge of, poverty. Those who had managed to scale down their regular budgets to the size of their pensions still faced the threat of sudden and heavy medical expense that could, in a matter of days, reduce self-sufficiency to pauperism. The need for a means of paying the high cost of medical care echoed throughout the hearings as the single greatest problem of America's retired generation. These excerpts from the testimony are illustrative:

A Tampa, Florida, retired workingman:

> I live with my wife and my income is $1500 a year. Well, we are old people and we don't require much. . . . We don't eat much so we get by in a manner. But I want to ask you . . . what do we do if something happens and we need medical care on $1500 a year? . . . I will have to seek some charity institution and submit to the humiliation of what they call a necessity, and pronounce to the whole world that I am only a pauper, a beggar. Now if I alone were involved in this personally, I might suffer it. I would take it and swallow it. But if my children are brought into that, then I say, "No, never." I would rather die than submit to that humiliation and that degradation.[3]

A Fort Wayne, Indiana, retired electrical worker:

> How many times have I heard them say, "We have savings, we took care of our money and we were getting along all right, but because Paw had that stroke and went to the hospital for 6 weeks, or months, had to have that operation . . . that took nearly all we had saved and now we don't know how we will manage.[4]

A seventy-five-year-old Boston woman:

> We cannot get medical care because we cannot afford to pay $5 and $7 for a doctor. They also would not come at night. They say go to the clinic. We go there in the morning. We stay in line like a lot of cattle. We pay $1.75 or $2 for a ticket to get in. . . . Then they write out a prescription. . . . $11 prescription. How in the world can I pay $11 for a prescription?[5]

A Ross, California, retired public accountant:

> I am now receiving, for my wife and myself . . . a total of $167 and some cents per month. On account of my heart condition, my drug bills and my

[3] Testimony of E. Pasternack, in *Retirement Income of the Aging*, Hearings before the Subcommittee on Retirement Income of the Senate Special Committee on Aging, 87 Cong. 1 sess. (Nov. 6, 1961), p. 266.
[4] Testimony of Arthur E. Shull, president, Retired Workers of America, in *The Aged and the Aging in the United States*, Hearings (Dec. 10, 1959), pp. 2090–91.
[5] Testimony of Mrs. Anna Flowers, in *ibid*. (Oct. 14, 1959), p. 434.

laboratory fees amount to $41.72 a month, one item of which is the California Physicians' . . . and we have just received notification from our doctors in Marin county that they have increased their fees . . . 25 percent. . . . You can see that the resulting amount of $167 less $40-odd is not very much to live on.[6]

A seventy-seven-year-old Malden, Massachusetts, man:

I don't care whether you call it socialized medicine or free medicine, or what, but something should be done. . . . The cost of hospitalization is enormous. It can wipe out all that we have in a short period of time.[7]

A Detroit retired mechanic:

We all need more health service than we can afford. Most of us are able to afford while we are working. Now we can't. We can't when we need it the most.[8]

A St. Joseph, Missouri, man:

I don't know what would happen should a large hospital bill and sickness come along. I do have some hospitalization but not enough to last any length of time.[9]

A St. Petersburg, Florida, retired insurance company employee:

Citizens of this country, over age 65 that have worked, saved, and sacrificed, during their productive years to accumulate a home and a few dollars for their old age should not be required to pauperize themselves to get health care.[10]

A seventy-five-year-old Oakland, California, retired painter:

Do these 150,000 members of the medical association have more power than the 16 million people on old age pensions, which are all voters, mostly, and citizens of the United States? What kind of democracy do we call this? . . . Most of our European states have a government health bill . . . and here, the richest country in the world does not take proper care of the old people.[11]

A seventy-nine-year-old Springfield, Massachusetts, retired railroad worker:

In my service I did have insurance cost coverage. Two of the insurance coverages, one of them especially has paid in 43 years, the other one 41 years.

[6] Testimony of Karl Fairfax, in *ibid.* (Oct. 29, 1959), p. 924.
[7] Testimony of a Mr. Palmer, in *ibid.* (Oct. 14, 1959), p. 451.
[8] Testimony of Enoch Jones, in *ibid.* (Dec. 10, 1959), p. 2099.
[9] Testimony of Harry Steidel, in *Retirement Income of the Aging*, Hearings (Dec. 11, 1961), p. 571.
[10] Testimony of Jesse W. Holmes, president, Prudential Retired Employees Society of West Coast Florida, in *The Aged and the Aging in the United States*, Hearings (Dec. 2, 1959), p. 1766.
[11] Testimony of Philip Ickler, in *ibid.* (Oct. 29, 1959), pp. 913–14.

When I reached the age of 70 they politely sent me notice, do not send any more premiums, you have already reached the age of 70.[12]

In the 1930's the builders of social security had considered health care for the aged only as part of the larger problem of health care for the entire population. Their solution was a program of universal health insurance as part of the social security structure, and bills were introduced to that end. President Roosevelt did not embrace the issue but President Truman did—and collided head-on with the American Medical Association (AMA). That body organized what became by far the most expensive lobbying campaign in history, aimed at "socialized medicine" and the Democratic politicians who supported the Truman plan.[13] In 1950 several Democratic candidates who had emphasized the health insurance issue went down to defeat. The party then backed away from the Truman position. The 1952 Democratic platform did not endorse the President's health insurance proposal, nor did Adlai Stevenson in the 1952 campaign.

The Republican party, meanwhile, joined forces with the AMA. Its 1952 platform roundly condemned "federal compulsory health insurance, with its crushing cost, wasteful inefficiency, bureaucratic dead weight, and debased standards of medical care," and General Eisenhower borrowed the AMA's own language in denouncing "socialized medicine" in his campaign.

But the issue would not die. After a half-dozen years of groping for a new position, the activists regrouped around a narrower proposal limited to health insurance for older persons. The next half-dozen years saw a political power struggle between those who claimed to speak for the 16 million people over sixty-five "which are all voters, mostly" in the words of the Oakland painter, and, on the other side, the 150,000 doctors and their allies. The two major parties aligned themselves on either side of the struggle. The strength of the issue helped bring about the ascendancy of the Democratic party in the 1960's and that ascendancy led in turn to enactment, in 1965, of what its sponsor called "the greatest social innovation since the passage of the original Social Security Act of 1935."[14]

---

[12] Testimony of Joseph Demers, in *Retirement Income of the Aging,* Hearings (Nov. 29, 1961), p. 492.

[13] See Richard Harris, "Annals of Legislation: Medicare," 4 pts., *New Yorker,* July 2, 9, 16, and 23, 1966, for a detailed study of the development and passage of the medicare bill, with particular emphasis upon the role and activities of the AMA. Harris estimates expenditures by the AMA and its affiliates and allies to have totaled $50 million by 1965 (*ibid.,* Pt. 1, July 2, 1966, p. 29).

[14] Senator Clinton P. Anderson, Democrat of New Mexico, quoted by Harris, *ibid.,* Pt. 1, July 2, 1966, p. 29.

Groping for Position *(1953–56)*

If the 1952 campaign saw a bipartisan repudiation of national health insurance, it also saw a bipartisan acknowledgment that a problem did exist. Accordingly, when the Republican administration took office, Federal Security Administrator Oveta Culp Hobby (who shortly became the first secretary of health, education, and welfare) set out to frame an Eisenhower administration alternative to "socialized medicine"—one that would cost no more than $25 million—and within a year had it ready. "It is unfortunately a fact that medical costs are rising and already impose severe hardships on many families," said the President in announcing the proposal. "The Federal Government can do many helpful things and still carefully avoid the socialization of medicine."[15]

The Eisenhower proposal was designed to speed the growth of private health insurance through a limited reinsurance service. Secretary Hobby had the assistance of eight insurance executives as consultants in reviewing the department's bill, she told a House committee, but it turned out that the industry was against it anyway. "Since the plan is so new and so many important details are yet unknown and therefore many uncertainties remain unresolved, we are not in a position to go on record in favor of the bill at this time," said the industry's spokesman, who had been one of her consultants.[16] The American Medical Association was more forceful: "We still do not see the need and we still are afraid it will be the opening wedge to . . . socialized medicine."[17]

Abandoned by the industries the plan was designed to help, the administration could hardly look to the Democrats for support. "A puny and totally inadequate 'gimmick' which all expert testimony at the hearings has demonstrated can accomplish virtually nothing," was the comment in House debate of Representative John D. Dingell of Detroit, long-time sponsor of the Truman national health insurance plan.[18] "The fires of

[15] State of the Union message, Jan. 7, 1954, *Public Papers of the Presidents, 1954,* p. 20.

[16] Testimony of Henry S. Beers, representing the American Life Convention and the Life Insurance Association of America, in *Health Reinsurance Legislation,* Hearings before the House Interstate and Foreign Commerce Committee, 83 Cong. 2 sess. (March 31, 1954), p. 210. Secretary Hobby referred to the participation of the consultants in her opening testimony, March 24, 1954. The executives of 17 life insurance companies later issued a statement favoring the bill's "general objectives" after a meeting with President Eisenhower.

[17] Testimony of David B. Allman, chairman, AMA legislative committee, in *ibid.* (April 5, 1954), p. 314.

[18] *Cong. Record,* Vol. 100 (July 13, 1954), p. 10424.

enthusiasm . . . which have been kindled in favor of this bill would probably freeze water, would they not?" asked conservative Democrat John
Bell Williams of Mississippi.[19] The health program, according to an
Eisenhower biographer, demonstrated the President's "middle of the
road" approach. "I feel pretty good when I'm attacked from both sides.
It makes me more certain that I'm on the right track," the President told
his legislative leaders.[20] But being attacked from both sides does not
necessarily produce majorities in Congress. The administration lost
seventy-five, or 38 percent, of its Republican votes in the House and
gained in return only fourteen Democratic supporters. The proposal was
overwhelmed, 238–134.

"There is nothing to be gained," said the President next day, "by
shutting our eyes to the fact that all of our people are not getting the kind
of medical care to which they are entitled. I do not believe there is any use
in shutting our eyes to the fact that the American people are going to get
that medical care in some form or other."[21]

The AMA, which claimed credit in its newsletter for defeating the
bill,[22] offered no alternative. For the next two years, neither did the administration. Then HEW Secretary Marion Folsom devised a plan for
relaxation of the antitrust laws to permit insurance companies to pool
their resources and efforts in order to extend coverage; but his proposal
received no warmer reception than had the earlier reinsurance plan.

The Democrats were even slower in evolving their alternative. As
early as 1950 the idea that ultimately blossomed into the medicare act
of 1965 had been conceived within the confines of the Federal Security
Agency. Demoralized by the strength of the AMA crusade against "socialized medicine," the agency's administrator, Oscar W. Ewing, and his
associates, among them Wilbur Cohen and I. S. Falk, had been exploring
new approaches to the problems of medical care. Among the groups least
well covered by the rapid postwar expansion of private health insurance
were retired people. They were generally ineligible for group plans designed for employed persons; if they had belonged to group plans during
their working years, their participation was often terminated upon retirement; to obtain coverage on an individual basis, they had to pay high rates
that were often prohibitive to those living on retirement incomes. Yet the

---

[19] *Ibid.*, p. 10399.
[20] Robert J. Donovan, *Eisenhower: The Inside Story* (Harper, 1956), p. 229.
[21] News conference, July 14, 1954, *Public Papers of the Presidents, 1954*, p. 633.
[22] *Congressional Quarterly Almanac, 1954*, p. 217.

need for health insurance increases in the retirement years, even as income declines; chronic illness has its highest incidence in the upper age brackets. Ewing and his staff hit upon the notion of making health care an added benefit for older people under social security through a simple amendment to existing law. Sixty days of hospitalization could be provided, they calculated, without raising the payroll taxes that finance social security benefits. In 1952 Democratic Senator James Murray of Montana, with Hubert Humphrey of Minnesota as a cosponsor, and Representative Dingell introduced a bill to that effect.

Despite a forceful endorsement by President Truman's Commission on the Health Needs of the Nation, which reported in December, the Murray-Dingell bill attracted little attention—even from the AMA. Dingell continued to introduce it in each succeeding Congress, without fanfare, but Murray and Humphrey filed it only once more in the Senate and then even they appeared to have forgotten about it. In 1956 the Democratic platform was silent on the entire subject of health insurance. Adlai Stevenson took note of the social security approach in a single sentence in his program paper on older citizens, in which he said he would urge a thorough investigation of the idea by Congress. But his program paper on health not only ignored but contradicted the proposal. In developing a plan to help people pay part of the cost of voluntary health insurance, he said, "the principle which should guide us . . . is, I believe, the historic principle embedded in our medical practice and our humanitarian philosophy of government, that those who can pay their own way should, that those who can pay a major part should pay that part, and that those who can pay little or nothing should pay what they can and should be assisted with the rest."[23] Thus he exalted to the status of a "historic principle" the very opposite of social insurance—government charity based upon a rigid means test. At this point, both parties recognized a problem but neither had anything that could be called a program.

A New Political Force: The Aging. It is significant that Adlai Stevenson's fleeting mention of hospitalization for the aging was contained not in his program paper on health but in his paper on the problems of older citizens. The tone of the former paper reflected the continuing reaction against the national health insurance movement of the 1940's; the latter mirrored the rising strength of another current of political thought and

[23] Adlai Stevenson, *The New America* (Harper, 1957), pp. 145, 134.

action centered upon what came to be called "problems of aging." The latter movement gave the health insurance issue its direction and much of its force after 1956.

The plight of the aged, as a group, came to national attention in the 1930's when Dr. Francis E. Townsend and others dramatized the fact that the hardships of the Depression were visited with especial weight upon the old. The overriding need of the aged was seen then as simply one of cash income, and two provisions of the Social Security Act were designed to help meet that need—federal grants for old age assistance for the needy, subject to a means test, and a system of compulsory, prepaid old-age insurance that would provide monthly cash payments as a matter of right rather than of charity and would eventually eliminate most of the need for direct assistance. Private pension plans also entered a period of rapid growth, propelled by the demands of a strengthened labor movement.

Other problems associated with the higher age brackets began to attract increased attention. The health professions recognized that the chronic diseases associated with aging had replaced infectious diseases, by then largely conquered, as the nation's foremost health problem. The American Geriatric Society and the Gerontological Society were formed in the 1940's. Between 1937 and 1950, six National Institutes of Health were established for research primarily on chronic diseases. But as research progressed, discussion of the problems of aging moved out of the separate contexts of health or income maintenance into a broader context of inter-related problems: low income, failing health, bad housing, lack of employment and recreation opportunities, withdrawal from family and community life, higher incidence of mental illness. As sociologists began to draw a picture of widespread neglect by an urbanized society of its older citizens, demographers were pointing out that the number of people over sixty-five was growing three times as fast as the number under that age, thanks to the advances in medicine. The three million "senior citizens" of 1900 would become fourteen million by 1955 and twenty million by 1975, and they would continue to be the lowest income group of the entire population.

In 1947 the New York legislature established the first official body concerned with the entire range of problems of the aging, a joint legislative committee which attracted national attention with its hearings and reports. The next year, following a recommendation of the National Health Assembly, the federal security administrator appointed a staff committee on aging. The Federal Security Agency convened a national conference on aging in 1950 which summarized the proceedings of its eleven sections in a 308-page report.[24] During the next four years, stimulated particularly by Clark Tibbitts, head of the agency's staff committee, and Sidney Spector, of the Council of State Governments staff, a score of states followed New York's lead by establishing an official state group—legislative committee, governor's commission, citizen advisory committee, or interdepartmental group—to be concerned with the spectrum of problems of the older population. Then the Governors' Conference sponsored a comprehensive study, which recommended a fifteen-point program of state action in employment, welfare, housing, rehabilitation, medical care, mental health, recreation, training, education, and research, to be coordinated in each state by a staff unit in the governor's office and an advisory council patterned after those established by Governor Averell Harriman in New York.[25]

Meanwhile, the activists of the aging movement were generating a variety of proposals for national action. Early in 1955 Senator Charles Potter, Michigan Republican, recited the compelling statistics defining the plight of the aging and proposed a national commission to undertake a comprehensive study. Although he had fifty-four cosponsors—well over half the Senate—he could not obtain administration support and his measure never emerged from committee. Several members of Congress, of both parties, proposed creation of a bureau or office of older persons to parallel the Children's Bureau in HEW; several congressmen urged a special committee in the House; others (including Senator John F. Kennedy) sponsored grants to states to assist their programs for the aging. Chairman John E. Fogarty (Democrat of Rhode Island) of the House Appropriations subcommittee responsible for the Labor and HEW departments chastised those departments for showing "very little awareness of the urgency" of the problems and demanded that they present a program.[26]

[24] National Conference on Aging, *Man and His Years* (Health Publications Institute, Inc., 1951); the report sketches development of awareness of the problems of aging (pp. 6–8).

[25] *The States and Their Older Citizens* (Council of State Governments, 1955), pp. xiii–xvii; Table 50 details organizational steps taken by the states prior to that time (pp. 161–64).

[26] *Cong. Record*, Vol. 102 (July 12, 1956), p. 12536. As a measure of the rising congressional interest, under the index heading "Older Persons" *Congressional Record* for 1953 contains six entries, for 1954 three, for 1955 a full column, and for 1956 and 1957 about a column and a half each; in 1960 the figure had reached six and a half columns. "Needs of Our Older Citizens" became a heading in the Democratic platform in 1952; the Republican platform had its first section on "Older Citizens" in 1960.

President Eisenhower's response to all of this congressional initiative came in March 1956 with the establishment of the Federal Council on Aging, an interdepartmental committee charged with advising individual agencies on their programs.[27] Later that year the Federal Council and the Council of State Governments joined forces in a planning conference.

The ground was thus well-prepared when the AFL-CIO's committee on social security met late in 1956 to talk about its legislative program.

The Rise of a National Issue   *(1957–60)*

The labor movement was riven on many issues, but social security was never one of them. When the leaders of the newly merged AFL-CIO sought subjects that would help to cement the uneasy combination, social security came immediately to the fore. In 1956 the entire labor movement had rallied behind legislation to authorize benefits under social security for the totally and permanently disabled. After that battle was won, the AFL-CIO social security committee scanned the remaining gaps in the nation's social insurance structure and found no disagreement on priorities: health insurance for retired persons must be the next objective.

There remained the question of the extent of benefits. The Murray-Dingell bill had been a modest measure, limited to sixty days of hospitalization financed without an increase in the payroll tax. But the contracts then being negotiated by the constituent unions of the labor federation went far beyond that, and the pressure from the membership was to gain for a man and his wife during retirement years the same protection they had had while employed. The discussion centered upon the coverage of surgical fees. Nelson H. Cruikshank, head of the AFL-CIO social security department, and his staff were mindful of the consequences of covering doctors' fees in any form and advocated their exclusion, but they were overruled by the policy-making committee of union executives. The decision was to cover hospitalization, nursing home care, and surgery, and this decision was ratified by the federation's executive council. Cruikshank then took the lead in working out a bill. For an increase in the tax rate of 0.5 percent of the covered payrolls (split between employers and employees), persons eligible for old age and survivors insurance benefits

[27] Announced in a letter to the ranking Republican on the Senate Labor and Public Welfare Committee, H. Alexander Smith of New Jersey, March 21, 1956, *Public Papers of the Presidents, 1956*, p. 53.

could be provided insurance protection for surgery, 60 days of hospitalization, and another 60 days of nursing home care in any one year (or any
combination of 120 days if fewer than 60 days of hospitalization were
required). The bill was offered to the ranking Democrats on the House
Ways and Means Committee, in turn. The fourth ranking member, Aime
J. Forand of Rhode Island, agreed with some reluctance to introduce it—
and a legislative star was born.[28]

The Gathering of Support. In less than three years the obscure Forand
bill, introduced without fanfare, would become what some considered
"the foremost issue in the presidential campaign."[29] It would be the
subject of more congressional mail, at least in some offices, than any other
bill.[30] A doctor-columnist for a Long Island newspaper would be "de-
luged" with mail after he wrote a column critical of the bill.[31] A news
magazine in May 1960 would say that "pressure for action . . . is . . .
assuming the proportions of a crusade."[32]

Yet all this would happen without benefit of any of the circumstances
that usually thrust a legislative measure into the national spotlight. No
presidential message or television appeal supported it; no crisis compelled
attention to it; it had no status as a party measure in Congress; its sponsor
there was a little-known congressman who could not bring national attention to it and, indeed, did not try; its existence was not reported on
the front pages of the newspapers until *after* it had become a major national political issue. Yet many thousands of people managed to learn of
the bill's existence and join the "crusade" for its enactment. Support for
the Forand bill began as a genuine grass roots movement—surely the most
phenomenal such movement of the period.

In the development of this movement, three groups of communicators
were important. First was organized labor. "We undertook no particular
promotional campaign," insists Cruikshank, "nothing expensive, just the
usual communicating process." Stories were provided to labor publications. Local unions passed resolutions and sought local publicity. Cruikshank and his staff wrote memoranda and made speeches. National or-

[28] Harris, "Medicare," Pt. 2, July 9, 1966, p. 36.
[29] *Baltimore Sun* editorial; inserted in *Cong. Record,* Vol. 106 (Aug. 20, 1960),
p. 16987.
[30] *New York Times,* March 23, 1960.
[31] H. I. Fineberg, *Long Island Press*; inserted in *Cong. Record,* Vol. 106 (March 23,
1960), p. 6421.
[32] *U.S. News and World Report,* May 2, 1960, p. 51.

ganizations identified with social issues were induced to pass resolutions, which were duly reported in organizational magazines and newsletters. Local organizations of retired persons—"golden age clubs," "senior citizen" organizations, pensioner social groups, few of which had any national affiliation—learned of the Forand bill through one or another means and spread the information among their members. In New York City, 3,040 delegates from senior citizen clubs met in Carnegie Hall and unanimously endorsed the measure.[33] "Our little efforts were just a catalyst," says Cruikshank. "The Forand bill caught on simply because it met a deeply felt need all over the country." One of the leading opponents of the bill, Representative Thomas Curtis, Missouri Republican, gave labor more credit. Even in the spring of 1960, he contended, the only significant congressional mail on the subject was that generated by labor's committee on political education.[34] Curtis cited, in particular, thousands of postcards bearing a picture of a careworn elderly couple and a biblical quotation, "Cast me not off in time of old age, forsake me not when my strength faileth." He considered the invocation of scripture on behalf of the bill "blasphemous."

The second group of communicators was made up of the bill's opponents, principally the American Medical Association. After the defeat of the Truman health insurance proposals, the AMA had gradually disbanded its lobbying and public relations apparatus. From a peak of $1.5 million in 1949, its expenditures for lobbying had declined to $50,000 in 1957.[35] But after the Forand bill made its appearance, the organization began again to rally its members and allied organizations. It joined with three other organizations—the American Dental Association, the American Hospital Association, and the American Nursing Homes Association—to form a joint council to improve the health care of the aged (an implicit acknowledgment that all was not satisfactory; further acknowledgment came that same year when the AMA convention adopted a resolution urging doctors to lower the fees charged elderly patients). The AMA publicized the arguments against the bill to its membership, and as state and county medical societies arranged debates and panel discussions and passed resolutions opposing the measure, more old people learned of the existence of the bill. "I want to pay tribute to the AMA

---

[33] *Social Security Legislation,* Hearings before the House Ways and Means Committee, 85 Cong. 2 sess. (June 27, 1958), p. 704.

[34] *Cong. Record,* Vol. 106 (May 2, 1960), p. 9142.

[35] Harris, "Medicare," Pt. 2, July 9, 1966, p. 36.

for the great assistance they have given me in publicizing this bill of mine," said Forand in 1960. "They have done more than I ever could have done." At the time, he noted, reports on file with the House showed the AMA to be spending more on lobbying than any other organization.[36]

The third communicating group consisted of Democratic politicians who sensed the potential of the Forand bill and began, one by one, to exploit it. As congressmen talked about the bill in their home communities, they not only capitalized on public sentiment but helped to create it. And as they reported to one another the growth of support at the grass roots—and as labor representatives talked with them—support for the measure spread within the Democratic party. In the 1958 House debate on social security amendments, half a dozen congressmen took occasion to endorse the Forand bill even though it was not before the House. Among them were such influential leaders of the activist Democratic Study Group as John Blatnik of Minnesota and Lee Metcalf of Montana. In the Senate, Wayne Morse of Oregon publicized the bill by offering it as an amendment to a pending social security bill, a gesture that was defeated on a voice vote. Senator Kennedy at that time endorsed the principle of the Forand bill in a Senate floor speech outlining a ten-point "bill of rights for our elder citizens."[37] The Democratic Advisory Council, made up of the party's leaders outside Congress, endorsed the proposal in December 1958.

The decisive influence on Democratic sentiment, however, was probably the McNamara subcommittee on aging of the Labor and Public Welfare Committee, created in 1959 by Chairman Lister Hill (Alabama Democrat) upon the urging of both McNamara and Kennedy. The subcommittee had no preconceived intent to make health insurance its first priority, according to Sidney Spector, who left the Council of State Governments to become its staff director, but the issue emerged as such from the testimony of the hundreds of old people and expert witnesses heard by the subcommittee as it moved around the country. The subcommittee's hearings generated publicity for the Forand bill wherever they were held, and its staff stimulated the interest of reporters and feature writers. At the end of its first year the subcommittee recommended health service benefits under social security as its top priority legislative measure for 1960, and McNamara and eighteen Democratic cosponsors, including all three of the northern senators seeking the Democratic presidential nomination—

---

[36] *Cong. Record*, Vol. 106 (June 22, 1960), p. 13820.
[37] *Ibid.*, Vol. 104 (Aug. 19, 1958), p. 18422.

Kennedy, Humphrey, and Stuart Symington—introduced a revised version of the Forand bill. Kennedy had introduced his own bill earlier.[88]

The Eisenhower administration took a position, initially, of outright opposition. "Health insurance is a matter for voluntary action," HEW Secretary Folsom told the House Ways and Means Committee in 1958. "I would hate to see us retard or destroy the great progress which is being made in the voluntary direction." The coverage of voluntary plans had grown by one-third since 1952, he said, and 36.5 percent of persons over sixty-five now had some insurance coverage.[89]

The American Medical Association denounced every aspect of the bill. Testified its spokesman, Dr. Frank H. Krusen: "The government would control the disbursement of funds; the government would determine the benefits to be provided; the government would set the rates of compensation of hospitals, nursing homes, and physicians; the government would audit and control the records of hospitals, nursing homes, and patients; and the government would promulgate and enforce the standards of hospital and medical care. . . . The professional relationship between the doctor and his patient would be hampered. Government regulations would be imposed on patient and physician alike." The bill would lead to "dangerous overcrowding" of hospitals with "personal and family financial responsibility eliminated."[40] The insurance industry also testified in opposition.

But even at this early date, the opposition of the party and the medical profession was not unbroken. Charles A. Wolverton of New Jersey, ranking Republican member of the House committee with jurisdiction over health, told his colleagues: "There is abundant evidence of the fact that under existing arrangements insurance against the cost of needed hospital and nursing home services is out of the reach of many, in fact of most, older people. The only question that remains unsettled is as to type of plan or program that should be adopted to accomplish the purpose."[41] A committee of the American Hospital Association, headed by James P. Dixon, had recommended in 1958 that the association accept social security as the most feasible longrun method of financing health care for the aged, but the association's policy-making bodies were not ready to break

[88] To eliminate some of the objections to the Forand bill, both Senate bills removed surgical fees from coverage and added some of the costs of home care.

[89] *Social Security Legislation*, Hearings (June 16, 1958), pp. 13–16.

[40] *Ibid* (June 27, 1958), p. 893.

[41] *Cong. Record*, Vol. 104 (July 31, 1958), p. 15768.

their alliance with the AMA. When Dr. Dixon testified before the House Ways and Means Committee in that year, all he could say was, "We have not seen the likelihood of a sufficient solution without the financial participation of the Federal Government," and that the "form and extent of the Federal Government's participation" should be studied.[42] The American Nurses Association went all the way in parting company with the AMA; it endorsed the principle of the Forand bill although not the details of the bill itself. Several small organizations of doctors, including the National Medical Association made up of Negroes, also supported the bill.

The Ways and Means Committee took no action on the Forand bill but it did ask the administration to make a study, as the American Hospital Association had proposed. When the findings of the study were reported by the new HEW secretary, Arthur Flemming, in the spring of 1959, the administration no longer argued that private insurance programs, unaided, could fill the need. "There is general agreement that a problem does exist," said the report. "Because both the number and proportion of older persons in the population are increasing, a satisfactory solution to the problem of paying for adequate medical care for the aged will become more rather than less important."[43] But the report made no recommendations, and when Flemming appeared before the committee three months later, he could only testify that proposals were under study. He was seeking an approach that would encourage rather than "bring to a virtual halt" the growth of private plans, which he said would reach 70 percent of older people by 1965; accordingly, HEW was restudying for application to the aging the reinsurance and pooling proposals advanced earlier for health insurance for all ages, and was considering also direct subsidies to enable private carriers to assume high-risk cases. Observed Forand: "If everybody who is interested in trying to find a solution to this problem had been devoting his time to finding a solution rather than fighting a

---

[42] *Social Security Legislation,* Hearings (June 16, 1958), pp. 862–64. The following year, Dr. Dixon, speaking this time for the Philadelphia Hospital Council, strongly endorsed use of the social security mechanism; AHA maintained its 1958 position while acknowledging that the Forand approach "may be necessary ultimately" (*Hospital, Nursing Home, and Surgical Benefits for OASDI Beneficiaries,* Hearings before the House Ways and Means Committee, 86 Cong. 1 sess (July 13 and 15, 1959), pp. 49, 357.

[43] *Hospitalization Insurance for OASDI Beneficiaries,* Report, by Secretary of HEW to House Ways and Means Committee, 86 Cong. 1 sess. (April 1, 1959), p. 1.

bill I introduced two years ago, perhaps we would have a solution by now."[44]

The Republican Counterproposal. For the next ten months Flemming struggled to develop a plan for health care that would be acceptable to the President, the Budget Bureau, and the Republican leadership in Congress. By October a task force headed by Assistant Secretary Elliot Richardson and made up largely of Public Health Service and Social Security Administration personnel had concluded that the social security system would be the most satisfactory means for financing the insurance benefits. Using the same social security tax increase of 0.5 percent of payroll that the Forand bill employed, the task force developed a range of alternative benefits that might be provided—lower benefits with no deductibility provision, as in the Forand bill, higher benefits designed to cover major expenses but with some deductible amount to be paid by the beneficiary, etc. The President encouraged Flemming in the social security approach, at least initially. But when the secretary checked with representatives of the insurance industry, he received no encouragement at all. The Budget Bureau and the Treasury Department were opposed. In mid-March Flemming's staff told him the Budget Bureau appeared to be "dug in" against any plan.

In the face of all this opposition, Flemming overruled his task force and came down on the side of a voluntary program, which he outlined to the President and the Republican congressional leaders at a White House meeting March 22.[45] Reading from testimony he had prepared for a Ways and Means Committee hearing, he said that a compulsory law "would represent an irreversible decision to abandon voluntary insurance for the aged in the hospital field and would probably mark the beginning of the end of voluntary insurance for the aged in the health field generally." Even if the program were limited to "catastrophic illnesses," it would be subject to these objections. He therefore proposed to tell the committee that the administration program, while not yet worked out in detail, would embody six principles: (1) it would be voluntary; (2) it would be open to all old people, rather than only those covered by social security; (3) it would cover comparatively long periods of hospital care,

---

[44] *Hospital . . . Benefits for OASDI Beneficiaries,* Hearings (July 13, 1959), p. 12.

[45] The account that follows is taken from notes on leadership meeting, March 22, 1960 (papers of Dwight D. Eisenhower, McPhee Files [in Dwight D. Eisenhower Library, Abilene, Kan.]).

with a portion of the cost to be paid by the beneficiary; (4) some fee would be charged the policy holder; (5) the states and the federal government would jointly finance that part of the cost not covered by the fees; (6) the states would administer the program and could contract with private groups to act for them.

But even this voluntary plan was rejected by the congressional Republicans. "This will be a small hole through which all will be driven, and the government will eventually be doing it all," Senator Everett Dirksen of Illinois told the meeting. He was echoed by House Minority Leader Charles Halleck of Indiana. "If people were dying right and left for lack of medical care you'd read about it in the papers," said Halleck. Barring such news, he argued, the whole problem should be left to state and local governments. Representative Charles B. Hoeven of Iowa observed that, "except for ten or twelve," Republicans in Congress "want to save the free enterprise system." The President said he was "fearful of a new federal program and thereby opening a new door," but he also agreed with Flemming that, "We can't say there is no problem and that we don't give a darn." He deferred decision, and Flemming was forced to cancel his appearance before the committee.

Flemming found a strong supporter in Vice President Richard Nixon. Though absent from the meeting, Nixon conveyed his views that day to *The New York Times.* "Nixon is said to believe," reported the *Times* correspondent, "that the party cannot afford to take a negative position on what has become a pressing social problem with major political implications."[46]

A week after the White House meeting President Eisenhower publicly espoused the Flemming position. He told a news conference that he had instructed the secretary to "get all the people that are interested—the insurance companies, the doctors, the older people, everybody that seems to have a real worthwhile opinion and conviction on this thing" and work out a voluntary program "that will show exactly where the federal responsibility in this field should begin and where it should end." He also laid down some criteria. The plan should provide for state participation: "There are lots of governments, and the thing I object to is putting everything on the federal government." It should be voluntary: "I have been against compulsory insurance as a very definite step in socialized medicine. I don't believe in it, and I want none of it myself." It should be built upon

[46] *New York Times*, March 23, 1960.

the private insurance system: "The number of people that have come under the voluntary health insurance programs has been very great, increasing rapidly."[47]

Not until May 4 did Flemming announce his plan—which he called "medicare," a name that remained attached to the legislation from that time on. Under the plan, coverage would be available to any person over sixty-five whose income was under $2,500 (or under $3,800 for a couple). For a fee of $24 a year,[48] and after paying the first $250 of costs in any year (or $400 in the case of a couple), the beneficiary would be covered for 80 percent of the cost of 180 days of hospital care a year, unlimited nursing home care, and virtually all other medical expenses. The states would administer the program, contracting with private carriers if they wished. The $24 enrollment fee would cover only an estimated 13 percent of the total cost, or $183 million, and the federal and state governments would each contribute $600 million, the federal share to be paid from general revenues. The states would be required to permit eligible persons, as one option, to buy private health insurance, with federal and state governments dividing half the cost up to a maximum subsidy of $60.

In the broad range of its benefits, and in the absence of ceilings on most types of expenses to be covered (after the deductible $250), it was tailored for "catastrophic illnesses," which the President had emphasized as his primary concern. It was broader than the Forand bill, too, in that it covered the 4.2 million persons over sixty-five who were outside the social security system.

But the Flemming plan attracted few supporters. From the left, the Democrats protested that fifty states would have to pass laws, negotiate with a multitude of carriers, and raise $600 million; they would act slowly, if ever. An income test, although at a high level, would still be required. Retired people would still be required to pay out of current income the $24 enrollment fee, all of the first $250 or $400 of medical expenses, and 20 percent of everything above that. The deductibility feature would serve as a barrier to early diagnosis and preventive medicine. And at least half of the plan's income, experience indicated, would

[47] *Public Papers of the Presidents, 1960–61*, p. 325.

[48] As presented by Secretary Flemming in the hearings, the plan called for a flat $24 fee for all enrollees regardless of income. However, when Senator Leverett Saltonstall, Republican of Massachusetts, introduced what he called the administration bill on June 30, it contained a sliding scale of fees ranging from $24 to $204 a year depending upon income.

go into insurance company overhead and profits rather than benefits.[49]
From the right, Republican Senator Barry Goldwater of Arizona condemned the Eisenhower plan as a "dressed up" version of "socialized
medicine."[50] So did the AMA. Noah M. Mason of Illinois, ranking Republican on the Ways and Means Committee, "was not just cold, he was
frigid," remarked one observer who was present when Flemming outlined the plan. The bill was not even introduced in the House. Some found
the Flemming plan no less "compulsory" than the social security approach. Wrote Walter Lippmann, in a much-quoted column: "For reasons which he has never explained, the President regards social security
taxes as unsound, socialistic, and rather un-American; on the other hand
he regards compulsory taxes to pay for doles based on a means test as
somehow more 'voluntary', sounder, more worthy of a free society and
more American."[51] The governors of the fifty states, assembled in their
annual conference, showed no interest in raising the money and administering the program. They rejected by an overwhelming 30–11 vote the
proposed federal-state system in favor of the all-federal social security
approach. Of the thirteen Republican governors who voted, six led by
Nelson Rockefeller of New York voted with the Democrats.

A Preelection Confrontation. Although scarcely anyone but its authors
liked the bill Flemming presented, he had at least succeeded in getting his
party finally and squarely on record that something needed to be done.
The parties now agreed on the necessity for medicare; what remained was
to agree upon how it would be provided. But that would not be easy.
Whatever might have been the merits of the administration bill, the
Democratic majorities in Congress—in the charged political atmosphere
of an election year—had no intention of considering it seriously. Yet the
Forand bill, while by this time overwhelmingly supported by northern
and western Democrats, still had not won the support of the southern
wing of the party. Among southerners still unpersuaded were those in the
key congressional positions—Majority Leader Lyndon Johnson and

---

[49] For a summary of the opposition arguments, see statement by Nelson Cruikshank;
inserted in *Cong. Record*, Vol. 106 (April 13, 1960), p. 7994 (his critique was directed
against a bill, introduced by Jacob Javits of New York and other Republican senators, that
followed the general lines of the subsequent administration bill); remarks of Senator
Joseph Clark, Democrat of Pennsylvania, *ibid.* (May 19, 1960), p. 10698, and Senator
McNamara, *ibid.* (June 2, 1960), p. 11661.

[50] *Congressional Quarterly Almanac, 1960*, p. 155.

[51] *Washington Post*, June 16, 1960.

Speaker Sam Rayburn of Texas, Chairman Wilbur Mills of Arkansas in the House Ways and Means Committee, and Chairman Harry Byrd of Virginia and Robert Kerr of Oklahoma in the Senate Finance Committee. Throughout the South the influence of doctors and insurance agents far outweighed the influence of organized labor. In Mills' second district of Arkansas, Cruikshank had noted, the largest town had a population of 7,500, and except for some railroad locals and one carpenters' local of seven members, organized labor was nonexistent.

A test vote in the Ways and Means Committee in March 1960 found only eight of the twenty-five members for the Forand bill—all northern and western Democrats—and only one more for a modified measure sponsored by Democrat Hale Boggs of New Orleans. Early in April, reports Harris, Rayburn reversed his position and urged Mills to have his committee reconsider. Mills agreed. But the Arkansan was firmly committed against the Forand bill. What he needed was an approach that was neither Flemming's nor Forand's—one that would respond to the pressures for action from Rayburn and others, yet leave him faithful to his Arkansas commitments.[52] He found it by returning to the old concept of public welfare—direct assistance for the indigent only, a course the AMA had suggested when it denounced the administration bill.[53] He proposed a new category of medically indigent persons over sixty-five who were not on public assistance but who could pass a means test establishing their inability to pay for medical care. The federal and state governments would share the cost of the health care, through either direct payments or purchase of private insurance, under plans that the states would develop. The federal share would be greater for lower-income states. The provision was approved quickly by the committee as part of a general measure liberalizing social security benefits, and the committee obtained its usual closed rule prohibiting floor amendments. Forand called the Mills proposal "a sham . . . a mirage . . . a watered-down version of a no-good bill that came from the White House,"[54] but the bill as a whole could hardly be opposed. It passed, 381–23.

[52] Harris, "Medicare," Pt. 2, July 9, 1966, pp. 66–70. Harris says that Johnson reversed his position at the same time as Rayburn but later rejected a proposal by Walter Reuther that he join the other Democratic presidential candidates in endorsing the bill publicly.

[53] *New York Times,* May 6, 1960. A comparable approach had been advocated by Republican Senator Robert A. Taft of Ohio in 1946 as an alternative to national health insurance proposals (Harris, "Medicare," Pt. 1, July 2, 1966, p. 46).

[54] *Cong. Record,* Vol. 106 (June 22, 1960), p. 13820.

In the Senate the bill reached the floor when Congress reassembled after the national party conventions. Although the Democrats had endorsed health care through social security in their platform and had nominated for President one of the leading advocates of that proposal, only five of the eleven Democrats on the Finance Committee supported an amendment by Senator Clinton Anderson of New Mexico embodying the Kennedy approach.[55] The others—all from southern or border states—voted with the Republicans for a modification, sponsored by Kerr, of the Mills provision for direct assistance to the medically indigent based upon a means test. But the Senate, unlike the House, could consider floor amendments. First, Jacob Javits, New York Republican, proposed an amendment based on his own earlier bill and the administration bill, but eliminating the deductibility feature of the latter. It received not a single Democratic vote and lost, 67–28. Then Anderson, with Kennedy as a cosponsor and with the support now of Majority Leader Johnson, offered his proposal, and the Republicans returned the compliment. Of thirty-three Republicans, only Clifford Case of New Jersey voted with the Democrats. The others joined nineteen southern and border state Democrats to defeat it, 51–44. Javits argued that it would be better not to try to write an insurance plan "at this time, under the intensely political circumstances of this brief session."[56] Besides, he contended, the Anderson amendment was by no means the best bill that could be written.

The President signed the Kerr-Mills bill,[57] and the issue thus entered the presidential campaign. Neither candidate stood on the Kerr-Mills act as the final answer. Kennedy berated the Republicans, in speech after speech, for giving his medicare amendment only a single vote in the Senate. "Ninety percent of the Republicans voted against the social security in the mid thirties and 95 percent in 1960 voted against the medical care for the aged tied to social security," was his line.[58] Nixon, again strik-

[55] The Anderson plan increased benefits to 120 days of hospitalization and 240 days of subsequent nursing home care but retained the 0.5 percent tax increase of the Forand bill by raising the eligibility age to 68 and making the first $75 of hospital costs deductible.

[56] *Cong. Record,* Vol. 106 (Aug. 20, 1960), p. 17213.

[57] President Eisenhower reportedly considered vetoing the bill because of the liberal matching formulas. The bill was especially favorable to the lower-income states (see *Congressional Quarterly Almanac, 1960,* p. 161), which included Oklahoma and Arkansas.

[58] Remarks at University of Southern California, Nov. 1, 1960, *The Speeches of Senator John F. Kennedy, Presidential Campaign of 1960,* S. Rept. 994, 87 Cong. 1 sess. (1961), Pt. 1, p. 844.

ing a defensive note, argued the superiority of the administration proposal. "The American people . . . do not want, they must not have, a compulsory health insurance plan forced down their throats, and we will not allow it," he told his audiences.[59] The Democrats for the first time in a presidential campaign created a special committee and headquarters staff unit to organize an appeal to "senior citizens." Aime Forand was chairman, and medicare was the center of the appeal.

The Struggle for Consensus   *(1961–65)*

President Kennedy lost no time in sending his medicare proposal to Congress. But Wilbur Mills was still chairman of the Ways and Means Committee, and Mills still represented rural Arkansas. He was "tentatively opposed" to the administration bill,[60] which was introduced by Representative Cecil R. King of California and Senator Anderson, but sent word to the President that "something can be worked out" if he were given time; he suggested that his committee be bypassed by initiating the measure in the Senate as an amendment to a House-passed bill.[61] The President "kept after" Mills but the latter did not move, and in April Kennedy suggested that initial action in the Senate might be the administration strategy.[62]

Meanwhile, both the proponents and the opponents organized for a show-down battle for public opinion. The advocates got the first break when a White House conference on aging, organized under the supervision of Secretary Flemming and held in January 1961, reported favorably on health insurance under social security after hearing Marion Folsom, Flemming's predecessor, advocate the approach he had rejected while in office. As the conference closed, 150 to 200 of the delegates held a separate meeting to form an ad hoc committee to set up a permanent organization of senior citizens that would, among other things, press for

[59] Speech at Cleveland, Oct. 6, 1960, *The Speeches of Vice President Richard M. Nixon, Presidential Campaign of 1960*, S. Rept. 994, 87 Cong. 1 sess. (1961), Pt. 2, pp. 477–78.

[60] The bill followed closely the Anderson-Kennedy amendment of 1960, but incorporated changes recommended by a task force headed by Wilbur Cohen, later assistant secretary and secretary of HEW.

[61] Theodore C. Sorensen, *Kennedy* (Harper & Row, 1965), p. 343.

[62] News conference, April 21, 1961, *Public Papers of the Presidents, 1961*, pp. 310–11.

enactment of medicare. Aime Forand, who had just retired from Congress, agreed to serve as chairman. In July the permanent organization, the National Council of Senior Citizens, was formed, and Blue Carstenson, who had worked with Forand in the senior citizens unit of the Kennedy campaign headquarters, became its executive director. By the year's end Forand reported 525,000 members, with an additional 900,000 supporters under sixty-five. Mammoth rallies were held late in 1961 in Miami, Detroit, and other cities. The council assembled mailing lists of organizations of retired people and distributed informational materials of all kinds, which were prepared by the administration, the AFL-CIO, and its own small staff, with the inevitable exhortation to "write your Congressman." Before the fight was over, the council was to distribute seven million pieces of literature—more, according to Carstenson, than on any other legislative issue in the country's history. By 1963 its outlets included senior citizen clubs affiliated with the council, either closely or loosely, with a total membership of two million. The labor federation, which underwrote about half the council's deficit (the Democratic National Committee covered the other half), was meantime distributing materials to constituent unions throughout the country and urging them to pass resolutions, obtain publicity, and stimulate letters to congressmen.[63]

The AMA kicked off its campaign early in 1961 by sending every member an advertisement-poster, designed for office display, entitled "Socialized Medicine and You." The doctors later received a supply of leaflets they were urged to hand their patients.[64] At a strategy meeting in April attended by representatives of state medical societies, the AMA organized a campaign of letters and visits to congressmen, with special attention to members of the Ways and Means Committee, and an advertising, direct mail, and speaking program. The meeting also emphasized the importance of solidifying the "united front" of health professions, and in particular of obtaining a reversal of the American Nurses Association endorsement of the bill.[65] The nurses' national headquarters later reported pressures upon their members from their doctor-employers in thirty-five states. "Rather unethical pressures," the nurses' president called

[63] This section relies upon a case study by Gary L. Filerman, "The Legislative Campaign for the Passage of a Medical Care for the Aged Bill" (Master's thesis, University of Minnesota, 1962).

[64] Harris, "Medicare," Pt. 3, July 16, 1966, p. 37.

[65] *Medical World News*, April 14, 1961, quoted in Filerman, "The Legislative Campaign for . . . Medical Care for the Aged Bill," p. 64.

them. The association lost some members, but it held its ground.[66] The "united front" was further broken when a physicians committee for health care for the aged through social security was formed, with prominent and respected names on its letterhead, and the health care section of the American Public Health Association endorsed the medicare proposal.

By summer the proponents appeared to be winning the contest for public opinion. A Gallup poll showed 67 percent of the voters favored medicare. But there was no sign of any shift of opinion within the Ways and Means Committee that would overturn the Republican-southern Democratic majority recorded against the Forand bill the year before. Mills did consent to hold hearings, and nine days of testimony in July and August served further to publicize the measure. But Congress adjourned with no further action.

During the fall, both sides stepped up their organizing and propaganda efforts. Medicare was made the central theme of a series of ten regional meetings at which Cabinet officers and other spokesmen presented the administration program and accomplishments to the public. Senator McNamara's special committee on aging set out on its ambitious series of field hearings which took testimony—and generated publicity and support—in thirty-one cities in thirteen states. The AMA meantime organized a political arm on the pattern of labor's committee on political education—the American medical political action committee—and by January corresponding bodies had been established in thirty-five states to wage the anti-medicare drive during the early months and then to enter the 1962 congressional elections in force. Estimates of expenditures by organized medicine during 1961 and the first half of 1962 ranged from $3 million to $7 million. The AMA reported lobbying expenses higher than those of any other group.[67]

The Health Insurance Institute was a second center of opposition, working through insurance agents throughout the country. But the AMA suffered an important loss when the American Hospital Association at a special meeting early in 1962 withdrew its opposition to social security financing. The hospital association still objected to the King-Anderson bill, however, holding that medicare should be administered through voluntary organizations such as Blue Cross.[68]

The administration, the AFL-CIO, and the National Council of Senior

---

[66] See Michael J. O'Neill, "Siege Tactics of the A.M.A.," *Reporter,* April 26, 1962, p. 31; Harris, "Medicare," Pt. 3, July 16, 1966, p. 46.

[67] *Congressional Quarterly Almanac, 1962,* p. 939.

[68] O'Neill, "Siege Tactics," p. 30.

Citizens—now coordinated by a special unit in the White House—agreed to bring their campaign to a climax with simultaneous rallies across the country on May 20 when Congress would presumably be approaching the showdown stage. President Kennedy would address the New York City rally at Madison Square Garden, and his appearance would be carried to the other rallies by closed-circuit television. When the networks arranged to cover the President's address as a news event, the AMA asked for equal time, hired the Garden for the following evening, and—when they were denied free time—purchased the time.

By all accounts, the AMA won the debate. The President gave a "fighting stump speech," as Sorensen described it, which was unpersuasive to the skeptical TV viewer at home and aroused editorial criticism for "hippodrome tactics" and "circuses."[69] Dr. Edward R. Annis of the AMA, with an empty arena as his backdrop, delivered an impassioned but effective plea to the viewers to trust their doctors' judgment on the "sacred" human relationships involved in the practice of medicine. Proponents were disheartened that their long-planned publicity coup had misfired. "The President's performance just let the steam out of the whole effort," said one afterward. At the same time the AMA brought its advertising campaign to a climax, with full-page displays in newspapers across the country urging readers to write their congressmen. Presumably as the result of these factors, the tenor of congressional mail abruptly shifted from favorable to unfavorable.

If the administration had ever had any prospects in the Ways and Means Committee, they faded now. HEW Secretary Abraham Ribicoff was ready to talk compromise, but his overtures failed. The lineup was reportedly ten Republicans and five southern Democrats, including Mills, against the bill, and ten Democrats in favor.[70] Senator Javits thereupon forced the issue by threatening to adopt as his own the administration's alternate strategy of initiating the measure as an amendment on the Senate floor. The senator proposed to use as his vehicle the so-called "Ribicoff bill" to amend the public welfare laws,[71] which had passed the House. The White House and Anderson agreed to move first.

Bipartisanship in the Senate. Since there appeared little chance for a significant increase in Democratic support in the Senate beyond the forty-

[69] Sorensen, *Kennedy,* p. 343; *New York Times* and *Wall Street Journal,* May 21, 1962.
[70] *Congressional Quarterly Almanac, 1962,* p. 193.
[71] See Chap. 4, pp. 129–30.

three who had voted for the Anderson-Kennedy amendment in 1960, the prospects of success lay in striking a compromise that would be acceptable to at least a half-dozen Republicans. Ten Republican senators, at least, were on record that some legislation was necessary. Led by Javits, they had introduced early in 1961 a bill embodying the administration-Javits plan of 1960. Perhaps the compromise that was beyond reach in the political heat of the post-convention session in that year could be achieved in the cooler atmosphere of 1962.

Javits had opened the door to negotiations by announcing that he would accept social security financing—in the belief that the outlook was dim for any plan that required financing from the general treasury—and in January he introduced a new bill and called for a "genuine bipartisan effort" to break the deadlock. His new bill differed from the administration measure, introduced by Senator Anderson and Representative King, in these major respects: It provided coverage for retired persons outside the social security system, with their benefits financed from the general funds. It restricted benefits for social security enrollees to those actually retired; the King-Anderson bill covered all persons over sixty-five eligible for retirement. While social security payroll taxes would finance the program, it would still be administered through the states. Health insurance moneys would be maintained in a fund separate from other old age, survivors, and disability insurance (OASDI) funds. It provided each beneficiary a choice of three plans—a "preventive" or "short-term illness" plan which covered fewer days of hospitalization but twelve visits to physicians, a "catastrophic" or "long-term illness" plan, or a $100 contribution to a private insurance program—instead of the single range of benefits in the King-Anderson bill. The "long-term illness" option of the Javits plan was closest to the King-Anderson bill; it provided 120 rather than 90 days of hospitalization and 360 rather than 180 days of nursing home care after discharge, the greater benefits offset by a higher deductibility ($125 instead of $90) and a requirement that the beneficiary pay 20 percent of all costs.

Senator Anderson met with representatives of the administration and the AFL-CIO to work out a line of compromise. They had no difficulty agreeing to accept from the Javits bill the benefits for those retired persons not under social security, and the provision for a separate fund. They also agreed, as the American Hospital Association had proposed, to utilize private nonprofit organizations such as Blue Cross in administering the benefits.[72] The most difficult point was the Javits insistence upon options, which the HEW technicians opposed as administratively undesirable.[73] Anderson then presented to Javits the conclusions of his strategy group. Except for the option question, which they agreed to discuss further, Javits found the compromise acceptable. But when he in turn presented the compromise to the nine cosponsors of his original bill, the group split. Some objected to the substance of the compromise bill; the negative shift in public opinion, as reflected in congressional mail, also had had its effect. Not more than four of the nine were willing to go as far as Javits. Anderson negotiated an agreement with Javits on a form of private insurance option—agreeing that a person holding a private insurance plan upon retiring could elect to continue it in preference to the social security health benefits—and their amendment was ready.

As the debate neared a conclusion, the prospect appeared close to a 50–50 split of the Senate. Pressure from both sides was concentrated upon the handful of uncommitted senators. Among these, unexpectedly, was Jennings Randolph, West Virginia Democrat. Randolph had supported the Anderson-Kennedy amendment in 1960 and still endorsed the principle, but he found himself in an awkward position in 1962. West Virginia had overspent its federal funds under another section of the public assistance law, and Senator Kerr had accepted in the pending welfare bill a retroactive provision covering West Virginia's deficit. Few believed that Kerr, who was known as a sharp trader, had solved West Virginia's problem out of sheer magnanimity, but in any case Randolph could explain that a fight over medicare might jeopardize the entire welfare bill to which the medicare amendment would be attached—and in which his state had an extraordinary stake. Moreover, he could argue that the medicare vote would only be a "gesture" anyway, since the amendment would never be accepted by the Ways and Means leaders in the House-Senate conference. West Virginia Democrats and labor leaders, alerted from Washington, inundated Randolph with communications, and Kennedy appealed to him, but in the end he cast his vote with Kerr.[74] Then Carl Hayden, Democrat of Arizona, who had promised his vote to Kennedy if it were

[72] However, in the course of the debate both the AHA and the Blue Cross Association announced their opposition to the Anderson-Javits amendment as written (Filerman, "The Legislative Campaign for . . . Medical Care for the Aged Bill," pp. 172–74).

[73] *Ibid.*, pp. 148–50.

[74] According to Sorensen, Kennedy responded by canceling a public works project in West Virginia (*Kennedy*, p. 345). See *Congressional Quarterly Almanac, 1962*, p. 195, for Randolph's explanation of his position.

needed to pass the bill, also voted in the negative and the Anderson-Javits amendment went down, 52–48. Every member of the Senate was on the floor and voted.

Few votes had been changed as the result of two years of some of the most intensive lobbying ever carried out on any measure. When the five unrecorded senators of 1960 are allocated according to their announced or probable positions,[75] the division that year was 53–47. Four Republicans—Javits and Kenneth Keating of New York, John Sherman Cooper of Kentucky, and Thomas Kuchel of California—switched to the affirmative in 1962. But one vote was lost when Republican John Tower replaced Lyndon Johnson as a senator from Texas, and Randolph and Hayden accounted for two more losses. The net gain, therefore, was only one.

"A most serious defeat for every American family," said President Kennedy. "The American people are going to make a decision in November as to whether they want this bill, and similar bills. . . ."[76]

The people's verdict was for medicare. Although the American medical political action committee spent $248,484 directly and estimated that doctors raised and spent five times that much locally,[77] organized medicine could not claim to have been instrumental in defeating a single pro-medicare senator or congressman. On the contrary, enough new Democrats were elected to the Senate to reverse that body's 1962 decision. Six Democrats, all supporters of medicare, defeated six Republican opponents of the measure, while three Democrats were beaten by Republicans—for a net gain of three. The National Council of Senior Citizens claimed that senior citizens' organized political action on the medicare issue was decisive in several close elections, including the defeat of Representative Walter Judd, Minneapolis Republican and physician, and the victory of former HEW Secretary Ribicoff as senator from Connecticut. "I traveled to every city and town in New Hampshire promising to support the medicare program if elected," said Senator Thomas J. McIntyre, one of the victors and the first Democrat sent to the Senate from New Hampshire in three decades. "Throughout my state . . . I found widespread approval of

---

[75] Two of the absent senators did not announce their positions; Thomas E. Martin, Iowa Republican, is assumed to have been against the bill, and Olin D. Johnston, South Carolina Democrat, for it, on the basis of his favorable 1962 vote.

[76] Statement of July 17, 1962, *Public Papers of the Presidents, 1962*, pp. 560–61.

[77] Harris, "Medicare," Pt. 3, July 16, 1966, pp. 65–66, quotes Representative King as estimating total political expenditures by physicians in 1962 at $7 million.

this program. I believe that this support is uniform throughout our nation, and it is now time to follow the mandate of the people. ..."[78]

But the outlook in the House was substantially the same. The opponents of the new King-Anderson bill, which closely paralleled the Anderson-Javits compromise of 1962,[79] still controlled the Ways and Means Committee, though by a slimmer margin. Of the fifteen-man opposition majority of 1962, Burr P. Harrison of Virginia had retired, and James B. Frazier, Jr., of Tennessee had been defeated in a primary in which his opposition to medicare had been the major issue. The Democratic caucus, in a revolt against Speaker John McCormack, had filled both vacancies with supporters of medicare,[80] but the majority against the bill was thus brought down only to 13–12. The three Democrats joining all ten Republicans in opposition were Chairman Mills, Sydney Herlong of Florida, and John C. Watts of Kentucky. Of these, Mills and Watts appeared, for a time at least, to waver. Mills indicated that he might switch if, in doing so, he would not cast the deciding vote. Watts, at one point, had given Mills his proxy, which could have been the deciding vote to which the Arkansan could then add his own.[81] But Watts later withdrew his proxy. The action came after the American Medical Association had lent its prestige to the embattled tobacco industry by suggesting that the surgeon general's report linking tobacco to lung cancer was inconclusive and accepting $10 million from the industry to study the question. Watts, it

[78] *Cong. Record,* Vol. 110 (Sept. 1, 1964), p. 21266.

[79] The new bill, which was introduced as recommended by the administration, had dropped the private insurance option but offered three alternative social security plans varying in numbers of days of hospitalization coverage and deductible amounts to be paid by the insured. Otherwise the features taken from the Javits bill were retained.

[80] Richard Bolling, *Defeating the Leadership's Nominee in the House Democratic Caucus* (published for the Inter-University Case Program by Bobbs-Merrill, 1965). McCormack supported the candidacy of Phil Landrum of Georgia for one of the vacancies. Bolling, one of the organizers of the revolt in the caucus, writes that the fate of medicare, which he considered "the most potent political measure in the President's program," was a prime consideration in deciding to make an issue of the Landrum election. The members chosen were Ross Bass of Tennessee and W. Pat Jennings of Virginia, each the strongest administration supporter within his state's delegation. McCormack himself, it should be noted, was a strong medicare supporter.

[81] It was widely reported in 1963 that President Kennedy and Mills had come to an understanding on medicare. Kennedy flew to Arkansas to dedicate some public works projects, with Mills much in evidence. When Mills opened hearings in November, just before the assassination, some observers thought they detected a change of heart on the chairman's part. In any case, the understanding—whatever it may have been—did not carry over to President Johnson (interview with Nelson H. Cruikshank, January 1968).

was pointed out, represented a tobacco district.[82] When Watts withdrew his proxy, King chose not even to press for a vote. That left the issue, once more, to initiation by the Senate.

In the Senate the outcome was assured. The 1962 election had switched three votes, Kerr's death had released his Democratic colleague from Oklahoma, Mike Monroney, and Randolph had returned to the fold and with him Hayden. On the Republican side, Javits had added Margaret Chase Smith of Maine to his small but decisive bloc. But Javits used his bargaining position to demand one more concession. Early in 1963 the senator had prompted the formation of an independent national committee for health care for the aged, consisting of prominent doctors and other leaders who were in favor of federal action but dissatisfied with the King-Anderson bill. Headed by former HEW Secretary Flemming, it had another former HEW secretary, Marion Folsom, among its members. In November it recommended a dual public-private approach—hospital and nursing home care through social security, as the King-Anderson bill provided, and other medical services through private insurance plans that would be "mutually reinforcing and mutually dependent" with the public insurance.[83] To facilitate the private insurance plans, Javits proposed exemption from the antitrust laws, exemption from taxation, and federal regulation of the companies involved. In hasty negotiations during the course of the debate, in 1964, the bill's Democratic sponsors accepted the antitrust exemption in order to permit the carriers to pool their risks, but rejected the other two provisions. With this change, the Javits "private enterprise" provision was added to the King-Anderson plan (which this time was the Gore amendment, sponsored by Senator Albert Gore of Tennessee) and the medicare amendment passed, 49–44—the first time the proposal had been approved by either house.

But that was as far as the bill could go. Mills and two Republicans comprised a majority of the five-man House delegation to the House-Senate conference, and they were adamant. Their position was supported by a vote count that showed the measure fell far short of majority support in the House. While the Senate conferees consisted of a majority who had voted against the Gore amendment, they supported the Senate's position even to the point of permitting the entire bill—which contained a substantial rise in social security cash payments—to die in a conference dead-

[82] Harris documents the "alliance" between AMA and the tobacco industry and quotes various allegations that the "deal" had cemented Watts' wavering position ("Medicare," Pt. 3, July 16, 1966, pp. 76–80).
[83] *Cong. Record*, Vol. 109 (Nov. 13, 1963), pp. 21737–39.

lock. One of the Senate Democratic conferees who had opposed the medicare amendment, George Smathers of Florida, is quoted as saying he held out for it in conference because "Lyndon told me to."[84] The White House saw the increase in social security cash benefits as useful and necessary leverage when medicare was sought again in 1965, and it feared that separate enactment of the higher cash benefits—which would bring the total social security payroll tax to the 10 percent long regarded as its practical limit—would bar the addition of health insurance for many years to come.

After the collapse of the conference, which occurred just a month before the 1964 election, Barry Goldwater tried to pin upon the Democrats the blame for the loss of the social security benefit increase. "The issue was whether to wreck the social security system by tacking on Johnson's medicare scheme," he said. Johnson asked the people once more to "pass judgment" on medicare in the election and give to the Congress and the President a "mandate."[85]

The People's Mandate. The 1964 Democratic landslide settled the question. Practically the entire Democratic "class of '64" in the House—numbering sixty-five, of whom thirty-seven represented a net replacement of Republicans—was committed to medicare. The National Council of Senior Citizens computed a net gain of forty-four votes for the bill. Lyndon Johnson named the issue his top priority legislative measure, and the congressional leadership responded by assigning the numbers H.R. 1 and S. 1 to the administration bill, introduced by King and Anderson.[86] The lopsided Democratic majority in the House entitled the Democrats to two more seats on the Ways and Means Committee, and two Democratic supporters of medicare replaced two opposition Republicans.[87] Polls showed a heavy popular majority for the bill. Mills quickly boarded the

[84] Harris, "Medicare," Pt. 3, July 16, 1966, p. 89. Another conferee who had opposed medicare, Russell B. Long (Democrat of Louisiana) was ambitious to succeed Hubert Humphrey as majority whip and depended upon medicare supporters for his votes. Harris asserts that Anderson had promised his support to Long if the latter held out for medicare in conference.

[85] *Congressional Quarterly Almanac, 1964*, p. 239.

[86] The 1965 administration bill dropped the optional benefits in favor of a 60-day hospitalization limit, with the first day's costs deductible. It included the Javits proposal for pooling of resources by private companies in developing supplemental plans.

[87] The National Council of Senior Citizens brought 1,400 old people to Washington at the opening of the Congress to make sure that the House Democrats reorganized the Ways and Means Committee to produce a pro-medicare majority. Two busloads from Boston kept vigil on Speaker McCormack until he announced his plan.

bandwagon. He scheduled executive hearings to begin January 29 and predicted a bill would be approved by March.

The AMA chose not to accept the inevitable. "We do not, by profession, compromise in matters of life and death; nor can we compromise with honor and duty," the association president, Dr. Donovan F. Ward, told the postelection convention of the organization in November.[88] The AMA announced an alternative to medicare which it called "eldercare"—an expansion of the Kerr-Mills act of 1960 to permit federal and state governments to purchase private health insurance policies for the needy aged—and launched an elaborate advertising and lobbying campaign to promote it.[89] But they could not even maintain their alliance with the House Republicans. Republican Representative Curtis of Missouri joined Democrat Herlong of Florida in introducing "eldercare," but the ranking Republican on the Ways and Means Committee, John W. Byrnes of Wisconsin, introduced his own measure which won official Republican Policy Committee support in the House.

"We all feel, Democrats and Republicans alike, that something should be done, that action is called for," said Byrnes in explaining his bill. "Our difference, and it is an important difference, is as to how."[90] Like the Herlong-Curtis bill, the Byrnes bill would authorize subsidies to enable elderly persons to buy private health insurance policies, but it would be wholly federal both in administration and in financing. Two-thirds of the cost of the policies would be paid from general revenues, one-third by the insured, and the social security system would be used indirectly by permitting OASDI beneficiaries to pay their one-third by means of deductions from their monthly checks. The means test as such was eliminated but the premiums, averaging $6.50 a month, would be varied according to the beneficiaries' incomes.

While the Byrnes bill would add $2 billion a year to the federal budget, its author could rightly claim that its benefits were far broader than those of the King-Anderson bill. The latter covered only hospital and nursing

[88] Quoted by Harris, "Medicare," Pt. 3, July 16, 1966, p. 91.

[89] According to Harris, the AMA distributed $4 million from its reserve funds to the state medical societies, which they were expected to match ("Medicare," Pt. 4, July 23, 1966, p. 37). *Congressional Quarterly Weekly Report*, Aug. 19, 1966, said that the AMA officially reported lobbying expenditures of $1,155,935 for 1965—an amount greater than the next nine highest-spending organizations combined. The reported amount had been exceeded only twice in history, in both cases by the AMA, which reported spending more than $1.5 million in 1949 and $1.3 million in 1950.

[90] *Cong. Record*, Vol. 111 (April 7, 1965), p. 7220.

home care up to a specified number of days, and some home care, but the Byrnes bill covered virtually all medical costs. The AMA in its advertising campaign had been stressing the fact that the administration's medicare plan did not cover doctors' bills. If the King-Anderson bill were passed, the Republicans would be able to say "we told you so" to every aged person who discovered, to his dismay, that his doctors' bills and drugs were not covered by the new law after all. Mills solved the problem by suddenly proposing a marriage of the two proposals. To the basic King-Anderson bill he added a supplementary voluntary program, which followed the approach of the Byrnes bill, to subsidize private insurance for surgery, physicians' services, and certain other health costs not covered by King-Anderson. At a cost of $3 a month to the beneficiary and $500 million a year to the treasury, the plan would cover 80 percent of the cost of the additional services beyond a deductible $50 each year. President Johnson happily accepted the additional budget item, and the bill came out of the committee on a straight party-line vote.[91] In its report the committee majority finally agreed that the Kerr-Mills program of 1960 did not meet the national problem of medical care for the aged "to the extent desired . . . because of the failure of some states" to implement it.

The House debate was desultory. "It is obvious that the House is not in a mood to debate and deliberate," complained Representative Curtis. "The decision which was made outside the well of the House, outside the deliberative process, is going to prevail. Members have already made up their minds. They are voting on a label."[92] Only one hundred and fifteen members of the House voted against the bill on final passage—seventy-three, or 53 percent, of the Republicans, forty southern and two non-southern Democrats. However, the vote on a motion to substitute the Byrnes bill was closer. It lost by only 236–191, and the division of 58–7 among the first-term Democrats made the margin of difference. Southern Democrats voted 60–38 against the administration and Mills. The elder-care proposal upon which the doctors had concentrated their heavy spending did not even come to a vote.

The tally on the Byrnes motion suggests that a social security approach to medicare would have been rejected by the House in any year before 1965, if the Ways and Means Committee had permitted a medicare bill to reach the floor. Defenders of the committee could claim, therefore,

[91] The bill also included a greatly expanded program of medical care for the medically needy of all ages, which came to be known as "medicaid."
[92] *Cong. Record*, Vol. 111 (April 7, 1965), p. 7229.

that that body had been only reflecting the views of the House when it bottled up the Kennedy and Johnson bills during the years from 1961 through 1964. Proponents could reply that with Mills' support, *some* bill would surely have been passed, and that an acceptable measure could have been worked out in the House-Senate conference. In any case, they could argue, the decision was properly one for the House itself to make.

The principal issue in the Senate was a proposal by Senator Ribicoff, the former HEW secretary, supported by Russell Long, the bill's floor manager, to remove the time limitation on hospital and nursing home benefits. The move was opposed by the administration as jeopardizing the bill by "overloading" it with benefits. The AMA supported the amendment—for the same reason[93]—and eight of the bill's last-ditch opponents voted for it. But it lost, 43–39, and a more modest liberalization was adopted. The final Senate vote for medicare was 68–21. In less than a year, Javits' little band of five Republican supporters of medicare had grown to fourteen, just two short of half his party's members in the Senate.

The House-Senate conference accepted some of the Senate's liberalization, adding thirty more days of hospital benefits to the original sixty but with $10 a day deductible in the added period. The original sixty days of nursing home care after hospitalization was extended indefinitely but with $10 a day deductible for the added period. The payroll tax increase was set at an initial 0.7 percent of payroll, rising to 1.6 percent by 1987. The wage base would rise from $4,800 to $5,600 initially and to $6,600 in 1971.

The final measure was the product of fifteen years of refinement and liberalization since the first medicare proposal was conceived in the Federal Security Agency, and eight years of continuous public debate since Forand presented his original proposal. Many of the major changes were made to meet Republican objections and embodied ideas that the Republicans could claim as their own. Thus, the extension of coverage to the 2.8 million persons over sixty-five outside OASDI, which Senator Anderson accepted from Senator Javits in their compromise of 1962, remained in the bill from that time on. The separation of medicare funds from those of OASDI had its origin in the same bipartisan compromise. So did the provision authorizing HEW to use private nonprofit organizations as intermediaries in dealing with hospitals. Most important of all, the sup-

[93] *Washington Post,* June 23, 1965; *Congressional Quarterly Weekly Report,* June 25, 1965, p. 1236.

plemental program covering surgical care and doctors' fees with a 50 percent federal subsidy was taken directly from the Republican bill sponsored by Representative Byrnes and is akin, except for the subsidy feature, to the proposal earlier developed by the Flemming committee and advanced by Javits. But no matter how great the contribution of individual Republicans, they did not speak officially for the party. "I still believe the majority is in error and I think the country will come to regret having pursued this course," said the House Republican spokesman on the issue, Mr. Byrnes, just before the final vote.[94] A majority of Republicans in the Senate and 49 percent of those in the House voted against the conference report.

President Johnson journeyed to Independence, Missouri, to sign the bill in the presence of Harry Truman. "No longer will older Americans be denied the healing miracle of modern medicine," the President said. "No longer will illness crush and destroy the savings that they have so carefully put away over a lifetime so that they might enjoy dignity in their later years."[95]

[94] *Cong. Record,* Vol. 111 (July 27, 1965), p. 17739.

[95] *Public Papers of the Presidents, 1965,* p. 813. From July 1, 1966, to June 1967, about four million persons received $2.4 billion in hospital services paid for under medicare, and another $640 million had been paid for physician's services in the voluntary medical insurance part of the program (article by HEW Under Secretary Cohen, "Medicare and Medicaid: A Progress Report"; inserted in *Cong. Record,* Vol. 113 [June 14, 1967], daily ed., p. H7261).

CHAPTER VIII

For All, a Better
Outdoor Environment

"A PRIME NATIONAL GOAL," Lyndon Johnson told the Congress in 1965, "must be an environment that is pleasing to the senses and healthy to live in."

In retrospect, one wonders why it took so long. As late as the 1950's, national policy relating to the outdoor environment had scarcely advanced from the point where Theodore Roosevelt had left it fifty years before—some public lands were to be preserved for recreation, but beyond that the nation would be content to let the forces of technology and economics, under such control as the states might exercise, determine the quality of the world in which its people lived.

In the early 1950's, hardly a word was spoken in the Congress to suggest that the beauty of countryside and city, the purity of air and water, the pressure of population upon outdoor open space were *national* concerns. Yet, a decade later the pages of the *Congressional Record,* reflecting to some extent the pages of newspapers and magazines, were filled with concern about the deterioration of the American environment. When President Johnson in February 1965 sent to the Congress the first presidential message ever devoted to natural beauty, the national government had adopted or was in the process of adopting a long series of measures declaring its responsibility for that environment. These measures, revolutionary in concept and in scope, were intended to cleanse the nation's water and air, create a network of recreation areas for urban populations, set aside wilderness areas in perpetuity, and beautify the nation's highways.

322

Thus did a long-standing national need burst suddenly upon the public consciousness. As the public mood changed from apathy to awareness, and then to alarm, national policies were proposed, refined, debated, and enacted. This chapter traces the development of both the mood and the measures.[1]

The Dispute over the Federal Role *(1953–60)*

"Water pollution is a uniquely local blight," said President Dwight Eisenhower in 1960. "Primary responsibility for solving the problem lies not with the Federal Government but rather must be assumed and exercised, as it has been, by State and local governments. . . . The Federal Government can help, but it should stimulate State and local action rather than provide excuses for inaction. . . ."[2]

These words from a message vetoing a Democratic bill to expand federal aid to localities for sewage treatment works—a program the President had earlier tried to abandon altogether—epitomized the continuing conflict of the 1950's. As demands for national action arose and grew, they collided with Eisenhower's faith in the principle of states' rights and states' responsibilities. And they clashed even more sharply with his views on public finance. If the issue were one that combined an increase in the federal budget with an expansion of the federal role, the President was steadfast. But most significant action proposals required money. During Eisenhower's eight years in office, consequently, the federal government undertook few major new departures to conserve or improve the outdoor environment.

Yet the problems did not go away. On the contrary, they steadily and visibly worsened. And as the bankruptcy of the states' rights principle in these fields became apparent, the agenda for national action in the 1960's was developed.

The Demand for Clean Water. Only in one six-year period since 1900 had construction of sewage treatment plants by the nation's cities kept pace with the growth of population. That was in the years 1933–39, when

---

[1] Much of this chapter is based upon the research of, and draft materials prepared by, Sandra Bennett.

[2] Message of Feb. 23, 1960, *Public Papers of the Presidents, 1960*, pp. 208–09.

the federal government, through the Public Works Administration, had paid a part of the cost of municipal public works.

So said a spokesman for the nation's mayors in telling Congress in 1956, "We are losing the battle against water pollution." "At the present rate of construction," he asserted, "in 1966 we will be twice as far behind as we are now."[3] The backlog of construction needs for sewage treatment plants and interceptor sewers was estimated at $1.9 billion, with another $3.4 billion needed in the next decade to replace obsolescent facilities and meet the needs of population growth. In all, more than $5 billion would be needed—yet expenditures were then running at only $200 million annually.

The federal government had entered the field of water pollution control in 1948, but on a limited scale. Under the Water Pollution Control Act, the Public Health Service (PHS) was authorized to conduct research and make research grants to the states. It was empowered to hold hearings and make recommendations on abatement problems on interstate streams, but could undertake enforcement only with the consent of the states involved. The act also authorized grants for the planning of sewage treatment plants and $22.5 million annually in low-interest loans for their construction. But no funds for the loan program were ever appropriated.

When the time came for renewal of that act in 1955, PHS was ready for the next step forward. It proposed amendments to strengthen its enforcement powers, and President Eisenhower recommended them to the Congress. The amendments would authorize PHS to initiate federal abatement action without the consent of the state in which the polluter was located if the action were requested by any other state adversely affected, and would empower PHS to set water quality standards for interstate streams if the states did not do so within a reasonable time.

Strong opposition from industry witnesses, supported by the states, persuaded the Senate committee to delete the provision for federal water quality standards. After that change, the bill moved easily through the Senate. Then the House Public Works Committee, which had been preoccupied with highway legislation, held a quick one-day hearing and sought to put the bill through the House just before adjournment. But the measure turned out to be more controversial than it had appeared.

[3] Testimony of R. P. Weatherford, Jr., mayor of Independence, Mo., for American Municipal Association, in *Water Pollution Control Act*, Hearings before the Subcommittee on Rivers and Harbors of the House Public Works Committee, 84 Cong. 2 sess. (March 13, 1956), p. 244.

Industries that feared federal enforcement stirred up so many members of the House that Speaker Sam Rayburn, Texas Democrat, decided to carry the bill over until the following session rather than attempt passage in the preadjournment rush. This unexpected development drew a sharp reaction from the bill's manager, John Blatnik, Minnesota Democrat. With the remark, "If the polluters don't like S. 890, let's give them a bill they really won't like," he assigned a staff aide, Jerome N. Sonosky, to spend the rest of the year considering what might go into a more effective statute.

By the time the new Congress met, in January 1956, Blatnik had decided upon the essential ingredient of a stronger bill: grants-in-aid to the states and cities to build sewage treatment plants. The idea had its origin, of course, in the Public Works Administration of the 1930's, and it had been kept alive ever since. In 1946 the House Rivers and Harbors Committee, predecessor of the Public Works Committee, had approved a grant bill. Senator Matthew M. Neely, Democrat of West Virginia, had introduced a similar bill in 1954, backed by labor, municipal, and conservation groups of the Ohio Valley, and Democratic Representative Lester R. Johnson of Wisconsin had a bill before Blatnik's subcommittee in 1955. The Outdoor Writers Association of America endorsed the idea at its 1954 convention. Late in 1955 the National Wildlife Federation summoned a meeting of conservation organization representatives to consider water pollution legislation, and they proposed grants for sewage treatment works, though for only 10 percent of the cost. It became clear that a distinctly Democratic measure could be drafted as a substitute for the Eisenhower bill, and that the new measure would appeal to a broad coalition of mayors, who wanted financial aid for municipal functions; sportsmen and conservationists, who wanted clean streams for recreation; and in a lesser role organized labor, which wanted jobs.

Blatnik asked the American Municipal Association to help Sonosky draft a bill and obtained help also from Murray Stein, a lawyer in the Department of Health, Education, and Welfare who had worked on the Eisenhower enforcement proposals. Their measure added to the enforcement features of the Senate bill a provision for $100 million a year in federal grants for municipal sewage treatment works. The grants would cover half the cost of a project, up to $500,000 in aid for any one project. Blatnik obtained consent of the House to return the pending bill to his committee, introduced his new bill, and reopened hearings. The coalition was now formalized. Its representatives began holding regular breakfast meetings to pool information and coordinate tactics—sessions that became known as "sewer breakfasts."

Party lines were drawn at once on the grant proposal. State responsibilities were not adequately recognized, argued the administration; cities did not need more money, they just needed to assign higher priority to waste-treatment works.[4] Not so, responded the mayors' spokesman; how could a community set aside "desperately needed" school classroom construction in favor of a sewage treatment plant?[5] Some state witnesses were favorable to grants; but the national organization of state public health officers was officially opposed. The health officers feared that some municipalities, awaiting federal grant funds, might delay projects that otherwise would go ahead. They pointed out that many communities had bonded themselves heavily to comply with sanitation standards but "the recalcitrant . . . or those who deliberately delayed . . . would now be blessed with a sizable fiscal gift despite their former actions." They suggested the grant funds be converted to loans instead.[6] But the American Municipal Association polled its members and received what a staff member called an "avalanche" of letters favoring grants, which were sorted by congressional districts and sent on to individual congressmen. The conservation organizations likewise rallied their members. "The purpose is to speed up lagging construction," Charles H. Callison of the National Wildlife Federation told the subcommittee. "Something is needed—and needed urgently —to speed up the overall program." With particular reference to enforcement, he added: "The people get a little impatient with theoretical arguments about the line between States rights and Federal jurisdiction. Unless we get some real action, the pollution program is going to get so smelly, the public health so endangered, and the water supply situation so critical, the public is going to demand a cleanup—and the public won't be particular about who swings the enforcement ax."[7]

After Blatnik accepted a series of compromises—reducing the authorization from $100 million to $50 million, the federal share from 50 percent to one-third, and the ceiling on individual grants from $500,000 to $300,000—the committee Democrats voted the bill out over a warning

[4] Testimony of Roswell B. Perkins, assistant secretary of HEW, in *ibid.* (March 12, 1956), p. 135.

[5] Testimony of George W. Dill, Jr., mayor of Morehead City, N.C., for American Municipal Association, in *ibid.* (March 14, 1956), p. 268.

[6] Testimony of Daniel Bergsma, New Jersey commissioner of health, president, Association of State and Territorial Health Officers, in *ibid.* (March 12, 1956), p. 151.

[7] *Ibid.* (March 15, 1956), pp. 366, 369.

by an eight-man Republican minority against the "new spending spree" that would follow. The party battle continued on the floor. Since "the debt of the Federal Government exceeds the debt of all the cities and of all the states and of all the other nations of the world combined," Republican Representative Gordon H. Scherer of Ohio contended, it is the cities who are "best able to pay."[8] To Blatnik, however, the bill without the grant provision would be "about as effective as a person rapping on the windowpane with a wet sponge; no one would hear him."[9] A motion to recommit the bill to strike the grant provision was defeated, 213–165. Republicans voted four to one for recommittal, Democrats seven to one against. Senator Robert Kerr, Oklahoma Democrat, manager of the Senate bill, was at first unhappy with the Blatnik amendments,[10] but finally, with only slight concessions—reduction of the federal share to 30 percent and the ceiling to $250,000—the bill was accepted by the Senate conferees. Then it passed both houses by voice vote. President Eisenhower concluded that the construction grants alone did not justify a veto of an otherwise good bill. In signing it, he expressed hope that municipalities would not postpone construction of needed projects because of the prospect of federal grants. The next year the Democrats defeated a motion supported by more than three-fourths of the House Republicans to kill the appropriation the President had dutifully included in his budget.

But the issue was not yet settled. In 1957 President Eisenhower put to a practical test the cardinal conviction of his political philosophy—that the trend toward centralized government must and could be reversed—and water pollution control became one of the principal testing grounds. In his address to the National Governors' Conference at Williamsburg, Virginia, he proposed creation of a joint committee of governors and federal executives to identify federal functions that could be assumed by the states and federal revenue sources that could be relinquished to finance them. By the end of the year, the Joint Federal-State Action Committee had settled upon grants for sewage treatment plants and vocational education as federal functions that could be discontinued and had agreed upon a portion of the temporary federal tax on local telephone service as the revenue source that could be relinquished to the states. To assure that the

---

[8] *Cong. Record,* Vol. 102 (June 13, 1956), p. 10237.

[9] *Ibid.,* p. 10245.

[10] M. Kent Jennings, "Legislative Politics and Water Pollution Control, 1956–61," in Frederic N. Cleaveland (ed.), *Congress and Urban Problems* (Brookings Institution, 1969). The Jennings study traces the history of water pollution legislation up to 1961.

states actually picked up the telephone levy when the federal government dropped it, the committee proposed that for the first five years the federal tax continue unchanged in those states that did not act. Governors on the committee who generally supported federal aid programs went along with the committee's recommendation, for reasons explained this way by Democratic Governor George M. Leader of Pennsylvania: "This federal program . . . was so limited that it was really holding back our program, rather than contributing to its rapid development. In other words, for each grant that was made in Pennsylvania, we had five or ten municipalities who were waiting in line for grants."[11]

President Eisenhower was unreservedly pleased with the committee recommendations. The governors, however, were not. The principle of states' rights, they discovered, interfered with another objective sometimes more deeply cherished—the redistribution of income through federal action. Specifically, the poorer three-fourths of the states, they learned, contributed only 30 percent of the telephone tax revenues but received 59 percent of the grants for sewage treatment plants and vocational education. More than half of the states and territories would actually receive less from the taxes than from the grants. At their 1958 conference the governors accepted the Joint Action Committee's plan only on condition that it be modified so that "the revenue source made available to each state is substantially equivalent to the costs of the functions to be assumed."[12]

Representative Blatnik was unreservedly displeased with the whole idea. To him the scheme was "a new gimmick . . . for torpedoing this most vitally needed Federal function . . . under the alluring mantles of economy and States rights." Only one state, he pointed out, had established a state aid program independent of the federal aid. "The reason we enacted section 6 [the grant provision] in the first place," he told the House, "is the fact that through the years the States have not assumed their responsibilities." And he found nothing in the committee report that gave assurance that the telephone tax, if relinquished, would be used by the states to finance pollution control.[13] But the criticism from Governor Leader and others that the federal program was too limited he happily accepted. He promptly introduced legislation to restore the annual authorization to the $100 million figure of his original bill and the ceiling on grants for individual projects to the original $500,000.

---

[11] *Proceedings of the National Governors' Conference, 1958* (Chicago: Governors' Conference, 1958) pp. 18–19.

[12] *Ibid.*, p. 164.

[13] *Cong. Record*, Vol. 104 (Feb. 13, 1958), pp. 2165–71.

Hearings on the new Blatnik bill in 1958 produced stronger support than in 1956. As in 1956, the American Municipal Association, the conservation organizations, and the AFL-CIO were favorable, the Eisenhower administration and the polluting industries opposed. But a decisive shift had occurred among the state pollution control agencies. Even though their governors were then weighing the proposal that federal aid be terminated, the men who dealt daily with pollution problems, like the chairman of North Carolina's stream sanitation committee, found the program "quite effective in accelerating sewage treatment works construction . . . and in many instances such projects could not have been undertaken" without the federal aid.[14] The Michigan water resources commission, a leading opponent of construction grants two years before, confessed in a letter to Blatnik that "apparently we were wrong and you were right."[15] The committee reported the bill, 21–7, in a gesture of defiance of the President. No attempt was made to pass it.

By the close of the year, the federal Water Pollution Control Advisory Board, created by the original Blatnik act, had climbed aboard the construction grant bandwagon. In its recommendations to the surgeon general, it labeled the Eisenhower-endorsed termination proposal "not feasible," expressed the view that few state legislatures would enact the telephone tax if the federal government relinquished it, and endorsed the objectives of the new Blatnik bill. Meanwhile, the House subcommittee on intergovernmental relations issued a report reflecting the Governors' Conference misgivings that the Joint Action Committee's plan favored the richer states, and the House Ways and Means Committee, which would have to initiate any action on the telephone tax, chose not to do so.

Despite these unfavorable omens, Eisenhower insisted on trying again in 1959. To counter the governors' criticism, however, he introduced an equalization feature for the initial five years. Each state would be assured new revenues equal to at least 140 percent of the amounts it would have received under the two grant programs nominated for termination. The incentive was substantial: the revenues relinquished by the federal gov-

---

[14] Testimony of J. V. Whitfield, in *Amend Federal Water Pollution Control Act*, Hearings before the Subcommittee on Rivers and Harbors of the House Public Works Committee, 85 Cong. 2 sess. (May 22, 1958), p. 199.

[15] *Ibid.*, p. 59. State, territorial, and interstate water pollution control agencies in a November poll voted 48–2 against the Joint Action Committee's recommendation to terminate the program. By overwhelming majorities, they reported the federal aid was stimulating sewage treatment plant construction and endorsed Blatnik's proposal to double the authorization (*Federal Water Pollution Control*, Hearings before the House Public Works Committee, 86 Cong. 1 sess. [March and April 1959], p. 126).

ernment would exceed by $50 million the total amount of the grants to be abandoned. But there was no way the federal government could be assured that the states would use any of the new revenues for water pollution control.

If Eisenhower was stubborn, so was Blatnik. He renewed his 1958 legislative proposals for expanding the grant program and added a provision transferring the water pollution control program from the Public Health Service to a new office reporting directly to the secretary of HEW. The latter move, however, alienated the Water Pollution Control Advisory Board and the state pollution control agencies, and after HEW went part way by raising the status of the program within PHS, Blatnik shelved his reorganization proposal.

Once again the Public Works Committee and the House itself split on party lines. The Republican motion this time was not to kill the program but to hold federal expenditures to the same level and achieve the doubled volume of construction by forcing the states to match the federal aid. Blatnik argued that the amendment would prevent municipalities from moving ahead "until that segment, which has been the slowest of all, the State government, moves."[16] The recommittal motion lost, 240–156. Republicans voted ten to one for it, Democrats eight to one against it. Only twenty-seven Republicans voted for the bill on final passage.

The proposal of the Joint Action Committee had one other powerful opponent—the telephone industry, which wanted the temporary telephone tax not transferred in part to the states and thus made permanent, but abolished outright. When the bill to extend for another year certain temporary taxes, including the one on local telephone service, was considered in 1959, the industry had enough strength to obtain repeal, but with an effective date of June 30, 1960. Thus the Democratic Congress removed the keystone from the Joint Action Committee's structure. The President had no choice but to accept the deferred repealer, since he could not afford to veto the tax extension bill as a whole. When administration witnesses appeared a short time later before the Senate Public Works Committee to oppose the Blatnik bill, they contended that there was still time in 1960 to transfer the tax to the states rather than repeal it, but Senator Kerr—ranking Democrat on both the Finance and Public Works committees—refused to look beyond the fact that the President had signed the repealer. "So that by his own action he has already approved the termi-

16 *Cong. Record,* Vol. 105 (June 4, 1959), p. 9906.

nation of this tax, without a condition, hasn't he?" Kerr demanded of the Budget Bureau witness, and drew an affirmative response.[17] That was the last that anyone heard of the Joint Action Committee and President Eisenhower's effort to roll back the centripetal tides of the federal system.

After the Senate in September passed the Blatnik bill handily—with a majority of Republicans again opposed—the Democrats postponed final action on the bill until the following year. The expected Eisenhower veto would then come in the presidential election year and a dramatic attempt could be made to override it to impress upon the country, as Blatnik had put it earlier, that it was the Democratic Congress, not the Republican administration, that was "concerned with their welfare."[18] The veto message duly came, with its characterization of water pollution as "a uniquely local blight." "Why is water pollution so exclusively local?" demanded Representative Edith Green, Democrat of Oregon. "Is the President aware of the fact that his own home state of Pennsylvania shares the Delaware river with New Jersey?"[19] A majority of the House voted to override, 249–157, but it fell twenty-two votes short of the necessary two-thirds majority. The partisan issue was clearly drawn: Democrats voted nine to one to override, Republicans nine to one against. And John Kennedy was able to say in the 1960 campaign: "I am not part of an administration which vetoed a bill to clean our rivers from pollution."[20]

The Demand for Clean Air. "The problem of air pollution," Republican Senator Thomas Kuchel of California told the Senate in 1955, "has become so widespread that no section of the United States is immune from it. It has posed a continually growing danger to the health and comfort of our people, a serious and increasing hazard to our Nation's agriculture, and a threat to the orderly growth of our industry."

Yet all that he proposed was a $5 million annual authorization for research. As his bill moved through both houses of Congress, not a voice was raised to suggest that a national problem of such magnitude should be dealt with more aggressively by the national government. Senator Kuchel assured his colleagues categorically: "It is not the thought that

[17] *Water Pollution Control,* Hearings before the Subcommittee on Flood Control of the Senate Public Works Committee, 86 Cong. 1 sess. (July 23, 1959), p. 39.

[18] *Cong. Record,* Vol. 105 (June 4, 1959), p. 9878.

[19] *Ibid.,* Vol. 106 (Feb. 25, 1960), p. 3491.

[20] Remarks at Warren, Ohio, Oct. 9, 1960, *The Speeches of Senator John F. Kennedy, Presidential Campaign of 1960,* S. Rept. 994, 87 Cong. 1 sess. (1961), Pt. 1, p. 535.

Congress has anything to do with control of air pollution through the proposed legislation or through any contemplated Federal legislation. That problem remains where it ought to remain—in the States of the Union, and in the cities and the counties of our country."[21] In the House, Representative John H. Ray, New York Republican, observed that when the wind was from the northwest, smoke from New Jersey industrial plants, "and all that is in that smoke," came over his Staten Island district. "In many cases the entire crop of the people who grow flowers for the market has been destroyed," he said. "Vegetable growers have often lost much of their crops overnight." Representative T. James Tumulty, Jersey City Democrat, countered that New Jersey studies showed that air pollution generally originated in New York. But that only proved Ray's point. "Local air pollution boards," said Ray, "cannot deal with the whole problem, because interstate features are involved. The States cannot cross State lines, and the cities cannot go outside their own jurisdiction."[22] But there the colloquy ended. In the same year that the administration was requesting, and the Senate approving, federal enforcement powers to control interstate water pollution, only research was proposed and authorized in the field of air pollution.

The first voice to suggest publicly that research was not enough was that of HEW Secretary Arthur Flemming three years later. From his experience in administering the Water Pollution Control Act, Flemming had concluded by the end of 1958 that comparable enforcement powers were needed to abate interstate air pollution. Opposition came, surprisingly enough, from his subordinates in the agency that would have been given the responsibility—the Public Health Service—and Flemming retreated part way. He gave up, for the time being, the idea of federal enforcement powers but suggested at a December news conference that the federal government should be empowered to hold hearings on interstate air pollution problems on its own initiative and make findings and recommendations. The Public Health Service had opposed even that step. "The advantages of such independent action," the surgeon general had argued, "would be likely to be outweighed by resentment and opposition engendered by what might be construed as an encroachment on state responsibilities."[23] Air pollution was not as serious an interstate problem

[21] *Cong. Record*, Vol. 101 (May 31, 1955), pp. 7249–50.
[22] *Ibid.* (July 5, 1955), p. 9924.
[23] Memorandum from Acting Surgeon General John D. Porterfield to Secretary Flemming, Feb. 16, 1959.

as water pollution, nor were scientific standards as clearly established as a basis for enforcement. And the opposition to federal hearings might jeopardize other features of the administration bill, which included removal of the $5 million limitation on research appropriations. But Flemming overruled the PHS objections to the proposed federal advisory role.

The Budget Bureau also had objections—and these Flemming could not overrule. Accordingly, when he presented his proposal to a House subcommittee on May 19, 1959, he was forced to add a caveat that the Budget Bureau "believes that the need for and desirability of" the legislation "require further study."[24] The Manufacturing Chemists' Association also registered opposition, calling air pollution "a matter which is peculiarly that of the community and State."[25]

The next year (by which time the Budget Bureau had withdrawn its objections) Senator Kuchel piloted the Flemming proposal through the Senate on the unanimous consent calendar, without debate, but the House subcommittee did not find time for hearings. Chairman Kenneth A. Roberts, Alabama Democrat, expressed doubts about whether "the great deal more authority" for the surgeon general was necessary. Kuchel vigorously protested Roberts' delaying tactics. "Since your subcommittee," he wrote Roberts, "already has held extensive hearings and acquired a wealth of information . . . I would think it feasible to reach a decision . . . in a rather short time."[26] But Roberts remained unmoved, and the bill was dead. The Congress did, however, pass a bill directing the surgeon general to make an "urgent" study of the problem of automobile exhaust pollution and report by 1962.

The Demand for Recreation Space. The pressure of people upon open space caught the nation unawares. Travel had been curtailed in the 1930's by the Depression and in the early 1940's by gasoline rationing. But when World War II was over, people had money to spend, plenty of gasoline, and more leisure time than ever before, and they took to the open road in unprecedented numbers. The national parks and the national forest recreation areas—still operated on constricted budgets—were inundated; so were state parks and private resorts.

[24] *Air Pollution Control,* Hearings before the Subcommittee on Health and Safety of the House Interstate and Foreign Commerce Committee, 86 Cong. 1 sess. (May 19, 1959), p. 7.

[25] *Ibid.,* p. 75.

[26] *Washington Post,* Aug. 26, 1960.

A series of articles in *The New York Times* in April 1954 deplored the condition of the national parks: obsolete roads and campgrounds, inadequate facilities, understaffing. Yellowstone National Park had twice as many visitors as in 1937 but seventeen fewer rangers to handle them; Yosemite 400,000 more visitors and fewer rangers; Great Smoky Mountains a million more and fewer man-hours devoted to management and protection. And there was no prospect for any letup in the pressure. Bernard De Voto used his *Harper's* column to paint the same gloomy picture.

To this welcome criticism, the National Park Service responded with a ten-year program to bring its facilities up to date. Christened "Mission 66," the program was approved by President Eisenhower and transmitted to the Congress early in 1956 with a supplementary budget request. In the campaign of that year the President was able to say that, "having inherited a declining system of national parks," he had launched a "bold new 10-year program" to rehabilitate them.[27] Encouraged by Sherman Adams at the White House, the Forest Service followed suit with a five-year development program for its recreation areas, whose visitors had doubled between 1947 and 1954. That program was approved by the President in 1957 as "Operation Outdoors."

But fulfilling established federal responsibilities was one thing, expanding them quite another. A proposal by the National Park Service to acquire large segments of undeveloped shoreline on the Atlantic and Gulf coasts was given a far less cordial reception within the Eisenhower administration. With private funds from anonymous donors, the service in 1954–55 had surveyed the 3,700 miles of Atlantic and Gulf shoreline and updated old studies. "Foreboding is the only word that adequately describes the situation," began the summary of the report, "Our Vanishing Shoreline," issued in July 1956. Of the 3,700 miles, only 240 were in public ownership and much of that—in the Acadia and Everglades national parks—was not beach frontage suitable for seashore recreation. Only 640 miles of beach were still available for public purchase, and they were rapidly being lost to private development. The Park Service suggested public acquisition of half the 640 undeveloped miles, so that 15 percent of the total coastline would be accessible to the public. The urgency was greatest in the Northeast, the most densely populated region of the United States.

[27] Campaign address at Portland, Ore., Oct. 18, 1956, *Public Papers of the Presidents, 1956*, p. 965.

With the report as his basis, Secretary of the Interior Fred A. Seaton proposed a bill authorizing $30 million for federal acquisition of 150,000 acres in five seashore areas, to be selected by the department, and another $15 million to pay half the cost of comparable acquisitions by the states. But the year was 1957, and the proposal perhaps foredoomed. Seaton argued that the speed with which the seashores were vanishing warranted making his proposal an exception from that year's budget stringency, and he had support within the White House and the Budget Bureau. But Budget Director Percival F. Brundage, while finding the proposal intrinsically "worthy," recommended its deferral. The Interior Department countered with a compromise: cut the number of national seashores to three, the acreage to 100,000, and the authorization to $15 million, plus $10 million for aid to the states. The answer, Brundage wrote Seaton, was still "no."

Meanwhile, the time seemed ripe for an idea that Joseph W. Penfold, conservation director of the Izaak Walton League, had first advanced in 1950: to dramatize the need for outdoor recreation development, establish a national commission to take inventory of the country's outdoor recreation resources and measure them against projected needs. Penfold flew to Washington with a draft bill and persuaded Senator Clinton Anderson, Democrat of New Mexico, to become its sponsor. The administration supported the proposal, as refined and introduced by Anderson, and the bill moved through Congress with little difficulty. President Eisenhower named Laurance S. Rockefeller chairman of the new Outdoor Recreation Resources Review Commission (ORRRC), and Anderson and Penfold were among the fifteen members. In late 1958 it held its first meeting, with a directive to report three years later.

In 1959 the Interior Department's attenuated proposal for a $15 million, three-seashore acquisition bill was accepted by Budget Director Maurice Stans, who had succeeded Brundage. "The few accessible and undeveloped beach sites that are left . . . are relatively small, and they are going fast," said Acting Interior Secretary Elmer F. Bennett's letter transmitting the bill to Congress. "Inaccessible sites, including islands, are almost the only hope for preservation today. Even many of these are now being purchased by real estate interests for subdivision purposes." To underline the inadequacy of the administration's bill, sixteen Democratic senators (joined by two Republicans) cosponsored a bill by Senator James Murray of Montana that authorized $50 million for acquisition of ten sea and lake shore areas, identified by name, and study of ten others. As in the administration bill, another $10 million would be provided for state land purchases. Echoing Bennett's note of urgency, Murray said, "If the need is not met by this Congress, it will have to be met a few years from now. Prices then will inevitably be many times higher. . . . It is my hope that this Congress will put an end to the enormously costly and foolish economy of postponing necessary expenditures."[28]

The political point having been made, the Senate Interior Committee then proceeded to the consideration of the sea and lake shore areas, one by one, through individual bills. Each proposal stirred up opposition from those whose property would be condemned, and the boundaries and terms of acquisition had to be negotiated. Hearings were held in 1959 on acquisition of the Cape Cod outer beach, Padre Island off the Texas coast, and the Oregon coastal dunes, but the laborious task of working out compromises that would leave the people of the affected areas reasonably happy could not be completed on any of the bills during the remainder of that Congress.

The Demand for Wilderness Preservation. The pressure of people upon open space aroused not only those who wanted to develop mass recreation areas in the wilderness but also those who wanted to leave a portion of the wilderness completely undeveloped—those who, in the words of Robert Marshall, would "repulse the tyrannical ambition of civilization to conquer every niche on the whole earth."

As early as 1924, the Forest Service had begun to set aside certain remote areas of the national forests to be preserved in their primeval state. In the national parks, roads and recreation development were authorized —although much of the acreage remained roadless—but logging, grazing, and mining were generally forbidden, as they were in the national wildlife refuges and designated "wild" lands within Indian reservations. But in all of these areas, wilderness was preserved by administrative regulation rather than by statute, and the administrative agencies could always reverse themselves. Moreover, their legal authority was limited; the Forest Service, for example, could not prohibit prospecting and mining even in areas designated as wilderness.

[28] *Cong. Record*, Vol. 105 (July 29, 1959), p. 14573. Both the administration and the senators were aware that shore areas could not be acquired for $5 million each, but both bills authorized private donations. All of the existing units of the national park system had been either set aside from public lands or donated by the states and private individuals; no federal funds for land purchase for the park system had ever been authorized by Congress.

Wilderness enthusiasts found themselves pitted not only against the lumbering, mining, and livestock interests whose potential resources would be "locked up" forever, but also against those who wanted to open primeval lands to mass recreation through development of roads and campgrounds. Even that much intrusion was incompatible with the concept of wilderness. In the language of one of the early wilderness preservation bills, a wilderness was "an area where the earth and its community of life are untrammeled by man, where man himself is a member of the natural community, a wanderer who visits but does not remain and whose travels leave only trails."[29]

The Wilderness Society and the Sierra Club, which had enthusiastically backed the Forest Service when it used its discretion to set aside wilderness areas, turned more and more to the notion that the discretion of that agency—as well as the discretion of the National Park Service and other Interior Department land agencies—should be limited to prevent a reversal of their actions. By 1951 the outlines of a bill had been drafted, but the latent sentiment for such a measure was not crystalized until two years later. Then a catalytic issue, a proposal to construct Echo Park dam within the Dinosaur National Monument in Utah, aroused the public as no conservation issue had in many years; Speaker Rayburn said in 1954 that congressmen had received more mail in protest against Echo Park dam than on any other subject.[30] The conservationists won the battle. In doing so, they demonstrated that the people wanted their wildernesses preserved. The time had come for action on a broad scale.

The drive for wilderness legislation began in earnest in 1955 and followed the classic pattern for developing support for a bill. Howard Zahniser, executive director of the Wilderness Society, advanced the general proposal in a speech before an American Planning and Civic Association conference in Washington.[31] Senator Hubert Humphrey, Minnesota Democrat, inserted the speech in the *Congressional Record*. The society mailed reprints to its members and to the mailing lists of other conservation groups under the franks of cooperative legislators. Humphrey inserted favorable replies in the *Record*, and these were again circulated.

[29] S. 1176, 85 Cong. 1 sess. (1957), sec. 1(c). The *Wildnerness Act*, P.L. 88–577, 88 Cong. 2 sess. (1964), sec. 2(c), contains some of the same phrases.

[30] Reported by Representative John P. Saylor (Republican of Pennsylvania), *Living Wilderness*, No. 59 (Winter-Spring 1956–57), p. 1.

[31] Speech delivered May 24, 1955; reprinted in *ibid.*, pp. 37–43.

In cooperation with other conservation leaders, Zahniser put the idea in legislative form. Humphrey and Republican Representative John Saylor of Pennsylvania agreed to be its sponsors. Neither was in an ideal position —Saylor was a minority member of the House committee and Humphrey not even on the Senate committee with jurisdiction. But wilderness was an unknown issue to most members of Congress and to the public; Zahniser's immediate need was for help not to pass a bill but to publicize one. For this purpose, zeal was more important than status, and Humphrey and Saylor could be counted among the zealots. Their bill was introduced in 1956, and the first hearings were held the following year.

The most comprehensive attack came, as expected, from commercial interests that would be excluded from the wilderness, or severely restricted in it. The American Mining Congress, the American Pulpwood Association, and the American National Cattlemen's Association were their spokesmen. They argued economics and western self-interest: wilderness meant locking up valuable resources that the country, and the West in particular, needed for economic growth. They argued administrative flexibility: the changing needs of the country for timber and minerals required changing policies. They appealed to the mass recreationists: it would be inequitable to dedicate vast acreages to the exclusive enjoyment of the hardy 1 percent who preferred to find their outdoor recreation without benefit of roads and campgrounds. They appealed to the administrative agencies: the bill implied that the agencies could not be relied upon to manage wisely the lands entrusted to them, and the proposed national wilderness preservation council (which with a majority of private citizens among its members would have the right to review and publicly advise upon administrative actions proposed by the agencies) would interfere with orderly administration. And they pleaded for delay: legislation should await the report of the Outdoor Recreation Resources Review Commission (ORRRC), then about to be created.

"It hurt our pride, to suggest we had to have our hands tied by law," a senior Forest Service official said some years later in explaining his agency's initial opposition to the wilderness bill. While expressing sympathy with the objectives of the measure, both the Forest Service and the Interior Department as spokesmen for the Eisenhower administration objected to those features that limited administrative flexibility and placed final determination of wilderness areas in Congress. The bill, said Richard E. McArdle, chief of the Forest Service, "would strike at the heart of the multiple-use policy of national-forest administration. . . . It would tend to hamper free and effective application of administrative judgment which now determines, and should continue to determine, the use, or combination of uses, to which a particular national-forest area should be devoted. If this special congressional protection is given to wilderness use, it is reasonable to expect that other user groups will subsequently seek congressional protection for their special interests."[32] The Interior Department found special objections to inclusion of wildlife refuge and Indian lands. Both the Interior Department and the Forest Service objected to the role of the proposed preservation council. The Department of Agriculture (in which the Forest Service is located) submitted an alternative bill that would recognize wilderness as one of the multiple uses of the national forests and establish criteria and procedures for establishment of wilderness areas by the President.[33] Interior had also sought to work out an alternative bill but could not reach agreement with the Budget Bureau; in its report it recommended referring the question to the proposed ORRRC.

In successive versions of the bill in 1958 and 1959, its authors made some concessions to the views of the Interior and Agriculture departments, particularly in regard to the proposed wilderness preservation council, but not enough to win their outright endorsement. President Eisenhower showed no personal interest in the bill, either favorable or unfavorable. The sponsors, meanwhile, continued to publicize the bill, and Senator Murray, as chairman of the Interior Committee, cooperated by calling hearings at appropriate intervals. But the opposition was organizing also. In a series of hearings in the West in 1958 and 1959, the most powerful voices were those of the resource-based industries and the state and local officials and chambers of commerce whose support they could command. "This portion of the United States has been left in a wilderness condition altogether too long now and it didn't begin to fulfill its purpose until the hand of man and his ingenuity were brought to bear upon it," was a typical expression by a cattlemen's association president.[34] Washington needed 12,500 new jobs a year, said the spokesman for that state; "we live in a raw materials economy. . . . Our new jobs . . . must come from greater

---

[32] *National Wilderness Preservation Act,* Hearings before the Senate Interior and Insular Affairs Committee, 85 Cong. 1 sess. (June 19–20, 1957), p. 93.

[33] *Ibid.,* pp. 8–17.

[34] Testimony of Alonzo F. Hopkin, president, Utah Cattlemen's Association, at Salt Lake City, in *ibid.,* 85 Cong. 2 sess. (Nov. 12, 1958), p. 755.

use of our raw materials. . . . We need greater access to these raw materials rather than less."[35]

The bill did not become more than a muted partisan issue in those years. Congressional support and opposition were both bipartisan. The Humphrey bill had nine Democratic and three Republican cosponsors, and the leading advocate in the House continued to be Republican Saylor. The principal opponent in the House was Democrat Wayne N. Aspinall of Colorado, Interior Committee chairman, but in the Senate committee, when the bill appeared to have a narrow majority in 1960, the "filibuster" that blocked it was led by Aspinall's Republican colleague from Colorado, Gordon Allott.

The partisan positions became clearer in 1960, when neither the Republican party's platform nor its candidate mentioned wilderness but the Democratic platform and candidate did. The Democratic plank sounded somewhat like the traditional platform straddle—endorsing creation of a wilderness system embracing areas already set aside for that purpose, with extension "only after careful consideration by the Congress of the value of areas for competing uses"—but the language reflected the actual terms of the Humphrey bill. Senator Kennedy confined himself to a simple endorsement of the platform proposal, with the comment that legislation need not await the ORRRC report.[36]

The Demand for Highway Beautification. As a free-lance journalist, Richard Neuberger had specialized in singing the scenic glories of his native Pacific Northwest. When he found himself, as a freshman Democratic senator from Oregon in 1955, on the subcommittee writing the act creating an interstate highway system, he saw an opportunity to strike a blow in defense of scenery. He offered an amendment written in his own language with, as he explained it, a single purpose: "namely, that in the case of the interstate system, which the American people are going to invest and are investing billions of dollars to construct, it should not be possible to plaster it with all kinds of advertising material, which would have no value whatsoever unless the American people had invested billions of dollars in the road system."[37]

[35] Testimony of H. DeWayne Kreager, director, Washington department of commerce and economic development, in *ibid.,* 86 Cong. 1 sess. (March 30, 1959), pp. 38–39.
[36] *The Speeches of Senator John F. Kennedy,* S. Rept. 994, Pt. 1, p. 1208.
[37] *Cong. Record,* Vol. 101 (May 23, 1955), p. 6788.

When Neuberger's amendment was recast in legal language by the Bureau of Public Roads and adopted by the Public Works Committee, it was a milder measure than his statement would suggest. Far from making highway advertising impossible, it merely authorized the federal government, acting as agent of the states, to acquire advertising easements along the interstate highway system as part of the land acquisition process when the states so desired. It contained no federal compulsion, nor any incentive beyond federal sharing of the cost of the advertising easements in the same 90-10 ratio that applied to the cost of land purchased for the highways. Yet even this limited amendment ran into a withering attack on the Senate floor as an invasion of states' rights. "I do not wish to have the federal government intervene and say what the states must do in reference to lands adjacent to the public highways running through the states," declared the patriarchal Walter F. George, Georgia Democrat, in leading the assault. The opposition to billboard regulation appeared strong enough to endanger passage of the highway bill itself. After a huddle with the bill's managers, Neuberger yielded, and the amendment was deleted by unanimous consent.

The episode marked the extension to the national capital of the contest that had raged for years in the state capitals between the billboard and antibillboard lobbies. On the one side were the outdoor advertising industry and roadside business groups, supported often by organized labor reflecting the views of the sign painters and allied unions. On the other side were conservation organizations, garden clubs, and miscellaneous women's and civic groups, supported usually by newspaper editorials that extolled beauty and safety without reference to the newspapers' own self-interest in suppressing a competitive advertising medium. In a few states, notably in New England, billboards had been kept from scenic areas by state legislation. But in most states the billboard lobby had prevailed.

After the 1955 incident, both sides organized for another showdown when highway legislation would again come before Congress, in 1957. Neuberger added to his proposal a directive to the secretary of commerce to promulgate recommended standards to prohibit billboards within 500 feet of interstate highways except in certain narrowly specified areas. Again, he proposed no federal compulsion nor any federal incentive beyond the 90 percent federal cost-sharing on the purchase of advertising easements. "The new highways, once built, will not be relocated in this generation," said Neuberger in introducing his bill early in 1957. "Unless we give thought now to the question of what the traveler is to see, as he cruises through the fields and forests and mountains and prairies of America, we know that he will see what we see along other highways today: Signs and billboards, large flat boards placed to capture his attention, designed with all the skill commercial artists can muster, to hammer into his consciousness the virtues of a cigarette, a whiskey, a brand of automobile or gasoline. . . . The motorist pays for the road with his fuel and vehicle taxes. He ought at least to have the right to glimpse the grandeur which the Almighty created throughout our countryside." And he quoted the Ogden Nash quatrain that was to echo and re-echo through the billboard debates during the next few years:[38]

> I think that I shall never see
> A billboard lovely as a tree.
> Perhaps unless the billboards fall
> I'll never see a tree at all.

Neuberger had strong allies in Bertram D. Tallamy, the federal highway administrator and former New York highway commissioner whose pride was the billboard-free New York thruway, and Commerce Secretary Sinclair Weeks, whose native Massachusetts had been a pioneer in billboard control legislation. A few weeks after Neuberger introduced his bill, they presented an alternative approach that not only contained a far stronger incentive to state action but also would achieve its goal at no cost to the federal treasury—a prime requirement in 1957. Instead of offering federal payment of 90 percent of the cost of advertising easements—which they estimated would cost the federal government $300 million—they proposed a penalty. The secretary of commerce would establish standards; noncomplying states would be required to pay 15 percent rather than 10 percent of the cost of interstate highway projects in their states. The states could comply either by buying land and easements or by exercising police power, or by a combination of these means, as New York had done in building its thruway. The Weeks proposal was presented in Senate hearings in March as "in accord with the program of the President,"[39] but Eisenhower at a news conference a month later expressed doubt that the federal government had any right to do anything. "So I think it is a very complicated question, and while I am against these

---

[38] *Ibid.*, Vol. 103 (Jan. 29, 1957), pp. 1129–30. Ogden Nash quatrain copyright 1932 by Ogden Nash (originally appeared in *The New Yorker*) ; from *Verses from 1929 On* by Ogden Nash, by permission of Little, Brown and Co.

[39] Statement of Secretary of Commerce Sinclair Weeks, in *Control of Advertising on Interstate Highways*, Hearings before the Subcommittee on Public Roads of the Senate Public Works Committee, 85 Cong. 1 sess. (March 18, 1957), p. 5.

billboards that mar our scenery, I don't know what I can do about it," he concluded.[40]

The opposing forces confronted one another in the hearings and then organized a deluge of mail to senators and congressmen. "We must look to our National Government to do that which we at the State level have been unable to do," the president of the Pennsylvania roadside council told the subcommittee.[41] The advocates made no clear-cut choice between the Neuberger and administration bills; they would gladly accept whichever the Congress preferred. But many thought both bills too weak and indecisive. They had fought their losing battles in their respective states and had little sympathy with the deference shown in both bills to the traditional rights of the states to make the regulatory decisions, subject only to financial incentives or penalties. Argued Albert S. Bard, counsel to the New Jersey roadside council: "It seems a little inconsistent to establish a national policy and then turn around and say to the States, 'Won't you please enforce our national policy?' I say that the federal government is not under any obligation to concede that it lacks the power to protect a . . . highway system that the Federal Government is proposing to create."[42]

Public opinion was with the enemies of billboards. Ten thousand Marylanders responding to an automobile club poll voted 95 percent to 5 percent in favor of prohibiting billboards on limited-access highways.[43] A Trendex telephone survey taken at the time of the hearings showed 66 percent in favor of billboard control, 26 percent against, and 8 percent with no opinion. The Trendex poll was "influenced by the public emotion of the times" which was "whipped up" by the press, responded the advertising industry spokesman.[44]

Except for the economic interests affected, no groups defended billboards. The advertising industry relied heavily upon the states' rights argument. "The states now have authority to enact any regulatory legislation which they desire or decide they need," contended Harley B. Markham, chairman of the Outdoor Advertising Association of America, Inc. "Legislation for federal control would not only preempt and usurp this

[40] On April 17, 1957, *Public Papers of the Presidents, 1957,* p. 292.
[41] Testimony of Mrs. Ernest N. Calhoun, in *Control of Advertising,* Hearings, (March 19, 1957), p. 74.
[42] *Ibid.,* p. 77.
[43] Testimony of Washington I. Cleveland, in *ibid.,* p. 75.
[44] *Advertising Agency,* Jan. 17, 1958.

right, but would assume that the States are unaware or unconcerned about their own resources," and the legislation would be "of doubtful constitutionality." He opposed "Federal regulation and control of business in general," and objected to singling out his industry for such regulation and control. Outdoor advertising was "a legitimate business use of land" subject only to the kind of local zoning controls applying to use of land generally.[45] "Outdoor advertising is a driving force in our economy," argued another of the association's spokesmen. "With the other major advertising media . . . it has its own key role in keeping the distribution of goods and services efficiently in high gear."[46] The painters, electrical workers, sheet metal workers, and carpenters unions joined in contending that their labor could "contribute materially toward the actual beautification of the countryside," and the parent AFL-CIO resolved that "highway users are entitled to full information disseminated in the American way"—from which premise it drew the conclusion that state and local restrictions on information were compatible with the American way but federal restrictions were not.[47] Roadside businesses on highways from which traffic would be diverted to the interstate system emphasized their competitive disadvantage if they were not allowed to let interstate highway travelers know of their existence.

From the beginning the subcommittee rejected the penalty approach advanced by Secretary Weeks. In the view of Chairman Albert Gore, Tennessee Democrat, to reduce the federal commitment from 90 percent to 85 percent would be "reneging" on a "moral commitment" made by the Congress when it passed the interstate highway act.[48] So the subcommittee stayed with the Neuberger approach but sought to strengthen the financial incentive. Instead of 90-10 sharing of the cost of advertising easements, it proposed to exclude such costs from federal aid but increase the federal share of all other costs of interstate highway projects from 90 to 90.75 percent in those states exercising billboard control. The effect would be to encourage the use of police power as against the procurement of easements. Police power would cost the states nothing, yet they would get the full 0.75 percent bonus.

Approved by one vote in subcommittee, the measure also carried by a

---

45 *Control of Advertising*, Hearings (March 26, 1957), p. 301.

46 Testimony of James E. McCarthy, dean emeritus, College of Commerce, University of Notre Dame, in *ibid.*, p. 296.

47 Letter from the four unions to the AFL-CIO president, Jan. 29, 1957, and resolution adopted by AFL-CIO executive council, Feb. 6, 1957, in *ibid.*, p. 156.

48 *Ibid.*, pp. 10, 390.

single vote in the full committee, after the committee accepted several amendments designed to meet specific objections and again altered the incentive formula—reducing the bonus from 0.75 to 0.50 percent but restoring cost-sharing on easement acquisition up to a limit of 5 percent of right-of-way acquisition costs. The committee vote on approval of the bill split both parties; three Democrats and four Republicans voted for the measure, four Democrats and two Republicans against.[49]

By the time the measure reached the Senate floor, as one provision of a broader highway bill, opponents of billboard control had mobilized far more letterwriters than had supporters, but the mail was discounted. "Obviously," said Senator Frank Lausche, Democrat of Ohio, "it comes from those who have a financial interest in perpetuating billboards along the highways" and "was artificially generated."[50] After an arduous debate, during which the bill's managers accepted several amendments designed to appease the opponents, billboard control survived by a vote of 47–41. Again, the parties split almost evenly, Democrats supporting the measure 24–21 and Republicans 23–20. The House accepted the Senate version. The President, who presumably had resolved his doubts of the previous year, signed the bill with a criticism of some of the concessions made in committee and on the floor "which might permit advertising to go unchecked in some areas."[51]

The following year Congress made one more concession. Senator Kerr, contending that the standards issued by the secretary of commerce violated the intent of Congress, persuaded the Public Works Committee, by an 8–6 vote, to approve a provision that all areas zoned for business use prior to that time would be excluded from control. Billboard control supporters protested that the action was taken without hearings and with little discussion and that it was an unwarranted restriction on state discretion, but the Senate sustained Kerr by a 44–39 vote, and the House went along with the Senate.

The Acceptance of Federal Responsibility *(1961–64)*

The major contribution of John F. Kennedy to national thinking about the outdoor environment was, perhaps, an open mind about the budget. President Eisenhower had evinced no great reluctance to expand the

---

[49] *Congressional Quarterly Almanac, 1958*, p. 143.
[50] *Cong. Record*, Vol. 104 (March 26, 1958), p. 5392.
[51] *Public Papers of the Presidents, 1958*, p. 323.

federal role in conservation and beautification—provided money was not involved. In water pollution control, in air pollution control, and in billboard regulation his subordinates had persuaded him to endorse extensions of the federal power to police and enforce; he had boggled only when they proposed additional expenditures. The consistency of the Eisenhower position on conservation is therefore to be found not so much in his oft-restated views about overconcentration of power in the federal government as in the moral precepts about federal spending to which he became increasingly dedicated as the years passed.

This presidential attitude was what Kennedy changed. As a senator, he had joined issue with President Eisenhower on federal grants for water pollution control, and shortly after his inauguration he urged an increase in federal aid for sewage treatment plants—noting that the rate of plant construction was barely half the need. He also recommended legislation for the procurement of certain seashore areas. For the first year he proposed only what he called "modest but symbolic increases" in expenditures for these purposes and for conservation and development of forests, parks, and recreation areas in general, but his messages contained a promise of more increases to come. On nonbudgetary matters, he endorsed the wilderness bill and followed Eisenhower's lead in calling for stronger federal enforcement powers in relation to pollution.[52]

Besides opening the budget gates, Kennedy offered a strong verbal commitment to the goals of the conservationists. "Our common goal," he told them, was "an America of open spaces, of fresh water, of green country—a place where wildlife and natural beauty cannot be despoiled."[53] His accession to the presidency, then, established a climate of greater receptivity to the demands for environmental improvement that had been growing during the Eisenhower years. These demands were given further impetus, as well as concrete form, by the landmark report of the Outdoor Recreation Resources Review Commission issued a year later. By the end of 1964 the disputes of the 1950's over the role of the federal government in the improvement of America's outdoor environment were on their way to being resolved—in favor of federal responsibility and leadership.

---

[52] Special messages on Natural Resources, Feb. 23, 1961, and on Budget and Fiscal Policy, March 24, 1961, *Public Papers of the Presidents, 1961*, pp. 114–21, 226.

[53] Remarks at the dedication of the National Wildlife Federation building, Washington, D.C., March 3, 1961, *ibid.*, p. 148.

Clean Water: Consensus for Federal Grants. When Kennedy assumed office, the drive for water pollution control had been stalled by President Eisenhower's veto of Representative Blatnik's 1960 bill. But even as that bill was working its way through Congress toward the veto, Blatnik and his staff aide Sonosky were working on a still bolder measure in anticipation of what they hoped would be a friendly new administration in the coming year.[54] In the summer of 1960 they circulated the bill for comment, and when the new Congress convened it was introduced. It expanded the sewage treatment grant authorization, for bargaining purposes, to $125 million a year from the $100 million in the vetoed bill and raised the maximum on individual projects from $500,000 to $600,000. It extended federal authority for pollution abatement to all navigable streams, rather than just interstate streams, but required state concurrence in any federal action on intrastate waters. And it renewed Blatnik's earlier proposal to remove pollution control from the Public Health Service and assign it to a new water pollution control agency in HEW.

Having denounced Eisenhower's 1960 veto, President Kennedy was committed at least to the bill that Eisenhower killed. But he was not prepared, at the outset of his administration, to go much further. The administration therefore recommended the grants be held to Blatnik's 1960 figure of $100 million a year. It proposed an even higher limit on individual projects, based on a sliding scale, and accepted the broader enforcement power. As for the reorganization, HEW Secretary Abraham Ribicoff asked for time to examine the situation.

In contrast to 1959, the proposed expansion of the grant program aroused only tepid dissent. The National Association of Manufacturers still contended "that the Federal grant program has resulted in Federal involvement and intervention in purely local situations; and that this program is part of an unfortunate trend toward federalization of all activities and responsibilities, no matter how local in character";[55] but at least one industrial group, the Manufacturing Chemists' Association, broke ranks to announce its willingness to accept the grant program.[56] On this point, however, the Congress was listening not to industry spokesmen but to city and state officials. While the rate of sewage treatment works construction had risen 62 percent since the initiation of the grant

---

[54] Jennings, "Legislative Politics."

[55] Testimony of Peter J. Short, Jr., in *Federal Water Pollution Control,* Hearings before the House Public Works Committee, 87 Cong. 1 sess. (March 15, 1961), p. 164.

[56] *Ibid.,* p. 180.

program in 1957, the state pollution control administrators argued that the $50 million grant level was holding back construction because municipalities had to wait their turn for the money.[57]

On the proposed expansion of federal enforcement authority, industry witnesses were united and forceful in their opposition while city officials and conservationists thought the provisions still too weak. The American Municipal Association wanted stronger federal sanctions even against its own member municipalities. "The level of enforcement should be prescribed by a Federal agency and Federal authority should be available when States or municipalities are unwilling or unable to act effectively," and the federal authority should extend to intrastate as well as interstate waters, the association's spokesman testified.[58]

When the bill emerged from committee, it reflected the administration position—a $100 million grant program, a higher ceiling on individual grants, the broadened enforcement powers, and no reorganization, although Blatnik did succeed in writing in a provision giving Secretary Ribicoff power to reorganize. On the House floor, Republicans faithful to the Eisenhower position sought first to eliminate and then to reduce the grants, but they were overwhelmed on each occasion by two-to-one margins. An assault on the broadening of enforcement powers lost by the same ratio. Then the bill passed, 308–110. Almost half the Republicans, 79 of 167, voted in the affirmative.

A slightly more conservative bill reported by the Senate committee encountered nothing but praise on the Senate floor and passed on a voice vote. The final measure, which Kennedy signed with "great pleasure," provided that the $100 million grant level would not be reached until the fiscal year 1964 and fixed the ceiling at $600,000 for any individual project.

Having thus overridden the Eisenhower veto of 1960 and settled finally the principle of federal responsibility, the enemies of water pollution hardly broke stride in advocating still further legislation. The cities wanted a bigger grant program, and they particularly wanted the $600,000 ceiling removed in order to permit full federal participation in major projects serving metropolitan centers. The conservationists wanted stronger enforcement and wanted the program taken away from the "medical men" and given independent status in HEW—an action the

[57] Testimony of Milton P. Adams, executive secretary, Michigan water resources commission, in *ibid.*, p. 56.
[58] Testimony of Justus H. Fugate, former mayor, Wichita, Kan., in *ibid.*, p. 14.

secretary had chosen not to take under the reorganization authority given him in the 1961 act.[59]

At this time the activists gained something they had badly needed—an effective champion in the Senate. As governor of Maine, Democrat Edmund S. Muskie had initiated a state program to upgrade the quality of water in Maine streams—an action propelled in part by the dependence of the Maine lobster industry on the purity of coastal waters. As a junior senator, Muskie had deferred to Robert Kerr of Oklahoma on water pollution control legislation, but Kerr died on January 1, 1963, and Muskie found himself the logical heir to Kerr's responsibilities in that field. He at once enlisted the aid of Hugh Mields of the U.S. Conference of Mayors,[60] Murray Stein of HEW, and others to draft a bill that would improve on the 1961 act. On the last day of January, Muskie introduced the bill and within ten days he had twenty-one cosponsors, twenty of them Democrats. Then Senator Patrick McNamara, Michigan Democrat, who as the new chairman of the Public Works Committee wanted to decentralize its activities, saw the opportunity to build a new subcommittee around Muskie and his bill. He created a special body with jurisdiction over both water and air pollution, and for the first time in a decade the Senate took the lead in water pollution control legislation.

The Muskie bill of 1963, which was cosponsored by Blatnik in the House, embodied the program of the activists. It again proposed transfer of water pollution control responsibility from the Public Health Service to a new agency in HEW. From Mields came two sections—one to raise from $600,000 to $1 million the ceiling on individual grants, the other to double the volume of grant aid by authorizing another $100 million annually to assist in separating storm and sanitary sewers in communities where they had been combined. From Stein came language reviving in stronger terms, and applying to all navigable streams, the proposal made by President Eisenhower in 1955 (but rejected by Kerr's subcommittee) that the federal government should set water quality standards. The bill also proposed, for the first time, to declare a "positive" national policy "of keeping waters as clean as possible."

The bill aroused no enthusiasm on the part of the Kennedy administration. The only provision the administration endorsed unqualifiedly, apart from the statement of policy, was the increase in the grant ceiling. It was

[59] See Jennings, "Legislative Politics," for a discussion of the reasons for the importance attached to reorganization by the conservationists.

[60] Mields had formerly been an American Municipal Association aide.

adamant against the reorganization proposal and against the $100 million for sewer separation. In the latter case it contended that more information was needed on the magnitude of the problem and the nature of alternative solutions before a commitment was made to aid that "very costly" program—estimated by the U.S. Conference of Mayors at $3 billion for ninety-two cities alone. It was agreeable to the section on water quality standards, provided the authority was made optional rather than mandatory.

Before taking his bill to the floor, Muskie sought to work out a broad consensus that would include the committee Republicans and the administration. He agreed to the need for better technical data before launching an ambitious sewer separation program and accordingly reduced that authorization to $20 million annually in demonstration grants. With Senator J. Caleb Boggs of Delaware, the ranking subcommittee Republican, he negotiated a milder standards section, which made the authority optional, restricted it to interstate waters, and required that the secretary give the states a chance to act first. With Assistant Secretary Wilbur Cohen of HEW, he compromised the reorganization proposal; a new water pollution control administration would be established but the research and grant programs would be retained by the Public Health Service. Then, aided by Representative John D. Dingell, Michigan Democrat, he persuaded President Kennedy to overrule the objections that still remained in HEW and the Budget Bureau and endorse the modified bill. It thereupon came from committee with only one Republican dissent and passed the Senate by a wide margin, 69–11.

The conservationists appealed to the House Public Works Committee to remove the Muskie compromises. But from the opposite direction industry trained heavy fire on the modified bill, particularly on what remained of the water quality standards section. "There is absolutely no need for such a drastic reversal of approach to water pollution regulation," testified the National Association of Manufacturers, and the Manufacturing Chemists' Association argued that "such a concentration of power in the hands of a single Federal official would be unwise."[61] Industry found strong support within the House committee, and Blatnik found it impossible to achieve the consensus that Muskie had worked out in the

[61] Testimony of Samuel S. Johnson, in *Water Pollution Control Act Amendments,* Hearings before the House Public Works Committee, 88 Cong. 1 sess. (Dec. 10, 1963), p. 328; testimony of Albert J. vonFrank, in *ibid.,* 88 Cong. 2 sess. (Feb. 17, 1964), p. 557.

Senate. Not until September 1964 did the committee report a bill—
which ten of the fourteen committee Republicans lambasted as "premature, unnecessary, and undesirable"—and by then it was too late for
action in a presidential election year. The issue thus went over until 1965.

Clean Air: Federal Enforcement Powers. As in the final Eisenhower
Congress, Representative Roberts remained throughout the first Kennedy
Congress the main obstacle to an expanded role for the federal government in air pollution control. As late as the end of 1962, he was saying,
"I do not think the Federal Government has any business telling the
people of say Birmingham or Los Angeles how to proceed to meet their
air pollution problems. This was made clear in the 1955 act. Even if
Washington attempted to exercise such authority, we would have a hard
time writing and enforcing regulations at long range. . . . Abatement and
enforcement programs to be effective must remain the responsibility of
local government." The only federal role he would accept was one of
research and dissemination of information.[62] Accordingly, he again
blocked the Kuchel bill for federal hearings and advisory recommendations on interstate air pollution problems, which the Senate passed with
administration endorsement in 1961, and he deferred action on an administration proposal of 1962 for federal grants to state and local air
pollution control agencies for developing, initiating, or improving programs. But he did promise full hearings on the subject in 1963.

Meanwhile, Hugh Mields, the ubiquitous lobbyist for the U.S. Conference of Mayors, had taken up the clean air cause and was seeking
ways either to move Roberts or to bypass him. He prepared a bill incorporating most of the administration measure of 1962 but adding a policy
statement directing the secretary of HEW to "mount a concentrated national effort to achieve the prevention and control of air pollution within
the next ten years," and persuaded Representative George M. Rhodes of
Pennsylvania, ranking Democrat on the Roberts subcommittee, to introduce it. Senator Clair Engle, Kuchel's Democratic colleague from California, sponsored the same bill in the Senate. Then, with technical assistance from HEW staff, Mields proceeded to draft an even stronger

---

[62] Speech to National Conference on Air Pollution, quoted in testimony on behalf of
National Association of Manufacturers, in *Air Pollution*, Hearings before the Sub-
committee on Public Health and Safety of the House Interstate and Foreign Commerce
Committee, 88 Cong. 1 sess. (March 18–19, 1963), p. 174.

bill, which would include federal enforcement powers along with research and grants-in-aid.[63]

Events in December 1962 focused public attention upon the question of federal enforcement powers, an issue that had lain quiescent since Arthur Flemming had advanced it four years before. A national conference on air pollution assembled in Washington, and even as it met, news came of a smog in London that killed 340 persons. At the conference Flemming reasserted his support of federal enforcement and denounced "those who put selfish economic interests ahead of the health of our nation and resent and resist the efforts of others who put the health of the nation ahead of all other considerations." Two staff members of the American Medical Association attending the conference decided it was time to put their association on record. They drafted a telegram declaring that "the federal government should engage in . . . enforcement in interstate or interjurisdictional difficulties in the manner of the successfully implemented Water Pollution Act" and sent it to AMA headquarters in Chicago, where it was dispatched officially to the conference.[64]

Within HEW a heated argument boiled up. Supporting enforcement powers were Wilbur Cohen and his assistant, Dean W. Coston; opposing them was the Public Health Service, consistent with its stand in Flemming's day. The PHS found an ally in the Bureau of the Budget, but Cohen had his opportunity when he presented the department's legislative program directly to President Kennedy in Palm Beach on December 26. Arguing that the administration could not well stand to the right of Republican Flemming and the American Medical Association, he succeeded in getting the President interested. Later, when the President's message to Congress on health was being drafted, Kennedy accepted the position of Cohen and Coston and recommended enforcement authority along the lines of the Federal Water Pollution Control Act. But the proponents of a strong bill were wary of trying to develop an administration measure that would have to be cleared with the Budget Bureau, so they agreed to leave the drafting to Congress.

Congress had competitive bills to consider. Senator Engle had reintroduced his bill of 1962, which lacked any enforcement provision. But

---

[63] This section relies upon Randall B. Ripley, "Congress and Clean Air: The Issue of Enforcement, 1963," in Frederic N. Cleaveland (ed.), *Congress and Urban Affairs* (Brookings Institution, 1968).

[64] The telegram was later "clarified" after industries allied with the AMA on such questions as medicare protested, but it was not retracted.

Senator Ribicoff, fresh from his service as HEW secretary, had decided to make air pollution his initial area of concern and had instructed his legislative assistant—the same Jerome Sonosky who had worked with Representative Blatnik on water pollution—to prepare a measure. Drawing upon the proposal Mields had been drafting and adding language of his own—some taken from water pollution bills—he assembled a "clean air act" that, besides the research and grant provisions, authorized the federal government to undertake pollution abatement upon request of any state, or of any municipality acting with state consent. He obtained nineteen cosponsors, compared to Engle's nine.

In the House, meanwhile, Kenneth Roberts had a change of heart. Only two months after his December speech rejecting federal enforcement, he introduced a bill paralleling closely the Ribicoff measure. "Consistency is a hobgoblin of little minds," he told those who reminded him of his earlier position. "Someone said, 'The wise man changes his mind and the fool never does.' . . . There have been some things that happened, particularly the recent London smog, which makes me feel that the Federal Government does have a responsibility in this field particularly when it involves the death and health of our people. Now I think there are some of these situations that we cannot reach other than by legislation of this type."[65] Many people, of course, had been in communication with Roberts —among them Coston, Mields, and Ed E. Reid of the Alabama league of municipalities—and he had received a firsthand report on the London smog from Richard A. Prindle of the Public Health Service.

The enforcement procedures set forth in the Roberts bill provided that HEW, upon request of a state or a municipality, would call a conference of representatives of the jurisdictions involved in a pollution problem and make recommendations for action. If, after a reasonable time, the actions had not been taken, the secretary of HEW could appoint a hearing board, on which the states involved would be represented. The recommendations of the hearing board would be enforceable through the courts, but only through a suit brought by a state. Roberts could contend, then, that "all this bill does so far as Federal enforcement is concerned is to give a State or the municipality of the State that is suffering from pollutants coming from over the line some opportunity to get some help."[66]

Hearings on air pollution legislation were almost a replay of the early water pollution hearings. The lineup of witnesses was much the same: on

---

[65] *Air Pollution,* Hearings, p. 184.
[66] *Ibid.*

one side were the mayors and the conservationists; on the other were spokesmen for the industries responsible for pollution, supported by the states. The industry spokesmen were especially solicitous of state and local rights. "Too much stress on Federal enforcement," contended the Manufacturing Chemists' Association, "will discourage State and local level enforcement people and impair their programs."[67] Air pollution was not "a mounting danger to national health" that justified "intrusion of the federal government into what has hitherto been strictly local and state affairs," argued the American Iron and Steel Institute.[68] Petroleum industry spokesmen even opposed the grants to states and local communities because they would encourage unnecessary regulation "simply because the money is there to be spent."[69] The National Association of Manufacturers feared the "stifling of local initiative."[70] A noteworthy dissenter from the industry position was the U.S. Chamber of Commerce, which generally endorsed the Roberts bill and described the enforcement provision as "an orderly process."[71] For the states, the National Association of Attorneys General argued that "a self-generating federal enforcement program seems premature, to say the very least."[72]

The mayors, on the other hand, welcomed the federal "intrusion" into their affairs. "The clearly national character of this problem is pinpointed by pondering the question, How local is air?" testified Mayor Joseph M. Barr of Pittsburgh on behalf of the American Municipal Association. "How do you prevent polluted air from passing from one political jurisdiction into another, from one county to another, from one State into a neighboring State? . . . National assistance is needed in meeting a problem which cannot be bottled up within a given region. . . . It is meaningless to establish effective control programs in one locality, if another locality across a State line is unable for whatever reason to control pollution. . . . The record will show that up to the present time, local governments and States, with a few notable exceptions, have not developed adequate programs for abatement and control of air pollution."[73] At its June meeting the U.S. Conference of Mayors urged passage of a bill authorizing the

[67] Testimony of Walker Penfield, in *ibid.*, p. 230.
[68] Testimony of Erwin E. Schulze, in *Air Pollution Control,* Hearings before the Special Subcommittee on Air and Water Pollution of the Senate Public Works Committee, 88 Cong. 1 sess. (Sept. 11, 1963), pp. 282, 283.
[69] *Air Pollution,* Hearings, p. 272.
[70] Testimony of Daniel W. Cannon, in *ibid.*, p. 170.
[71] *Ibid.*, pp. 286–87.
[72] Testimony of Attorney General David P. Buckson of Delaware, in *ibid.*, p. 85.
[73] *Ibid.*, p. 97.

Public Health Service to "take action to abate interstate air pollution when state or local governments fail to do so."[74] Thus the mayors were ready to accept a bill stronger even than the Ribicoff and Roberts measures, which made federal action dependent on state initiative or consent. So were conservationist spokesmen, who found the enforcement provisions of the pending bill too weak and cumbersome.[75]

But the Democrats did not attempt to strengthen their bill. After making a few minor changes to lessen industry opposition, Roberts brought his proposal out of committee. House Democrats voted for it, 206–10. The Republicans were closely divided, sixty-seven voting for the bill and ninety-two against. Industry representatives, now resigned to the inevitability of a bill, worked with the Senate subcommittee on what amounted to minor amendments. Then the bill passed in that body by voice vote.

President Johnson made far-reaching claims for the final Clean Air Act of 1963. "Under this legislation," he predicted, "we can halt the trend towards greater contamination of our atmosphere."[76]

Outdoor Recreation: Federal Funds and Leadership. In January 1962 the outdoor recreation advocates were at last provided the springboard they had been awaiting—the report of the Outdoor Recreation Resources Review Commission. In a twelve-inch shelf of handsomely produced volumes, ORRRC elaborated in text, charts, and diagrams two fundamental points: "Outdoor recreation activity, already a major part of American life, will *triple* by the year 2000," and "the conventional approach to providing outdoor recreation is not adequate for present needs, and it will certainly not be adequate for the future." The first task ORRRC saw was to provide recreation for the great population centers. National and state policy alike had been to acquire park land in rural areas—in "far-away places"— but "the need is far more urgent close to home." "Large-scale acquisition and development programs are needed; so is money— lots of it," but "the effectiveness of land, not sheer quantity, is the key." Existing recreation areas needed to be opened to more effective use. Recreation must be made an integral part of future metropolitan growth; the environment as a whole must be shaped to serve recreation needs.[77]

---

[74] *Air Pollution Control,* Hearings (1963), p. 102.

[75] See, for example, statement of Spencer M. Smith, Jr., secretary, Citizens Committee on Natural Resources, *Air Pollution,* Hearings, pp. 293–95.

[76] On Dec. 17, 1963, *Public Papers of the Presidents, 1963–64,* p. 60.

[77] *Outdoor Recreation for America* (Outdoor Recreation Resources Review Commission, 1962) ; quotations from pp. 47, 81, 82.

While awaiting the report, Congress had pushed ahead in 1961 with two measures. One created the Cape Cod National Seashore, the first unit of the national park system in history to be acquired with appropriated funds. The second established a new program of grants to local governments for the acquisition of "open space." Taking his cue initially from a report of the Regional Plan Association on the need for open space in the New York metropolitan area, Senator Harrison A. Williams, Jr., New Jersey Democrat, had conceived the idea of a grant program, enlisted the support of the housing and urban lobby groups, and with the backing of the administration succeeded in incorporating it into the 1961 housing act.

But 1961 had been, essentially, a year of temporizing. Now, the ORRRC report called for "vigorous, cooperative leadership" by the federal government in a nationwide recreation effort. To provide the leadership, it proposed a Bureau of Outdoor Recreation in the Department of the Interior. The bureau would administer a program of grants to the states for planning recreation programs and acquiring and developing land, the money to come from the general funds of the treasury. The ORRRC also endorsed the wilderness bill, the acquisition of additional shoreline recreation areas, the preservation of certain rivers in their free-flowing state, and the new open space program.

President Kennedy followed with a message to Congress in which he said, "The need for an aggressive program of recreational development is both real and immediate."[78] His program, however, departed in major respects from that of the ORRRC. The Bureau of Outdoor Recreation was established, as recommended, in the Department of the Interior, but the President recommended grants to the states only for preparation of recreation plans, not for land acquisition or development. His major emphasis was upon federal land purchases. For that purpose, he proposed a "fiscally responsible" plan through which recreation users would pay for the land. He asked for broad authority to impose fees upon the users of federal land and water recreation areas; the new fees—along with existing ones, like admission charges at the national parks—would be paid into a land conservation fund to be used primarily for land acquisition. In particular, a new annual tax would be imposed on recreation boats. "The services that boat owners receive from the federal Government are of great value and,

[78] Message of March 1, 1962, *Public Papers of the Presidents, 1962*, p. 178.

for the most part, no compensation is paid for these services," the President observed.[79]

But this innocent-sounding proposal brought into being a whole new lobby, made up of boat manufacturers, distributors, and users. Members of Congress were surprised to learn how many of their constituents had a direct, personal, and hostile interest in the proposed new tax. Moreover, the general proposal to authorize user fees stirred fears in many other breasts. Would commercial vessels traveling inland waterways be charged new fees if they passed through an area developed for recreation? Would the fifteen million visitors a year who had had free access to Corps of Engineers reservoirs in Oklahoma now be charged admission? Would Sunday drivers have to pay tolls on the Blue Ridge Parkway? Would hunters and fishers in the national forests be obliged to obtain federal as well as state licenses? Would motorists have to pay a toll to cross national forest land between two towns?[80]

The bill also raised sectional issues. The user charges would be assessed largely in the West but the money would be spent mainly in the East. From the viewpoint of westerners, should not the money be used for developing existing federal recreation land as well as for acquiring new lands? Westerners even worried that improvement of recreation facilities in the East through the federal expenditures would decrease income in the West from the tourist industry.[81]

It took nineteen months for the House Interior Committee to work out an acceptable bill. The new boat tax was dropped at once. Then the House committee went back to the ORRRC recommendations and allocated 60 percent of the moneys in the new fund (renamed the land and water conservation fund) for grants to the states. The states could use the money for land acquisition and development as well as for recreation planning. Forty-six of the fifty states thereupon officially endorsed the bill. The House committee also wrote a series of clarifying and restrictive amendments to limit the application of user fees, but at the insistence of Chair-

[79] Letter transmitting bill to create a land conservation fund, April 4, 1962, *ibid.*, pp. 291–92.

[80] For a summary of these and other questions and "misunderstandings"about the user fee proposal, see speech by Edward C. Crafts, director of the Bureau of Outdoor Recreation, before the National Audubon Society, Nov. 11, 1963; reprinted in *Cong. Record,* Vol. 109 (Nov. 19, 1963), pp. 22282—84.

[81] See comments of Senator Peter H. Dominick, Colorado Republican, in *Land and Water Conservation Fund,* Hearings before the Senate Interior and Insular Affairs Committee, 88 Cong. 1 sess. (March 7, 1963), p. 73.

man Aspinall retained the principle. The chairman held his ground against his fellow westerners who wanted to divert a part of the federal share of the funds from acquisition to development—and he rejected the proposition in conference after the Senate had approved it. With the restrictive amendments, more of which were added by the Senate, the bill passed both houses in 1964 with only token opposition. It made available about $200 million a year for the first nationwide recreation land purchase program in the nation's history.

"We will begin, as of this day, to acquire on a pay-as-you-go basis, the outdoor recreation lands that tomorrow's Americans require," said President Johnson on signing the bill.[82]

Meanwhile, the Congress had authorized, in separate measures, three additional national seashores—Point Reyes, California; Padre Island, Texas, and Fire Island, New York—the Ozark National Scenic Riverways, in Missouri, and Canyonlands National Park in Utah. Commenting on all of these enactments, in addition to the Wilderness Act (see below), Johnson was able to say that the Eighty-eighth Congress had made a record in conservation equaled by "no single Congress in my memory."[83]

Wilderness: The National Wilderness Preservation System Is Established. President Kennedy's commitment to wilderness legislation made the difference. The Agriculture and Interior departments, which had been allowed to take a "yes, but" attitude during the Eisenhower years, became all-out enthusiasts for a strong wilderness bill in 1961. Clinton Anderson, the new chairman of the Interior Committee, assumed leadership in the Senate. The President endorsed the bill introduced by Anderson—the Humphrey bill revised on the basis of the extensive field hearings of 1958 and 1959—and the drive for legislation was underway.

Realizing that a wilderness bill of some kind was bound to pass sooner or later, the opponents of previous years now shifted their strategy from outright opposition to qualified support—the qualification being amendments designed to protect western economic interests. Most important of the amendments was one sponsored by Senator Allott of Colorado to require congressional action to set aside any wilderness beyond the 8.6 million acres in forty-six Forest Service areas designated as wilderness by the bill. This was in contrast to Anderson's procedure under which the President would designate such areas subject only to a veto by either house

[82] On Sept. 3, 1964, *Public Papers of the Presidents, 1963–64*, p. 1033.
[83] *Ibid.*

of Congress within sixty days.[84] "I know of but few people who are trying to kill this bill," said Allott; "If we can get the proper protection in a bill, I will vote for a wilderness bill." But the arguments he used in pressing for his amendment were essentially those used in earlier years by those seeking to kill the whole idea. "I believe," he said, "that in the West we cannot exist unless we develop the land, unless we provide means of conserving water, build dams, and take means toward conservation that are not provided for in the bill. The future of the West is still great, but it can be great only if it is allowed to grow." Then he concluded, "I do not want these areas tied up without giving Congress an opportunity to study their use."[85] The managers of the Anderson bill argued that since the executive branch already had complete authority to set aside wilderness areas and had been using that power, the proposed procedure for a congressional veto actually reclaimed congressional authority. A majority of Republicans supported Allott, 20–10, but the Democrats held their lines and the amendment was smothered, 53–32. After other amendments were rejected, the bill passed, 78–8.

In the House, however, the Allott view had powerful support on the Democratic side, notably that of Chairman Aspinall. At a White House conference on conservation, he had predicted: "Congress will continue to equate conservation with wise use; will not put out of reach resources that may be required for our national continuance; and . . . all the resources will be managed for the benefit of the many and not the few."[86] Accordingly, his committee outdid Allott in embracing weakening amendments. It not only proposed the requirement for affirmative congressional action that the Colorado senator had advanced, but also incorporated a proviso that mining and prospecting could continue in wilderness areas for twenty-five years and another requirement that each wilderness area be reviewed each twenty-five years to determine whether it should be continued in that status. The provision for a twenty-five year review, observed Howard Zahniser, was "as dubious in a Wilderness Act as in a marriage vow." "This is indeed a substitute bill," commented Representative Saylor

---

[84] New wilderness areas would be established within national parks, wildlife refuges, and game ranges or created from those primitive areas in national forests not yet reclassified as wilderness areas by the Forest Service. The forty-six areas already reclassified would be automatically incorporated in the wilderness system under both the Anderson bill and the Allott amendment.

[85] *Cong. Record*, Vol. 107 (Sept. 6, 1961), pp. 18357, 18365.

[86] *White House Conference on Conservation, Official Proceedings, May 24–25, 1962,* p. 65.

in his minority report. "For the preservation of wilderness it substitutes protection for exploiters of our wilderness areas."[87]

To guard against floor amendments that might restore the bill to its original form, the committee decided to seek its consideration under a suspension of the rules, which bars amendments and requires a two-thirds vote. But the indignant outcry from the conservationists led Aspinall and the House leadership to conclude that they could not muster the necessary two-thirds majority.[88] Under pressure to bring the measure to the floor under normal procedures, the chairman simply went home to Colorado. His committee colleagues—most of whom disliked the bill anyway— would not "slap [him] down" by acting in his absence, which continued until Congress adjourned.[89] The administration reacted with mixed feelings—disappointment at the delay but satisfaction at the frustration of what it considered a bad bill. President Kennedy told a conference of business editors that the House bill was "not very satisfactory" and that he hoped eventually for a "good bill" akin to the Senate version.[90]

Senate handling of wilderness legislation in 1963 was a near rerun of its 1961 performance. The precedent of the House bill had strengthened the proponents of weakening amendments to a degree, but they were still defeated. The congressional initiative amendment lost by a margin smaller than before, 49–34, with only six Republicans opposed, and some procedural safeguards for western economic interests were incorporated. An amendment by Allott and his Colorado Republican colleague, Peter H. Dominick, to allow mining and prospecting in wilderness areas for fifteen years was defeated 56–26. Democrats voted 48–9 against it, Republicans 17–8 for it. The bill, essentially the same as the measure passed in 1961, was approved by almost as great a margin, 73–12.

But Aspinall still gave no sign of bringing a bill out of the House committee except on his own terms. And the bill depended wholly upon him; he was, if anything, less anti-wilderness than the other westerners who made up a majority of the committee. If at any time he had taken a stand of outright opposition, those close to the House committee agreed, his colleagues would gladly have shelved the bill. But Aspinall, who had gone

---

[87] *Providing for the Preservation of Wilderness Areas, and for the Management of Public Lands, and for Other Purposes,* H. Rept. 2521, 87 Cong. 2 sess. (Oct. 3, 1962), p. 118; Zahniser quotation in *ibid.,* p. 129.

[88] *Cong. Record,* Vol. 108 (Sept. 20, 1962), pp. 20202–03.

[89] Robert Bendiner, *Obstacle Course on Capitol Hill* (McGraw-Hill, 1964), pp. 62–63.

[90] On Sept. 26, 1962, *Public Papers of the Presidents, 1962,* p. 714.

along with other members of ORRRC in endorsing wilderness legislation, argued that it was inevitable eventually and that the western objective should therefore be to write a bill with which western economic interests could live.

President Kennedy asked the Bureau of the Budget to take the lead in working out a compromise, and negotiations were completed just before the President's death.[91] The result was hardly a compromise—it was, rather, an acceptance of Aspinall's terms. The House committee dropped only the provision for the twenty-five year review; otherwise the bill was the same as the committee bill of 1962. Yet the atmosphere this time was one of utter harmony—wilderness advocates realized that the choice was between Aspinall's idea of a bill and no bill at all. "A significant step forward," said Representative Saylor, the bill's sponsor, in accepting as amendments the same provisions he had denounced two years before. "A highly reasonable approach," Representative Dingell agreed.[92] The bill passed the House with only one dissenting vote. What emerged from the House-Senate conference was essentially the House measure. The requirement for congressional initiative had been accepted by the Senate conferees; the permission for mining in wilderness areas had been reduced from twenty-five to nineteen years, but it was still there. Senator Anderson assured his colleagues that administrative regulations could prevent "serious depreciation of wilderness values" as a result of prospecting and mining. "A great forward step," Senator Humphrey called the Wilderness Act.[93] "Imperfect but vital," the Wilderness Society described it.[94] "The wilderness bill preserves for our posterity, for all time to come, 9 million acres of this vast continent in their original and unchanging beauty and wonder," intoned President Johnson.[95] And another fifty million acres would be reviewed for possible inclusion within ten years.

Beauty for America   (1965–66)

When Lyndon Johnson proclaimed the goal of a "Great Society" in 1964, he defined it as a new and qualitative dimension of the national

---

[91] As reported by Aspinall, *Cong. Record*, Vol. 110 (July 30, 1964), p. 17427.
[92] *Ibid.*, pp. 17431, 17434.
[93] *Ibid.* (Aug. 20, 1964), p. 20602.
[94] *Living Wilderness*, No. 86 (Spring-Summer 1964), p. 2.
[95] On Sept. 3, 1964, *Public Papers of the Presidents, 1963–64*, p. 1033.

objective. "We have the opportunity," he told the graduating class of the University of Michigan, "to move not only toward the rich society and the powerful society, but upward to the Great Society." That Great Society "is a place where the city of man serves not only the needs of the body and the demands of commerce but the desire for beauty and the hunger for community. . . . It is a place where men are more concerned with the quality of their goals than the quantity of their goods."

Into each strand of the President's expression of his vision of America was woven the word "beauty"—surely for the first time in any presidential message. "We have always prided ourselves on being not only America the strong and America the free, but America the beautiful," he said. "Today that beauty is in danger. The water we drink, the food we eat, the very air that we breathe, are threatened with pollution. Our parks are overcrowded, our seashores overburdened. Green fields and dense forests are disappearing. A few years ago we were greatly concerned about the 'Ugly American.' Today we must act to prevent an ugly America. For once the battle is lost, once our natural splendor is destroyed, it can never be recaptured. And once man can no longer walk with beauty or wonder at nature his spirit will wither and his sustenance be wasted."[96]

The President announced a series of "working groups" to "assemble the best thought and the broadest knowledge" on the problems of building the Great Society and to prepare a series of White House conferences and meetings. One of these working groups, he said, would be on "natural beauty." Appointed in July, it reported in November, and its findings and recommendations (which were never made public) were the starting point for the drafting of the first presidential message to Congress in the nation's history on the subject of natural beauty. The message[97] was followed by a White House conference on natural beauty in May 1965, which published its proceedings under the heading "Beauty for America."

The phrase and the concept of "natural beauty," the presidential message, and the White House conference—these unified and dramatized as a major national objective the separate and narrower objectives that had been pursued independently during the previous decade. On each of the subsidiary objectives—water pollution control, air pollution control, recreation development, wilderness preservation, highway beautification—the President presented new and challenging proposals. They comprised an

[96] On May 22, 1964, *ibid.*, pp. 704–06.
[97] Message of Feb. 8, 1965, *Public Papers of the Presidents, 1965*, pp. 155–65.

agenda for national action to preserve, improve, and beautify man's natural environment for the enjoyment of man.

Clean Water: "We Begin To Be Masters of Our Environment." When the new Congress with its overwhelming Democratic majority met after the Johnson landslide, Senator Muskie was in no mood to await a presidential message on natural beauty before passing his water pollution control bill. He had passed a bill in 1963 by a 69–11 margin, only to be frustrated by the chemical industry and its allies in the House. This time he proposed to move before the national temper had a chance to change. With thirty-one cosponsors he introduced a bill only slightly modified from the Senate-passed bill of 1963, held a single day of hearings, brought it to the floor, and passed it on January 28, 1965, barely three weeks after Congress convened. The vote was 68–8; three Republicans who had opposed the measure two years before now joined the bandwagon.

So did the administration. In contrast to the Kennedy administration's reluctant support of the Muskie position in 1963, the Johnson administration proposed to go even further. The key proposal in the "clean water" section of the President's February message on natural beauty dealt with water quality standards; it proposed to "provide, through the setting of effective water quality standards, combined with a swift and effective enforcement procedure, a national program to prevent water pollution at its source rather than attempting to cure pollution after it occurs." The compromise provision on water quality standards that Muskie had negotiated in the previous Congress and had just put through the Senate anew fell short of this objective. It did not contemplate a *national* program; it was for the express purpose of avoiding the obligation to proceed on a nationwide basis that the Kennedy administration had insisted that the standards-setting authority be made optional. The states were to be given "reasonable time" to adopt their own standards before the federal government moved. And the federal authority would be limited to interstate streams.

At the request of Muskie and Blatnik, however, the administration withheld its new and stronger recommendations on standards and enforcement in order not to upset the course of the pending bill, which had foundered on the enforcement issue the year before. The HEW report to the House committee merely noted that the standards section fell short of carrying out the President's recommendation. The department promised to submit new proposals but urged that action on the pending bill not be delayed.[98]

In the House committee, Blatnik put the emphasis on those parts of the legislation with which he, rather than Muskie, had been originally identified. The committee raised the grant ceiling on individual sewage treatment projects to $1.2 million and the total authorization to $150 million annually (compared to $600,000 and $100 million in the 1961 law and $1 million and $100 million in the Senate-passed bill). It also placed all, rather than some, of the water pollution control activities of the Public Health Service in a new water pollution control administration. But yielding to industry threats to kill the entire bill, as in 1964, if federal water standards were retained in it, the committee developed a new approach to that problem. No power to set standards would be given the federal government; the states would retain that responsibility, but the federal government would coerce them into exercising it. In order to remain eligible for the federal grants, each state would have to file notice by June 30, 1967, of its intention to establish water quality criteria.[99] This compromise satisfied the critics, and the bill was approved by the committee and by the House by unanimous votes.

To Muskie, however, the compromise looked like surrender. For several weeks he refused even to request a conference, despite pressure from the administration and even some of the conservation groups to yield on the standards issue. All told, Blatnik calculated, it took almost four months to resolve the dispute.[100] And, he revealed, it took a presidential "nudge in the ribs . . . about as hard as you'd get from a hockey player" to get the two sides together.[101] But Muskie won his point. When the conference met, it adopted a compromise worked out by the Senate subcommittee staff that restored federal authority to impose standards. They would be imposed on any of three conditions: if the state failed within a year to file a declaration of intent to establish standards; if the standards were not established by June 30, 1967; or if the secretary of HEW con-

[98] HEW report dated Feb. 18, 1965, *Water Pollution Control Hearings on Water Quality Act of 1965*, Hearings before the House Public Works Committee, 89 Cong. 1 sess. (1965), pp. 85–86.

[99] Criteria were not standards, but rather a preliminary classification upon which standards would be based, it was explained by a committee source (*Congressional Quarterly Almanac, 1965*, pp. 749–50).

[100] *Cong. Record*, Vol. 111 (Sept. 21, 1965), p. 24587.

[101] *Evening Star* (Washington), Aug. 27, 1965.

sidered the standards inadequate.[102] Procedural safeguards were written to assure state participation in standards-setting; in exchange, procedures for abatement action under established standards were simplified. The grant and reorganization provisions followed the House bill. Muskie acknowledged that the stalemate and the long negotiations had resulted in improving the original Senate bill.

"This moment makes a very proud beginning for the United States of America," said Lyndon Johnson in signing the Water Quality Act of 1965. "Today, we proclaim our refusal to be strangled by the wastes of civilization. Today, we begin to be masters of our environment. . . . Additional, bolder measures will be needed in the years ahead. But we have begun."[103]

Senator Muskie was already at work on his version of the additional bolder measures. During the period of the House-Senate deadlock in 1965, the Muskie subcommittee set out on a series of Washington and regional hearings to take the measure of the country's water pollution problem, and in January 1966 it released its findings. It estimated the backlog of needed municipal sewage treatment facilities at $20 billion, and if the federal share of 30 percent were to be retained, a total of $6 billion in federal expenditures should be authorized. Without waiting for presidential recommendations, nearly half the Senate, forty-eight members in all, joined Muskie in introducing a bill authorizing the $6 billion over a six-year period. Among the cosponsors was the Senate subcommittee's ranking Republican, Caleb Boggs, who said that in the field hearings "it became abundantly clear to me" that the federal government must increase its aid "if we are ever going to be in a position to control and prevent water pollution."[104] The Muskie bill also removed the dollar ceilings on individual grants and provided an incentive for state matching by raising the federal share from 30 to 40 percent in those cases where the states assumed half the remaining cost. Moreover, if states proceeded before federal money was available, they would be reimbursed later—a provision designed to accommodate New York state, where under Governor Rockefeller's leadership a $1 billion bond issue for state aid for sew-

102 All fifty states met the 1967 deadline for establishing standards. The Department of the Interior (to whom the authority had been transferred from HEW) then began the process of reviewing and approving the standards, state by state.

103 On Oct. 2, 1965, *Public Papers of the Presidents, 1965*, p. 1034.

104 *Water Pollution Control—1966*, Hearings before the Subcommittee on Air and Water Pollution of the Senate Public Works Committee, 89 Cong. 2 sess. (April 19, 1966), p. 25.

age treatment facilities had been approved by a "thunderous" four to one vote in a referendum.[105]

The President's own version of the needed bolder measures, submitted to Congress in February 1966, was a reorganization plan transferring the Federal Water Pollution Control Administration to the Department of the Interior and a clean rivers restoration bill that would authorize Interior to provide financial aid not just for individual sewage treatment plants but for "the management of pollution control activities on a whole river, lake, or other body of water."[106] The river basin plans would be prepared by either existing or new federal-state water resources planning agencies.[107] The plans would include water quality standards, enforcement authority, and basin-wide sewage treatment programs. For works proceeding under approved plans, grant ceiling limitations would be removed. But the expenditure level was to be raised by only $50 million a year.

The administration saw the Muskie bill as not just bold but downright audacious. Its spokesmen warned that it might render the river-basin approach ineffective, cautioned that to proceed so rapidly without comprehensive planning could result in "gross errors," and pleaded for time to consider the $6 billion authorization. "More money is needed," said HEW Assistant Secretary James M. Quigley, "but just more money is not the answer."[108] But Muskie was not deterred. He retained his $6 billion figure, conceding only that it might be used to finance a modified river-basin program as well as the existing program. At the instance of the cities, the federal grant level was raised from 30 to 40 percent for all projects, not just for those in states that shared the local cost. At the instance of the administration, which still sought an incentive to encourage river-basin planning, the federal share was raised to 50 percent for projects carried out under approved river-basin programs. The bill passed the Senate 90–0.

[105] Testimony of Hollis Ingraham, New York commissioner of health, April 28, 1966, in *ibid.*, p. 236.

[106] Interior Department letter to Senator Muskie dated May 25, 1966, *ibid.*, p. 138b.

[107] The Water Resources Planning Act, passed in *1965*, authorized establishment of federal-state river basin commissions to develop comprehensive water utilization plans, encompassing plans for flood control, water supply development, pollution control, and enhancement of fish and wildlife and water-based recreation. The act grew out of the work of the Senate select committee on water resources, chaired by Senator Kerr, which reported in *1961*.

[108] *Water Pollution Control—1966*, Hearings, p. 127.

At this point the administration hastily recalculated the total grant needs and arrived at $3.45 billion over six years, compared to Muskie's $6 billion. Of this amount, $2.45 billion would be spent in the first five years, ending in 1971, compared to $4.5 billion in the Muskie bill. The House committee accepted the administration's figures for a five-year program, and its bill passed the House by a vote of 313–0. The House-Senate conference split the difference, authorizing $3.55 billion for a five-year program which would begin at $150 million for the first year and rise by annual steps to $1.25 billion in the fifth year (1970–71). The final bill retained the 30 percent federal share where states did not participate but allowed 50 percent wherever a state assumed half of the remaining cost and established enforceable water quality standards for the waters into which the sewage treatment project discharged. Thus the Clean Water Restoration Act of 1966 established the administration's program in a modified form. It also finally removed the dollar ceiling on individual grants.

The country had come a long way. Only six years after President Eisenhower had vetoed a federal aid bill on the ground that water pollution was "a uniquely local blight," the Congress—without a dissenting vote in either House—had approved a program for full national leadership and participation in eradicating a national blight, with an ultimate spending rate twelve times as great as the level contemplated in the vetoed bill. In his budget for the fiscal year 1968, however, the President requested only $203 million, less than half the $450 million authorized for that year.[109]

Clean Air: "We Intend To Rewrite History." "Smog wasn't invented in Los Angeles but it was here that the fight against it was born," Governor Edmund G. Brown of California told the Muskie subcommittee in 1964. For twenty years the battle had been underway. Yet, as the governor spoke, in January 1964, it was still a losing fight. "We are not reducing the total amount of smog," he testified. "We are only keeping even with growth."

The reason: the omnipresent automobile, numbering 3.5 million in the Los Angeles basin. Oil refineries and industrial smokestacks had been brought under control, backyard trash-burning had been outlawed, but these gains had been offset by the increase in emissions from motor cars.

[109] The President requested only $225 million for the fiscal year 1969, compared to the authorization of $700 million.

This problem, too, California had attacked, with laws requiring "crank-case blowby devices" on all automobiles sold in the state. But these would eliminate only 20 percent of the tonnage of hydrocarbons emitted by automobiles.

The governor appealed for federal help. "The automobile manufacturer is no different from the maker of any other product," he argued. "His product should not be injurious to health, nor a threat to the safety of the individual. We do not permit manufacturers to add dangerous preservatives to the food we eat. . . . And we can no longer permit the automobile to contaminate the air we breathe." Then he added: "The automobile industry is in interstate commerce and the Federal Government clearly has jurisdiction."[110]

In five other cities and in five days of technical hearings in Washington, the Muskie subcommittee heard the same story. Pollutants were being added to the atmosphere faster than they were being brought under control. Automotive exhaust accounted for about half the nation's air pollution problem. After automobiles came trash-burning in municipal dumps and smoking incinerators, and the burning of coal and oil for domestic heating. Research was needed, but far more was known about air pollution control than was being applied. Citing these findings, based upon 1,408 pages of testimony and exhibits, the subcommittee in October 1964 —less than a year after passage of the Clean Air Act of 1963—recommended additional federal legislation.[111] By January 1965 the new bill was ready, and Muskie introduced it.

The bill's primary focus was the automobile, its secondary focus the municipal dump. It prescribed standards of exhaust emission for gasoline-powered vehicles and directed the secretary of HEW to develop criteria for diesels. It also authorized $25 million in grants to the states for programs of inspection to insure compliance. To cope with the problem of municipal dumps, it authorized $100 million annually in grants for construction of facilities for solid-waste disposal. On all of these problems, as well as on the problem of sulphur oxides, it authorized an accelerated program of research centered in a federal air pollution control laboratory.

HEW, which had followed the Muskie hearings, presented to the

110 *Clean Air,* Hearings before the Special Subcommittee on Air and Water Pollution of the Senate Public Works Committee, 88 Cong. 2 sess. (Jan. 27, 1964), pp. 6–7.

111 *Steps Toward Clean Air,* prepared by the Special Subcommittee on Air and Water Pollution for the Senate Public Works Committee, 88 Cong. 2 sess. (October 1964); the recommendations are summarized on pp. 5–6.

White House a comparable proposal for enforceable federal standards on automotive exhaust. But when it reached President Johnson, he had questions. Had the automotive industry been consulted? Industry had just demonstrated that it was willing to "reason together" with the government on fiscal legislation—indeed, Henry Ford, II, had been a leader of the business committee supporting the President's tax reduction program—would they not be willing to reason on pollution? Was a federal "crackdown" in order before the companies had had opportunity even to consider with the President a course of voluntary action? The proposal was dropped. In its stead the President in his February message to Congress on natural beauty announced only, "I intend to institute discussions with industry officials and other interested groups leading to an effective elimination or substantial reduction of pollution from liquid fueled motor vehicles."

But the President was a busy man. Two months went by with no discussions. Senator Muskie, who had already probed the automotive industry to his own satisfaction, was impatient to move. He called HEW for a witness on his bill on Tuesday, April 6. HEW was ready to move also, but the Budget Bureau ruled that the department was still bound by the President's February decision. When Assistant Secretary Quigley appeared before the subcommittee, all he could say was that the administration opposed the bill until it had had the benefit of two developments: first, further testing of control devices under the California law and on government vehicles throughout the country; second, the President's meeting with industry to explore "what can be done to cope with this problem on a voluntary basis." He also objected, pending further research, to the construction grants for solid waste disposal facilities. As for the new research authority conferred by the bill, he considered it unnecessary because existing authority was sufficient.[112]

Muskie came down hard. His bill, he said, had been "reduced to nothing." "You recommend giving the President authority to find new pollution problems but you don't recommend doing anything about the ones we know about," he told Quigley. "You recognize a problem, you recognize that it is a national problem, you say that a technological potential now exists for meeting the need and dealing with the problem. Frankly I just can't make the next jump in your reasoning. You say that having

[112] *Air Pollution Control,* Hearings before the Special Subcommittee on Air and Water Pollution of the Senate Public Works Committee, 89 Cong. 1 sess. (April 6, 1965), p. 29.

said all this we don't recommend doing anything now. . . . The tune is the same but we don't come up with the same words."[113] Other subcommittee members made clear they shared the chairman's disappointment. Next day, Muskie asked Quigley to appear again before the subcommittee, on Friday, April 9.

Perhaps more important, the newspapers came down hard. *The New York Times* said that the administration's "feeble statement" bore the "odor" of politics. It reported in its news columns that President Johnson had personally determined the administration position and that Quigley was "not happy" with it. *The Los Angeles Times* deplored the "love affair" between the President and industry. On the same theme, *The Washington Post's* cartoonist Herblock portrayed a clinching couple— the administration and the automotive industry—zooming off in a limousine spewing exhaust fumes on a jilted girl labeled "legislation to control air pollution." The President, who presumably had thought little about the subject since February, was startled to discover that the administration had blundered. He ordered HEW to extricate itself, and him, from their predicament, and now a happier Quigley found himself liberated to negotiate with Muskie the words they would sing in harmony to their common tune.

The objective was easily accomplished. Quigley reappeared before the subcommittee to say that his Tuesday testimony had "unfortunately been completely misinterpreted that we are against any legislation and all legislation to control automobile exhaust." "We favor all action that is appropriate," he went on, "and if it is the judgment of the committee that legislation is appropriate at this time we want to work with the committee in making sure that that legislation is . . . the most effective piece of legislation that we are able to put on the books." The main requirement was that the standards not be written into statute but be left for administrative determination.[114]

The automotive industry was by no means adamant either. It had made its peace with California and it was aware of the rumblings in other state capitals. A bill had been introduced in the Pennsylvania legislature. In New York a state senator was boasting that his bill imposed standards higher and tougher than those of California. This was what the industry feared most: state regulations as diverse among the fifty states as, say, the early state standards governing the size and weight of trucks. At hearings

[113] *Ibid.*, pp. 27, 28, 74.
[114] *Ibid.* (April 9, 1965), p. 295.

in Detroit, on April 7, the industry spokesmen had protested for the record that air pollution was not a national problem and that automotive exhaust was being blamed for an undue share of the trouble, but they put most of their emphasis upon asking for additional time beyond the 1966 deadline in the Muskie bill. General Motors could comply in two years, said Harry F. Barr, a vice president, assuming "that a national standard rather than diverse State or regional standards could be established and that any such national standard would be no more stringent than that now required in California."[115]

Senator Muskie was satisfied to trade a year of time for acceptance of his principle. He conceded the administration's request for administrative flexibility, moved the deadline back to 1967, and converted his solid waste disposal grant program to a research and demonstration program. Then he moved the bill through the Public Works Committee and the Senate without dissent.

The automotive exhaust provisions encountered no opposition in the House either, after the committee removed the specific 1967 deadline from the bill and left that matter, also, to administrative discretion.[116] The solid waste disposal research and demonstration program, however, drew a dissent from seven committee Republicans who, in familiar language, insisted that "no case has been made for Federal action" in what was "primarily the function of . . . local agencies."[117] But when they moved deletion of the program by the House, they were beaten by a three-to-one margin. Republicans supported the motion, 61–32, but Democrats smothered it, 188–19. The Senate accepted the House amendments.

In signing the bill, President Johnson quoted Rachel Carson: "In biological history, no organism has survived long if its environment became in some way unfit for it, but no organism before man has deliberately polluted its own environment." Added the President: "We intend to rewrite that chapter of history. Today we begin."[118]

Outdoor Recreation: "A Parks-for-America Decade." In his message on natural beauty, President Johnson proposed a "Parks-for-America dec-

[115] *Ibid.*, p. 127.

[116] As it developed, this change made no difference; the standards were announced by HEW on March 29, 1966, to take effect with 1968 models going on sale in the fall of 1967.

[117] *Clean Air and Solid Waste Disposal Acts*, H. Rept. 899, 89 Cong. 1 sess. (1965), p. 66.

[118] On Oct. 20, 1965, *Public Papers of the Presidents, 1965*, p. 1067.

ade." Using in full the moneys authorized for the land and water conservation fund, he proposed adding to the nation's system of parks and recreation areas a dozen new units scattered from coast to coast. He also proposed a companion measure to the national wilderness preservation system—a national wild rivers system that would preserve scenic stretches of water in their free-flowing state.

Four of the twelve proposed new parks and recreation areas met no local opposition and were approved quickly in 1965. Another four areas were approved in 1966, and Congress added an area not on the President's list.[119]

With that, the Eighty-ninth Congress had approved nine new park and recreation areas, for a total of fifteen since 1961. For the first time in a generation, more land was saved for permanent preservation as open space than was developed for homes, businesses, and highways. In addition, the President recommended approval of three more areas, including a redwoods park in California. These, plus the four remaining from his original 1965 list, provided an agenda for the Ninetieth Congress, and prospects were favorable for at least some of them.[120]

The proposal for a national wild rivers system appeared to have a course ahead of it as tortuous as that of the Wilderness Act. The President proposed that portions of six streams—the Salmon and Clearwater in Idaho, the Green in Wyoming, the Rogue in Oregon, the Rio Grande in New Mexico, and the Suwannee in Georgia and Florida—be designated immediately as wild rivers on which dams would be prohibited, and that nine others be studied for possible inclusion. The Senate passed the bill after restricting condemnation power, removing two rivers (the Green

---

[119] The four approved in 1965 were the Assateague Island National Seashore in Maryland and Virginia and three national recreation areas—Delaware Water Gap in Pennsylvania and New Jersey, Spruce Knob-Seneca Rocks in West Virginia, and Whiskeytown-Shasta-Trinity in California. The four approved in 1966 as recommended by the President were the Guadalupe Mountains National Park in Texas, the Bighorn Canyon National Recreation Area in Montana, the Cape Lookout National Seashore in North Carolina, and the Indiana Dunes National Lakeshore in Indiana. The Congress added the Pictured Rocks National Lakeshore on the Michigan shore of Lake Superior.

[120] The four remaining from the 1965 list were Sleeping Bear Dunes National Lakeshore in Michigan and Great Basin National Park in Nevada, both of which were delayed by boundary questions raised by local interests; the Oregon Dunes National Seashore, blocked by the opposition of Senator Wayne Morse, Oregon Democrat, to granting condemnation power; and the Flaming Gorge National Recreation Area in Utah and Wyoming. The new proposals, in addition to the Redwood National Park, were the North Cascades National Park in Washington and the Apostle Islands National Lakeshore in Wisconsin.

and the Suwannee), adding three others, (the Eleven Point in Missouri and the Cacapon and Shenandoah in West Virginia), and increasing to seventeen the number to be studied. "It is imperative," Chairman Henry M. Jackson (Democrat of Washington) of the Senate Interior Committee had urged upon the Senate; "We must act now. . . . Once gone, they are lost forever."[121] But Chairman Aspinall of the House committee said that his committee had "no interest in this bill"[122] and that ended the matter for the Eighty-ninth Congress.

In the face of this deadlock, advocates of wild rivers turned to individual bills, as they had done successfully in the case of the Ozark National Scenic Riverways, but results were sparse. A bill for a national scenic riverway on the St. Croix, the boundary river between Wisconsin and Minnesota, passed the Senate but not the House. No other bill passed either house. The state of Maine enacted a measure to protect the Allagash, but that was all that could be claimed by the end of 1966.

In response to the President's recommendations regarding urban recreation areas and beautification programs, Congress without controversy took several steps in 1965. It increased the federal share of acquisitions under the open space land program from 20 percent (or 30 percent in some instances) to 50 percent, broadened the program to include landscaping of public property and clearance of urban land for open space, authorized a new program of 50 percent grants for acceleration of community beautification activities, and added another $235 million in grant authorization for all these purposes.

Highway Beautification: "A First Step." President Johnson's embrace of natural beauty as a prime national goal came at a time when one of the most important congressional enactments to that end—the billboard control legislation of 1958—was conceded to have failed. By 1965 only half the states had passed enabling legislation and qualified for the bonus offered in the 1958 act to states undertaking to control billboards on the interstate highway system. Only 194 miles of the system, or less than 1 percent of the total mileage completed, had been brought under control. The legislation, said Secretary of Commerce John T. Connor, had proved "definitely . . . ineffective."[123]

---

[121] *Cong. Record,* Vol. 112 (Jan. 17, 1966), p. 420.
[122] *New York Times,* Jan. 19, 1966.
[123] *Highway Beautification,* Hearings before the Subcommittee on Roads of the House Public Works Committee, 89 Cong. 1 sess. (July 20, 1965), p. 4.

When President Johnson directed Secretary Connor to prepare the highway components of the national beautification program in early 1965, the billboard control advocates in the Bureau of Public Roads were prepared to state what a serious highway beautification effort would entail. It would require making effective the intent of the 1958 act by compelling, rather than merely inviting, the states to adopt stringent controls on outdoor advertising on the interstate system. It would require applying the compulsion not only to the 41,000 miles of that system but also to the 225,000 miles of federally aided roads already built in the primary system, which included some of the most notorious "billboard corridors" in the country. It would require not only preventing new billboards, but removing those not complying with beautification standards. It would require extending advertising easements more than 660 feet beyond the rights-of-way. And it would require removing or limiting the exemptions for municipalities and commercial areas written into the legislation of 1958 and 1959.

While the administration was mulling over suggestions like these, the Outdoor Advertising Association of America—by definition, a public relations-conscious group—was shifting its position. In the opinion climate of 1965, it bowed to the inevitability of federal regulation and abandoned its ideological and constitutional stance of 1958. Now it rested its case upon what had been a secondary argument earlier—a demand that advertising be treated just as any other legitimate business use of land. On this basis it was willing to accept confinement to business areas, provided that the Kerr amendment of 1959—which excluded from regulation only those areas already zoned for business—was broadened to exclude areas that would be so zoned by local authorities in the future and areas used for business in jurisdictions that had no zoning regulations. In short, it would give up its interest in scenic areas in exchange for unrestricted access to business areas, including whatever areas it could persuade local governments to open up to it in the future.

During the spring of 1965 the administration and the association entered into a series of discussions. By the time the White House conference on natural beauty convened in May an understanding, if not an agreement, had been reached, and the administration bill—which came to be known as "Lady Bird's bill" because of the First Lady's identification with the natural beauty campaign—was put in final form. It extended coverage to the primary as well as the interstate system. Reviving the penalty approach first suggested by the Eisenhower administration, it withheld all federal highway funds, after January 1, 1968, from any state that did not exclude billboards from the noncommercial areas of the covered highways (except on-premise signs, which would be regulated in conformance with national standards). Noncomplying billboards would have to be taken down by 1970. Control would extend to 1,000 feet on each side of the pavement's edge. Billboards would be allowed in all industrial and commercial areas, unzoned as well as zoned, future as well as present.

The administration bill also required removal or screening of junkyards, and it required the use of 3 percent of primary and secondary road funds for beautification purposes, without state matching—a mandatory and broader version of an option that had lain virtually unused by the states since its enactment in 1940.

At the White House conference, Philip Tocker of Waco, Texas, chairman of the board of the Outdoor Advertising Association, was able to tell fellow members of the panel on roadside control that his organization "pledges its enthusiastic and aggressive support" to legislation that would limit billboards to industrial and commercial areas and would assure "equitable and appropriate" regulations for the removal of noncomplying signs. In addition, the association promised voluntary efforts to keep billboards out of scenic and historic areas. His remarks fell on skeptical ears. "I am glad to hear," responded Democratic Senator Maurine B. Neuberger of Oregon, widow of Congress' first billboard control activist, that "they have finally and reluctantly been dragged in. . . . I have heard this old story about self-policing by various industries for all of my legislative life, which goes back only to 1950. . . . These people don't police themselves. They don't remove billboards. They don't control them. But when they see that we mean business, then of course they want to come around."[124] Mrs. J. Melvin Nelson, president of the Arizona roadside council, was even less gracious. "Why is it," she demanded to know, "that there is a representative of the outdoor advertising industry sitting on this panel, considering their defamation of scenic views? . . . Why didn't you call in representatives of the strip miners? . . . Why don't we have a junk car dealer, or water polluter, or beer can maker, or litterbug sitting on the panel? Surely, they, too, have some ambiguous statements that they could have made to defend themselves."[125] The chairman cut off the discussion, but not before another conference participant observed, "I believe that

---

[124] *Beauty for America,* Proceedings of the White House Conference on Natural Beauty (Washington, May 24–25, 1965), pp. 254–55.
[125] *Ibid.,* p. 266.

you had a true statement of honest indignation from the ladies of America. . . . The Outdoor Advertising Association . . . just doesn't understand the indignation of Americans against being exploited forever."[126]

A majority of the eight panelists refused to accept the administration compromise. They voted to recommend that all advertising except on-premise signs be outlawed on the entire interstate and primary highway systems, including commercial areas. Only Mr. Tocker, Senator Neuberger, and the representative of the Department of Commerce who had handled the industry negotiations, Lowell K. Bridwell, would go so far as to approve general advertising billboards even in business areas.[127]

Backed by this show of support for a strong law, the President sent his draft legislation to Congress the day after the conference adjourned. The central issue became, at once, removal of the myriads of signs located in rural, unzoned areas along primary highways advertising motels, restaurants, service stations, and other roadside businesses whose survival depended upon the highway trade. "The bill will destroy my business," wrote thousands of small businessmen to their congressmen. They were joined by the small advertising concerns who served them—and who wanted it understood that the Outdoor Advertising Association of America did not speak for them. "We are well aware that in May of this year our President talked to a small segment of the advertising industry," one of their spokesmen told the House subcommittee; "but did you know that the OAAA has less than 700 members out of the more than 6,000 licensed sign companies in the United States? And most of these members operate in urban areas which are already zoned commercial and industrial."[128]

The plea by small businessmen for survival was one to which members of the Senate Public Works Committee were bound to listen. By a unanimous vote they agreed that signs that were legal when erected should not be removed under state police power without compensation. They voted to require full compensation of both the sign owner and the owner or leaseholder of the land on which the sign stood, the cost to be shared by the federal and state governments. This made compensation necessary even in states that preferred to use police power and had used it in the past. Any loss to the advertising companies was thus averted; but what

[126] Comment of Marvin B. Durning, chairman, Inter-Agency Committee for Outdoor Recreation, Seattle, Washington, *ibid.*, pp. 269–70.

[127] *Ibid.*, p. 653.

[128] Testimony of Don Barbour, president, Florida Outdoor Advertising Association, in *Highway Beautification*, Hearings (Sept. 7, 1965), p. 386.

of the needs of roadside businesses for highway signs in unzoned areas? The decision of the committee was to retain the principle of the administration bill but leave the decision wholly to the states by letting them determine what constituted business areas in jurisdictions that had no zoning.

These changes were enough to evoke cries of "emasculation" from the enemies of billboards. "Some conservationists and beauty lovers feel that no bill at all would be better," Senator Margaret Chase Smith, Republican of Maine, told the Senate. "They contend that the committee bill gives billboard interests a virtual carte blanche by allowing them to erect signs in areas zoned commercial and industrial by state legislatures and point to the power of the billboard lobby with State legislatures."[129] The administration agreed. Before the debate began, it persuaded Democratic Senator Jennings Randolph of West Virginia, the bill's manager, to accept an amendment that would restrict the states' carte blanche by providing that the secretary of commerce must approve the state determinations regarding unzoned areas. The amendment also introduced new authority for the secretary to concur in state criteria governing the lighting, size, and spacing of signs in business areas.[130] Now it was the turn of the roadside businesses to cry "foul." Senator Spessard Holland, Florida Democrat, told the Senate that his constituents felt the amendment violated an understanding reached twelve days earlier by the national representatives of their industry and the Public Works Committee. Senator Muskie hotly denied that any such agreement had been reached,[131] but the amendment was held over for a day. After further consultation between Randolph and the administration, the senator offered still another version, this time providing for "agreement" between the secretary and the states, rather than "approval" by the secretary, regarding the designation of unzoned business areas. The new amendment "places both parties on an equal footing," he argued, while his opponents contended that it meant the same as the previous version.[132] The revised amendment squeaked through, 44–40, although the Republicans—billboard oppon-

---

[129] *Cong. Record*, Vol. 111 (Sept. 15, 1965), p. 23869. In 1967, Wyoming zoned all agricultural land within 660 feet of primary highways as commercial, Transportation Secretary Alan S. Boyd told Congress (*Washington Post*, May 3, 1967).

[130] For a review of the legislative history of this amendment, see statements by Senator Muskie, *Cong. Record*, Vol. 112 (Feb. 16, 1966), pp. 3127–29, and Senator George Murphy, Republican of California, *ibid.* (April 6, 1966), pp. 7915–17.

[131] *Ibid.*, Vol. 111 (1965), p. 23876.

[132] *Ibid.*, pp. 24113–15.

ents and supporters alike—united to vote 22–1 in favor of states' rights and against the amendment.

Then it was the Republicans' turn to try to tighten up the bill. Senator John Sherman Cooper of Kentucky contended that the bill, both before and after the amendment, would relax the standards set in 1958 and 1959 for the interstate highway system by permitting even those states that had qualified for bonuses to open up the interstate system to "strip zoning" for advertising. He proposed an amendment to preserve the earlier stricter standards where they had been applied. The Senate was plunged into a fog of legal argumentation, but one thing was clear—any such amendment would lose the hard-won and crucial support for the bill from the Outdoor Advertising Association of America. The Republicans again held their lines, 22–1, this time against states' rights and for the stricter standards, but the Democrats united, 44–7, to support the administration and defeat the amendment. Once this dispute was settled, the bill passed on a bipartisan basis with only token opposition, 63–14.[133]

The Randolph amendment survived two votes in the House. A motion by Representative William Cramer, Florida Republican, to give the states complete control over the unzoned areas was defeated on a teller vote, 157–115, and later on a roll call, 230–153.[134] Protesting White House pressure for "Lady Bird's bill" and contending the measure was not carefully written, House Republicans, unlike their Senate counterparts, voted against the bill on final passage, 89–26. But overwhelming Democratic support carried it to passage, 245–138.

"This bill will bring the wonders of nature back into our daily lives," declaimed President Johnson as he signed it into law with "America the

133 The Senate made a number of other changes in the administration bill. As the penalty for noncompliance, only 10 percent (rather than 100 percent) of the state's federal aid for highways could be withheld. All costs of the bill would come from general appropriations in order to preserve the highway trust fund for road construction. Controls were restricted to 660 feet on each side of the right-of-way, as provided in the 1958 act. The requirement that states use 3 percent of their secondary road funds for beautification was deleted. Junkyards in industrial areas were exempted from federal control.

134 The House made several other changes in the bill. It provided that junkyard owners would receive full compensation for landscaping or screening junkyards outside of industrial areas. It required that the federal-state standards for billboards in permitted areas, governing size, lighting, and spacing, conform to "customary use." The latter amendment also made explicit that the states' powers to zone areas for commercial or industrial purposes was not impaired by the bill. This language presumably made no substantive change in the bill, however, because the administration bill had been so interpreted by Secretary Connor as had the Randolph amendment by the bill's managers in the Senate.

Beautiful" as background music. "This bill will enrich our spirits and restore a small measure of our national greatness." Then he added, somewhat surprisingly in view of the fact that Congress had given him essentially what he asked: "This bill does not represent everything that we wanted. It does not represent what we need. It does not represent what the national interest requires. But it is a first step, and there will be other steps."[135]

The Never-Ending Race with Despoliation. The surge of legislation in the decade ending in 1966 asserted, for the first time through the national government, the principle that man would be, in Lyndon Johnson's phrase, the master of his environment. But assertion of the principle did not establish it. The basic laws had created only the means. The end would depend upon a steadfastness of purpose that the country had yet to prove, and upon a proportion of the national resources that the country had yet to dedicate.

Environmental improvement was not a field of legislation, like civil rights or medicare, where the issue once settled would remain settled. It was, rather, a field where the constantly accelerating pressure upon living space generated by the forces of population growth and technological development would have to be countered by an equally constant acceleration of public action. Public policy developed rapidly in the early 1960's— rapidly enough to suggest that the race with despoliation could indeed be won—but at the end of 1966 it remained at least an open question whether the rate, or even the direction, of policy development could be maintained. In some fields the race was clearly being lost. In a message to Congress asking for further legislation on air pollution, for example, President Johnson in January 1967 said that despite three laws since 1963, pollution was "getting worse."

The accumulated needs alone were enormous. By the time the national government bestirred itself, almost everywhere the water was already fouled, the urban air poisoned, the seashores and lakeshores occupied, the coal fields stripmined, the wild rivers dammed, the wetlands drained, the highways blighted. The forces making for destruction of the environment had not merely to be resisted but to be pushed back. What had been allowed to happen over the decades had now to be undone.

But the spoilers of the environment could be counted on not to relax

[135] On Oct. 22, 1965, *Public Papers of the Presidents, 1965,* p. 1074.

for a moment. They were not merely inanimate forces; they were real, live people—and people with power. Their livelihood sometimes depended on continuation of the practices that had caused the trouble. And they had powerful arguments. They provided jobs and payrolls. They were the backbone, if not of the national economy, of many local economies—in the case of outdoor advertising they had even claimed "a key role" in keeping the entire economy "in high gear." They were symbols of American freedom, of property rights, of states' rights, of local autonomy, even of struggling small business. They could plead technological uncertainty and demand more research. They had learned how to contribute to campaigns, to muster votes, to dominate state and local governments.

Despoliation could be combated in two ways. It could be regulated through the police power, as the air and water pollution control agencies were trying gingerly to do—and as Congress refused to permit in the case of billboards. Or federal money could be used—to finance sewage treatment plants, to purchase offending billboards, to buy the redwood groves and recreation land. Police power led to long-drawn-out legal processes which had yet to prove their effectiveness on a national scale, and the economic costs of its use—crankcase devices, for instance—would have to be borne by consumers. And mastery of the environment through the federal budget would require sums so enormous as to sternly test the country's dedication to the cause.

In early 1967, for example, the secretary of transportation chilled congressional enthusiasm for billboard control when he computed at $558 million the cost of compensating advertising companies for the one million signs to be removed under the 1965 act. The stringency of wartime budgeting held the allocation for sewage treatment plants to less than half the sum Congress had authorized; yet the ultimate cost of purifying the country's air and water was estimated at many tens of billions—$30 billion just for complete separation of storm and sanitary sewers. To win industry cooperation, it was being argued, substantial sums would have to be paid by the federal government through tax abatement for pollution control expenditures.

Land costs spiraling from speculation were delaying, and could ultimately limit, the purchase program under the land and water conservation fund; for this reason the redwood park would be, at best, a compromise with the aspirations of its advocates.

To complete the gloomy picture, it was evident as the decade ended that public and congressional interest could wane as well as wax. The Congress of 1967 had a different composition than that of 1965. The White House conference on natural beauty represented a peak, not a plateau, of public enthusiasm; the zeal mobilized at that gathering could not be sustained even for the few months that the billboard control legislation was under consideration in Congress, and the beautification advocates—who had only psychic income at stake—scarcely even tried to compete with the lobbies representing those whose money income was in the balance. The political weight of the beautifiers and the spoilers was even more disparate in 1967.

As in the case of other problems—poverty, discrimination, substandard education, the manifold problems of the urban ghettoes and the rural backwaters—one could see grounds for hope, but none for certainty, that the ability of institutions to respond would be commensurate with the magnitude of the challenges.

PART II

The Institutions

CHAPTER IX

Ideas and Parties

PEOPLE ALWAYS HAVE unmet needs. And always some say that the nation should do something about those needs—that "there ought to be a law." And others are opposed. Out of this conflict political issues are born and political party alignments are formed.

As the chapters of Part I have shown, the proponents of national action to deal with the major domestic problems of the period 1953–66 were a diverse lot. What they had in common was a desire to act and a readiness to take *national* action through the national political and governmental processes. The desire to act seems basically to be a quality of temperament —"to feel strongly, to be impatient, to want mightily to see that things are done better," as Adlai Stevenson put it.[1] The national government was an instrument to be used, if that were the quickest and surest way to the solution of the problem. It was not to be used for the sake of using it, but neither was it to be avoided for the sake of avoidance. The advocates of national action were therefore less ideological than anti-ideological— resisting the ideologists who condemned in advance any national solution—and they are perhaps best described not as "liberals," a word with ideological connotations, but as "activists," a term that suggests both their temper and their pragmatism.

Opposing the activists, in each instance, were those who were less impressed with the severity of social problems than with the danger of injurious side-effects from the proposed solutions. Alleviation of evils like unemployment, poverty, discrimination, or pollution would be desirable

[1] Speech in Green Bay, Wis., Oct. 7, 1955, reprinted in Adlai E. Stevenson, *What I Think* (Harper, 1956), pp. 30–37.

enough as goals in themselves, but to use the instrumentalities of the national government to those ends would bring other, and worse, evils in its train: bigger federal budgets, a larger federal debt, higher taxes, and inflation; aggrandizement of the national government at the expense of state and local institutions; and growth of the "welfare state," resulting in injuries to individual initiative and private enterprise. Moreover, the federal government was a remote, rigid, and clumsy apparatus to be used for the solution of problems that might take an infinite variety of forms in a vast country. The conservatives, therefore, tended to look to other institutions—states, communities, the family, private enterprise, private groups of various kinds—for any necessary collective action. Depending upon the nature of the particular issue, they argued that a series of local problems, no matter how widespread, was still only just that—a series of *local* problems, not necessarily a national problem (underpaid teachers, polluted air and water); that private disadvantage was a *private* problem not necessarily requiring public action (depressed areas, discrimination, poverty); that the problem was not as bad as the activists painted it and, in any case, was being or would be met without the intervention of the national government (economic recessions, the school construction "crisis," health care for the aged).

Thus was the conflict joined. And it was this collision of views that marked the essential cleavage in American political life during the period 1953–66. It formed the basis of the party struggle. Activists and conservatives were found within each party, but throughout the period the activists dominated the Democratic party and the conservatives the Republican party. In the case of the Democrats, the activist control became increasingly pronounced during the fourteen-year span.

As the parties entered the period covered by this study, the Democrats had an activist program on domestic issues inherited from twenty years of the Franklin Roosevelt and Truman administrations. President Truman had advanced specific proposals on many of the major questions—aid to education, national health insurance, a comprehensive civil rights program. These were carried into the 1952 platform, in more general terms. But all had been defeated in Congress, and Adlai Stevenson's voice did not ring on these issues in the campaign. He was forced upon the defensive on the Democratic record—the inconclusive and unpopular war in Korea, inflation, price and wage controls, and charges of corruption and communism in the government—and it was not the time to advance either an old or a new Democratic legislative program.

Nevertheless, Stevenson made his own major contribution to Democratic party doctrine. During much of the preceding sixty years, activist programs had been redistributional in character—proposing in one way or another to help the "have nots" at the expense of the "haves." Strong third parties during that time had been openly based upon the agricultural and urban "have not" classes. Only the restraining influence of sectionalism, which held so many southern conservatives in the Democratic party and northern activists in the Republican party, seemed to be keeping the two major parties from realignment as class parties on the European pattern. But World War II demonstrated the enormous potential of the American economy to produce abundantly for everybody. The arguments for redistributional measures suddenly lost their economic base; through continuous and rapid economic expansion, all classes could climb the economic ladder together without the need to haul one another down. Truman, influenced particularly by Leon H. Keyserling, chairman of his Council of Economic Advisers, embraced the objective of the expanding economy, but he could not bring himself to abandon the anti-big business rhetoric inherited from Franklin Roosevelt. Stevenson did abandon it.[2] When Truman left the White House, such phrases as "economic royalists" and "malefactors of great wealth" passed from the Democratic vocabulary. To Stevenson and his successors the activist philosophy did not mean using the powers of government *against* any class but rather *for* all classes, "have nots" and "haves" alike, by solving social problems of all kinds— the only redistributional consequence being that the poor might be the principal beneficiaries and the upper and middle classes the greater contributors of the necessary taxes. In such an activist party the wealthy and the powerful could find themselves at home, if by temperament they were impatient to find remedies for social ills, and increasingly, in the 1950's and 1960's, the Democratic party attracted support from the upper economic classes.

If Stevenson were the man who made the Democratic party safe for the rich, Dwight Eisenhower was the leader whose mission was to make the Republican party appealing to the poor. But in this he failed. He elected not to use his imposing personal prestige to develop new policy positions

---

[2] For example, in an article in *Fortune* (October 1955) he labeled talk about a basic antagonism between American business and government as "nonsense." "If it is expected that . . . one sometimes close to government—particularly a Democrat!—must inevitably be . . . slanted against 'Big Business,' I promise disappointment" (reprinted in *What I Think*, pp. 3–17).

that would give the party, as such, a permanent broader base of support. Although his defeat of Robert A. Taft at the 1952 convention had been billed as a decisive victory of the party's progressive elements over the "Taft conservatives," a clear shift in party direction was evident only in foreign affairs. "In almost all domestic matters," Eisenhower later wrote, ". . . he [Taft] and I stood firmly together." After a discussion of federal aid to education and old-age pensions shortly after his inauguration, he told Taft, "Why, Bob, with those views you're twice as liberal as I am."[3]

Eisenhower was not the leader, then, to divert the Republican party from the conservative course it had steadfastly followed ever since the party split of 1912. As the domestic issues of the 1950's developed, the President for the most part stood aside and permitted them to become Democratic issues. Republican activists who had looked hopefully for a reconstruction of their party on progressive lines were to face eight years of frustration.[4] In the fields covered by this study, what had become the modern pattern of executive-legislative relations was reversed—it was the Congress, through its Democratic majorities, that proposed and the executive who disposed.

Table 1 divides, by party of origin, the major legislative measures of the period 1953–60 discussed in Part I. Except in civil rights, the initiative was almost wholly with the Democrats. The Republicans could claim only the Hobby bill for aid to school construction, which died for lack of support from any quarter, one of the two simultaneous versions of the national defense education bill, and two modest conservation proposals. Broad proposals for federal aid to education all carried the Democratic label—even the college aid proposal that originated in an Eisenhower-appointed committee. Legislative measures to deal with unemployment and medicare were exclusively of Democratic origin. As shown in the table, the administration in some cases came forward, after a year or two, with countermeasures that characteristically took a "middle of the road" position between the original Democratic proposal and none at all. In contrast, in the three instances where Republican initiative led to Democratic countermeasures, the latter were bolder and broader, particularly

---

[3] Dwight D. Eisenhower, *Mandate for Change* (Doubleday, 1963), p. 219.

[4] On the other hand, he disappointed those conservatives who had been waiting two decades for the Republican party to assume power and repeal the New Deal. Eisenhower had no intention of attempting anything so drastic—but neither did Taft, whose views on such matters as public housing and aid to education were to be frequently quoted by Democrats during the Eisenhower years.

in terms of federal expenditures, and it was the new Democratic initiative that became the center of debate.

The party battle on domestic issues during the Eisenhower period, then, can be discussed under two headings: Democratic initiative, and Republican response.

Democratic Initiative

Unlike the party in power, which speaks through the president, the party out of power always speaks with many voices. Leaders and factions struggle for ascendancy and control. The basic confederal structure of the national party asserts itself. And members of Congress, with their eyes fixed on their states and districts, may go in directions quite opposite from those of national party leaders whose interests are centered upon the next presidential election.

All of these were Democratic problems in 1953—just as they became Republican problems eight years later. The Truman-Stevenson split of 1952, more personal than ideological but nonetheless pronounced, continued to divide the national leadership of the party, and as 1956 approached the ambitions of presidential candidates divided it further. But these divisions were secondary to the fundamental cleavage between the party's northern and southern wings—or "presidential" and "congressional" wings, as they have been called—that reflected the incomplete realignment of the American party system from the post-Civil War sectionalism. One wing of the Democratic party was activist, the other predominantly conservative; one was dominant in the national party, the other disproportionately powerful in Congress; one was urban-centered, the other rural-based; one was intent upon preparing for forthcoming presidential elections, the other upon the maintenance of the relatively comfortable and secure one-party politics of the southern states.[5]

---

[5] Sidney Hyman has described the attitudes of the Democratic party's congressional wing in these words: "Since they know that men from their section have been barred from the Presidency for almost a hundred years, regardless of personal talent, they may well ask themselves why they should fight to install a Democrat in the White House when *they* cannot be that Democrat—and when the waging of such a fight might imperil their local position." On the other hand, "the winning of the White House becomes the transcendent aim of Northern Democratic politics" ("Can a Democrat Win in '60?" *Reporter*, March 5, 1959, p. 12). James MacGregor Burns regarded the split between the presidential and congressional wings in each party as amounting to "four-party politics in America," the subtitle of his book, *The Deadlock of Democracy* (Prentice-Hall, 1963).

Table 1. *Party Initiative and Response, Major Legislative Measures, 1953–60[a]*

Issue and measure	Primary source	Date initiated[b]	Response[c]
REPUBLICAN INITIATIVE—DEMOCRATIC RESPONSE			
Education			
Aid for school construction (Hobby bill)	Department of HEW–banker consultants	1955	Countermeasure, 1955 (Kelley bill)
National defense education	Department of HEW	1958	Simultaneous bill
Civil rights			
Power to initiate enforcement (Part III)	Department of Justice	1956	Support in House and by national party;[d] opposition in Senate
Federal registration of voters	Civil Rights Commission	1960	Support
Outdoor environment			
Water pollution control (enforcement)	Department of HEW	1955	Countermeasure, 1956, including grants
National seashores	Department of Interior	1959	Countermeasure, 1959
DEMOCRATIC INITIATIVE—REPUBLICAN RESPONSE			
Unemployment			
Area redevelopment	Senate	1955	Countermeasure, 1956
Youth Conservation Corps	Interest group (conservationists)	1957	Opposition
Manpower development and training	Senate–interest group (AVA)	1960	None
Education			
Aid for school construction (Kelley bill)	House	1955	Countermeasure, 1956
General aid, including teacher salaries	Interest group (NEA)	1958	Opposition

Table 1. *Continued*

Issue and measure	Primary source	Date initiated[b]	Response[c]
National defense education	Senate	1958	Simultaneous bill
Aid for college construction	Presidential committee	1958	Countermeasure, 1959
Medicare (Forand bill)	Interest group (AFL-CIO)	1957	Countermeasure, 1960
Outdoor environment Water pollution control (grants)	House	1956	Countermeasure, 1958[e]
Billboard control	Senate	1955	Countermeasure, 1957

[a] The only measure in the fields studied that began under bipartisan sponsorship was the wilderness bill, introduced in 1956.
[b] Date of first measure to receive substantial and sustained attention. Both the Douglas area redevelopment bill and the Forand medicare bill were later versions of earlier proposals.
[c] In the case of the Democrats, response by the main body of Democrats in either or both houses of the Congress. In the case of the Republicans, response by the administration. (In the instances where the two houses disagreed, response of the national party policy-making bodies is shown.)
[d] Approval by Democratic Advisory Council; adoption in 1960 platform.
[e] Joint Federal-State Action Committee recommendations.

Writing in 1950, the committee on political parties of the American Political Science Association, headed by E. E. Schattschneider, asserted that "an effective party system requires, first, that the parties are able to bring forth programs to which they commit themselves...."[6] Can a party as deeply divided as the Democratic party of the 1950's bring forth a program and commit itself to that program? Or does one have to accept the earlier view of Pendleton Herring, based perhaps upon observation of that same Democratic party before and after 1932, that "parties cannot be pictured realistically as coming foward with a program, winning office, and then putting their platform into effect"?[7]

As it happened, the Democratic party in the 1950's and 1960's did exactly those things the Schattschneider committee said should be done and Herring said could not be expected. It *did* develop a program to which it committed itself—and which it put into effect after winning office. This section outlines the processes by which the out-party in the 1950's initiated, developed support for, and adopted the major elements of what became the domestic program of the in-party in 1961. While the discussion is limited to issues covered in Part I of this volume, these were by definition the domestic questions that dominated political debate

[6] American Political Science Association, Committee on Political Parties, *Toward a More Responsible Two-Party System* (Rinehart, 1950), pp. 17–18.
[7] Pendleton Herring, *The Politics of Democracy* (Norton, 1940), p. 112.

during 1953–66, and measures to deal with them formed the core of the Democratic party program.

Initiation of Program Measures. While the Democratic program of the 1950's incorporated many old ideas—federal aid to education and health insurance, for example, were live issues in the 1930's—the measures themselves were new. The old proposals advanced by President Truman had been killed in the Congress, and the remains had been buried by the Eisenhower landslide. The Democratic activists had to assess the new political circumstances, the new public attitudes, and the new problems of the time and begin afresh.

Who did the assessing? As Table 1 shows, the major new proposals can be about equally divided between those conceived within Congress and those originated by outside interest groups. But this division of credit applies only to the earliest stage of the initiation process. Once the germ of an idea had appeared, its development came perhaps more from interaction between congressional activists and outside groups than from either source independently. Neither side could get far without the other; therefore, the quicker they could reach a meeting of minds the better.

After the initial conception, then, the legislative measures listed in Table 1 can be seen as arrayed along a spectrum according to the *relative* degrees of participation by congressional and private groups. At one end would be the medicare bill; it was carried by the AFL-CIO all the way to the bill-drafting stage, and for the first few months, at least, it had only nominal sponsorship by a congressman who had doubts about it and did little to promote it. Aime Forand became, when all was over, surely one of the more inadvertent heroes of the day. At the other end of the spectrum would be aid to higher education; no interest group could be found to marshal outside support during the early years, and the senator spearheading the congressional drive was forced to the extraordinary length of trying to organize such a group. At the center would be the Manpower Development and Training Act, which arose directly out of communication between an interest group and a senator. Most measures would be nearer the center than the extremes. Activist politicians looking for public support and interest groups looking for political support were natural allies, and alliances were formed almost automatically. While maintaining their official nonpartisan stance, the Washington representatives of such groups as the National Education Association, the AFL-CIO, the conservation organizations, the American Municipal Association, and the United States Conference of Mayors were admitted to full participating status in the Democratic party's inner councils on matters within their fields of interest and remained in continuous consultation.

To a considerable extent the individual alliances overlapped, and the participants in a very real sense formed a single institution, unorganized and amorphous but self-conscious and cohesive. Its members were bound together by a common interest in legislative strategy, tactics, manipulation, and brokerage, a common responsibility in these matters, a common activist temperament, and a common political partisanship—although the last of these could be set aside on those issues, like civil rights, where Republicans and Democrats worked actively together. They made up a highly developed Washington-centered communications and intelligence network, exchanging information and plotting strategy over luncheon tables and in informal meetings and social gatherings. The nongovernmental organizations designated themselves as "public interest groups"—as distinct from "private interest groups" or "lobbies"—to gain their own collective identity.

This unique Washington institution had its nonresident members, but its operations were in the capital. Its function was to transform general ideas into specific, practical, and timely legislative proposals. The key words are "practical" and "timely." Practicality is attained by fitting an idea into the habit patterns of the legislative process, by clothing novel ideas in familiar garments. Thus medicare was presented as just another application of the "time-tested" social security principle, and aid for college construction first reached the Senate floor as a simple extension of the college housing program, treating academic buildings as a kind of subcategory of dormitories. Timeliness is achieved by designing a measure to ride with, rather than against, the currents of public opinion—currents that are often set in motion by specific events, as sputnik created the climate for a national defense education bill. At the seat of government is concentrated expertise in the legislative process, intimate knowledge of the variety of legislative means to a given end, and sensitivity to the drifts of political and public opinion. There legislative strategists and tacticians can assemble and probe, test, jockey, and negotiate until they have transformed a general legislative objective into a concrete proposal around which political support can be mobilized.

Table 1 does not show the academic community—often the presumed source of legislative ideas—as the originator of any proposal. Individual academicians made their contributions—for example, Wilbur Cohen, temporarily a professor, in the development of medicare—but they were effective not because they were members of the academic community but because they were of the circle of Washington-based legislative strategists and tacticians. They were, as a rule, among those whom Richard Neustadt has labeled "in-and-outers." Their legislative expertise they had gained in government service—which in Cohen's case amounted to more than twenty years—and they had retained their interest and their Washington associations after leaving the government. Perhaps it can be said that, while the academic community has a responsibility for defining social problems and developing data bearing upon their solution, the responsibility for devising the legislative solutions themselves belongs to the Washington legislative community. Few men live simultaneously in both.

Mobilization of Support. With few exceptions the congressional initiators of Democratic measures during the Eisenhower period were not members identified with the leadership of either house. They were, rather, individual activists—usually members of the committees with jurisdiction over the bills they sponsored but sometimes, as in the case of Senator Hubert Humphrey and the Youth Conservation Corps, not even that. Their problem was to mobilize broad support within the party without benefit of control over the party machinery of the Congress.

The national leaders of the Democratic party's presidential wing had a related concern. As they saw it, the party could retain—or regain—its voter appeal only if it presented a clear, liberal image, and for the most part the image would depend upon what happened in the Congress. But party leadership there was in the hands of the congressional wing, which was not only more conservative in its outlook but was not inclined to openly oppose the popular Eisenhower.

Among those who earliest felt the need for a means of formulating a Democratic party program were the veterans of presidential campaigning. In 1954, Senator Estes Kefauver of Tennessee, a presidential candidate two years earlier, urged Minority Leader Lyndon Johnson to call a party caucus to adopt a program. Adlai Stevenson spoke of the need for a "system of consultation" whereby he as titular head of the party might "be advised of party policy" and might "help to shape that policy."[8]

But the congressional leadership showed no interest in any such proposals. Johnson "let it be known through newspaper leaks" that he was rejecting Kefauver's request for a caucus.[9] None was held for purposes of

---

[8] *What I Think*, p. ix.

[9] Rowland Evans and Robert Novak, *Lyndon B. Johnson: The Exercise of Power* (New American Library, 1966), p. 71.

policy discussion in either house. No other machinery for party policy making existed. Democrats in the House of Representatives had no policy committee like that of the Republicans, and the Senate Democratic Policy Committee was a misnomer. That body had the function of clearing for floor action the bills approved by committees; if it ever discussed basic policies, it made no pronouncements on them. The leaders preferred a flexible party strategy that left initiative largely to President Eisenhower and preserved their freedom to deal with each issue as it arose.

If this strategy was not satisfactory to the presidential Democrats in 1954, it was even less so after the party's victory in the congressional elections that year. Once the Democrats gained control of both houses, the record of the Congress itself became the party record that would be taken into presidential and congressional campaigns. Therefore, argued the presidential Democrats, the Congress should be used for purposes of record-building, of establishing a clear, liberal image that would appeal to voters in the two-party, urbanized states which they represented and which, in 1956, would cast the decisive votes in the electoral college. This meant taking a party position, maintaining it against undue compromise, and carrying it to a showdown in the two houses, where the consequence would be either a dramatic victory or a dramatic defeat to be appealed to the people at the next election.

"I have become convinced through rather sad experience," said Stevenson, "that real issues cannot be developed, nor even effectively presented, during a political campaign. They must be sharpened and clarified largely through the legislative process between elections."[10]

But the congressional leadership was not to be persuaded. The activists were constrained to proceed independently to organize their own bloc in each house of the Congress, rally support for specific measures inside and outside the legislature, and press for action on them. They could also work with the Democratic National Committee, which remained in the hands of the Stevenson Democrats under Chairmen Stephen A. Mitchell (1953–54) and Paul Butler (1955–60), and particularly with the Democratic Advisory Council established by Butler late in 1956.

The Senate activist bloc, the corresponding House bloc (organized as the Democratic Study Group), and the national committee and advisory council came to comprise a triangle of communication[11] and mutual re-

[10] Quoted by Kenneth S. Davis, *A Prophet in His Own Country* (Doubleday, 1957), p. 439.

[11] For reasons given below, the Democratic Study Group avoided establishing formal direct communication with the Democratic Advisory Council, but indirect and informal channels were always open.

inforcement that bypassed the party's leadership in Congress. By 1960 it had come close to isolating that leadership.

The Senate Activist Bloc. When Lyndon Johnson rejected Kefauver's proposal for a party caucus in 1954, he was concerned that a liberal program, even if it could be adopted by his divided party, could not be passed. "Should that happen," explain Evans and Novak, "the Democrats, not Eisenhower, would be blamed for stalemating Congress. The chief blame-takers would be the Democratic leaders; and the chief Democratic leader was Lyndon Johnson." "Without a program of his own and committed deep down to no ideological doctrine," he preferred to wait for the Eisenhower proposals and maintain his flexible strategy, opposing some on a selective basis when a consensus of Democrats could be found.[12]

As a matter of personal style and taste, notes Johnson's more worshipful biographer, William S. White, the Senate Democratic leader distrusted "doctrinaire solutions to political problems, and . . . absolute, all-or-nothing stands which are good theater but bad politics." Johnson rejected "opposition for opposition's sake" and "frantic and purely partisan assaults upon Eisenhower."[13]

In any case, it can be argued that Johnson's was the inevitable course for the Democratic leader—any Democratic leader—of the Senate in the early and middle 1950's. The body of Senate Democrats did not reflect, in its geographical and ideological makeup, the national Democratic party. Senators from the one-party states of the then-solid South made up nearly half the membership of the Democratic caucus which chose the leader, and by virtue of seniority they exercised an influence disproportionate to their numbers. Moreover, senators from the border and mountain states, not moved by the same issues that motivated their colleagues from the urban northeast, often found the southerners more congenial ideologically as well as personally. Thus the activist senators who reflected the main body of Democratic opinion in the country as a whole appeared in the unrepresentative Senate party as extremists, not just as liberal but as "ultra-liberal" and "doctrinaire," to use some of White's adjectives. A man who represented their point of view would not be elected to party office by the whole body of Senate Democrats in the first place—not in the absence of intervention by a Democratic president. Once elected by all of the Senate Democrats, the leader's obligation was to lead and represent them all. Northern critics of Lyndon Johnson's

---

[12] Evans and Novak, *Lyndon B. Johnson*, pp. 72–73.
[13] William S. White, *The Professional* (Houghton Mifflin, 1964), pp. 55, 173, 174.

leadership were not reasonable in expecting him to adopt and thrust upon the Senate Democratic party as a whole a liberal program distasteful
to half or more of its members—including many of the committee chairmen upon whom Johnson had to depend for any kind of party record at
all. But neither was the leadership reasonable in expecting those who
represented the national party and who themselves faced tough reelection
contests to abandon their demands in the interest of party harmony. The
result was constant and growing tension between the majority leader and
the presidential Democrats.

Sporadically, after 1954, the latter renewed their demands for a party
program. But except in 1955, when he announced in a Texas speech a
thirteen-point "program with a heart," Johnson would go only as far as
an annual "state of the union message" which avoided commitments or
promises on matters where a consensus of Senate Democrats had not
already been reached.

The presidential Democrats, left to their own devices, experimented
in 1953 with biweekly dinner meetings as a means of coordinating their
efforts in opposition to President Eisenhower's offshore oil bill (a measure
Johnson favored). These sessions, chaired by Lister Hill of Alabama,
proved so useful that some senators talked of continuing them for purposes of coordination on other issues, but that hope died when it became
apparent that the makeup of the "liberal" bloc varied, often drastically,
depending on the issue under discussion. What developed in the Senate,
therefore, was a series of ad hoc arrangements with a leadership and participation that differed with each question that arose.

The central unifying device for the activist Democrats was the cosponsorship of bills. When a senator had ready a particular measure, he could
identify his allies and organize them to join in introducing and supporting it. The activists inevitably traded support for one another's bills in
a tacit log-rolling operation, and while the sponsoring groups varied from
bill to bill, they came to have an overlapping membership which loosely
defined the composition of the liberal bloc as a Senate institution—a bloc
with uncertain and intermittent membership at the fringes but a continuing core. Prior to 1959, the core consisted of only a dozen senators
or so, with others joining on particular issues, but after the 1958 election
perhaps two dozen members could be said to give the bloc consistent and
reliable allegiance. It was recognizable as a distinct entity in internal Senate politics, and one with which the majority leader had constantly to
contend.

Table 2 illustrates the makeup of the activist, or liberal Democratic

Table 2. *Adherence of Democratic Senators to Activist Bloc, 1957–60[a]*

| | | Percentage of bills cosponsored by each senator | | |
		85th Congress[b] (1957–58)	86th Congress[c] (1959–60)	Both Congresses (1957–60)
Senator	State			
NORTHEASTERN REGION				
Hubert H. Humphrey	Minnesota	100	89	94
Joseph S. Clark	Pennsylvania	86	78	81
Philip A. Hart	Michigan	—	78	78
Jennings Randolph	West Virginia	—	78	78
Robert C. Byrd	West Virginia	—	67	67
Paul H. Douglas	Illinois	57	67	63
Patrick V. McNamara	Michigan	57	67	63
John O. Pastore	Rhode Island	57	56	56
Eugene J. McCarthy	Minnesota	—	56	56
William Proxmire[d]	Wisconsin	100	33	54
Thomas C. Hennings, Jr.	Missouri	43	56	50
John F. Kennedy	Massachusetts	43	44	44
Theodore Francis Green	Rhode Island	29	44	38
Thomas J. Dodd	Connecticut	—	33	33
Harrison A. Williams, Jr.	New Jersey	—	33	33
Edmund S. Muskie	Maine	—	22	22
Stephen M. Young	Ohio	—	22	22
Vance Hartke	Indiana	—	22	22
Stuart Symington	Missouri	14	22	19
Frank J. Lausche	Ohio	14	11	13
J. Allen Frear, Jr.	Delaware	14	0	6
WESTERN REGION				
James E. Murray	Montana	86	100	94
Richard L. Neuberger[d]	Oregon	86	100	93
Wayne Morse	Oregon	71	89	81
Ernest Gruening	Alaska	—	67	67
Warren G. Magnuson	Washington	71	56	63
Mike Mansfield	Montana	57	67	63
Henry M. Jackson	Washington	57	56	56
Clair Engle	California	—	44	44
Frank E. Moss	Utah	—	44	44
John A. Carroll	Colorado	29	44	38
Gale W. McGee	Wyoming	—	33	33
Frank Church	Idaho	14	44	31
Dennis Chavez	New Mexico	29	22	25
Howard W. Cannon	Nevada	—	22	22
Clinton P. Anderson	New Mexico	14	22	19
E. L. Bartlett	Alaska	—	11	11
Alan Bible	Nevada	0	11	6
Carl Hayden	Arizona	0	0	0
Joseph C. O'Mahoney	Wyoming	0	0	0

Table 2. *Continued*

		Percentage of bills cosponsored by each senator		
Senator	State	85th Congress[b] (1957–58)	86th Congress[c] (1959–60)	Both Congresses (1957–60)
	SOUTHERN REGION			
Estes Kefauver	Tennessee	43	33	38
Ralph W. Yarborough[d]	Texas	50	22	31
John J. Sparkman	Alabama	57	0	25
A. S. Mike Monroney	Oklahoma	29	22	25
J. W. Fulbright	Arkansas	43	0	19
Lister Hill	Alabama	43	0	19
Robert S. Kerr	Oklahoma	14	11	13
Russell B. Long	Louisiana	29	0	13
Olin D. Johnston	South Carolina	0	11	6
George A. Smathers	Florida	14	0	6
Harry F. Byrd	Virginia	0	0	0
James O. Eastland	Mississippi	0	0	0
Allen J. Ellender	Louisiana	0	0	0
Sam J. Ervin, Jr.	North Carolina	0	0	0
Albert Gore	Tennessee	0	0	0
Spessard L. Holland	Florida	0	0	0
Lyndon B. Johnson	Texas	0	0	0
B. Everett Jordan	North Carolina	0	0	0
John L. McClellan	Arkansas	0	0	0
A. Willis Robertson	Virginia	0	0	0
Richard B. Russell	Georgia	0	0	0
John Stennis	Mississippi	0	0	0
Herman E. Talmadge	Georgia	0	0	0
Strom Thurmond	South Carolina	0	0	0

[a] Senators who served less than one full Congress are omitted. On each of the bills except medicare, one or more Republicans joined as cosponsors. Senator Langer of North Dakota cosponsored ten measures, registering a higher score than all but a few Democrats. Senator Javits of New York cosponsored five and Senators Cooper of Kentucky and Smith of Maine cosponsored four.

[b] Based on civil rights bill introduced by Humphrey (S. 501-10), area redevelopment by Douglas (S. 964), wilderness by Humphrey (S. 1176), national defense education by Hill (S. 3187), aid for elementary and secondary schools by Murray (S. 3311), aid for community facilities by Fulbright (S. 3497), and aid for college construction by Clark (S. 3713).

[c] Based on aid for elementary and secondary schools bill introduced by Murray (S. 2), aid for college construction by Clark (S. 194), area redevelopment by Douglas (S. 722), civil rights by Douglas (S. 810) or by Humphrey (S. 1997-2013) (the sponsoring blocs are considered as one), Youth Conservation Corps by Humphrey (S. 812), wilderness by Humphrey (S. 1123), temporary unemployment compensation by McNamara (S. 1323), shoreline preservation by Murray (S. 2460), and medicare by McNamara (S. 3503).

[d] Senators Proxmire and Yarborough did not become members until after the Eighty-fifth Congress had begun and Senator Neuberger died before the expiration of the Eighty-sixth Congress. Thus their scores for their partial years, as well as their scores in the final column, are based upon a smaller number of bills.

bloc, as measured by cosponsorship of major bills in the fields covered by this study, during the last two Eisenhower Congresses. On sixteen occasions in those four years, sponsors of important bills made a serious effort to obtain cosponsors for their legislation. No Democratic senator joined in cosponsorship on all occasions but eighteen joined on at least half of the occasions when they had the opportunity. Cosponsorship, of course, understates the total support for particular bills among Senate Democrats, as well as the degree of attachment of individual senators to the liberal bloc. Senators may, for a variety of reasons, not be listed as cosponsors of bills they support—some, wary of identification with any "bloc," decline as a matter of principle to cosponsor bills (Johnson was among those senators); some may object to a particular feature of a bill or prefer an alternate version; others may be omitted simply because the sponsor of the bill fails to communicate with them before its introduction. Nevertheless, as applied to the Senate Democrats of the period 1957–60, the table presents an accurate picture of a bloc that was highly cohesive at the center, was less cohesive away from the center, and had an indistinct and mobile boundary.

The regional character of the activist bloc is shown by the fact that not a single southerner was among the eighteen with at least 50 percent adherence. Conversely, the median figure for the northeastern group was 50 percent. Among the westerners, the influence of latitude is clearly evident; northwesterners tended to have a high degree of adherence, southwesterners a low degree.

Fourteen of the sixteen measures were sponsored by five senators at the center of the activist bloc—Hubert Humphrey, Paul Douglas, James Murray, Joseph Clark, and Patrick McNamara. None of these senators was a part of the official party leadership, only Murray operated from a post of authority as committee chairman, and only Humphrey could be considered a member of the Senate's "inner circle" or "club."

The response of the Senate leadership to the activist-initiated legislation, in the absence of anything resembling a party program, was not unlike its response to Eisenhower measures. Majority Leader Johnson took a wait-and-see attitude. If a proposal developed substantial support, if it were the kind of measure that tended to unite rather than divide the party, and if it were likely to be approved by the legislative committee, he might give it his personal support. Similarly, if a floor amendment to a committee bill appeared likely of victory, it too might receive his support. But the expectation of victory was the key condition. As White makes clear, the majority leader had no affinity for lost causes; if a bill or an amendment were destined to die, it rarely carried any of his prestige with it. For the same reason, he did not intervene—publicly, at least—in the substance of committee affairs (as distinct from questions of scheduling). If he attempted to lead a committee and failed, his standing as leader would suffer. But "because he spurned the hopeless fight, he was able to fashion a myth of invincibility which was itself mightily persuasive," as one scholar has observed.[14]

Tension between the activist wing and Johnson reached its climax after the 1958 election. Senate Democrats had been augmented by fifteen new members from the North and West, most of whom had run on activist platforms. A presidential election was approaching, with Johnson a potential candidate. It appeared to the activists that their hour at last had come. The majority leader, who for so long had contended that his policy of "moderation" faithfully reflected the preponderance of Senate Democratic opinion, would presumably shift his policy to reflect with equal fidelity the new balance of opinion. But the activists were to be disappointed. They hopefully sought greater representation for the North and West on the party's policy and steering committees—but were rebuffed.[15] They sought to amend rule 22 to limit debate—but Johnson fought and defeated them. They advocated other changes in the Senate rules—and received no support. They looked for him to help push their program through committees—and were often disappointed, as Senator McNamara stated so forcefully in his outburst against Johnson over his handling of the unemployment compensation issue.[16] They sought to pass uncompromised Democratic bills to be sent to the President on a take-it-or-leave-it basis—but he sought to make the measures "veto-proof."

While the senior rebels were pondering how to marshal their forces to seek greater influence in the leadership structure, Senator William Proxmire of Wisconsin launched a one-man assault on the Johnson leadership in a series of speeches on the Senate floor—the first of which was delivered while Johnson was absent from the city. Unable either to follow Proxmire's ill-timed lead or to dissociate any efforts they might undertake from his, the other members of the activist bloc abandoned any serious attempt to force significant formal concessions from the leadership and concentrated instead upon using their greater numbers to get their program measures through committees and through the Senate itself. In this undertaking, Johnson expedited Senate procedures for their bene-

[14] Ralph K. Huitt, "Democratic Party Leadership in the Senate," *American Political Science Review*, Vol. 55 (June 1961), p. 338.

[15] The former screens committee-approved bills for floor action; the latter assigns Democratic senators to committees.

[16] Chap. 3, pp. 78–79.

fit even if he sometimes took the lead in compromising the substance of their measures.[17]

Throughout the Eisenhower years, then, the development of a program for Senate Democrats was initially the self-assigned responsibility of the activist bloc. If it succeeded in getting its bills out of committee, it could count on the considerable weight of Johnson's support to gain as broad a consensus as possible, and negotiation of floor amendments to broaden the consensus was a Johnson specialty. In no instance did he oppose a major liberal measure that cleared its committee, or prevent its consideration. (Civil rights measures, of course, did not reach the floor from the hostile Judiciary Committee.) Thus, the senator who held the title of Democratic leader was in many respects a follower. Others made the program and initially mobilized the support; the leader joined the movement only after it was well underway. But this may be in the nature of legislative leadership in the party that does not hold the White House. Power comes only from those who are led; the party leader must stand somewhere near the middle of the party spectrum in his legislative body if he is both to gain and hold power and to use that power effectively.[18] If the party spectrum in the legislature differs from the party spectrum in the nation—as it did in the Senate in the 1950's—then the successful legislative party leader will be out of step with the national party, as Johnson found when he ran for president in 1960. The leader of the out-party in a legislative chamber cannot be both the champion of causes and the builder of consensus. The word "leader" has, in fact, two meanings—program leadership and floor leadership, trail-blazing and consensus-building—that were often confused by those who expected a different kind of Senate leadership from Lyndon Johnson. And, accordingly, two kinds of leaders served separate functions in the Senate of 1953–60—the activist bloc and the majority leader—and it would have been impossible, under the circumstances of the time, for one man to have filled concurrently both leadership roles.

[17] See Evans and Novak, *Lyndon B. Johnson,* pp. 199–208 for an account of the conflicts of this period. After the crisis passed, Johnson did add three freshman senators to the policy committee, but the Democratic conference (or caucus) in 1960 defeated a motion to make that committee elective by the conference and to broaden its role; several conferences were held in January and February 1960 to discuss policy measures, but none after that time (Huitt, "Democratic Party Leadership in the Senate," p. 343).

[18] The evidence bearing upon this proposition, which has been advanced by David B. Truman and others, is discussed by Samuel C. Patterson in "Legislative Leadership and Political Ideology," *Public Opinion Quarterly,* Vol. 27 (Fall 1963), pp. 399–410.

The House Activist Bloc: The Democratic Study Group. On the House side of the Capitol, Speaker Sam Rayburn faced the same problems that Lyndon Johnson faced in leading a divided party, and he adopted the same tactics. Like Johnson, he avoided party caucuses where program issues that divided the party might be discussed. Like Johnson, he avoided setting forth a program, preferring to wait for Eisenhower proposals and then to seek an opposition posture around which a degree of Democratic unity could be achieved. He concentrated, wrote Neil MacNeil, on "minimizing" the "divisiveness" of his party. "The avoidance of open controversy is his genius," said Representative Lee Metcalf of Montana.[19]

And, as in the Senate, the activist Democrats became restive early under that kind of party leadership. In the Eighty-third Congress (1953–54), while their Senate counterparts were coalescing on the tidelands oil issue, House Democratic liberals had found common cause in combating some Republican measures affecting conservation.[20] Throughout the first Eisenhower administration they continued to function as a bloc on an ad hoc basis, collaborating on particular issues under various leaders. By the end of 1956, however, they had concluded that more systematic organization was essential if they were to communicate effectively with one another and mobilize their maximum strength on individual issues.

Meeting in Washington in advance of the opening of Congress in 1957, their leaders—among them Eugene McCarthy and John Blatnik of Minnesota, Chet Holifield of California, and Lee Metcalf—decided as an initial step to draft a statement of objectives. The statement, which was released on January 8, 1957, and promptly labeled the "Liberal Manifesto," was specific and forthright, but broke little new ground. It endorsed measures on which the party position in the House was already established, including the area redevelopment bill, federal aid for school construction, and civil rights legislation in the fields of voting, employment, and protection of personal security. By the end of January, eighty House Democrats had adhered to the statement, all of them from the North and West, three-fourths of them from urban constituencies. With a view to keeping their strong civil rights language uncompromised, McCarthy and his colleagues had not sought signatures from any southern Democrats.

[19] Quoted in MacNeil, *Forge of Democracy* (McKay, 1963), pp. 107–08.

[20] This section relies upon Kenneth Kofmehl, "The Institutionalization of a Voting Bloc," *Western Political Quarterly*, Vol. 17 (June 1964), pp. 256–72, the most complete account of the early years of what became the Democratic Study Group.

As in the Senate, the liberal bloc spread outward from its central core, with varying numbers of additional Democrats joining on particular issues. But, in contrast to the Senate, it had a continuing leader—McCarthy—and it developed a whip system under Frank Thompson, Jr., of New Jersey. On key votes, Thompson alerted a dozen assistant whips who in turn made contact with the rest of the original eighty signers and with other Democrats who might share their views on the particular issue. The group also organized briefings and seminars.

Rayburn neither approved nor opposed the activists' organizing efforts. Had he opposed them, they would assuredly have called off the undertaking. They took pains to keep him informed of their activities, often through Representative Richard Bolling of Missouri, a Rayburn confidant.[21] Bolling in turn counseled them on the speaker's views and reactions. Majority Leader John McCormack of Massachusetts, while reportedly offended originally at not being notified in advance of the "Liberal Manifesto," privately urged House members to join the group once he was satisfied it was in responsible hands.[22]

When the Eighty-sixth Congress convened, in January 1959, the activist bloc looked forward confidently to the enactment of its program. The Democrats had gained forty-nine new nonsouthern members and now held almost a two-to-one majority. For the first time in a generation, the House of Representatives appeared to have a liberal preponderance. As in the Senate, they looked first to a redistribution of power within the formal structure of the House—specifically to a curbing of the power of the Rules Committee—but they failed to persuade Rayburn to undertake that battle. By the end of the summer the liberals had demonstrated only impotence. The civil rights bill and the school construction bill were buried in the unreformed Rules Committee. On the preeminent liberal-conservative issue of the session—labor reform—the conservatives had won a stunning victory with passage of the Landrum-Griffin bill. Particularly concerned were those first-term Democrats who had campaigned on liberal platforms and faced the prospect of running for reelection with few or none of their measures passed. The leaders of the activist bloc decided that the time had come to act. They invited their colleagues to a meeting on September 5, 1959, to discuss "the most effective operation

---

[21] Bolling, for example, suggested Rayburn be shown a copy of the "Liberal Manifesto" in advance of its release. Rayburn's comment was, "There is nothing here I disagree with" (Bolling, *House Out of Order* [Dutton, 1965], p. 56).

[22] Kofmehl, "Institutionalization of a Voting Bloc," p. 272.

next year on imperative issues of concern to an effective party program."

One recipient of the invitation alerted Rayburn with a report that "your troops are revolting," and Rayburn summoned Lee Metcalf, who had succeeded McCarthy as leader of the liberal bloc when McCarthy was elected to the Senate. Metcalf assured Rayburn that they were not opposing the speaker; rather, they were seeking to strengthen him in his struggles with Rules Committee Chairman Howard Smith of Virginia. Rayburn expressed no objection, and on September 9 the liberals established what was to become probably the most elaborately organized "party within a party" in the history of the House of Representatives—the Democratic Study Group.

The group defined its program only in the most general terms. It listed seven areas of concentration for 1960, including "effective civil rights legislation," aid to elementary and secondary schools, area redevelopment, and medicare. "On the basis of experience with more precisely defined goals in the Liberal Manifesto," writes Kofmehl, "the group left the statement of these legislative objectives deliberately vague."[23] Task forces were appointed in each of the program areas to prepare background materials and develop policy positions, but the main objective was to organize for parliamentary action. In the large and unwieldy House the compelling need of the activists was for an effective communication system, particularly a whip organization to assure that their full voting strength—numbering on some occasions one-third or more of the House membership—was mobilized for crucial votes. Debates over program specifics could only weaken the internal cohesion of the group and thus detract from its effectiveness in its primary role. Once it evolved into a body with many of the characteristics of a party within the House, the group confronted the same problem faced on a broader scale by its parent legislative party—the problem of "minimizing divisiveness" by avoiding specific program declarations on matters of controversy within the party ranks. Lacking even the device of cosponsorship, which was at that time forbidden by House rules, the House activists had to leave to others the definition of the program of the Democratic party as a whole.

The Democratic Advisory Council. When the 1956 election returns were in, the Democratic presidential party had suffered a crushing defeat, but the Democratic congressional party had actually won its election.

[23] *Ibid.*, p. 271.

Despite the Eisenhower landslide, the Democrats had retained control of Congress. Lyndon Johnson and Sam Rayburn saw the results, naturally enough, as a vindication of the congressional leadership and its philosophy of "moderation" and "responsible" opposition. But the leaders of the presidential party could see only defeat, and they ascribed it to two causes: the Democrats had not undermined the Eisenhower prestige by forcefully pointing out to the country the mistakes and folly of his policies, and they had not developed and presented to the country a distinct and liberal party program that would have given the voters a clear and attractive alternative to Eisenhower. And, as Stevenson insisted, neither of these objectives could be served by the speeches of a presidential candidate during a single autumn each four years. The attacks on the Republicans had to be made, and the program had to be assembled and presented to the public, day by day and week by week in the long years between presidential elections— and the only place where that could be done was on Capitol Hill. Failure to achieve those objectives was the direct consequence of the Johnson-Rayburn approach to legislative leadership, reasoned the presidential Democrats. The "responsible" compromises which were the pride of the congressional leaders might be necessary to get bills passed but they blurred the image of the Democratic party. Better to stake out a party position and go down fighting than to try to share the "middle of the road" in a bipartisan embrace with the conservative Republican President.

In the days following the election, the thoughts of presidential Democrats moved in the same direction: some mechanism had to be designed to give the party as a whole a means of adopting policies that would be presented to the country and, hopefully, pursued in Congress in the years leading up to 1960. It is impossible, says Charles Tyroler, II, who later became the executive director of the Democratic Advisory Council, to determine who originated the idea of the council—"lots of people wanted to do something, and many people take credit for it." The 1950 report of the Schattschneider committee of political scientists had provided a model in its proposal for a "party council" for each party, constituted along lines close to those the council eventually took—a model frequently cited by those struggling with the Democratic problem of 1957. In any case, on November 27, Democratic National Chairman Paul Butler presented to the executive committee of the national committee a plan to constitute an advisory body to which the national committee would delegate the policy-making power which it officially holds between the quadrennial party conventions. The new council would be made up of the party's national leadership—the leaders of each house of Congress, four governors, the 1956 ticket of Adlai Stevenson and Estes Kefauver, former President Truman, a mayor, and the members of the executive committee. The executive committee approved, and Butler immediately issued the invitations.

Lyndon Johnson appeared to go along with Butler. He suggested the names of the other Senate participants, including that of John F. Kennedy, who had narrowly missed winning the vice presidential nomination in 1956. But when Sam Rayburn was reached in Texas, the speaker exploded. He would have nothing to do with any outside group who would purport to set policy for the Democratic leadership in Congress. He also persuaded his House colleagues to decline Butler's invitation—including one who had already accepted. Thereupon Johnson reversed himself and declined to serve. So did the other Senate invitees, except for Hubert Humphrey. Humphrey and Kefauver, who was on the council not as a senator but as the 1956 vice presidential nominee, were the only members of Congress to participate until the fall of 1959, when all presidential hopefuls were invited and Kennedy and Stuart Symington agreed to join.

Not only did Butler lose the congressional leadership but he also failed initially in his quest for a southern governor who would serve. When the council held its first full meeting, therefore, it was quite a different body from the one Butler had envisaged. Instead of an all-party council, it was virtually an all-northern and -western, all-liberal council.[24] It could, and did, thus become exactly what most leaders of the presidential wing of the party had wanted—a clear voice for *their* "party" that could state positions different from, and if necessary in defiance of, those of the congressional leaders.

In its very first action, on January 4, 1957, the council threw its weight behind the northern activists and against the Johnson leadership in the fight over rule 22 in the Senate. A month later it called for passage of "pending legislation introduced by Democratic members" relating to voting rights, fair employment practices, and other aspects of discrimination—in other words, the Humphrey bills and the corresponding House measures which went far beyond what Johnson, and presumably Rayburn, would publicly support. In February 1958, a few months after Johnson

---

[24] The only southern members at the outset were Kefauver and three members of the national committee's executive committee. The latter regularly dissented from the council's statements on civil rights. Subsequently, Governor LeRoy Collins of Florida joined the council; he, like Kefauver, was not a regular dissenter on civil rights.

had joined in killing Part III of the civil rights bill, which would have authorized federal initiation of enforcement procedures, the council proposed in general terms that it be considered anew. In April it urged a tax cut to end the recession, a position both Johnson and Rayburn were resisting.

The following year, when the Johnson leadership was under attack from the Senate activists, the Democratic Advisory Council joined the fray in a formal statement:

> . . . Time-consuming efforts have been made to water-down proposed legislation to the limits of what the President might accept, or to what might win the support of the two-thirds majority in each House necessary to override a Presidential veto.
>
> The record should be clearly written. The Congress should not be intimidated by threats of Presidential veto. The American people are entitled to have the lines definitely drawn.
>
> It is our considered judgment that the interests of the nation and the people would be best served by passing the legislation the Democratic majority knows the country needs, and by putting it in the President's hands to sign or veto. We believe that this will have two beneficial results. First, more good legislation will be enacted than would otherwise be the case. Secondly, when and if bills actually are vetoed, the differences between the Democratic and Republican parties would be even more sharply brought into focus so that the voters will understand them clearly in the election of 1960.[25]

Retorted Johnson:

> In a government which is divided, we can either do something or do nothing. . . .
>
> I think the Senate has acted wisely. I think it has demonstrated that it is reasonable and fair, that it is not hard-headed, that it is not adopting a "me too" attitude. It believes that if we cannot do all we desire to do, we should at least do what can be done. . . . We can either do something or do nothing. As for myself, speaking for the party which I attempt to represent, I prefer to do something.[26]

While Butler was disappointed when the congressional leaders and a southern governor declined to serve, their refusal turned out to be fortuitous from his own standpoint. It is clear that the council would have been quite a different kind of body if they had served. The congressional leaders, immersed in the struggles on Capitol Hill, surely would have

[25] "The Current Legislative Situation," statement adopted June 14 and issued June 15, 1959.

[26] Statement in news conference of June 15, 1959, quoted by *Congressional Quarterly Weekly Report*, June 19, 1959, p. 830; included in remarks on an airport aid bill, which had been greatly reduced to avoid a threatened presidential veto.

prevailed on the other national leaders not to "rock the boat" or repudiate the congressional party position on controversial matters. At the least, they would have subjected the council continuously to the same pressures they themselves felt to avoid open controversy on matters that divided Democrats, and the pronouncements of the council would have tended to convey the same blurred and "moderate" image that the council was conceived in order to dispel. At the most, the congressional leaders would have immobilized the council.

It has been correctly said that the Democratic Advisory Council, as constituted, had little influence on the party in Congress.[27] But it well served its other purposes. From the beginning, and especially after it entered the Little Rock desegregation controversy with a blast at President Eisenhower for failing "to use the prestige and power of his office to rally the moral force of the country against the defiance of law," it was an effective attention-getting device, regularly obtaining front page space for forceful statements of the position of the presidential Democratic party. It carried on a running attack on the policies of the "Eisenhower-Nixon administration," thus presumably weakening the Republican position as the 1960 campaign approached. While it did not pioneer the development of the party's program—it rarely pronounced upon a measure until after a substantial consensus had already been attained among the activist Democrats in Congress—it did contribute a vital element to the solidification of the Democratic position. In December 1958, and again a year later, it issued comprehensive "state of the union" messages, and in its later years it approved program statements in a dozen specialized fields. Before the council acted, a measure may have had the support of a bloc of Senate and House Democrats, but even a large bloc did not amount to the *official* support of the *national party*. The council's status as the party's official policy-making body, as well as the prestige of its members, gave weight to its pronouncements both within and outside the party.

The greatest contributions of the Democratic Advisory Council to program formulation, in the fields covered by this study, were twofold: First, with former Senator Herbert Lehman of New York as its goad and conscience, the council took an uncompromisingly liberal stand on the most divisive issue of the day—civil rights.[28] It made clear that on this issue the "moderation" of Lyndon Johnson, as well as the outright defiance of the big southern wing of the Democratic party, was not the Democratic

[27] See, for example, *Congressional Quarterly Weekly Report*, Dec. 5, 1958, p. 1499.
[28] When the council established a committee on civil rights, Eleanor Roosevelt was its chairman and it consisted entirely of strong advocates of the Negro cause.

party's position. In so doing, it paved the way for the bold declarations of the 1960 platform and the even bolder legislative proposals of 1963 and later years.[29] Second, one of its principal committees, the economic policy group headed by John Kenneth Galbraith of Harvard University, played a significant role in making the "new economics" the basis of the party's economic policy. In a steady flow of council policy statements, it maintained a drumfire attack upon "tight money," high interest rates, and the slow rate of economic growth. The Democratic Advisory Council thus helped to make respectable the economic analysis that subsequently underlay the tax reduction act of 1964.

Adoption of the Party Program. By the time the Democratic platform writers assembled in Los Angeles in July 1960, the contents of their document had been largely settled. The major elements of the Democratic program for the 1960's had been established.

At some point in the mobilization of support for each of the issues that made up that program, a proposal ceased to be simply the idea of an individual or a bloc within the party and became identified, in the public press and by party workers generally, as a *Democratic party* measure. It was to establish an official procedure for the adoption of party measures by the "out" party that the Schattschneider committee had proposed a party council. But, like the platform committee in Los Angeles, the Democratic Advisory Council at its meetings tended to confirm party positions that were already recognized as such. The decisive action had already, at some point, been taken. Table 3 is an attempt to identify the processes by which the Democratic party actually—rather than formally—adopted program measures during the 1953–60 period. The final column of the table represents a judgment as to when and how a proposal in fact crossed the threshold of adoption as a party measure.

---

[29] Chairman Butler personally carried the fight for a strong civil rights position to extraordinary lengths. In the midst of the 1958 off-year campaign, on Oct. 19, Butler predicted on a national television show that the 1960 Democratic convention would adopt a "no compromise" plank and said that Democrats who "don't want to go along on the racial problem and the whole area of human rights . . . are going to have to take political asylum wherever they can find it, either in the Republican party or a third party. . . . I certainly hope they would take leave of the Democratic party." These remarks drew violent protest from southern Democrats, but on Dec. 6 the Democratic National Committee, by a vote of 84–18, endorsed Butler's forthright utterances on civil rights (*Congressional Quarterly Weekly Report,* Oct. 24, 1958, p. 1364, and Dec. 12, 1958, p. 1523). Some contend that Butler, whose tenure as chairman was not secure, fanned the civil rights issue in order to make himself a symbol of the party's pro-civil rights position and thus make it difficult for northerners to join his southern enemies to dislodge him.

Of the major legislative measures listed in Table 1, ten that had been initiated or supported by the Democrats remained to be enacted in 1960. To these can be added the wilderness bill, which is not listed in Table 1 because it was bipartisan in its initial sponsorship. Each of these eleven proposals was specifically and emphatically endorsed in the platform. Each had earlier been officially endorsed by the Democratic Advisory Council. And of those eleven, six had been the subject of decisive action on Capitol Hill that had clearly identified them as party measures supported not just by the liberal wing but by the central element represented by the leadership. In the main, therefore, it was as Speaker Rayburn had held it should be—the party's elected officeholders, the Democrats in Congress, established the party program through their votes.

It was in those instances where, for one reason or another, the Democratic activists on Capitol Hill were unable to make the party record that the Democratic Advisory Council was especially useful. The outstanding example was medicare. By 1958 the Forand bill had not mobilized decisive support among Democrats in either house of Congress. Both the House committee (Ways and Means) and the Senate committee (Finance) were overwhelmingly against it. Because Ways and Means Committee bills are considered on the House floor under "closed" rules barring amendments, House members had no opportunity to offer the bill as an amendment to the social security bill of 1958. Nor, since social security measures originate in the House, had the Senate Democratic activist bloc followed its usual practice of introducing a measure with wide cosponsorship.[30] When Wayne Morse proposed a medicare amendment to the 1958 social security bill on the Senate floor, discussion had not advanced far enough for the bill's backers to make a serious effort. Nevertheless, in December 1958 the Democratic Advisory Council gave medicare a categorical endorsement, and the action undoubtedly contributed to the solidification of support for the proposal throughout the Democratic presidential party. Not until 1960 could medicare be said to have received general Democratic party support—as distinct from bloc support—on Capitol Hill.

---

[30] Social security bills originate in the House because they include tax provisions. While senators usually do not bother to introduce social security measures, Senator McNamara did assemble 19 Democratic cosponsors to introduce a medicare bill in May 1960, partly for purposes of general publicity and Democratic record-building and partly to draw attention to specific features of the bill that differed from those of earlier medicare bills.

Table 3. *Process of Adoption by Democratic Party of Major Legislative*

| Issue and measure | Date first intro- duced | Party endorsement in Senate | |
		Bloc support (Date and size)	Adoption (Date and means)
Unemployment			
Area redevelopment	1955	1955; 8 senators	1956; passage
Youth Conservation Corps	1957	1959; 20 senators	1959; passage
Manpower development and training	1960	—	—
Education			
Aid for school construction	1955	—	—
General aid, including teacher salaries	1958	1958; 11 senators	1960; passage
Aid for college construction	1958	1958; 14 senators	1958; passage
Civil rights			
Power to initiate civil rights enforcement (Part III)	1956	—	—
Fair employment practices; elimination of poll taxes and literacy tests	—	—	—
Medicare	1957	1960; 19 senators	1960; Democratic majority support in floor vote
Outdoor environment			
Expansion of water pollution control grants	1958	—	1959; passage
Wilderness preservation	1956	1956; 6 senators	—
National seashores	1959	1959; 16 senators	—

Proposals in Its 1960 Program

Party endorsement in House		Democratic Advisory Council endorsement (Date)	Adoption as party measure (Date and instrumentality)
Democratic Study Group support (Date)	Adoption (Date and means)		
1957	1956; House committee approval	1958	1956; Senate passage; House committee approval
—	—	1959	1959; Senate passage
—	—	1959	1959; Democratic Advisory Council
1957	1955; House committee approval	1958	1955; House committee approval
1960	1959; House committee approval	1960	1960; Senate passage
—	1958; House majority approval	1959	1958; Senate passage; House majority approval
—	1956; passage	1958	1958; Democratic Advisory Council
—	—	—	1960; party platform
1960	—	1958	1958; Democratic Advisory Council
—	1959; passage	1959	1959; passage by both houses
—	—	1959	1959; Democratic Advisory Council
—	—	1959	1959; Democratic Advisory Council; Senate bloc bill

The other domestic proposals that the Democratic Advisory Council endorsed in advance of decisive support by the party in the Congress were the retraining of unemployed workers, as proposed in legislation that had not been introduced but was then being drafted; Part III of the civil rights bill of 1957, which had been approved by most House Democrats but rejected by a majority of the party in the Senate; the wilderness bill, which had not come out of committee in either house; and national seashore legislation, which the Senate committee was handling through individual bills.

Of the six proposals that were established as party measures by action of the Democratic majorities in Congress, five were brought to a test on the Senate floor and passed, with decisive majorities from the Democratic side; four were approved by either the House or one of its committees. In each case the council action came concurrently or later and only ratified the party action in the Congress. Sometimes the council lagged well behind the liberal Democratic bloc in the Congress in supporting specific measures. It did not endorse aid to institutions of higher education in its December 1958 "state of the union" message even though the House as well as the Senate had given majority approval to the idea in the housing bill that had died that year in the House Rules Committee; not until a year later did the council adopt the proposal. Again, the council was still supporting only construction aid for elementary and secondary schools long after the Democratic presidential party on Capitol Hill had coalesced behind the Murray-Metcalf bill, which provided aid also for teacher salaries. It did not endorse salary aid until January 1960, after the House Education and Labor Committee had reported the Metcalf bill and just before the Senate went on record for such aid by adopting an amendment to its school construction bill.

Only in the field of civil rights was a substantial initial contribution made by those who drafted the 1960 party platform. Democratic activists in Congress, accepting the legislative priorities set by the Eisenhower administration, had temporarily shelved such old liberal favorites as fair employment practices and anti-poll tax legislation, and the Democratic Advisory Council had not gone beyond the bipartisan legislative program. But the Democrats who assembled at Los Angeles were not deterred by any considerations of bipartisan cooperation or even of legislative practicality. The platform committee wrote into its civil rights plank bold commitments on housing, voting restrictions, public accommodations, employment practices, and school desegregation. The platform specifically endorsed legislation on fair employment practices, poll taxes, literacy tests for voting, and Part III; on other major topics the ends were stated but the means left undefined.

What emerges from a study of Democratic program development in the 1953–60 period is a picture of block-by-block building under the leadership of those making up the activist triangle in the Senate, the House, and the Democratic Advisory Council. Individual activists on Capitol Hill took responsibility, often working closely with interest groups, for molding particular blocks. One resourceful and tireless backer, like a Douglas on area redevelopment or a Clark on aid to higher education, could almost single-handedly add a major element to the Democratic program. These activists developed general public support and mobilized backing within the Democratic presidential party. In sequence, although not always in the same order, the three corners of the triangle endorsed the measure. When the issue could be forced to a vote, which was usually in the Senate, the congressional party ordinarily gave the measure enough additional support to establish it as a *party* measure—the outstanding exceptions being civil rights measures. When the issue could not be forced to a vote, the Democratic Advisory Council, with its national prestige and its official grant of party authority, acted as a legitimating body. In any case, the Democratic program that was presented to the country in 1960 was truly a *party* program. The platform writers and the presidential nominee contributed emphasis, style, and form, but the substance of the program had been written with unusual precision and clarity during the eight years out of power—eight years that at the time seemed endlessly frustrating but that were, it is clear in retrospect, extraordinarily fruitful.

In a two-party system, the Schattschneider committee wrote, "the opposition party acts as the critic of the party in power, developing, defining and presenting the policy alternatives which are necessary for a true choice in reaching public decisions." Despite its deep internal division, the Democratic party in its opposition years did fulfill its role—it succeeded in defining a concrete program that presented the voters with a true choice in reaching their public decision in November 1960.

Republican Response

Adoption of a party position by the "in" party is a simple process: the party program is what the President says it is. The contest between competing elements of the party is therefore a contest for the President's attention and allegiance. The party's internal debates take place not in the open, as is the case with the "out" party, but within the confines of the White House and the upper echelons of the executive branch. And a discussion of the development of party policy must be a discussion of the evolution of one man's thought, and an attempt to discern the influences that played upon him.

Materials bearing upon the internal struggles of the Eisenhower administration are still sparse. The best published sources are Robert Donovan's *Eisenhower: The Inside Story,* which covers only the first three years, and Sherman Adams' *Firsthand Report,* which terminates in 1958. Reliable secondary source material on the final years is almost nonexistent. President Eisenhower's own memoirs are disappointing; insofar as they touch upon the subjects covered in this volume, they shed little light on the questions of who influenced him and how he arrived at his positions. Most of the significant White House files were not open to researchers when this book was being written.

But while the forces that influenced the President may be obscure, the development of his views during his eight years in office is mirrored with unusual clarity in the *Public Papers of the Presidents.* Eisenhower held news conferences weekly, when his health permitted, and he responded often and at length—and, from all indications, candidly—to questions about his conception of the Republican party, its program, and his own goals. A president must exercise his party leadership role to a large extent in public, and Eisenhower as a party leader is revealed in his exhortations to Republican rallies and his campaign speeches, as well as in his news conference remarks. The references to the Eisenhower philosophy in this section are based primarily on an analysis of his own statements, messages, and speeches.

The Search for Party Unity. More than most presidents, Dwight Eisenhower was the target of contending forces within his party. Not since the time of some of the Civil War generals in the White House had any president entered office so uncommitted on domestic issues. And he was a political innocent; not until 1952 did he ever declare a party affiliation, and the leaders of the party that he then joined were, to a large degree, strangers to him.

As Part I made clear, the election of 1952 by no means healed the party rift that had been conspicuous since 1912. The Republican party was divided along the same activist-conservative lines that separated the two major parties themselves. In the traditional states of Republican dominance, the GOP—like the Democratic party in the South—necessarily was the political home for leaders of both points of view. In the urban states where the social problems of a complex society were concentrated, both parties tended to produce activists; it is hard to detect much difference in the approach of a Dewey or a Rockefeller and that of a Harriman to the governing of New York.

Like the Democrats, the Republican activists were willing to accept a federal solution to a national problem, if that appeared to be the most feasible solution. They were pragmatic rather than doctrinaire, interested more in solving problems than in expressing absolutes. They might take pains to give their solutions a distinctively Republican cast—a bigger role for the states, perhaps, than the Democrats offered, or a larger role for private enterprise—but these were differences of degree, and were negotiable with the Democrats in the legislative process. On Capitol Hill, activist Republicans and Democrats commonly cosponsored one another's bills.

The Republican conservative wing, on the other hand, consisted of the intellectual descendants of those who had opposed, year by year and measure by measure, the principal proposals of twenty years of Democratic administrations. Not all in 1953 would have tried to turn back the clock, but they were united in opposing further innovation. They abhorred "me too-ism." Their goal for federal policy was retrenchment—in the size of government, its budget, its debt, its impact on private enterprise, and its tax rate. Their strength was centered in the one-party rural sections of the Midwest, where urban problems were remote.

As the administration took form, representatives of both wings found a place in it. The nucleus of the White House staff was the president's personal campaign organization, headed by Sherman Adams, the former New Hampshire governor, and drawn from the Dewey progressive wing of the party which had drafted Eisenhower as its candidate. As the staff was filled out, it retained a distinctly progressive coloration. The Cabinet, however, covered almost the whole spectrum of the party. It included Herbert Brownell, Thomas E. Dewey's 1948 presidential campaign manager, and John Foster Dulles, whom Dewey had appointed to the Senate, but it also included such staunch conservatives as George Humphrey in the Treasury Department and Ezra Taft Benson in Agriculture. Under Eisenhower the Cabinet functioned as a collective advisory group on major issues, so the President was subjected continuously to the contending views.

The most conspicuous activists, as it developed, were those who came to the administration from political life—Adams, Brownell, Vice President Richard Nixon—augmented by others who were activist by temperament, like HEW Secretaries Marion Folsom and Arthur Flemming, Chairman Arthur Burns of the Council of Economic Advisers (CEA), and Labor Secretary James Mitchell (who later entered political life as a candidate for governor of New Jersey). The conservative forces were grouped around the leading businessmen in the administration—Humphrey and later Robert Anderson in Treasury, Sinclair Weeks and later Frederick Mueller at Commerce, Benson at Agriculture, Postmaster General Arthur E. Summerfield (who had been in politics, too, as Republican National Committee chairman)—backed by other nonpoliticians like Budget Director Maurice Stans and Raymond Saulnier, who succeeded Burns as CEA chairman. While the activists argued that as a political matter the Republican party must avoid negativism and be identified with problem-solving, the businessmen looked with disdain on "politics" when the political considerations ran counter to basic principles, particularly the principles of fiscal orthodoxy with their overtones of public morality. In the long run, they argued, good government would be the best politics —political rewards would go to the party that balanced the budget, prevented inflation, and stabilized the value of the dollar. The businessmen were not looking for careers in politics, however; as Marquis Childs wrote, "They came with the conviction that the mess in Washington could be tidied up in a year or so, and then they could return to their businesses." The antipathy between the businessmen and the politicians, he adds, was considerable.[31]

Republicans in Congress were split, too, but there the preponderance had long been on the conservative side. The sympathies of Speaker Joseph Martin of Massachusetts may at times have been with the party's urban progressive wing, but the more forceful rising figures in the House, notably Charles Halleck of Indiana, who succeeded Martin as minority leader in 1959, stood squarely with the conservatives. So did Senate Republican Leader William Knowland of California.

On the United States' role in world affairs, the President's philosophy was formed. His long army career, capped by his military-diplomatic experience as commander of coalition forces in war and in postwar Europe, had made him a convinced internationalist—a believer in the United Nations, in the North Atlantic alliance, in foreign aid, in a liberal trade policy. Here he recognized his differences with the Republican

[31] Marquis W. Childs, *Eisenhower, Captive Hero* (Harcourt, Brace, 1958), p. 174.

irreconcilables, and he sought, with considerable combativeness and with marked success, to lead the Republican party out of its isolationist past. But, as Sherman Adams notes, Eisenhower was more "confident and incisive" in dealing with global strategy than with "detailed debates on domestic issues."[82]

His career had at no time immersed him in domestic matters. Confronting the nation's internal economic and political problems, he could not fall back for guidance upon experience, as he could in dealing with external affairs; he turned instead to a set of basic convictions that had developed over a lifetime but that had their roots, still discernibly, in the relatively simple life of turn-of-the-century Kansas.

The President sought, for most of his eight years, to express those convictions in words that would appeal to both wings of his party and thus help to bridge the gap between those wings and unify the party. His statements of philosophy had therefore a dual ring. In a ceremony at Garrison Dam, in North Dakota, in 1953, he first used a quotation from Lincoln which he repeated or paraphrased incessantly throughout his presidency: "The legitimate object of government is to do for a community of people whatever they need to have done but cannot do at all or cannot do so well. In all that the people can individually do so well for themselves Government ought not to interfere."[83] On this basis, a Republican could speak kindly of Garrison Dam—as Eisenhower did—but a Democrat could justify his party's program too. By the end of his first year in office, Eisenhower was associating the Lincoln dualism with one of his own: "In all those things which deal with people, be liberal, be human. In all those things which deal with the people's money or their economy, or their form of government, be conservative. . . ."[84] He explained that this philosophy differed from that of the New Deal because the Republicans would be liberal in human affairs while still reducing the expenditures of the government.[85] By the following year he had reduced his dualism to two words, "progressive moderates," which he later supplanted with "dynamic conservatism."[86] He was also fond of the phrase "middle

---

[82] Sherman Adams, *Firsthand Report* (Harper, 1961), p. 7.

[83] On June 11, 1953, *Public Papers of the Presidents, 1953*, p. 395.

[84] Lincoln Day speech to a Republican dinner, Washington, D.C., Feb. 5, 1954, *Public Papers of the Presidents, 1954*, p. 242.

[85] On Jan. 27, 1954, *ibid.*, pp. 210–11.

[86] Remarks to a Republican meeting, Feb. 17, 1955, *Public Papers of the Presidents, 1955*, p. 270.

of the road": "I feel pretty good when I'm attacked from both sides," he told a news conference. "It makes me more certain I'm on the right track."[37]

It was easy for Eisenhower's critics to point out that these statements of philosophy begged the hard questions. The Lincoln dictum was unarguable; it could be, and was, quoted by Democrats as well as Republicans, since it left to anybody's judgment the definition of what individuals could "do so well for themselves." When human problems could not be solved without money, the president still had to decide, on a given issue, whether to solve the problem or save the money. Adlai Stevenson commented acidly: "I am not even sure what it means when one says he is a conservative in fiscal affairs and a liberal in human affairs. I assume what it means is that you will strongly recommend the building of a great many schools to accommodate the needs of our children, but not provide the money."[38]

President Eisenhower's actions, like his words, had a dual character. During his first term, each State of the Union message outlining his program had a major section devoted to what, in 1955, he called "the third great purpose of our government" (after peace and prosperity) and in 1956 entitled "the response to human concerns." In this section each year he had presented his proposals for health reinsurance, school construction, minimum wage increases, improvements in social security and unemployment insurance, civil rights, extensions of hospital construction and public housing programs, and so on. But while he appealed to liberals by accepting and proposing extensions in established New Deal and Fair Deal programs like social security, he appealed to conservatives by resisting the establishment of any major new programs on the same patterns. He supported civil rights, but Brownell's bill went too far for him. He cleared Folsom's school construction bill, but withheld his backing at the crucial moment. He appointed the Josephs committee on higher education, but did not accept its findings. He favored area redevelopment, but not to the point of entering into serious negotiations with the Democrats on a compromise bill. On many matters his duality seemed to take the form of proposing a bill but not doing much thereafter to get it passed.

Many observers have commented on Eisenhower's "Whig" concept of

[37] See Chap. 7, p. 292.
[38] News conference in the fall of 1955, as quoted by Davis, *A Prophet in His Own Country*, p. 462.

a "weak presidency."[39] "I am not one of the desk-pounding type that likes to stick out his jaw and look like he is bossing the show," he told a news conference on one occasion when he had been accused of not taking personal leadership to get his program through the Congress. "I would rather try to persuade a man to go along, because once I have persuaded him he will stick. If I scare him, he will stay just as long as he is scared, and then he is gone."[40] Adams points out that the President temperamentally found it impossible to use the sanctions of his office to discipline recalcitrant Republicans.[41] But to attribute Eisenhower's detachment from domestic legislative struggles wholly to his concept of the presidency would be to ignore the considerable evidence that he did assert forceful personal leadership over Congress on issues of foreign policy, like foreign aid and reciprocal trade. On these matters, congressmen sometimes complained of presidential pressures and "arm-twisting" in Eisenhower's time as in the years before and after. On these matters the President felt so strongly that when he was frustrated by the Republicans in Congress while finding support among the Democrats, he speculated with Adams about starting a third party.[42] His reluctance to battle equally hard for the measures that embodied his "liberal" position on "human" issues suggests the absence of any deep conviction about them. Indeed, after the fiasco on the Folsom school construction bill, when Eisenhower's support could not be obtained at the crucial moment, the President admitted that the original Hobby bill was the only school proposal he really "believed in."[43] The evidence supports an interpretation given to me by one of the President's close associates on the White House staff: the President's deeply-held personal convictions were conservative; a Brownell or a Folsom could get him to accede to a civil rights or a school construction bill, but when the showdown came he would "snap back" to his fundamental position.

In any case, his "middle of the road" posture on domestic issues, with its elements of ambiguity and disinterestedness, failed totally to achieve the aim of reconciling the party's divergent wings. Rather than possessing

[39] See, for example, Ivan Hinderaker, "The Eisenhower Administration: The Last Years," in *American Government Annual, 1959–60* (Holt, 1959), p. 90.

[40] On Nov. 14, 1956, *Public Papers of the Presidents, 1956*, pp. 1,103–04.

[41] *Firsthand Report*, p. 27. See also Robert Donovan, *Eisenhower: The Inside Story* (Harper, 1956), p. 224, for an account of Eisenhower's attitude during his first year in office.

[42] Adams, *Firsthand Report*, pp. 9, 27–29.

[43] Chap. 5, p. 173.

appeal to both sides, in many cases it appealed to neither. The original Eisenhower initiatives in the fields of health insurance and school construction, for example, were among the most conspicuously unsuccessful presidential proposals of modern times. They were condemned by the activists as inadequate to solve the problems and by the conservatives, at the same time, as unwarranted extensions of government activity. In the absence of support from any quarter, both proposals had to be abandoned.

The President's posture also conceded to the Democrats exclusive possession of the activist role on most of the pressing domestic issues. Once they obtained control of Congress, in the 1954 election, they proceeded to assert initiative and exploit the opportunity the President gave to them.

Republicans on the Defensive. The "cold war of partisan politics," which the President had predicted if the Democrats won control of Congress,[44] did not develop on foreign policy. His problems there lay with the Republicans. The Congressional Quarterly box score of support for the President's position on foreign affairs in the House for the year 1955 showed 69 percent support from the Democrats but only 50 percent support from his own party. The President was clearly striving to lead his predominantly conservative congressional party to new positions on foreign policy, but he was failing to do so and found himself leading the Democrats instead—the circumstance that gave rise to his musings about the need for a new party. But on domestic issues he found himself not out of line with the House Republicans. They supported him—or, perhaps more accurately, he supported them—64 percent of the time, while the Democrats registered only 47 percent support.[45]

As shown in Table 1, only a half dozen major legislative efforts of the Eisenhower period can be credited to Republican initiative, and in none of these instances was the credit clear and exclusive. One was the ill-fated Hobby school construction bill, which the administration was forced to

[44] In a campaign speech at Denver, Colo., Oct. 8, 1954, *Public Papers of the Presidents, 1954,* p. 898.

[45] The corresponding figures for the Senate showed a more nearly normal degree of support for the President—75 percent from the Republicans and 71 percent from the Democrats on foreign issues, 68 and 36 percent on domestic questions (*Congressional Quarterly Almanac, 1955,* Vol. 11, p. 67). The percentages are based on total membership rather than the number actually voting; since 10–15 percent of the members were, on the average, absent, the figures understate the actual percentage of support, but they are valid for purposes of comparison between parties.

abandon. The second Republican education proposal—the national defense education bill—was essentially a bipartisan achievement growing out of cooperative and simultaneous action of the Republican administration and Democratic congressional leaders. The two measures relating to the outdoor environment were, as he originally proposed them, limited in scope and impact.

In the field of civil rights, where the Democrats were largely immobilized by their strong southern wing, the administration had its clearest opportunity. The two proposals upon which debate centered during the Eisenhower period—Part III, to authorize broad enforcement powers, in 1957 and federal registration of voters in 1960—were distinctly of Republican origin, the one being conceived in Herbert Brownell's Justice Department and the other by the Eisenhower-appointed Civil Rights Commission. Yet on both issues the Republicans missed the chance to draw a sharp line between the two parties. Part III was killed through bipartisan cooperation—at the hands of the Democratic leadership during a southern Democratic filibuster, but not until the Republican President had publicly withdrawn his support. Similarly, while the proposal for federal registration of voters originated in the Civil Rights Commission, an agency of the executive branch, President Eisenhower did not give the idea his approval until after activist Democrats in both houses had had ample time to claim the proposal as their own. By the time the bill was enacted, Lyndon Johnson's Senate leadership in breaking the southern Democratic opposition had given the bill more of a bipartisan than a Republican image.

With these cloudy exceptions, all of the major legislative proposals of the time were of Democratic origin. And the Republican response to the Democratic initiative, as shown in Table 1, reflects the inevitable dilemma of the responding party. As soon as the Democrats had seized upon a popular issue, the Republicans had two choices, each of them painful. They could take a stance of outright opposition by either denying the existence of the problem or contending that the problem was inappropriate for federal action. Or they could counteract the Democratic proposal with one of their own, which necessarily appeared as a pale shadow of the Democratic measure, at the same time that it conceded to the Democrats the credit for having recognized the problem first. The choice, for the responding party, tended to be between a posture of negativism and one of "too little and too late."

In the first category are four measures. When the Democratic party joined forces with the National Education Association to press for federal aid to raise teacher salaries, the Eisenhower administration stood its ground that federal assistance should be given only for construction and only for a strictly limited period of time. Eisenhower's personal views hardened on this point as time went on. In regard to unemployment, the Republicans had no counterparts for the Democratic-sponsored Youth Conservation Corps, manpower training, and public works acceleration bills. In these areas, then, the Democrats could exploit the political advantage of having a concrete and aggressive program to cope with problems the Republicans did not even recognize.

When in other cases the administration acknowledged the problem and came forth with an alternative measure, the Democrats also reaped advantage. In each case, one to three years elapsed between the time of the first substantial Democratic initiative and the announcement of the administration proposal. During this period the Democrats could exploit Republican inaction. Once the Republican administration made its proposal, the Democrats could shift to a we-told-you-so line, at the same time attacking the Republicans for the inadequacy of their alternative remedy. Caught in the awkward choice between negativism and "me too-ism," Eisenhower was forced on the defensive—and the Democratic assault grew ever more forceful as the Democrats built consensus around specific program measures. Eventually, the President was driven to counterattack.

Republicans on the Attack. The shift in presidential strategy was a gradual one, but the turning point can be dated some time in 1957. That was the year of the "battle of the budget," launched by Treasury Secretary George Humphrey's extraordinary assault on the spending plans of his own President. On the very day that the President sent to the Congress a budget embodying his new "modern Republicanism," Humphrey responded to a news conference question by saying that if the country's expenditures and "terrific tax take" continued "over a long period of time, I will predict that you will have a depression that will curl your hair." Earlier, he had said, "I think there are a lot of places in this budget that can be cut."[46] The President, at his next news conference, compounded the issue by saying that "with the thought behind the Secretary's

---

[46] Richard E. Neustadt, *Presidential Power* (Wiley, 1960), pp. 64–85, 108–23, 153–54, 159–61, 169–71; Neustadt gives a vivid account of the Humphrey statement, its antecedents, and consequences. See also *Basic Papers of George M. Humphrey* (in Western Reserve Historical Society, Cleveland, Ohio, 1965), pp. 252, 243.

statements I am in complete agreement" and said it was the "duty" of the Congress to cut the budget if it could.[47] Thereafter the budget-spending-inflation debate raged on Capitol Hill and the public spotlight played upon the issue with a glare that obscured every other domestic question.

In the President's State of the Union message, which had preceded the budget by a few days, the usual "human concerns" section had shriveled to a bare mention of school construction and civil rights bills, but the President continued for a time his statements to news conferences and party gatherings expressing his conception of Republican philosophy—which he had labeled "modern Republicanism"—in dual terms. "I think I have grown more conservative," he told his news conference in May of that year, expressing alarm at government spending and at "trifling with our financial integrity." But then he went on with a statement that was anything but conservative, calling upon his party to "study carefully the needs of the people today"—their need for security against the hazards of an industrial economy, for security in old age and sickness—and to take leadership in responding to those needs.[48] A month later, in a speech to a Republican national conference, he denounced "easy-spending, paternalistic, business-baiting inflationists" and the "New-Deal Fair-Deal toboggan of loose spending, centralization, punishment of business and fiscal irresponsibility," but he insisted that the Republicans "adapt our basic convictions imaginatively to current problems" and cited emergency school construction aid as an example.[49] It was at this time, too, that he took to national television to defend his mutual security program against attacks arising mainly from his own party in Congress.

But as the year wore on, the potency of the spending issue became plain. Democrats and Republicans in Congress, responding to the challenge

[47] On Jan. 23, 1957, *Public Papers of the Presidents, 1957*, pp. 73–74.

[48] On May 15, 1957, *ibid.*, pp. 354–55. See also his news conference comments on "modern Republicanism," Nov. 14, 1956, *Public Papers of the Presidents, 1956*, pp. 1,102–05. He had earlier endorsed *A Republican Looks at His Party* (Harper, 1956), an amplification of the Eisenhower dual approach by Arthur Larson, under secretary of labor, as expressing his (Eisenhower's) philosophy of government "as well as I have seen it in a book of that size" (news conference, Aug. 31, 1956, *Public Papers of the Presidents, 1956*, p. 193). Larson's term, "new Republicanism," to denote the Eisenhower philosophy was presumably the origin of the phrase, "modern Republicanism," which the President introduced on election night in 1956. The President's speech accepting his party's renomination in 1956 is still another balanced expression of appeals to conservative "long-range principles" with appeals to activist sentiment (Aug. 23, 1956, *ibid.*, pp. 705–09).

[49] On June 7, 1957, *Public Papers of the Presidents, 1957*, pp. 450–58.

from the administration and an avalanche of antispending mail from home, vied with one another to cut the Eisenhower budget. Spending was not just an abstract good-government issue; it could be brought home to every family in terms of inflation, high prices, the declining value of the dollar. Here appeared to be the weapon Eisenhower had been seeking. With this issue he could counterattack the Democratic activists and regain, with interest, the political advantage that their espousal of popular spending measures had won for them. Some time in the latter part of 1957 the choice was made—and that was the end of dualism. The 1958 and later State of the Union messages no longer dwelt on "human concerns." In 1958 the President vetoed Democratic bills on area redevelopment, rivers and harbors, civil service retirement, and agriculture—all on the spending issue—and he proposed to repeal the Democratic-initiated water pollution control grant program. In addition, a housing bill the President opposed died in the House Rules Committee. Eisenhower gave his news conference a one-sentence statement of his 1958 campaign plans: "I will tell you what I am going to stress, if that is good enough: getting down these deficits and keeping our money sound so that America can have a good, healthy, thriving, progressive economy."[50] His campaign was a series of slashing attacks on the Democratic "extremists" and "radicals" who had "mangled or mushroomed" his bills. "Either we choose left-wing government or sensible, forward-looking government—spendthrift government or efficient government able to keep its promises to America," he told his television audience.[51]

When the election was over, the people had overwhelmingly endorsed the President's opponents.

At a news conference on the morrow of the election, Eisenhower dwelt at length on the fiscal policy issue. He was rueful ("talk about the spender-wing of the Democratic Party . . . apparently . . . didn't make any great impression"), puzzled ("the United States did give me, after all, a majority of I think well over nine million votes. Here, only two years later, there is a complete reversal; and yet I do not see where there is anything that these people consciously want the administration to do differently. And, if I am wrong, I'd like to know what it is . . ."), and

[50] On Aug. 27, 1958, *Public Papers of the Presidents, 1958*, p. 644.

[51] From his Los Angeles speech, Oct. 20, 1958, *Public Papers of the Presidents, 1958*, pp. 757–65. See also his other major televised addresses, from Chicago on Oct. 22, Pittsburgh on Oct. 27, and Baltimore on Oct. 31, *ibid.*, beginning on pp. 786, 802, and 819, respectively. In *Waging Peace* (Doubleday, 1965), pp. 377–81, Eisenhower gives his own account of his campaign tactics.

still in a fighting mood (". . . they obviously voted for people that I would class among the spenders, and that is what I say is going to be the real trouble. And I promise this: for the next two years, the Lord sparing me, I am going to fight this as hard as I know how. And . . . in the long run, everybody else that is responsible has got to fight it. The conservative Democrats, the newspapers, every kind of person that has got brains to see what is happening in this country with our loose handling of our fiscal affairs has got to fight it. . . . If we can get this whole country just awakened to this particular danger and ready to do their part about it . . . if we can do that, then this defeat in the long term of history will be completely forgotten and unimportant, because what we need is understanding").[52]

Other Republicans—like the Democrats two years earlier—clashed over the reasons for the defeat: the activists, not unexpectedly, contended that the party had not been activist enough, the conservatives that it had not been conservative enough. The one thing they agreed on was that the party's image had not been clear enough. "I'm sick and tired of going around the country and having good, honest Republicans coming up to me and saying, 'For what does the Republican party stand?' " Representative Richard M. Simpson of Pennsylvania, chairman of the Republican congressional campaign committee, told a Republican National Committee post-mortem meeting in January. He asked President Eisenhower for "a statement of principles for which we can stand." Similarly, Senator Barry Goldwater of Arizona said that "the elephant will come out of hibernation when he knows in what direction to point his trunk." He offered the direction: "Quit copying the New Deal."[53] At a White House meeting a month earlier, the same criticism of lack of direction had arisen from the party's progressive wing, notably from Charles H. Percy, a young Chicago industrialist. So this was the end to which President Eisenhower's six years of philosophy-building had led—"dynamic conservatism" had left the party neither appealingly dynamic for the Percys nor satisfyingly conservative for the Simpsons and the Goldwaters. The "middle of the road," it turned out, was neither a direction nor a destination.

The President himself had noted "a mysterious apathy" among Republicans—for which, he writes, he has never been able "to develop a logical

---

[52] On Nov. 5, 1958, *Public Papers of the Presidents, 1958*, pp. 828, 836.
[53] *Congressional Quarterly Weekly Report*, Jan. 30, 1959, p. 137.

explanation or even an excuse that sounded plausible."[54] Perhaps it was his own groping for a sense of direction that led him, in early 1959, to establish his privately financed President's Commission on National Goals, headed by Henry M. Wriston.[55] He also initiated, after the White House meeting with Percy and others, a committee on program and progress headed by Percy to clarify the objectives and responsibilities of the Republican party.[56] But these were longer-range undertakings. The President still had to set the course of both the party and the government for the last two years of his administration. Percy may have seen his committee "as an opportunity to liberalize the Republican Party,"[57] but the President unmistakably cast his lot with the conservatives and, true to his post-election pledge, continued to fight the spending battle. By the end of July 1959 he had referred to the fiscal issue twenty-two times, by actual count, in his news conferences.[58] In that year he vetoed two housing bills, two public works appropriation bills, and a wheat bill, and in 1960 an area redevelopment bill, a federal employee pay increase bill, and a bill to expand the program of grants for sewage treatment plants, all on the spending issue.

Within the administration the balance of the President's advisers followed the rightward course of his philosophy. Sherman Adams, consistently a voice for political pragmatism in the inner councils, took his leave in 1958. At the Treasury, George Humphrey had been succeeded by Robert Anderson, perhaps no more conservative but reportedly more influential with the President. Raymond Saulnier had brought a stolid conservatism to the Council of Economic Advisers as Arthur Burns' successor, and the most aggressively conservative of all of Eisenhower's budget directors, Maurice Stans, was in that office. Even in this hostile setting, however, the activists managed to salvage something—largely through HEW Secretary Arthur Flemming. Almost single-handedly— although with encouragement from Nixon and from some members of the White House staff—Flemming got President Eisenhower's assent to put

[54] Eisenhower, *Waging Peace*, p. 377.

[55] On Nov. 16, 1960, the commission issued its report, *Goals for Americans* (Prentice-Hall, 1960).

[56] For an account of the origins and work of the committee, see Cornelius P. Cotter and Bernard C. Hennessy, *Politics Without Power* (Atherton, 1964), pp. 195–204. See also Philip S. Wilder, Jr., *Meade Alcorn and the 1958 Election*, Eagleton Foundation Case Studies in Practical Politics (Holt, 1959), pp. 2–4, 16.

[57] Cotter and Hennessy, *Politics Without Power*, p. 199.

[58] Cabell Phillips, *New York Times Magazine*, Aug. 16, 1959, p. 76.

the Republican party on record for some kind of program in the fields of medicare and aid to public schools and colleges, even if his specific proposals had to be rendered unacceptable and perhaps even unworkable by the contrivances chosen to avert a major impact on the federal budget. To the degree that Eisenhower could be persuaded in these last years to accept an activist position, he was—like Lyndon Johnson in the Senate but far more reluctantly—within his party a follower rather than a leader.

As long as Eisenhower remained in office, his position on the issues defined his party's position. The Percy committee ploughed no new ground. When it reported, in October 1959, it merely ratified and publicized positions already taken by the party through its policy-making process—that is, positions taken by decision of the President. It could, and did, emphasize more than he did the affirmative proposals he had advanced on education, medicare, civil rights, and related issues, but it could not go beyond those proposals without repudiating the President, and this it did not do.[59]

Nixon, in the campaign, was in the same position. He had used his influence upon the President to give the Republican party something of an activist program of its own, but once the campaign began, that program as defined by the President was as far as he would go. He could determine the tone and emphasis of the presentation, but not the substance of the program. In contrast to Eisenhower, who in the campaign continued his denunciation of Democratic spending and "currency debasement," Nixon placed considerable stress upon the positive Republican alternatives to the Democratic proposals for health care, aid to education, and area redevelopment. The Nixon speeches thus captured an echo of the old dualism that Eisenhower had abandoned. But they also impaled him on the horns of the political dilemma of that dualism—if one concedes that the opposition has been right all along about the problem, how can he be persuasive that they are wrong about the answer? The response of public opinion to the issues of the period, and to the activist-conservative struggle in general, is the subject of the next chapter.

---

[59] The report, "Decisions for a Better America," is reprinted in *Congressional Quarterly Almanac, 1959,* pp. 753–57.

CHAPTER X

Ideas and Elections

THE YEARS OF the Eisenhower administration were a period of rising fortunes for the Democratic party. Having discharged the Democrats from national office in 1952, the voters reversed themselves in three of the next four elections. In 1954 they gave Congress back to the Democrats. In 1958 they gave the Democrats control of both houses by landslide proportions. And in 1960 they chose a Democratic President.

This period of rising Democratic fortunes coincided with the period when that party—as Chapter 9 has shown—was developing an increasingly clear and concrete alternative to the domestic policies of President Eisenhower and the Republicans in Congress. Were those events related? Were the elections of 1954, 1958, and 1960 great acts of proprietorship by which the people expressed a clear and growing preference for Democratic policies and programs? Were those elections a mandate to the government to pursue a course of activism on domestic problems, rather than the course of conservatism to which the Republican President and his party in Congress were committed?

To answer those questions in the affirmative would require evidence, first, that the Democratic position on the domestic issues was more popular than the Republican position and, second, that the popularity of that position on those issues, singly or collectively, had a significant impact on the election results. Evidence, primarily from public opinion surveys, is available on both points but stronger on the first; it is easier to find out how a voter feels on an issue than to find out whether that feeling actually contributes to his voting decision, but there is some data bearing on the latter point too.

430

This chapter summarizes what appear to be most significant of the available data.

The 1953–54 Recession—and the Democratic Resurgence

Before as well as since the Depression, as Louis H. Bean and others have shown, "hard times" have always been blamed by the voters upon the party in power and have cost it support on election day.[1] But the 1953–54 recession was relatively mild and brief. Could so brief a downturn in the economy have a major political impact?

If the answer is affirmative, it would be reflected in a decline of confidence in the party in power during the period of the business slump. The trend lines in Figure 1 indicate that such a decline did in fact occur. During the recession year 1954, the proportion of the electorate expressing disapproval of President Eisenhower's conduct in office reached and remained at what was, for Eisenhower, an unusually high level. Figure 1 plots three trend lines for the years 1953–55—the actual rate of unemployment, month by month; the percentage of the adult population expressing an expectation of increased unemployment, as measured by the American Institute of Public Opinion (the Gallup poll), and the percentage disapproving Eisenhower's conduct in office, also recorded by AIPO. All three lines rose sharply in the late months of 1953, peaked or leveled off in 1954, and declined through most of 1955.

The evidence from 1953 alone is not conclusive. Any president begins his term of office with a high rate of voter approval, as the AIPO polls over the years have shown, and he begins to lose ground gradually as he is forced to make decisions that cannot please the whole electorate. But the similarity of the contours of the three lines for the entire period 1953–55 is impressive. The peaking of the "disapproval" votes when actual unemployment—and the fear of more unemployment—were at or near their heights, and the simultaneous decline of the two lines through most of 1955 appear to be more than coincidence. The concurrence of the lines is even more impressive if one accepts George Gallup's interpretation that the abrupt drop in the President's "disapproval" rating in early 1954 was due to the initiative taken in his "atoms for peace" speech to the United Nations. After this event had faded into the background, disapproval of

[1] See Bean, *How to Predict Elections* (Knopf, 1948), especially Chap. 6.

Figure 1. *Trends in Unemployment, Fear of Increased Unemployment,
and Disapproval of Eisenhower Performance, 1953–55*

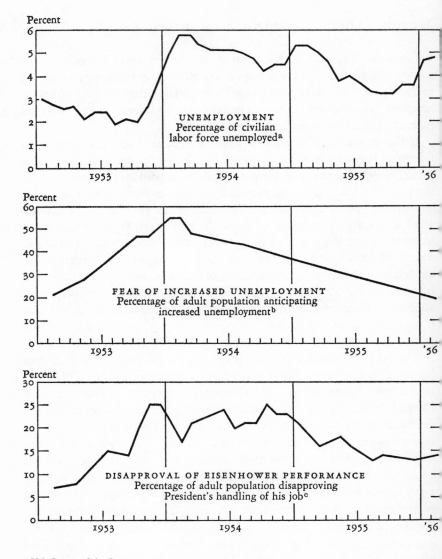

a U.S. Bureau of the Census.
b Based on responses to: "Do you think unemployment will increase during the next six months, decrease,
or remain the same?" (AIPO releases, relevant dates).
c Based on responses to: "Do you approve or disapprove of the way Eisenhower is handling his job as
President?" (AIPO releases, relevant dates).

Eisenhower rose again and remained high during the remainder of 1954, then declined during 1955 as unemployment—and the expectation of unemployment—fell.

It should be noted that the expectation of unemployment coincides more closely than does actual unemployment with disapproval of the President. In 1953 the rise in disapproval actually preceded the rise in unemployment, but it did not precede the rise in the anticipation of hard times. In November, when actual unemployment was still at the prosperity level of 2.7 percent, the Gallup poll found that 47 percent of its respondents answered "more" to the question, "Do you think there will be more people out of work, or fewer people out of work, in this community in the next six months?" Only 14 percent answered "fewer" (the rest either responded "about the same" or expressed no opinion). The 47 percent compared to 21 percent in February, nine months earlier.[2] Recession jitters were clearly developing during the autumn months.

That the relation between the three trend lines is more than a random one is indicated by other findings of the Gallup interviewers. In October 1953, when the rate of disapproval had climbed to 20 percent, the AIPO found that, in the view of those disapproving, Eisenhower "hasn't fulfilled promises . . . hasn't displayed leadership; hasn't accomplished anything . . . hasn't improved economic conditions; has caused unemployment . . . hasn't helped the working people . . . hasn't helped the farmer . . . vacations, golfs too much. . . ."[3] In December, in response to the question, "Would you say you and your family are better off, or worse off, financially than you were a year ago?" only 18 percent reported themselves better off, 24 percent worse off.[4] And in February 1954, when asked, "Do

[2] Since unemployment rises seasonally in the winter and declines in the spring, public awareness of this phenomenon might be assumed to account in part for the higher expectation of increased unemployment in November than in February. However, the "expectation" line as a whole does not show a seasonal pattern, which suggests that this factor can be discounted. On the assumption that what affects political decisions is the actual level of unemployment rather than the seasonally adjusted figure, I have used the former.

The reader is also cautioned that AIPO data are difficult to ascribe precisely by months. Some polls are taken partly in one month, partly in another. Where the data are taken from AIPO releases, I have used the release date, unless the release itself indicates the actual date of the poll. Where the data were obtained directly from the tabulations of particular surveys, I have used the dates on the questionnaires.

[3] AIPO release, Oct. 25, 1953. The official unemployment figure for October was a very low 2 percent. The rise did not begin to show in the Bureau of the Census count until November. The comments reported by Dr. Gallup appear to reflect expectation rather than actuality.

[4] *Ibid.*, Dec. 23, 1953.

you think business conditions would be better or worse today if the Democrats had won the presidential election in 1952?" the Gallup respondents voted 28 percent "better," 18 percent "worse" (the remainder said "about the same" or expressed no opinion). Voters identifying themselves as independents gave the nod to the Democrats, 23–17 percent.[5]

By March 1954, one of every five voters in the AIPO sample named unemployment and the business recession as "the most important problem facing the country." In June, when the question of intervention in Indo-China had captured the headlines, the number naming unemployment remained high, at 14 percent. Most important, 45 percent thought the Democratic party was "best able to solve this problem," compared to only 15 percent for the Republicans. Of all the major issues named, only unemployment was working in favor of the Democrats. On the other issues —maintaining peace, solving the Indo-China problem, handling communism in the United States—voters expressed more confidence in the Republican party than in the Democratic party.[6] "As of today," wrote Gallup as the 1954 campaign began, "the best talking point to get a person to vote Democratic, the voters say, is unemployment and the fear of a depression under a Republican administration."[7] After the election, when Eisenhower disapproval was still at a high point, unemployment was cited first in the AIPO's list of reasons, and the number of persons naming unemployment as the most important problem facing the new Congress stood at 10 percent.[8]

If it can be accepted that unemployment was the principal issue working for the Democrats throughout 1954, the question remains: was a significant number of voters in the congressional election actually influenced by the issue? In an attempt to shed light on this question, I have adapted to the off-year election an approach used by V. O. Key, Jr., in his analysis of presidential elections.[9] Key sought out the "switchers"— those whose movement from one party to another accounted for the partisan swing between elections—to determine whether they, as a body, held views different from those of the voters who did not switch. He found that they did. His little volume was a demonstration that, as he put it, "voters are not fools"—there are "quite marked correlations between policy

[5] *Ibid.*, Feb. 5, 1954.
[6] *Ibid.*, June 6, 1954.
[7] *Ibid.*, Aug. 27, 1954.
[8] *Ibid.*, Nov. 28, 1954, and Jan. 5, 1955.
[9] *The Responsible Electorate* (Belknap Press of Harvard University Press, 1966).

attitudes and vote switching." This chapter attempts to go a step further to determine which policy or program issues are most influential and to assign relative weights to them.

Thus, if unemployment were the major issue causing a swing in party preference toward the Democratic party in 1954, one would expect to find a higher proportion of switching among those voters who identified unemployment as a problem of major concern than among voters who were more concerned with other problems. This is exactly what is shown by the analysis in Table 4 of AIPO data for March 1954: the "switchers" who desired to restore control of Congress to the Democrats were most heavily concentrated among those voters who were especially sensitive to the unemployment problem.

Table 4. *Switches in Voting Preference, November 1952–March 1954, in Relation to Issues*[a]

Problem identified as most important	1952 Eisenhower voters		1952 Stevenson voters		Other voters[c]		Index of relative pulling power to Democrats[d]
	No.	Percent switching to Democrats in 1954[b]	No.	Percent switching to Republicans in 1954[b]	No.	Percent supporting Democrats in 1954	
Unemployment, recession, depression, inflation	126	29	105	4	78	76	1.3
Other problems	643	22	319	8	270	60	—1.3

[a] Vote cast for president in 1952 compared to party preference indicated for the 1954 congressional election. Based on 1,562 responses to: "What do you think is the most important problem facing this country today?" and "If the elections for Congress were being held today, which party would you like to see win in this state—the Republican party or the Democratic party?" (AIPO 528-K, March 17, 1954). Tabulated responses exclude 1952 voters who did not indicate for whom they voted and "other voters" who were undecided, unrecorded, or preferred a third party in 1954. Respondents who gave more than one answer to the "most important problem" question are recorded as a separate respondent for each answer, which inflates the total slightly.

[b] Those not switching include both those whose party preferences remained constant and those who were undecided, unrecorded, or supported an "other" party.

[c] Those who did not vote in 1952, did not remember how they voted, or voted for an "other" party candidate.

[d] The index is computed by comparing the number preferring the Democrats (or the Republicans) on each line with what the number would have been if the respondents on that line had expressed their preferences in the same proportions as the total sample. The index figure is the percent of the total sample that the difference constitutes. In this case, if the voters designating either unemployment, recession, depression, or inflation as the most important problem had switched in the same proportions (and "other voters" had divided their votes in the same proportions) as the sample as a whole, the Democratic share of the total would have been smaller by 1.3 percentage points.

The greatest percentage of defections of Eisenhower voters was among those whose responses to the "most important problem" question were coded under the headings, "unemployment" or "depression-recession-inflation."[10] Among those voters, the defection rate was 29 percent, compared to 22 percent among Eisenhower voters who identified other problems—primarily those having to do with war and peace, the Soviet Union, and "communists in U.S." Similarly, the rate of defection to the Republicans among 1952 Stevenson voters was only 4 percent for those most concerned with unemployment and recession, compared to 8 percent for those naming other problems. And the Democratic leaning among new voters or 1952 nonvoters was 76 percent in the former category, compared to 60 percent in the latter.

These figures are mutually consistent in showing that those voters who considered the problem of unemployment more important even than problems of foreign relations—numbering 20 percent of the total sample —were drawn more strongly toward the Democratic party than were those who were less concerned with unemployment. If we were to assume that, in the absence of a recession and an unemployment issue, the 20 percent would have been drawn to the Democratic party only at the same rate as the sample as a whole, then the Republican party would have been the preference of an additional group of voters adding to 1.3 percent of the total sample. This figure, which I have labeled an "index of relative pulling power," is an indicator of the relative strength of an issue and the direction of its political impact.

A 1.3 percentage-point shift attributable to the differential behavior of the unemployment-sensitive segment of the voters would be significant, particularly in view of the fact that the actual shift in the party vote for the House of Representatives which restored control of that body to the Democrats in 1954 was only 2.7 percentage points—from a 49.9 percent Democratic share of the two-party vote in 1952 to a 52.6 percent Democratic share two years later. Any measure of the pulling power of the unemployment issue must be evaluated, however, in the light of the

[10] Voters mentioning "recession" and "inflation," grouped together in the AIPO tabulation, might have different political responses. However, in this particular survey, taken at the bottom of the recession, "unemployment" and "depression-recession-inflation" show parallel pro-Democratic reactions, which indicates that the recession and its consequent unemployment were the primary concern of the second category as well as the first and they are properly combined in considering the political impact of the recession.

peculiar circumstances of the period.[11] The Democratic voters who had switched to the Republican column to bring about the Eisenhower landslide of 1952 had not changed their basic party preference, as many studies have shown. They voted Republican in 1952 "just this once" to express their disapproval of President Truman, of the stalemate in Korea, of "the mess in Washington," or of sundry other circumstances of the time, but they remained Democrats—at most, "Eisenhower-Democrats." The election of 1952 was thus a "deviating" election, in Angus Campbell's terminology, rather than a "realigning" election like those of the early 1930's when Republicans who crossed the party line assumed an enduring allegiance to the Democratic party.[12] Many of the "deviating" Democrats could be expected to return to their normal voting patterns in 1954, when Eisenhower was not himself a candidate and the pressing considerations that had prompted their defection in 1952 had disappeared. Insofar as the 2.7-point shift is not attributable to the unemployment issue, it presumably is accounted for mainly by the return home of deviating Democrats, since from all the AIPO evidence most voters were satisfied with the way the Republicans were handling other issues—foreign affairs, internal communism, and so on.

[11] A number of statistical difficulties also suggest caution in interpreting calculations in this chapter based on AIPO polls. The computation of party switches in the off-year elections of 1954 and 1958 is based upon the expression of congressional preference in those years and the remembered presidential vote of two years before, because the survey did not include a question about congressional voting in the earlier years. Thus, there is no way of identifying and excluding those "switching" voters who were in fact consistent in their congressional preferences. Moreover, reliance upon people's memory as to their presidential vote tends to overstate the number reported as having voted for the winner. In the March 1954 sample, 64.4 percent of the respondents who recalled voting for one of the major party candidates in 1952 said they voted for Eisenhower, whereas his actual percentage of the two-party vote was 55.3 percent. (For a discussion of this and related technical problems in analyzing switching, see Key, *The Responsible Electorate*, Chap. 2.) Other deficiencies are mentioned in Table 4, note a. These statistical discrepancies would appear, however, to have essentially a random effect upon the comparisons made in this chapter among groups of voters sensitive to various issues.

[12] See Campbell, "A Classification of the Presidential Elections," in Campbell and others, *Elections and the Political Order* (Wiley, 1966), pp. 63–77; the book is based on data compiled by the Survey Research Center of the University of Michigan. See also Philip E. Converse, "The Concept of a Normal Vote," in *ibid.*, pp. 9–39; he discusses in theoretical terms the concept that the actual vote for a party in any election consists of that party's normal share of the electorate derived from basic party allegiance, plus or minus the deviates who shift parties temporarily because of the circumstances of the particular election.

It can be further argued that the deviating Democrats of 1952 contained a disproportionate share of the unemployment-conscious group, because they were presumably the least secure elements of the population—skilled and unskilled workers and their families, and low-income groups generally—among whom the Democratic party had its greatest basic strength. The higher proportion of switching shown in the third column of the table among the unemployment-sensitive voters might simply be accounted for, then, by the greater proportion of deviating Democrats—as distinct from basically Republican voters—in that group. A case can be made, then, that the Democratic gains indicated in the poll of March 1954 reflected almost entirely the return home of Democrats from their 1952 excursion, uninfluenced by the recession or any other current issue.

The argument is persuasive but not conclusive. Party allegiances of some voters do change, in every election—if not in massive numbers, then on a smaller scale. Few of the Democrats who defected in 1952, outside the South at least, were strong partisans; as Campbell has pointed out, most had a relatively weak identification with the Democratic party.[13] They had decided to give Eisenhower—and, in many cases, his Republican running mates for Congress—the benefit of the doubt for one election; had the Republican record been free of major shortcomings, would not that period of grace have been indefinitely extended? In other words, had the administration been able to maintain unalloyed prosperity throughout its first two years, would not the return to normal voting patterns of many of the defecting Democrats have been deferred—for as long, at least, as good times continued? And would not some of those who voted for Eisenhower in 1952 but stayed with the Democratic candidates for Congress have heeded their President's plea this time to support him with a Congress of his own party?

It is significant that the AIPO poll in the prerecession month of May 1953 showed no automatic return to normal voting patterns; the respondents expressed a 53–47 percent preference for the Republicans in answer to the standard question on congressional preference—a margin substantially exceeding the 50.1 percent actual vote for Republican House candidates in the 1952 election.[14]

As it happened, the Republican failure occurred on the very issue on which the party was most vulnerable. The identification of the Republican party with hard times—like the identification of the Democratic party with war—is deeply embedded in the consciousness of the electorate. The

[13] Campbell, *ibid.*, p. 70.
[14] AIPO 515–K, May 7, 1953.

loss of confidence in the Republican party reflected in the 1954 switches, as well as in the drop in the Eisenhower approval rating, was not simply automatic and predictable; it may have been latent, but it was triggered by the increase in unemployment—and, even earlier, by the fear of increased unemployment. The percentage of voters who had switched their party preference in early 1954 because of the unemployment issue may have been something less than 1.3 percent but it was surely something more than zero.

By the time of the election, economic recovery was underway, but not rapidly. Discontent with farm prices had, indeed, worsened. Vice President Nixon, the leading Republican campaigner, had the impression that the slump which "contributed" to his party's losses "hit bottom early in October."[15] In any event, the Republican party did not succeed in recovering the confidence it had lost at the onset of the recession the previous winter. The preelection AIPO poll, in October, obtained the following responses to the question: "If control of Congress should go over to the Democrats, what do you think will happen to business and employment? Just your best guess—will conditions get better or worse?"[16]

Response	*Percent of total*
Better	43
Worse	18
No difference	28
No answer or no opinion	11
	100

The Survey Research Center (SRC) of the University of Michigan asked its respondents, at the same time, to relate the election to their individual and family welfare, with this question: "Do you think it will make any difference in how you and your family get along financially whether the Democrats or Republicans will win?"[17] This was the result:

Response	*Percent of total*
Better off if Democrats win	22
Better off if Republicans win	11
No differences, about the same	59
No answer or no opinion	8
	100

[15] Richard M. Nixon, *Six Crises* (Doubleday, 1962), p. 310.
[16] AIPO 538–K, Oct. 13, 1954.
[17] University of Michigan, SRC study 623, October 1954.

After the election, in November 1954, the Gallup interviewers again asked the "most important problem" question, this time in terms of problems facing the incoming Congress. The unemployment issue was listed as highest priority by only 12 percent of the voters compared to 20 percent in March. But a related recession issue—low farm prices—had risen to the position of top concern with 8 percent of the voters, compared to only 1 percent in March. Those who identified these two issues contained a disproportionate share of the switchers who had just restored control of Congress to the Democrats. So did other groups, smaller in number, who mentioned problems in several other domestic fields—civil rights, housing and rent, social security, and schools, youth, and juvenile problems—which had not been significant in the March poll (perhaps because the March question had not focused specifically on legislation). All of these domestic issues, then, were exerting a pro-Democratic influence on the electorate. One or another of these issues was named as the "most important problem" by 35 percent of the respondents, as shown in Table 5.

Table 5 indicates the relative pulling power of the domestic issues that worked for the Democrats in the 1954 election. The Republicans suffered a loss of support—either to the Democrats or to nonvoting—of 52 percent of the 1952 Eisenhower voters most concerned about those issues, compared to a 40 percent loss among those who gave highest priority to other problems—principally foreign policy, communism, and strikes and

Table 5. *Switches in Voting Preference, November 1952–November 1954, in Relation to Issues*[a]

| Problem identified as most important | 1952 Eisenhower voters | | | 1952 Stevenson voters | | | Other voters | | Index of relative pulling power to Dems.[b] |
	No.	Percent switching to Dems., 1954	Percent not voting, 1954	No.	Percent switching to Reps., 1954	Percent not voting, 1954	No.	Percent supporting Dems., 1954	
Democratic domestic issues[c]	152	23	29	147	6	27	23	78	.9
Other issues	372	17	23	219	9	19	35	60	—.9

[a] Based on 1,473 responses to: "What is the most important problem you would like to see the new Congress take up in the new session starting in January?" and "In the election last month . . . for Congressman, did you vote for the Republican candidate, or for the Democratic candidate?" (AIPO 540-K, Nov. 30, 1954). See Table 4, notes a-d, for basis and method of computation.

[b] The index in this case is the average of the pull *from* the Republicans and the pull *to* the Democrats (the difference being accounted for by nonvoting).

[c] Issues shown as "more jobs—employment—unemployment," "segregation—discrimination," "housing—rent," "farm—stabilize farm prices," "more social security benefits—more old age benefits—unemployment security," "schools—youth—juvenile problems."

labor policy. The Democrats won 78 percent of the new voters identifying the domestic issues, compared to 60 percent of the others. The percentage of 1952 Stevenson voters most concerned with the enumerated issues that defected to the Republicans was smaller than those most concerned with other issues (although the loss of Democrats to the nonvoting category was actually larger—reflecting a heavy drop in the off-year vote, as might be expected, among the unemployment-sensitive group and the discontented farmers). The enumerated issues as a group show an index of relative pulling power to the Democrats of .9. This figure is roughly comparable to the 1.3 pulling power index of the recession issue in March, if one makes allowance for the heavier falloff in voting among those concerned with the pro-Democratic issues.

The evidence summarized in this section points to a conclusion that the decisive swing in voter preference that resulted in the restoration of Democratic control of Congress occurred when the recession struck, in the winter, and that the voters whose loyalties were then switched remained on the Democratic side. Enough of them stayed switched through 1956 also, in congressional voting, to prevent Eisenhower from carrying a Republican Congress into office with him, as he had done in 1952, even though the voters preferred him to Adlai Stevenson by an even greater margin than in his first campaign.

Public Response to Activism

As every politician knows, the average voter feels no compulsion to be consistent. Asked whether he feels that the government should take action to solve a pressing social problem—be it unemployment, civil rights, a school shortage, or whatever—he is likely to answer in the affirmative. But asked whether the federal government is doing too much—whether it should cut spending and cut taxes and return governmental functions to the states—he is apt to answer in the affirmative also. During President Eisenhower's second term, as the party division became increasingly sharp and clear, the two parties appealed to these opposite facets of the voters' collective intelligence—the Democratic party to their latent activism, the Republican to their basic conservatism. Each party's appeal had its basis in doctrinal principle and honest conviction but it reflected, also, the party's faith that what it believed to be best for the country could be "sold" to the electorate and thus made to pay political dividends as well.

On the latter score, the Democrats had the better of the argument. A review of public opinion polls of the period makes unmistakably clear that the Democratic program was genuinely popular. In all of the published national polls, direct questions regarding the specific legislative issues in the fields covered by this study brought forth, almost without exception, expressions in favor of the activist position. Data from the national polls are corroborated by evidence from surveys of constituency opinion made by members of Congress. This section reviews the available data on public reaction to the activist issues during the Eisenhower years. The following section assesses public reaction to the conservative counter-arguments. The final section of the chapter attempts to appraise the influence of these issues upon the election returns of 1958 and 1960.

Attitudes Toward Unemployment Action. In its 1958 and 1960 election surveys, the Survey Research Center asked its respondents whether they agreed or disagreed with the proposition, "The government in Washington ought to see to it that everybody who wants to work can find a job."[18] The results were as follows:

	Percent of total	
Response	*1958*	*1960*
Agree strongly	44	47
Agree but not very strongly	12	11
Not sure;–it depends	7	8
Disagree but not very strongly	9	7
Disagree strongly	17	16
Don't know; no opinion; no answer	11	11
	100	100

The number agreeing with the proposition outnumbered those disagreeing by better than two to one, and the ratio increased between the two surveys.

On specific legislative measures to deal with unemployment, the polls show further support for the activist position. The Youth Conservation Corps drew a 63 percent endorsement in an AIPO poll in 1957, with only 28 percent opposition.[19] In the midst of the 1957–58 recession, 54 percent of the sample thought the government should take action, against 35 percent who thought the recession would cure itself. Those who wanted action

[18] *Ibid.*, study 431, Sept.-Nov., 1958, and study 440, Sept.-Nov. 1960.
[19] AIPO release, Oct. 11, 1957.

were about equally divided between tax reduction and public works as the remedy.[20]

Attitudes Toward Education Legislation. The most substantial body of public opinion data on domestic issues during the Eisenhower period relates to federal aid for school construction. On three occasions the AIPO asked a direct question on this issue: "Some people say that the Federal Government in Washington should give financial help to build new public schools, especially in the poorer states. Others say that this will mean higher taxes for everyone and that states and local communities should build their own schools. How do you, yourself, feel—do you favor or oppose federal aid to help build new public schools?"[21] From two-thirds to three-fourths of the national sample gave an affirmative response, as these results show:

	Percent of total		
Response	*1956*	*1957*	*1960*
Favor	67	76	65
Oppose	24	19	25
No opinion	9	5	10
	100	100	100

The polls showed that support for federal aid for school construction was spread rather evenly throughout the population. Republicans as well as Democrats, Catholics as well as Protestants, showed solid majorities in each of the polls; support for the legislation to aid public schools was, in fact, stronger among Catholics than non-Catholics. In the 1960 poll, for example, Democrats favored the legislation by a 68–24 percent margin, Republicans by 57–35 percent, independents by 69–18 percent, Catholics by 68–22 percent. Surveys taken at intervals since 1938 indicated that public support in the general range shown above had been consistent for at least two decades.

[20] *Ibid.*, April 19, 1958, inserted in *Financial Condition of the United States,* Hearings before the Senate Finance Committee, 85 Cong. 2 sess. (April 22, 1958), pp. 1876–77. The results of this poll were more strongly in favor of governmental action than those of a survey taken during the 1953–54 recession; then 44 percent of the sample favored a public works program, while an equal proportion felt that unemployment was not yet severe enough (AIPO release, May 26, 1954).

[21] Jan. 22, 1956; Feb. 10, 1957; Feb. 19, 1960.

In its election surveys of 1958 and 1960, the SRC also found that those who favored federal aid for school construction outnumbered opponents by the same two to one or three to one ratio. In response to the statement, "If cities and towns around the country need help to build more schools, the government in Washington ought to give them the money they need,"[22] it obtained the following results:

Response	Percent of total 1958	1960
Agree strongly	46	37
Agree but not very strongly	17	15
Not sure; it depends	6	10
Disagree but not very strongly	7	8
Disagree strongly	14	17
No answer or no opinion	10	13
	100	100

Finally, a Roper poll in the spring of 1957 showed 73 percent of the public in favor of federal aid, 16 percent opposed.[23]

While the cause of aid to school construction never lost its majority support, the conservative campaign against it in the late 1950's did appear to reduce the degree of that support. Both the Gallup and SRC surveys show a 10-point drop in the percentage of public support for federal aid, and a somewhat smaller increase in opposition, in 1960 compared to 1957 and 1958. An analysis of 289 polls taken by members of Congress among their own constituents during the period 1953–60 provides further evidence of the subsidence of popular support. Of those polls, 114 included questions bearing upon federal aid for school construction. As shown in Table 6, a decisive majority of the constituencies polled approved federal aid in the period 1953–57 while an equally decisive majority opposed the legislation in the years 1959–60.

It should be emphasized that congressional polls must be interpreted with great care. The questions are frequently "loaded," the samples used are not scientific cross-sections of the population, and far more Republican

[22] SRC studies 431 and 440.

[23] Quoted in testimony at *Science and Education for National Defense*, Hearings before the Senate Labor and Public Welfare Committee, 85 Cong. 2 sess. (1958), pp. 488–89. The poll was taken by the Elmo Roper polling organization.

Table 6. *Majority Responses to Congressional Constituency Polls on Federal Aid for School Construction, 1953–60*[a]

(Number of polls reporting majority indicated)

Year	Republicans' polls			Northern Democrats' polls		Southern Democrats' polls	
	For	Against	Tied	For	Against	For	Against
1953	4	0	0	0	0	0	0
1954	1	0	0	1	0	0	0
1955	5	1	0	3	0	0	0
1956	14	3	0	2	0	0	1
1957	11	3	0	2	0	1	2
1958	7	5	0	0	0	0	0
1959	4	11	1	1	1	0	1
1960	8	13	2	3	0	0	3
Total	54	36	3	12	1	1	7

Source: *Congressional Record*.
[a] Results of 114 polls (5 taken by senators, 109 by representatives).

congressmen than Democrats make use of the polling device.[24] Nevertheless, the figures in Table 6 show a convincing trend, if Republican constituencies only are considered, from support to opposition in the last two years of the Eisenhower period.

[24] Congressmen usually conduct their polls by mailing questionnaires, but a few simply print questionnaires in newspapers in their districts. Mailed questionnaires may be sent to all households in the district or in selected areas, to addressees taken from voters' lists or from telephone directories, to lists of business, civic, and other leaders, or to persons on the congressman's regular mailing list. In addition to the distortion resulting from methods of sample selection, the polls are biased by the self-selection of those electing to return the questionnaire. The "loading" of questions results in still further bias. These compounded distortions tend to skew the results in favor of a conservative position and the congressman's own position. While congressional polls cannot be considered valid as a measure of *absolute* support, they can be used, with care, to indicate *trends* in support of or differential degrees of support for an issue. They can also be given special weight where they show support of positions contrary to those of the poller. For further discussion of congressional polling techniques, see Leonard A. Marascuilo and Harriet Amster, "Survey of 1961–1962 Congressional Polls," *Public Opinion Quarterly*, Vol. 28 (Fall 1964), pp. 497–506; and "Congressional Use of Polls: A Symposium," *Public Opinion Quarterly*, Vol. 18 (Summer 1954), pp. 121–42.

The 289 questionnaires analyzed in this chapter were those inserted in the body of the *Congressional Record* during the period 1953–60, plus three inserted in the *Record* appendix during 1953. Tabulations of the questions and responses were prepared by Constance Holden. In a few instances, answers to questions that appeared on their face to be ambiguous or misleading were not included in the tabulations.

A closer examination of the public opinion data appears to confirm the thesis advanced by Munger and Fenno that the overwhelming support for federal aid shown in the national surveys was not a matter of deep conviction on the part of many respondents.[25] If the indicated support were largely superficial, it would presumably be shaken as federal aid became increasingly a controversial partisan issue; and the loss of support would be especially marked among Republican voters, who would reflect the views of their party leaders as those views became more widely known. Both the national and congressional constituency polls indicated that this is what happened.

In the AIPO polls, the falloff in support between 1957 and 1960 is heaviest among Republicans. Their 74 percent favorable vote in 1957 declined to 57 percent three years later—a 17-point drop. Democratic support, in the same period, fell by only 11 points, from 79 to 68 percent, and support among independent voters by 8 points, from 77 to 69 percent. In the two SRC polls summarized above, the increase between 1958 and 1960 in the number who "disagree strongly" may reflect the sharpening of the political debate.

In only a few instances did the congressional surveys ask the same or comparable questions in successive polls in the same district, but in each such case the support trend was downward. The findings are shown in Table 7.

Despite the downward trend, public opinion nonetheless clearly supported federal aid for school construction throughout the decade—and by decisive margins. At the end of the period, to refer again to the SRC 1960 poll on page 444, supporters outnumbered opponents by more than two to one, and of the supporters 70 percent classified themselves as agreeing "strongly" with the proposition put to them.

The Democrats were in accord with public opinion on this issue, but on the related question of aid for teacher salaries they may very well have outrun public opinion. The only national survey bearing upon this point was the 1957 Roper poll referred to earlier. Of the 73 percent who favored federal aid to education, 30 percent favored aid for construction only, leaving only 43 percent in support of aid for both construction and salaries. To put it another way, of those persons favoring aid for construction, 41 percent declined to support assistance for the other purpose.

---

[25] Frank J. Munger and Richard F. Fenno, Jr., *National Politics and Federal Aid to Education* (Syracuse University Press, 1962), pp. 92–93.

Table 7. *Response to Repeated Polls of Congressional Constituencies on Federal Aid for School Construction, 1956–60*

Member's district and party	Year	Percentage of respondents			
		For	Against	No opinion	Total
Ohio, 23rd; Republican[a]	1957	45	52	3	100
	1958	45	51	4	100
	1959	37	58	5	100
Washington, 2nd; Republican[b]	1956	70	30	—	100
	1959	57	43	—	100
	1960	50	50	—	100
Washington, 6th; Republican[c]	1957	65	32	3	100
	1958	49	46	5	100
	1959	42	58	—	100
Michigan, 6th; Republican[d]	1957	45	51	4	100
	1959	42	42	16	100
	1960	39	49	12	100
Ohio, 17th; Republican[e]	1957	58	42	—	100
	1958	41	59	—	100
Illinois, 13th; Republican[f]	1959	29	48	23	100
	1960	26	39	35	100
Florida, 6th; Democratic[g]	1957	59	41	—	100
	1959	45	55	—	100
	1960	49	51	—	100

Source: *Congressional Record.*
[a] "Do you favor federal aid for local school construction?"
[b] "Do you favor federal aid for school construction?" On this and the three following polls the wording of the questions was changed slightly between years, but probably not in such a way as to invalidate comparison.
[c] "Do you approve direct federal grants to states to help build schools?"
[d] "Should Congress provide financial aid for school construction?"
[e] "Do you approve federal aid for construction of school buildings?"
[f] "To meet educational needs do you approve . . . federal grants to states for school construction?"
[g] "Do you favor federal aid to education?" (1957). "Do you favor federal aid for school construction?" (1959). "Do you favor using federal funds for school construction?" (1960).

Congressional constituency polls, from districts of every kind, were unanimous in confirming the weakness of the salary issue. An analysis of eleven polls in 1960 that asked comparable questions on the issues shows a differential ranging from 6 to 42 percentage points in the favorable vote as between the questions, with an average differential of 19 percentage points. These polls are summarized in Table 8. The differential amounts to a net loss of support for salary aid, on the average, of 38 percent of the voters who favored construction aid, a figure remarkably close to the 41 percent shown by Roper. If either figure is applied to even the

highest percentage shown in the national polls as supporting aid for
school construction, then support for aid for teacher salaries drops below
50 percent. Thus, making whatever allowance may be appropriate for the
weaknesses of congressional constituency polls, it is unlikely that public
opinion, as of the end of 1960, supported the principle of federal aid for
teacher salaries embodied in the Murray-Metcalf bill and the Democratic
platform.

Table 8. *Support for Federal Aid for School Construction and for Teacher
Salaries, as Shown in Congressional Constituency Polls, 1960*
(Percentage of respondents favoring action indicated[a])

Member's district and party	Construction aid	Salary aid	Difference
South Dakota, 2nd; Republican	50	27	23
Minnesota, 9th; Republican	45	21	24
Florida, 6th; Democratic	49	34	15
Kansas, 1st; Republican	44	31	13
Texas, 21st; Democratic	33	27	6
Oregon, 1st; Republican	45	22	23
Washington, 2nd; Republican	50	29	21
Illinois, 13th; Republican	40	24	16
Indiana, 3rd; Democratic	68	58	10
Massachusetts, 1st; Republican	65	23	42
Illinois, 11th; Democratic	50	38	12

Source: *Congressional Record.*
a Percentages only of those with opinions.

Attitudes Toward Civil Rights Legislation. Evidence from the available public opinion polls of the 1950's shows strong public support for
the general principle of civil rights and for at least some of the specific
legislative proposals under discussion during the period.

The 1958 and 1960 studies of the Survey Research Center found
stronger support for governmental action against discrimination in jobs
and housing than for action against school segregation, but found a favorable majority in all three areas in 1960. Since the national figures conceal
the strong difference in sentiment by regions, they should be read as
showing an even more decisive level of support for civil rights action
among voters outside the South. In response to the statement, "If Negroes
are not getting fair treatment in jobs and housing, the government should
see to it that they do,"[26] the following results were obtained:

26 SRC studies 431 and 440.

Response	Percent of total	
	1958	*1960*
Agree strongly	47	45
Agree but not very strongly	16	17
Not sure; it depends	6	7
Disagree but not very strongly	5	5
Disagree strongly	13	13
No answer or no opinion	13	13
	100	100

In response to the statement, "The government in Washington should stay out of the question of whether white and colored children go to the same school,"[27] the following results were obtained:

Response	Percent of total	
	1958	*1960*
Agree strongly	35	32
Agree but not very strongly	8	6
Not sure; it depends	5	7
Disagree but not very strongly	7	8
Disagree strongly	34	33
No answer or no opinion	11	14
	100	100

It will be noted that a slight shift in sentiment between 1958 and 1960 converted a majority in favor of the government's staying out of the school integration question into a majority favoring intervention.

The AIPO asked no questions during the period bearing directly upon civil rights legislation. At intervals, the poll tested voter approval of the Supreme Court's school integration decision and found margins of approval, in the North, in the two-to-one and three-to-one range. It also recorded a 49–35 percent margin in January 1957 in favor of a change in Senate rules to permit "a simple majority" to close debate.

Congressional constituency polls, which asked questions covering a wide variety of civil rights legislative proposals, invariably obtained a negative response in the South and almost always a strongly favorable response in the North. The 289 questionnaires examined in this chapter included 37 questions soliciting views on civil rights legislation. Five

[27] *Ibid.* It may be that the negative wording of this question caused the responses to be less favorable, from an activist standpoint, than responses to the jobs and housing question.

questions asked in southern constituencies provoked heavy margins against such legislation. Of the 32 questions asked of northern constituencies, 29 received favorable replies. Legislation to protect voting rights and to outlaw bombing of schools and churches received the strongest support, with approval ratios ranging from 80 to 95 percent, but questions relating to the enforcement of the whole range of civil rights or to the need for "stronger civil rights legislation" in general also received substantial favorable majorities.

Attitudes Toward Medicare Legislation. The first AIPO poll on medicare was not taken until 1961, but the strong support shown at that time—67–26 percent in favor of medicare[28]—must have been building during the 1950's. A Minnesota poll taken in 1960 found a 55–40 percent majority in favor of the Forand bill.[29] When the Survey Research Center asked its respondents in 1960 whether they agreed with the statement, "The government ought to help people get doctors and hospital care at low cost," nearly half the sample "agreed strongly." Those who agreed outnumbered those who disagreed by a three-to-one ratio.[30]

Some of the most impressive evidence of support for medicare comes from congressional constituency polls. Of the 289 polls studied, 39 contained questions relating directly to the question of health care for older persons under social security. All but one were taken in 1959 and 1960. The results are summarized in Table 9.

While a majority of the polls showed a preponderance of sentiment against the Democratic approach to medicare, an analysis that takes into account the nature of the constituencies leads to the opposite conclusion. In the northern Democratic districts, all but one—a normally Republican rural Ohio district held by a one-term Democrat—showed promedicare majorities in the range of two-thirds to three-fourths. Republican districts, at the same time, showed surprisingly strong support for the Democratic position on the issue, especially in urban areas and particularly in the election year of 1960. Thus, Representative Frances P. Bolton, Republican representing a suburban Cleveland district, found a 60–32 percent majority of her respondents favored medicare, an increase from a 49–39 percent majority in the previous year. "During the past year," she told the House, "it is apparent that many people have become more aware of the

---

[28] AIPO release, June 9, 1961.
[29] Minnesota Poll, April 24, 1960, conducted for *Minneapolis Star* and *Tribune*.
[30] SRC study 440.

Table 9. *Majority Responses to Congressional Constituency Polls on Medicare, 1958–60*
(Number of polls reporting majority indicated)

Year	Republicans' polls		Northern Democrats' polls		Southern Democrats' polls	
	For	Against	For	Against	For	Against
1958	0	1	0	0	0	0
1959	3	9	0	0	0	0
1960	10	10	4	1	0	1
Total	13	20	4	1	0	1

Source: *Congressional Record.*

problem that our senior citizens face in the matter of hospital and medical care. The results of my 1959 and 1960 polls indicate this increased concern...."[31] Of Republican Representative Walter Judd's Minneapolis respondents, only 11.5 percent identified themselves as Democrat-Farmer-Laborites, but 59 percent favored medicare, while only 33 percent opposed it. Constituents marking the questionnaire of Representative Harold C. Ostertag, whose district included part of Rochester, New York, were 59 percent for Nixon and only 8 percent for Kennedy, but they were 49–46 percent in favor of amending the social security law to "increase the social security taxes to provide for a program of hospital and medical benefits for eligible retired persons." Urban and suburban Republicans throughout the North and West were thus finding that questionnaires returned mainly by their own Republican supporters were preponderantly in favor of the Democratic approach to health care through social security. Only the Republican rural and small-town heartland of the North and, probably, most or all of the South—although survey evidence from the South is scant—were holding out against it.

Attitudes on the Wilderness Bill. The wilderness bill found strong backing among urban residents. The question, "Do you favor legislation to preserve wilderness areas in our national parks, forests, wildlife refuges and other public lands?" drew 91 percent backing in 1960 in the suburban Chicago district of Republican Marguerite Stitt Church, with only 4.4 percent opposed. A San Francisco suburban congressional poll in the same year showed 77–14 percent support. Respondents voted against it, how-

[31] *Cong. Record*, Vol. 106 (1960), p. 5226.

ever, in Republican districts in Idaho and Washington where potential wilderness areas existed.

Public Response to the Republican Appeal

If the activist programs espoused by the Democrats were popular with the voters, how deep-seated was the antispending, anti-inflation sentiment to which the Republicans sought to appeal? The available evidence, while not voluminous, indicates that the Republican campaign on behalf of limited government aroused little popular excitement.

At the very peak of that campaign, in 1959, when President Eisenhower was striving to alert the country to the peril of the "spenders," an AIPO release carried the headline, "Few Voters Worked Up over Government Spending Debate." In response to the question, "Do you think there is anything the government should be spending more money on than it is at present?" and a corresponding question about things on which the government should be spending less money, domestic spending came out a little better than even. Almost half the respondents—48 percent— named no purpose for which spending should be cut, while 26 percent named foreign aid or defense. Only 26 percent proposed cutting either specific domestic programs or government spending in general. On the other hand, 29 percent identified government programs (other than defense) that they felt deserved more spending—11 percent specifically naming education.[32]

The SRC's 1960 survey bears out the Gallup findings. In response to a question as to how money saved through disarmament should be used, only one person in six—221 of 1,304 with opinions—felt that cutting taxes was highest priority. Another 277 named debt reduction as top priority, but 763 proposed to use the funds for increased spending for welfare, schools, and highways.[33]

Congressional polls during the same period showed overwhelming voter allegiance to the general principles that the budget should be balanced, that it should be balanced by cutting spending rather than by raising taxes, and that debt reduction should come ahead of tax reduction in the event of a surplus. But while the voters emphatically endorsed spending reductions if necessary to balance the budget, they tended to respond quite

[32] AIPO release, May 1, 1959.
[33] SRC study 440.

differently when the proposal was for reductions in particular areas of expenditure, or when they were asked to consider government spending in a question that did not mention deficits or debt. In addition to the questions on aid to education, summarized earlier, five Republican polls asked about expenditures for health, welfare, and public works, with results, as shown below, that portrayed no general pattern of hostility to the spending programs:

Minnesota, 5th district (1957): "Welfare programs such as social security, old-age assistance, unemployment and disability compensations, etc., have been expanded substantially during recent years, with corresponding increase in costs. Do you favor further expansion of these programs?"
Response: yes, 55 percent; no, 39 percent; no opinion, 6 percent.

Pennsylvania, 29th district (1958): "Do you believe that the federal government should reduce its efforts in the fields of health, education, and welfare to save money?"
Response: yes, 24 percent; no, 76 percent.

North Carolina, 10th district (1959): "Do you favor increase or decrease in federal grants to states and local communities for public works such as sewage disposal works?"
Response: increase, 27 percent; decrease, 60 percent.

Idaho, 2nd district (1960): "On public welfare programs: Do you believe government spending is [one of the following]?"
Response: insufficient, 23 percent; about right, 32 percent; too much, 33 percent.

New York, 42nd district (1960): "Do you believe in increasing or decreasing spending in . . . public works, harbors, flood control, etc.?"
Response: increase, 66 percent; decrease, 34 percent.

New York, 42nd district (1960): "Do you believe that the proposed budget expenditures of $70.8 billion are [one of the following]?"
Response: about right, 58 percent; too low, 9 percent; too high, 33 percent.

Most of the Republican polls endorsed the Eisenhower proposal of 1957–58 to transfer certain federal grant programs to the states, along with tax sources to finance them. One conspicuous exception, however, was a statewide poll taken by Iowa Senator Thomas E. Martin. He received a 65–35 percent negative response to the question: "Do you approve transferring to the states all vocational education, waste-treatment plants, advance planning for slum clearance, and disaster relief for damage to public facilities, with power to levy part of the tax on local telephone service to meet the cost?"[34]

If the public even in Republican districts was not aroused about spending, the survey evidence suggests that it also was not upset about high taxes. A Gallup poll question asked over the years showed that voter resentment against taxes faded markedly from its high point in the election year of 1952. Responses to the question, "Do you consider the amount of federal income taxes which you have to pay as too high, too low, or about right?"[35] indicated the downward trend:

Response	Percent of total				
	1951	*1952*	*1953*	*1957*	*1959*
Too high	52	71	59	61	51
Too low	1	—	—	. . .	1
About right	43	26	37	. . .	40
No opinion	4	3	4	. . .	8
	100	100	100	. . .	100

Herbert McClosky and his associates at the University of Minnesota provide a particularly intriguing body of evidence showing that the Democratic party position on the issues in the 1957–58 period coincided much more nearly with general public opinion than did the Republican party position. They distributed questionnaires containing questions on twenty-four current issues to party leaders, using 1956 convention delegate lists, and to a national sample of rank and file party members. From the returns they constructed an index showing the degree of support within each sample for the government program indicated. They found that the support ratios of the rank and file Republicans were close to those of rank and file Democrats and that the scores of Democratic leaders were close to both. The fourth group—the Republican leaders—held views decidedly different from those of the other three, including those of their own followers. Following are the support ratios shown on five issues in a category labeled "equalitarian and human welfare," which roughly parallels the scope of this study.[36]

[34] *Cong. Record*, Vol. 104 (1958), p. 5872.

[35] AIPO releases, March 9, 1953; April 15, 1959.

[36] Herbert McClosky, Paul J. Hoffmann, and Rosemary O'Hara, "Issue Conflict and Consensus among Party Leaders and Followers," *American Political Science Review*, Vol. 54 (1960), pp. 406–27. The index figure is derived by allowing 1 if the respondent favored an increase in the program, 0 if he favored a decrease, and .5 if he favored continuing the program at its existing level; the scores were averaged for the sample.

Support ratio

Issue	Leaders		Followers	
	Democratic	Republican	Democratic	Republican
Federal aid to education	.76	.40	.85	.78
Slum clearance and public housing	.86	.59	.87	.82
Social security benefits	.78	.55	.83	.77
Minimum wages	.73	.52	.78	.69
Enforcement of integration	.59	.47	.57	.59

The average gap between Democratic leaders and their followers on these issues was only .04. But the difference between Republican leaders and followers was a startling .22. The Democratic leaders were much closer to the Republican rank and file, with a difference of only .02. Indeed, the Democratic leaders scored even closer to the Republican followers than to their own followers.

For all twenty-four issues, the average differences were:

Between Democratic leaders and their followers	.07
Between Republican leaders and their followers	.15
Between Democratic and Republican followers	.04
Between Democratic and Republican leaders	.21
Between Democratic leaders and Republican followers	.08
Between Republican leaders and Democratic followers	.20

McClosky and his associates observed:

. . . there is substantial consensus on national issues between Democratic leaders and Democratic and Republican followers, while the Republican leaders are separated not only from the Democrats but from their own rank and file as well. . . . Whereas Republican leaders hold to the tenets of business ideology and remain faithful to the spirit and intellectual mood of leaders like Robert A. Taft, the rank and file Republican supporters have embraced, along with their Democratic brethren, the regulatory and social reform measures of the Roosevelt and Truman administrations. . . . Thus, in addition to being the preferred party of the more numerous classes, the Democrats also enjoy the advantages over their opponents of holding views that are more widely shared throughout the country. . . . It is conceivable . . . that the Republican party has come to be the minority party partly because the opinions of its spokesmen are uncongenial to a majority of the voters.[37]

[37] *Ibid.*, p. 423.

The Issues and the Elections, 1958 and 1960

Looking back upon the 1958 election, that tireless campaigner Richard Nixon assessed the reason for the Democratic landslide: "The power of the 'pocketbook' issue was shown more clearly perhaps in 1958 than in any off-year election in history. On the international front, the Administration had had one of its best years. . . . Yet, the economic dip in October was obviously uppermost in the people's minds when they went to the polls. They completely rejected the President's appeal for the election of Republicans to the House and Senate."[38]

The evidence from public opinion data supports the Nixon conclusion. Throughout his eight years in office, the President and his party maintained the confidence of the people on international issues, but on the "pocketbook" issue the recession of 1957–58—following the less severe downturn of 1953–54—dealt the Republicans a setback in public confidence that contributed decisively to their loss of governmental power.

Figure 2 depicts the public view of the two parties—the Republicans as the party of peace and the Democrats as the party of prosperity—during the second Eisenhower term, as reflected in AIPO polls. At no time during that period, as shown in the peace chart, did the Republicans fail to register an advantage over the Democrats in response to the question, "Which political party do you think would be more likely to keep the United States out of World War III?" Conversely, at no time during the period could they match the Democrats' appeal, as shown in the prosperity chart, in response to the question, "Which political party do you think will do the best job of keeping the country prosperous?" Any substantial Democratic advantage on the prosperity issue, however, was the direct outgrowth of the 1957–58 recession. Prior to the beginning of the slump in the fall of 1957, the Democratic advantage was negligible, but by the time unemployment had reached its peak, in March, it had widened to a gap of 25 percentage points. As the economy recovered, the gap narrowed but it remained substantial throughout 1959 and 1960.

[38] *Six Crises,* p. 310. Nixon's timing of the "economic dip" is imprecise. The bottom of the recession was reached in the early months of 1958 and recovery was underway by spring. Unemployment reached its peak in February and March on an unadjusted basis and in August on a seasonally adjusted basis. By all measures, recovery was underway when the voters went to the polls but the unemployment figures, in particular, responded slowly. See Chap. 2, p. 28.

Figure 2. *Prosperity and Peace Images of the Democratic and Republican Parties, 1957–60*

(Percentage of poll respondents indicating each option)

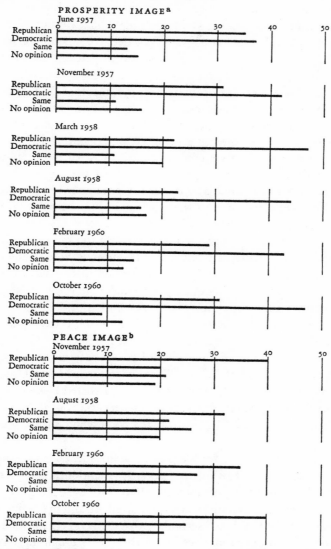

PROSPERITY IMAGE[a]

PEACE IMAGE[b]

Source: Various AIPO releases and AIPO survey data on file at Roper Public Opinion Research Center, Williams College, Williamstown, Massachusetts.

[a] Responses to: "Looking ahead for the next four years, which political party—the Republican or the Democratic—do you think will do the best job of keeping the country prosperous?"

[b] Responses to: "Which political party do you think would be more likely to keep the United States out of World War III—the Republican party or the Democratic party?"

Figure 3 compares party preference on the prosperity and peace issues with the party preference for Congress. While the chart suffers from certain gaps in the data, since the issue questions were asked only occasionally, it nonetheless suggests a strong relationship between the prosperity issue, in particular, and the congressional elections—on a pattern markedly parallel to that of 1954. The decisive 5-point rise in Democratic preferment for Congress, from 53 to 58 percent, occurred at the time the economy was dipping to the recession low reached in the winter and early spring. It was in March 1958, too, that Dr. Gallup noted that the Democratic party was in its strongest position since the AIPO had first asked a question about party preference in 1944. Of voters identifying themselves with one or the other party, 63 percent preferred the Democrats—a 6-point rise in four months.[39] And in April the proportion of poll respondents expressing approval of the President's conduct of office reached the lowest point in his entire eight-year tenure—49 percent—and the number expressing disapproval reached its highest point, at 35 percent. At that time, 42 percent of the poll's respondents—equivalent to 22 million households—answered affirmatively the question, "Has the present business situation affected you and your household in any way?"[40]

Two other events that had been emblazoned in the headlines at the same time that the slump began helped to shake the voters' confidence in the Republican administration. The Soviet Union orbited its sputnik in October 1957, and the Democrats seized upon the occasion at once to spread alarm about the "missile gap." And the President had sent the Army to Little Rock, likewise in the fall of 1957, to enforce integration of that city's Central High School. That action turned some Eisenhower-Democrats in the South back to ordinary unhyphenated Democrats; in the North the President was credited for acting decisively but at the same time blamed for letting the situation drift to the point where such a drastic step was necessary.

In analyzing the reasons for the ebb in the President's popularity in the winter, Dr. Gallup noted all three issues. He mentioned first "a dissatisfaction with his handling of domestic affairs—in particular, the South's segregation problem, the Midwest's farm problem, and the nation's growing unemployment problem"; second, "a dissatisfaction in the men around Mr. Eisenhower and the manner in which he is maintaining leadership over his advisers"; and, third, "a dissatisfaction with our national defense

[39] The question was: "Suppose you couldn't register as anything but a Democrat or a Republican. If this were the case, how would you register?" (AIPO release, March 23, 1958).
[40] Ibid., April 21, 1958.

Figure 3. *Relation of the Peace and Prosperity Issues to Preference for Democrats for Congress, 1956–60*
(Percentage of poll respondents preferring Democratic party)

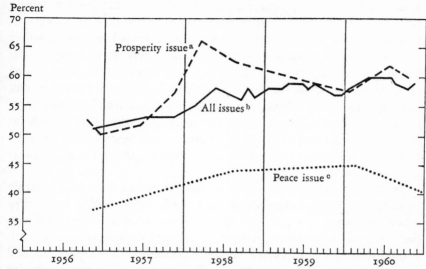

Source: AIPO releases and AIPO survey data on file at Roper Public Opinion Research Center. "No opinion" responses are eliminated, as are "undecided" responses, on the congressional preference question; responses judging the two parties "about the same" on the "peace" and "prosperity" issues are counted at half-votes for the Democrats.
a Responses to: "Looking ahead for the next four years, which political party—the Republican or the Democratic—do you think will do the best job of keeping the country prosperous?"
b Responses to: "If the elections for Congress were being held today, which party would you like to see win in this state—the Democratic party or the Republican party?" The November entries for 1956 and 1958 are the results of the actual vote rather than the poll results.
c Responses to: "Which political party do you think would be more likely to keep the United States out of World War III—the Republican party or the Democratic party?"

program and a feeling that we are losing out in the arms race with Russia."[41]

An analysis of the March 1958 AIPO poll indicates, however, that unemployment was by far the strongest of all these issues. In that survey, 40 percent of the respondents identified "unemployment" as the nation's most important problem, compared to fewer than 10 percent who mentioned the arms race, missiles and space, or national defense. As shown in Table 10, the Eisenhower voters of 1956 who indicated in March 1958 that they were switching to a Democratic preference for Congress were disproportionately heavy among those most conscious of these two issues, but the greater number concerned with unemployment gives this issue a much stronger relative pulling power. The number mentioning "integration" or "segregation" as the most important problem was fewer than 4 percent, so that the pulling power of this issue registers as negligible.

[41] *Ibid.*, Feb. 26, 1958.

It will be noted, from Figure 2, that the Republican party suffered a loss of confidence on both the peace and prosperity issues simultaneously, and to about the same degree, during the winter of 1957–58. The Democratic party enjoyed a concurrent gain in confidence, but more decisively on prosperity than on peace. It can be assumed that the simultaneous movement of the two lines reflects to some extent a mutual interaction rather than independent causation—a voter reacting adversely to the Republican handling of the 1957–58 recession would probably suffer some loss of confidence in the administration's handling of other matters as well, and one who felt that the President and his advisers were alarmingly complacent about sputnik might come to question the administration's judgment on domestic issues. Similarly, a loss of confidence arising from the Little Rock crisis would act to reinforce the antiadministration attitudes on the other issues.

By the time of the election, unemployment had lost its immediate urgency as a national problem. In the October AIPO survey, fewer than 8 percent named unemployment as the nation's most important problem. Race relations and civil rights were mentioned by almost twice that number. So were high prices and high taxes. Concern with the space race and preparedness had also faded. But the October survey was noteworthy for the uniformity of the distribution of the switchers among all the major issue categories, as shown in Table 10.

The remaining unemployment-conscious voters were switching to the Democrats in a slightly higher proportion than other voters,[42] and the much larger number of persons concerned with foreign policy and peace were switching in lower proportions, but there was no single current issue outstanding among all others in pulling voters toward the Democrats. The uniformity in the proportion of Republican defectors among the categories—all within the narrow range of 28 to 35 percent—is perhaps to

---

[42] Voters mentioning integration, segregation, racial disputes, and civil rights were also switching in disproportionate numbers to the Democrats, but this probably should be disregarded as reflecting one of the weaknesses of the data. Since "switchers" are computed by comparing the 1956 presidential vote with congressional preference in the voter's own state, the category includes Eisenhower-Democrats in the South who supported Democratic candidates for Congress in both 1956 and 1958 and, hence, were not congressional switchers. Since southern voters were especially conscious of the problem of integration and racial disputes in the period after the use of troops in Little Rock in 1957, it is probable that the Eisenhower-Democrats listed as switchers account for most of the .4 index figure shown in the table. The figure therefore should not be interpreted as showing pulling power toward the national Democratic party in the districts where the Democratic gains in Congress took place in 1958.

Table 10. *Switches in Voting Preference, 1956–58*[a]

Problem identified as most important	1956 Republicans		1956 Democrats		Other voters		Index of relative pulling power to Democrats
	No.	*Percent switching to Democrats in 1958*	No.	*Percent switching to Republicans in 1958*	No.	*Percent supporting Democrats in 1958*	
PREFERENCE EXPRESSED IN MARCH 1958[b]							
Unemployment	252	35	244	2	129	73	1.4
Arms race, missiles, space, national defense	70	34	43	5	38	71	.2
All others	369	23	193	5	196	70	—1.6
PREFERENCE EXPRESSED IN OCTOBER 1958[c]							
Keeping the peace, foreign policy issues in general	341	29	184	7	133	65	— .9
Unemployment	55	33	33	0	23	83	.4
Economic problems, high cost of living, high taxes	103	28	66	6	44	68	— .3
Integration, segregation, racial disputes, civil rights	84	35	60	5	65	74	.4
National defense, preparedness, sputnik, nuclear testing	21	33	10	0	11	82	.2
All other issues	83	30	36	3	35	74	.2

[a] See Table 4, notes a-d, for basis and method of computation.
[b] Based on 1,610 responses to: "What do you think is the most important problem facing this country today?" and "If the elections for Congress were being held today, which party would you like to see win in this state—the Republican party or the Democratic party?" (AIPO 596-K, March 4, 1958).
[c] Based on 1,553 responses to questions shown in note b, above (AIPO 606-K, Oct. 13, 1958).

be explained in either, or both, of two ways. The unemployment-conscious voters of the March survey and the smaller number concerned with the "missile gap," who had switched in large numbers to the Democrats, remained switched even though they no longer saw unemployment or space competition as the nation's foremost problem. Or the 1956 Eisenhower voters, in the period since the March survey, had become equally disillusioned over the Republican handling of other issues. The data do not provide a basis for a conclusive judgment as to the relative influence of these two factors, but since major new issues had not developed, it appears likely that the former explanation is nearer the truth. Dr. Gallup himself expressed this view in his interpretation of the October preelection poll:

"The current Democratic advantage . . . dates back to the effect of the launching of Sputnik I. . . . While the campaign issue of unemployment has now lost much of its impact, it too added to the Democratic strength during the past winter and spring. . . ."[43]

In any event—in contrast to 1954—it is not possible to make a case for dismissing all the issues and attributing the 1958 Democratic congressional victory to a normal return of Democratic voters to the party of their basic allegiance. Campbell, in analyzing the comprehensive SRC data on the 1958 election, concludes that "the partisan movement in 1958 cannot be entirely attributed to a normal decline toward standing party loyalties after the displacement of the vote in a surge year." Indeed, of his switchers who in 1956 had voted for Eisenhower but in 1958 for a Democratic congressional candidate, 8 percent classified themselves as "strong" Republicans and another 20 percent as "weak" Republicans. Almost half of the total number of "weak" Republicans who voted and one out of seven of the "strong" Republicans supported the Democratic candidate.[44] It is of such massive defections—especially from a minority party—that landslides are made. Deviations from normal party allegiance of such magnitude in presidential elections can be ascribed, sometimes, to the impact of the personalities of candidates, but in an off year they can be explained only in terms of the political and governmental issues of the time.[45]

[43] AIPO release, Nov. 1, 1958.

[44] Angus Campbell, "Surge and Decline: A Study of Electoral Change," in Angus Campbell and others, *Elections and the Political Order* (Wiley, 1966), pp. 55–57.

[45] Both the victorious and defeated candidates referred to issues in explaining the 1958 election. Answering questions asked by *U.S. News and World Report* (Nov. 14, 1958, pp. 44–48, 100–08), candidates commented as follows:

Democrats who unseated Republicans

Harrison A. Williams, Jr., New Jersey, Senate: "It seems to me that economic problems were overriding in the minds of most of the people in this state; questions of inflation, cost of living—whether it was high rents or high cost of money and the interest they had to pay, mortgages and other things. . . . And of course, the recession at the same time with its impact—you have 200,000 unemployed in New Jersey."

William T. Murphy, Chicago, House: "Voters appeared chiefly concerned with recession, unemployment, high cost of living, blundering in foreign affairs."

Denver D. Hargis, Kansas City, Kan., House: "Our district has been plagued with unemployment."

R. Vance Hartke, Indiana, Senate: "I found that people were definitely and vitally interested in the economic issues of the day—that is, in just plain figuring out how to make ends meet."

Frank Kowalski, Connecticut (at large), House: "Two things combined to produce a Democratic sweep: the political personality of Governor Ribicoff, and the dissatisfaction of the people. I found the people unhappy about unemployment, high prices, and the business slump."

In 1959 and 1960, the Republicans made a partial comeback from their 1958 loss of public confidence on both the peace and prosperity issues—but only a partial comeback, as Figure 2 shows. The party regained about half the advantage it had held on the peace issue before sputnik and cut in half the advantage the Democrats had gained on the prosperity issue during the 1957–58 recession.[46] But analysis of the AIPO polls of the period shows that the Democratic advantage was strong and broad not only on the prosperity issue alone but on the entire range of domestic questions.

Table 11 is a cross-tabulation of answers to two questions on two 1959 polls. The questions were the familiar one, "What is the most important problem facing this country today?" and a follow-up, "Which political party do you think can do a better job of handling the problem you have just mentioned?" The problems mentioned were grouped under a dozen headings, identical in the two polls. One of these covered the entire range of questions of foreign policy, relations with Russia, and war and peace. Another concerned nuclear testing. These were the only two categories on which those identifying the issue in question gave the Republican party a stronger vote of confidence than the Democrats, and in each case the

---

Republicans defeated by Democrats

Fife Symington; Baltimore County, Md., House: "The national trend with its overtone of recession influenced the independent voter away from Republicans."

Albert P. Morano, Greenwich, Conn., House: "Most difficult issue was the recession and unemployment in Connecticut. Republican Party has had to suffer for economic dips ever since the 1929 depression."

John D. Hoblitzell, West Virginia, Senate: "West Virginia's loss was due to the recession, efficient labor organization, technological unemployment in the mining areas. . . ."

Reelected Democrats

John D. Dingell, Detroit, Mich., House: "The campaign issues in my district, as in most other districts, were Republican lack of concern and inaction in the face of a severe nation-wide recession."

G. Mennen Williams, Governor of Michigan: "The largest issue in the Michigan campaign was the situation of unemployment and recession. This was particularly acute here in Michigan because of our automobile industry suffering from a lack of market due to the national recession."

[46] The SRC election poll of 1960 generally confirmed the AIPO findings as of the time of the election. Its question on the peace issue, almost identical with AIPO's, was, "Now looking ahead, do you think the problem of keeping out of war would be handled better in the next four years by the Republicans, or by the Democrats, or about the same by both?" It showed a 29–15 percent advantage in favor of the Republicans, a difference about equal to that found by AIPO; a greater percentage, however, saw no difference between the parties or expressed no opinion. The question on the prosperity issue, while worded somewhat differently, confirmed the Democratic advantage (SRC study 440).

margin was relatively narrow. On every other issue the Democratic party maintained the advantage, and in some cases—as on the 1958 questions of unemployment and the missile gap, as well as farm policy, education, and juvenile delinquency—the advantage was overwhelming.

Table 11. *Voters' Confidence in Parties' Handling of Important Problems, 1959*[a]

	Num-ber of re-spon-dents	Percent of respondents indicating choice[b]				
Problem		More confidence in Republicans	More confidence in Democrats	No difference between parties	No opinion or no answer	Total
Keeping the peace, dealing with Russia, foreign policy, external communism	3,633	31	28	29	12	100
Unemployment	404	14	46	25	15	100
Integration, racial disputes, civil rights	401	16	35	30	19	100
National defense, preparedness	89	8	35	35	22	100
Economic problems, including high prices, high taxes, inflation, recession	1,033	26	40	27	7	100
Space, sputnik, missiles	96	21	50	20	9	100
Education	99	12	31	45	12	100
Farm problems	102	5	69	20	7	100
Nuclear testing	168	23	21	37	19	100
Juvenile delinquency	249	11	32	33	24	100
Labor union problems, strikes	276	34	38	17	11	100
All others	413	20	32	31	17	100
No answer, don't know	552	—	—	—	—	—
All problems[c]	7,515	25	31	27	18	100

[a] Based on 7,515 responses to: "What do you think is the most important problem facing this country today?" and "Which political party do you think can do a better job of handling the problem you have just mentioned—the Republican Party or the Democratic Party?" (AIPO 612-K, March 31, 1959, and 618-K, Sept. 16, 1959).
[b] Percentages sometimes do not add to 100 because of rounding.
[c] Includes those who did not identify a problem but did respond to confidence question.

The unkindest cut of all, from the standpoint of the Republicans, must have been the voters' views on the GOP's own chosen issue—inflation.

Insofar as the Republicans had been able to arouse public concern about "spending," deficits, taxes, and inflation, the evidence that they gained any political benefit is, at best, doubtful. The responses between 1956 and 1960 to a series of AIPO questions on price inflation indicate that the

Republicans were actually being penalized as the party in power and the benefits were redounding to the Democrats.

In response to the question, "Which political party. . .do you think is most interested in keeping prices down?" or a similar question,[47] the following choices were indicated:

Response	Sept. 1956	Dec. 1957	March 1959	July 1959	May 1960
			Percent of total		
Republican	26	19	28	23	39
Democratic	30	40	35	38	45
No difference	25	20	26	27	16
No opinion	19	21	11	12	—
	100	100	100	100	100

Asked about one of the 1959 polls, President Eisenhower gave what may be a reasonable explanation. He pointed out that, although the cost of living had risen only 7 percent in seven years, each fractional increase was headlined in the press as "a new high" even if it were as tiny as one-tenth of 1 percent.[48]

By 1960, however, the Survey Research Center found that the onus of being the party of high prices rested on the Democrats. Of its national sample, 30 percent thought prices would be more likely to increase under the Democrats, and 17 percent under the Republicans (the remainder thought the election would make little or no difference or had no opinion).[49]

On the unemployment-prosperity issue there could be no question that the Democratic advantage continued through 1960. As Figure 2 indicates, in mid-1960 the Democratic rating as "the party of prosperity" was only slightly under the peak reached during the 1957–58 recession. The AIPO obtained similar answers when the question was phrased differently. In July 1960 the query, "What about business conditions next year—do you think they will be better if a Republican is elected president, or better if a Democrat is elected president?" drew a 39 percent vote for the Democrats

[47] AIPO releases, Sept. 28, 1956; Dec. 31, 1957; March 18, 1959; July 25, 1959; and "The Polls," *Public Opinion Quarterly*, Vol. 25 (Spring 1961), p. 132. Variants of the wording were: "Which party—the Republican or Democratic—do you think is best able to solve this problem [keeping prices down]?" and, "Which of these two men, Nixon or Kennedy, if elected President, do you think would do the most effective job of handling this problem [dealing with the threat of inflation and increases in the cost of living]?"
[48] On July 29, 1959, *Public Papers of the Presidents, 1959*, p. 552.
[49] SRC study 440.

against 19 percent for the Republicans, with 42 percent neutral or without an opinion.[50] And a few weeks later, a similar question found the Democrats favored by 44–31 percent.[51] Asking the question again in individual and family terms, the SRC found 19 percent of its respondents thought they would be better off financially if the Democrats won, and 12 percent if the Republicans won, with a big majority seeing no difference between the parties.[52]

An analysis of the switchers between the 1956 and 1960 presidential elections, based upon the October 1960 preelection AIPO poll, shows that the net gains by the Democrats were disproportionately heavy among voters most concerned with unemployment and with the missile gap and related national defense questions, as in 1958, and disproportionately light among voters most concerned with foreign policy. The Democrats also gained substantially from voters mentioning economic problems other than unemployment, a further indication that the Kennedy campaign appeal to end "economic stagnation" and "get the country moving again" had a stronger effect than Republican warnings about Democratic spending and inflation. In addition, education had finally emerged as an effective Democratic issue, and the question of American prestige abroad, which Kennedy labored to develop in the campaign, may have been making a tiny contribution to his candidacy. The relative pulling power of the principal issues most favoring the Democrats and the other issues, principally of foreign policy, favoring the Republicans are shown in Table 12.

The Kennedy Mandate

"The voter emerges," wrote Key, "as a person who appraises the actions of government, who has policy preferences, and who relates his vote to those appraisals and preferences."[53] The analyses in this chapter of the period 1954–60 confirm the conclusion Key reached from his study of a longer period. In short, issues do count. By their votes the people do

[50] AIPO release, July 29, 1960.

[51] *Ibid.*, Sept. 2, 1960. The question was: "Suppose that between now and the election it begins to look as if business is going to be bad the next two or three years. In that case would you prefer to have the Republicans in office or the Democrats?"

[52] SRC study 440.

[53] *The Responsible Electorate*, pp. 58–59.

Table 12. *Switches in Voting Preference, 1956–60*[a]

Problem identified as most important	1956 Republicans		1956 Democrats		Other voters		Index of relative pulling power to Democrats[b]
	No.	*Percent switching to Democrats in 1960*	No.	*Percent switching to Republicans in 1960*	No.	*Percent supporting Democrats in 1960*	
Unemployment	48	63	83	7	61	84	.9
Other domestic economic problems, including inflation, high prices	124	29	106	4	110	68	.3
Defense, preparedness, missile lag	58	59	45	7	30	53	.5
Education problems	21	81	15	20	18	67	.3
American prestige	8	75	10	0	6	33	.1
All other issues[e]	1,168	25	634	8	645	58	—2.2

[a] Based on 2,944 responses to: "What do you think is the most important problem facing this country today?" and "If the presidential election were being held today, which candidates would you vote for—the Democratic candidates Kennedy and Johnson, or the Republican candidates Nixon and Lodge?" followed by another question to the undecided: "As of today, do you lean more to Kennedy and Johnson or more to Nixon and Lodge?" (AIPO 637-K, Oct. 18, 1960). See Table 4, notes a-d, for basis and method of computation.
[b] Total in this column does not add to zero because of rounding.
[e] Primarily foreign policy (other domestic issues were either minor or approximately neutral in terms of relative pulling power).

exercise their right of proprietorship and determine the policy and program direction of their government.

But, as in other years—like 1932 and 1952—when the people changed party tenure in the White House, the mandate of the voters was clear only in its general outlines, obscure in its particulars. If the campaign issues are divided into three broad categories—domestic issues, international and foreign issues, and the quasi-issue of Kennedy's Catholicism—then Kennedy's mandate grew almost wholly from the first of these. Indeed, the mandate for a redirection of the course of government on domestic problems had to be strong enough to offset his losses on the other issues. By all the evidence, the people were not dissatisfied with the Republican handling of international matters; their confidence in the GOP as the party of peace was still evident after Eisenhower gave way to Nixon as its leader. And Kennedy lost heavily on the religious issue, as the analysis by Philip Converse, in particular, has shown.[54] But on domestic affairs the people had already rebuked the Republicans in 1954 and castigated them in 1958. There was no sign that the electorate had changed its mind. The message was simply repeated in 1960.

Among the domestic issues, the clearest expression was, of course, on unemployment. The people said, in their votes as in their responses to survey questions, that they would not tolerate recessions. They wanted sustained economic growth and the reemployment of the idle. They did not specify the means—fiscal policy, monetary policy, structural measures —that was for the experts to figure out. An exception was the Area Redevelopment Act: Kennedy had made that twice-vetoed bill the symbol of his promises to deal with unemployment, and the response from the depressed areas of the nation was decisive enough to comprise a mandate from those areas alone.

On education, too, the voice of the people was plain. Every public opinion study had revealed a broad majority endorsement of the principle of federal aid for school construction. By 1960 the impact of the issue on the election was measurable, and in Kennedy's favor. In the light of the narrowness of his margin, any issue that gave him a few thousand votes could be construed as *the* issue that made the difference in his election. Education, like area redevelopment, was such an issue.

On civil rights the voice of the people was not so clear. A southern minority spoke vociferously in one voice, a northern and western majority less forcefully in another. But the majority had written the powerful civil rights platform pledges on which Kennedy ran; that was the major policy issue that split the Democratic convention at Los Angeles, and the majority there did not compromise. If the people were not ahead of Kennedy, assigning him a mandate, the party that chose him was.

Despite the emphasis in the Democratic campaign on medicare, there is almost no evidence in public opinion data that the issue influenced the election. This is due, perhaps, to the wording of the question used in the surveys analyzed in this chapter: a person might feel that health care was the most important problem facing him, or his parents—and might be intending to cast his vote on the basis of that issue—but still not bring himself to tell a polltaker that it was the most important issue *facing the country.* The popular strength of the issue became clear enough in the

[54] "Religion and Politics: The 1960 Fiction," in Angus Campbell and others, *Elections and the Political Order* (Wiley, 1966), pp. 96–124. See also Key, *The Responsible Electorate*, pp. 114–23.

early Kennedy years to perhaps justify its being judged retroactively as a part of the Kennedy mandate.

That much, at least, the people voted for in 1960. But, it should be added in deference to the promises of both candidates, the people wanted these things done without unbalancing the budget, without inflation, and with a reduction, sooner or later, in the national debt.

To say that the election was that much of a popular expression on the issues is not to discount two other election factors of undoubted impact—personality and habitual voting patterns.

There is no question that the Kennedy personality proved appealing, and in a sense decisive. But the personality of a candidate is more than his youth, his poise, his voice, and his smile. It is the combination of these with what he stands for. Kennedy's personality registered as dynamic and vigorous, which suited the mood of the people in 1960; but if by chance he had been cast in Nixon's role, of defending the record of a conservative administration and striking only half-heartedly in new directions, would he have made the same impression of vigor and dynamism? When he promised to "get the country moving again" the people responded, but the response was not just to the unfamiliar accent in which the words were spoken. It was also to the content of the words themselves.

Much the same can be said of voting habits. It was true in 1960—as in 1954—that a Democratic victory would have been no more than the normal expression of the country's Democratic majority. But to argue that, for that reason, the election was automatic and issues were not decisive would be, essentially, to beg the question. If the straying Democrats were simply coming home after their eight-year excursion with Eisenhower, they were still not coming home blindly. They knew what awaited there. They understood, if not all of the specific actions the party promised, at least its general approach to government.[55] As McClosky and his associates so lucidly pointed out, the Democratic party may be the majority party for no other reason than that most of the people agree with its basic philosophy. It became the majority party some time ago, it is true, when Roosevelt wooed an earlier generation with the program and philosophy of

[55] As Donald E. Stokes and Warren E. Miller have written, "Especially on the broad problem of government action to secure social and economic welfare it can be argued that the parties have real differences and that these have penetrated the party images to which the electorate responds at the polls" ("Party Government and the Saliency of Congress," in Angus Campbell and others, *Elections and the Political Order* [Wiley, 1966], p. 210). Their argument as a whole is that the specific policy content of congressional elections is decidedly limited.

the New Deal, and it may be that many Democrats had not thought much since that time about the reasons for their party loyalty. But the policies and programs of Democratic leaders since that time, down to and including Kennedy, were faithful to the Roosevelt tradition. If the election of 1960 were no more than an unthinking return of Democrats to the faith of their fathers, that in itself would be a mandate to the Democratic victors—to do what was expected of them, to apply the Roosevelt-born tradition to the issues of the 1960's.

The Democratic tradition the voters endorsed was, in a word, one of activism. It was the activist approach to public problems—open-minded, innovative, willing to employ the powers of government (or, as seen from the opposing point of view, rash)—that characterized the Democratic program developed in the 1950's and both the attitude and the substance of the Kennedy campaign. The election cannot be interpreted as a clear endorsement of all of the specific policy proposals in the Democratic program. But it was a clear endorsement of an approach to domestic problems, of a governing temper—and tempo. That was the mandate Kennedy asked for. That was the mandate he was given.

CHAPTER XI

Ideas and Laws

THE VOTERS' MANDATE to the Democratic party in 1960 was not one that could be promptly and smoothly executed. The election had been one of the closest in American history. What Kennedy had gained on the domestic issues he had all but lost on the other factors that influenced the voting—on his Catholicism surely, and probably on issues of foreign policy as well. In the House of Representatives the Democratic party actually had won twenty-one fewer seats than it had carried two years earlier. And while it still held a 262–174 majority, by the nature of the Democratic party that was not a sufficient margin to enable Kennedy to fulfill the promises of his campaign.

"For government to function," wrote V. O. Key, "the obstructions of the constitutional mechanism must be overcome, and it is the party that casts a web, at times weak, at times strong, over the dispersed organs of government and gives them a semblance of unity."[1] But, as Key was careful to say, the web may be either strong or weak; it is only as strong as the governing party is itself unified. The Democratic presidential party was unified enough in 1961 around its activist philosophy and program, but the congressional party was something else again. In the once-solid South, all men had been Democrats, whatever their views on public policy. When a new member came to Congress, no ideological tests were imposed. If the member called himself a Democrat, that sufficed: he automatically assumed his share of the party's legislative power, and if he remained in Congress, his power grew with seniority.

Accordingly, when President Kennedy assumed office, he confronted

[1] *Politics, Parties, and Pressure Groups* (5th ed.; Crowell, 1964), p. 656.

471

in his congressional majorities a body of men and women ranging the whole ideological spectrum of each house. The elected party leadership—the speaker, the majority leaders and their assistants—represented the mainstream of party thinking, but occupying many of the key committee chairmanships were men who possessed little more than a sentimental attachment to the national party and who were hostile to much or all of the party's program. Enactment of the program depended, then, upon persuading these Democrats to yield to the majority view, bypassing them through procedural devices, or stripping them of their power. Beyond that was the problem of the rank and file; Kennedy's eighty-eight-vote Democratic majority in the House included too many Democrats-in-name-only, uncommitted to the party program as presented in the platform and the campaign.

Kennedy had lived long enough in both houses of Congress to be thoroughly aware of the pitfalls. There were those who urged that he begin his term with a frontal attack upon the seniority system in order to put the machinery of Congress in the hands of those who believed in the party program—as Woodrow Wilson had done successfully in 1913 but no president had attempted since. But, observes Sorensen, Kennedy "knew he lacked the votes to put through any of the sweeping reforms required to enable a majority to work its will in each house."[2] He had to rely upon the normal presidential arts of pressure and persuasion and upon lesser reforms in congressional organization. Most important, among the latter, was the reform of the House Rules Committee, which had wreaked such havoc upon the Democratic program during the Eisenhower administration.

The Rules Committee had an 8–4 Democratic majority, but two of its members, Chairman Howard Smith of Virginia and William Colmer of Mississippi, were among the most unreconstructed Democrats in the entire House. Unless something were done, Smith and Colmer had the power to bottle up any part of the Kennedy program in the committee by 6–6 tie votes. "Nothing controversial would come to the floor of Congress," said the President; "our whole program would be emasculated."[3] Speaker Sam Rayburn, with the President's backing, assumed tactical command of the battle to strip Smith and Colmer of their veto power. He first threatened to purge Colmer from the committee for his failure to

---

[2] Theodore C. Sorensen, *Kennedy* (Harper & Row, 1965), p. 346.
[3] Quoted by Sorensen, *ibid.*, p. 340.

support Kennedy in the 1960 election, then retreated, in discussion with moderate southerners, to a preplanned compromise position—the committee would be enlarged by the addition of two Democrats and a Republican. Two additional administration supporters would give Kennedy and Rayburn a narrow but reasonably reliable 8–7 margin.

The new administration threw all of its resources into the struggle. The Republicans and southern Democrats mobilized their strength also. Lobbyists representing conservative and liberal organizations reinforced the two sides. Rayburn entered the well of the House for one of his rare floor speeches. Yet the popular speaker and the Kennedy administration— in its "honeymoon" period—could win for this relatively moderate and modest procedural reform only a five-vote margin. It carried 217–212.[4]

The vote reflected, more accurately than any other tally in the Eighty-seventh Congress, the fundamental alignment of the House of Representatives between activists and conservatives. Indeed, in view of the extraordinary pressure applied by Kennedy and Rayburn, it may even have overstated the activist strength. All northern and western Democrats, but barely one-third of the southern Democrats followed their party leadership.[5] Twenty-two Republicans—one-eighth of their party membership— voted for reform. In planning legislative strategy for his entire program, Kennedy could never forget that his basic margin in the House of Representatives consisted of just five votes.[6]

The Democratic Program Blocked

Nevertheless, the President methodically sent forward to Congress in 1961 most of the program measures to which his party was committed. The priority accorded a particular measure depended on many factors— the emphasis given to it in the Kennedy campaign; its political strength; the extent to which it had been considered, refined, and agreed upon by

---

[4] The story of the 1961 House rules fight is well told in Neil MacNeil, *Forge of Democracy* (McKay, 1963), Chap. 15; William R. MacKaye, *A New Coalition Takes Control: The House Rules Committee Fight of 1961* (Eagleton Institute Case 29; McGraw-Hill, 1963); and Richard Bolling, *House Out of Order* (Dutton, 1965), pp. 210–20. The unsuccessful Senate fight in the same year to modify rule 22, in which the President took no part, is told in Alan Rosenthal, *Toward Majority Rule in the United States Senate* (Eagleton Institute Case 25: McGraw-Hill, 1962).

[5] Two Democrats from border districts voted with the southern majority.

[6] Sorensen, *Kennedy*, pp. 340–42.

Democratic legislators during the Eisenhower years; the relative standing and degree of impatience of the prospective congressional sponsors; the existence or nonexistence of any substantial challenge from within the President's official family. On these bases, area redevelopment won the coveted designation as S. 1 of the Eighty-seventh Congress—introduced with the Kennedy blessing even before the inauguration—and aid to education and medicare quickly followed the swearing-in. The Youth Conservation Corps and manpower retraining were delayed, primarily by administrative and cost-effectiveness questions raised by career staff of the Bureau of the Budget, and they were substantially revised from their pre-1961 form before they were ultimately submitted. Only on civil rights measures did the President renege on his own and the party's program.[7] On fiscal measures to reduce unemployment—as distinct from structural measures like area redevelopment—the party and the President had no clear commitment. The accelerated public works bill was recommended in 1962, but tax reduction as the major fiscal initiative of the Kennedy administration had to await the President's "education in the White House" and the precipitating influence of the stock market collapse of May 1962 —although one can certainly speculate that he would have moved sooner in response to his economic advisers if the congressional climate had been more hospitable.[8]

The presidential party thus fulfilled its commitment to the party's legislative program. But the same cannot be said of the congressional party. When the Eighty-seventh Congress adjourned, the Kennedy domestic program was in shambles. It was almost as though the Democratic party had not presented in the campaign of 1960 a concrete and specific program and won from the people the mandate that it sought.[9]

[7] See Chap. 6, pp. 256–58.

[8] See Carroll Kilpatrick, "The Kennedy Style and Congress," *Virginia Quarterly Review*, Vol. 39 (1963), pp. 4, 10. "Congress through Chairman Mills had in effect dictated the President's position to him," argues Kilpatrick, referring to Wilbur Mills of the House Ways and Means Committee.

[9] Sorensen, in *Decision-Making in the White House* (Columbia University Press, 1963), p. 47, observed that Congress "has consistently enacted four-fifths" of the Kennedy program. This, however, is a quantitative measure that gives the same weight to minor as to major proposals, and the Sorensen appraisal covers foreign policy legislation as well as domestic proposals. In 1962 Kennedy gave highest priority to a foreign policy measure—the trade expansion act—and successfully steered it through Congress. For a complete listing of successes and failures in the Kennedy program, see *Congressional Quarterly Almanac, 1962*, pp. 82–91. See also Arthur M. Schlesinger, Jr., *A Thousand Days* (Houghton Mifflin, 1965), p. 713.

Table 13 sets forth the progress in the Eighty-seventh Congress of the measures identified in Chapter 9 as principal elements of the Democratic party program evolved during the Eisenhower era. Of the eleven measures, only three—the Area Redevelopment Act, the Manpower Develop-

Table 13. *Disposition of Major Democratic Party Measures by the Eighty-seventh Congress, 1961–62*

Issue and measure	Date adopted as party measure[a]	Date recommended by President Kennedy	Disposition
Unemployment			
Area redevelopment	1956	January 1961	Enacted
Youth Conservation Corps	1959	June 1961	Killed by House Rules Committee
Manpower development and training	1959	May 1961	Enacted
Education			
Aid for elementary and secondary schools	1955, 1960	February 1961	Killed by House Rules Committee
Aid for college construction	1958	February 1961	Killed by House Rules Committee in 1961, by House in 1962
Civil rights			
Power to initiate civil rights enforcement (Part III)	1958	Not recommended	—
Fair employment practices; elimination of poll taxes and literacy tests	1960	Not recommended	—
Medicare	1958	February 1961	Defeated in Senate; killed by House Ways and Means Committee
Outdoor environment			
Expansion of water pollution control grants	1959	February 1961	Enacted
Wilderness preservation	1959	February 1961	Died in House
National seashores	1959	b	b

a From Table 3, pp. 412–13.
b Each seashore acquisition was handled as an individual bill; three were enacted in 1961–62.

ment and Training Act, and expansion of grants for water pollution
control—had become law by 1962. A part of the seashore acquisition
program had been enacted. (The Accelerated Public Works Act, embraced by the President early in 1962, also had passed.) All the others
had died somewhere along the way. Three of the eleven were killed in
the House Rules Committee. Medicare was killed on the Senate floor, as
well as in a House committee. Wilderness preservation died in the House.
The party's civil rights program—redefined, expanded, and emphasized
in the party platform—never left the White House.

Where, in the institutional structure, did the failure lie? It is easy to
point the finger at the House Rules Committee as the chief culprit, and
observers at the time did not hesitate to do so. But if the Rules Committee
had released the three measures it killed, it is far from certain that they
would have passed. The committee, once it was reconstituted with its
8–7 Kennedy-Rayburn majority, reflected with some precision the makeup
of the House as a whole; if anything, it was more favorably disposed toward the Kennedy program than was the full body, if one takes the 217–
212 vote on the Rules Committee reform as defining the basic House
posture on domestic issues. A proposal that could pass the House could,
in all probability, clear the Rules Committee with equal or greater ease.

The evidence is clearest in the case of aid for elementary and secondary
schools. In 1961 no majority existed for any specific aid bill. Even though
popular support stood at 60 to 70 percent for federal aid to education as
an abstract issue, that majority dwindled as soon as the terms of treatment
for Catholic schools were specified. One segment of supporters preferred
no bill to one that helped the parochial schools; another, no bill to one
that excluded them. A third group in the electorate was, of course, opposed to any bill. The nation had not a workable consensus but a three-
way split among groups whose views were, in 1961, irreconcilable. And
the division in the country was reflected with far greater intensity in Congress, where the pressures were focused. The review of the 1961 fight in
Chapter 5 leads to the conclusion that if the Catholic, Republican, and
southern Democratic opponents of the Kennedy aid to education bill had
not killed it in the Rules Committee, the same combination of forces would
have killed it on the House floor.

In the case of aid to colleges and universities, the evidence is less conclusive but still persuasive. In the heated battle over the elementary and
secondary school bill, the higher education bill had been little noticed,
and when the Rules Committee killed both in a single motion, the latter

measure appeared to have been stricken as an innocent bystander. Yet the Rules Committee coalition knew what was in the bills and knew what it was doing; if no Rules Committee had existed and the two bills had reached the floor by other procedures, would not the House as a whole have reacted in 1961 just as its committee did and disposed of both in the same way? The defeat of the college aid bill in 1962, when it was presented to the House on its own merits as a separate measure, suggests that it could not have been passed in 1961 either.

Much the same comment can be made in the case of the Youth Conservation Corps. Backed only half-heartedly by an administration divided over its merits, it was eventually buried in the Rules Committee in 1962 because it endangered the political future of one member of the eight-man majority on that committee—Carl Elliott of Alabama. But how many moderate southerners were in the same position as Carl Elliott? If the bill had reached the floor by other means, would it not have been defeated by a combination of Republicans, southern Democratic opponents of the program, and a score or so of Elliotts who would find that voting for integrated youth camps might jeopardize their careers?

The death of the wilderness bill can be attributed to the unrepresentative character of the House Interior Committee, which overrepresents the western states and their industries dependent upon exploitation of the public lands. The only version of a wilderness bill the committee would approve was one that was unacceptable to the original bill's conservationist backers, and the bill therefore was allowed to die without being brought to a vote in the House.

While the defeat of medicare occurred ostensibly in the Senate, it can more properly be attributed to the House. If the House had passed the bill, or if its passage had been possible, it is likely that the votes necessary for Senate approval would have been provided by Senators Jennings Randolph, Carl Hayden, and possibly others who under the circumstances of 1962 voted nay.[10] The House Ways and Means Committee was therefore the measure's true burial place. But, like the Rules Committee, the Ways and Means Committee accurately reflected the makeup of the House itself. Chairman Wilbur Mills was representative not just of the second district of Arkansas but of his region; medicare had little backing anywhere in the South. And such vote counts as were taken indicated that the bill did not command majority support in the House in 1962.

[10] See Chap. 7, pp. 313–14.

Those who argue that approval by the Ways and Means Committee would have led to the passage of medicare base their argument on the assumption that the prestige of Wilbur Mills and the committee majority would have been sufficient to sway a critical number of votes. But the consequence would have followed from the fact that a *conservative* chairman and committee were recommending the bill. If the hypothesis assumes a committee chaired by a Kennedy liberal and controlled by administration supporters—in other words a committee unrepresentative of the House—its recommendations would carry little weight beyond that already provided by the President himself.

The Ways and Means Committee is, of course, a powerful body in itself. It not only writes major legislation but its Democratic members determine the committee assignments of the party's House members. Thus the committee and its chairman, had they been determined backers of medicare, could conceivably have used sanctions to coerce Democratic members opposed to medicare to vote against their convictions. But to argue thus is not to demonstrate that the Ways and Means Committee in the Eighty-seventh Congress thwarted the will of the House. It is, rather, to posit that a differently constituted committee could have used its power to thwart the will of a House that, in the absence of such pressure, would have rejected medicare.

On the basis of the evidence from these five measures, it is neither fair nor accurate to blame the failure of the Kennedy domestic program in the Eighty-seventh Congress primarily upon congressional organization or procedure—the power of the reformed House Rules Committee,[11] the seniority system, or any other of Congress' internal processes. The failure of Congress to enact the Kennedy program is chargeable, rather, to the simple fact that the voters who elected Kennedy did not send to Congress enough supporters of his program. His razor-thin popular majority was reflected in a Congress formally Democratic but actually narrowly balanced between activists and conservatives. If the machinery of both houses had been entirely controlled by supporters of the Kennedy program, that in itself would not have changed the convictions of the members so as

[11] The reform of the Rules Committee, however, was highly important to enactment of that part of the program that did pass. In the debate on the accelerated public works bill in 1962, for example, Representative William H. Avery of Kansas, a Republican member of the Rules Committee, noted that the bill was cleared by only an 8–6 vote and pointed out that if the committee had not been "packed" at the beginning of 1961 the bill "would have met a very logical and a very quiet rejection in the House Committee on Rules" (*Cong. Record,* Vol. 108 [Aug. 28, 1962], p. 17925).

to produce a dependable administration majority. The machinery might have been used more effectively to coerce Democratic congressmen into voting in opposition to their convictions—but that is another matter.

There remains the question of the Kennedy leadership. Some frustrated supporters of the Kennedy program, surveying the wreckage, fixed a share of the blame upon the President himself. He had been diffident in dealing with the leaders of Congress, so the criticism went; his aides had been clumsy; the President had not appealed over the head of Congress to the people. The criticisms were accurate enough as to the President's leadership style. "Kennedy, particularly in his first year . . . felt somewhat uncomfortable and perhaps too deferential with these men who the previous year outranked him," writes Sorenson. He "generally resisted urgings of disappointed partisans who would have him stir up the public against . . . Congress."[12] "There is no sense," Schlesinger quotes Kennedy as saying, "in raising hell, and then not being successful. There is no sense in putting the office of the Presidency on the line on an issue, and then being defeated." Kennedy quoted Jefferson: "Great innovations should not be forced on slender majorities."[13]

Certainly the public was not stirred. It is not the president's leadership directly of the lawmakers so much as the public reaction to that leadership that wins congressional votes. The polls (summarized below) showed that the people supported the President's program but, lulled by prosperity and the absence of crisis, they were not clamoring for action. In 1962 Majority Leader Mike Mansfield blamed the ineffectiveness of Congress on the "strangely quiescent" mood of the country. "I haven't noticed this year any real desire on the part of the country as a whole for any specific legislation," he said. "It isn't stirred to any degree. It isn't demanding much of this or that."[14]

Whatever the merit of the criticisms of Kennedy's leadership, they beg the essential question. Should it be the normal expectation that a

[12] Sorensen, *Kennedy*, p. 345, and *Decision-Making*, p. 47; he goes on to discuss the President's leadership style in each book.

[13] Schlesinger, *A Thousand Days*, p. 709; he devotes a section to a discussion of Kennedy's relations with Congress (pp. 707–13) and a chapter to his use of the presidency as a "bully pulpit" (Chap. 27). For a critical account of presidential leadership, see Carroll Kilpatrick, "The Kennedy Style and Congress." For a summary of the charges of inept congressional liaison, see Meg Greenfield, "Why Are You Calling Me, Son?" *Reporter*, Aug. 16, 1962.

[14] *U.S. News and World Report*, Sept. 17, 1962. Six months later the magazine found the Congress still reflecting public complacency in a round of congressional interviews reported in, "Why Congress Doesn't Give JFK What He Wants," March 18, 1963.

president must put his office "on the line," must appeal over the heads of Congress to the people, to get his program through? Granted that congressmen can be coerced on occasion through presidential pressures—and his powers of coercion are severely limited, as every student of the presidency has pointed out—is an institutional structure sound that depends for its success upon such use of presidential power? And if the president coerces Congress to act against its will, is the president necessarily right? Would an institutional structure that enhanced his power to impose his will be an improvement in the long run? Is he necessarily a better judge of legislative right and wrong, necessarily more representative of the popular will, than Congress? Most of those who argued in the affirmative, in 1961 and 1962, would have argued in the negative just two years before—and vice versa.

To repeat, the fundamental trouble in the Eighty-seventh Congress was not presidential leadership, just as it was not House organization. The trouble was the ambiguity of the 1960 election. That election did not resolve the partisan conflict between the executive and legislative branches that had wracked the Eisenhower administration in its last two years. It merely reversed the terms of that struggle. In 1959 and 1960, the conservatives controlled the administration and the activists the Congress; after 1960, the activists held the presidency but they had lost enough seats in the House of Representatives to restore effective control of that body, on most controversial domestic issues, to the conservatives. The possibility of control of the two branches of government by opposing political forces is, of course, a hazard peculiar to American democracy. But following elections as narrow as the Kennedy-Nixon contest of 1960, European parliaments can stalemate too, with unstable, caretaker governments. On either side of the Atlantic, decisive government is difficult to achieve if the electorate chooses to express itself indecisively.

Yet the year 1963 was to suggest that the difficult can, on occasion, be achieved. The voters were hardly more decisive in 1962 then they had been two years earlier. The usual off-year reversals to the party in power were held to a minimum, but the Democrats still lost five seats in the House while the Republicans gained three (the House membership was reduced by two seats).[15] In the Senate the Democrats gained two seats.

---

[15] Congressional Quarterly calculated that while Kennedy did not gain in total support in the House, he gained in "hard-core" supporters, so that the House was on balance slightly more favorably disposed toward his programs (*Congressional Quarterly Weekly Report*, Nov. 9, 1962, p. 2133).

The composition of the Eighty-eighth Congress was therefore much like that of the Eighty-seventh. Nevertheless, the new Congress behaved quite differently.

The Democratic Program Unblocked

Looking back upon the legislative successes of the middle 1960's, what appears remarkable is not the prodigious output of the post-Goldwater Eighty-ninth Congress (1965–66) but the achievements of the pre-Goldwater Eighty-eighth (1963–64). The Eighty-ninth Congress performed about as expected. After the 1964 Democratic landslide, it was a foregone conclusion that medicare, aid to education, and the other remaining elements of the stalled party program would be passed. The obstacles to that program had simply been washed away by the Goldwater debacle. But the performance of the Eighty-eighth Congress was not at all what might have been expected upon the basis of the previous record of its members. The Democratic program was unblocked in 1963 and 1964 by a Congress substantially the same in makeup as the one that had blocked that program two years earlier.

The most profound influence upon the new Congress was, of course, the assassination of the President and the country's reaction to that tragedy. Nevertheless, the ice-jam of stalled legislation had been thawing in the months preceding Dallas. In the field of education, Congress had set aside the President's proposal for general aid to elementary and secondary schools, but it had made marked progress upon less explosive items of education legislation. By November the college aid bill had been passed by both houses and the outlook in the conference committee was favorable. Agreement had been negotiated on a wilderness bill. The President was also pressing successfully for bold action in two areas where, in the previous Congress, he had not sought legislation. One was the tax reduction bill, which by November had passed the House. The other, the civil rights bill, had cleared the House Judiciary Committee; the force of public opinion and an incipient petition to discharge the Rules Committee assured it of that committee's clearance in due time and then of prompt House passage.

After the accession of President Johnson, all of these measures completed their way through Congress. In addition, a third major program initiated by Kennedy but put in legislative form by his successor—the

Economic Opportunity Act—was passed. The end result was a notable record of accomplishment for a Congress that, when it assembled, was assumed to be predisposed *against* the Kennedy legislative program.

No one can calculate how much of the result was attributable to the wave of emotion that followed the assassination. Nor can one calculate how much of the result depended upon the skill, energy, and resourcefulness with which President Johnson applied himself to pushing his precedessor's legislative legacy through Congress. Yet the considerable progress of the Kennedy program prior to November suggests strongly that most of what happened would have happened—more slowly, perhaps, but ultimately—if Kennedy had lived.[16] The record of the Eighty-eighth Congress would have been, under any circumstances, strikingly different from that of the Eighty-seventh. Clearly, the members of that body were responding in 1963 to forces not present in the political atmosphere two years before.

What were the forces? Schlesinger emphasizes the cumulative impact of presidential leadership. Kennedy did not hope for immediate results, in many cases, when he sent his recommendations to Congress in 1961. "But he knew that if he sent up a message and bill, there would be debate and hearings; Congress would begin to accustom itself to unfamiliar ideas; the legislation would be revised to meet legitimate objections; the opposition would in time expend itself and seem increasingly frantic and irrelevant; public support would consolidate; and by 1964 or 1965 the bill would be passed."[17] This language could apply as well, incidentally, to the pre-Kennedy years. It describes the hope and expectation of all of the activists in and out of Congress who had put forward in the lean Eisenhower years the measures that Kennedy adopted as his program. It is another way of saying that, if a problem truly exists, time is on the side of those who propose to solve it. But where individual members of Congress, or even blocs of senators and congressmen, have difficulty being heard, the president of the United States is always heard and—when his popularity in the country is high—is given the benefit of the doubt. Thus a Congress that could withstand the power of presidential advocacy for

---

[16] Alan L. Otten has written: "Few well-informed members of Congress or administration lobbyists doubt that Mr. Kennedy would have won from the 1964 session much the same tax, civil rights, education and other vital measures won by Mr. Johnson, and on much of the same timetable" (*Wall Street Journal*, Oct. 19, 1967). See also Rowland Evans and Robert Novak, *Lyndon B. Johnson: The Exercise of Power* (New American Library, 1966), p. 364.

[17] Schlesinger, *A Thousand Days*, p. 710.

two years was bound to have difficulty sustaining its resistance as it faced two more years of leadership and pressure.

But there were other factors. In 1963 many of the influences that had served to weaken the President's position in the previous Congress had faded or disappeared. The narrow election of 1960 had receded into the background, superseded by another election that showed, on balance, none of the usual mid-term reaction against the President. His conservative approach to fiscal policy in his first two years had won him an essential measure of confidence from the business community. He had earned further confidence by his courage and firmness in the 1962 Cuban missile crisis, which now superseded the earlier Bay of Pigs fiasco as the symbol of the administration's mastery of foreign policy. The President was riding high in the presidential popularity polls.[18] And both the administration and the Congress—as well as their allies outside the government—had learned from two years of deadlock. Notably in the field of education, legislative strategy was skilfully designed to skirt the pitfalls that had beset the Kennedy program earlier.[19] White House liaison practices that had ruffled sensitive congressmen were altered.[20] The approach of the 1964 election also had its influence: Kennedy would be heading the Democratic ticket in every congressional district, and to weaken the President by defeating his program would be to weaken the entire ticket. Not having been accorded in 1961 the "honeymoon" with Congress to which a new president is traditionally entitled, Kennedy seemed on his way to being granted, under the pressures for party unity, a kind of compensatory period of grace.

The Democratic leadership in the crucial House was also more effective in the Eighty-eighth Congress than in the Eighty-seventh. The year 1962 had been the "shakedown cruise," as one observer has put it, for the new speaker, John McCormack, the new majority leader, Carl Albert of Oklahoma, and the other members of their leadership team. The McCormack-

[18] In January 1963 the American Institute of Public Opinion found that 76 percent of its sample approved of the way Kennedy was handling his job, with only 13 percent disapproving. From this high point, his popularity fell to a 59–28 approval-disapproval ratio in November. The decline was largely in the South and was attributed to his stand on civil rights.

[19] See Chap. 5, pp. 210–11. See also Sorensen, *Kennedy*, p. 359.

[20] For a discussion of the liaison organization and its methods, see interview with Lawrence F. O'Brien, chief liaison officer under Presidents Kennedy and Johnson, *U.S. News and World Report*, Sept. 20, 1965, pp. 68–73. Also see MacNeil, *Forge of Democracy*, pp. 255–69.

Kennedy relationship had been complicated by the Massachusetts senatorial contest between the speaker's nephew and the President's brother—which, while it did not spill over into hostility between the Washington members of the families, nevertheless did not make for intimacy in planning legislative maneuvers. By 1963 that issue was settled and the McCormack-Albert leadership had more firmly established itself. Moreover, the Democratic Study Group had converted itself from a "guerilla band," as its role in the Eisenhower years has been described, to a disciplined ally of the House leadership in mobilizing supporters of the Kennedy program. Finally, public opinion polls continued to show that the people supported the principal elements of the Kennedy program—with the probable exceptions of aid for teacher salaries and, at least until late in 1963, of the tax cut.

Public Opinion and the Kennedy Program. By 1961, medicare had become the most popular Democratic legislative measure. A pre-inauguration poll by the American Institute of Public Opinion (AIPO) that asked what the new President and the new Congress should do found that 52 percent of the respondents mentioned federal aid for medical care of the aged—a number second only to the 63 percent who mentioned holding down prices and preventing inflation. Nearly half, or 46 percent, said the government should "do more to end segregation" and 40 percent proposed federal aid to education. Each of these figures exceeded the 37 percent who wanted the government to balance the budget by cutting spending.[21] In June the poll found a 67–26 percent majority in favor of "having the social security tax increased in order to pay for old age medical insurance," with 7 percent undecided.[22] By the next year the effects of the invigorated American Medical Association campaign against medicare could be measured in the polls, but they still gave the social security proposal a majority. In March the AIPO respondents voted 55–34 percent in favor of the social security approach over a voluntary alternative plan, and in June 48–41 percent, with 11 percent undecided in each case.[23]

[21] AIPO release, Jan. 8, 1961.

[22] *Ibid.*, June 9, 1961.

[23]*Ibid.*, July 1, 1962. The question was: "Two different plans are being discussed in Washington for meeting hospital costs for older persons: One plan would let each individual decide whether to join Blue Cross or buy some form of voluntary health insurance. The other plan would cover persons on Social Security and would be paid by increasing the Social Security tax deducted from pay checks. Which of these two plans would you prefer?"

While the public disagreed over the terms of federal aid to education, support for the objective continued to be overwhelming. An AIPO poll in 1961 showed a pro-aid majority of 73 percent,[24] and a Survey Research Center (SRC) inquiry the following year showed that 69 percent of those with opinions favored aid for school districts that needed help in building schools. The proponents split almost evenly, however, on the question of whether religious schools should be included.[25]

The 1963 civil rights legislation had powerful backing outside the South. A poll in June on the public accommodations question showed support among northern whites at 55 percent, with 34 percent opposed and 11 percent undecided. Two months later another poll showed the favorable ratio even higher.[26] The SRC in its 1962 poll showed a majority of 51–32 percent in agreement with the statement, "The government in Washington should see to it that white and colored children are allowed to go to the same schools" (with 17 percent undecided or without an opinion).[27] The following year an AIPO question, "Should each state have the right to decide what it will do about integration, or not?" showed a majority, except in the South, favorable to national action.[28] These findings reflected a dramatic long-term shift in white attitudes toward the Negro and toward integration shown in a series of studies by the National Opinion Research Center at the University of Chicago. Between 1942 and 1963, the NORC found, the proportion of northern whites supporting school integration rose from 40 to 75 percent, and the proportion accepting neighborhood integration from 42 to 70 percent. "In the minds and hearts of the majority of Americans the principle of integration seems already to have been won," the NORC analysts concluded.[29]

The most popular item in the Kennedy program appeared to be the Youth Conservation Corps. "Few issues in polling history have recorded such overwhelming support," said Dr. Gallup in releasing a 1963 tabulation showing 89 percent support with only 6 percent opposed and 5 per-

[24] Frank J. Munger and Richard F. Fenno, Jr., *National Politics and Federal Aid to Education* (Syracuse University Press, 1962), p. 92.

[25] Survey Research Center study 714, Fall 1962.

[26] AIPO releases, July 10 and Sept. 4, 1963. The second release did not break the national total into southern and nonsouthern components, but the national ratio had risen from 49–42 percent to 54–38 percent, with much of the increase registered in the East.

[27] SRC study 714.

[28] AIPO release, Nov. 13, 1963.

[29] Herbert H. Hyman and Paul B. Sheatsley, "Attitudes Toward Desegregation," *Scientific American*, July 1964. Also see Sheatsley, "White Attitudes Toward the Negro," *Daedalus*, Vol. 95, No. 1 (Winter 1966), pp. 217–38.

cent undecided. A similar poll a year earlier had shown a support ratio of 79–16 percent.[30]

Views on the tax cut, at least prior to 1963, appeared to depend on whether the cut were explicitly associated with an increase in the national debt. A 1962 AIPO poll found the public four to one against a tax cut "if a cut meant that the government would go further in debt."[31] But late in 1963 the simple question, "Do you favor or oppose a cut in income taxes now?" showed 60 percent favorable, 29 percent opposed, and 11 percent undecided.[32]

Beyond the specific measures, the pollsters found a favorable reaction to the administration's general tone of activism. "The differences cited by those who favorably compare the course of the present administration with the previous one," wrote Gallup in early 1962, "are sometimes in terms of legislation passed or attempted. More often, however, preference is shown the Kennedy administration in terms of its *approach* to problems. The new regime appears to have caught the mood of many Americans in conveying an impression of forthrightness, directness, energy, and optimism. . . . In brief, an important element behind the current popularity of the Kennedy administration is the feeling that it is a 'do something' administration."[33]

Congressional constituency polls during the Kennedy years bear out the findings of the national surveys that public opinion supported activist domestic measures. Table 14 summarizes the data contained in 145 such polls inserted in the body of the *Congressional Record* during the years 1961–63. Because polls taken by congressmen in their districts are liable to be biased toward the position of the congressman and his party,[34] the favorable attitudes toward Democratic measures found in Republican districts are particularly noteworthy.

The table shows clearly the partisan split within the population. Northern Democratic constituencies (or, more correctly, those portions of the constituencies in communication with the congressmen) were solidly be-

---

[30] AIPO release, Sept. 6, 1963.

[31] *Ibid.*, Aug. 1, 1962.

[32] *Ibid.*, Sept. 29, 1963.

[33] *Ibid.*, Jan. 24, 1962 (italics in the original). The comment was offered on a poll that showed a 50 percent affirmative response to the question, "Have you noticed any marked differences between the Eisenhower administration and the Kennedy administration, or not?" and a 4 to 1 agreement among that 50 percent that "the changes have been generally to the good."

[34] See Chap. 10, pp. 444–45, especially note 24.

Table 14. *Majority Responses to Congressional Constituency Polls on Domestic Legislative Measures, 1961–63*

(Number of polls reporting majority indicated)

Issue and measure[a]	Republicans' Polls		Northern Democrats' Polls		Southern Democrats' Polls	
	For	Against	For	Against	For	Against
Unemployment						
Area redevelopment	7	2	4	0	1	0
Manpower development and training	6	2	1	0	—	—
Public works acceleration	0	6	6	0	0	1
Youth Conservation Corps	7	5	7	0	0	3
Tax cut not offset by spending cut	1	22	2	2	0	2
Education						
Aid to education (phrased generally)	0	32	7	1	0	2
Aid for school construction	15	20	9	0	1	3
Aid for teacher salaries	0	32	6	5	0	4
Scholarships for higher education	11	7	3	1	—	—
Aid for college construction	8	9	7	0	—	—
Medicare						
1961	7	12	3	0	1	0
1962	6	23	12	0	0	2
1963	0	23	4	2	0	4
Civil rights						
Stronger civil rights legislation in general	1	3	2	0	—	—
Stronger voting rights legislation	3	0	2	0	—	—
Fair employment legislation	1	0	3	0	—	—
1963 civil rights bill (or sections thereof)	3	0	2	0	0	2
Outdoor environment						
Wilderness preservation	1	0	3	0	—	—
Expansion of recreation areas	1	0	1	0	—	—

[a] Some questions referred only to a general legislative objective, others to a specific bill. These have been combined, except in the case of medicare, where favorable majorities include only those that specifically supported the mandatory social security approach proposed by Kennedy. A few questions were eliminated from the tabulation because of ambiguity. The data were obtained and tabulated by Constance Holden.

hind the Kennedy program, with the exception of aid for teacher salaries
—a weakness noted in the earlier analysis of the polls of the 1950's—and
the 1963 tax cut. The few southern Democratic constituencies surveyed
were just as solidly opposed to it. On the Republican side, the figures
reflect the division in the party. For those legislative objectives that had
won the endorsement of the Eisenhower administration and of Vice President Nixon before and during the 1960 campaign, the Republican constituencies gave substantial support—majority support for civil rights and
aid to depressed areas, mixed support for education measures. In the 1961
and 1962 polls on medicare the Republican voters in thirteen surveys went
further than the party leadership and embraced the Kennedy proposal for
medicare under social security. By 1963, however, after the AMA campaign against the bill was in full force, every Republican constituency
had fallen into line with the party leadership to reject medicare and support, at most, a voluntary alternative. A majority of the Republican samples also supported the Youth Conservation Corps, which did not win
Republican majority support in Congress.

Taken as a whole, the constituency surveys showed a substantial readiness among Republicans and Democrats alike to embrace activist solutions
to domestic problems. Most voters who opposed a specific Democratic
measure, as in the case of medicare, did so because they preferred a Republican alternative. That segment of the public that remained steadfast
in opposition to any governmental initiative at all had been reduced by
the 1961–63 period to a lonely minority—a circumstance that seems to
have been clear to all except those Republicans who, a short time later,
engineered the nomination of Barry Goldwater.

Favorable public attitudes both set the stage for and were the consequences of presidential leadership. Although Kennedy's initial program
was tempered by his judgment of the mood of Congress and the country,
he still put forward far more measures than Congress would accept and
pressed them selectively where he could find support, all the while carrying on—albeit in restrained style—his task of public education. For the
rest, he bided his time until the public mood changed—or he found opportunity to change it. "The presidential secret was timing," writes Schlesinger.[35] Kennedy's bold initiative on fiscal policy waited the stock market
collapse of 1962, and his civil rights initiative was launched from the
springboard of events in Alabama. The President was criticized for not

[35] *A Thousand Days*, p. 721.

stepping forward on these and other issues earlier, to jolt the country out of its "strangely quiescent" mood; his defenders respond that to have done so would have been futile and would have frittered away his influence. In any case, at the moment when the nation turned to Washington in anxiety and alarm, Kennedy spoke. In doing so, he crystalized and mobilized public opinion—and unblocked his legislative measures.

Development of New Measures

After January 20, 1961, nobody talked any longer about "the Democratic party program"—they talked about "the Kennedy program" and after that "the Johnson program," for the in-party's program is what the president says it is. President Eisenhower may have flirted, in moments of weariness, with the Whig notion that the legislative branch should legislate and the executive branch should execute—although in practice he sent to Capitol Hill a legislative program virtually as complete, in the areas where he believed Congress should act, as that of any other president—but to John Kennedy and Lyndon Johnson the Whig conception of a "weak presidency" had not even fleeting charm. Both explicitly believed in a strong presidency, and both consciously used the vast resources of the office to establish the president firmly in his role of legislative leadership. With the exception of antipollution measures, the major legislative impulses of the 1961–66 period came from a single source—the White House. Members of Congress could retard, accelerate, or deflect those impulses, and they could expand, limit, or modify the specific proposals initiated from the White House. But they could not set in motion the legislative stream itself. Constitutionally, they had every right to do so. Theoretically, perhaps, they had the opportunity. Practically, they did not.

There were many reasons. First of all, Kennedy let it be known before his inauguration that he expected Congress to await his messages. He had appointed responsible Cabinet officers, and they should have the opportunity to examine the measures that were pending when Congress adjourned in 1960 and improve upon them. Only rarely, as in the case of the Area Redevelopment Act, did the President exempt a measure from this process. When, in the other cases, he asked for time to make recommendations, the responsible committee chairmen could hardly do the President the discourtesy of refusing to grant the time. Moreover, the chairmen might as well wait, because without the support of a presidential endorsement a measure had little or no chance of getting leadership clearance for floor consideration.

Even when a Republican occupied the White House, the Democratic leaders and committee chairmen normally awaited White House messages before proceeding with legislation, if they knew that messages were forthcoming. The creative record of Congress in legislative initiative in the 1955–60 period was made in areas where the president did not choose to lead. But the vacuums into which Congress had moved in the 1950's were few in the next decade. Kennedy and Johnson were as eager for new laws as the most activist members of Congress, and they preempted with their initiative the fields where Congress may have been ready to proceed.

Instead of taking independent initiative, therefore, activist members of Congress spent much of their energy in "lobbying" the administration, much like any private citizen or interest group, to advance their particular measures in the scale of presidential priorities or to influence the content of presidential messages and bills. This subordination the members of Congress had difficulty accepting philosophically, even as they recognized its inevitability. Many grumbled openly at their exclusion from deliberations in the executive branch, fretted at the delays in getting presidential recommendations, and complained of what they regarded as capricious changes in bills that had been considered carefully before the transition. One consequence was occasional arbitrary, and sometimes petty, actions by legislators to assert authority. But while the friction may have made the legislative process less enjoyable for the participants in both branches, especially during the transition period, there is no evidence that it resulted in the death of any major presidential measures that otherwise would have lived.

The Dual Legislative Process. When the principle of presidential initiative prevails, a new legislative idea must surmount not one legislative process but two. The procedures within the executive branch for adoption of a proposal are scarcely less elaborate, and sometimes are more deliberate, than the processes of Congress. In both branches, information is gathered and appraised, experts are consulted, formal or informal committees are created to draft bills, political prospects and consequences are weighed, and finally decisions are made. The difference lies less in the procedures than in the setting: in the executive branch the legislative process is for the most part secret and the decisions are the responsibility of a single person; in Congress the proceedings are for the most part in the open and the decisions are the responsibility of many men. Each process has its strengths and weaknesses, but special stresses grow from the circumstance that the two must coexist.

One difficulty is that the legislative process in the executive branch can be taken to foreclose a thorough, open process in the legislative branch. In the 1950's, when the congressional majority felt free to reject or ignore the president's leadership, Democratic measures were considered and refined with extensive participation of the public. Members introduced new ideas tentatively, often explicitly for purposes of discussion, circulated the proposals widely, and put them through successive stages of refinement on the basis of suggestions made in open hearings. Presidential proposals were subjected to the same kind of public review. But congressional chairmen are inhibited from processing in the same manner the proposals of a president of their own party. After all, a strong president does not suggest party policy—he *proclaims* it. Senators and congressmen who challenge the presidential decision risk the suggestion of disloyalty to the party that elected them. They also risk the suggestion—since the president is presumed to represent *all* the people—that the challenge is motivated by only a local, a narrow, or a special interest. And the suggestion carries weight because, sometimes, it is.

The president, for his part, finds it awkward to advance a measure tentatively, for purposes of discussion. He is expected to know what he wants and where he stands. When he presents the product of his legislative process, he presents not suggestions but decisions. "The President's policies emerge in speeches and messages to Congress as holy writ, to be defended stubbornly against criticism and change," observes Alan Otten.[36] Executive officials have little latitude to negotiate the president's recommendations with the Congress. To the extent that the Congress accepts the presidential legislative process as final, or even presumptively final, the basic strength of the legislative process in the Congress—which arises from wide public discussion and democratic participation in decision making—is sacrificed. Yet a review of the presidential decision in an openminded fashion, ab initio, can be seen as an affront to the president and a rejection of his leadership.

Among those who felt most keenly the subordination of the Congress were the public interest groups who had become full partners, in the 1950's, in the formulation of the Democratic legislative program. In 1961

[36] *Wall Street Journal*, Dec. 7, 1966.

they, like the congressmen themselves, became outsiders to the more important legislative process—the one within the executive branch. Like the congressmen, they were consulted not as a matter of right but as a matter of agency discretion—selectively, sporadically, haphazardly. They came no longer as members of the Democratic family but as supplicants to it. They too grumbled at their exclusion, chafed at the delays, and complained that their ideas were not incorporated. Yet often they could not effectively appeal to Congress because neither they nor the legislators wanted to appear in the position of conspiring together against the president.

The secret legislative processes of the executive branch have the very real advantage of bringing together persons who are expert and public spirited, and permitting them to think and work in some degree of insulation from political pressures. But what the executive branch can gain in expertise and disinterestedness it sometimes loses in imagination and flexibility; executive agencies, too, can be vested interests, with a stake in old ways of doing things. Both Presidents Kennedy and Johnson sought systematically to broaden participation in their legislative processes by creating task forces made up largely of private citizens, but these usually operated in secrecy also and were no substitute for a truly public legislative process as a means of refining ideas, testing their workability and acceptability, and winning public support. While some observers— the Washington press corps in particular[37]—may contend that the executive branch has lately carried secrecy on these and other matters to the point of fetishism, it nevertheless is clear that the president could not make his legislative processes wholly open, through the equivalent of public hearings, without subjecting himself and his staff to unbearable pressures and further irritating Congress by appearing to usurp its methods as well as its functions.

Finally, the legislative process in the executive branch can suffer from its domination by a single man. A good idea initiated on Capitol Hill cannot be killed by the judgment, or the whim, of any individual; it is in the public domain, it will gain support on its merits through public awareness and discussion, and if a committee chairman refuses to hold hearings, there are many safety valves: a second house, other committees that may assert jurisdiction, the opportunity to initiate action on the Senate floor. Granted, a Howard Smith may exercise great obstructive power as

[37] See *ibid.*, for example.

an individual, but this is not in the nature of the legislature; the power granted him can be withdrawn by the body granting it. But by the very nature of the executive branch, no corrective mechanism exists. The president has the power to stifle consideration within the executive branch of legislative ideas with which he does not agree, and to shut off the flow of information about those ideas that is needed for intelligent public discussion. When he promulgates his program, as Democratic Representative John Brademas of Indiana has pointed out, "not only does the executive fail to call attention to the full range of possible actions; it resents public reports that debate [within the administration] is even taking place."[38] Presidents, of course, are usually politicians with sensitive antennas, but they are also capable of complacency and shortsightedness.

The Legislative Product. Having said all this about the processes, what can be said of the effectiveness of legislative initiative in the six years after the transition compared to the six years before? Through the legislative procedures of Congress, the measures listed in Table 13 were well advanced by 1961. After the transition, most of these measures were substantially altered by the executive branch, and impressive new initiatives were taken. The latter included major departures in three areas—the tax reduction act of 1964, the war on poverty, and the civil rights acts—as well as several measures that rounded out the attack on structural unemployment, and the land and water conservation fund and other proposals in the field of conservation and natural beauty.

Of these enactments, the war on poverty represents the most extreme case of legislative initiative by the president almost to the exclusion of Congress, and as such it illustrates both the strengths and the weaknesses of the dual process. The President did not ask Congress to declare war on poverty; he announced, in his State of the Union message, that "this administration" had already declared the war. A task force, insulated from congressional influence, then prepared the battle plan. When the plan was ready, committee chairmen and prospective sponsors of the bill were given notice of its contents but no real opportunity to study and advise. Then the President put the full force of his leadership behind a demand for immediate hearings and action, and staked his own prestige and the party's position in the coming presidential campaign upon the outcome. Congress was forced to "rubber stamp" the measure. Compared to the

[38] Address at Princeton University, April 15, 1966.

consideration that had been given other major measures—medicare, for example, over a span of nearly a decade—congressional consideration of so major an undertaking as a war on poverty was almost cursory.

This process produced, in record time, a legislative achievement of historic scale. But the manner of its passage left the program with uncertain underpinning. It was the President's program, and Sargent Shriver's program—not the country's. Initially at least, its standing was no greater than the President's, and Sargent Shriver's, personal standing in the country. Nobody in either house of Congress nor any leadership group outside the government felt a sense of paternity toward the Economic Opportunity Act or the Office of Economic Opportunity; and accordingly the program had no organized and vigorous defense in its early years when it came under fire. Republicans felt free to make the war on poverty a partisan issue, since it had been presented as one. But Democrats in Congress felt little responsibility to defend it.

Perhaps no other course of action would have succeeded. To have brought Congress into the planning process might have been to engender conflict prematurely. To have allowed Congress a leisurely period for the program's consideration might have been to dissipate the public support aroused by the presidential rhetoric and to delay the legislation beyond the psychological moment for its passage—while incidentally tarnishing the President's image as leader and master of Congress. Yet the course of action chosen left the program without the base of reliable and continuing congressional and public support accorded those measures that were the product of the legislative branch's own initiative and tedious processes of refinement.

The tax cut of 1964 represents the opposite kind of hazard of the dual legislative process—too much, rather than too little, consideration. For two years, beginning even before President Kennedy's inauguration, his advisers gave the question of a tax cut the most intensive consideration. In mid-1962 the President finally made his decision, and the next six months were devoted to working out the details of the measure. But this was only the beginning. Wilbur Mills and Harry Byrd—not members of the Democratic presidential party—did not respond for John Kennedy as did the committee chairmen who handled the Economic Opportunity Act for Lyndon Johnson. Hearings were long, leisurely, and complete. So was the deliberation of the Ways and Means Committee. More than nine months were required for the House to act, and another four months for the Senate—the latter period foreshortened by Johnson's extraordinary pressure upon that body during his initial weeks in office. The bill was passed, but not until two years beyond the point in time when President Kennedy and his advisers were satisfied beyond any doubt that the time when a tax cut was needed had arrived. By contrast, as noted in Chapter 2, the simpler legislative process of Great Britain enables the government to enact a tax reduction within a few weeks after its economic analysts and its governing party are agreed that one is necessary. Fiscal policy, where timing is of the essence, appears to be one area of legislation where a simplification of the cumbersome dual legislative process of this country is emphatically needed.

The civil rights acts of 1964 and 1965 perhaps showed the dual legislative system at its best. The President made his proposals with somewhat less than the usual air of finality; the Congress added its own initiative; the public was heard, and through effective collaboration between the two branches of government a genuine consensus was reached—a consensus strong enough to survive the filibuster and to give the administrators of the new laws the solid footing their tasks required.

In the fields of air and water pollution, in particular, Congress demonstrated that it had not lost its capacity to initiate where the administration, for one reason or another, lagged. In these areas it was Congress that led and the administration that followed. Moreover, on many measures where the President led, the contribution of Congress was still substantial. Major sections of the Civil Rights Act of 1964 and of the medicare act were of legislative origin. Congress initiated the grant features of the college assistance legislation. The Johnson proposal for assistance to elementary and secondary education was built around an approach that, in its initial form at least, can be credited to Senator Morse. The Accelerated Public Works Act and the Manpower Development and Training Act were recast by Congress. Only on a minority of the measures enacted did Congress relinquish wholly the legislative role. And in 1966, as the President and his administration became steadily more preoccupied with the war in Vietnam and the budget stringency brought on by that conflict, the initiative for devising new and effective measures to meet the crisis in the Negro ghettoes appeared to be moving from the executive branch to activists on Capitol Hill.

If the separation of powers in the American system makes the processes of action cumbersome and sometimes tediously slow, it also contributes vitality through assuring a series of independent centers for the generation of ideas and creative energy.

Ebbing of the Tide

Of the entire Democratic party program evolved to meet the domestic problems covered in this study, only one major piece of unfinished business remained when the Eighty-ninth Congress adjourned—the 1966 civil rights bill with its fair housing provisions. But every measure that had been before the Congress for a year or more had been enacted. It was accomplished, after the Johnson landslide of 1964, by "the simple tread of marching numbers," as one reporter put it.[39]

The voters liked the activist legislative measures even better in retrospect than they had in prospect. On specific bills, pollster Louis Harris found the approval-disapproval ratio as follows:[40]

Measure	Percentage approving	Percentage disapproving
Voting rights for Negroes	95	5
Cutting excise taxes	92	8
Federal aid to education	90	10
College scholarships	89	11
Medical care for the aged	82	18
Highway beauty	79	21
Antipoverty program	73	27

Harris placed President Johnson's popularity rating at 67 percent, Gallup at 66 percent with only 21 percent disapproving. The President's record as a legislative leader was clearly the decisive factor. In response to the query, "What are the things President Johnson has done that you like best?" the Gallup respondents named medicare first, then civil rights legislation, then the antipoverty program. "Favorable responses far outweighed unfavorable responses," observed Dr. Gallup.[41]

Yet, just one year later the tide had ebbed. The inconclusive war in Vietnam preempted public attention. Consumer prices rose 4 percent in a year's time. The summer's riots—thirty-eight separate disturbances were counted—cast a pall over the very concept of the Great Society. President Johnson suffered his most crushing legislative defeat with loss of the 1966 civil rights bill. His approval ratio in the Gallup poll slipped by more than 20 points, from the 66–21 percent of November 1965 to 44–42 percent in October 1966. The proportion of voters calling themselves Democrats fell to the lowest point in twenty years—44 percent, compared to 53 per-

[39] Dan Cordtz, *Wall Street Journal*, Aug. 11, 1965.
[40] *Washington Post*, Jan. 9, 1966.
[41] AIPO release, Nov. 5, 1965.

cent as late as 1964.[42] And the voters replaced forty-seven Democratic congressmen and three Democratic senators with Republicans.

Explanations were plentiful for the Democrats' precipitous decline. Dr. Gallup called the Vietnam war "probably the prime reason why the GOP did so well" in the election. Republican victors offered their own interpretations. Said House Minority Leader Gerald Ford of Michigan: "I view the election as a repudiation of the President's domestic policies."[43] Senator-elect Charles Percy of Illinois: "They are frustrated by the war in Vietnam, burdened by rising prices, disturbed by the whole civil rights-civil disorder question." Governor-elect Ronald Reagan of California: "I think the people now have shown they want a pause, a chance to ask: 'Where are we going? How fast? How far?' " Governor George Romney of Michigan: "I think they were saying several things—that at this time, when we are involved in a war in Asia, the federal government is trying to do too much, and this is reflected in higher prices and inflation; that we have too much of a government-oriented society, not enough of a people-oriented society; that we need to put more reliance on state and local governments, and on private institutions." Senator-elect Edward W. Brooke of Massachusetts: "I think that this was more of a protest vote against what the President has been calling the 'Great Society' at a time when the nation is at war and we have inflation and housewives are marching to protest spiraling food costs. There is protest, too, against the riots in urban centers. The administration in power, of course, is being held accountable for all these things."[44]

A Harris poll in September indicated that the loss of confidence in the President extended nearly uniformly across the range of his responsibilities. The proportion of voters giving him a positive rating had declined from a majority to a minority in each of six areas, as follows:[45]

Issue	*Percentage approving President's handling*	
	September 1966	*October 1965*
War in Vietnam	42	65
Keeping the economy healthy	49	69
Civil rights	43	60
The war on poverty	41	60
Labor-management problems	37	69
Taxes	31	56

[42] *Ibid.*, Dec. 20, 1966. The Republican proportion had risen since 1964 from 25 to 29 percent and those calling themselves independent from 22 to 27 percent.

[43] *Newsweek*, Nov. 21, 1966, pp. 32, 38.

[44] Quotations from interviews in *U.S. News and World Report*, Nov. 21, 1966, pp. 55, 59, 62, 94.

[45] Harris surveys, reported in *Newsweek*, Sept. 26, 1966, p. 27.

Rarely has the short span of voter gratitude been more vividly demonstrated. Economic prosperity was now taken for granted. The legislative triumphs of 1965 had faded into the past. In the words of Alben Barkley's apocryphal citizen, the voters were asking the President, "What have you done for me lately?" And lately he had given them only Vietnam, inflation, and riots. Civil rights, the once-popular cause, was now in Percy's phrase "the civil rights-civil disorder question," and the President who had so fully committed himself to the Negro revolution in the day of its flowering remained no less identified with it when the bloom was gone. The war on poverty, since Negroes numbered large among its beneficiaries, caught some of the onus of civil disorder; by September a majority of voters with opinions thought the program was unsuccessful, and 60 percent of white voters expressing a view believed it would not get at the causes of racial unrest.[46] Finally, these were the very government programs that could be blamed for the rise in the cost of living. To quote Alan Otten once more, "Voters didn't really know what the Great Society was—they just knew it was spending too much of their money, was all fouled up, was trying to do too much for the Negroes." The President, responding to public reaction, had even abandoned the phrase.[47] As the voters reacted adversely to the issues, they also responded less favorably to the President's personality, and the two negative factors appeared to reinforce each other.

The political danger of the civil rights issue had been apparent for some time. Despite the general public approval given to the 1964 and 1965 rights bills, Governor George Wallace of Alabama had entered the Democratic presidential primaries in Wisconsin, Indiana, and Maryland in 1964 as the candidate of the "white backlash" and had won from 25 to 43 percent of the Democratic vote, carrying many white working-class precincts —and some whole counties—against slates of Johnson supporters. The Gallup poll had consistently shown that a substantial proportion of northern white voters thought that the Democratic presidents were pushing racial integration too fast, and by the fall of 1966 that proportion had become a majority. Following are the responses by northern whites to the question, "Do you think the Kennedy administration [or President Johnson] is pushing racial integration too fast, or not fast enough, or about right?"[48]

---

[46] Harris survey, reported in *Washington Post*, Sept. 5, 1966.

[47] *Wall Street Journal*, Jan. 12, 1967.

[48] AIPO releases, May 30, 1962, June 16, 1963, Feb. 26, 1964, April 11, 1965, Aug. 6, 1965, July 20, 1966, Sept. 28, 1966.

	Percentage responding		
Date	Too fast	Not fast enough	About right or no opinion
May 1962	27	11	62
June 1963	35	13	52
February 1964	28	13	59
April 1965	28	17	54
August 1965	36	10	54
July 1966	44	6	50
September 1966	52	8	40

A Theory of Party Alternation. The sudden emergence of new issues fixed 1966 as the date of the reversal of fortunes of the two political parties, but history tells us that the reversal was bound to come sooner or later. The cyclical, or pendulum, character of American politics has often been commented upon.[49] For a century the Republican and Democratic parties had been alternating in the control of government. Neither had been able to hold the presidency for a continuous period of more than twenty years, and sometimes the office had been relinquished to the opposition party after only a single four-year term.

The period covered in this volume appears to have measured one arc of the cycle—from the peak of Republican strength after the election of 1952 to the peak of Democratic strength in 1964 and 1965—followed by one year of what appears to be the return swing of the pendulum toward the Republicans. From an analysis of this fourteen-year span, a theory can be constructed that appears to account for the cyclical nature of American politics during that period—and that also appears useful to an interpretation of at least some of the political history of the last half-century.

It is noteworthy that many of the comments upon the 1966 election were expressed in terms of tempo: Johnson was moving "too fast," doing "too much"; the people desired "a pause." The voters were reacting against the speed of the President's movement toward his goals, not against his ultimate objectives.

Arthur W. Macmahon made the point more than twenty years ago, in his presidential address to the American Political Science Association: "In the setting of such a society as the United States, electoral campaigns

[49] Donald E. Stokes and Gudmund R. Iversen have demonstrated statistically that forces exist that make for two-party competition and equilibrium between the parties, although they do not seek to identify the forces. "On the Existence of Forces Restoring Party Competition," *Public Opinion Quarterly,* Vol. 26 (Spring 1962), pp. 159–71.

are concerned with the tempo rather than the trend—in other words, the main course of development or the direction—of public policy. Principles once enacted are seldom repealed; steps firmly taken are seldom retraced. . . . So tempo, not direction, is actually in dispute . . . the important question of destination is largely fictitious in any campaign. A decision to go more slowly, or to go no farther, or even to withdraw a little, does not involve a marked deviation from the course already traced."[50]

The basic cleavage in American politics between the activists and the conservatives can be defined, then, as a matter of tempo. It is a division, essentially, between those who want to move rapidly toward their vision of a good society, even at the risk of errors of commission, and those who would minimize that risk—but in turn risk errors of omission—by moving more slowly. The basic cleavage between the two major parties can be seen as a division of voters along the activist-conservative spectrum, with the party identifiers overlapped but clearly centered on either side of the spectrum's mid-point, as in this schematic diagram:

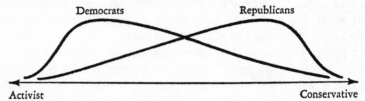

Democrats   Republicans

Activist   Conservative

Other factors influence party identification, so that persons who on the activist-conservative scale would belong in one party may actually identify with the opposite party. However, as Schattschneider argues, at any given time one cleavage in the electorate is *dominant*, the others are subordinated. The dominant cleavage divides parties, the subordinated cleavages cut across party lines. A party realignment takes place when one conflict supplants another as the dominant cleavage in the political system.[51] Since the dominant cleavage during most of this century has been between the activist and conservative approaches to domestic issues, the diagram illustrates the single most important basis of party identification.

Party policy and party leadership are determined, of course, by the views and desires of the party's active members, not by the views and wishes of the whole electorate. It follows, then, that—barring a basic

[50] Address of Dec. 28, 1947, *American Political Science Review*, Vol. 42 (February 1948), p. 3.
[51] E. E. Schattschneider, *The Semi-Sovereign People* (Holt, Rinehart and Winston, 1960), especially Chaps. 4 and 5.

realignment of the parties—the leadership and program of one party, the Democratic, will be on the activist side of the mid-point, or "left of center," and the leadership and program of the other party, the Republican, on the conservative, or "right of center," side. A Republican president, like Eisenhower, might seek the "middle of the road," or a Democratic president, like Johnson, might talk of "government by consensus," but the dynamics of the party system suggest that each must fail. The leader must stand somewhere near the mid-point of his party; one who does not is unlikely to attain party leadership in the first place, but if by some accident he is chosen at his party's convention, he cannot retain leadership for long unless he moves to a position that reflects the views of the main body of his followers. Barry Goldwater was one who did not so move, and he lost the effective leadership of his party on the very day he accepted it, by openly identifying himself with the extremists in the party and defying those who counseled moderation. Lyndon Johnson, in contrast, did move. When he was named by John Kennedy as the Democrats' vice presidential candidate, his first act was to reassure his party—which would not have selected him in an open contest—by embracing those elements in the party's program that he had rejected as its Senate leader. Only after he became president did he talk of "consensus" government, and even then his notion of consensus was Republican acceptance of the Democratic program, not the abandonment or modification of that program.

But because the governing party stands either left or right of center, it finds itself in a state of permanent disequilibrium with the electorate. It is either moving too fast and doing too much—the pitfall of the Democrats —or moving too slowly and doing too little, the bane of the Republicans. At the point of party change, the electorate is correcting the current disequilibrium by the only means available to it—by transferring power to the other party. During the "honeymoon" period of a new administration, the electorate enjoys the satisfaction of feeling the old tensions removed— as when the country began "moving again" under Kennedy. But gradually the voters become aware of the new disequilibrium. The party out of power drums away at the new tensions; the party in power can only call up memories of the tensions of the past. Sometimes memories linger long, as with those of Herbert Hoover and the Depression. But eventually they fade. They fade fastest when the opposition party rallies behind leaders who cannot be identified with the tensions of the past—as Eisenhower could not be identified with Hoover conservatism.

Thus the pendulum swings. The particular issues, and personalities, of each election determine the speed of the pendulum movement—may slow or even halt it for a time, as in 1956, or accelerate it, as in 1958. It is a pendulum of fits and starts, but the direction of its movement is constant. Once a party firmly establishes its power, it is already on its way to losing that power. It is only a matter of time.

This theory provides a basis for interpreting the shifts in party fortunes during the period 1953–66. The elections of 1958 and 1960 can be seen as reactions by the electorate against the staticism of the conservative party, and the election of 1966 can be understood at least in part as a reaction against the tempo of the activist party. The theory also provides an interpretation for at least two of the previous occasions in this century when control of the government was passed from one party to the other. The elections of 1912 and 1932, like those of 1958 and 1960, were expressions of a popular demand for more vigorous governmental action in relation to domestic matters.

A review of the first half of the century does not, however, present a clear illustration of the opposite swing of the pendulum—that is, a reaction against excesses of the activist party in domestic affairs. As it happens, all of the elections in which Republicans wrested control from the Democrats occurred during, or in the immediate aftermath of, war. As Donald Stokes has emphasized, party competition is multidimensional, and the dimensions have different weights at different times.[52] In 1920, 1946, and 1952, the voters reacted against the activist party, true enough, but more against its identification with war—and the domestic disruption arising from war—than against its position on domestic issues in general. Even the 1966 election did not turn solely on domestic issues; the war in Vietnam clearly contributed to the dissatisfaction of the electorate. One may speculate, of course, about the relationship. If activism and conservatism are matters of temperament, then one would expect a party leadership that is activist at home to be activist—or interventionist—abroad. It may therefore be no accident that it has been the Democratic party that has been in power when the country has become most deeply involved in world affairs, including military involvement.

In any case, one can only guess whether, or when, the activist domestic policies of the Democratic party during its previous periods of ascendancy would have exceeded the tempo the voters were willing to tolerate. The 1948 election is particularly instructive: even after sixteen years of Demo-

[52] Donald E. Stokes, "Spatial Models of Party Competition," *American Political Science Review*, Vol. 57 (June 1963), p. 370.

cratic control of the presidency, the voters reacted in that election not against the Democrats but against what Harry Truman called the "do nothing" Republican Congress, then only two years old. Moreover, the survey evidence indicates that in 1952 the domestic policies of the Democratic administration were not unpopular.

Prior to 1966, then, the theory of disequilibrium had been demonstrated primarily on one side. Repeatedly, the electorate had turned to the activist party to speed up the tempo of the government in its handling of domestic problems, but when it turned the Democrats out of office the party's domestic program was not the primary cause. The party in power has been penalized far more often for doing too little than for doing too much. This bears out the evidence from public opinion surveys that a majority of the electorate is clustered on the activist side of the activist-conservative spectrum.[53] In other words, a disequilibrium powerful enough to drive the Democrats from office requires a tempo well beyond that the Democratic party is usually able to attain. After the 1964 landslide, however, President Johnson had the majorities in Congress that enabled him to attain such a tempo. When that tempo was expressed in measures and programs, like open housing and the war on poverty, that bore upon the emotion-laden field of race relations, the reaction occurred.

If the disequilibrium theory is helpful in explaining at least some of the elections of the past, down to and including that of 1966, what is its predictive value for the future? The theory rests on the proposition that the conservative party is compelled, by its internal dynamics, to choose conservative leaders and pursue conservative policies, and that the opposite is true of the activist party. But let us consider this proposition further. Can either party move toward the center of the spectrum, to the point where the tempo of its policies is approximately in balance with the mood of the electorate as a whole, and remain there? In other words, can the historic pattern of alternation be interrupted by the kind of "middle of the road," "consensus" government that presidents of both parties have dreamed about? Some writers have suggested that the parties not only can move toward the center but are positively impelled to do so. Anthony Downs, for example, concludes that in a two-party democracy the parties "try to be similar" by moving toward the center—in much the same way

[53] See especially the findings of McClosky and his associates, Chap. 10, pp. 454–55, above. See also Lloyd A. Free and Hadley Cantril, *The Political Beliefs of Americans; a Study of Public Opinion* (Rutgers University Press, 1967), especially Chap. 2.

that competing merchants tend to cluster together in a location that is central in relation to the buying public.[54]

But parties are not free to move toward the center of the spectrum merely because their leaders judge that they might gather more votes that way. Parties cannot adopt their policies in quite the detached and calculating manner of a merchant selecting a location for his store—for it is policies that determine party groupings in the first place. Many active politicians, and assuredly a large segment of the voters, look upon parties as instruments for advancing principles to which they are committed— not as ends in themselves. Thus, an attempt by a party leadership to move away from the position held by its followers—whether toward or away from the center—leads to a party split. The split may result in nothing more than a splinter, like the Conservative party that was formed in New York when the Republican leadership in that state moved toward the center; or it may produce a chasm as wide as the ones that rent the Republican party in 1912 and again in 1964 when its leaders moved abruptly to the right.

A shift in the position of the Democratic party toward the center would at once raise the prospect of a party split. To be significant, a move in that direction would have to challenge activist positions that have proved unpopular, in particular the party's position of sympathy toward the demands of the militant Negroes. Any overt move to abandon the Negroes could hardly fail to touch off a struggle within the party that would either restore it to its former activist position or split it. The potential for such a struggle was clearly shown in the Maryland gubernatorial contest of 1966, when the effort of Democratic candidate George Mahoney to move the party away from its commitment to open housing legislation led to a schism that elected his Republican opponent. A party's necessity for cohesion, then, tends to keep its policies near the center of *its own* spectrum, not the spectrum of the electorate as a whole. So the Democratic party will remain activist. Not since 1892 has it elected a conservative president, not since the 1920's has it nominated a candidate who could be so classified, and not since that time has a conservative candidate come even within striking distance of the nomination.

[54] Anthony Downs, *An Economic Theory of Democracy* (Harper, 1957), especially Chap. 8. Key, *Politics, Parties, and Pressure Groups*, pp. 218–20, also emphasizes the influences that "tend to pull the party leaderships from their contrasting anchorages toward the center." Among the influences he cites is the diversity of views within each party. Key's analysis seems to predate the recent period in which the Democratic party has emerged as consistently activist with its conservative wing increasingly submerged.

By the same token, Republican presidential candidates are most likely to be chosen from among persons who stand near enough to the center of the Republican spectrum to be able to bridge the division between its ultraconservatives and its moderates. If such a candidate is elected, he will stand to the right of the center of the electorate as a whole—as did Dwight Eisenhower—and the potential for disequilibrium will exist as it existed throughout the Eisenhower years. It is not inconceivable, of course, that a Republican convention hungry for victory—and one looking closely at the public opinion polls—might nominate a candidate so far on the activist side to be unrepresentative of the party as a whole. What then? If the disequilibrium theory has validity, it suggests that a party leadership could not survive if it took and held a position substantially to the left of the bulk of the party's active supporters. The disequilibrium then would be *within* the party—between the party and its leaders rather than between the electorate and its governing party—but the corrective forces would work in much the same way. By McClosky's definitions, nearly one-quarter of the voters are "extreme conservatives."[55] Those voters, not to mention the moderate conservatives, are bound to have a political instrument. If the Republican party, through some accident of politics, were to find itself one day with its first activist president since 1908, there is no reason to expect that the party would tolerate a successor who followed in the same direction. After Theodore Roosevelt, it will be recalled, came William Howard Taft.

New forces may arise some day that will align the parties on a basis other than the present activist-conservative cleavage, but such forces are not on the horizon yet. Indeed, as will be developed at greater length in Chapter 12, the trend for several decades has been away from old bases of party division toward an ever clearer activist-conservative alignment. So the prospect is that one party will continue to be activist and the other party conservative—most of the time. The electorate as a whole will presumably continue to move steadily in the activist direction as yesterday's activism becomes today's conservatism, but wherever the mid-point of the spectrum stands at any given time, the parties will find themselves on either side. Both parties, after all, cannot be on the same side of the issues that determine the basic alignment of a two-party system.

---

[55] See Herbert McClosky, "Conservatism and Personality," *American Political Science Review*, Vol. 52 (March 1958), p. 27.

CHAPTER XII

Toward More
Responsive Government

THE PERIOD 1953–65 may be seen as one swing of the political pendulum, from a peak of Republican strength to a peak of Democratic strength. But the pendulum denotes more than just the ebb and flow of party fortunes. It describes the cyclical nature of the policy-making process itself.

The chronology of governmental response to the problems reviewed in Part I was remarkably parallel in all the areas of concern. During the early years of the period, when the pendulum was starting slowly, the problems were being identified and the initial forms of remedial action were being devised. In the middle years, as the pendulum gathered speed and momentum, political support was being mobilized and the measures themselves were being refined in public debate. At the mid-point in the period they had become the central issues that divided the activist and conservative parties. The Democratic party assembled the measures as its program and then, taking those measures to the people, won its mandate. The late years of the period were a time of rounding out the program with additional proposals, of solidifying popular support, and of maneuvering the program through the policy-making institutions of the government. When the period ended, all of the items of the Democratic program of more than one year's standing had been enacted—some of them, to be sure, in compromised form. The promises had been kept, the pledges fulfilled; and the activists were starting at the beginning again—identifying the new problems that had arisen or the old that had been inadequately dealt with, preparatory to carrying them to passage on the pendulum's next swing in the activist direction.

The policy-making cycle just completed is impressive not only in its rhythm but in the aura of inevitability about the outcome. The ultimate results were, in a sense, compelled by the circumstances of the problems themselves. Though the imagination and skill and doggedness of the political actors were indeed remarkable, these men nevertheless seem as actors, following a script that was written by events.

The script suggests that where a problem is real in its impact upon the people, and where a national solution is indicated by the failure of all other solutions, then time is on the side of the activists. Unless the problem itself vanishes or abates, the pressure for the national solution will grow. The issue will gather political support, and through a circular process the issue and the activist politician will reinforce each other—the politician will publicize the issue, and the issue in turn will strengthen him and attract other politicians to its support. During a period of conservative ascendancy, as in the Eisenhower years, the simultaneous development of a series of issues through this circular process will strengthen the appeal of the opposition party as a whole at the same time that the party strives to enhance the appeal of the issues. Eventually the party and its program attain the strength to elect a president, and at that point the power of the presidency to publicize issues is added to the resources of the proponents. The circular process continues until the president and the program have the force to push past the obstacles in the institutional machinery.

The cases in Part I reveal a pattern of steady growth of support for the activist measures from their conception to their enactment, with the seeming inexorability of a swinging pendulum. Sometimes the movement was speeded by events—as civil rights legislation by the violence in Alabama—but rarely was ground lost. Even one of the most lavishly financed lobbying campaigns in history, by the American Medical Association against medicare, did not interrupt for long the momentum of that proposal.

Public opinion is molded through innumerable channels that intersect and overlap—expert to opinion leader to follower; political leader to ward politician to voter; lobbyist to local organization to member; commentator or columnist to viewer and reader. It is the business of the political activist and his allies to exploit all these channels. In the descriptions of parliamentary maneuvering in Part I, the long process of publicizing problems and building public sentiment may sometimes have been submerged. Enormous expenditures of time and energy inside and outside the Congress went into the accumulation and distribution of information. The speeches of politicians, the resolutions of national and local interest groups, the insertion of dreary statistics into the *Congressional Record,* the duplication of the arguments and the statistics and their distribution to the mailing lists of cooperating organizations, the constant letter-writing between politicians and their constituents are the substance of the circular process by which the politicians and their activist proposals build support for one another. A bill is introduced, hearings arranged, the measure brought to a test vote in committee or on the floor—not always with a view to immediate enactment but often just to dramatize the issue, lay the groundwork for campaigning, and obtain publicity. As this process of "building the record" is pursued systematically, an issue gradually moves from the shadows to the light.

The processes of communication involve a combination of factual education and emotional advocacy, and the dialogue has several levels that are distinguished by the relative proportions of those ingredients:

1. The expert level, where the nature of the problem and the adequacy of the solution are analyzed in factual terms.

2. The political leadership level, where factual analysis is blended with emotional appeal. This is the language in which the politicians and their allies build the record.

3. The campaign level, where the weight of the dialogue is upon emotional appeal and the factual argument may be reduced to a few symbolic words and numbers. This is the language of communication between the politicians and their constituents.

The national debate on the issues covered in Part I can be judged to have fulfilled the purpose of debate. In each case the validity of the claims of the activists was put to the test. They were forced to establish that the problem they described was indeed real; they had to demonstrate that it was not being solved in the absence of national action, that the states, the local communities, and private enterprise were collectively failing to cope with it. In the course of the debate the problem itself was perhaps redefined, and in almost every case the remedial measures themselves were altered and improved. At some point, however, positions crystalized, arguments and even facts became frozen, and the debate became repetitive. Such a hardening is essential to the smooth working of the publicity mechanisms. Public support can be generated best around an issue and a solution that remain reasonably constant; when proponents switch signals they derail their followers. Once the terms of the debate become hardened, the antagonists are no longer talking to each other but to the public, and the contest of ideas becomes submerged in a contest of pressure organizations, with substantive arguments giving way to instrumental ones.

Very few of the activist measures were passed without the organizing efforts of a national interest group. The pattern varied: some were ad hoc groups established for the purpose, like the Area Employment Expansion Committee for area redevelopment; others were long-established general-purpose groups like the National Education Association or the AFL-CIO. But in either case their methods were the same. They organized local support. They conducted research and fed information to the political sponsors of the measures. They disseminated publicity through the media. They identified the key senators and congressmen and concentrated pressure on them, directly and through the members' constituencies. They stimulated a flow of mail from home to the members whose votes they needed. In this process they formed an intimate alliance with the activists of the Democratic party, both in the formulation of the measures and in the tactical maneuvers and struggles on the way to passage. With varying degrees of effectiveness the interest groups provided political support, including campaign contributions, to the politicians who embraced their cause. On the other side, of course, interest groups opposed to the activist measures established the same alliance with the Republican party.

In any case, at some point in the course of building public support, the opposition became divided—and this was the key to victory. In many of the cases reviewed in Part I, the turning point appeared to come when a significant element of conservative opinion yielded to the compulsion of the facts that pointed to national action as essential to the solution of a national problem. In the case of the tax cut, it was the United States Chamber of Commerce that provided the crucial measure of conservative support. In area redevelopment, it was the local chambers of commerce in the areas affected. In aid to colleges and universities, it was the Eisenhower-appointed committee on higher education. In medicare, it was the American Hospital Association and other medical groups that broke ranks with the American Medical Association. In water pollution control, it was the state administrative agencies and the governors. In aid to education, medicare, and area redevelopment, the ultimate outcome was assured when a conservative administration was itself compelled to acknowledge that some kind of national action was essential.

The opponents, it turned out, could not succeed just by opposing, because with the passage of time the recognition of the problems was bound to be more widespread. Indeed, the opponents themselves publicized the problems even in the act of denying they existed. Nor could the opposition prevail by warning of the danger of side effects—like, say, the evils of government spending. Those dangers were at most speculative. In the long run, not the conjectural evil but the real one persuades.

If the enactment of the measures of 1964–65 was really as inevitable as it appears now to have been, then the course of wisdom for the opposition would have been to join in recognizing the problems and in working out solutions. In the early stages the proponents of action are open to compromise; after they gather strength, they need not be. The American Medical Association could have had a version of medicare much more acceptable to it, if it had been willing to negotiate; the South could have had a milder civil rights bill. Indeed, President Eisenhower could in all probability have saved the Republican party from defeat in 1960 by something less than adamant opposition on a few key issues, and Nixon in all likelihood could have won by aggressively standing *for* something instead of emphasizing his opposition to Democratic initiatives.

If these, then, are the processes by which the government responds to its domestic problems, what can be said of their efficiency? By what standard, indeed, should they be judged?

Democratic theory begins with the principle that the majority should rule, but goes at once beyond it. The majority can be wrong, too. It can act impulsively; it can act in passion. Majority rule is therefore offset with an opposing principle—the majority should be restrained from misusing its power to oppress the minority. All democratic systems strike a balance between the principles of responsiveness and restraint.

But what is the proper balance?

The United States is unique among the world's democracies in the extent to which the institutional system is weighted on the side of restraint regardless of the mandate of the people. The Constitution defines actions that the majority can at no time take. An independent Supreme Court interprets and applies the Constitution. An independent president and Congress restrain each other, through a mutual veto power. The two houses of the legislature likewise restrain each other. Some decisions of the majority must, under the Constitution, be taken by a two-thirds vote. Powers are divided, or shared, between the federal government and the states. To all these constitutional limitations, Congress has voluntarily added other elements of restraint, by granting to groups and individuals within each house what can amount to a power of veto over the majorities of the houses. The total effect can be not just to delay action in the interest of full and free debate, but to forbid action. To the extent that the American institutional system cannot respond to a popular mandate for a change in the general course and direction of the government, as translated into specific measures by the president and his legislative majorities, it must be judged defective—unless one is to borrow from nondemocratic theory the notion that those who lose an election may have an intellectual or moral superiority that gives them an inherent right to rule.

On the basis of its actions over the fourteen-year period surveyed in this volume, the United States government can be characterized as less than fully responsive to the popular mandate during a period of more than six years—from November 1958 to January 1965. Before the election of 1958 its performance was consistent with a mandate for conservatism, but after the voters changed their minds in 1958, six years elapsed before the activist course could come to full fruition.

Perhaps six years is not an unreasonable lag. Perhaps new departures as bold as those of 1964 and 1965 should not be made before the mandate has been confirmed through three or four elections. Those propositions are arguable—although I would argue on the other side. But what is truly disquieting is the persistent suspicion that—despite the very real progress that the Kennedy program was making in the fall of 1963—the barriers to responsive government would not have been completely swept away except for an assassination, which profoundly affected the national mood, and the subsequent nomination by the conservative party of a presidential candidate so unappealing as to destroy his party's strength in Congress. Must governmental competence depend upon events so extraordinary?

The answer for the immediate future lies in whether the legislative successes of the recent period have left a residue of structural change that will make the American system permanently more responsive—as has happened in previous periods of activist ascendancy. The crisis of the 1930's, as one conspicuous example, shattered the constitutional limitations that were then the most formidable barrier to governmental action.

There are indications that in this period, too, some major barriers to change have been, or are being, swept aside.

In the optimistic mood of 1965 many observers saw the Madisonian system itself as having been permanently altered. "The old, traditional system of checks and balances within the governing structure has played itself out," exulted columnist Eric Sevareid. "With Johnson the era of undisputed executive government has arrived in America."[1] "The old system," wrote Joseph Kraft, referring to the organization of Congress against the White House, "is now dead."[2] Stephen K. Bailey discerned a "revolution"—propelled by basic political, economic, and sociological changes—that had created "a new electorate," which in turn had created a "new Congress." "It will never again be the same," predicted Bailey; the balance toward responsive government had been tipped "inexorably."[3]

Less than three years earlier James MacGregor Burns, scanning the same horizons, had found only repetitive cycles of "deadlock and drift" as far ahead as he could see. One may surmise that professors, like columnists, are not insulated from the general gloom or euphoria of the times and that, if they had been writing somewhat later, Burns might have been more sanguine and Bailey less so. Nevertheless, while it may be too soon to proclaim Bailey's "revolution," the general thesis that profound structural changes are in the making seems supportable.

The most important of those changes appear to be congressional reform, with which Bailey deals, and the realignment of the American party system.

Congressional Reform

Much of the current discussion of congressional reform is couched in terms of the relations between the president and the Congress—how to make the Congress responsive to presidential leadership or, conversely, how to preserve its independence. Writers on both sides of the question equate a "strong" Congress with one that obstructs the president, and a responsive Congress with one that submits to presidential leadership.[4]

[1] *Evening Star* (Washington), Jan. 10, 1966.

[2] *Ibid.*, Aug. 9, 1965.

[3] *The New Congress* (St. Martin's, 1966), especially pp. vii–ix.

[4] The writings of Samuel P. Huntington and Alfred de Grazia are illustrative. Huntington writes: "Apparently Congress can defend its autonomy only by refusing to legislate, and it can legislate only by surrendering its autonomy. . . . Congress can assert its power or it can pass laws; but it cannot do both" ("Congressional Responses to the Twentieth Century," in David B. Truman [ed.], *The Congress and America's Future* [published for the American Assembly by Prentice-Hall, 1965], p. 6); choosing between these alternatives, Huntington advocates congressional surrender. De Grazia makes the opposite choice: "Without a strong Congress the major problems of the country will be handled in ways that will become excessively majoritarian, often arbitrary, usually collectivist, and in the

But the basic question, from the standpoint of responsive government, is not whether Congress is responsive to the president, but whether, in Douglass Cater's phrase, it is responsive to its own majorities[5]—not whether it acts in obedience to the president, but whether it can act at all. The weakness of Congress has not been that it has failed to assert itself against the president, but that it has failed to assert its will over its own minorities.

The principal instruments of minority rule in the period 1953–66 were three in number—the House Rules Committee, the Senate filibuster, and the relinquishment of power to autonomous legislative committees and their chairmen chosen by seniority. To a considerable extent, however, these barriers to majority action have been weakened or eliminated. To this extent the country has, indeed, a "new Congress."

The House Rules Committee. In 1960 alone, the House Rules Committee was responsible, directly or indirectly, for the death of three major pieces of Democratic legislation—the omnibus housing bill, the minimum wage bill, and federal aid to education—and area redevelopment was passed only through the use of difficult procedures to circumvent the committee.[6] Clearly, in 1961, the Kennedy program was not going anywhere if each measure had to receive the majority vote of a committee split 6–6 between the program's supporters and its diehard opponents. Accordingly, curtailment of the extraordinary power of the Rules Committee was the one congressional reform on which the President-elect was willing to risk his prestige when Congress met in 1961.

The narrow victory of 1961 that enlarged the committee made it more

---

end suppressive of the American ideal of individuality" ("Toward a New Model of Congress," in de Grazia [ed.], *Congress: The First Branch of Government* [American Enterprise Institute for Public Policy Research, 1966], p. 7); his description of a "strong" Congress parallels Huntington's description of an obstructive one.

[5] *Power in Washington* (Random House, 1964), pp. 168–76. The 1960 and 1964 Democratic platforms also stated the objective simply: "Majority rule after reasonable debate."

[6] James A. Robinson, *The House Rules Committee* (Bobbs-Merrill, 1963), p. 74. The committee denied the housing bill a rule for floor consideration after it had been approved by the Senate and by the House Banking and Currency Committee; it declined to grant a rule to permit the education bill to go to a House-Senate conference; and it refused to permit the minimum wage bill to go to conference until it had exacted from the House conferees a promise to agree to no more than $1.15 an hour, a figure that was unacceptable to the conferees. Area redevelopment was brought to the floor through "calendar Wednesday" procedures (see Chap. 3, p. 71, above).

responsive to the House majority, with an 8–7 majority behind the leadership on most issues[7]—that is, provided the committee met and the issue
was scheduled. But Chairman Howard Smith retained the very important
power of calling meetings and scheduling committee business, subject
only to the entreaties of the House leadership and awkward procedures by
which the committee majority could, in extreme cases, schedule meetings
over the chairman's opposition. So it was that when the Eighty-seventh
Congress adjourned in 1962, the Rules Committee had failed to grant
rules on thirty-four significant measures. Attempts were made to bypass
the committee on nine of these, but only four were successful. Among the
casualties were the education bills, the Youth Conservation Corps, aid for
mass transportation, and a number of civil rights measures.[8] The Rules
Committee therefore continued to be the prime target of those reformers
who sought a more responsive Congress. Finally, in 1965, they had the
votes. Then the committee was at last humbled, with relative ease.

Two changes in the House rules stripped the Rules Committee of its
arbitrary power. One, the so-called "twenty-one day rule," authorized the
House speaker to recognize any member of a legislative committee to bring
a bill to the floor for action if the Rules Committee had not cleared it
within twenty-one days. The other eliminated the power of the Rules
Committee to prevent a bill passed by both houses from going to a House-
Senate conference. The twenty-one day rule was abandoned by the
Ninetieth Congress, in 1967, but other circumstances then made such
a rule no longer necessary. In the preceding November the very symbol
of Rules Committee autocracy, Chairman Smith, had been defeated in the
Democratic primary in Virginia. That left only one conservative Democrat, William Colmer of Mississippi, on the committee. Colmer was
scheduled to become chairman, by right of seniority, but before acceding
to his election, the Democratic leadership exacted from him a promise to
hold regular weekly meetings.[9] Since then the Rules Committee has been
no barrier to congressional responsiveness. Conceivably, the Howard
Smith brand of Rules Committee tyranny can one day be restored, but it
will not happen soon. The nine Democrats who flank the septuagenarian

[7] See Chap. 11, pp. 472–73.

[8] Walter Kravitz, "The Influence of the House Rules Committee on Legislation in
the 87th Congress," in Joseph S. Clark (ed.), *Congressional Reform: Problems and
Prospects* (Crowell, 1965), pp. 127–37. Kravitz lists the 34 measures and details the
disposition of each. He also records instances of delay in granting rules and instances
where the committee forced substantive concessions before granting rules.

[9] *New York Times*, Jan. 27, 1967.

Colmer on the Democratic side of the committee table all identify with the national party. The southern seats are held by moderates or liberals— John Young of Texas, Claude Pepper of Florida, and William R. Anderson of Tennessee. The young southern congressman who might be the Howard Smith of another generation has not yet even begun his climb up the Rules Committee seniority ladder. Moreover, after the experience of this generation with Smith and Colmer, the Democratic leadership and caucus are hardly likely to acquiesce soon again in assignment of any extremely conservative Democrat to the committee. If the Republicans gain control of the House, the new members they name will make the committee representative of their majority. For all these reasons, one can predict without being oversanguine that the Rules Committee, at least, will not be the same again.

The Senate Filibuster. In the Senate the most celebrated device through which the will of the minority has been allowed to prevail over that of the majority is rule 22, which requires a two-thirds vote to close debate. In hailing his "new Congress"—just after the Senate had twice succeeded in voting cloture on civil rights bills in the two preceding years—Bailey composed what turned out to be a premature epitaph to the filibuster. "Essentially, this decade witnessed the end of the power of a militant Southern minority to block or emasculate civil rights legislation," he wrote; by 1965, "what had been the shattering of an unbroken tradition the year before had become virtually routine."[10] But in 1966 the filibuster succeeded. A militant southern minority was not in itself sufficient, but a minority composed of southerners plus some northerners sufficed.

Essentially, it can just as readily be argued, the events of that decade showed that a militant southern minority was able to have its way except on the two occasions when there was enough televised violence in the South to solidify the rest of the country. In the absence of such extreme provocation, the national majority sentiment in favor of civil rights could not find expression. The combined forces of the President, the House majority, and the Senate majority in favor of the civil rights bills of 1966 were frustrated by the militant minority in the Senate.

The theoretical defense of rule 22, by its supporters, rests on the proposition that under some circumstances a majority should not be allowed to prevail. The Constitution requires a two-thirds majority for

[10] Bailey, *The New Congress,* pp. 65, 78. A filibuster against another civil rights bill, with open housing provisions, was broken in 1968.

certain kinds of actions—Senate approval of treaties, congressional overriding of vetoes, and Senate action in impeachment cases. To this list
should be added, they contend, any piece of ordinary legislation on which
a minority feels strongly enough to engage in endless debate. Speaking
to his fellow liberals, Daniel K. Inouye, Democrat of Hawaii, put it this
way in a Senate floor speech:

> American democracy does not necessarily result from majority rule, but
> rather from the forged compromise of the majority with the minority. . . .
> . . . I do seriously doubt whether any legislation which would arouse the
> stubborn opposition of one-third of this body, or that could be stopped simply
> by threatening a delay, could necessarily be very effective legislation. After all,
> ours is a government by consent; and its powers are divided, so that what is
> legislated may not be administered, may not be funded, may not be supported
> by the courts. Our task is to anticipate and reconcile conflicting pressures in
> this society as we formulate its laws. . . .
> . . . Since when is a simple majority an infallible indication of wisdom and
> right? We hear much talk about the tyranny of the one-third. I am just as
> fearful of the tyranny of the majority.[11]

What has been the practical effect of rule 22? In the fields covered by
this study, only civil rights aroused enough passion to provoke the filibuster. No "forged compromise" between the majority and minority
proved possible—not just for years, but for decades—because the minority, standing behind rule 22, found no need to make significant concessions. Eventually, the aggrieved Negroes took their case away from
a paralyzed Congress and into the streets. Mass demonstrations, police
dogs and fire hoses, and assassinations of civil rights workers finally accomplished what quiet testimony before congressional committees had not
alone been able to achieve.

The consequences of rule 22 may thus have been, curiously, exactly the
opposite of what its defenders, like Senator Inouye, have contended. If
Congress had been allowed to legislate by majority rule in the 1950's, or
even earlier, the measures passed would have been more substantial than
the bills enacted in 1957 and 1960 but would still in all probability have
been far milder, from the standpoint of the southern whites, and less
satisfactory from the standpoint of the Negroes, than those that were
passed under pressure of the violence of the 1960's. Even in 1964, if rule
22 had not given the southern senators a false sense of security, they
would have been moved to seek a compromise and would probably have
been able to settle for a milder bill. Thus, without rule 22, there would

[11] *Cong. Record*, Vol. 113 (Jan. 25, 1967), daily ed., p. S854.

have been more compromising between North and South, not less—since in the end, as it happened, there was very little. A frustrated majority, if it is prevented by arbitrary barriers from asserting its will, can impose that will more harshly—even "punitively"—if it is compelled finally to shatter the barriers by brute force.

The theoretical argument defending rule 22 on the ground that an extraordinary Senate majority should be required to enact stubbornly opposed legislation also overlooks the fact that a form of extraordinary majority is built into the American system for all legislation. No bill can be passed without the concurrence of the president, a majority of the House, and a majority of the Senate, all chosen from different constituencies—or, if the president does not concur, by two-thirds of each house. The bicameral system is a substantial barrier to hasty or ill-considered action by the majority, and the presidential veto is yet another barrier. Rule 22, by adding a two-thirds vote requirement for any bill whenever the minority so insists, actually demands a more substantial majority to enact ordinary legislation than to take the extreme step of removing a president from office. The chief executive can be removed through impeachment proceedings by a majority of the House and two-thirds of the Senate, but passage of a civil rights bill requires the concurrence of those majorities plus approval of the president as well.

Over and over, of course, in the biennial efforts to revise rule 22, a majority of the Senate has sustained the rule. The voluntary relinquishment by the majority of its right to prevail might appear to give the filibuster a kind of democratic sanction. But the decisions have been suspect as a true expression of the majority view on rule 22 itself. The key votes have been taken on a different issue—whether the Senate is a continuing body and consequently has continuing rules. The notion of continuity, which strikes very near the heart of the Senate's self-image, attracts more support than the substance of rule 22 itself. In January 1963, for instance, only forty-two of ninety-five Senate votes could be mustered to support the position that the Senate is a new body in each Congress and therefore able to adopt new rules by majority vote, but a few days later fifty-four senators supported a cloture motion to permit them to vote on changing rule 22 (the fifty-four votes, while a majority, fell ten short of the two-thirds that remained necessary, because of the earlier vote, to close debate). Moreover, the potential support of Democratic senators for a change in rule 22 has undoubtedly been held down by strong leadership pressure. A Democrat's votes on the question of adopting new rules have been treated, more than any other votes, as a test of fealty by the party leadership in the Senate. Observers have long noted a relationship between a Democratic senator's votes on rule 22 and his committee assignments.[12]

Despite the adverse procedural circumstances, however, the interest in revising rule 22 has repeatedly brought the Senate close to judging itself to be not a continuing body. In 1957 a switch of nine votes would have given the Senate the opportunity to consider rule 22 on its merits; in 1961, three votes; in 1963, six votes. The reserve power of the Senate to change its mind serves as a counterpoise to the filibuster itself. Surely one factor in persuading the southerners to accept the weak and compromised civil rights bill that was passed in 1957 was the strong showing of the anti-filibuster forces earlier that year. The same influence was undoubtedly at work during the civil rights debate of 1960. Just as the majority can be cowed by the minority if it threatens filibuster, so the minority can be restrained from abusing the filibuster by the knowledge that one such abuse could be the last.

Some day, no doubt, the necessary combination of circumstances will occur—the minority will abuse its filibuster privilege on an issue that the public at large, the president, the Senate leadership, and a majority of that body consider vital, and the Senate will withdraw the privilege. The strenuous and nearly successful efforts of recent years, supported by Vice President Nixon's interpretation of the Senate's constitutional right to change its rules by majority vote, have prepared the ground.[13] In the meantime, it can at least be said that the successful imposition of cloture in 1964 and 1965 may have set precedents that will make it easier for the majority to impose cloture and crush filibusters in the future despite rule 22.

Committees and Their Chairmen. When the Senate Judiciary Committee refused to report the civil rights bills referred to it, the Senate leadership found alternative procedures. In one instance it initiated legislation on the Senate floor in the form of an amendment; in another it declined to send a House-passed bill to the committee; in still another it sent the bill to the committee with instructions to hold hearings and report the bill. But such extraordinary steps cannot be taken routinely. They are confined

[12] See comments of Joseph Clark, Democrat of Pennsylvania, and other senators in *The Senate Establishment* (Hill and Wang, 1963). For an account of the rule 22 dispute, see John Bibby and Roger H. Davidson, *On Capital Hill* (Holt, Rinehart and Winston, 1967), pp.146–49.

[13] See Chap. 6, p. 231.

to issues of high visibility and public interest, like civil rights, where the committee's abuse of its prerogatives has been thoroughly established. In the House, procedures for bypassing the legislative committees are even more difficult; only one such instance—a tax extension bill in 1953—occurred in fields covered by this study. Except in extraordinary cases, then, committees of Congress have life-or-death power over legislation within their jurisdictions. They have the power to veto measures supported by the majorities of the houses they represent.

Whether a committee in fact uses that veto power depends upon the existence of one of two circumstances. Either the committee must be so unrepresentative of the parent house that a majority of the committee thwarts the majority will of the house, or the committee must be so undemocratically run that the minority within the committee can impose its views on the majority.

Each of these circumstances occasionally prevails, but perhaps less frequently than is supposed. Often when a measure is bottled up in committee, the action is taken by a committee majority that reflects accurately the views of the majority of the parent body; in other words, measures are killed that otherwise would be defeated on the House or Senate floor. Probably the most conspicuous example is medicare, which was held in the House Ways and Means Committee for half a dozen years after it became a major element of the Democratic party program. But, as noted in Chapter 7, it is probable that during most of those years the measure could not have commanded a majority on the House floor. When the membership of the House was drastically reconstituted, in the 1964 election, the makeup of the Ways and Means Committee was similarly altered and the will of the House majority was faithfully expressed through the committee majority.

Some committees, of course, are far from representative of the full membership of the parent bodies, for either of two reasons. First, the nature of the committee's jurisdiction may cause the imbalance; for instance, the two agriculture committees overrepresent rural constituencies and the two interior committees overrepresent the West because members from those areas seek service on those committees while members from other constituencies do not. Second, committees on which membership is widely sought, like Senate Finance or Appropriations, can be unrepresentative because the party group making assignments is itself unrepresentative.

Of the four systems employed for making committee assignments—

each party in each house has its own method—the only one seriously attacked in recent years has been that of the Senate Democrats, who entrust the job to the party's steering committee. After the 1958 election, when new Democratic senators from the North and West took their seats, committee assignments were in the hands of a steering committee that counted seven southerners among its fifteen members, although southerners numbered fewer than one-third of all Senate Democrats. Northern senators were rebuffed by Majority Leader Lyndon Johnson when they demanded proportionate representation for their region, but Mike Mansfield as Johnson's successor accepted the principle of a representative steering committee and gradually made it so by appointing northerners to fill vacancies.[14]

From the fields covered in this study, the outstanding example of a veto by a nonrepresentative legislative committee is the long delay of the wilderness bill by the House Interior Committee. Through that committee, the western timber, mining, and livestock industries exercised the controlling influence, while the interest of the eastern multitudes in wilderness preservation was represented through barely half a dozen eastern members. In the end the committee bowed to the national pressure for action but only with compromises that in all likelihood would have been rejected by a truly representative committee.

Instances of veto of a committee's majority by its minority are even rarer. Such a veto can occur if an unrepresentative subcommittee fails to act, or an adamant chairman overrides the sentiment of the majority of his committee. The only case of the former type encountered in this study was the rejection of the area redevelopment bill by an allegedly "stacked" subcommittee of the Senate Banking and Currency Committee—a barrier

[14] Senator Clark, who led the drive for equitable representation of northern Democrats on the steering committee, describes the negotiations in *Congress: The Sapless Branch* (Harper & Row, 1964), pp. 9–10, 119–23. Clark himself was appointed to the committee by Mansfield. Highly critical of its work in 1963, he could find no fault with its actions in 1965. "The performance . . . was largely in accord with equity. There was no discrimination against liberal Senators," he wrote in 1965 ("Coda: Making Congress Work," in Clark [ed.], *Congressional Reform: Problems and Prospects* (Crowell, 1965), p. 359). Senate Republicans adhere generally more strictly to seniority in making committee assignments. House procedures are discussed in Nicholas A. Masters, "Committee Assignments in the House of Representatives," *American Political Science Review*, Vol. 55 (June 1961), pp. 345–47. The two House parties use committees on committees which are chosen on the basis of geography. The Republican committee has been criticized because it operates through an executive committee that underrepresents the smaller states.

that was ultimately surmounted by parliamentary maneuvering in the full committee.

Defiance of their committees by arbitrary chairmen is also, not surprisingly, rare. Chairman Howard Smith of the House Rules Committee delighted in the exercise of autocratic power in defiance of everybody; James Eastland of the Senate Judiciary Committee used all of his chairman's privileges to block majority action on civil rights legislation within his committee, and Graham Barden of the House Education and Labor Committee refused to ask for a rule for consideration of a juvenile delinquency bill that had been approved by his committee. The Rules and Judiciary cases, of course, have been dealt with—the former through curtailment of both the powers of the committee and the prerogatives of the chairman, the latter through development and use of effective procedures for bypassing the committee entirely. The committee that Barden headed has also adopted rules to restrain its chairman, and in any case it will be led, for many years to come, by chairmen who are in tune with the committee's bipartisan liberal majority. Thus, the seniority system for selecting committee chairmen, in those instances where it proved to be a substantial barrier to expression of the majority will in Congress, is no longer a serious obstacle. As long as seniority practices and committee powers remain unmodified, of course, new instances of obstruction of committee majorities by their chairmen can always occur.

Short of actually vetoing the majority, moreover, the chairman has many ways of making life difficult for them. He can delay proceedings, he can set priorities so that bills he dislikes are disadvantaged, he can "stack" subcommittees and control assignment of bills to them, he can hamper staff work through his control of appointments and committee funds, and he can force compromises and exact concessions as the price of action. But a chairman is normally restrained in the exercise of power by the principle of comity; he needs to retain the cooperation and respect of his committee colleagues because he too will want something from them sometime. Ultimately, he risks losing his power if his abuse of it is flagrant and prolonged. What happened to the House Rules Committee is one object lesson; another is the series of revolts by House committee majorities that resulted in assumption of power, either temporarily or permanently, from several chairmen, including Graham Barden and Adam Clayton Powell of Education and Labor, Clare Hoffman (Michigan Republican) of Government Operations, Wright Patman (Texas Democrat) of Banking and Currency, and Tom Murray (Tennessee Democrat) of Post Office and Civil Service.[15] Senators and congressmen appear to agree that committee operations are becoming increasingly democratic in both houses.[16]

In order to eliminate what remains of the abuse of power by committee chairmen, various reformers have proposed to alter the seniority system by which chairmen are selected. Among suggested remedies are forced retirement of chairmen at a specified age, election of chairmen by the committee members or by the majority caucus, and rotation of the chairmanship among members of the majority. None of these proposals has attracted appreciable support in Congress.[17] Some might eliminate one evil only to introduce another; thus, many members oppose election of chairmen on the ground that divisiveness and factionalism would be fostered within a majority party which needs cohesiveness to be effective. The more productive direction of reform effort would appear to lie not in schemes for deposing arbitrary chairmen but rather in systems for removing the arbitrariness through procedures assuring majority rule in committee. Most important is the right of the majority to call meetings when the chairman refuses to do so, and to transact business in his absence. The majority's right to full participation in major administrative decisions,

[15] The revolt against Barden is mentioned in Neil MacNeil, *Forge of Democracy* (McKay, 1963), p. 173. The new rules adopted by the Education and Labor Committee after the uprising against Powell appear in *Cong. Record*, Vol. 112 (Sept. 26, 1966), daily ed., pp. 22851–52. The dispute between Patman and other members of the Democratic majority, which resulted in rules for the majority's conduct, is discussed by Rowland Evans and Robert Novak, *Washington Post*, March 1, 1967. For an example of a chairman's "quiet and subtle" use of his prerogatives to restrain the majority of his committee, see Bibby and Davidson, "The Senate Committee on Banking and Currency," in *On Capitol Hill*, pp. 176–79; the discussion is of Senator Willis Robertson's chairmanship.

[16] For views of House members, see Charles L. Clapp, *The Congressman: His Work as He Sees It* (Brookings Institution, 1963), pp. 222–29. Senators who participated in a series of discussions in 1965 had relatively little complaint about committee operations, and there was little dissatisfaction expressed during the Senate debate on the legislative reorganization bill in 1967 (forthcoming book by Randall B. Ripley, based in part upon senators' "round table" discussions at the Brookings Institution).

[17] Roger H. Davidson, David M. Kovenock, and Michael K. O'Leary found in interviews with 118 members of the House of Representatives that various proposals to substitute another method for seniority in selecting committee chairmen drew support varying from 14 to 29 percent, with the more senior members, as might be expected, overwhelmingly opposed to any change (*Congress in Crisis: Politics and Congressional Reform* [Wadsworth, 1966], pp. 100–03). Senator Clark's proposal for election of committee chairmen was given scant consideration by the Senate and defeated on a voice vote when he presented it as an amendment to the legislative reorganization bill in 1967.

such as those pertaining to subcommittee structure, staff appointments, and the committee's work schedule, should be assured in the rules of each house.[18] "The power of the chairman is a more fundamental issue in sound committee operations than is his method of selection," concluded the Joint Committee on Organization of the Congress.[19] Ultimate power should rest with the majority of the committee, it held, and the chairman should be its "agent." Accordingly, the joint committee's first recommendation was for what it called a "committee bill of rights" to "insure that the members always have an opportunity to work their will." Adoption of those recommendations, which were eliminated when the Senate passed the legislative reorganization bill in 1967, would go far toward solving what remains of the problem of the seniority system. If democratic processes can be made to prevail in the actual conduct of committee affairs, then it matters little who presides at the meetings.

Party Realignment

When Congress has allowed itself to be vetoed by its own minority, it has not been the *official* minority—the Republicans—who caused the trouble. The rules and practices of Congress guard against that. Members of the minority party are allowed to talk and to vote but, beyond that, only to kibitz; the majority party retains for itself the right to control all committees and schedule the business of Congress in committee and on the floor. But there is nothing in the rules of Congress that prevents the majority from letting itself be obstructed by its *own* minority. The troubles with the Rules Committee and with recalcitrant committee chairmen chosen by seniority have all been troubles not *between* parties but *within* the majority Democratic party.

The deep cleavage in the Democratic party has sapped the capacity to govern not only of the Democrats but of the Republicans as well. During much of the past thirty years, conservatives have comprised a majority of one or both houses of Congress but because their ranks were split between

[18] The rules should also guarantee to the committee minority a fair share of staff resources. While a "fair" share does not necessarily mean half, it assuredly means more than the tiny remnant now allotted by the Democratic majorities to their Republican colleagues.

[19] The committee, headed by Senator A. S. Mike Monroney and Representative Ray Madden, issued its final report July 28, 1966.

Republicans and southern Democrats, a conservative majority has not been able—except for two periods of two years each—to organize the Congress. They have had the numbers to obstruct a liberal program, but without control of the formal machinery available to the official majority, they could not present and enact a program of their own. The result was a separation of responsibility and power—and mutual impotence.

The Democratic "solid South" has been a feature of the political map for a hundred years. But parties based on region rather than on principles or programs are unnatural in a unified country—and could only arise from so searing and disunifying an experience as a Civil War. In time, regional parties are bound to dissolve before the unifying and nationalizing forces of society and the gradual substitution of live issues for those long since dead. The time for the dissolution of the "solid South" appears now to have arrived. The Republican party has been gaining strength there at an astonishingly rapid pace. At a certain critical point a realignment becomes irreversible, and that point may already have been reached. If that is the case, almost all of the critiques of Congress and of the American party system written in this century will be obsolete. Proposals for reform of Congress will be largely moot. The implications of party realignment for responsive government are so significant that the prospects deserve careful examination at this point. And the examination should begin with a review of the process of realignment in the North, because what is happening in the states that lost the Civil War can best be understood if it is seen as something like a mirror image of what has already happened in the states that won.

Realignment in the North. In the North, two-party competition was restored in most states within a generation after the Civil War. That conflict left the North a predominantly Republican area, just as it left the South predominantly Democratic, but in few northern states was the Democratic party wiped out as a serious competitive force. Table 15 shows how the northern states established, one by one, what today is the "normal" two-party system of alternation of state administrations between the Republican and Democratic parties. The three states of the Far West and three eastern states—Connecticut, New York, and Indiana —quickly returned to a two-party system closely balanced between the parties. By 1882 another six states had elected a governor at least once on the Democratic ticket but remained preponderantly Republican. By 1892 another four states had elected their first post-war Democratic governors.

Table 15. *Restoration of Two-Party Politics in Republican States after the Civil War*

State	Date of election of first Democratic governor	Number of years governorship held, by party, 1867–96		
		Republican	Democratic	Other
California	1866	16	14	—
Connecticut	1866	17	13	—
New York	1868	9	21	—
Oregon	1870	10	20	—
Nevada	1870	16	12	2 (Silver)
New Hampshire	1870	28	2	—
Indiana	1872	14	16	—
Wisconsin	1872	22	6	2 (Democratic-Greenback)
Ohio	1873	22	8	—
Massachusetts	1874	25	4	1 (Democratic-Independent)
Pennsylvania	1882	22	8	—
Kansas	1882	26	2	2 (Populist Democratic)
Rhode Island	1886	28	2	—
Michigan	1890	26	2	2 (Democratic-Greenback)
Nebraska	1890	26	2[a]	2 (Populist)
Illinois	1892	26	4	—
Minnesota	1898	30	—	—
Maine	1910	27	—	3 (Democratic-Greenback)
Iowa	1932	30	—	—
Vermont	1962	30	—	—

Source: Joseph V. Cirieco, "State Governors 1789 to Present" (Legislative Reference Service, Library of Congress, 1958, processed).
[a] Democratic governor elected for two-year term served less than one year because his eligibility for office was contested in the courts.

At the time of the McKinley-Bryan presidential contest, in 1896, only four states—Minnesota, Iowa, Maine, and Vermont—had a Democratic party so weak that it had not been able to elect a governor at least once since the Civil War, and in one of those states—Maine—a coalition between the Democratic and Greenback parties had been successful twice.

Just as two-party politics were being restored in most northern states, a second shattering event occurred. In the Democratic convention of 1896 the rising forces of agrarian revolt in the West and South seized control of the party from the conservative Cleveland Democrats, and nominated William Jennings Bryan on a "silver" platform. The consequence was what Schattschneider calls "one of the decisive elections of American history," involving a massive shift in party allegiance in the North. The Populist party dissolved and its support, for the most part, was attracted by Bryan into the Democratic party. But Bryan's Populist platform was as unappealing in the East as it was alluring in the West. Thousands of men of substance in the North and East fled the Democratic party, and with them went thousands of others who were not men of substance but were subject to the influence of those who were. The activist issues of a new day had at last, after a generation, supplanted the issues of the Civil War and Reconstruction periods as the basis of party alignment in the North, but the result was a far from equal party competition. The Democrats became the majority party in a few of the Rocky Mountain mining states; elsewhere throughout the North the Republican advantage was reinforced and solidified. Northern states that had been predominantly Democratic during the previous twenty years, like New Jersey and Delaware, now became preponderantly Republican. States that had been closely balanced, like Connecticut and Indiana, became part of the solid Republican North; and in some of the states that had already been solidly Republican, the Democratic party was all but decimated. Again it required a generation, as shown in Table 16, to gradually restore two-party competition. The Democrats gained particularly during the period 1910–16, with the progressive movement and the Roosevelt-Taft split in the Republican party, but the GOP was dominant—as measured by victories in state elections—in every single state outside the South, the border states, and a few Mountain states until the Depression and Franklin Roosevelt. From that time forward, the two-party system in the North has been essentially in balance. The Democratic party held the edge in the more urban eastern states, where immigrants had seen their opportunity in the minority party and made it theirs; the Republican party held a continuing advantage in the Midwest. But in every state the party split reflected the cleavage of the national parties, and state elections followed the cyclical pattern of genuine two-party politics. Even Vermont—the last holdout of the once one-party Republican North—elected its first Democratic governor in 1962 and reelected him in 1964 and 1966.

Realignment in the South. As in the North, two-party politics developed in the South after the Civil War. The Democrats were the dominant party everywhere, as they had been since Jefferson, but as Schattschneider

Table 16. *Restoration of Two-Party Politics in Republican States after the Party Realignment of 1896*

State	Date of election of first Democratic governor or popularly elected Democratic senator	Number of years governorship held, by party, 1897–1930		
		Republican	Democratic	Other
Minnesota	1898	27	7	—
Oregon	1902	20	14	—
Rhode Island	1902	28	6	—
Massachusetts	1904	28	3	3 (Progressive-Democratic)
Ohio	1905	18	16	—
North Dakota	1906	28	6	—
Indiana	1908	26	8	—
Wyoming	1910	23	11	—
New York	1910	16	14	—
New Jersey	1910	19	15	—
Maine	1910	30	4	—
Connecticut	1910	30	4	—
Michigan	1912	30	4	—
Washington	1912	24	6	4 (Populist-Democratic)
New Hampshire	1912	30	4	—
South Dakota	1914[a]	22	4	4 (Populist-Democratic)
Wisconsin	1914[a]	34	—	—
California	1914[a]	34	—	—
Utah	1916	24	10	—
Delaware	1916[a]	30	4	—
West Virginia	1916	30	4	—
Kansas	1922	30	2	2 (Populist-Democratic)
Iowa	1924[b]	34	—	—
Illinois	1930[a]	34	—	—
Pennsylvania	1934	34	—	—
Vermont	1962	34	—	—

Source: Cirieco, "State Governors 1789 to Present"; "The Governors of the States 1900—1966" (Chicago: Council of State Governments, 1966).
[a] Senator.
[b] Senator; seated by the Senate in 1926 after contesting the election of his Republican opponent.

points out,[20] in 1884 the Republicans received one-third or more of the presidential vote in all of the southern states but three. Then the western Populist movement spread into the South. In 1890 the Populists won control of eight southern legislatures. The conservatives responded with the poll tax and other electoral laws and practices that reduced participation in elections in some states by well over 50 percent. The Republican party was all but destroyed outside the mountain counties; a one-party system may be unnatural in a society where everybody votes, but it may be downright inevitable in a society where only one class votes.[21] Gradually the restrictive electoral laws were softened, but only with the Voting Rights Act of 1965 did the nation take strong action to compel open elections in the South.

The influences that helped to strengthen the Democratic party in the North and thus restore the party balance aided the Democrats in the South too—but there, of course, they had the opposite effect on the party system. Wilsonian progressivism, liberal Democratic trade policies, and—most important by far—the "Hoover Depression" reinforced Democratic hegemony. For all these reasons the development of two-party competition in the South has been retarded.

But the main factors making for one-party politics in that region have now been removed. The Negroes and the poor whites have been reenfranchised, and electoral participation is rising spectacularly. Only the older generation remembers the Depression; the younger voters see the party struggle in terms of new national issues. In 1964 in particular, the voter of the deep South saw racial integration as the overriding issue and the Republicans under Barry Goldwater as closer than Lyndon Johnson's Democratic party to the southern point of view.

The recent resurgence of the Republican party in the South is not, therefore, a temporary phenomenon. Indeed, as experience in the North has shown, once genuine two-party competition is established in a state, the trend toward a balance in that competition tends to accelerate. Sixty-six years had to elapse between the realignment of 1896 and the election of a Democratic governor in the last of the Republican states—Vermont—but now every single state of the North is a genuine two-party battleground with a party division corresponding, with individual variations, to the national activist-conservative cleavage. Now that the political isolation of

[20] E. E. Schattschneider, *The Semi-Sovereign People* (Holt, Rinehart and Winston, 1960), pp. 83–84.
[21] See tables, *ibid.*, p. 84, and accompanying discussion.

the South has been shattered, the same acceleration of competition can be expected there. It will be stimulated by many factors—the steady urbanization of the region, the in-migration of northerners, the reapportionment decisions of the Supreme Court, the nationalizing influences of television and other communications media, and perhaps most important, the pressures of the two national parties. Both parties have a stake in realignment that they can scarcely overlook—the Republican party to gain the numbers necessary to organize the Congress, the Democratic party to gain the capacity to control it in fact when they organize it in form.

As the numbers of southern conservative Democrats in Congress dwindle, they will have a lessening power to force compromises from the dominant activist wing of the party. The Democratic national party, in its platforms and in the operation of its national committee, has long since ceased to be conciliatory; and in the House of Representatives the Democratic Study Group in 1965 found the strength to insist upon stripping seniority from two southerners who had backed Goldwater—John Bell Williams of Mississippi and Albert Watson of South Carolina, the latter of whom resigned from Congress, changed party affiliation, and returned to the House as a Republican. By the same token, the Republican party has abandoned its live-and-let-live policy toward the conservative Democrats. House Republican Leader Gerald Ford has formally denounced the Republican-southern Democratic coalition that was the center of his predecessors' legislative strategy.

Table 17 presents one measure of the growth of Republican strength in the South—the rise in congressional representation from the states of the Confederacy since 1950.[22] The elections of 1966 offer further dramatic evidence. For the first time in history, Republican governors were elected in Florida and Arkansas and, for the first time since Reconstruction, Republican senators in South Carolina and Tennessee. In Texas the first Republican senator since Reconstruction was reelected. Of the states of the once-solid South, only five—Alabama, Georgia, Louisiana, Mississippi, and Virginia—have yet to elect a Republican senator or governor. But

---

[22] Another measure would be the number of "safe" Democratic seats in the House of Representatives from the South. They declined as strikingly—from 91 in 1950 to 60 in 1964 (safe seats are defined as those won by 65 percent or more of the vote; Raymond E. Wolfinger and Joan Heifetz, "Safe Seats, Seniority, and Power in Congress," *American Political Science Review*, Vol. 59 [June 1965], pp. 337–49). In 1966, 62 seats were safe.

Table 17. *Growth in Number of Republicans Elected to the House of Representatives from the South, 1950–66*

State	Number of Republicans elected								
	1950	1952	1954	1956	1958	1960	1962	1964	1966
Alabama	—	—	—	—	—	—	—	5	3
Arkansas	—	—	—	—	—	—	—	—	1
Florida	—	—	1	1	1	1	2	2	3
Georgia	—	—	—	—	—	—	—	1	2
Louisiana	—	—	—	—	—	—	—	—	—
Mississippi	—	—	—	—	—	—	—	1	—
North Carolina	—	1	1	1	1	1	2	2	3
South Carolina	—	—	—	—	—	—	—	—	1
Tennessee	2	2	2	2	2	2	3	3	4
Texas	—	—	1	1	1	1	2	—	2
Virginia	—	3	2	2	2	2	2	2	4
Total southern Republicans	2	6	7	7	7	7	11	16	23
Total southern representatives	105	106	106	106	106	106	106	106	106
Republican percentage	2	6	7	7	7	7	10	15	22

Georgia came very close to choosing a Republican governor in 1966; and Alabama, Georgia, and Virginia all sent Republicans to Congress from districts that were reliably Democratic a decade or two earlier. Republicans gained state legislative seats as well. The Democratic party will no doubt remain dominant in at least the rural areas of the South for a long time to come, as the Republican party will remain dominant in the rural North, but—barring a national collapse of Republican fortunes—competition will be strong enough to permit the minority party to make a serious challenge at every election and to win in some of them. This has been the pattern in the border states since the realignment of 1896, as shown in Table 18.[23]

[23] For an analysis of survey data bearing upon political realignment in the South, see Philip E. Converse, "On the Possibility of Major Political Realignment in the South," in Angus Campbell and others, *Elections and the Political Order* (Wiley, 1966), pp. 211–42. Writing from data through 1960, before the recent acceleration of the pro-Republican trend, Converse found a "slow convergence" between southern and non-southern patterns of voting behavior.

The Stages of Realignment. A review of the stages in the transition from one-party to two-party politics in the Midwest and the more rural states of the Northeast[24] after the realignment of 1896, and a comparisan of those stages with current developments in the South, may shed light on the general process of realignment.

Initially, before two-party politics could be a possibility in the Republican North, the minority Democratic party had to achieve *respectability,* so that a person identifying with it was not looked upon—as Dwight Eisenhower once said his home town of Abilene looked upon a Democrat —as "the town drunk." Throughout the rural and small-town North, respectability was not fully achieved by the Democrats until the Depression discredited the Republican party and the New Deal attracted some of the pillars of the communities into the Democratic party's ranks. They provided the minority party a necessary foundation for growth, but even that period was not marked by any mass shift in party allegiance by persons identified and active as Republicans. The "Roosevelt Republicans" in the North still considered themselves Republicans, even after some of them had voted for Roosevelt four times. The Republican leaders and functionaries, whatever their views, were bound to their party by the rewards of status and the knowledge that, if they were to transfer to the other party, they would have to begin again at the bottom of the political ladder. On rare occasions, an officeholder might change parties without losing his

Table 18. *Restoration of Two-Party Politics in Border States after the Civil War*

State	Date of election of first Republican governor	Number of years governorship held, by party, 1897–1966	
		Democratic	Republican
Delaware	1894	18	52
Kentucky	1894	50	20
Maryland	1895	51	19
West Virginia	1896	34	36
Missouri	1907	50	20
Oklahoma[a]	1962	56	4

Sources: "The Governors of the States 1900—1966"; Cirieco, "State Governors 1789 to Present."
[a] Admitted to the union in 1907.

[24] The comparison is limited to the rural states of the Northeast because in the urban centers the Democratic party was built on immigrant ethnic groups, principally Catholic and Jewish, who were numerous enough to bring the two parties into balanced competition.

office, as did Wayne Morse in Oregon—but even in that case Morse had to begin his seniority climb on U.S. Senate committees all over again.

Politically minded younger people, however, were bound by no established party ties. They were attracted to the revived minority party not just by its principles and policies but also by the very emptiness of its political ladder—as a Democrat, one would not have to wait long before aspiring to public or party office. And the newcomers had little reason to wait. In their eyes, the older generation of Democratic leaders who had guided the party during its long years of impotence was worn out, defeatist, and content with minority status. The outcome was inevitable. After a decade or two of tension, the new generation supplanted the old in positions of party leadership and from its ranks came candidates whose youth, freshness, and vigor had enough appeal for sustained success. The Democratic party could arrive at full competitive status with Hubert Humphrey in Minnesota and G. Mennen Williams in Michigan in the 1940's and with Edmund Muskie in Maine, William Proxmire in Wisconsin, and George McGovern in South Dakota in the 1950's.

As the minority party grew, a critical point was reached when the internal balance of the majority party was upset—and this accelerated the development of a two-party system. When enough of the agrarian progressives of the rural North, or their sons and daughters, had drifted across the party line into the Democratic party, the hold upon the Republican party of those progressives who remained Republicans was destroyed. No longer could they contest with the conservatives for control of the Republican party, even in the upper Midwest and Plains states where they had been strongest; there the mantle of GOP leadership passed from the Norrises, the Brookharts, and the Shipsteads to the Wherrys and Hickenloopers of more modern times, while the leadership of the old progressive cause passed to the rising generation of Democrats. The generational process can be observed within single families: Democratic Senator Quentin Burdick of North Dakota is the son of Usher Burdick, the long-time progressive Republican congressman; and the current bearer of the LaFollette name in Wisconsin politics is the Democratic attorney general of the state. The basic policy questions that had divided the Republican party have thus become the basis for interparty competition between two relatively homogeneous parties.

The one-party South is about two decades behind the one-party North in the development of two-party politics. In the South the Republicans achieved their respectability in the moral fervor of Eisenhower's "crusade." Again, direct conversions of established Democratic politicians were few. The party switch of Senator Strom Thurmond of South Carolina, like that of his counterpart Wayne Morse, was exceptional. The minority party was built for the most part by young lawyers and businessmen and their wives who were attracted, like their earlier northern Democratic counterparts, both by the principles of the national party and by the opportunity for rapid political advance. After a decade or so, the young and ambitious newcomers displaced their elders in positions of leadership. Many assumed party office or became candidates while still below the age of forty. They have given the party a fresh, dynamic image in many of the southern states, and it may well be that their successful young candidates—like Howard Baker in Tennessee, Claude Kirk in Florida, Albert Watson in South Carolina, and John Tower in Texas—will prove to have the staying power of the Humphreys and Williamses of the North. Like the older "Roosevelt Republicans," the older generation of "Eisenhower Democrats" will for the most part go to their graves as Democrats, but the younger generation of conservatives will find it natural and normal to identify openly with the Republican party. The process can, of course, be interrupted—a George Wallace third party could temporarily attract the major share of Democratic defectors, just as the Minnesota Farmer-Labor party and the Wisconsin Progressive party attracted Republican defectors during the Depression years. The effect on the majority party, however, would be the same.

Already, the critical point has been reached in many states and districts where the internal balance of the Democratic party has been upset. Enough conservatives have been drained from the Democratic party to leave the activists dominant in such major cities as Norfolk, Atlanta, Miami, Nashville, and San Antonio; and the same trend appears to be proceeding in Houston, Memphis, and Richmond. Florida Democrats in 1966 nominated a gubernatorial candidate (an unsuccessful one) far removed from the southern tradition and closely aligned with the national party. As the Democratic party becomes less and less hospitable to conservatives, their drift—and that of their sons and daughters—out of the Democratic party is bound to accelerate. Their places will be taken in part by new voters added through expansion of the voting rolls. In the first two years after passage of the Voting Rights Act of 1965, 550,000 Negroes were registered in the South,[25] and—as in the North—most of

---

[25] Justice Department announcement, reported in *New York Times*, July 10, 1967.

them cast their votes in the Democratic primary. This will in turn drive out more conservatives, in an accelerating spiral.

So far, then, the process of erosion of one-party hegemony in the South has proved to be almost the mirror image of the earlier process in the North. Eventually, the realignment seems destined to proceed to its final stage when the last of the southern Democrats of the conservative tradition will be as lonely as was William Langer of North Dakota during his last years in the Senate—before he died and the Republican agrarian progressive movement died with him.

The Consequences of Realignment. Party realignment—even if carried to its theoretical ultimate—still will not mean the end of stalemate in the American system of divided powers. After a close election, like that of 1960, the president may still be of one party and the majority of Congress of the other, or the majority party in Congress may have a margin so thin that it can pass its program only with the aid of defectors from the minority. But such periods of stalemate will be the exception, not the rule that they were during the decade from 1955 to 1965. When the people give a Republican president an overwhelming majority, as they did Eisenhower in 1956, he will be able to work with a Congress organized and led by his own party instead of by the opposition. Conversely, when they give their mandate to the Democrats, that party will no longer be hamstrung by the seniority rights of senators and congressmen who oppose their party's program. When the electorate is indecisive, so will be the government, as it is in any democratic country. But when the voters are decisive, the government will have the capacity to respond to the expressed will of the people.

Those who have written of party realignment have often assumed that homogeneous, "responsible," and "disciplined" parties will be homogenized by, responsible to, and disciplined by the president. "The decline of the Southerners will be accompanied by a Democratic president's greater ability to get his way with Congress," said the authors of a recent article on power shifts in Congress.[26] But this tells only half the story. The decline of the southerners will also be accompanied by an enhanced ability

[26] Wolfinger and Heifetz, "Safe Seats, Senority, and Power in Congress," p. 348. See also Bibby and Davidson, *On Capitol Hill,* pp. 261–66; Huntington, "Congressional Responses to the Twentieth Century"; and de Grazia, "Toward a New Model of Congress," for discussions of the issue of executive versus legislative supremacy.

of Democratic senators and congressmen who adhere to the national party to get *their* way with Congress. The southern conservatives obstruct not only the president but their own colleagues. Who is obstructed depends upon the source of the proposal being obstructed, and the realignment of the parties will not of itself lessen the initiative of legislators.

Those who fear—or hopefully expect—the subordination of the Congress to an all-powerful president after party realignment cannot have looked closely at the present relationship between a Democratic President and the members of Congress from the northern presidential wing of his party. That relationship does not amount to a pattern of subordination. While the legislators do not obstruct, neither do they surrender. At times, it has been they who led and the President who followed. The substantial contributions of members of Congress to legislation on air and water pollution, civil rights, education, medicare, and other measures summarized in Part I come nearer to genuine partnership than to subordination. In 1966 and 1967, leadership in publicizing the problems of the cities and devising remedies was assumed by Senators Ribicoff and Robert Kennedy at a time when the President was resting on the status quo.

The discipline of a homogeneous majority party in the new American system will be supplied not by the imposition of one man's will but by the cohesive power of the party program, fashioned through processes summarized in Chapters 9 and 11 in which members of the party from the executive branch, the Senate, the House, and party organs outside the government all take part. What passes will be passed not by direction of the president but by consensus of the party—a consensus that becomes achievable once those who are opposed in general to the party's program are, by definition, outside the party.

Given the federal structure of American parties, the constitutional separation of powers, and the tradition of assertiveness of American legislators, there is no reason to conjecture that even with homogeneous parties senators and representatives will ever be reduced to the spectator status of the back-benchers of a European governing party.

Ideally, what will come out of party realignment will be the best of both the parliamentary and presidential worlds. From the presidential system will be retained the multiple centers of legislative initiative that gives the American system its unique vitality. From the parliamentary system will be drawn its great advantage—the capacity of a united majority party to act, and to act quickly and decisively.

The Agenda of Activism

When the climactic congressional session of 1965 adjourned, a decade of ardor had finally produced a battery of measures that brought the country, in some respects, abreast of the major social problems of the time. But much of the new legislation fell short of the hopes—and, in the hyperbolic climate of campaigns, the boasts—of those who sponsored it. Area re-development did not redevelop much. The problem of poverty proved far more complex and intractable than the optimists had anticipated. The Elementary and Secondary Education Act was not general aid to education. The civil rights acts did not alter the way of life in northern ghettoes. In the flames of Watts, and later of Hough and Detroit and Newark, it was clear that nothing had been finally solved. From the activist standpoint, the country's problems—even in the halcyon years of 1964 and 1965—were mounting faster than they were being met. And since those years the country has been losing ground.

One problem is that of scale. The magnitude of the commitments that are implied in the stated goals—to wipe out poverty, unemployment, slums, pollution, and a host of other evils—far outstrips the expenditure of public funds, and the gap between promise and performance is itself a source of frustration and of cynicism.

A second problem is administration. Many of the new goals that have been proclaimed by the national government have to be achieved through the initiative and the administrative expertise of other governments, state and local, that legally are independent and politically may be even hostile. The transformation of the federal system seems to have been accepted, but the mechanisms that will make it work have yet to be perfected. How can the resources of states and local communities be mobilized for national purposes, and how can the tangle of relationships between a multitude of federal agencies and thousands of state and community bodies be ration-alized and simplified? What are the administrative processes that can penetrate the urban ghetto and the rural backwater and reach the "hard to reach"? If and when a new "Hoover commission" is created, these are the questions that need attention.

But the basic problem is knowing what to do. The agenda of the 1950's has been swept clean; the nation has yet to define the new goals, and the new means for achieving old goals, that can command widespread accept-ance. The country is in the period of pause that marks the return swing of the pendulum toward the beginning of a new cycle. In the normal alternation of political moods, the pause would continue through a time of consolidation while the activist forces designed the measures that would be enacted in the next burst of creative legislative energy. The question this time is whether the crises of race and poverty and violence that press in upon the country will tolerate a pause. The triumphs of responsive government in 1964 and 1965 leave the need for responsive institutions only more compelling than before.

Index

Index

Academic community, 393–94

Accelerated Public Works Act: passage of, 92–97, 476; popularity of, 105, 106, 109; superseded, 110, 495

Ackley, Gardner, 53n, 55n

Activists: in Congress, 473, 478; development of support, 507–09; in political spectrum, 500–03, 505; program of, 8–9, 482, 490, 506–09; views of, 385, 386–87; voter response to program of, 430, 441–52. *See also* Democratic party; Republican party

Adams, Sherman, 16n, 17, 18, 19n, 66, 224n, 227, 235, 237n, 334, 416–21 *passim*, 428

ADC. *See* Aid to dependent children

Administered prices, 32, 33

Advertising easements, 341–45, 374. *See also* Billboard control

Advisory Council on Public Assistance, 126–27

AFL–CIO, 3, 509; on billboard control, 344; on civil rights, 79; on education, 165; on medicare, 296–98, 299, 309, 310, 312, 392; political education committee, 298–310; on recession, 23, 26; social security committee, 296; on water pollution, 329. *See also* Labor, organized

Aged and aging, the: and medicare 6, 287–321 *passim*; problems of, 293–96; and social security, 126; state agencies on, 294–95; and unemployment, 81, 82

Aged and aging, Senate subcommittee on problems of the, 287, 299

Aging, Senate Special Committee on, 287, 288n, 310

Aging, White House conference on, 308

Agriculture Committee, House, 519

Agriculture Committee, Senate, 74, 519

Agriculture, Department of, 133, 144, 339, 358

Aid to dependent children (ADC), 126–30

Aiken, George D., 236–37

AIPO. *See* Polls, American Institute of Public Opinion (AIPO)

Air pollution control, 331–33, 351–55, 367–71, 495, 535

Albert, Carl, 483–84

Albright, Robert C., 3n

Alcorn, Meade, 69n

Alinsky, Saul, 118

Aller, Curtis C., 59n, 88n, 91n

Allott, Gordon, 163, 237, 340, 358–60

Alter, Karl J., 189

American Assembly, 200, 201n

American Association of School Administrators, 204, 219n

American Bankers Association, 48

American Council on Education, 195, 198n, 201

American Dental Association, 298

American Federation of Labor–Congress of Industrial Organizations. *See* AFL–CIO

American Friends Service Committee, 239n

American Hospital Association, 298, 300–01, 310, 312, 313n, 509

American Institute of Public Opinion (AIPO). *See* Polls, American Institute of Public Opinion (AIPO)

American Iron and Steel Institute, 354

American Jewish Committee, 213

American Medical Association (AMA), 484, 488, 507, 509, 510; on air pollution control, 352; lobbying expenses of, 290n, 298, 299, 310, 314, 318n; on medicare, 290–93 *passim*, 298–301 *passim*, 305, 306,